SAS
ENCYCLOPEDIA

STEVE CRAWFORD

igloo

This revised edition published in 2005 by **igloo**
Igloo Books Ltd
Henson Way
Telford Way Industrial Estate
Kettering
Northants NN16 8PX

ISBN 1-84561-123-3

Editorial and design by:
Amber Books Ltd
Bradley's Close
74-77 White Lion Strett
London N1 9PF
United Kingdom
www.amberbooks.co.uk

Printed in Singapore

Extracts taken from 'Looking for Trouble' by Peter de la Billière (HarperCollins, London 1994),
'SAS: The Jungle Frontier' by Peter Dickens (Arms & Armour Press, London 1983),
'SAS: Operation Oman' by Tony Jeapes (William Kimber, Northampton 1983),
'Immediate Action' by Andy McNab (Bantam Press, London 1995)

Contents

Contents

THE SAS

AT

WAR

WORLD WAR II

North Africa

The SAS was the brainchild of a young Scots Guards officer, Lieutenant David Stirling, and though it got off to a shaky start at the end of 1941, its subsequent behind-the-lines actions had a significant impact on the outcome of the North African campaign.

For some time after the evacuation of Dunkirk in the summer of 1940, the British military hierarchy was quite naturally preoccupied with the defence of the British Isles against German invasion. However, one far-thinking officer, Lieutenant-Colonel Dudley Clarke, managed to persuade his superiors to consider setting up special forces units to undertake lightning strikes upon the enemy. The idea was passed on to Prime Minister Winston Churchill, and approval to raise such units was quickly granted. Over the next few months several Special Service Battalions, or Commandos, were raised.

By the end of November 1940 all members of No 2 Commando had been parachute trained, and it was decided to rename this unit No 11 Special Air Service Battalion. This was partly to differentiate the unit from the seaborne commandos of the other special service battalions, but was also aimed at confusing the Germans into believing that Britain had a larger parachute capability than actually existed. The first operational drop was carried out by X Company of 11 SAS Battalion in February 1941, when it attacked an aqueduct over the River Tragino in Italy.

RAIDS IN NORTH AFRICA

The para-commando concept had hardly had a chance to prove itself before the Germans invaded Crete in May 1941, causing the British high command to re-evaluate the potential of large airborne units. The following September, 11 SAS Battalion became the nucleus of the 1st Parachute Brigade. A 2nd Parachute Brigade was also formed in India from British, Indian and Gurkha battalions. A consignment of parachutes destined for this brigade would later be put to good use in Egypt by a daring young officer who had managed to persuade his superiors to create a special raiding unit under his command. This officer was David Stirling, the founder of the SAS.

Lieutenant David Stirling had been commissioned into the Scots Guards and then, in June 1940, volunteered for No 8 Commando. Later that year Nos 7, 8 and 11 Commandos, plus a small unit known as the Special Boat Section, were assembled into a brigade under Lieutenant-Colonel Laycock for operations in North Africa. Known as Layforce, it should have been used for coastal raiding and harassing operations, but a shortage of naval craft severely curtailed its effectiveness. Somewhat bored, Stirling persuaded Laycock to allow him to experiment with parachuting as an alternative method of delivery however, a heavy landing damaged his spine and put him in hospital for the best part of two months.

As he lay in bed, Stirling set his mind to expanding his ideas on airborne and commando operations. At that time commando operational thinking called for units of anything up to 200 men to be used for each operation. Getting them to the target caused all sorts of logistical problems, and at the landing site a large proportion of the commando had to be

Left: Parachute training at the SAS's first base, at Kabrit near the Suez Canal, in mid-1941, in preparation for the first mission.

used just to secure the beachhead. Stirling believed that smaller units inserted deep behind enemy lines would be able to inflict disproportionately high damage on soft targets. He concluded that the best solution was for the assault unit to parachute in for surprise, being collected after the attack by a second unit dispatched overland with wheeled transport.

On his release from hospital in July 1941, Stirling took his written plan to Middle East Command Headquarters and attempted to deliver it to the Commander-in-Chief, General Sir Claude Auchinleck, but was refused entry. Not one to give up easily, he slipped over the perimeter fence and hobbled into the building, eventually barging into the office of Major-General Neil Ritchie, the Chief of Staff. Ritchie was so impressed by Stirling's ideas that he presented them to Auchinleck. Soon after Stirling was promoted to captain and ordered to raise a new unit of 60 men and six officers.

L DETACHMENT, SAS BRIGADE

Stirling's new unit was given the name L Detachment of the Special Air Service Brigade. Within a week he had recruited all his men, mostly from No 8 (Guards) Commando, and assembled them near Kabrit in the Suez Canal Zone.

When the men arrived at their new camp, they found only a few old tents. That night, after a quick briefing and recce, they mounted their first operational raid – against a large New Zealand camp a short distance away. By first light the next morning a new tented camp stood on L Detachment's pitch.

Due to the lack of proper facilities in the region, all training had to be carried out in-house with improvised equipment. Emphasis was placed on desert navigation, familiarity with all types of weapons, including German and Italian models, movement at night, and a high degree of physical fitness. As the only parachuting schools were in England or India, all initial drop training was improvised. To practise landings, Stirling's men would jump backwards off moving trucks. However, as a result of the unacceptably high rate of ankle injuries, a proper jump trainer was constructed from scaffolding towers.

Once the basics of parachute drills had been mastered on the improvised training towers, the detachment was trucked to Cairo to jump from RAF Bristol Bombay transport aircraft. On the first day tragedy struck when attachment rings in the aircraft broke during a jump. Two troopers, Duffy and Warburton, were killed and training immediately ceased. The RAF resolved the problem and next morning the SAS lined up again. First man out of the aircraft was Stirling himself.

By November 1941 the unit was ready. On the 16th, after weeks of planning, the detachment launched its first operational mission, against five frontline Axis airfields. The entire detachment, but for five men,

Above: Trucks of the Long Range Desert Group (LRDG). The LRDG transported SAS teams to and from their targets in 1941-42.

was to be dropped in groups of 12 men about 30km (19 miles) from their designated target airfields. After destroying as many aircraft on the ground as possible, each group would rendezvous with a Long Range Desert Group (LRDG) patrol for transport back to Kabrit.

That night the region was hit by the worst storms in three decades, and all the aircraft carrying the SAS were blown off course, but the drops went ahead anyway. None of the patrols were able to find their target airfields, and all subsequently

David Stirling

The founder of the SAS was born in 1915. A rather restless spirit in his youth, he had studied architecture at Cambridge, but still loved the outdoor life, particularly mountaineering. After dabbling with the idea of being an artist, when war broke out in 1939 he was in the Rockies brushing up on his mountaineering skills for a climb on Mount Everest. His par-

ticipation in a number of ineffectual large-scale raids on the North African coast convinced him that small-scale units would be more effective. He managed to convince his superiors that SAS troops should be used strategically: to attack priority targets deep behind enemy lines and not immediately behind the front. Another of Stirling's gifts was his ability to enlist men of talent into the new unit, men such as 'Paddy' Mayne, Reg Seekings and 'Jock' Lewes. With men like these the unit thrived despite Stirling's capture in January 1943. Stirling died in 1990, being knighted in the New Year Honours list of that year.

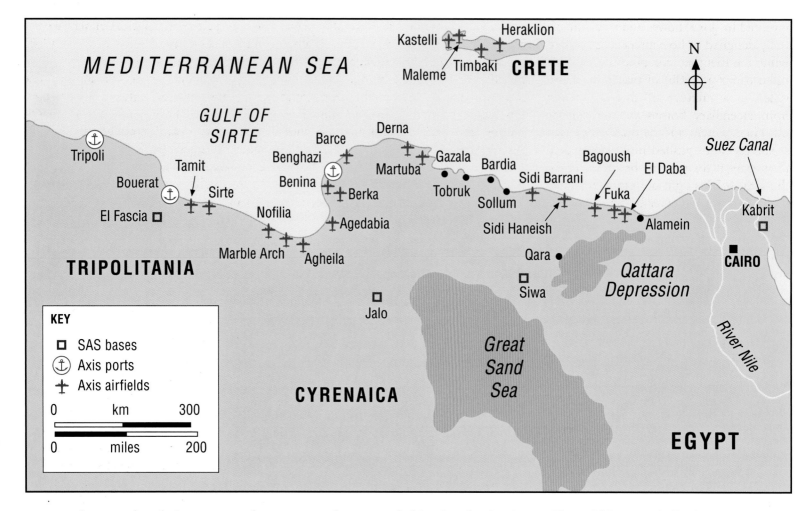

MEDITERRANEAN SEA

GULF OF SIRTE

KEY

- ☐ SAS bases
- ⚓ Axis ports
- ✈ Axis airfields

| 0 | km | 300 |
| 0 | miles | 200 |

TRIPOLITANIA

CYRENAICA

CRETE

Great Sand Sea

Qattara Depression

EGYPT

Above: SAS targets in North Africa in 1941-43 included all Axis airfields behind the lines, plus the ports of Benghazi and Bouerat.

attempted to make their way to the LRDG rendezvous. After marching all morning through incessant rain, which left the desert awash, all afternoon under the searing sun, which came out after the storm, and then through the evening by starlight, 'Jock' Lewes's patrol and half of 'Paddy' Mayne's patrol reached the rendezvous. The only others to arrive were David Stirling and one of his men. Of the 62 officers and men who set out, only 22 returned. The first mission had been a complete failure.

Although this first raid had been a disaster, Stirling was determined not to give up. Even on the way back in the LRDG trucks, the survivors were analysing their performance and discussing what lessons could be learned. Rather than parachuting into action in future, it was decided that delivery into the area of operation by the LRDG, followed by an overland hike to the target, was more likely to be successful. When Stirling reported back to Auchinleck in Cairo (L Detachment had no parent unit, so Stirling answered directly to the Commander-in-Chief), he

managed to persuade him that despite the high losses his command still had a future – it was just the fine detail which needed a little tuning.

FIRST SUCCESSES

After the briefest of rest periods, the remains of Stirling's command were flown to the oasis of Jalo deep behind enemy lines, where the LRDG had established a patrol base. From here, on 8 December 1941, Stirling and 'Paddy' Mayne would lead a raid against an Italian Air Force base. A few days later, 'Jock' Lewes and Bill Fraser would lead their men in attacks on two different targets. For four days, the LRDG transported Stirling's and Mayne's patrols across the open and uncharted desert, until at last they were about 80km (50 miles) south of the town of Sirte. A recce team in one vehicle then went ahead to observe the airfield, but when they got closer they discovered a second and more active airfield nearby at Tamit.

After some discussion it was decided that the two patrols, one of four men and the other of five, would each attempt to

attack one of the airfields. Stirling took Sirte and Mayne took Tamit. Due to minefields and heavy defences encountered near the Sirte airfield, Stirling's patrol was not able to mount its attack, but placed charges on trucks in a parked Italian road convoy instead. Mayne and his men found Tamit airfield to be much less well defended and planted all of their charges on aircraft, and then attacked the pilots' mess with grenades and machine guns while aircraft exploded in the background. Before the enemy had collected its senses, the patrol was heading back into the desert. Shortly after the SAS's return to the operational base at Jalo, RAF reconnaissance aircraft confirmed that the Tamit raid had resulted in the destruction of 24 aircraft. The other patrols had even greater success, taking out no less than 37 aircraft at Agedabia.

The explosive charges used on these raids, known as Lewes bombs, had been invented by 'Jock' Lewes and were specifically designed to hole aircraft wings then ignite the fuel they contained. They consisted of 500g (1.1lb) of plastic explosive rolled in a mixture of thermite filling from incendiary bombs and old engine oil. Time pencils and detonators, carried separately, were pushed into each charge to prepare it for use just before reaching the airfield. This light but efficient multi-use device subsequently became standard issue on all SAS operations.

The success of the Tamit and Agedabia raids confirmed beyond all doubt that Stirling's theories were sound. Within days other attacks were launched on the same airfields, Tamit once again suffering badly, with 'Paddy' Mayne accounting for 27 more aircraft. Once again the trucks of the LRDG were used for transport, but unfortunately one returning patrol was caught in the open by a Messerschmitt. 'Jock' Lewes, by now just as famous as David Stirling, was killed by a cannon shell in the attack.

OPERATIONS IN EARLY 1942

In just a couple of weeks 21 members of L Detachment had destroyed over 100 Axis aircraft, which was more than the RAF could claim in several months. As a result that sector of the desert was too full of enemy troops to operate in for a while and they returned to their Kabrit base to plan new ventures. They returned to Jalo in the first week of January 1942, suitably refreshed and with plenty of new ideas. Their first mission in this phase was to be against shipping and fuel dumps in the Italian-controlled port of Bouerat.

Once again the LRDG provided the transport, with all patrol members actually riding right into the town on one of the trucks. Charges were laid in warehouses and on numerous full fuel bowsers in the port area before the team withdrew without having alerted any of the sentries. As they drove quickly away the dock side erupted in flames.

Stirling had now been promoted to the rank of major, and with his new rank, and his connections, was able to requisition more and better equipment for the SAS. In addition to being given a higher rank, Stirling was also empowered to

enlarge L Detachment. His subsequent recruiting drive gathered more British soldiers, as well 50 Free French troops and the Greek Sacred Squadron. Over the next six months countless raids were mounted against enemy airfields, fuel dumps and port installations, all with great success.

SAS JEEP MISSIONS

At the beginning of July 1942 a batch of American Willys Jeeps became available and Stirling snapped them up. Vickers 'K' machine guns, pintle-mounted heavy calibre Brownings, and racks for copious petrol and water jerrycans were all added to the vehicles to make them suitable for SAS desert operations.

The patrols now had their own all-terrain transport to take them further afield. The Jeeps were also faster and more manoeuvrable than the LRDG trucks, so it was now possible to drive right through an airfield or installation, shooting up and grenading everything in sight before the enemy could reply. This Jeep-strafing technique came about more by accident than design when, during a raid on Bagoush airfield on 7 July 1942, only half of the 40 Lewes bombs placed on aircraft exploded. Before the enemy had collected their senses, Stirling raced through the dispersal area, his vehicle shooting up undamaged aircraft. Seeing his actions the crews of two other vehicles followed him, with all guns blazing. As the results were so successful, this method of attack was

used in preference to sneak attacks whenever possible, as it had an even more demoralising effect on the enemy.

No Axis soldier or airman now felt safe from attack at night, no matter how far behind the front line he was stationed. In October 1942, L Detachment was formally renamed 1st SAS Regiment, but even before this the SAS name was feared by the Italians and Germans across the deserts of North Africa. So great was the impact that this small band of men had on Axis morale that special units were set up specifically to track and capture patrols after raids. These hunter units on the whole had little success, but in January 1943 they did manage to catch David Stirling himself. He was to end up in Colditz Castle after making several daring escape attempts.

'Paddy' Mayne, who had served under Stirling since the beginning and was one of his closest friends, took over the Regiment and continued in the same style. A second SAS regiment was also in the process of being formed at this time under the command of Lieutenant-Colonel William Stirling, David Stirling's brother. The 2nd SAS Regiment became fully operational in May 1943, but by this stage in the war the Desert Campaign was over. However, the SAS was required for the Allied invasion of Sicily.

Below: SAS soldiers mounted on Willys Jeeps behind enemy lines in North Africa in July 1941 on their way to Sidi Haneish.

Sicily and Italy

The conclusion of the war in North Africa in 1943 created a number of doubts about the SAS's continued existence. Its creator had been captured and some wondered if its only use was in the desert. However, the campaigns in Sicily and Italy were to show the SAS's worth.

The end of the North African campaign saw the SAS in some turmoil. It had lost its leader, David Stirling, and no one was sure whether it would be disbanded. Stirling had always kept his plans for the future of the SAS to himself, and so when he disappeared from the scene none of his officers knew what to do.

Another problem was the loss of Stirling's influence. During the war in North Africa he had met both Churchill and Montgomery. He was able to see the most important people and convince them of his views. As a result Middle East Headquarters tended to leave him alone. This meant the SAS had a more or less free hand to develop as a strategic unit that operated inside enemy territory. However, with Stirling gone there was no one to protect the SAS's interests.

Another problem was manpower. In January 1943 the SAS had totalled nearly 700 men. This consisted of the 1st SAS Regiment (390 men), the French squadron (94 men), the Greek squadron (114), the Special Boat Squadron (55 men) and the Special Interrogation Group. The latter consisted of 12 Jewish immigrants to Palestine who could speak German. They were trained to infiltrate behind enemy lines dressed in German uniforms and driving captured vehicles to spread disorder behind the lines and gather intelligence.

After Stirling's capture the whole of the SAS was reorganised. In mid-March 1943, the Special Boat Squadron (SBS) was formed into a separate unit and put under the command of Major the Earl George Jellicoe. One of the early SAS recruits, Jellicoe took part in many of the early raids in North Africa. The SBS was shipped off to Athlit in Palestine to prepare for work in the eastern Mediterranean. The Greek and French squadrons were returned to their respective national formations fighting for the Allies.

The 1st SAS Regiment had also been reduced in numbers, as B Squadron had received a mauling from the Germans that had killed and captured many others. The regiment was therefore formed into three troops, and also renamed the Special Raiding Squadron (SRS). The man chosen to lead the 250-strong unit was 'Paddy' Mayne.

Mayne was a wild Irishman who was probably the bravest man to wear SAS uniform. On the battlefield he was absolutely fearless, and with his fiery temperament and natural leadership he was an inspiration to those around him, and therefore a logical choice to lead the SAS. However, he did not have David Stirling's influence or political skills. Mayne was a fighter, not an administrator. And he had a fearsome temper. During a period of leave in North Africa, he had taken a particular dislike to the many journalists in Cairo. He despised them for being deskbound warriors, who wrote about war but had never experienced it. He especially disliked the BBC correspondent Richard Dimbleby, and while he was drunk decided to hunt him down and beat him up. He searched the bars and hotels of Cairo but was arrested before he found his prey. He knocked out the Provost Marshal and six military policemen before being locked up for the night.

PREPARATIONS FOR SICILY

The SRS and SBS were grouped under the HQ Raiding Forces and were kept on a tight leash. A second SAS regiment – 2 SAS – had been formed by Stirling's brother Bill, but many of its men were very green.

Despite its inexperience, both 2 SAS and the SRS were committed to the Allied invasion of Sicily, codenamed Operation 'Husky'. Both Mayne and Bill Stirling were now lieutenant-colonels, but many SAS veterans were not happy with the way they were to be used in the invasion. Though parties from 2 SAS were to be dropped by parachute behind enemy lines, the SRS, under the command of British XIII Corps, was to be used as shock infantry. The men were to be landed by boat and attack targets near

'Paddy' Mayne

One of the leading figures in the SAS hall of fame, 'Paddy' Blair Mayne had been a rugby international and boxer before the war. Originally a member of No 11 Commando, Mayne was one of the first recruits to L Detachment. A fearless leader, at the end of 1941 Mayne, by now a captain, took part in the SAS's first operation. Though it was a failure, throughout 1942 he took part in many successful raids behind enemy lines, leading SAS units against enemy airfields at Tamit, Bagoush, Fuka and Sidi Haneish. He commanded 1 SAS through Sicily and Italy as a lieutenant-colonel, and then in northwest Europe in 1944-45. By the end of the war bravery in battle had won him an incredible four Distinguished Service Orders. He was killed in a car crash in Ireland in 1955 aged 40.

the beaches. If David Stirling was still in command he would no doubt have had something to say about this. But he was in a prisoner-of-war camp.

Mayne's men were transported to the Sicilian coast in the ship *Ulster Monarch*. Their target was an Italian shore battery on top of Capo Murro di Porco. Its 150mm guns could do great damage to the invasion fleet lying offshore, so they had to be knocked out.

The SRS landed on the night of 9 July 1943, and within hours had captured the guns and 500 Italian soldiers. Mayne simply walked around the battlefield, pistol in hand, issuing orders. Another enemy battery was discovered, and that too was captured. The SRS then marched into Syracuse to link up with the 5th Division. The *Ulster Monarch* then steamed into the harbour and the SAS soldiers re-boarded her. As far as they were concerned their part in the invasion was over. However, there was more work to be done.

THE CAPTURE OF AUGUSTA

Mayne and his officers were ordered to take the port of Augusta, which was held by enemy troops. On 12 July the SRS steamed into the harbour and stormed ashore. In the face of enemy fire the SAS soldiers raced onto the beach and into the town. There were several firefights with enemy snipers before the port was cleared. The enemy was not finished, however: there were still hostile troops in the hills surrounding the town.

Sporadic fighting continued into the evening. Then the SAS soldiers decided to have a party. A piano was found and dragged out into the street, along with dozens of bottles of wine. Then followed a great sing-song and drunken dancing, with enemy gunfire all around.

With the capture of Augusta the SRS's war in Sicily was over. The SAS men had fought well, and Mayne's leadership had been inspiring (he won a second DSO for his actions).

Bill Stirling's 2 SAS did less well on Sicily, taking part in two operations code-

Right: 2 SAS behind German lines in Italy in 1944. Note the Union Jack on the ground – a precaution against strafing by Allied aircraft.

named 'Chestnut' and 'Narcissus'. Operation 'Narcissus' involved 40 SAS soldiers of A Squadron led by Major Sandy Scratchley. The men were landed by landing craft on the southeast coast of the island with orders to seize a lighthouse, where the Allies suspected there might be an enemy artillery battery.

On 10 July 1943, the men scrambled ashore and then clambered up the rock face below the lighthouse. Tension was high as they edged closer to the top of the cliff – no one made a noise. When the first few men reached the top of the cliff they

Above: Soldiers of 2 SAS photographed after their bruising action at Termoli in October 1943. The officer is Major Sandy Scratchley.

rushed forward and stormed into the lighthouse, weapons at the ready. Other parties searched for the enemy guns. The search was futile. Both the lighthouse and the surrounding area were deserted.

A frustrated A Squadron made its way back down the cliff face and then boarded the waiting landing craft. At least there had been no deaths among the would-be mountaineers.

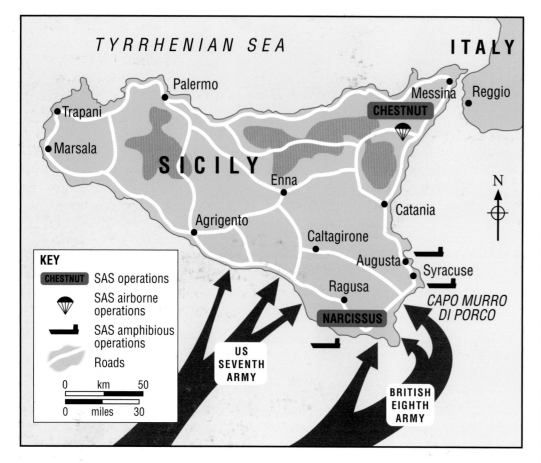

Left: Of all the SAS operations on Sicily in 1943, the airborne drop of Operation 'Chestnut' was the least successful.

gratulated themselves. There wasn't much time for back-slapping, though, the invasion of Italy was about to begin.

The British and American invasion of the Italian mainland in early September 1943 opened up a new theatre of operations for the SAS. Its first operation was conducted by the SRS and was codenamed 'Baytown'. Mayne's men were tasked with disrupting German communications in southern Italy. The high command hoped this would interfere with enemy attempts to stop the Allied advance (British and American forces had crossed the straits of Messina from Sicily on 3 September 1943).

The first objective for the SRS was the port of Bagnara. Mayne's men seized the port on 3 September, though not before the Royal Navy had dropped them in the wrong place. Meeting only light resistance, the soldiers quickly took Bagnara itself. However, they then came under heavy mortar and machine gun fire from the surrounding hills. The SRS lost five killed and 17 wounded before linking up with Allied troops advancing from Reggio. It was a foretaste of things to come. With a somewhat bloody nose, Mayne's troops were pulled back to Sicily for a much-needed rest.

OPERATION 'SPEEDWELL'

Bill Stirling's 2 SAS, meanwhile, was having a much better time of it. After all the unit's five squadrons took part in the capture of Taranto (which should have been allotted to regular troops), Stirling's regiment undertook Operation 'Speedwell'. This was a classic SAS-type operation, and showed what small parties could do if inserted deep behind enemy lines and left to operate for long periods.

Two seven-man parties were dropped by parachute on the night of 7 September into the Genoa/Spezia area of northeast Italy with orders to destroy the railway lines that were taking enemy reinforcements to the front farther south. After landing the two groups split up into smaller units and began hitting targets.

Farther north, other members of 2 SAS were also landing on Sicily. Operation 'Chestnut' involved two teams being dropped by parachute in the north of the island to cut enemy communications.

'Pink' party, led by Captain Pinckney, was ordered to sever roads and telephone lines on the northeast coast of the island. In addition, the SAS soldiers were told to destroy the Catania-Messina railway line. 'Brig' party, led by Captain Bridgeman-Evans, was to attack enemy convoys and an enemy headquarters near Enna.

Both parties were dropped on the night of 12 July, and both got into trouble straight away. First, the containers packed with the radios and equipment for 'Pink' party were smashed to pieces on landing. This wrecked the radios and other gear. In addition, it was very windy and the men themselves were scattered all over the Sicilian countryside. For most of those dropped it was their first operational jump, and they had trouble finding their comrades.

'Brig' party fared even worse. The SAS men were dropped too near enemy outposts, and had to fight their way out of trouble as soon as they had landed. Several

were captured, including Bridgeman-Evans, but he escaped almost immediately. Far from destroying enemy communications, the SAS soldiers were like fugitives fleeing from their pursuers.

As Captain Pinckney struggled to gather his men, he saw that he would have to abandon the mission. A reinforcement drop scheduled for the night of 13 July failed to materialise because the SAS soldiers on the ground could not contact the pilots of the transport planes.

The lessons were learned for future missions. The reasons for the failure of 'Narcissus' and 'Chestnut' are not hard to find: there were no rehearsals, the men were inexperienced and the plans had been changed several times, confusing everyone concerned.

Despite these setbacks, overall the SAS had performed well in Sicily, especially Mayne's SRS. As well as his medal mentioned above, several of his men got gallantry awards. Harry Poat and Johnny Wiseman won Military Crosses and Sergeant Sillito and six other men won Military Medals.

Bill Stirling intensified training for 2 SAS, while 'Paddy' Mayne's veterans con-

Very soon railway lines were cut and enemy trains derailed.

October 1943 witnessed a number of SAS operations, but again the results were mixed. Bill Stirling was determined to keep the SAS operating along the lines his brother David had envisaged: operating deep inside enemy territory. The high command, however, did not have the same enthusiasm for what they regarded as a bunch of glorified bandits roaming around Italy unchecked.

THE FAILURE OF 'JONQUIL'

An example of the type of muddled thinking that surrounded how the SAS should be used was Operation 'Jonquil' at the beginning of October 1943. B Squadron, 2 SAS, was detailed to land by sea between Ancona and Pescara on Italy's Adriatic coast to act as guides for the large numbers of Allied prisoners of war (POWs) who had been released as a result of Italy's surrender.

A number of small fishing vessels were assembled for the operation and were landed at Termoli. However, a German counterattack meant they had to be moved back to Bari. Meanwhile, the POWs started to gather on he beaches to be evacuated. When the SAS finally managed to get to the beaches, the POWs had moved on. The mission was a complete disaster, made worse by the fact that 2 SAS had not been allowed to take part in the planning of it.

After its rest in Sicily, the SRS, along with two Commandos and support units, was ordered to take Termoli as a way of aiding the Eighth Army's attempt to breach the Termoli Line. The amphibious assault took place on 3 October, and at first things went well. The town was soon cleared and around midday forward detachments of the Lancashire Fusiliers and 2 SAS arrived. It all seemed too good to be true – it was. On 5 October the Germans counterattacked in force, driving in the Allied units. A grim battle of attrition began, in which the SRS suffered many casualties.

The arrival of a detachment of Royal Irish Rangers and some Canadian Sherman tanks saved the day and pushed the Germans back, but the men of the

SRS had been badly shaken. Termoli was to be their last action in Italy: they were sent back to Britain to prepare for the forthcoming Allied invasion of France. Only Bill Stirling's 2 SAS remained to carry on the fight.

Farther up the coast, after the SRS had been mauled at Termoli, four parties from 2 SAS were put ashore by torpedo boat to cut the railway line between Ancona and Pescara. Under the codenames 'Candytuft' and 'Saxifrage', the men were landed on 27 October. The weather was abysmal

Above: During the SAS campaign in Italy (1943-45), the railway line between Ancona and Pescara was cut on many occasions.

– it rained continuously – but under the able leadership of Major Roy Farran the railway line was cut in a number of places and the coast road mined.

Greater successes would come for 2 SAS in Italy during the next 18 months as small parties operated behind enemy lines. And Italy proved that the SAS could operate in any theatre of war.

Northwest Europe

The SAS campaign in France, the Low Countries and Germany in 1944-45 was one of the most spectacular periods in the Regiment's history. Dozens of operations were carried out behind enemy lines, causing thousands of enemy casualties and widespread disruption.

By January 1944, the SRS had reverted back to being 1 SAS and, together with 2 SAS, was placed under command of 1st Airborne Division to return to the UK to prepare for the invasion of France. In March they were joined by two French Parachute Regiments, 2 RCP and 3 RCP, who became 3 SAS and 4 SAS respectively, plus an independent Belgian Para-Commando Squadron, which later became 5 SAS. The last part of the jigsaw was the clandestine intelligence and signals unit known as Phantom Squadron, which joined what was now the Special Air Service Brigade as F Squadron, GHQ Liaison Regiment.

Now 2000 men strong, the SAS Brigade was retrained for operations in France in support of the forthcoming D-Day invasion. At this stage William Stirling resigned his command as he believed that the SAS was no longer being used in its proper role. Even the by now traditional beige SAS beret was ordered to be discarded in favour of the maroon of airborne forces, but many old troopers and officers ignored the directive, including 'Paddy' Mayne. It was also directed that 'airborne' wings be worn on the right shoulder, but those men who had earned the privilege of wearing SAS 'combat' wings on the left breast after three operational jumps in the early desert campaign, continued to wear them.

Eventually, after much procrastination by the high command, which did not really know how to employ such an unconventional unit, a minor role was found for the SAS, though half of the brigade was held back as a conventional parachute-trained reserve. Prior to D-Day only a few SAS troops were individually deployed in France, but on and just after D-Day this changed.

SAS operations in France fell into two broad categories. On the one hand, SAS groups provided small-scale tactical support to General Bernard Montgomery's 21st Army Group. This entailed cutting enemy lines of communication and providing intelligence about the movement and locations of German forces. In addition, SAS teams immediately after the D-Day landings (6 June 1944) were ordered to do everything they could to stop German reinforcements reaching the beachhead. The second category of operations was the dropping of SAS teams deep behind enemy lines to establish bases, link up with the Resistance and disrupt enemy movements.

SAS soldiers were called upon to work with the Resistance and Special Operations Executive (SOE) people, who were already on the ground gathering information. There were to be problems with both organisations. Operations in France carried out by the SAS and SOE were supposed to be coordinated, but the latter tended to regard the SAS soldiers as being under its command, and also jealously guarded its missions. Nevertheless, after several months of comparative inactivity the SAS was glad to be back in business.

THE *MAQUIS*

The problems that the SAS had were nothing compared to those of working with the French Resistance. The latter were called *Maquis*, after a Corsican word meaning 'bush'. Following D-Day the SAS worked closely with the *Maquis*. But the latter were split between the supporters of General de Gaulle's Free French and the communists. As a result, many groups hoarded weapons for use against each other after the war. The *Maquis* were motivated, and had excellent local knowledge, which was put to good use by SAS teams planning raids, but their security was poor and their ranks contained traitors. The SAS soon learned that it was better to operate separately.

Left: A converted RAF bomber drops a Willys Jeep to a waiting SAS team on the ground in central France in August 1944.

Left: SAS Jeeps in northwest Europe in 1945. Note the armour plate shields and the bullet-proof glass to protect crew members.

In the first two weeks after D-Day, the entire A Squadron of 1 SAS was parachuted into hilly country around Dijon to blow up railway lines and organise the *Maquis* into raiding parties. Codenamed 'Houndsworth', this operation was to last two months and would tie down hundreds of German troops who might otherwise have been committed against the Allied advance out of Normandy. In addition to nearly 150 troopers, the squadron also had nine armed and armoured Jeeps and two anti-tank guns. The kill tally for the operation was six re-supply trains derailed, 70 trucks destroyed, over 20 rail lines cut and in excess of 200 German soldiers killed or seriously wounded.

THE FRENCH SAS REGIMENTS

Meanwhile, in Brittany 160 men from 4 (French) SAS parachuted in on D-Day under the codename 'Dingson' to set up a major operating base and to help organise the local *Maquis* (three battalions were eventually equipped). The following day three 18-man patrols from the same regiment were dropped to cut rail lines serving the port of St Malo and the German reserves stationed in that area. Having successfully completed their tasks, the three patrols then joined the rest of the regiment at the main operating base.

To the south, also on D-Day, two officers from B Squadron of 1 SAS dropped near Vienna to contact the local *Maquis*. Five days later, four patrols from the same squadron were dropped in the area to attack specific targets before linking up with the *Maquis*. The strategic railway line into Poitiers was cut in two places and a train was derailed on the Saumur to Bordeaux line, but the most successful part of the mission was the discovery of fuel trains in sidings at Chatellerault. RAF ground-attack aircraft were called in by radio and the trains destroyed. The fuel they carried had been meant for a panzer division heading for Normandy, and the loss of this fuel severely delayed deployment of those tanks.

Jeeps were parachuted in to give B Squadron a limited degree of mobility, but by the beginning of July 1944 their base had been compromised. The Germans surrounded the area and attacked in force, killing some troopers, though 17 escaped. However, 33 members of the SAS were captured alive, and after torture and interrogation by the Gestapo all were executed. During the desert campaign, Hitler had decreed that any members of the SAS should be executed as they posed such a danger, but Rommel and his officers had generally disregarded this so-called Commando Order. In France, however, the German Army had to turn over all prisoners to the Gestapo, who showed no mercy to the SAS.

From D-Day onwards, the Allied campaign in northwestern Europe steamrollered its way through France and the

Anders Lassen

Anders Lassen was a Danish member of the SAS and the Special Boat Squadron (SBS) in World War II, and a soldier of quite extraordinary bravery. Originally in the Danish Navy, he had joined the British Army in 1940 and then volunteered for the Commandos. He was assigned to the Small Scale Raiding Force, and in May 1943 transferred to the Middle East as a member of D Squadron, 1 SAS, which then became part of the SBS. He quickly gained a reputation for being a fighter, and took part in many SBS operations in the Aegean in 1943-44. In April 1945, Major Lassen was fighting around Lake Comacchio in northern Italy. He single-handedly took on three German pillboxes, and succeeded in knocking two of them out before he was cut down. He then covered the withdrawal of his men before dying. He was 25 years old. For his courage he was posthumously awarded the Victoria Cross.

UNITED KINGDOM

HOLLAND

BELGIUM

GERMANY

LUXEMBOURG

FRANCE

SPAIN

LONDON

Southampton Portsmouth

Calais
Boulogne
Abbeville
Dieppe

Cherbourg

St Malo
St Brieuc
Brest

Pontivy

Lorient

St Nazaire

Nantes

La Rochelle

Rochefort

Angoulême

Bordeaux

Mayenne

Angers

Caen

Rouen

Le Mans

Blois

Vierzon

Châteauroux

Limoges

Aurillac

Cahors

Montauban

Toulouse

Arras

Amiens

St Quentin

Rheims

Orléans

Nevers

Montluçon

Clermont-Ferrand

Montpellier

BRUSSELS Namur
Liège
Mons

Verdun

Châlons-sur-Marne

St Dizier

Troyes

Auxerre

Dijon

Vesoul

Lyons

Avignon

Nîmes

Marseilles

Meuse
Somme
Seine
Aisne
Marne
Loire
Rhône

PARIS

GOBBO
FABIAN
CALIBAN
BERGBANG
BRUTUS
NOAH
WOLSEY
BENSON
DEFOE
TRUEFORM
TITANIC
GAFF
DERRY
SAMWEST
COONEY
GROG
DINGSON
COONEY
DUNHILL
HAFT
BUNYAN
CHAUCER
SHAKESPEARE
RUPERT
GAIN
HARDY
LOYTON
KIPLING
WALLACE
ABEL
SPENSER
HAGGARD
HOUNDSWORTH
NEWTON
BARKER
HARROD
BULBASKET
JOCKWORTH
MOSES
SAMSON
SNELGROVE
MARSHALL
DICKENS

N

KEY

TITANIC	1 SAS
DEFOE	2 SAS
DICKENS	3 SAS (3 French Para Battalion)
GROG	4 SAS (4 French Para Battalion)
BENSON	5 SAS (Belgian Independent Para Co)
WOLSEY	Phanton Signals Section

0   km   100
0   miles   60

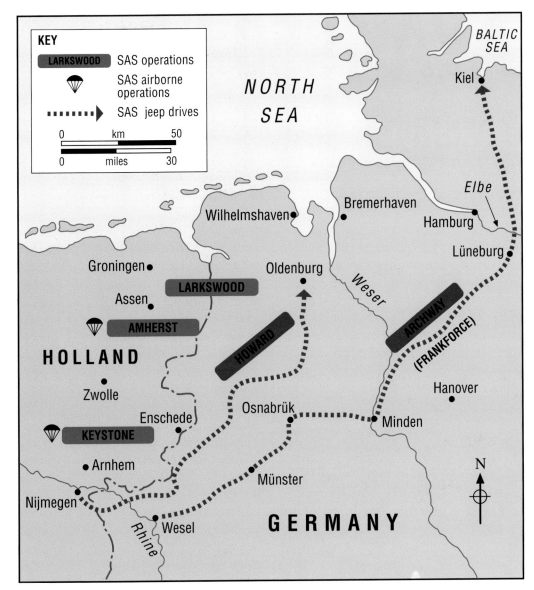

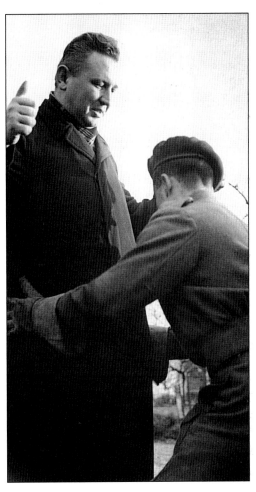

Above: An SAS soldier searches a German civilian after the war's end during the Regiment's attempts to find those responsible for the murder of its men during the conflict.

Above: SAS Jeep operations in Germany in 1945 were large-scale affairs. 'Archway', for example, involved 75 vehicles.

Low Countries, until the Allies found themselves knocking on Germany's front door. Throughout the advance, the SAS was always in the vanguard, organising resistance behind the German front lines and attacking lines of communication.

Crossing into Germany in the early months of 1945, the SAS undertook a number of reconnaissance operations. Two squadrons from 1 and 2 SAS took part in a reconnaissance mission east of the River Rhine at Wesel codenamed Operation 'Archway'. The Belgians of 5 SAS mounted Operation 'Larkswood',

Left: Prior to D-Day the SAS Brigade numbered 2500 men, enough to mount many operations in France and the Low Countries.

which entailed gathering intelligence for the advancing Canadian 4th Armoured Division as it moved into northwest Germany. The Belgians, together with 1 SAS, took part in the Canadian assault on Wilhelmshaven. 1 SAS had a hard time of it during its approach, its 40 Jeeps being constantly ambushed by German parties in a series of hit-and-run actions. Though the SAS men inflicted some damage on the enemy, they too had received casualties and were rather discomfited.

In general SAS operations in the final moths of the war in Europe were ill-conceived. SAS teams were restricted mainly to the reconnaissance duties for regular formations. As such, they operated near or just beyond the front line, and were subjected to ambushes. This attritional type of warfare was not the role David Stirling had envisaged for his unit, but he was a prisoner and the war was drawing to a

close. In fairness, as German-occupied territory shrank, there was physically not the room for SAS parties to roam far behind the lines.

Another problem was the population. In France and the Low Countries SAS teams had found the locals to be largely friendly and sympathetic to their cause. In Germany this was not the case, and the general hostility of the population served to aggravate the SAS's problems.

Despite all the problems, by the spring of 1945 the SAS had fulfiled its role and the war in Europe was virtually over. All SAS units were back in Britain by the end of May 1945. The SAS Brigade was officially disbanded in October 1945, though in 1947 a Territorial Army SAS Regiment was formed. For all intents and purposes, however, the regular Special Air Service was just another of those wartime units which had been consigned to history.

MALAYA 1950-60

The Malayan Scouts

The Malayan 'Emergency', which began in June 1948, was to result in the reformation of the Special Air Service and the expansion of its wartime role. It was a far cry from the deserts of North Africa and northwest Europe, but it was a challenge the Regiment rose to.

For much of World War II, the British colonies on the Malay peninsula were occupied by Japan. In an effort to dislodge the Japanese invaders, Britain had armed and supported the Malayan People's Anti-Japanese Army (MPAJA), the military wing of the mainly Chinese Malayan Communist Party, but in the immediate post-war years this policy backfired disas-

trously. The MPAJA hid its weapons in secret caches, later to be unearthed and used against the British.

After the war, most of the educated populace of Malaya wanted independence from Britain, but the two main ethnic groups had different ideas about how their country should proceed. Those of Malay stock, some 49 per cent of the population, plus the

minority Indian community, tended to favour the Malaysian Federation of States route advocated in 1948 by the British. The other 40 per cent, however, who were of mainly Chinese stock, were totally opposed to the idea of any Federation which could be dominated by the majority Malays, many of them preferring the Chinese Communist ideology instead.

In June 1948 the Malayan Races Liberation Army (MRLA), which was essentially the post-war military wing of the Malayan Communist Party (MCP), commenced a violent campaign to try to oust the British.

The first targets of the MRLA were British rubber planters and their families living in relatively isolated areas. The campaign started on 16 June with the murder of three rubber estate managers in the Sungei Siput area in the northern Perak province, which bordered Siam (modern-day Thailand). That evening a State of Emergency was declared in the district, and within two days this was extended to cover the entire country. What became known as the Malayan 'Emergency' was to last 12 years in all, and would lead to the rebirth of the regular SAS.

The guerrillas, or communist terrorists (CTs), in Malaya were led by their World War II commander Chin Peng, who had been awarded the OBE by Britain in the World War II Victory Honours List for the part he played in the defeat of Japan. Using tried and tested procedures which had helped in the downfall of the Japanese, Chin Peng's men operated from

Left: In fencing mask with an air rifle, a Malayan Scouts recruit practises jungle warfare techniques at Johore in mid-1950.

bases at the edge of the dense jungle, which covered more than two-thirds of the peninsula. From these hidden bases, they were at first able to operate unchallenged, striking fear amongst both the British rubber planters and the Malays who worked for them.

Though only 7-8000 strong, even at the height of the campaign, the CTs were able to rely on the support of more than half a million Chinese-race squatters, who provided the bulk of the CTs' recruits and food. These largely uneducated Chinese had been displaced from the towns by the Japanese during the war, and had taken to squatting in small communal settlements on low-quality agricultural land reclaimed from the jungle, or on the edges of established Malay villages. To these squatters, the Chinese brand of communism represented their only real hope for a prosperous future.

MIKE CALVERT'S PROPOSALS

Over the next two years, the CTs murdered nearly 500 policemen and soldiers plus more than 850 civilians, for the loss of about 1100 of their own. Everything was not going the terrorists' way, though, as the Malayan Police Force and the British Army had also captured 1000 guerrillas. That said, by no means were the British resolving the situation. So, in 1950, a former wartime SAS brigadier, Mike Calvert, was asked to analyse the situation and write a report on all aspects of the war and how it could be won.

'Mad Mike' Calvert, had fought with Orde Wingate's legendary Chindits, who had campaigned deep behind enemy lines against the Japanese in Burma, so he was eminently qualified to find a solution to the problem. After several months of extensive research, much of it spent actually in the jungle assessing the current situation, he submitted detailed proposals to the Commander-in-Chief Far East Land Forces, General Sir John Harding.

Calvert came to two main conclusions. He recommended, firstly, that vulnerable natives should be moved into protected villages to keep them out of the clutches of the CTs, who had been forcing many to provide food and shelter; and, secondly, that a specialist force of

'Mad Mike' Calvert

Mike Calvert is well known for his exploits during the Malayan Crisis. However, he first joined the SAS in World War II after a series of adventures in the Far East. He joined the Royal Engineers in 1933, and when war broke out six years later was in Military Intelligence Research. He helped to organise guerrilla units to fight in the event of a German invasion. He was then posted to Burma, and there met Orde Wingate. Together they raised the Chindits, troops trained to fight behind Japanese lines. By 1944 he commanded the Chindits' 77th Indian Infantry Brigade and had won the DSO and US Silver Star. He returned to Europe, and was given command of the SAS Brigade in March 1945. His ideas on how to combat the Communist Terrorists in Malaya, particularly winning 'hearts and minds', led to the formation of the Malayan Scouts in 1950, and its success was to lead to the reformation of 22 SAS in 1952.

jungle fighters should be raised to take the war to the communists on their own ground. The General Staff quickly accepted both proposals, which formed the basis of the so-called 'Briggs Plan' (Lieutenant-General Sir Harold Briggs was the Director of Operations), and 'Mad Mike' himself was tasked with raising the specialised jungle unit.

Known initially as the Malayan Scouts, this new unit was free to poach suitable recruits from all Army units stationed in the Far East. Individuals with jungle experience were actively sought. A few

Below: A group of Malayan Scouts take a breather while on operation. All officers for the unit were selected by Calvert personally.

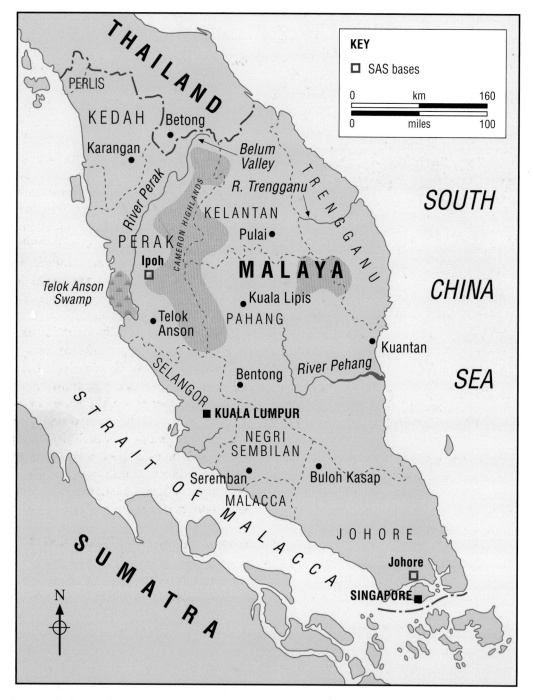

KEY

☐ SAS bases

0   km   160

0   miles   100

Left: The SAS launched many operations in the Cameron Highlands and the Belum Valley during its jungle war in Malaya.

SAS veterans were recruited. In addition, 21 SAS (Artists), a Territorial Army unit which was preparing some of its number for service in Korea, would also later provide men, and the Rhodesians offered a company-sized unit of volunteers.

The prime candidates, however, were former members of Force 136 and men from Ferret Force. The men of Force 136 had trained and led units of the MPAJA during World War II, so they were able to bring a wealth of knowledge of their former allies' tactics. Ferret Force, on the other hand, was a highly skilled band of volunteer British, Gurkha or Malay soldiers and some policemen, who acted as scouts for the regular infantry battalions chasing the CTs. All of these men were expert at operating and fighting in the oppressive conditions of the jungle.

THE SCOUTS' FIRST ACTIONS

On formation, the Malayan Scouts had an operational strength of just 100 men. Initial training took place at the Jungle Warfare School in the southern province of Johore, but almost immediately they were deployed nearly 500km (310 miles) northwest to Perak province to act as forward air controllers for RAF bombing raids and to ambush fleeing CTs. Due to their reputation for indiscipline and their lack of cohesive training prior to operational deployment, many of the original members of what was known as A Squadron would eventually find themselves 'returned to unit'. However, their initial successes proved Calvert's basic idea to be sound.

Up in Perak province, to the west of the Cameron Highlands, 12-man patrols of Scouts and Malay Police, accompanied by Chinese-speaking liaison officers, penetrated deep into the jungle to establish communication bases. From these bases, four-man teams could cover large areas of jungle and lay ambushes along CT

Left: A group of Scouts in the Ipoh area in November 1950. One patrol spent 103 days in the jungle searching for enemy units.

Above: Malayan Scouts in the Cameron Highlands. In this area the Scouts set up bases from where patrols hunted the enemy.

approach and re-supply routes. One patrol during this phase of the war lasted a record-breaking 103 days.

In addition to staking a claim to areas of previously hostile jungle, the Scouts also established contact with the local tribespeople. For many of them this was their first close encounter with Europeans, but rather than bring disease, as often happens when natives first meet Westerners, the British brought medicines. Simple administrations such as penicillin helped clear up eye infections and skin disorders, which affected many of the natives. Slowly and patiently, the soldiers built up trusting relationships in the process that was to become known as 'winning hearts and minds'.

EXPANSION OF THE SCOUTS

In due course a second squadron of Malayan Scouts was formed, primarily from the TA and reserve volunteers from 21 SAS. Unlike A Squadron, the men of the new B Squadron were more traditional in their approach to soldiering.

Many were veterans of the European SAS campaign and had trained together in a conventional manner for some time, so they were much more disciplined. They were also able to train in Johore province for their new role for a longer period of time than their predecessors, and as a consequence unit discipline was better.

In March 1951, a third squadron joined the men of A and B Squadrons at their base camp at Dusun Tua. Raised in Rhodesia as the Far East Volunteer Unit, for what most thought would be United Nations service in Korea, the new squadron had an established complement of 100 men. All but 10 of the volunteers were completely new to military service, but they were the cream of Rhodesia's youth, and for every successful applicant at least 10 more had been rejected.

Soon after they arrived at their jungle camp, the keen young Rhodesians met some of the men of A Squadron returning from a long operational jungle patrol. With their long hair, beards, threadbare clothing and shredded canvas jungle boots, the Scouts looked more like a bunch of tramps than élite fighting men, but appearances can be deceptive. Round his neck, every member of the returning

patrol sported a sweat stained kerchief of yellow parachute silk. When one of the new boys asked if this was a typical British dress tradition, the curt rebuke shocked him. Allegedly the reply was, 'My arse! It's to stop us shooting each other.' In the close confines of jungle warfare, the man who shoots first lives – the wearing of a yellow neck scarf instantly identified friend from foe. Rough and ready the men of A Squadron may have been, and on occasion the squadron had a reputation for being a bit of an undisciplined rabble, but at that time they were probably the best Caucasian jungle soldiers in service anywhere. To this day, the skills learned on these long jungle patrols are taught to every SAS soldier.

By the second half of 1951, the Malayan Scouts (SAS), as the formation was now formally known, had been expanded to three full squadrons and a battalion headquarters. Their main task at this time was not the deep penetration raids into the jungle to which they were best suited. Instead, they were used to assist the police in patrolling the edges of the jungle and to defend the new forts being built to protect the villagers.

SLOANE TAKES OVER FROM CALVERT

Around this time, Calvert was invalided back to the UK to recover from malaria, dysentery and other unpleasantnesses he had picked up during several years of jungle and hostile-territory soldiering. Command was passed to Lieutenant-Colonel John Sloane, nicknamed 'Tod' by the SAS, who came from a traditional infantry background and who had served in Korea. He had no prior experience of special operations, but was widely considered to be a superb tactical officer.

The new commanding officer, who had previously been second-in-command of the much respected Argyll and Sutherland Highlanders, detested indiscipline and soon set about reorganising attitudes. His appointment came like a breath of fresh air to most of his command, with the exception of the wild men of A Squadron. One result of his appointment was that many good officers and men who had put their name on the transfer list decided to stay with the SAS.

22 SAS is Formed

In 1952, 22 SAS was formed. During the next eight years the Regiment perfected its jungle warfare skills and, perhaps more importantly, developed its 'hearts and minds' ideas. In this way SAS soldiers became experts at counter-insurgency warfare.

Under Lieutenant-Colonel Sloane's leadership the wheat was sorted from the chaff, and a period of retraining and reorganisation was begun. By the end of 1951 the Malayan Scouts title had been dropped, and the command was renamed 22 Regiment, Special Air Service, or just plain 22 SAS. The regimental base was now more centrally located at Sungei Besi near Kuala Lumpur, on the western side of the peninsula.

In February 1952, the SAS squadrons returned to jungle operations with a vengeance. One of their first major missions was an airborne and overland operation into a virtually inaccessible valley near the Thai border to clear it of communists. Despite their initial opposition, the unarmed Malay tribesmen in the valley had been coerced into supplying the CTs with food and shelter, and now a 100-strong group of Chinese terrorists controlled the area.

One squadron of nearly 60 SAS troopers, including some Rhodesians, parachuted into the Belum Valley to protect the locals and block off a CT escape route. Although the drop zone was theoretically in a small clearing, all but four of the troopers actually landed in the branches of trees some 30m (98ft) high, but miraculously there were no casualties. Meanwhile, a combined force of two more SAS squadrons, Gurkhas, Royal Marines and Malay Police, hacked their way cross-country to join them. In due course the CTs were put to flight from the valley, and at long last the SAS was participating in the type of operation which Calvert had originally envisaged.

NEW JUNGLE TACTICS

Although this particular operation in the Belum Valley was not spectacularly successful, and no large numbers of CTs were killed or captured, it did show that the basic procedures and tactics were sound. However, the fact that so many men had become caught up in the trees did cause some concern, and so it was decided that a method of self-rescue had to be developed. After much considera-

tion, the simple 'solution' to the problem was to issue each man with a 50m (164ft) length of knotted rope and a supply of pain-killers. The rope would be carried coiled on the chest above the reserve parachute, and could be tied to a tree branch and then used to descend the tree. To prove the concept, the second-in-command, Major Freddie Templar, plus two other officers would each make at least two drops onto the jungle canopy.

On the chosen day, Major Templar exited the Dakota transport aircraft first and landed cleanly in the trees. He was followed out by Major Peter Walls, who was later to become Rhodesia's top soldier, but he stumbled in the doorway after hitting his head. Behind him Lieutenant Johnny Cooper, who had been one of David Stirling's original L Detachment volunteers and the driver of the 'Blitz Buggy', gave him a helping push, only to have his own arm caught up in the static line as Walls fell out the door. Cooper's upper left arm was broken in three places and his helmet was ripped off his head, but incredibly he made a safe if painful landing in the tree tops. His problems were far from over, though, as he was trapped 60m (200ft) up in the air with only one usable arm. Fortunately Roger Levett, his troop sergeant, quickly located him and the medical officer scaled the tree twice to effect a rescue. For his bravery Freddie Brunton, the MO, was awarded the MBE. A few months later, almost fully recovered, Cooper was promoted to captain and returned to 22 SAS as motor transport officer.

In spite of Cooper's accident, the technique known as 'tree jumping' had been proven for operational use. The Regiment was now able to insert patrols as and

Left: Members of 22 SAS and regular British Army personnel before Operation 'Helsby' in the Belum Valley in February 1952.

where required to cut off fleeing CTs or to assist police and infantry under attack.

In addition to military operations against the terrorists, the British had also been slowly converting the natives away from communism. They started by issuing identity cards to everyone over the age of 12, and then used the Emergency Powers to restrict food distribution and other aid to card holders only. Safe settlements, protected primarily by the local police and backed up by company-sized infantry units, were then set up to give the squatter population somewhere decent to live. In this way the communists, who tended to take rather than give, were alienated and access to food and accommodation was denied them.

At first small SAS patrols were used to provide security to the police posts in the safe settlements, but as the situation slowly normalised the troopers were transferred to the deep penetration duties to which they were best suited. The tribespeople who were the original occupants of the Malay peninsula had been pushed farther inland by successive waves of invaders and settlers. These tribespeople were now being picked on by the CTs, who were desperate for food. So the SAS was dispatched deep into the jungle both to gain their trust and to protect them.

EARLY FOUR-MAN PATROLS

By March 1953 the 10 Sikorsky helicopters of 848 Naval Air Squadron were being used to deliver and re-supply patrols deep in the jungle. Small troops of SAS personnel, usually numbering 12-16 men, were flown deep into the interior by helicopter to establish contact with the mainly nomadic Sakai and Semam tribes. Each SAS troop was sub-divided into four teams of three or four men, who lived in primitive conditions alongside the tribespeople for up to three months at a time. One man in each team was a trained medic, and the first aid which he administered helped cement the bond between soldiers and natives. The troopers also helped to build protected settlements and lay on fresh water to improve the quality of life. Even landing strips were carved out of the jungle to allow aid to be delivered in bulk and produce to be air-

lifted to market. Living among these primitive tribespeople, some of whom had been cannibals only a few years before, was no easy feat for white Europeans, but the SAS troopers adapted as best as they could. Slowly, the 'hearts and minds' campaign turned the proud tribes into staunch allies.

Above: Operation 'Termite' in July 1954. Three SAS squadrons were dropped into Perak to wrest control of the area from the guerrillas.

The Rhodesians of C Squadron were deployed to Malaya for a tour of duty which lasted for nigh on two years, but eventually their government called them

'Tree Jumping'

This was an SAS parachute technique used by the Regiment in Malaya. Because Communist Terrorist (CT) camps were often located deep in the jungle, reaching them on foot was time-consuming. However, because the guerrillas had to grow their own food, and therefore had to clear patches of the jungle nearby, these camps could be easily spotted from the air. Two members of the SAS, Johnny Cooper and Alistair MacGregor, believed men could be dropped by parachute onto the jungle canopy, from where they

could lower themselves to the floor by ropes. The first operational jump took place in February 1954. The 54 men who were dropped suffered few casualties, and the technique was judged a success. However, subsequent operations revealed 'tree jumping' to be fraught with hazards. During Operation 'Sword' in January 1954, for example, three SAS soldiers died after smashing into trees. 'Tree jumping' was abandoned soon after.

Left: The rivers that cut through the Malay jungle provided a more speedy means of travel than on foot, though more dangerous.

home. To replace them, a new squadron commanded by Johnny Cooper was hurriedly recruited from available camp personnel, including clerks and drivers, plus an intake of new recruits. In his memoirs, Cooper refers to his new command as C Squadron, though other sources contradict this. Only 80 strong, including just 15 experienced men, the new squadron was tasked with penetrating the Pahang mountains and establishing a fortified settlement to protect the local tribes.

THE ESTABLISHMENT OF FORT BROOKE

In October 1953 Johnny Cooper led his men into virgin jungle at the start of what was to become a 122-day operational patrol. As well as clearing an area of jungle to build what became Fort Brooke, alongside the Sungei Brok River, they also built a helicopter landing ground and

conducted offensive patrols against the CTs. On one such patrol, Trooper Wilkins and Corporal Bancroft were killed in an ambush, but the other troopers drove off their attackers with loss using a typical SAS-style counterattack.

When the men from the hurriedly cobbled together new squadron eventually emerged from the jungle at the beginning of February 1954, they were down to half their original strength. Diseases such as leptospirosis caught from rats, jungle fevers and extreme fatigue had taken their toll on nearly 40 men, who had to be helicoptered back to civilisation, but the ad hoc formation had successfully completed its task. Much to the Regiment's embarrassment, Cooper's men became Fleet Street heroes.

To replace the Rhodesians and bring 22 SAS back up to strength, a New

Zealand SAS Squadron was deployed, but they did not inherit the C Squadron designation. After the Malayan 'Emergency', this title was placed in suspended animation as a mark of respect to the Rhodesians, who had been held in such high esteem despite their relatively short service with the Regiment. To this day a C Squadron has never been resurrected by the Regiment in honour of their old comrades. Formed in 1954 as part of the Commonwealth Strategic Reserve, the New Zealand SAS (NZSAS) only selected men of high physical and mental stamina. In mid-1955 a company-sized independent squadron was formed specifically for service in Malaya and after six months specialist and jungle training, it was deployed operationally in the border provinces of Perak and Kelantan.

THE NEW ZEALAND SAS

The well-trained and adaptable Kiwis quickly blended in with the personnel of the established squadrons, who appreciated the new skills and methods which they brought with them. Among their ranks were a fair number of Maoris, who had been experienced hunters and trackers before joining the army, and their skills were much in demand. The Maoris also soon established a close empathy with the interior tribes.

The New Zealand squadron's training had been deliberately concentrated on the specialist skills required for long-range interdiction by small, tight-knit patrols. During their two-year tour, they carried out many 13-week search-and-destroy missions in the remotest of areas, and achieved a high success rate. It was their last operation in the southwest, however, which gained them the most fame.

For weeks they trailed a group of over 30 CTs around the hilly province of Negri Sembilan, eventually killing or capturing almost the whole band. The final patrol tally was eight dead terrorists, two wounded and 19 captured. By the end of their 24-month operational tour, the NZSAS Squadron had lost only two

Right: Dropping supplies to SAS patrols on the ground. RAF Valettas and Beverleys were invaluable for sustaining patrols.

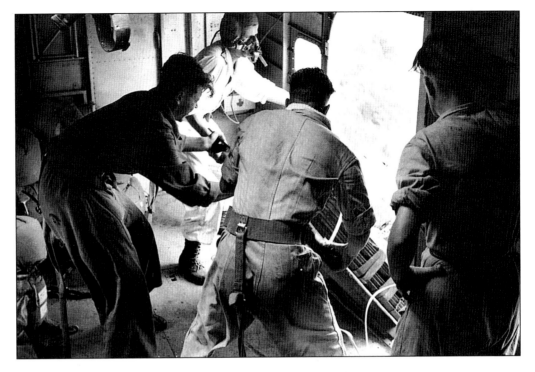

Right: Dropping supplies to SAS patrols on the ground. RAF Valettas and Beverleys were invaluable for sustaining patrols.

of its men. On return to New Zealand the squadron was disbanded, but was to be reactivated in 1959, though it never returned to Malaya.

Another British squadron was formed in 1955 from members of the Parachute Regiment. Known rather unimaginatively as the Parachute Regiment Squadron, these men formed a fully cohesive fighting unit who, like the Kiwis, required jungle training on arrival in Malaya, but had the advantage of being already fully parachute trained.

SAS JUNGLE WEAPONS IN MALAYA

The effective combat strength of 22 SAS was now almost 600 officers and men. To the conventional troops whom the Regiment supported, however, the difference between officers and men was sometimes difficult to ascertain. On operations, for example, SAS men never used soap or toothpaste as the smell carried for miles, but their weapons were kept spotless. In his memoirs, D Squadron veteran Lofty Large describes how rifles were stripped and cleaned thoroughly every night. 'All the woodwork was taken off, cleaned and oiled with linseed oil. The weapons were never more than an arm's length from us until they were handed back to the armoury after an operation.'

Shotguns and Patchet carbines were the favoured weapons for jungle fighting, where engagements often happened at point-blank range. Frequently patrols spent weeks on end searching the jungle without finding any trace of their quarry, but when they did strike lucky the encounter was usually over in seconds. The man who fired first invariably lived, so hip shooting was actively practised. When Sergeant Bob Turnbull finally caught up with the notorious CT leader Ah Tuck, whom he had been diligently tracking, they came face to face at only 20m (66ft). Turnbull killed Ah Tuck on the draw before the latter could even raise his weapon, much less fire it.

By about 1956 the British were winning the war against the CTs, in what was the first major defeat of communist terrorism by a conventionally structured army. Not only were the town-dwelling Malays and Chinese, plus the nomadic tribespeople, firmly on the British side, even most of the Chinese squatters had turned against the terrorists.

Full independence within the British Commonwealth was granted to Malaya on 31 August 1957, but the British Army stayed on to help the Malaysians for three more years. However, the communists would not give up until the bitter end and the violence went on, albeit at a much lower intensity, with the State of Emergency continuing until 31 July 1960. For the SAS, however, the job was nearly over by mid-1958, as Malayan troops and police were by then well in control. SAS soldiers started to return to England, but D Squadron was soon to find its skills needed in another theatre.

Below: SAS soldiers search for Communist Terrorists in Tregganu. On average it took 1800 man-hours of patrolling for one kill.

THE JEBEL AKHDAR

The Jebel Akhdar operation is a masterful example of how adaptable SAS soldiers can be. A and D Squadrons were plucked from the humid jungles of Malaysia and immediately went into action in the mountainous region of northern Oman, where they achieved a great victory.

In Malaya the men of the SAS had proved themselves to be superb jungle fighters, but the barren desert uplands of Northern Oman would show just how adaptable the ordinary trooper was.

Oman in the 1950s was a desperately poor country, being ruled over by a despotic Sultan, Said bin Taimur. The British had signed a treaty of friendship with the Sultan of Muscat in 1789, giving the East India Company commercial rights in exchange for the protection of the Royal Navy. Both sides benefited from the treaty: Oman was a seafaring nation which had interests in East Africa, Zanzibar, Socotra and Baluchistan, but its commercial concerns were threatened by the multitude of pirates who sailed the seas. The presence of the Royal Navy did much to make the seas safe for trade, which the Omanis were grateful for.

By the twentieth century the pirates had gone, but the British were more than happy to maintain the ties that had been built up with the numerous rulers of

Oman. Then a new factor entered the equation: oil.

By the 1950s the discovery of more and more oil under the Arabian sands was turning this huge desert peninsula into one of the richest regions of the world. Oman's position suddenly made it very important to the British, and the West in general. Northern Oman overlooks the Straits of Hormuz, through which oil tankers have to pass (the country across the straits is Iran, which in the 1950s was sympathetic to Western interests, but is now in the hands of an extreme Islamic, anti-Western regime, thus making it doubly important that Oman has rulers that are kindly disposed to the West).

In 1952 neighbouring Saudi Arabia invaded parts of Abu Dhabi and Muscat, which were rich in oilfields. Britain, ever eager to avoid having to take military action, at first advised negotiation, but when the Saudis started to organise a rebellion in Oman, the British government felt it had no alternative but to hon-

our its treaty obligations to the Sultan. The Trucial Oman Scouts, recruited in what is now the United Arab Emirates and led by British officers, were brought in to expel the Saudis. The Sultan then sent in his armed forces to garrison the few small towns in the region.

REBELLION IN NORTHERN OMAN

In 1957, however, an open rebellion was mounted by the Imam Ghalib bin Ali of Oman and his brother, Talib, along with Sheikh Suleiman Bin Hamyar, whose tribe inhabited the northern Jebel Akhdar region. The Sultan's troops were attacked by a well-organised enemy armed with modern weapons and land-mines, and they were all but wiped out. The Sultan, somewhat alarmed, immediately requested military help from Britain, invoking the mutual assistance treaty between the two countries.

A troop of Hussars with Ferret armoured cars was drafted in from Aden and two infantry companies were flown down from Bahrain. The Trucial Oman Scouts were also redeployed to help drive back the rebels. RAF jets based in neighbouring states provided top cover and ground support. In next to no time the out-gunned rebels withdrew to the near inaccessible plateau of the Jebel Akhdar. This bleak, sun-bleached granite outcrop rose sheer from the desert sands to a height of several thousand metres, very much like Ayers Rock in Australia. The name translates as 'Green Mountain', but other than for a brief few weeks after the spring rains, when a profusion of desert plants live their short lives, it is almost entirely devoid of vegetation.

Left: A far cry from the jungles of Malaya. The terrain of the Jebel Akhdar meant that the SAS had to battle the rebels and geography.

Right: Captain Peter de la Billière (left) is appraised of the tactical situation on the jebel by Major Johnny Watts, December 1958.

Peter de la Billière, then a young captain with D Squadron, describes the geography of the Jebel Akhdar thus: 'The plateau measured some 20 miles by 10, and formed a phenomenal natural fortress, protected by the precipitous steepness of its sides and by the fact that there was no road leading to the top. Only half a dozen paths, negotiable by men and donkeys, wound their way up wadis, or dry valleys, so steep and narrow that each could be effectively guarded by a small detachment. On any track half a dozen men with rifles and a machine gun could keep a company at bay and inflict severe casualties. Even without opposition, the sheer physical difficulties of climbing seven or eight thousand feet in very high temperatures would have been formidable: other units trying to patrol the mountain had lost several casualties to sniper fire but more to heat-stroke. Small wonder that no foreigner had conquered the top of the jebel since the Persians in the tenth century.'

THE TACTICAL SITUATION

With the rebels confined to the high ground and the Sultan's Forces pretty much in command, most of the British troops were withdrawn. A small number of Army and Air Force loan officers remained along with some specialists, such as medics and signallers and an armoured car troop. During 1958, land mines laid by rebels damaged or destroyed many of the British armoured cars, and RAF aircraft overflying the jebel repeatedly came under heavy machine gun fire. As the Sultan's forces were unable to take on the rebels in their mountain hideouts, the British would clearly have to lend a hand to bring the campaign to a successful conclusion. But to do what?

Though only numbering around 200 properly trained soldiers, backed up by about 500 hill tribesmen, the rebel force was not going to be a pushover. The soldiers were armed with 0.5in machine guns and 81mm mortars, in addition to modern rifles, and the tribesmen were all good marksmen with older but well-maintained rifles. They had plentiful supplies of ammunition for most of their weapons, and knew the area like the backs of their hands. To complicate matters further, the Jebel Akhdar plateau had reputedly never been successfully assailed in the previous millennium (as mentioned by de la Billière above).

The British government decided that the SAS was the unit to resolve the situation (a small-scale affair was infinitely preferable to a large-scale, and expensive, commitment). In mid-November 1958, therefore, D Squadron was dispatched from Malaya to help clear the rebels from the Jebel Akhdar. The squadron consisted of four troops (16, 17, 18 and 19) plus a small headquarters. Each troop had a fighting strength of about 10 or 12 men rather than the 16 they should have had. They were armed with the Belgian 7.62mm FN rifle [predecessor to the Self Loading Rifle (SLR)] and a few light machine guns.

But the fighting would be very different to that experienced by the men in Malaya. The jebel required a new set of operational and survival skills. The rock of the Jebel Akhdar is hard and metallic, which makes silent movement very difficult, the more so because initially the SAS soldiers wore nail-shod boots that generated a lot of noise. The plateau is cut by deep-sided ravines, which took many hours of hard climbing and descending to traverse. Living off the land is impossible, so SAS soldiers were faced with the prospect of having to carry all their rations and equipment on their backs. In addition, the weather was quite severe: alternating between sub-zero conditions at night to scorching heat during the day.

D SQUADRON'S ACCLIMATISATION

As soon as they arrived, the men of D Squadron began a short acclimatisation regime to make the changeover from jungle to mountain operations as soon as possible. A corporal in the squadron records the procedure: 'We set up a series of hard marches with bergens, weapons and ammunition, and at the end of each march there was more and more range work, more and more open work, as opposed to work which we'd always done in jungle, and longer marksmanship, well over the 25 or 30yds which we had previously engaged in.'

Soon after their arrival in theatre, and really before they had even had the chance to acclimatise properly, they were pressed into action. The squadron's first feat was to put men on top of the seemingly unassailable jebel a mere 4km (2.5 miles) from the rebel stronghold of Aquabat al Dhafar in the northwest. Desperately short of manpower, the squadron was split into two units. To the north, 16 and 17 Troops attempted an

Left: The geographic feature codenamed Sabrina, which SAS soldiers, led by Captain Rory Walker, seized in mid-November 1958.

approach from the rear of the enemy position. The second formation, consisting of 18 and 19 Troops, made its way in from the south.

The first clash with the rebels took place in the shadow of the jebel, when a joint patrol from 18 and 19 Troops closed with the enemy in daylight. Unfortunately Corporal Duke Swindells, who had earned the Military Medal in Malaya, was killed by a sniper in this encounter, but the patrol killed at least one rebel in return. From then on, most patrols were carried out in darkness to avoid the danger of lone snipers hiding in the rocks.

From the north the men of 16 and 17 Troops managed to scale the plateau unopposed, with the help of a local guide, by an ancient route known as the Persian Steps. Supposedly thousands of years old, this narrow, stepped track had reputedly allowed a few men to hold back an entire army of Persians hundreds of years before. Despite the route being well covered by enemy sangars (improvised walls of rocks), the rebels had not manned them, on the assumption that no ordinary soldier could possibly make the climb in darkness. They did not appreciate that SAS troopers were not ordinary soldiers!

FOOTHOLD ON THE JEBEL

Having reached the top undetected and well ahead of schedule, the officer in command, Captain Roderic 'Red Rory' Walker, decided to consolidate the position on the grounds that they would be unlikely to pull off the stunt quite so easily a second time (Walker's most famous exploit was to take place in the Indonesian capital, Jakarta, when a stone-throwing mob rioted outside the British Embassy following Sarawak and Sabah's decision to join the Malaysian Federation – Walker marched up and down in front of the building playing the bagpipes).

As the ascent had been made in belt order, the men from 17 Troop went back down to collect their packs, leaving less than a dozen men of 16 Troop on the plateau. It took 17 Troop a full day and night to descend the 2000m (6566ft) to the village where their stores had been dumped, collect all their kit and supplies, then re-ascend the Persian Steps route. During that first day, the men of 16 Troop laid up and watched for signs of enemy activity, then sent out recce patrols in the late afternoon.

No rebels were spotted and 16 Troop bedded down for some much-needed sleep, though naturally a sentry was posted at all times. Shortly after midnight, the trooper on 'stag' noticed some movement and woke his mates. Out in the darkness, four villagers with donkeys were breaking curfew to use an old and uncharted trading route over the jebel. Fortunately for them, the SAS asked questions before opening fire. The villagers were so grateful to have been spared their lives that they not only showed the SAS their route, but even offered to work for them by transporting water, supplies and ammunition. On the second morning, 17 Troop arrived with their kit to relieve 16 Troop, who headed off back down the Steps to collect their packs. 'Lofty' Large was one of these troopers and he remembers that it was one 'hell of a climb and took all night'. The ascending troopers were accompanied by about half a dozen donkeys laden with supplies and jerrycans of water, led by friendly Arab handlers.

SKIRMISHES WITH THE REBELS

Now firmly established on the Jebel, albeit only in a small area, the SAS put out patrols to locate the enemy, but at all times tried to avoid contact. An observation post, with a sergeant and five troopers manning it, was set up some 2000m (6566ft) forward of the main location to give advance warning of any enemy attack. Just before dusk on the first day the OP was attacked by 30-40 well disciplined rebels, but the SAS men managed to kill five and fatally wound four more with their FN rifles. The attack petered

Above: The remains of the village of Saiq on the Jebel Akhdar. The inhabitants of the jebel were in a wretched state by January 1959.

out and the patrol withdrew under cover of darkness as planned. Next morning the patrol returned to the OP expecting to have to fight to retake the position, but the rebels had decided that discretion was the better part of valour.

This early period was fraught with danger for SAS patrols. A troop commander wrote of his experiences during one reconnaissance: 'We got to the top and we found positions that the enemy had obviously occupied, so we decided to get into their positions rather than make new ones of our own, because we knew enough about them to realise that they would spot a new position on the skyline the

Right: By using deception and raw courage, the rebels were totally outwitted during the SAS's final assault on 26-27 January 1959.

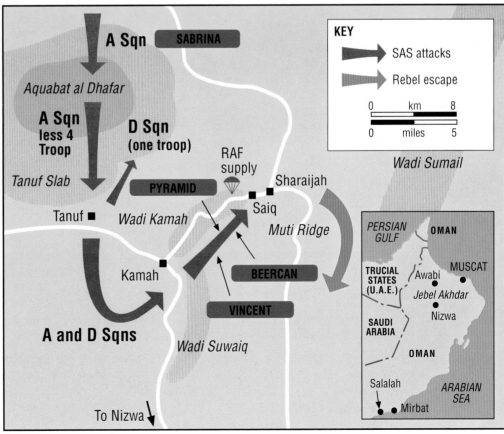

Above: With victory in sight, 16 Troop, D Squadron, 22 SAS, poses for the camera just before the final push onto the jebel.

same as we would if it was our area. At about 0639 hours the sun came up and we fried and fried and fried. We had two extremes. At night it was cold enough on top of the mountain to freeze the water bottle, and we weren't as well equipped then as we are today. All we had were OG [olive-green] trousers and jacket and a very thin standard-issue pullover. We didn't take sleeping bags on a 24-hour recognisance all they did was slow you down, and anyway, we didn't intend to sleep, not knowing whether they had established night picquets.

'Around about 1400 hours I had another three men with me in my patrol and we were looking down and covering an area when, lo and behold, I saw this Arab start making his way up. He got to within 300yds of us when he must have spotted some sort of movement because he shouted up at me, obviously thinking I was one of them. So we shouted down, but then he decided, having had his rifle on his shoulder in the sling position, that something wasn't quite right here, so he took it off, whereupon I shot him. My mate alongside me shot him as well and we just blew him away. Within 30 seconds we were under fire from numerous places.

They were hyperactive and their reactions were perfect, and they started shooting from all areas and concentrating on us. Further along the ridge, the other half of our troop was trapped.'

The SAS soldiers soon learned to respect the guerrillas, as a machine gunner from D Squadron remembers: 'As de la Billière's troop had done the recce, they would do the nearest bit and put a 66mm rocket or Carl Gustav [rocket launcher] rocket into the [rebel] cave – several in fact. Our troop was designed to cover them and we were on a slightly higher ridge about two or three hundred yards above them. We climbed up that night; early morning came and I was behind the Browning. I had persuaded John Watts [the major in command of D Squadron] that the ideal weapon for Oman was the 0.3in Browning, where you had the range you didn't have with the LMG [light machine gun], but, like all machine guns, it attracts a lot of attention

'We set the gun up overlooking the cave and then, first thing in the morning, several men came to the entrance of the cave and were about to start leading the donkeys out, whereupon, three rounds rapid from the Carl Gustav went straight in the middle and whoosh, they blew the cave in and a fair number of them to pieces. Once again, within a minute and a half, we were all under attack. They were

amazing in their reactions plus their knowledge of the local ground. They were born for it and their reactions were fast. We were under attack from their mortars. We were under attack from their LMGs and from individual tribesmen, who were all spoiling for a fight. But, with the help of my machine gun and the RAF who arrived, we extracted ourselves without loss.'

Having now established their presence on the jebel, the SAS decided to set up a more easily defended patrol base on an area of dominating higher ground which they called Cassino. After their bad experience in trying to take on the six-man OP, the rebels ruled out an assault on this larger and better defended position. Instead they resorted to relatively ineffectual long-range mass sniping and machine gun attacks on the SAS positions, plus late afternoon mortar attacks. Although they had an 81mm mortar which could outrange the smaller-calibre weapons of the SAS, ammunition must have been low as they seldom fired more than two or three rounds a day.

BRITISH ARMY AND OMANI SUPPORT

To provide fire support to the lightly armed troopers, about 20 men from the Lifeguards, along with some signallers, medics and REME fitters, were sent to Cassino. The Lifeguards brought machine guns from some of their scout cars which had been disabled by the American mines given to the rebels by the Saudis. A little later, an infantry company from an Omani regiment joined them to secure the camp, while the SAS troopers were out on patrol.

STORMING SABRINA

The forward enemy defensive line on the jebel was a well-guarded cliff which had a 25m-(80ft-) wide re-entrant giving access to the fortified twin peaks nicknamed Sabrina (the name derived from a well endowed television presenter of the time) by the British. About 50 rebels, well located in a cave system, defended this major access route to the main rebel positions in this sector of the jebel. Nonetheless, despite the size of the task, it was the next SAS target.

With 17 Troop making a diversionary flank attack, 16 Troop set out, on Christmas Eve 1958, to climb the cliffs and assault the forward defensive positions from the rear. As the Lifeguards and Omanis laid down covering fire and a mortar barrage, the troopers scaled near impregnable cliffs to attack the rebels in their caves. In virtual darkness they inflicted many casualties in hand-to-hand fighting, but took none themselves. However, some of the rebels had been tenacious fighters and it was decided that more than one SAS squadron would be required if the jebel was to be cleared.

To the south, the second group from 18 and 19 Troops had managed to push their way up about 1000m (3280ft) to a plateau above the village of Tanuf. Patrols from this southern group located a position being used to guard the main approach the Jebel Akhdar. This deep cave, which was also being used to store weapons and ammunition, would have to be taken out sooner or later if the Jebel was to be captured.

The task of clearing the cave was given to the young Captain (now General Sir) Peter de la Billière, who would later command Operation 'Desert Sabre' in the 1991 Gulf War. Under cover of darkness, de la Billière led his men on a 10-hour route march through occupied territory to get them into the only position from which it was possible to attack the cave. At dawn, as the rebels emerged into the sunlight, the troopers opened up with rifles, Bren guns and anti-armour missiles.

Although the attack killed and wounded a good many of the enemy, the survivors held ranks and returned fire. From their sangars, every rebel within range opened up on the exposed troopers, and they had to withdraw under fire. However, a ground-attack aircraft overhead strafed the cave with rockets and from high ground behind them a lone trooper was able to cover their withdrawal with a 0.3in Browning medium machine gun. No major British casualties were suffered and the attack was consid-

Right: One of the donkey handlers who played a part in the SAS deception plan during the Jebel Akhdar operation.

ered to have been a success, but it was now clear that more than one understrength SAS Squadron would be needed if the operation was to be quickly wrapped up.

On New Year's Day 1959, the Commanding Officer of 22 SAS Regiment, Lieutenant-Colonel Tony Deane-Drummond, arrived in Muscat with an advanced party to set up a Combined Headquarters. Within 10 days A Squadron, now commanded by Major Johnny Cooper, arrived from Malaya. They deployed immediately and acclimatised from jungle tepidity to the clear Arabian air on the job. Two weeks later a full attack on the Jebel was mounted by the combined squadrons.

JOHN WOODHOUSE

The SAS's ability to transfer from one terrain type to another with seeming ease is testimony to the calibre of recruits the Regiment was producing, and the man responsible for this was John Woodhouse. Now regarded as the father of the modern SAS, he was one of the original members of the Malayan Scouts. Together with Major Dare Newell he set about reorganising the Scouts to fight in the jungle on long-duration operations. Woodhouse insisted on the highest levels of professionalism, discipline and physical fitness.

In the summer of 1952, he returned to England to organise SAS recruitment procedures. The course he subsequently came up with formed the basis of the current SAS Selection and Continuation used by the Regiment. By the end of the 1950s the courses were sifting out those who were unsuitable to be SAS soldiers, and ensuring that only the best got to wear the Winged Dagger badge. The courses ensured that the Regiment could tackle jobs such as the Jebel Akhdar operation. The Special Air Service owes much to John Woodhouse.

Meanwhile, on the Jebel Akhdar, in an attempt to draw as many rebels as possible away from the highest peaks commanding the jebel and the villages in their shadows, the SAS first mounted an elaborate diversionary attack on Sabrina. They also confided in their Arab donkey handlers that the main attack would come from Tanuf in the southwest and, as expected, within 24 hours this information was passed on to the rebel command. De la Billière explains the ruse: 'On the evening of 25 January Deane-Drummond gave four of the leading [donkey] handlers a special briefing. He opened by saying that the information which he was about to divulge was top secret, and that they were not to pass it to anyone else, on pain of death. He then told them that although a

Johnny Cooper

Johnny Cooper was one of the 'Originals' of L Detachment in North Africa. He took part in many SAS missions in the desert, before being sent to officer training school in 1943. By D-Day he was a troop commander in A Squadron, 1 SAS, taking part in Operation 'Houndsworth' and the crossing of the Rhine. After World War II he was demobbed, but rejoined the regular Army in 1951 and was posted to Malaya. There he joined 22 SAS, and went on to command A, B and C Squadrons. He saw much service, including the storming of the Jebel Akhdar. By this time a lieutenant-colonel, Cooper then served with the Omani Northern Frontier Regiment beginning in 1960, before becoming second-in-command of the Muscat Regiment. He became involved with the SAS again in 1963, when he led a secret mission into the Yemen to aid royalist rebels. In all he had three spells in the Yemen before finishing his career in 1966.

feint was to be made up the Wadi Kamah, the real assault was to be launched from Tanuf, and the donkey-trains would be going up that way. (Our knowledge of the local intelligence system suggested to us that this information would reach the top of the jebel in very short order – and so it proved. We learnt later that an accurate account of our phoney plan reached the rebels within six hours.)'

To give D Squadron a bit of a break, and to allow A Squadron to train in an operational environment, the new arrivals took over positions and patrol duties at Cassino. The morning after their arrival in northern Oman, Cooper's men therefore set off carrying their 27kg (60lb) packs to climb the 2000m (6560ft) ascent to the Persian Steps, which they reached before sundown. After a night in their sleeping bags in the chill desert air, they set off to climb the Persian Steps for the first time. The were met at the top by Captain de la Billière, who guided them to the sangars on Cassino and briefed Cooper on the current situation.

The men of D Squadron then redeployed to the Tanuf Slab area and mounted operations in the area to the south of Sabrina. They also took the opportunity to maintain or change weapons and kit at the SAS headquarters near Tanuf.

A SQUADRON'S ATTACK

This major increase in military activity in the area also helped convince the rebels that the expected big push would be coming in this sector. After dusk on the evening of 25 January 1959, the now acclimatised A Squadron moved forward to the start line near Cassino for the northern assault on Sabrina as part of the diversion plan. At 0300 hours, three troops commenced their ascent of the mountain by different routes, while the fourth troop covered them from the right flank with machine guns.

By first light both peaks were cleared and, despite an intensive firefight followed by fierce hand-to-hand combat, only one trooper had to be evacuated with a bullet wound. As part of the deception 4 Troop

stayed behind on Sabrina, but the rest of A Squadron descended to low ground, where trucks were waiting to take them to Tanuf by road. Meanwhile, D Squadron also launched a diversionary attack, but they came up against much stiffer resistance. Once again a single troop was left in the area to convince the rebels that the main push was coming from the western sector, but the bulk of the squadron had assembled back at Tanuf by late afternoon. That evening the combined force of six SAS troops was trucked round to the village of Kamah to begin the main attack.

LOGISTICS OF THE ATTACK

Although they were about to embark on a nine-hour, 2500m (8200ft) ascent in darkness along what was little more than a mountain goat track, each man carried an incredible amount of ammunition, in addition to full belt order and pack. A typical trooper's load was five 20-round rifle magazines, 100 rounds in a bandolier, a 250-round box of 0.3in machine gun ammunition, eight hand grenades, six white phosphorus grenades, four rifle-launched grenades and two 3.5in anti-armour rockets. This pack tipped the scales at 44.5kg (98lb) and belt order weighed another 10kg (22lb), making a total of 55kg (120lb) plus rifle!

D Squadron was first off the start line, but A Squadron was right behind them. It could have given the game away if the SAS had attempted to reconnoitre their proposed route in advance, so instead they used long-range surveillance and photo reconnaissance techniques. Fortunately the route proved to be just climbable, although for one particularly precarious traverse men had to be roped together for safety. Just before the final summit they also had to descend a 15m (50ft) cliff, but by this stage the prospect of finally reaching the top spurred the men on.

For D Squadron the ascent was relatively uneventful, though just as hard, as de la Billière makes clear: 'Away we went, climbing hard, not up any of the wadis, but straight up the face of the slab above us, our first objective being a feature known as Pyramid. Two troopers ranged ahead to warn of any enemy and make sure that the bulk of the squadron did not waste time by going up blind alleys. The first or so was the most daunting. We were all carrying very heavy loads – some bergens weighed 40kg (90lb) – and we knew we would have to keep climbing all night, without any chance of a proper rest, still less a restorative brew. At first the air was very hot, and we poured sweat.'

As the climb continued the scouts did come across one unmanned but loaded machine gun in a nest near the top of the climb. Two members of 16 Troop found the gun crew asleep in a cave nearby and silenced them permanently. At daylight other isolated machine gun positions opened up on D Squadron as they neared the summit, but nobody was hit. RAF ground support aircraft were called up to help suppress some enemy gunfire, but on the whole the SAS assault was pretty much unopposed.

A SQUADRON'S PROGRESS

Unfortunately the men of A Squadron, who were still climbing as daylight broke, did not get off as lightly as their colleagues. A single long-range shot from a sniper hit a grenade in a trooper's pack and detonated it. Troopers W. Carter and A. Bembridge died as a result of their wounds and a third trooper was injured. Other than this incident, there were no other serious SAS casualties on the assault. Later that morning, a re-supply parachute drop convinced the few remaining rebels on this part of the jebel that an airborne invasion was taking place and they melted away. Behind them they left all their heavy weapons and masses of incriminating documents. As the word got back to the main body, who had rushed off to counter what their command perceived as the major offensive, they too fled – the battle was all but over, and the SAS had won it.

The assault had brought the SAS onto the plateau and within striking distance of the main rebel base at Saiq. At that moment dozens of supply containers began to float down to earth, dropped from RAF aircraft. The rebels believed

that a full-scale airborne operation was taking place, and that was enough to convince them to give up the fight. The Imam hastily seized some camels and fled with a number of followers in the direction of Saudi Arabia.

THE SAS VICTORIOUS

For the loss of just three men, two under-strength squadrons of the SAS, supported by the Lifeguards and loyal members of the Sultan's Forces, had taken the supposedly impregnable Jebel Akhdar in less than 10 weeks.

Why had the SAS been so successful? Johnny Cooper was in no doubt as to the reasons for the triumph: 'It had to be done quickly. If you'd sent in a battalion of infantry it would have cost a lot of money. Here you were sending only a small gang. It was an SAS job because we had the ability to carry pack-mule loads and we were all very fit.'

London was not slow to offer its gratitude; after all, it had not only been saved a lot of money but also political face (very important not long after the Suez debacle). Deane-Drummond had deservedly been awarded a DSO for his planning of the operation, as well as his overall leadership, while Military Crosses went to Rory Walker, Tony Jeapes (a lieutenant with A Squadron), Watts and de la Billière.

With the jebel safely in British and Omani government forces hands, the SAS set about addressing the problems of the jebelis themselves. Peter de la Billière was one of those who had this task: 'The inhabitants of the plateau were in a wretched state: their villages had been wrecked, their fields left untilled, the ancient *falaj*, or water-conduit, system was in ruins, and the people themselves had been living miserably in caves. For the next three weeks the SAS carried out a programme of flag-marches, trekking all over the jebel in half-troops, each accompanied by a couple of donkeys and an officer from one of the native regiments.'

More importantly, the Jebel Akhdar operation had ensured the continued survival of the Regiment. It had proved itself to be a formation that could deploy anywhere in the world at a moment's notice, and that it contained excellent soldiers. This had gone a long way to dispel the poor reputation of the Malayan Scouts, (see the previous chapter), and had shown that the SAS was now cast in the highest professional mould.

Ironically, after all this excitement, the Regiment faced a quiet period after the Jebel Akhdar. For the men this meant lengthy training courses, in driving, parachuting and physical fitness. By the time the SAS was needed in Borneo in 1963, the Regiment had a pool of highly trained soldiers ready and fully prepared to undertake any mission. By now the SAS was an elite, a unit that was full of professionals and a key part of the British Army's arsenal.

Right: Lieutenant-Colonel Anthony Deane-Drummond with captured rebel weapons on plateau of the Jebel Akhdar, February 1959.

BORNEO 1963-66

Back to the Far East

When President Sukarno of Indonesia threatened the formation of the British-sponsored Federation of Malaysia, the government in London organised a military force to be sent to the island of Borneo. Among the units dispatched was the SAS, Britain's jungle warfare experts.

The end of the Malayan and Omani campaigns brought lean times for the SAS, as the British Army concentrated on its NATO commitment in Germany.

As a result of the post-Suez reorganisation of the Army, 22 Regiment SAS was formally integrated into the Order of Battle, which assured its future once more, but it did not escape the defence cuts unscathed. At the height of the Malayan 'Emergency', the Regiment consisted of a Headquarters Squadron and four Sabre or fighting squadrons. The Sandys Report of 1957, however, proposed that in due course only two sabre squadrons be included in the peacetime British Army Order of Battle.

When not at war, the Headquarters Squadron was reduced to a small core supported by personnel from the Sabre squadrons. The Rhodesian C Squadron had, of course, returned home, so it was out of the picture, thus the Regiment was at first left with three operational squadrons. However, at the end of 1959, when most personnel had returned to the UK at the end of their operational tours, B Squadron was disbanded. As both A and D Squadrons were operating below full establishment, most troopers from B were transferred, but some experienced officers were forced to return reluctantly to their original regiments. Major Johnny Cooper, for example, who had served the SAS for the best part of two decades, was offered a boring desk job in Whitehall, but opted to join the Northern Frontier Regiment in Oman as a company com-

mander instead. Others also offered their services elsewhere.

On their return from Malaya and northern Oman in 1959, the SAS had been temporarily based at Merebrook Camp in Malvern, which had been a World War II hospital camp. After reorganisation in 1960, the Regimental Headquarters and the two surviving squadrons moved to Bradbury Lines in Hereford, which was to be the SAS's home for the next three decades.

Soon after the move, D Squadron went to Kenya on a three-month training exercise. Although well versed in operating procedures for Far East jungle and high-altitude desert environments, the Regiment as a whole had little experience of the African theatre. To remedy this, D Squadron spent a great deal of time learning different techniques required for patrolling and tracking in the African jungle, the bush and on the slopes of Mount Kenya. Even today, Kenya is a key training area for the Regiment because of its wide range of terrain and climatic conditions.

THE FIRST HOSTAGE-RESCUE DRILLS

In keeping abreast with the changing world order, the Regiment also taught itself numerous new skills. During that intensive training period in Kenya, the first 'killing house' was constructed, mainly of sandbags, to allow troopers to practise room clearing and hostage-rescue techniques. The following year, each of the four troops in each of the 'Sabre' Squadrons received training in its allotted

Left: An SAS detachment being briefed prior to being sent on a long-range patrol in Sarawak in the winter of 1963-64.

speciality. Members of Freefall Troop (now called Air Troop) became proficient in combat sky-diving, Boat Troop learned all aspects of boatmanship and clearance diving, Rover Troop (later renamed Mobility Troop) specialised in long-range vehicle patrols, and Mountain Troop became expert climbers and abseilers.

For a short period in 1961, the services of D Squadron were put to good use in persuading Saudi troops occupying the Baraimi Oasis on the borders of Oman and the Trucial States that it was time to go home. However, despite all the various skills learned by the Regiment in Europe and Africa during the early 1960s, it was the humid jungles of Borneo which were to provide the next major challenge.

HISTORICAL BACKGROUND

The island of Borneo lies on the equator midway between the Chinese mainland and Australia, with the Malay peninsula to the northeast and Indonesia to the south, southeast and southwest. Most of Indonesia had formerly been under Dutch rule, and the southern part of Borneo, known as Kalimantan, became part of an independent Indonesia in 1949. The northern parts of the island, Sarawak, Sabah and Brunei, however, remained part of the British Commonwealth, as did neighbouring Malaya.

In the early 1960s, with British approval, Malaya suggested that the Commonwealth territories of Brunei, Sabah, Sarawak and Singapore join her in a new Malaysian Federation. The Indonesians, however, who had expansionist designs in the region, specifically their leader, President Sukarno, objected and set about trying to destabilise northern Borneo. As the Sultan of Brunei also preferred to retain his independence from all of his larger neighbours, Sukarno decided to try to exploit this weak link in the Malaysian Federation chain.

At this time Lieutenant-Colonel John Woodhouse was the commander of 22 SAS, and he had foreseen that the Regiment might have to conduct another campaign in the Far East. He thought it might be in Thailand, which would be the next in line if the communists succeeded in Vietnam (this was part of the

Above: An SAS soldier sends a Morse message back to headquarters from a native kampong near the border with Kalimantan.

so-called 'domino theory', a doctrine that was popular among Western military and political analysts in the 1960s). In fact, the immediate threat came from Sukarno. Far from being a communist, 'The Mad Doctor' as he was known, dreamed of emulating the Japanese in World War II by attempting to unite the whole of Southeast Asia under his leadership. If the rest of region did not share his dream, well, no matter. He had the military muscle to back up his ambitions.

He had already embarked upon a propaganda campaign in the region, issuing threats and orders against the Malaysians to close the British bases on their land. When they refused that served only to make Sukarno more determined to fulfil his ambitions. The revolt that broke out in Brunei in December 1962 was a strictly local affair, but it was backed by Sukarno

in the belief that it could further his aims. However, it also furthered the aims of John Woodhouse.

Unfortunately for Sukarno, his machinations on the island of Borneo aroused the interest of the commanding officer of the SAS, who petitioned the Ministry of Defence in London to be allowed to send some of his men to the island. He argued that not only would it brush up 22 SAS's jungle skills, but that the Regiment could use long-range Morse communications on the new radios it had just been issued with. In this way London could be kept abreast of developments as they happened. London was interested – the SAS was on its way.

The Jungle Campaign

The first SAS unit to arrive in Borneo was A Squadron in early 1963. At first the high command wanted to use the Regiment as a kind of mobile reserve, but the commanding officer, Lieutenant-Colonel John Woodhouse, had other, much more effective ideas.

On 8 December 1962, an Indonesian-backed group calling itself the North Kalimantan National Army (NKNA) launched a revolt against the Sultan of Brunei, who instantly requested help from Britain. Inside a week British and Gurkha troops, shipped and flown in from Singapore, had taken care of most of the trouble-makers, though it did take nearly six months in total to mop up the last of the rebels. Thanks to the rapid and timely British intervention, the Brunei affair was not the success which the Indonesians expected. It did, however, give them the excuse they were looking for to decry the Federation as the 'accomplices of neo-colonialist and neo-imperialist forces pursuing a policy hostile to Indonesia'. On 20 January 1963, the Indonesian Foreign Minister announced a state of confrontation with Malaya.

As regional politicians and international mediators attempted to find a solution to the problem, bands of Indonesian 'volunteers' infiltrated the border regions of Brunei, Sabah and Sarawak to prepare for a campaign of attacks on police posts and to carry out sabotage missions. Although supposedly these 'volunteers' were all Kalimantan irregulars, many were clearly Indonesian Army soldiers, though this was denied by their government at the time. On the morning of 12 April 1963, the Indonesians launched their first major sortie in the west of Sarawak.

The police post in the border town of Tebedu was a soft target, manned only by a handful of policemen more used to frightening off smugglers and keeping the peace than fighting trained soldiers. Around 30 'volunteers' launched a dawn attack on the post, taking the occupants completely by surprise. Hopelessly outgunned, the police officers tried to fight back, but one was killed and two were wounded. Afterwards the Indonesians, or Indos as the Brits called them, looted the town market before fleeing to safety over the border. The British responded by dispatching a troop of Royal Marines to the scene, but all that the attackers had left behind were propaganda leaflets claiming that they were from the NKNA.

THE SAS ARRIVE ON BORNEO

By the time of the Tebedu attack, the SAS already had a squadron deployed operationally in the region, though its presence was not widely known. In late December of the previous year, after the Brunei rebellion had been put down, a new command known as British Forces Borneo Territories (BFBT) had been set up under Major General Walter Walker. Lieutenant-Colonel Woodhouse, who now commanded 22 SAS, immediately spotted the opportunities which a Borneo deployment would offer the Regiment, and actively campaigned for this.

Within days of BFBT being formed, Woodhouse and his signaller arrived at Walker's headquarters to demonstrate their brand new Morse radio sets, which were the only method of communications that could be relied upon for jungle

Left: An SAS trooper with an Iban tracker on patrol in Borneo. The Ibans, skilled in warfare and tracking, were a great asset.

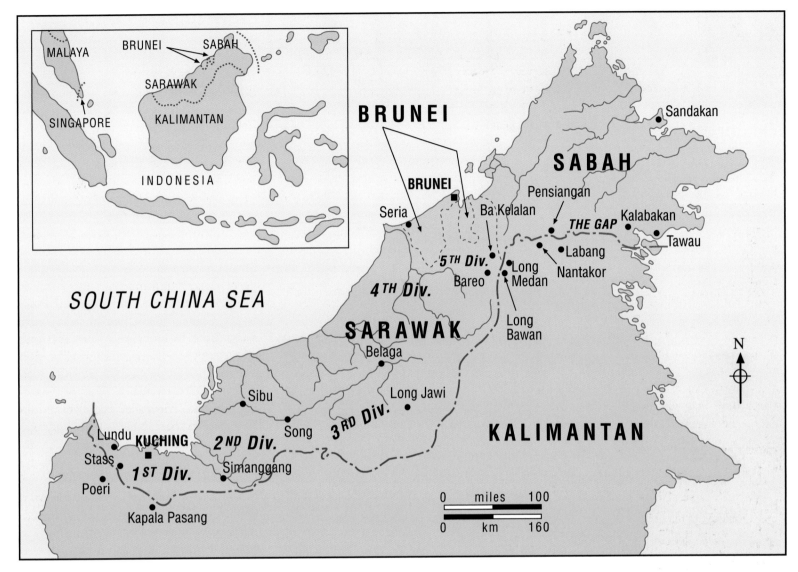

operations. Even without the new radios, the general would have been happy to accept the offer of an SAS squadron under his command. He had previously commanded the Gurkhas in Malaya and was an admirer of the jungle exploits of the SAS during the 'Emergency'. Three days after Woodhouse's visit, A Squadron deployed back to the equatorial jungle.

The border across Borneo between Indonesian Kalimantan in the south and the Malay provinces of Sabah and Sarawak in the north stretched over nearly 1500km (930 miles). Brunei was theoretically shielded from direct infiltration by Sarawak, but the intervening jungle was dense enough to hide a dozen invading armies. The only way that the British could intercept advancing or retreating attackers would be to set up a sort of defensive early warning line along the length of the border. This was where the SAS would prove its worth.

The men of A Squadron numbered less than 100, including headquarters and logistic support personnel, so they were going to be stretched very thin indeed along the border. However, there were no roads through the jungle and very few established tracks, so the job was not as impossible as it might at first appear. With the help of local tribesmen, vast areas could be supervised by a four-man team who understood the jungle and its limitations. When signs of Indonesian military activity were located, even if the tracks were a couple of days old, overland progress in the jungle was so slow that the enemy could not have gone far. Reinforcements, called up on the SAS's Morse transceivers, could quickly be brought in by helicopter to set up an ambush ahead of the infiltrators.

The majority of Borneo jungle tribesmen were on the whole friendly to the British, so gaining their cooperation in

Above: Only by spreading itself very thinly could the Regiment hope to cover the whole of the border with Indonesian Kalimantan.

monitoring for Indonesian cross-border movement was not to be too difficult. Malay was widely spoken by both natives and troopers, so communication was relatively easy. The rest of the native population was not exactly unfriendly, they had just never seen many white men before, so the SAS first had to gain their confidence.

SAS TACTICS ALONG THE BORDER

Split into patrol teams of four men, the troopers spread out along the length of the border to establish contact with the locals. Frequently single patrols were responsible for 10km (six miles) of border, so the eyes and ears of the tribesmen were invaluable to them. This is where the 'hearts and minds' lessons learned in Malaya really bore fruit.

other tribesmen and inform them of the threat from the south. These 'bad men from over the mountains', who would come with their guns one day soon, were no friends of the villagers. They would eat their food, take their young women and bring bad luck on the kampong, but the British Army would protect the villagers if they asked the SAS for help. Of course there were some kampong headmen who did not believe these white outsiders, but the troopers had the perfect sales pitch. If the headman would just get some of his men to make a small clearing in the jungle, warriors would arrive from the skies to protect their friends. As the tribesmen chopped down the trees, the patrol called up a helicopter-borne company of Gurkhas who were waiting on standby and they duly arrived on cue. The villagers were impressed by the show.

FIRST CONTACTS WITH THE 'INDOS'

When the Indonesians mounted that first major raid into Sarawak to attack the police post at Tebedu, A Squadron was already living in the kampongs. In this instance the SAS was not in the position to block the retreat, but this would soon change. One two-man SAS team in a remote location was instructed by radio to dig in as news of the Tebedu attack broke. Their typical reply was, 'What, both of us?'

By mid-May the men of A Squadron had been relieved by their colleagues from D Squadron, who took over the village locations on a one-for-one basis. During this first of three tours, the troopers from D Squadron continued the 'hearts and minds' campaign begun by their predecessors, spreading out to bring more border villagers into the fold. What little support the Indonesians had among the tribes was fast evaporating.

However, the SAS was stretched to the limit, for there was no way that the 60 or so troopers in the field at any one time could provide even a token presence in every kampong near the border. Unlike in Malaya, there were too many tribesmen even to consider moving them into

Each team located the largest village, or kampong, on its patch and set up a hide near it from where they could monitor comings and goings. When they were satisfied that the Indonesians did not have a presence in the area, they then introduced themselves to the village headman and paid their respects. At all times the customs and rituals of the tribesmen were honoured to avoid alienating them. The troopers accepted food and hospitality from their hosts, but always retreated to their hides afterwards. Rather than bringing cheap trinkets as gifts for the natives, the SAS repaid their hosts' hospitality with manpower and medical aid. One man in each patrol was a trained medic and his

skills were put to good use in clearing up minor ailments and dressing wounds. In time, as mutual trust built up, the patrol would move out of its hide and move in to the edge of the kampong to live and work among the natives. In the early stages, the troopers were intelligence gatherers not fighters, and when not out and about they would help the villagers with their crops and daily chores. It was usual for a patrol to live on their patch for anything from three to five months, by the end of which time they looked more like natives than soldiers, but for their height.

With their base firmly established in the kampong, members of the team would move further afield to contact

Right: An SAS trooper on a village walkway. The Regiment's good relations with the locals helped achieve ultimate victory.

fortified settlements, so a means of self-protection needed to be found for them. The immediate answer to this problem seemed to be to train some of the young men, all volunteers, in the use of firearms and defensive tactics.

The British Army supplied these eager young tribesmen with rifles and ammunition. This native self-defence force became known as the Border Scouts. After three weeks of training, they returned to their home regions, to be led by small Gurkha teams posted with them. The Border Scouts were ideal as trackers and information carriers, but three weeks of basic training was insufficient to turn a former head-hunter into a soldier capable of defeating highly trained regulars.

DEFEAT AT LONG JAWI

One such formation was a platoon-sized grouping of 21 Border Scouts, three police radio operators and six Gurkhas manning a garrison post at the village of Long Jawi in central Sarawak, at least 50km (30 miles) from the border. On 28 September 1963 some 200 Indonesians, mostly regular soldiers, attacked the post without warning. All but three of the garrison were killed and the village was looted before being razed to the ground. Due to poor atmospheric conditions, the lack of radio communications from the post did not unduly worry headquarters. Four days later, though, the two surviving Gurkhas and a lone Border Scout walked out of the jungle to raise the alarm. Ambush parties of Gurkhas were immediately helicoptered out to the border to cut off escape routes plotted by the SAS, and many of the Indonesians were killed before they could reach the sanctuary of Kalimantan.

The conflict in Borneo was now clearly escalating rapidly, and it became clear that more SAS troops were needed on the ground. During the last quarter of the year, the Indonesians launched a number of raids along the border. At Hereford, selection was stepped-up in preparation for the re-formation of B Squadron, which became operational in January 1964.

Border Scouts and Cross-Border Scouts

The Border Scouts were irregular forces raised and trained by the SAS. They were created by the Director of Operations Borneo, Major-General Walker, as part of an effort to establish a defensive intelligence network along the border with Indonesian Kalimantan. They were recruited from the indigenous tribes of the region. The SAS men were responsible for all aspects of training, discipline and administration. But they could not hope to stand up to regular troops, and a detachment was wiped out by Indonesians at Long Jawi in September 1963. Afterwards their role was changed to purely intelligence gathering. In addition, one or two Scouts were often added to SAS patrols to facilitate contacts with locals. The Cross-Border Scouts was a 40-strong unit raised by the SAS in the summer of 1964. Recruited from Iban Dyaks, its role was to mount operations into Kalimantan. Thereafter they were active along the border in western Sarawak and around Bemban.

Cross-Border Raids

To pre-empt the build-up of Indonesian forces in Kalimantan, the SAS decided to mount a series of top-secret cross-border raids into Indonesian territory. Codenamed 'Claret' Operations, the first one was mounted in June 1964.

In late December 1963, an Indonesian force of over 100 men, with a nucleus of at least 20 regulars, penetrated well into Sabah to attack the village of Kalabakan. The half-company garrison of the Royal Malay Regiment was caught completely off-guard in the midnight attack and lost eight men, including their commanding officer. Nineteen more were wounded in the battle. Once again the Gurkhas were brought in to cut off the Indonesians' escape, and by the end of January all but six of the attackers were killed or captured.

After the Kalabakan incident, the British decided to take the war to the enemy instead of waiting for him to make the first move. In January 1964, a force of Indonesians was detected camped on the Sabah-Sarawak border, and a small patrol of British infantry moved in to attack. Seven of the enemy were killed and the remainder fled, leaving their weapons and equipment behind. The British now had concrete evidence that the Indonesian

Army was, at the least, lending support to these operations. At this point President Sukarno announced a ceasefire and called for negotiations.

The talks only lasted for a few weeks before Indonesia pulled out, but in the meantime Sukarno's military commanders fully re-appraised the situation. When the Indonesians broke their ceasefire, they dropped all pretences and their army openly took over the operation (formerly guerrilla groups such as the Clandestine Communist Organisation, a Chinese group based largely in Sarawak, had been fronting the Indonesian effort). From March 1964 onwards conventional army units, rather than irregulars with regular support, launched a series of attacks on Malay, British and Commonwealth forces.

The first major attack by an Indonesian regular army unit took place on 7 March 1964, when Gurkhas were fired upon near the border in southwest Sarawak. They lost two of their number

before the 40-strong Indonesian force fled back over the frontier. A few days later the Indonesians attacked again a few kilometres further along the border, but the Gurkhas beat them back once more, though they needed to call on artillery support and helicopter-launched missiles to finish the job.

By this stage in the campaign, British and Commonwealth forces were established in strength all along the border in fortified settlements. Each settlement was in direct communication with its neighbours, and artillery support was mutually available. With infantry units now more accustomed to jungle patrolling, the SAS was primarily engaged on covert cross-border operations.

THE FIRST CROSS-BORDER RAIDS

Now that there were two squadrons, B and D, operational in Borneo, sufficient manpower was available to launch covert probes over the border into Kalimantan. At first the four-man SAS patrols, sometimes accompanied by a local guide, only slipped a few hundred metres into enemy territory as the lie of the land was unknown. In these days before satellite mapping, the central area of Kalimantan was virtually uncharted by the Malays or British, and the scantily detailed Indonesian maps of the area were, of course, not available to the SAS.

Just in case the patrol was compromised, normal British Army uniform was worn and standard-issue Self-Loading Rifles (SLRs) were carried. This way the British command could claim they were lost soldiers rather than clandestine infiltrators. Slowly but surely, the SAS charted the land south of the border and mapped out all the approach routes which could

Left: An SAS four-man patrol test-fires its weapons prior to a covert 'Claret' Operation into Kalimantan in the autumn of 1964.

be of use to any Indonesian units intent on crossing the border.

Later, when the situation deteriorated to the point of open warfare, much deeper patrols were mounted and the SAS reverted to using its specialist weapons, such as pump-action shotguns and Armalite rifles. On regular operations a four-man patrol would consist of a lead scout armed with a shotgun, followed by the commander and then the radio operator, both with Armalites, with a Bren gunner bringing up the rear. The General Purpose Machine Gun (GPMG) was by now in widespread service with the British in Borneo, but the SAS retained the Bren as it was lighter to carry on long-range patrols.

The SAS now had two specific tasks to undertake. First, long-range patrols consisting entirely of the most experienced troopers deployed well behind the lines to undertake in-depth reconnaissance missions. Second, slightly less experienced and resting troopers were used as guides for cross-border operations by conventional foot soldiers. The deep-penetration recce patrols were tasked with finding the Indonesian lines of communication and supply, locating their jungle bases and reconnoitring suitable ambush sites. As these bases could well be 20-30km (12-18 miles) from the border, and in a totally hostile jungle environment occupied by possibly unfriendly tribesmen, this was no easy task.

THE NATURE OF JUNGLE WARFARE

To find the enemy, the troopers had to use all of their tracking skills. In the dank, dark jungle the snakes, insects and even some of the plants were all potential hazards, not to mention the skilled jungle soldiers of the Indonesian Army. Patrols usually lasted around three weeks, and everything needed in the way of supplies and rations had to be carried, as re-supply across the border was out of the question. As the patrols moved deeper and deeper, loads were reduced to a minimum to allow them to strike fast at any enemy encountered, then retire quickly before taking casualties. Eventually each trooper carried no more than 15kg (33lb) of dehydrated rations in his pack, with water

Above: One of the 'Tip Toe Boys' on a 'Claret' job. Both A and B Squadrons undertook cross-border raids in the second half of 1964.

bottles, survival kit and ammunition being carried on the belt.

Because of the shortage of skilled manpower, troopers returning from three hard weeks behind the lines had less than a week to recuperate and build up their reserves before the next mission. By the end of a three-patrol tour, SAS men looked worse than prisoners released from a dungeon at the end of a 10-year sentence with only bread and water to survive on. They were usually flown back to Hereford to recuperate for a few weeks before being put back on the treadmill.

It was not initially intended that the SAS deep-recce patrols should attack Indonesians on the Sarawak side of the border, but when targets of opportunity arose, the troopers responded. To keep British casualties to an absolute minimum, especially as cross-border helicopter casevac was clearly out of the question, all engagements had to be brief. Much to the annoyance of the troopers, it was decreed from on high that all encounters must be limited to 'shoot and scoot' actions. However, when the SAS shot they usually took out a lot more targets before scooting than ordinary soldiers would have.

The main weapon of the SAS on cross-border raids was stealth. Even the

Gurkhas, who themselves had a fearful reputation for materialising silently out of nowhere to strike down their enemy, respected the skills of the light-footed troopers. As stories of their ghost-like ambushes on skilled Indonesian jungle soldiers spread throughout the British forces, SAS covert operators were nick-named the 'Tip Toe Boys'.

'CLARET' OPERATIONS IN FULL SWING

In an attempt to spread the war to the Malay peninsula, the Indonesians mounted an airborne assault on Johore province at the beginning of September 1964. This was backed up by infiltration from the sea on the west coast. All of the invaders were quickly captured, however, so Sukarno turned his attentions back to Borneo.

Full cross-border operations by British infantry units, guided by SAS troopers, commenced in June 1964. Due to the political sensitivity of putting soldiers into a country which technically was not at war with Britain, these missions remained top secret for a long time. Known as 'Claret' Operations, these attacks could have proved to be very diplomatically

on the scene. Claymore mines would be positioned at each end of the line and fired electronically when all of the patrol was in the frame. The hail of lethal ball-bearings usually mowed down most of the party, and the troopers then opened up with rifles and machine guns to finish the job. Minutes later the SAS forces had melted away into the jungle, usually before any survivors had the chance to work out what had hit them.

PROTECTING SABAH AND SARAWAK

The Claymore could also be used as a sleeping soldier by the SAS. A single mine, hidden a few metres back from a well-used track or sited to cover the end of a log bridge, could be rigged with a trip wire or remote pressure switch. It would then hibernate until the next patrol to pass tripped it, with devastating consequences. Of course mines and booby-traps laid by the SAS could also have killed friendly forces, so this was another reason for the SAS to guide in the infantry and for only one 'Claret' raid being mounted at any one time.

Occasionally Indonesian troops would bounce the SAS patrol instead – it was their territory, after all – despite the troopers taking every possible precaution. Usually the men who fire first in the jungle have the upper hand, but the superior fighting skills of the SAS could often turn the tables. However, some troopers were inevitably injured and a small number were killed; one is believed to have been captured alive and unfortunately to have later been tortured to death.

Military Indonesian incursions into Sabah and Sarawak were severely curtailed during the last quarter of 1964 and the first quarter of the following year as a direct result of the 'Claret' Operations. Every successful attack by the SAS and the Gurkhas forced the Indonesian Army to pull back their operating bases further from the border. Despite this, though, as they were well armed and equipped, they were still able to launch the occasional raids on kampongs and army posts. The

---

embarrassing to the British had news got out. However, because of their success even the Indonesians kept quiet for fear of loss of face.

At first the Claret raids were limited in range to 5 km (three miles) across the border, to give troops a much better chance of getting any casualties out overland. Later, as the Indonesians pulled their camps farther back to escape British attacks, permission was granted for troops to penetrate up to 20km (12 miles) against definite targets. Each raid had to be authorised by the General Officer Commanding, Major-General Walter Walker, and no more than one operation could be undertaken at any one time. The four-man SAS reconnaissance patrols were not strictly classified as being 'Claret' Operations, however, so they usually carried on regardless.

Most of the early 'Claret' raids were carried out by Gurkhas, as General Walker had stipulated that only infantry with at least one full jungle tour under their belt could go behind enemy lines. Usually their guides were SAS troopers taking a well-earned break from deep-recce duties. Typically the Gurkha raids would be directed at Indonesian base camps, where the enemy troops thought they were well out of harm's way. Usually a

couple of anti-armour rockets and a hail of GPMG fire at dawn or dusk were the first signs they got that their positions had been compromised.

GURKHAS AND CLAYMORES

The Gurkhas were also adept at ambushing Indonesian patrols aiming to cross into the north. The fastest method of transport in the jungle was often boat, and the SAS soon located the regular Indonesian water transit routes. After planning suitable ambush sites, they would lead in larger groups of Gurkhas, who went to ground until the next boatloads of troops appeared. Few of the enemy would swim alive out of the killing zone once the Gurkhas opened fire.

One of the new pieces of kit which became available around this time was the American Claymore mine. Weighing just a few kilos, this highly effective weapon quickly gained favour with the SAS. It consisted basically of several hundred ball bearings embedded in an explosive charge encased in steel. It could be triggered either electronically or by a trip wire, and was lethal over a wide arc. If an SAS recce patrol located a regularly used track, they would position themselves alongside and overlooking it then go to ground until the next enemy patrol came next major Indonesian attack was to occur in late April 1965.

In the extreme west of Sarawak, the British 2 Para had an under-manned company base at the village of Plaman Mapu. At dawn on the morning of the 27th, a large Indonesian Army force attacked the base, supported by mortars and anti-armour missiles used as bunker busters. They easily breached the outer defences, but after more than an hour of close combat they were routed, mainly as a result of the company sergeant major picking up a machine gun and rallying his men. Two of the 10 paratrooper casualties died of their wounds.

The attack on Plaman Mapu proved the final straw for the British, and the general staff now authorised overt cross-border operations against the Indonesian Army. Over the next few months, several Gurkha and British Army battalions pen-etrated into Kalimantan to kill the best part of 100 enemy soldiers for the loss of only four men. From this point on the writing was on the wall for President Sukarno. After one final invasion towards Brunei by about 50 Indonesian soldiers in March 1966 ended with the loss of 37 men, the Indonesian General Staff removed much of the President's authori-ty and began negotiations with Malaysia. A peace treaty was subsequently signed on 11 August 1966.

THE CAMPAIGN IN RETROSPECT

The development and expansion of the SAS also continued. During the Borneo troubles the Regiment trained the Guards Independent (Pathfinder) Company of the Parachute Brigade to undertake SAS-type cross-border raids. And in 1966, before the end of the Borneo campaign, G Company 22 SAS was formed from the ranks of this Guards formation and from volunteers from 2 Para.

Without the sterling service of the SAS in Borneo, especially their early 'hearts and minds' campaign and the later deep-recce patrols, the Confrontation could so easily have had a different end-ing. The signing of the 1966 Agreement between Malaysia and Indonesia has since brought over three decades of peace to this region of the world. As Walker him-self said of the Regiment: 'I regard 70 troopers of the SAS as being as valuable to me as 700 infantry in the role of "hearts and minds", border surveillance, early warning, stay behind, and eyes and ears with a sting.' Once again the SAS had achieved spectacular results.

Below: SAS soldiers carry out their final checks before a patrol in Sarawak. By 1965 the SAS had destroyed Indonesian ambitions.

ADEN 1964-67

The SAS was committed to the conflict in Aden in April 1964. It fought two distinct kinds of war: against the tribesmen of the mountainous region of Radfan, and against terrorists operating in the port of Aden itself. But political mistakes made the SAS's job very hard.

In the 1950s and early 1960s, what is now the country of Yemen was divided between the independent North Yemen and a British Protectorate based around the port of Aden in the south. In an attempt to stabilise a precarious political situation in the run-up to British withdrawal from the region, a federation of the 18 western tribal areas and three larger eastern territories in the south was proposed, but it never really got off the ground because of the politicians. Egypt, which at the time was pro-Soviet and anti-British, while being at the same time being strongly pan-Arab under its charismatic leader, Nasser, then aided a coup in North Yemen and assisted the Yemenis and anti-British tribesmen in the Protectorates to destabilise Aden.

In truth the British had done little to help themselves in their affairs with the inhabitants of the region around Aden, and when they found themselves in an armed struggle they displayed the sort of political weakness that made defeat almost inevitable.

Aden had been a British possession since 1839. For the maritime British Empire it was an important port. The opening of the Suez Canal had shortened communications between Britain and her colonies in the Far East and Australia, but she still needed coaling stations around the globe so that her steam ships could refuel. These stations were located along the main sea routes from Britain. Aden was in an ideal position, being at the entrance to the Red Sea.

Appreciating its importance, Britain annexed Aden in 1839 and administered it from India. By 1900 the Royal Navy

had a large base there, and Britain also acquired large tracts of the hinterland around the port. In 1937, Aden became a crown colony, and in February 1959 six of the emirates, sultanates and various 'states' of the Western and Eastern Aden Protectorates came together to form the Federation of South Arabia (FSA) under the auspices of the British government. Another 10, together with the colony of Aden, had joined by the end of 1963. The small states had agreed to federate on the understanding that the British would stay until after full independence, scheduled for before 1968.

The theory was a diplomat's dream, but the reality was very different. The

British had done little for the inhabitants of the region, and had never encouraged any loyalty towards the Crown. They had been content to buy off local warlords and rulers with guns, ammunition and money. When pan-Arab and communist ideologies arose, the inhabitants of the hinterland quickly began to desert their nominal British rulers.

THE OPENING OF HOSTILITIES

The Radfan area of Dhala, to the north of the main British staging post of Aden, is populated by the Queteibi hill tribe of fearsome reputation, who had traditionally extracted 'tolls' from all travellers and caravans travelling on the main road

Right: An SAS machine gunner on a mountain-top observation post keeps watch for the enemy in the Radfan Mountains in mid-1964.

through Thumier to Dhala town. With the help of finance and weapons from Yemen and Egypt, these tribesmen set about closing the road and harassing federal troops in the area. By late 1963, the security situation in the Radfan had deteriorated to such an extent that the British had to do something.

In January 1964, Operation 'Nutcracker', involving two battalions of the Federal Regular Army (FRA) supported by British helicopters and ground-attack aircraft, penetrated deep into the Radfan in a show of strength. Unfortunately, the FRA was soon needed elsewhere, and the area was allowed to slip back into rebel control. Throughout the months of February and March 1964, the rebels reoccupied all of the high ground and recommenced attacks on the Dhala road to such an extent that the British had to mount a second operation to clear the Radfan.

RADFORCE

As at the time there was no suitable formation available in the region, a Joint Reaction Force, to be known as Radforce, had to be cobbled together from Royal Marines and garrison troops. The core of this scratch brigade was provided by the resident infantry battalion of the East Anglian Regiment from the Aden garrison, local soldiers from the Federal Regular Army, 45 Commando RM and one company from 3 Parachute Battalion, who were flown in from Bahrain. In support they had an armoured car squadron (4 Royal Tank Regiment), a battery of pack howitzers (Royal Horse Artillery) and two squadrons of RAF Hunter ground-attack aircraft.

Back at Hereford, meanwhile, the men of A Squadron were recuperating from their second five-month jungle tour in Borneo, but they had been scheduled to re-train in desert warfare in the Protectorates that May. As luck would have it, their commanding officer was in Aden conducting the usual pre-exercise recce as Brigadier Hargroves was assembling his task force. The squadron commander offered the assistance of his men to the brigadier, who accepted it on the spot. By mid-April A Squadron had flown into Aden for acclimatisation, but on security

Above: Trucks and Land Rovers transporting members of Radforce in April 1964. The force contained Captain Edwards' ill-fated patrol.

grounds the men's wives and families were told they had gone on exercise to Salisbury Plain.

On arrival in Aden, A Squadron immediately headed 100km (60 miles) north to the small desert town of Thumier, where they established their base. Being less than 50km (30 miles) from the North Yemeni border, Thumier was right in the lion's den and in the shadow of the Radfan Mountains. In spite of the huge difference in temperature between England and Thumier, the squadron mounted its first patrol in the foothills of the Radfan that evening.

OPERATIONS FROM THUMIER

Within two weeks of its arrival, A Squadron was earmarked to spearhead the main operation to expel the rebels from the Radfan. The basic plan of this operation was to occupy the two highest peaks to the northeast of Thumier, which dominated the enemy re-supply routes from the border to the north. The company of paratroopers would drop onto the southern objective, which was codenamed Cap Badge, and the Royal Marines would 'yomp' 10km (six miles) east from the Dhala Road to take Rice Bowl, the more northerly objective.

As the paras only had one company in the country and no pathfinders were available, 3 Troop of A Squadron was given the job of marking the drop zone

(DZ) for the paras. This nine-man patrol left Thumier on the evening of 29 April to march overnight to the DZ, where they would go to ground to watch the area before guiding in the paras the following night. Although this scouting role was not a task which the SAS was usually called on to undertake for the paras, it was one which every trooper who had served with an SAS freefall troop was well trained to carry out.

There are conflicting reports on how 3 Troop reached its start line on the 29th. One published account says they were deposited by helicopter under cover of an artillery barrage, but this seems very unlikely. Other reports state that the men travelled up the Wadi Rabwa inside Saladin armoured cars and slipped away under cover of darkness when the going became too tough for the vehicles. Bearing in mind that the entire area was awash with rebel gunmen who fired on anything that moved, the armoured car option seems the more plausible.

Captain Robin Edwards, who had only just joined the SAS from an infantry regiment, but who was well regarded by his men, commanded 3 Troop. Despite having contracted polio after Selection Training, the young officer had fought off

Above: Early morning in the Radfan, 1965. An SAS patrol prepares for another day's work in the stifling heat after a freezing night.

Yemen

The Yemen was the scene of a covert mission involving SAS soldiers. In September 1962, North Yemen's ruler, Imam Mohammed al-Badr, was toppled by a coup led by Colonel Abdullah Sallal, who then proclaimed the Yemen Arab Republic and started to receive aid from the Egyptians. The British and French were alarmed at this spread of Arab nationalism in the Gulf, and thus decided to send a secret unit to North Yemen. The party, commanded by SAS veteran Johnny Cooper and including three SAS soldiers, arrived in June 1963, and linked up with royalist forces near Sana (Badr had fled into the mountains and organised an army). Cooper's men trained the royalists, supplied them with weapons and confirmed that Sallal's regime relied on Egyptian support. Cooper spent the next three years in Yemen, training royalists and organising supply drops.

the disease and brought himself back to full operational fitness inside a year, which was no mean feat. His hand-picked team for this operation consisted of two four-man patrols, each of which was led by a sergeant with a corporal and two troopers under him. All but the signaller, Trooper Warburton, were veterans of at least one Borneo tour of duty.

THE EDWARDS PATROL

The plan was for 3 Troop to march about 12km (7.5 miles) to their objective under cover of darkness on the night of the 29th. Had the route been free from rebel forces as intelligence reports suggested, this would have posed no problem to the experienced troopers. As soon as they started out, though, it became clear that the hills were alive with riflemen, so progress had to be slow and careful. Before long, Trooper Warburton began to lag behind because of severe stomach cramps, and the rest of the patrol had to distribute his kit among themselves, including the 20kg (44lb) radio set. The ailing soldier was put in the middle of the group so that an eye could be kept on his progress, but eventually he slowed down so much that the file nearly split into two.

About three hours before first light, Captain Edwards decided that at the current rate of progress, even if they made it

the last few kilometres to the objective, it was unlikely that they would find suitable hiding places before sunrise. However, as there were a couple of rock sangars on high ground in the immediate vicinity, which would hide the troop from prying eyes during the day, it made sense to go to ground there. And from these sangars the Drop Zone and the surrounding area could be kept under discreet observation. If all went well they could depart at dusk the next evening, rested and, Edwards hoped, with his signaller fully recovered and the DZ marked.

THE PATROL IS COMPROMISED

At dawn the troopers discovered that their hiding place was only about a kilometre from a small hamlet. As the sun rose, armed tribesmen climbed the high ground to mount pickets, though fortunately none came near the sangar. All went well for the first five hours or so of daylight, then the troop had the same bad luck which would strike 'Bravo Two Zero' over a quarter of a century later. To Europeans, the deserts of Arabia and Asia are barren places, but to the tribes who inhabit them they provide a meagre living. Arable crops may be difficult to grow, but far-ranging mountain goats can survive on the sparsest of vegetation. Unfortunately, goats come with goatherds.

As a herd of goats slowly nibbled its way up a wadi close to their position, the troopers pressed themselves into the rocks and held their breath. Behind them a goatherd kept stragglers on the move and held a distant conversation with a woman making her way up from the village. It was inevitable that sooner or later the goatherd would discover them and, if they tried to silence him, his female companion was bound to see.

When the expected alarm was finally raised by the goatherd, a single shot took him out, but not before his and the woman's cries alerted every tribesman in the village. In this region possession of a rifle was regarded as the first sign of adulthood, so every male villager was both armed and fully capable of using his weapon. In the first disorganised couple of minutes, the highly trained troopers shot down a good number of the advan-

cing horde, but soon the tribesmen went to ground to appraise the situation.

The lessons learnt from generations of banditry and inter-tribal strife were not lost on the tribesmen. Slowly and carefully they crawled to fire positions on a low ridge overlooking the sangars, from where they could snipe at the soldiers. However, Edwards had anticipated their actions and as the first shots rang out, he called down an air strike from a pair of RAF Hunters circling high overhead. As cannon fire raked the ridge, the tribesmen quickly retreated to the shelter of the rocks below. The pinned-down troopers, however, had no escape route during daylight hours.

For the next few hours the tribesmen continued to fire at any part of the soldiers' bodies which they inadvertently exposed. About an hour before sunset one of the corporals was hit twice in the leg, but as the enemy were using home-made bullets in refilled cartridge cases, he suffered only flesh wounds. At about the same time, another trooper suffered a flesh wound across his shoulders. Though in pain, neither man was incapacitated.

Further deadly accurate air strikes, called down by signaller Warburton, kept the attackers at bay until the sun started to drop over the jebel, but just before the light faded the rebels tried to rush one of

the sangars. The first attackers to reach the position were cut down at point-blank range, and the others wisely withdrew to await nightfall. With darkness now fast approaching and the aircraft returning to their base, Edwards and his men prepared for a staggered withdrawal. The main radio set was smashed to prevent the enemy later using it to monitor British channels, and the packs were dumped. A delayed artillery strike was also ordered as a surprise for any eager enemy who chose to explore the position after the SAS soldiers had retreated.

The group was split into two teams to allow for mutual support as they withdrew. As the first team, commanded by Edwards, prepared to leave, it was discovered that Trooper Warburton had been killed by several rounds and his secondary radio had been destroyed. Reluctantly it was decided that his body had to be left behind. With the second team, commanded by a sergeant, laying down covering fire from positions in the rocks behind the sangars, Edwards and three others attempted to escape. Within the first few metres, though, the captain was hit by several shots and crumpled to the ground, whereupon most of the tribesmen turned their rifles on him to ensure his death. The other three made it into cover and then laid down suppressive fire to allow

Above: A Belvedere helicopter operating from the Habilayn airstrip drops off supplies to an SAS patrol fighting Egyptian-backed rebels.

the second group to move away from their hiding place in the rocks in a classic leap-frog movement. The less tactically proficient tribesmen, meanwhile, continued to fire on the sangars and Captain Edwards' body.

For the next three or four hours the seven survivors, two of them wounded, slowly and carefully picked their way through the rocky terrain towards their base at Thumier. At one stage the two back markers realised that they were being followed and went to ground, leaving the other five to continue walking uninterrupted. When four trailing tribesmen reached the hidden back-markers, one of whom was the wounded corporal, they were dispatched in a hail of bullets. When, a short while later, another group of tribesmen almost caught up with the troopers, the same two back-markers carried out an identical and equally successful ambush.

About seven hours after evacuating the sangars and without a radio to contact base, the troopers reached the Dhala Road then went to ground until dawn, fearful that nervous friendly troops might open up on them in the dark. Just after

Above: SAS soldiers in the Radfan. The procedure was for small teams to watch for the enemy from high observation posts.

ally took place in a hostile operational environment. In the early days duties normally consisted of deep recces to gather intelligence or long periods spent in desert hides on observation, but in the closing stages of the campaign the emphasis switched to urban intelligence gathering and covert operations.

In July 1964, Britain agreed to grant independence to the Protectorates by 1968, though it was still intended that military bases would be retained in Aden State. From this point onwards, two of the three opposing nationalist organisations launched concerted campaigns to prove their superiority and fitness to rule after independence, mainly against the British but also against each other. The Soviet-controlled National Liberation Front (NLF) was the most active through 1964 and 1965, but the Egyptian-backed Front for the Liberation of South Yemen (FLOSY) resorted to widespread terrorism in 1966 (President Nasser of Egypt had seen his support for adjoining Yemen result in the Yemen Arab Republic being proclaimed in September 1962; he hoped to establish another Arab nationalist state to the south, and so provided FLOSY with weapons, training and camps). From late February 1966, when the new Wilson Government in Britain announced complete withdrawal, the power struggle between FLOSY and NLF caused anti-British violence to escalate rapidly. Often this violence was directed at easy targets, such as the families of servicemen.

'KEENI MEENI' WORK

The maze of narrow alleyways of the Crater district of Aden town was every bit as hostile to the British Army as the streets of Belfast would become a few years later. Gunmen and grenade-throwing terrorists, who knew the area like the backs of their hands, used the twisting passageways for hit-and-run ambushes or as escape routes. British Intelligence used many informers, but plainclothes agents and army officers working the district were wide open to attack, as Europeans stood out like a sore thumb. To take the war to the terrorists, the SAS was called in to set up covert intelligence-gathering and anti-terrorist squads.

dawn they flagged down a passing armoured car, which picked up the two wounded men. The other five marched back into camp behind it. The wounded corporal who had detected and then ambushed the tribesmen following the survivors was later deservedly awarded the Military Medal.

POLITICAL EMBARRASSMENT

While 9 Troop had been lying-up in the sangars on the morning of the 30th, a task force of East Anglians and armoured cars from 4 RTR had launched a diversionary raid up the Wadi Rabwa, but they met with stiffer resistance than had been expected. At this stage it was realised both that the intelligence available was woefully inadequate and that the Radfan tribesmen were much tougher adversaries than had been at first thought. As the SAS had not been able to reach and mark the DZ,

that night's parachute drop was called off, even though 3 Para volunteered to jump in blind. Subsequently it took the combined might of Radforce over a month to clear the region of rebels.

Although 9 Troop had not achieved its task, partly through bad luck but mainly because of one man's incapacity slowing it down, the patrol fought gallantly and its members lived up to the traditions of the SAS. The bodies of Captain Edwards and Trooper Warburton were later recovered, but the rebels had cut off their heads and displayed them publicly on poles in the Yemen. Regrettably, the first that their families knew of the deaths was through media coverage of this incident, at a time when they still thought their loved ones were just on exercise on Salisbury Plain.

Until the final British withdrawal from Aden, all three operational SAS squadrons served short periods in the Protectorates between their operational tours in Borneo. Seldom more than a few weeks long, these periods were ostensibly desert warfare training exercises, but they gener-

Above: When watching SAS teams in the mountains spotted rebel tribesmen, they would request air and artillery strikes against them.

Known in the Regiment as 'keeni meeni' jobs, these operations involved troopers with suitable facial features dressing appropriately and passing themselves off as Arabs (see box). This was not as difficult as it sounds because most troopers were deeply tanned after years of working in the open and many spoke passable Arabic. As most of the troopers were of sinewy build, even those with fair hair could make themselves look Arabic by growing beards and dyeing their hair if they had long straight noses.

By the end of December 1967, after much political fudging and needless loss of British lives, the Protectorates were abandoned to the Marxist NLF, who established the pro-Soviet People's Democratic Republic of Yemen (which was neither democratic nor for the people). For the SAS, however, the lessons learned in close-quarter combat techniques and experience of conducting urban clandestine missions were to stand the Regiment in good stead as the international terrorism of the 1970s changed the emphasis of much of its work.

But it was not much reward for three years of fighting, and the war in Aden was to come back and haunt Britain. The new regime in Aden immediately began to try and de-stabilise neighbouring Oman, which Britain was obligated to by treaty. In Oman, however, the SAS was to have a freer hand, and would ensure a very different outcome.

'Keeni Meeni'

During the Aden conflict the Yemenis infiltrated killer squads into the port of Aden itself, where they then assassinated local politicians who were friendly towards the British administration. In response, the SAS became involved in urban counter-insurgency in an effort to stop them in what was called 'keeni meeni' work, after the Swahili phrase that was used to describe the undulating, sinuous movement of a snake in long grass. In early 1966, Major Peter de la Billière of A Squadron established a close-quarter battle school to teach accurate handgun shooting techniques. He then chose a group of his men who could go into the Crater and Sheikh Othman districts of the port disguised in native Arab dress. The Fijians who served in the squadron at that time proved particularly adept at this kind of work, as their dark skin colour was similar to that of the locals. The 20-strong 'Keeni Meeni' unit operated from Ballycastle House, a block of flats in the Khormaksar military district of the port.

OMAN 1970-76

The 'Five Fronts' Campaign

In 1970, the Sultan of Oman was in deep trouble. His country was about to fall to communist rebels, and in despair he turned to his British allies. The British government, ever aware of political sensitivities, sent the SAS, a unit that could do the job in secret and in small numbers.

The short peaceful interlude between withdrawal from Aden at the end of November 1967 and the deployment of troops on the streets of Ulster in August 1969 was one of the very rare occasions since before Queen Victoria's reign when the British Army has not been engaged on a campaign somewhere or other in the world. With nowhere left abroad to train 'on-the-job' in combat conditions, the SAS turned its attention to more mundane exercises in support of the British Army of the Rhine (BAOR), though when opportunities to work outside western Europe arose, the Regiment snapped them up.

As the Regiment had played a major part in clearing up the Jebel Akhdar in Oman a few years previously, its credit was good with the Sultan, Said bin Taimur, who was only too happy to have them train in his backyard. Never ones to miss out on new challenges, the SAS Intelligence Cell at Hereford (nicknamed the 'Kremlin') constantly kept themselves well abreast of political developments worldwide, and when potential trouble loomed again in northern Oman in 1969, they had men on hand to assist.

The Persian (or Arabian) Gulf, through which most of the region's oil is exported, narrows considerably through the Straits of Hormuz before reaching the Gulf of Oman and thence the Indian Ocean. To the south of the Straits is the Musandum Peninsula, which belongs partly to Oman and partly to the United Arab Emirates, known at that time as the

Trucial States. To the Iraqis, who relied on safe passage of their oil exports through the Straits to sustain their economic growth, it made sense to befriend the fiercely independent hill tribesmen of the Musandum, so in 1969 they infiltrated military personnel into the area to train the natives.

FIRST DEPLOYMENT

At the request of the British-officered Sultan's Armed Forces, a reinforced Boat Troop from the SAS squadron training in Oman at the time went ashore by inflatables as a show of force in the area. The squadron's Air Troop then parachuted into the interior with the intention of cutting off any Iraqis' fleeing from the Boat Troop. The operation was reasonably successful in that the troop moving in from the sea made contact and took prisoners,

but inland one of the freefallers, 'Rip' Reddy, was killed when his parachute failed to open. This action is believed to have been the first operational HALO (High Altitude, Low Opening) deployment by the Regiment.

For the previous five years, Egypt and the Soviets had also been fomenting revolt against the Sultan among the hill tribes of Dhofar Province in the southwest. Their job was made much easier by the Sultan's almost complete lack of interest in his people, despite the vast wealth being generated from oil in the region. The ageing monarch saw the country and its riches as his private property, and its population as mere chattels. Medical care and education were virtually non-existent, except for members of the extended royal family. In the Sultan's view, the people of his backward nation were not ready for Western

Right: Under SAS guard, supplies for civil aid projects are off-loaded from an RAF transport in Dhofar, southern Oman.

ways, so foreigners were brought in to run the oilfields and the economy.

The native population was ruled with a rod of iron, and the Sultan had to grant his personal permission for any changes in lifestyle, no matter how small. No political opposition was allowed and dissenters were flogged or imprisoned. If their crime against the monarchy was regarded as serious, they were executed as traitors without right of appeal. Family and friends of offenders were also punished, and it was not unusual for the Sultan to have the life-sustaining water supply to a traitor's home village cut off or destroyed as a reprisal.

Clearly Britain could not allow an ally to continue in this fashion, so when the Wali (Sheikh) of Dhofar and the Sultan's western-educated heir decided to mount a peaceful coup, the new Conservative government promised its support. On 23 July 1970, the Wali confronted the Sultan in his private apartments and, after a scuffle in which both men were injured by the Sultan's pistol, the old man agreed to abdicate in favour of his son, Prince Qaboos (Said bin Taimur was banished to London, and lived out the two remaining years of his life in great luxury; it is said that when anyone mentioned the coup, he burst out laughing).

STOPPING THE ROT

No sooner had the news of the abdication broken than an SAS team flew out to Oman to act as bodyguards for the new Sultan. Educated in England and trained at Sandhurst, Sultan Qaboos favoured change and the introduction of basic human rights, realising full well that it was the only way of keeping his kingdom together. Coincidentally, only a few months before at one of their think-tank sessions, senior SAS officers had studied how the situation in the region could be stabilised. They now had the opportunity to put their plans into operation and, based on the experiences of Malaya and Borneo, the SAS proposed another 'hearts and minds' campaign.

To bring lasting stability to any region, the local populace must first be on the side of authority. The easiest way to ensure this is to improve their quality of

life and prove that the actions of the government are more benevolent and tangible than the vague promises made by those trying to exploit the masses. If the peasant farmer and his family are happy with their lot and feel secure, the 'freedom fighter' will soon lose support.

The SAS strategy in Oman was based on the 'Five Fronts' Campaign. This was devised by the commander of 22 SAS, Lieutenant-Colonel Johnny Watts, and entailed the Regiment waging war on five 'fronts': the establishment of an intelligence cell; the setting up of an information cell to ensure that the locals had reliable and truthful information concerning the Omani government's civil aid programme, and to counter the enemy's Radio Aden; a medical officer backed up by SAS medics; a veterinary officer to treat the locals' animals; and raising Dhofari units to fight for the Sultan.

The plan was primarily a catalyst, whereby the SAS would train the Omanis in the five tasks, with the ultimate aim of leaving them to do everything themselves. Watts knew that the success of the plan depended upon the Omani government wanting to improve the lot of the Dhofaris, otherwise it would be stillborn.

Fortunately, Sultan Qaboos was very different from his father. Soon after the

Above: SAS with firqat **troops near Salalah in Dhofar. The** firqats **were an integral part of the 'hearts and minds' campaign.**

new young Sultan took power, the SAS drafted out propaganda leaflets to be dropped by the RAF over rebel areas. These leaflets promised that the new regime would help make life more bearable for the hill tribes, and offered a personal amnesty from the Sultan for any rebel fighter who changed sides.

The rebels, or *adoo* as they were known (the Arabic word meaning 'enemy'), consisted of the Dhofar Liberation Front (DLF) and the People's Front for the Liberation of the Occupied Arabian Gulf (PFLOAG). The fighters of the DLF were Dhofaris and essentially traditional. The PFLOAG, on the other hand, was a communist group which was based in neighbouring Yemen. It had an abundance of Russian- and Chinese-supplied weapons and money, and it suggested a merger with the DLF. The latter was at first reluctant, but the PFLOAG's resources were too good to resist, and soon the DLF had been dominated. However, the Moslems in the ranks of the rebels were soon alienated by the radicalism of the PFLOAG, and they were therefore receptive to the amnesty.

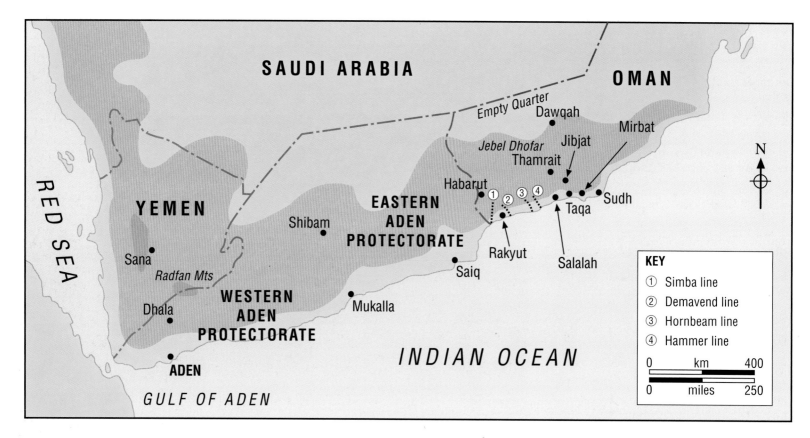

Incredibly, one of the first men to take up this offer was a top guerrilla leader, Salim Mubarak. This exceptional soldier, who had formerly served with the Trucial Scouts and had been sent for advanced military training in Britain, had become deeply disillusioned by the previous regime and defected soon after his return from Aldershot. A senior figure in the DLF, he and 24 men had fought their way out of a communist encirclement on the Jebel Dhofar. The SAS and Army Intelligence were quick to make use of his extensive knowledge. In addition, Mubarak advocated the raising of an anti-rebel unit called a *firqat* (the Arabic word for 'company').

'HEARTS AND MINDS'

To keep their promise to raise living standards, rather than just chasing rebels, the SAS set about providing civil aid to the villagers in the foothills of the Dhofari Mountains. Although at this time there was only one troop available, pairs of troopers established themselves in the villages where they administered basic medical treatment, surveyed and drilled for wells, provided security and generally helped in any way that they could. Within six months of the 'hearts and minds' cam-

paign getting off the ground, more than 200 rebels had changed sides.

The best and most trustworthy of the defectors were then recruited into the *firqats*, trained and led by small SAS teams. Usually one trooper in each four-man SAS patrol was a linguistic specialist who would know the rudiments of Arabic, but as the Omanis were on the whole illiterate it was necessary for every British soldier to learn their language. After retraining, the *firqats* were sent back to patrol bases in their home areas accompanied by their SAS trainers, who were usually officially referred to as British Army Training Teams or BATTs.

More SAS operatives were drafted into the country as and when they became available until, by the second half of 1971, both B and G Squadrons were fully deployed. By now several *firqats* had been trained and established in camps along the Salalah coastal plain south of the desert highlands known as the Jebel Massif. This 1300m (4250ft) high plateau ran parallel with the coast for about 250km (150 miles) from the western border with what was now the Marxist state of South Yemen. The jebel was, of course, the perfect stronghold for the communist-backed hill tribesmen.

Above: When Aden fell and became the Republic of Yemen, it was easy for the adoo to ship arms and men into Dhofar Province.

Down on the Salalah Plain, the newly established *firqat* camps were beginning to prove their worth. When the British set up a camp, they first flooded the area with British and Sultan's troops to drive away any rebels. Royal Engineers then laid access roads, built an airstrip or helipad, drilled a well for fresh water and constructed a small strongpoint. When the camp was finished, the SAS training team and the *firqat* would set up shop inside the perimeter and the other troops would move on to the next location.

THE *FIRQATS*

When Salim Mubarak defected from the DLF, he first approached the SAS's Major Tony Jeapes with the idea of forming a military unit containing ex-rebels. Jeapes took up the idea and began training the men at Mirbat. The first *firqat* was called the Firqat Salahadin after the great Islamic leader. It was an inspired move, and soon the SAS was training other *firqats*.

The initial number of men in each *firqat* was between 30 and 40 men, though they rapidly grew in size following mili-

tary success. The *Firqat Salahadin*, for example, numbered 68 men by late April 1972, and at the end of the war the total *firqat* strength was 2000 men.

The *firqats* were not conventional infantry, far from it, but they were excellent in the reconnaissance role, acting as a forward screen and for gathering intelligence (which often entailed nothing more than picking up gossip from the next village).

From day one, locals were positively encouraged to come into the base to collect fresh water and the SAS medics operated a simple clinic. Medicines, treatment and bandages were dispensed free and at first even food was distributed without charge. Later, a nominal price was put on government supplies to encourage the population to become more self-sufficient by bartering and trading produce to vary their diet. Slowly the new regime won over the locals, and as the benefits of supporting the government became clearly visible, more rebels were persuad-

ed by their relatives in the hills to desert and join the *firqats*.

This is not to say that the military situation was at all favourable, despite the people's acceptance of what the SAS was doing for them. The whole of the Jebel Dhofar was in the hands of thousands of PFLOAG fighters, who were busy shipping weapons and ammunition across the border from Yemen.

THE SULTAN'S FORCES

The Sultan's Armed Forces on their own were totally inadequate to deal with the rebels militarily. Consisting of the Muscat and Northern Frontier Regiments, they were at first able to contain the rebellion, but as rebel numbers increased they were thrown onto the defensive. In addition, the tactics of the Sultan's Air Force were disastrous. If any rebel units were reported to the Air Force, the latter usually dispatched one or two aircraft to try to find them. When they arrived at the reported spot the

Above: Civil aid in action. Water gushes from a freshly dug well, courtesy of Britain's Special Air Service Regiment.

rebels had invariably melted away, so the pilots simply bombed and strafed the nearest village. This naturally alienated the villagers and threw them into the arms of the rebels.

Johnny Watts decided that the time had come to take the war to the enemy. By February 1971 the position along he coastal strip in Dhofar had been stabilised. There were 200 men in *firqats*, and the civil aid programme was going well. He decided that the *firqats* needed blooding, and chose the small fishing village of Sudh for this purpose. It was taken on 24 February with little opposition. Their morale suitably boosted, Watts decided to use them again in March, when the SAS and *firqats* mounted a successful probing action onto the jebel. It was now time for the SAS to establish a firm foothold on the Jebel Dhofar itself.

Operation 'Jaguar'

Operation 'Jaguar' was the codename for the SAS-led assault on the Jebel Dhofar in October 1971. It was ultimately successful, though the antics of the firqats nearly drove the SAS commander, Lieutenant-Colonel Johnny Watts, to despair.

With five *firqats* operational by September 1971, it was decided that a major offensive could now be launched against the rebel tribesmen, or *adoo*, to establish a firm government foothold on the Jebel Dhofar itself. Code-named Operation 'Jaguar', this operation would involve both SAS squadrons, the *firqats*, a platoon of loyal Askari tribesmen from northern Oman and two companies of British-led soldiers of the Sultan's Armed Forces.

In all, the commander of 22 SAS, Lieutenant-Colonel Johnny Watts, had assembled 800 men for the operation. The only problem was that the attack was due to start in October. However, Ramadan was due to begin on the 20th of that month, which would severely curtail the fighting effectiveness of Watts' Omani soldiers and *firqats*. However, a dispensation had been granted by religious leaders to allow the troops to fight through Ramadan in what was considered a battle against atheistic communism. Johnny Watts had taken care of everything – or so he thought.

THE OPERATION BEGINS

B Squadron, the Askaris and two *firqats* would start the operation by recapturing an old government airstrip on the jebel to the east of Jibjat. Once the landing strip had been secured, the remainder of the Operation 'Jaguar' Task Force, including complements of mortars and pack howitzers, would be flown in by transport aircraft and helicopter.

The attack phase of the operation commenced on 2 October 1971. Armoured cars escorted the truck-borne assault troops from a base camp some 90km (56 miles) north of the jebel until the roads ran out in the foothills. The soldiers then moved up a wadi to the start line and rested until last light. From this point on they would have to march with

full kit uphill in darkness and in the sweltering desert night air for nearly 12 hours until they reached their objective next morning. The SAS soldiers who took part were each carrying 1000 rounds of machine gun ammunition, four SLR magazines, SLR rifle and three full water bottles. No wonder it was nicknamed 'the death march'.

To the south, a small contingent of troopers from G Squadron launched a diversionary attack to draw the *adoo* away from their colleagues. As daylight broke, the near exhausted assault force was just short of the objective, but the diversionary attack had drawn the enemy away and the airstrip was taken unopposed.

Once the immediate perimeter was secured, SAS patrols scaled the high ground nearby and built themselves sangars in the rocks, overlooking possible routes which the *adoo* could use to attack the airstrip. Below the troopers the airborne build-up of men, materiel and sup-

Above: Troops of the Sultan's Armed Forces (SAF) on their way to take part in Operation 'Jaguar' in October 1971.

plies continued, until by mid-afternoon more than 800 troops had been deployed. When the expected enemy counter-attack finally commenced on the west flank sangar just before last light, one of the SAS patrols held off the 20–30 attackers without loss.

On the evening of 3 October, it was realised that another airstrip on the edge of Jibjat and some 7–8km (4–5 miles) distant, actually offered better facilities for long-term re-supply. The following morning the entire force moved location and by that afternoon the new airstrip was secure and open to aviation traffic. The SAS force was then split into two battle groups, each accompanied by a *firqat*, to probe the surrounding area. During the next week, the easterly group came under sustained attack by rebels and an SAS sergeant was killed. On the 6th a patrol from the westerly group was bounced by rebels controlling a major water hole, but three days later the battle group occupied the position after a heavy firefight. One of the Fijian troopers was injured in this assault, but fortunately no SAS lives were lost.

It was at this point that the *firqats* decided they would stop fighting and observe Ramadan. As this involved a period of not eating or drinking, this would drastically reduce their effectiveness. Watts was enraged, and was forced to abandon some positions and re-group at a place called White City. He then informed the *firqat* leaders that he was considering withdrawing all SAS support for them. As they relied on the Regiment for their training, weapons and supplies, the *firqats* decided they would fight after all.

THE *ADOO* COUNTERATTACKS
By the 12th the troops committed to Operation 'Jaguar' had advanced 25km (15 miles) into enemy territory and had set up a well-defended forward base only 8 km (5 miles) from the main rebel stronghold. The *adoo*, however, were not accepting their presence gracefully, and frequently mortared the base and ambushed patrols. They also launched a fierce counterattack, which resulted in a fierce firefight. Soldier 'I' was one of those who fought in it: 'I clipped a fresh belt of 200 rounds on to the old belt and began feeding the beast. Stream after stream of tracer zapped into the area of the [enemy] heavy machine gun, the sound of the GPMG drumming in my ears.' Over the next three months, however, the British, Omani regular and *firqat* troops slowly forced the rebels off the high ground.

Isolated *adoo* attacks on government or British patrols and installations continued through 1972 without too much success as the British 'hearts and minds' campaign gained results. As ever-increasing numbers of rebels were persuaded to change sides by their now prospering relatives on the coastal plains, the rebel command was

forced to find a way of saving face. Simply killing a number of government troops or *firqat* personnel out on patrol on the jebel would achieve little as word would not get out. The logical answer to their problem was to try to wipe out a *firqat* post completely, thereby proving that they were still in control. However, to ram the message home, their success needed to be in public and witnessed by what the *adoo* considered to be turn-coat villagers.

'Jaguar' was, by any reckoning, a great success. The government had established a presence on the Jebel Dhofar, and had also reinforced its control over the coastal plain and its towns. In addition, government policies for the improvement of agriculture, medical facilities and education could be put into effect. Wells could be drilled on the jebel itself, bringing fresh water to the locals. The effect of the well-drilling programme should not be underestimated. The effect on the locals of seeing clear blue water gush from what had been bare rock moments before was a powerful symbol. The only blemish concerning 'Jaguar' was the firqats, who proved they could be headstrong and infuriating to work with.

The *adoo*

*A*doo is an Arab word meaning 'enemy'. It was used by the SAS during the war in Oman to describe the guerrillas of the People's Front for the Liberation of the Occupied Arabian Gulf (PFLOAG) and the Dhofar Liberation Front (DLF). The fighters of the latter were raised from Dhofari tribesmen. They were organised along tribal lines and were armed with mostly obsolete weaponry. Over the border in Yemen, however, the Russian- and Chinese-backed young revolutionaries of the PFLOAG had money and modern weaponry. These, combined with high motivation, soon absorbed the DLF fighters and forced the Sultan's forces onto the defensive. Throughout the war the *adoo* fought with determination and courage, and it took six years of hard fighting for the SAS and Omanis to finally defeat them.

Right: A transport aircraft brings in rations and ammunition to the airstrip at Jibjat during the first phase of Operation 'Jaguar'.

The Battle of Mirbat

The Adoo attack on Mirbat on 19 July 1972 was aimed at destroying the credibility of Sultan Qaboos' regime in Oman, as well as teaching the SAS a bloody lesson. However, the nine-man SAS BATT team at Mirbat destroyed the rebel assault in a stunning one-day action.

The place chosen for the *adoo* attack that was designed to persuade the people that their cause would eventually triumph was the coastal hamlet of Mirbat, about 65km (40 miles) to the east of Salalah. Being right at the end of the road from Salalah and close to the foot of the Jebel Dhofar, it appeared to be perfect for the job. The local police, the Dhofar Gendarmerie, and the SAS were garrisoned on the northern outskirts of the village, which meant that the *adoo* could easily approach them without alerting the dogs or firqat personnel in the village. The attack was timed to begin at first light on 19 July 1972.

The *adoo* had planned their attack well, for the rainy period would ensure that the Sultan of Oman's Air Force (SOAF) would be unable to provide air support because of low cloud. In addition, the blanket of drizzle and low cloud that hung over Mirbat and the surrounding hills meant that the SAS soldiers in Mirbat could not see the build-up of enemy forces that was frantically going on around them.

The arrangements at Mirbat were virtually no different to those at any other *firqat* camp, though there was a small detachment of around two dozen gendarmes permanently stationed in a small fort to the northeast of the hamlet. Some 30 Askari tribesmen, who were loyal to the Wali of Dhofar and who provided perimeter security for the camp, were garrisoned in a fortified house to the northwest. The British Army Training Team (BATT), in reality nine men from 8 Troop of B Squadron 22 SAS, operated out of a large house between the Wali's fort and the village. Nearly all of the *firqat* men lived with their wives or families in the village houses. The entire area was bounded by the sea on two sides and a barbed wire fence on the others.

The *adoo* may have been illiterate hill tribesmen, but that did not mean that they were poor soldiers. Generations of inter-tribal strife and adherence to the principle of 'an eye for an eye', meant they were all totally fearless fighters. They also had to be pretty good shots and trackers to survive in the hostile wilderness of the jebel. Their leaders, too, had been trained in guerrilla tactics by the communists, and they were all well supplied with modern weapons and ammunition. In addition to Kalashnikov assault rifles and RPD machine guns, they also had 12.5mm heavy machine guns, light and medium mortars, rocket-propelled grenades and even at least one 75mm recoilless rifle, and possibly two.

WEAKENING THE GARRISON

Like the SAS, the *adoo* had a good intelligence gathering set-up, probably including some informers amongst the *firqat*. They almost certainly knew that the BATT was right at the end of its tour and due to hand over to its replacements within days. It was highly likely, therefore, that the soldiers in this quiet outpost would be more relaxed than usual.

To ease the odds, a small number of armed tribesmen had made themselves highly visible at the extremity of the Mirbat area of operations a couple of days before the planned attack. As expected, about 60 of the *firqat* were dispatched to look for them, which reduced the number of defenders by a third. This action may also have been to protect informers and possibly some *firqat* who were not 100 per cent sure where their loyalties lay. It is even possible that *adoo* military activity had been deliberately scaled down in this sector to heighten the boredom for the British. In fact other than occasional snipe-and-run or snap mortar attacks on the post (usually in the early mornings), neither of which were particularly effec-

Left: The SAS BATT house at Mirbat. During the battle the two machine guns on the roof inflicted many casualties on the adoo.

Right: The focus of the adoo attack during the battle was the Dhofar Gendarmerie fort to the northeast of the village of Mirbat.

tive, recent rebel activity in the immediate area had been minimal.

A small section of gendarmes mounted a night picket on a low rise known as Jebel Ali, just under 1000m (3280ft) outside the wire compound, to the north of their fort. Just before dawn *adoo* scouts silently climbed the hill and slit their throats, but one alert gendarme managed to loose off a shot before the hill was overrun. Assuming that they had now lost the element of surprise, the *adoo* mortar line set up to the north of Jebel Ali at a range of about 2000m (6566ft) from the fort and opened fire.

Inside the BATT house, the young Captain Mike Kealy (he was 23 years old and nicknamed the 'baby Rupert' by the men) and the eight troopers under his command were starting to stir when the first mortar round landed. At first they did not pay too much attention, as from time to time the *adoo* would loose off a few rounds at dawn then disappear before being detected. However, as the individual crumps turned into a barrage, the SAS headed for their stand-to positions.

THE BATTLE BEGINS

At the BATT-house, four men manned the 7.62mm General Purpose Machine Gun (GPMG) and the 0.5in Browning heavy machine gun, which were emplaced with sandbags at the northern corners of the roof. To one side of the building three more troopers, including one of the patrol's two Fijians, manned an 81mm mortar in a sandbagged position. The eighth man, Fijian Corporal Labalaba, had sprinted over to the old Dhofar Gendarmerie (DG) fort to command the World War II-vintage 25-pounder artillery piece which was emplaced beside the front door there. All held their fire, awaiting the now inevitable infantry advance from the north as the *adoo* mortars ceaselessly pounded the perimeter

Right: The Dhofar Gendarmerie fort at Mirbat. Beside the fort was positioned the gunpit containing the 25-pounder field gun.

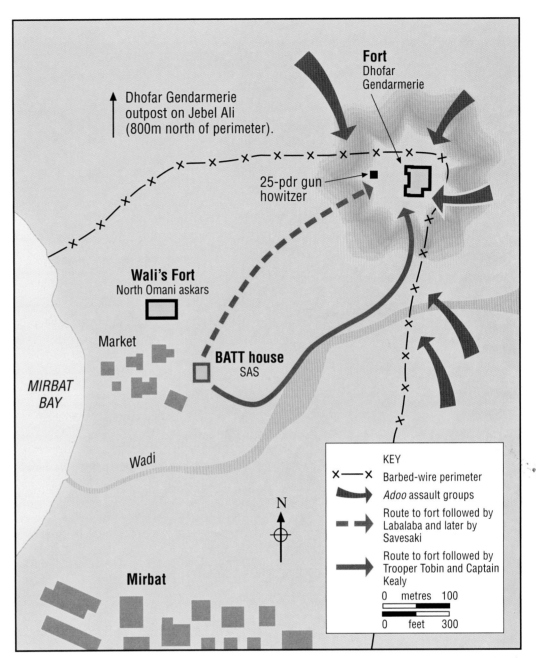

Dhofar Gendarmerie outpost on Jebel Ali (800m north of perimeter).

Fort
Dhofar Gendarmerie

25-pdr gun howitzer

Wali's Fort
North Omani askars

Market

MIRBAT BAY

BATT house
SAS

Wadi

N

Mirbat

KEY

×——× Barbed-wire perimeter

Adoo assault groups

Route to fort followed by Labalaba and later by Savesaki

Route to fort followed by Trooper Tobin and Captain Kealy

0   metres   100

0   feet   300

Left: Corporal Labalaba, the hero of the Battle of Mirbat, whose actions manning the 25-pounder blunted the adoo *assault.*

ammunition for each man in the relief party. All the men at Mirbat had to do was hold on until they arrived.

But at Mirbat the situation was deteriorating fast, with the Gendarmerie fort bearing the brunt of the enemy mortar and machine-gun fire. As mortar rounds, machine-gun fire and rockets slammed into the BATT house and DG fort, Kealy realised this was no probing attack. To the southeast of the fort, a well-drilled party of about 40 *adoo* suddenly broke cover from the wadi which had been concealing their approach and moved towards the gaps mortared in the wire. The gendarmes on the ramparts opened up with everything that they had, and the Browning gunner on the BATT house roof joined in the fray.

THE ATTACK ON THE GUNPIT

The 25-pounder gun outside the fort was a key target for the *adoo*, and its Omani gunner was soon put out of action. Corporal Labalaba was determined to keep the gun firing, though, and he continued to load, lay and fire on his own. Eventually, however, he too was hit, but, although his jaw was smashed, he managed to call for help on a walkie-talkie radio. His request for assistance was answered by one of his Fijian buddies, who sprinted the 400m (1312ft) between the BATT house and gunpit under intense rifle and machine gun fire to take charge of the gun.

In the gunpit Savesaki applied a field dressing to Labalaba's wound to stop the flow of blood. But shortly after Savesaki was himself wounded, and he fell back against the sandbags which surrounded the gun. By this time the *adoo* fire against the gunpit had intensified, and the gun's shield had been riddled with bullets. Corporal Labalaba was still firing the gun on his own, but then he took another hit which was to prove fatal.

The Askaris and the gendarmes were giving as good as they got, but their forts were under intensive fire from an enemy who had now well and truly breached the

wire into the desert sand. Both fortresses and the BATT house were now coming under intense fire from the advancing horde of over 200 men.

Captain Kealy quickly appraised the situation and sent one of his men down to the radio room to call for reinforcements. The trooper was just about to encode his signal when a recoilless rifle round struck the BATT house and he threw caution to the wind by keying the message in plain English. In his reminiscences the trooper remembers thinking, 'Fuck the Rule Book, the *adoo* know we're here anyway!' Back at the base camp at Um Al Gwarif, just outside Salalah, the day suddenly kicked off for the men of G Squadron, who had been preparing to relieve their B Squadron colleagues at Mirbat and Taqa .

Some of G Squadron's officers and senior NCOs had already left the base camp on recces or to liaise with their outgoing opposite numbers. Those who were not already in the field had been programmed for a morning of live firing to give them a chance to zero their weapons on the camp range. When the balloon went up at Mirbat, therefore, 23 fully tooled-up troopers, complete with no less than nine GPMGs, were fortunately on hand to reinforce the defenders. To fly them along the coast in low cloud, drizzle and poor visibility would not be easy, but the helicopter pilots of the Sultan's Armed Forces rose to the challenge. Three Omani Hueys were scrambled as the G Squadron troopers headed in trucks for the airfield with 1000 rounds of

Right: The fishing village of Mirbat, which on 19 July 1972 marked the turning point of the SAS's counter-insurgency war in Oman.

perimeter fence (they were also out-gunned, being armed mostly with bolt-action rifles). The *firqat* men still in the village had also joined the fray from the south, and were doing their best to drive out any *adoo* who breached the perimeter, in spite of the mortar rounds landing among them. Many *firqat* members became casualties as the battle unfolded, and the downstairs room of the BATT house had to be turned into a dressing station to cope with the ever-increasing numbers of wounded. At this point one of the SAS troopers manning the GPMG took a radio and headed for the helicopter landing zone on the beach, in the hope that he could talk in the casualty evacuation helicopter promised by HQ.

THE BATTLE'S CRISIS POINT

In the gunpit one Fijian lay dead and the other lay wounded. If the 25-pounder were to fall into *adoo* hands, it could be turned against the BATT house and the battle would be lost, so Mike Kealy decided to attempt to reach the gun himself. Trooper Tobin, one of the two trained medics, volunteered to go with the captain to tend to the two injured Fijians and anyone else still alive in the gunpit (radio contact had been lost with the gunpit earlier). For the first couple of hundred metres of their sprint, both men were out of sight of most of the enemy, but inevitably they soon came under a hail of gunfire. The troopers manning the BATT house roof GPMG and Browning laid down covering fire for them, and both men reached the safety of the sandbagged emplacement without injury. Shortly later, however, Trooper Tobin was killed outright by a round as he tended to one of the wounded.

As the still-advancing *adoo* reached within grenade-throwing range of the gunpit, it looked certain that they would overrun the position, but without warning a sheet of lead spewed from the skies. Through the low cloud and mist, a pair of British-piloted SOAF Strikemaster jets swept low over the battlefield to strafe the

attackers. Their first pass, which arrived just in the nick of time to save Mike Kealy, was directed in by the trooper on the helicopter landing zone by radio. Despite the atrocious flying conditions and the curtain of bullets fired into their path, the Omani Strikemasters continued to gun, rocket and bomb the *adoo* until they eventually stemmed the flow of the attack. One jet was damaged quite badly by gunfire, but the pilot managed to nurse it back to base.

THE TIDE IS TURNED

Throughout the battle, the SAS mortar team and machine gunners had been firing until the barrels of their weapons were so hot that the rain was turning to steam on them. Indeed, so high was the rate of fire that the 0.5in Browning could only be used on single-shot mode towards the close of the battle. When the mortar first opened up, its targets had been a couple of kilometres distant, but after the first wave of jets left it was engaging targets virtually alongside the DG fort. In fact, so close were the enemy at this stage that the mortar commander had to clasp the barrel to his chest and raise the bipod legs to achieve the required short range.

Roughly three hours after the attack was launched, the SAS troopers from G

Squadron arrived on board three Hueys and launched an immediate counterattack from the beach landing zone. With two GPMGs to every five troopers, the weight of fire brought to bear on the *adoo* was overwhelming, and they soon turned tail.

The Battle of Mirbat had been conclusively won, though two troopers, some of the *firqat*, the Omani gunner and a Dhofari gendarme lost their lives, and several men were wounded in a few short hours. On the other hand, in addition to losing about 40 of their most experienced fighters on the battlefield, plus those who died of their wounds in the days and weeks after the battle, the loss of face to the *adoo* was considerable.

In Britain the battle received no publicity. For this reason the gallantry awards given to those who fought there only became known four years later. Kealy won the Distinguished Service Order for his leadership that day, while two of the others received a Military Medal and Distinguished Conduct Medal. Surely the most miserly award was a Mention in Despatches for Labalaba. It has been opinioned that in a more overt conflict his actions at Mirbat would have won him the Victoria Cross. He undoubtedly single-handedly prevented the fall of the gunpit, and therefore saved the battle. A Mention in Despatches seems an insult.

The SAS Victorious

The SAS victory at Mirbat was not the end of the war in southern Oman – there was still another four years of fighting left – but it did mark the beginning of the end. Slowly but surely, the adoo were forced onto the offensive, and the SAS won the battle for 'hearts and minds'.

Over the three years following the battle of Mirbat, government troops, supported by Iranian and Jordanian Special Forces, consolidated the ground won by the *firqat* and their SAS trainers. The *adoo* had lost many men at Mirbat, but far more important than these physical losses was the loss of prestige. The fact that they had outnumbered the defenders by so many resulted in a severe loss of face. Far from convincing the Dhofaris that the Sultan and his British advisers were finished, the battle reinforced the credibility of Sultan Qaboos. In addition, the civil aid programme designed to improve the living standards of the Dhofaris was stepped up. Here was physical proof that the Sultan was as good as his word. The results were not long in coming: there were many more defections from the *adoo*.

THE *ADOO* ON THE DEFENSIVE

Slowly but surely, the *adoo* were forced farther back towards the Yemeni border as a series of patrol bases and defensive lines were established. These lines consisted of barbed wire, booby traps, mines and ground sensors designed to cut the *adoo* off from their supply centres in Yemen.

In the central and eastern areas of the jebel, constant *firqat* patrolling had virtually wiped out all rebel resistance, and in the west conventional troops had cut many of the *adoo* lines of supply. The only major rebel stronghold left was the near-deserted coastal town of Rakyut less than 40km (25 miles) from the Yemeni border, and which the communists were claiming was the capital of the 'freed territories'.

A few kilometres to the north of Rakyut, on the edge of the jebel escarpment, the *adoo* had a major supply dump in a series of caves above the Wadi Shershitti. On 4 January 1975, a battalion group of the Sultan's Armed Forces, supported by three SAS troops and 40-50 *firqat* members, launched the first phase of an assault on the heavily defended cave system. One SAS troop split into four-man patrols to accompany each regular company, and the other two troops joined the *firqat* as spearhead for the attack. During the first day, the SAS and *firqat* spearhead advanced for 3 km (1.8 miles) through the dense brush under sustained machine gun fire to capture an area of high ground and establish a supply base. By late afternoon, despite many *firqat* casualties, the objective was seized and the first helicopters had started to arrive. The *adoo* counterattacked at dusk, but were easily beaten back.

TAKING THE SHERSHITTI CAVES

The main phase of the assault on the caves commenced at dawn on the 5th, with three Omani companies advancing through the cover of thick brush in a long sweeping attack. Unfortunately, due to the thickness of the vegetation, the officer commanding the lead company misjudged his position and the entire battalion ended up to the west of the objective instead of to the north. When the second Omani company was then forced to advance over an open area, *adoo* machine gunners hidden on overlooking high ground mowed many of them down. The situation was only recovered by the actions of the four-man SAS patrol seconded to the lead company manning its machine guns and opening up on the *adoo* position. The SAS officer in overall charge of the operation dispatched his second in command, a Fijian sergeant, to lead from the front. Once in position he called down air and mortar strikes to force the *adoo* to abandon their positions. Under a hail of fire the *adoo* attack slackened off somewhat.

With the element of surprise now well and truly lost, there was no way that an assault on the caves could go ahead. As the Omani forces still held the high ground overlooking the caves, however, all was not lost. Heavy machine guns were set up to cover the caves and the access road from long range, and a little later two

Left: SAS soldiers on the Jebel Dhofar in mid-1975. By this time the adoo had been forced back to the Yemeni border.

recoilless rifles were also put into position. Finally, a Saladin armoured car with a 76mm gun was brought up into position, and for five days fire was poured into the caves to make them unusable. With their major stores depot now destroyed, the *adoo* were unable to continue fighting in the area to any great extent.

Technically the operation around the Shershitti Caves had been a defeat, but as the *adoo* were now denied their use, and the fighting had allowed the Iranians to capture Rakyut, allowing a new defensive line to be constructed to stop *adoo* infiltration along the coastal plain, it was turned into a long-term victory.

THE END IN SIGHT

Other than a few isolated incidents, the remainder of 1975 passed off relatively peacefully for the SAS in Oman. Seven *firqats* were fully operational by this stage of the war, and their military capability was such that the four-man SAS patrol attached to each was really only needed for liaison duties. One final big push on the western borders was planned for mid-October, but in the end a diversionary move by Omani forces from the mountain-top positions in Sarfait met with virtually no resistance, and therefore the main operation was not needed.

By early December 1975 the entire Dhofar region was declared free of rebels and, with the peace holding, the SAS were withdrawn early in the new year. To this day, however, the Regiment continues to train in desert and jebel operations with the Sultan's blessing. Despite the ferocity of the Omani campaigns and the harsh conditions endured over six years, only 12 members of the Regiment lost their lives. In return for the Regiment's sacrifices, plus of course that of the Omanis and their allies from Iran and Jordan, the spread of communism in the region was finally halted.

So the war in Oman was over, and its conduct has left a superb example of how a modern counter-insurgency war should be fought by government-backed forces. The size of the SAS commitment was never large – it never exceeded 80 men at any one time – but the soldiers' attitude and conduct had been the deciding fac

tor. Though individual SAS units had fought well during the war, as the Battle of Mirbat showed, the Regiment's 'hearts and minds' campaign, which had been patiently conducted by four-man patrols throughout Dhofar, had been the key to victory. Little things had made the difference, such as the ability of individual troopers to converse with the Dhofaris in their own tongue, to treat their sick and livestock, and the subsequent bond established between civilians and soldiers, had laid the basis for military victory.

THE CAMPAIGN IN RETROSPECT

Of course there had been difficulties. Many among the Omani armed forces, for example, looked upon the Dhofaris with disdain, and this never entirely disappeared. In particular, Omani regular officers were scathing about the value of the *firqats*. However, the SAS convinced them of the wisdom of having them on operations. In addition, practices that were anathema to the waging of a counter-insurgency campaign, such as the indiscriminate bombing of Dhofari villages were stopped.

Nor should the effect of modern drugs and well-drilling equipment be underestimated. Dhofar Province in the 1960s resembled a medieval fiefdom, being poor, barren, having an inhospitable cli-

Above: SAS men with Arab tribesmen in Dhofar. The ability of individual troopers to speak local languages helped their cause.

mate and being ruled over by an autocratic despot. The drilling of wells and the administration of modern medicines brought about a change in the quality of life to the average Dhofari that is difficult to conceive. This contrasted sharply with the empty words of the adoo.

Of course, the calibre of the SAS soldiers who fought in Oman was also a significant factor in bringing victory. Men such as Johnny Watts were almost visionary in formulating a strategy for winning the war. Tony Jeapes, who also commanded the Regiment in Oman after Watts, paid tribute to his predecessor: 'More than anyone else, it was the strategy he had devised and the groundwork he had completed that was to lead to the ultimate defeat of the enemy.'

The SAS had also won a strategic victory, for its efforts had ensured that Oman remained in the hands of a ruler that was friendly towards the West. While the Yemen and Iran were torn apart by rebellions, Oman was allowed to develop peacefully. It did not, and has not, turned into a Western democratic state, but it is not in the hands of a Marxist dictatorship which is opposed to the West's interests.

NORTHERN IRELAND

Early Operations

The war in Oman (1970-76) meant the SAS did not have the manpower to maintain a sizeable presence in Northern Ireland. However, it did help form a British Army intelligence-gathering unit, and also participated in the general war against terrorism.

The years of civil unrest and violence in Northern Ireland, known as 'The Troubles', started in earnest in January 1969 when a civil rights march by members of the minority Roman Catholic community was broken up by Protestants. Police officers escorting the march made little effort to stop the violence, and that night barricades went up in the Catholic Bogside area of Londonderry.

The situation was kept under control, just, by the politicians until the following August, when a Protestant parade in Londonderry and a counter-demonstration by Catholics turned into a full-scale riot. Within three days, the inter-communal violence had spread to towns throughout the Province and the British Army was put on the streets to try to keep the peace. The long-standing Republican movement and its paramilitary wing, the Irish Republican Army (IRA), took full advantage of the chaos, and mounted a long and bloody campaign against the security forces, the agencies of government and the Protestant Loyalist movement.

FIRST SAS DEPLOYMENT
The first recorded involvement of the SAS in Ulster came in September 1969, when D Squadron was dispatched to the east coast of the Province. Based in Newtownards to the east of Belfast, its area of responsibility was the coastal region of the counties of Antrim and Down. The squadron's prime function over the next couple of months was to check for gun-running, particularly from Scotland, where the Loyalists had strong support. In addition to openly watching ports and undertaking occasional searches of suspect boats, SAS men also patrolled inland

in the more rural areas. When on patrol, the troopers wore standard Army uniform with Winged Dagger cap badge. By November, however, the SAS was needed in Oman and it left the Province.

Individual members of the Regiment did serve in Ulster in the early days, particularly in intelligence gathering and advisory roles, but they would have been seconded to other outfits, such as Military Intelligence. One specialist unit to which it is known that individual troopers and officers were posted was the Military Reconnaissance Force (MRF), whose operatives worked in civilian clothes. However, most members of the MRF were drawn from the Intelligence Corps, the Royal Signals or even the Military Police, and their role was mainly information gathering rather than offensive action. Their main task when away from their desks was to photograph suspected terrorist 'players' from both sides of the divided community, though at this stage the Republicans were the prime targets.

To photograph an IRA 'player' and his contacts, it was necessary for the men of the MRF to blend into the area so that they were not 'pinged' and turned into targets themselves. For this reason, soldiers with genuine Irish accents were much in demand and the SAS had its fair share of those. Naturally, working in such a potentially hostile environment, MRF operatives were armed for self-defence and occasionally they had recourse to their weapons, but they were not 'death squads' as some sectors of the Republican movement have on occasion claimed.

One MRF operation, often wrongly attributed to the SAS, was the running of the Four Square Laundry in Belfast in the

latter half of 1972. This outfit used an actual laundry as a screen for covert intelligence gathering, complete with a van collection service in Republican areas. In addition to watching the movements of suspects, the laundry was able to gather forensic evidence of weapons and explosives handling from residues left on clothes sent in for cleaning. All of the staff were police and soldiers raised in the Province, and able to blend in well with the local community. Eventually, the team's cover was blown, and on 2 October 1972 the driver was shot to death but his female assistant managed to escape.

INTER-AGENCY RIVALRY
After an inquiry into the Four Square Laundry incident and a couple of other controversial operations which had involved the MRF, it was decided that the unit had to be disbanded. Its responsibilities were passed onto the Intelligence Corps, as the Army required its own sources of information free from the inter-departmental politics and squabbles of MI5 (counter-intelligence), MI6 (intelligence gathering) and the RUC's Special Branch. Due to a lack of trust, each of these agencies on occasion withheld information from the others which they felt might jeopardise their sources or undercover operatives. The Army had often, therefore, been kept in the dark. Naturally it took a while for the new military information gathering unit to establish itself in the Province, and experienced SAS officers were drafted in to help train it. However, without men on the ground the Army was blind, so towards the end of 1974 some experienced troops from B Squadron were brought in to

cover until the new formation was fully up and running.

Under the cover designation of 4 Field Survey Troop Royal Engineers (4 FST RE), but in reality 14 Intelligence Company, the new unit deployed in the spring of 1974. Its headquarters was in Lisburn, but its frontline operatives were stationed in the 'bandit country' of Armagh alongside a real Royal Engineers unit for extra cover. The officer in command of this team, Captain Ball, was a former paratrooper who had risen through the ranks via the SAS to be commissioned into an infantry regiment. He was credited with having set up the first covert observation post (COP) in Republican West Belfast on a prior posting to Ulster with the King's Own Scottish Borderers in 1971, so was well qualified to lead 4 FST in its covert observation role.

From its inception, 14 Intelligence Company, or '14 Int' as most British soldiers refer to it, worked closely with the SAS, and in the early days B Squadron personnel helped with on-the-job training. Indeed, so close was the relationship

between 14 Int and the SAS over the next two decades that many journalists were unable to differentiate between the two units. In general terms, 14 Int is responsible for both overt and covert intelligence gathering and collation, whereas 22 SAS is tasked more with close observation in areas of great danger and direct action against armed terrorists. Of course sometimes the roles have to overlap.

PARTIAL SAS WITHDRAWAL

By the end of the summer of 1974, with 14 Int now up and running successfully, B Squadron was withdrawn from the Province, though its departure was hastened by the embarrassing arrest of two of its members for an attempted armed robbery. For the next 15 months it is believed that only officers and troopers on attachment to other units served in Ulster. With both the Dhofari campaign and re-training for the anti-terrorist role stretching the SAS to the limit, withdrawal from Ulster was regarded as a godsend.

Over the 1974/75 Christmas period the IRA had held a ceasefire, which broke

Above: The corpse of SAS Captain Westmacott lies on Belfast's Antrim Road, May 1980, after being hit by IRA fire.

on 16 January following the assassination of a senior IRA man south of the border a few days earlier. Republicans blamed the SAS for his murder, but though a British soldier may have been involved, this suspect (now dead) was not under SAS command at the time. The ceasefire was re-instituted in February 1975, but sectarian murders continued, though 'only' four British soldiers were killed over the next seven months. There was also considerable in-fighting between the more politically minded Official IRA (OIRA) and the more violent Provisional IRA (PIRA). With hindsight it is clear that this period of relative quiet during 1975 was required to allow PIRA to sort out its differences with the Officials, then re-group and re-arm. It is now also clear that Libyan arms and explosives had arrived in vast quantities the previous autumn, and a major fund-raising campaign was also under way in America.

South Armagh

It is nicknamed the 'bandit country' on account of its high terrorist activity, but from 1976 the SAS was deployed there in strength to take the sting out of the IRA's tail. Thus began a deadly cat-and-mouse game that carried on into the 1990s.

The pretence of an IRA ceasefire was dropped in November 1975, and on 5 January 1976 the round of tit-for-tat sectarian attacks came to a head with the murder of 10 Protestant workers in South Armagh, though the Catholic driver of their bus was not harmed. This atrocity was in reprisal for the killing of five Catholics in two separate attacks the previous day, these murders in turn being in revenge for previous Protestant deaths.

In response, Britain's Labour Prime Minister Harold Wilson announced on 7 January that the SAS would be operationally deployed to South Armagh to target terrorist assassination squads. So sudden was this decision, that even the duty officer at Hereford was taken unawares, and some people claim that the Ministry of Defence had no prior warning of what was essentially a political decision.

The few SAS troopers available, probably less than 12, were dispatched to Ulster as an advance party. One source claims they were from D Squadron, which had just returned from Dhofar, but in his memoirs 'Soldier I' claims that a team drawn from all four troops of B Squadron left for covert operations in Belfast at this time. Either way, the Regiment was clearly back in Ulster.

Once sufficient troopers were in-theatre and all available local intelligence had been absorbed, four-man covert patrols were put on the ground. These men usually moved by night and laid-up by day to observe unauthorised border crossing points or suspect buildings. If intelligence had been received about a specific threat or action, they would go to ground for days at a time in hides until their target appeared. Unlike that of 14 Int Coy, though, the SAS brief was geared more to direct military action than general intelligence gathering.

Troopers not on rural patrols cruised urban areas in civilian cars, tracking known PIRA players, gathering intelligence and looking out for potential ambushes on the more conventional security forces in the area. They were only armed with 9mm Browning automatic pistols and a couple of spare 13-round magazines for personal protection if compromised. Their vehicles had ever-changing number plates and false tax discs, marked in such a way that an RUC officer inspecting closely at a checkpoint would realise who the suspicious-looking, scruffy, long-haired occupants were and not blow their cover. As covert operations became more widespread, the SAS were even able to call on the services of their own plainclothes tow truck, should

Left: The Irish Republican Army (IRA) has been the SAS's most persistent foe since the Regiment first went to Ulster in 1969.

one of these typically ageing and rusty Q-cars break down on operations.

The first operational SAS success after its announced deployment, other than the almost instant cessation of sectarian attacks and a temporary reduction of the level of Republican activity in rural areas, came early in March 1976. A four-man patrol arrested known PIRA terrorist Sean McKenna near the border in controversial circumstances. In court the soldiers said that he had bumped into their patrol just north of the border after a drinking session. McKenna, on the other hand, claimed that he had been dragged from his bed in a cottage south of the border at gunpoint by an SAS patrol and was then bundled over the border before being formally arrested. Either way, he ended up being convicted of 25 separate terrorist charges and a good many innocent people slept safer in their beds.

THE CAPTURE OF PETER CLEARY

The next successful SAS operation was the capture of leading IRA member Peter Cleary on 15 April. This incident was controversial, as it ended in the captive losing his life. For the best part of a week prior to his arrest, an SAS team had been on the lookout for him in the Crossmaglen area, and were closely observing the homes of his known acquaintances, including that of his girlfriend's sister, some 50m (164ft) from the border. When Cleary turned up at this house he was arrested, and a helicopter was called in to transport him away as travel by road was considered to be too dangerous. Five men escorted Cleary to a nearby field, but with four of the team employed in marking the landing site, he allegedly tried to overpower the lone soldier guarding him, in the hope that he could run to sanctuary over the border. Cleary was shot in the chest and died instantly of his injuries.

The Regiment hit the headlines again in early May, when a four-man covert patrol in a car strayed over the border at night on a dark country lane. As luck would have it, they ran straight into a *Garda* checkpoint little more than 500m (1640ft) into the Republic, and ended up being escorted to the local police station. Three hours later, a second SAS patrol

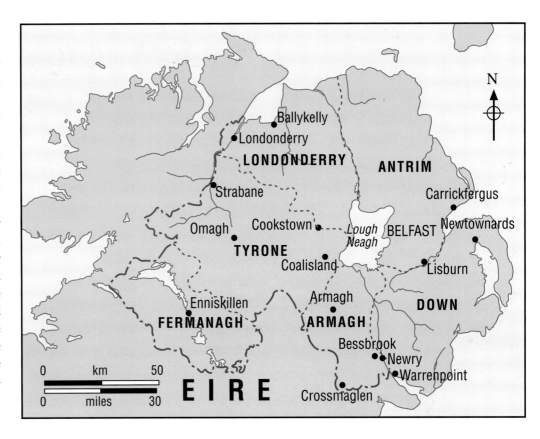

out searching for their missing colleagues ran into the same checkpoint – they too ended the night in custody. Next morning the Dublin government ordered their release, but in the meantime the soldiers had been charged with being in possession of firearms and they had to be bailed before release. A diplomatic row between governments ensued, but in due course the fuss died down, although the soldiers were later fined on weapons offences by a Dublin court.

REDUCTION IN VIOLENCE

As a result of the SAS operations in South Armagh, plus Republican claims at the time that the 'lost patrol' was actually a cross-border death squad, IRA activity in both the Crossmaglen and Forkhill areas reduced quite considerably for the rest of the year. Early the following January, however, the terrorists launched a mortar attack on an infantry patrol near Crossmaglen, killing a lance-corporal. But the terrorists were spotted fleeing south of the border in a distinctive vehicle, and the security forces were all briefed to report all future sightings of it. Less than three weeks later, it was spotted again north of the border and an ambush was laid to catch its occupants.

Above: The SAS was first deployed in strength to Ulster in 1976, when a full squadron was despatched to South Armagh.

Local IRA member Seamus Harvey walked into the ambush zone at dusk carrying a sawn-off shotgun and, when challenged, raised his weapon. He was shot by the challenging trooper before he could fire. On the other side of the hedge, two of Harvey's colleagues fired blindly before running away into the darkness. Later, it was discovered that two of the bullets which struck Harvey came from terrorist 5.56mm Armalites, and not from the 7.62mm FN rifles used by SAS patrols at this time. For the whole of 1977, offensive IRA activity was virtually non-existent in the area, despite being at a much higher level throughout the rest of the Province.

The IRA has never been slow to change its tactics to gain maximum publicity for its cause, and so in 1978 the focus was placed on disrupting commerce in the Province. This phase of the campaign offered the triple advantages of maximum disruption, good publicity and low casualty figures among their band of 'volunteers'. After all, factories, offices and shopping centres cannot shoot back, unlike troops or the police. A typical soft

Left: Crossmaglen, near the Irish border, a town noted for its high incidence of IRA activity in the 1970s and 1980s.

target chosen at this time was the Transport & Engineering Depot of the Post Office in Belfast.

Based on information supplied by an informer within the IRA, a 'tout' in IRA parlance, six troopers, backed up by RUC officers, staked out the depot off Ballysillan Road late on the evening of 21 June 1978. Within about an hour of their arrival, four IRA men arrived by stolen car, which they parked in a cul-de-sac behind the depot.

INNOCENT DEATHS

The driver remained with the vehicle, but the other three entered a lane running alongside the depot and threw satchel bombs over the wall. The SAS troopers and an RUC constable covering the lane then opened fire, killing all three. The car driver waiting around the corner fled on foot when he heard gunfire, unseen by the main SAS ambush party. Unfortunately, at the same time two innocent men on their way home walked into the virtually unlit lane and one was shot to death after making a sudden movement. The trooper who shot him thought that he was the fourth IRA man from the car. The dead man's friend, who had dropped to the ground on hearing gunfire, and who offered no resistance to the SAS, was handed over unharmed to the RUC even before his identity had been confirmed.

To Republicans the killing of three of their 'volunteers' was unacceptable, even though they were undertaking an active operation. Not for the first time, they bleated that the SAS was operating a 'shoot-to-kill' policy. The fact that the second of the two innocent men was totally unharmed by the SAS shows quite the opposite to be the case. The people guilty in such a situation are the IRA men, who try to claim the protection of a democratic system that they themselves are out to destroy. They are the men, and sometimes women, who do not identify themselves but claim the status of soldiers in the secret army of a mythical republic, yet demand to be gently apprehended and put before a court whose authority they do not even recognise, after being caught in the act of pulling a trigger, throwing a bomb or firing a mortar.

The death of another innocent man in July 1978 brought more adverse publicity to the Regiment, though it was primarily a breakdown in communications which led to the tragedy. Teenager John Boyle discovered weapons and a military uniform under a gravestone in the local cemetery, and told his parents, who in turn informed the police. An SAS patrol was immediately drafted in the same evening to lay a trap for anybody returning to empty the cache. Before deployment, the team was told that a child had

discovered the weapons, and they requested that the RUC contact the family to warn him to keep away. Unfortunately the message was not passed on until the following morning, but just before the police arrived the 'child' – 16-year-old farmworker John – returned to the graveyard for another look at his find. As he picked up the rifle and turned unknowingly in the direction of one of the troopers, they shot him. The two troopers who opened fire were charged with murder but later acquitted.

In the late 1970s the SAS was more geared to operating in rural areas than in the major cities, but occasionally, because of the Regiment's unique anti-terrorist training, teams were called in to undertake close-quarter operations in built-up areas. For example, in November 1978 a patrol positioned themselves in an unoccupied house being used by PIRA to store guns and ammunition for use against the security forces. When a known 'player' turned up to check the weapons, he was killed before he could fire the gun he was holding.

THE DEATH OF CAPTAIN WESTMACOTT

Over the next 18 months, the Regiment seemed to be maintaining a low profile, but the four troops dispersed throughout Northern Ireland were seldom idle. Each troop usually comprised 16 personnel operating in four patrols of four men. Permanent troop locations were Belfast, Londonderry and South Armagh, with areas of responsibility matching the local Army Brigades. The fourth troop was held as a mobile reserve under direct command of Army HQ at Lisburn.

In May 1981, Captain Richard Westmacott became the first SAS officer to lose his life on an operation in Ulster, though Staff Sergeant David Naden had died in a road accident in the Province three years earlier. The captain was leading seven of his men in a rapid response raid against an IRA ambush squad, lurking in a house on Belfast's Antrim Road. With four men guarding the rear, the rest

Left: A British Army observation post in the 'bandit country' of South Armagh, where the SAS has conducted many operations.

driver drove off, but was wounded during his getaway.

As usual, family and supporters of the dead men protested that they should have been arrested not shot. When their rifle was subsequently examined, it was discovered that it had been used to kill four off-duty members of the Ulster Defence Regiment on different occasions. Unlike the PIRA gunmen, the unarmed UDR soldiers had not been given the opportunity to surrender, but had been shot down in cold blood. Such is the hypocrisy of the Irish Republican movement, which expects leniency from the SAS but shows no mercy to its victims.

of the SAS patrol drove right up to the house and jumped out to storm the front door before the gunmen realised what was happening. Unfortunately, they had been given the number of the house next door to where the gunmen actually were, and just after their car pulled up it was fired upon from an upstairs front window. The captain fell mortally wounded, hit by a burst from an American M60 machine gun. Realising that they were surrounded, the eight gunmen then hung out a white sheet and called for a Catholic priest to negotiate their surrender to the RUC.

NEW BATTLES IN THE 1980s

Although the services of the SAS were much in demand throughout the Province, other anti-terrorist duties, both at home and abroad, were stretching the Regiment to the limit. To relieve the strain, 14 Int Coy plus highly trained Royal Marine and Parachute Regiment recce troops, gradually took over most of the covert observation duties and patrols. The SAS also took on the task of training other military personnel plus RUC operatives in intelligence gathering, both in Ulster and at Hereford itself. However, SAS teams were still kept available throughout the Province to take charge of particularly tricky operations.

By the end of 1981, for the first time in six years, a full 'Sabre' Squadron was no longer permanently stationed 'over the water'. Instead, an enhanced independent troop of about 20 men, known as Ulster Troop, was deployed with one team always on a few minutes' standby to move into action. Many of the men posted to Ulster Troop from the squadrons had special skills or assets which were in demand in the Province, and consequently they could volunteer for extended tours or semi-permanent postings if they wished.

One operation where the skills of Ulster Troop were needed arose in December 1983, when the RUC was made aware of a hidden arms cache in the countryside near Coalisland. Due to the time of year and the fact that the operation could easily last several days, it was decided that only the SAS could tackle the job. A six-man team, deployed in pairs to cover all approach angles, constructed hides and settled down for a long wait. After a couple of days, on a Sunday afternoon, three men drove up to the field where the guns were hidden.

The driver of the car stayed with the vehicle, but the other two made straight for the cache. The first pulled out an AR-16 Armalite rifle and handed it to his colleague, then reached down to withdraw a shotgun. As he did so he was challenged by one of the SAS soldiers and, when he turned and raised the shotgun, he was shot along with his companion. The

Ulster Troop

In the 1980s the Army recognised that the effectiveness of the SAS in Ulster was being lessened by spreading men over a wide area. Thus a new organisation – the Intelligence and Security Group (Northern Ireland) – was set up. This saw a reduction in the number of SAS soldiers in Ulster from a full squadron to a troop of just over 20 men, called Ulster Troop. SAS soldiers served for a year in Northern Ireland, not including prior training, and worked closely within the Group and the 14th Intelligence Unit. In the Group the SAS contingent and 14th Int were commanded by a single officer, and the actions of the Group and the Royal Ulster Constabulary (RUC) special units were also integrated. This means that although there were fewer SAS men in Northern Ireland, they were used much more effectively. It also meant that there was the Regiment could maintain its other specialist skills, which in the early 1980s were suffering because of its commitments in Northern Ireland.

The Loughall Ambush

In May 1987, the SAS achieved one of its greatest victories against the IRA when the terrorists' notorious eight-man East Tyrone Brigade was wiped out in a spectacular ambush at Loughall RUC police station in County Armagh.

After the Brighton bombing of 12 October 1984, when the IRA attempted to assassinate Prime Minister Margaret Thatcher and her cabinet as they slept in their hotel beds, there appeared to be an increase in SAS-style ambushes of IRA gunmen. Many were not actually carried out by the Regiment, as other organisations such as 14 Int Coy, and even the recce troops of infantry battalions, were now well trained in covert observation and follow-through tactics. To the IRA, though, every death blamed on an SAS 'death squad' made good propaganda, and it also reminded its members of the need for operational security. When

the SAS did strike, however, the results of their handiwork usually left no doubt as to just who was responsible.

NEW WEAPONS FOR THE IRA

A few weeks before the Brighton bomb, Libya's leader, Colonel Gaddafi, had re-supplied the IRA with a huge quantity of guns and ammunition, plus at least two tonnes of Semtex plastic explosive. The new guns were of the most modern design, but, much worse, the Czech Semtex military explosive was so powerful that only half a kilo (1lb) was required to destroy a car. With so much explosive and weaponry now available to them, the

IRA could increase the number and variety of its operations. As well as attacks on off-duty security force personnel in Ulster, it carried out numerous hit-and-run mortar and grenade attacks on police stations or Army posts, and bombed or shot 'soft' targets in Britain and on the continent. Because of this increase in operational activity, though, it had to involve more men and as a result its own security suffered. The security forces took full advantage and scored numerous suc-

Below: The scene after the Loughall ambush on 8 May 1987, the mangled remains of the mechanical digger can be clearly seen.

cesses over the next couple of years, culminating in the Loughall ambush.

The security forces received a godsend when routine surveillance overheard an IRA member on the telephone talking about a planned attack on the RUC station at Loughall, County Armagh. The IRA team detailed to carry out the attack was the East Tyrone Brigade. Known as the 'A Team', it had carried out a series of attacks against the Army and RUC. In December 1985, for example, it had attacked Ballygawley RUC barracks with assault rifles, killing two guards in the process. They also attacked the RUC station at the Birches, County Tyrone, using a bomb in the shovel of a mechanical digger to blow the barracks up.

LOUGHALL – THE SOFT TARGET

The predominantly Protestant village of Loughall, lying half-way between Armagh and Portadown on the B77 minor road, had been relatively violence-free during the Troubles, but that was to change on the evening of Friday 8 May 1987. The village's small police station, like hundreds of others in small rural communities across Great Britain and Northern Ireland, had started life as a pair of police houses with a small office open for public enquiries. However, as police stations across Ulster had become prime targets for the IRA, a 4m- (13ft-) high chain-link security fence enclosed what had been the police house gardens. Inside this compound, the white-painted police houses looked like any others on the mainland, but for a 2m- (6.5ft-) high blast wall outside the front doors.

Manned only by one sergeant and three constables, this small RUC station in a generally law-abiding and close-knit community only operated during the day, and was not considered to be a prime terrorist target. To the East Tyrone Brigade of the IRA, however, who considered themselves to be an elite, it offered a great opportunity for a headline-grabbing attack with little personal threat. The station formally closed at 1845 hours, and the officers usually locked up by 1900 hours on Fridays, leaving it unmanned for the night. If the attack were to take place after this, there was little chance of return

fire, but the IRA could claim to have taken out a police station in the heart of a Loyalist area. It is propaganda such as this which keeps IRA support high in the Republican ghettos.

Unfortunately for the terrorist team undertaking the attack, the aforementioned unguarded telephone conversation was monitored by the security forces. A major surveillance operation was mounted, with both the target and timing for the attack being discovered well in advance. By the time that the raid was launched, a troop from G Squadron had been flown in from Hereford to supplement Ulster Troop, and the target was surrounded by SAS teams.

SAS DEPLOYMENTS AT LOUGHALL

From intelligence gathered, it was known that a vehicle-mounted bomb was going to be used against the station, but for it to have had any major effect, the SAS reckoned that it would have to be driven inside the compound. The weak point in the perimeter fence was clearly the main gate at the east end, which gave access to the car park behind the station, so the small SAS team hidden in the police station kept to the west end of the building. Some reports suggest that one trooper actually waited outside the building with

Above: The Toyota van offered little protection to the IRA terrorists who took refuge inside it, nor did their body armour.

only the blast wall for protection; an action which must have taken considerable nerve.

At a location some 15km (nine miles) from the target IRA men loaded 100kg (220lb) of explosive into the bucket of a mechanical excavator, which was the means by which they hoped to break into the compound. In addition to Declan Arthurs (the driver), two armed terrorists – Gerald O'Callaghan and Tony Gormley – were to ride shotgun on the digger as it approached Loughall. Ahead of the digger, five more terrorists – Patrick Kelly, Jim Lynagh, Padraig McKearney, Seamus Donnelly and Eugene Kelly – cruised through the village in a van to check that the coast was clear and then pulled up with wheels on the pavement, across the road from the police station. As the digger with the rubble-covered bomb in its bucket approached, the men in the van dismounted. The IRA fully expected the station to be unmanned, but just in case there was still anyone inside who could have fired on the digger team, they sprayed the building with gunfire in a mad act of bravado.

Rules Of Engagement

The SAS has, on occasion, been accused of being out of control, of operating without rules or concern for the rule of law, even of having a licence to kill. In fact, the SAS operation in Gibraltar in March 1988, codenamed 'Flavius', was a tightly controlled affair. The rules of engagement for the Gibraltar operation were made public by one of the SAS men, Soldier 'F', at the inquest held into the shootings in September:

OBJECTIVES
1. These instructions are for your guidance, once your participation in Operation 'Flavius' has been duly authorised. You are to issue orders in compliance with these instructions to the men under your command.
2. You are to operate as directed by the Gibraltar Police Commissioner or by the officer(s) designated by him to control this operation.

Should the latter request military intervention, your objectives will be to assist the civil power to arrest members of the IRA, but subject to the overriding requirement to do all in your power to protect the lives and safety of members of the public and of the security forces.

COMMAND AND CONTROL
3. You will be responsible to the Governor and Commander-in-Chief, through his Chief of Staff, for the way in which you carry out the military tasks assigned to you. You will act at all times in accordance with the lawful instructions of the senior police officer(s) designated by the Gibraltar Police Commissioner to control this operation.

USE OF FORCE
4. You and your men will not use force unless requested to do so by the senior police officer(s) designated by the Gibraltar Police Commissioner, or unless it is necessary to do so in order to protect life. You and your men are not then to use more force than is necessary in order to protect life, and you are to comply with rule 5.

OPENING FIRE
5. You and your men may only open fire against a person if you or they have reasonable grounds for believing that he/she is currently committing, or about to commit, an action which is likely to endanger your or their lives, or the life of any person, and if there is no other way to prevent this.

FIRING WITHOUT WARNING
6. You and your men may fire without a warning if the giving of a warning or any delay in firing could lead to death or injury to you or them or any other person, or if the giving of a warning is clearly impracticable.

WARNING BEFORE FIRING
7. If the circumstances in paragraph 6 do not apply, a warning is necessary before firing. The warning is to be as clear as possible and is to include a direction to surrender and a clear warning that fire will be opened if the direction is not obeyed.

AREA OF OPERATIONS
8. Under no circumstances are you or your men to enter Spanish territory.

Unknown to the terrorists, however, they were surrounded by SAS soldiers armed with GPMG machine guns, Heckler & Koch G3 and M16 assault rifles. In addition, there were also two cut-off groups in the village and another SAS unit close to the village church.

THE AMBUSH IS SPRUNG
From inside the station and from positions in a copse on high ground just 100m (328ft) from the van, SAS troopers mowed down the van team with assault rifle and GPMG fire. However, the digger outriders managed to ignite the bomb fuse before they too were gunned down by an SAS stop group as they tried to flee. The digger driver was hit too. The bomb detonated just outside the compound, but the three troopers inside the station escaped with only minor injuries. All eight terrorists were killed, outright. So, regrettably, was one of two innocent passers-by in what another stop group wrongly identified as a back-up vehicle.

As a direct result of the SAS success at Loughall, the IRA did not launch another major direct attack on the security forces in Ulster for more than two and a half years. Instead, they resorted to low-risk rocket and bomb attacks on police vehicles, sniping attacks mainly in the border areas, incendiary bombing of commercial premises, door-stop assassinations of police and soldiers, and sectarian killings. One of their most despicable acts took place on Remembrance Day in 1987, when a bomb exploded during the ceremony in the town of Enniskillen, an act that attracted worldwide condemnation. Frequently, however, through good observation and intelligence work by all sectors of the security forces, many were caught in the process of committing their crimes or soon afterwards.

With operations in Ulster becoming increasingly difficult, the IRA also stepped up their campaigns on the mainland and overseas, but within a year of Loughall the SAS scored another major victory against the IRA when it shot and killed three of it terrorists – Mairead Farrell, Danny McCann and Sean Savage – in March 1988 during their operation in Gibraltar.

Of course the war against the IRA continued into the 1990s. Some of the organisation's best terrorists have been killed by the SAS while attempting to carry out bombings or assassinations. Martin Corrigan was killed in Armagh in April 1990 while attempting to murder an Army reservist; Desmond Grew, the 'widow maker', and Martin McCaughey were shot and killed at Loughall while moving Kalashnikov rifles from one arms cache to another (Grew was a suspect in the murder of six-month-old Ruthy Islamia in Germany); and Peter Ryan, shot by the Regiment in June 1991 in Coagh while on the way to murder someone. One of the most spectacular actions was the ambushing of Kevin Barry O'Donnell, Sean O'Farrell, Patrick Vincent and Peter Clancy, all shot in Clonoe, Coalisland, after machine gunning a police station.

AN END TO HOSTILITIES?

At the end of 1994, however, the IRA, quickly followed by Loyalist terrorists, called a ceasefire in Northern Ireland. And as the politicians seemed to be getting close to a settlement, it appeared that the SAS would no longer have a role in Ulster. Perhaps nearly 30 years of service in the Province was coming to an end.

The talk of peace was intoxicating, but as time went on and no progress was reached ominous noises started coming from the terrorists of both sides. With the politicians dragging their feet, the IRA called off its ceasefire. Having had time to reorganise its structure and resources, the Republican movement was well placed to commence a new campaign. The worst fears of the security forces were confirmed as a series of bomb attacks were carried out on the British mainland, of which the Manchester bombing in 1996 was one of the largest. For the SAS, Ulster was back on the agenda.

Above right: The damaged RUC station at Loughall. The IRA was also damaged in the operation, losing eight of its key men.

Right: To some sections of the Nationalist movement the terrorists who died at Loughall were heroes to be mourned.

COUNTER-TERRORISM

Rescue at Mogadishu

The international terrorism of the 1970s resulted in Western governments forming crack anti-terrorist units. In Britain the SAS was given a counter-terrorist brief, and was thus well placed to assist its West German counterpart, GSG 9, at Mogadishu in 1977.

In the relatively quiet period between the return from Aden (1967) and deployment to Ulster (1969) and Oman (1970), the SAS was not officially employed on active operations. However, as the Regiment's skills had to be constantly honed to perfection to prepare for as yet unknown threats and challenges, every opportunity to train in the most realistic of conditions was actively sought.

On the continent, the annual round of NATO exercises gave plenty of scope for deep-penetration missions to practise intelligence gathering, to breach security cordons around prime installations or just

to test the readiness and reactions of allied troops. Compared to the jungle and jebel, though, training exercises in Germany, Denmark or Norway did not offer much of a challenge. The hospitality of friendly governments in Africa, Central America, the Middle East and Southeast Asia, however, gave the SAS the opportunity to practise for operations in hostile climatic environments. In return, the Regiment's experienced personnel imparted their specialist knowledge and skills to the host country's soldiers.

In addition to conventional exercises, exchange tours with the special forces of

Britain's allies and service on British Army Training Team missions around the world, troopers were also loaned to other governments for specialist duties. In many Third World countries, rulers and monarchs, irrespective of whether they are democratically elected or their position of power is hereditary, often live in fear of the assassin's bullet. The use of highly skilled SAS personnel to train bodyguards for heads of state not only helped main-

Below: The hijacked Lufthansa Boeing 737 airliner stands on the tarmac at Mogadishu airport in October 1977.

tain stability in Commonwealth and other friendly countries, but created worthwhile jobs for men who might otherwise have been twiddling their thumbs. Intelligence on political developments worldwide gleaned by these well-placed servants of the Crown, plus information passed on by British intelligence agencies, was collated by the Operations Planning and Intelligence Cell at Hereford, usually referred to by troopers as the 'Kremlin'. If one of Britain's allies was going to be subject to a coup or revolution, the SAS wanted advance notice.

COUNTER-REVOLUTIONARY WARFARE
At the beginning of the 1970s, the 'Kremlin' was just coming to terms with the implications of Irish Republican Army (IRA) terrorist activity in Ulster when the September 1972 Munich massacre of Israeli Olympic competitors finally threw international terrorism into the world media spotlight (the Palestinian group 'Black September' took hostage and then murdered 11 Israeli athletes during the games). In addition to watching for relatively conventional uprisings and coups in friendly countries, the SAS now had to keep its eye on a growing international brotherhood of political extremists and fundamentalist groups out to strike at Western democracies. Behind them, these highly motivated activists had both the finance of the communist global revolution and the patronage of dictators with an axe to grind. To monitor this situation, therefore, a separate team known as the Counter Revolutionary Warfare (CRW) Wing was established at Hereford within a few months of Munich.

The only apparent common objective of the shadowy revolutionary organisations, which originated from both extremes of the political divide, was the eventual downfall of the current world order to further their own blinkered aims. They were fully prepared to assist each other, irrespective of political differences, and their financing by third parties allowed them the best weaponry and communications to carry out their aims. Arab groups were in the vanguard, many supporting basically just causes which could not be settled through the ballot

box as they had no vote, but German, Japanese and, to a lesser extent, Irish activists all cooperated. The 1970s was to become the decade of the international terrorist and hijacker.

The SAS has never been particularly keen on publicity, and since Munich it has tried whenever possible to avoid the camera almost completely. However, as international terrorism spread around the globe, the British government did leak enough information on the Regiment's new role to let the terrorists know that Britain had no intention of becoming an easy target. Other European countries, particularly France and West Germany, formed specialist anti-terrorist paramilitary units at this time, and it was no great secret that the SAS trained alongside and exchanged information with them.

By the end of 1974, the SAS Counter-Terrorism Team (CTT), was now a permanent squad, equating roughly in size to a troop and drawn from the four Sabre Squadrons, with its own headquarters, communications and transport cell at Hereford. As the terrorist threat was now so great, the CTT had complete freedom to choose the most suitable weaponry for its roles, irrespective of cost, country of origin, or lack of commonalty with the rest of the armed forces. It also had access to the funding necessary to enable procurement of exactly what equipment it needed to get the job done without having to fight against civil service bureaucracy. This meant, for example, that the best and latest communications and eavesdropping equipment available on the international market could be bought.

FIRST OPERATIONS
Speed, too, was of the essence if the CTT was to confront armed hijackers and hostage-takers effectively, so it is to the credit of the government that the team was given instant access both to fixed-wing aircraft and helicopters. On the ground it had its own fleet of Range Rovers, which offered the perfect combination of high road speed and excellent off-road mobility. All that the SAS seems to have lacked in the transport department was its own submarine, but of course their cousins in the Special Boat Service (SBS)

had the necessary contacts to lay one of these on if required.

The next time that the SAS hit the headlines in an anti-terrorist role, it did not even have to go into action to achieve the desired outcome. In September 1975, the IRA launched a major bombing and killing campaign in London. Underground stations were targeted to create maximum disruption, and small bombs left in restaurants caused numerous casualties. On 6 December, however, a four-man IRA team was detected in Mayfair and their car was chased into a cul-de-sac in a residential area. With no avenue of escape and carrying only handguns, the terrorists forced their way into an occupied flat and took the middle-aged couple inside as hostages. What became known as the Balcombe Street Siege was to last for nearly six days.

THE BALCOMBE STREET SIEGE
The siege was primarily a police operation, handled almost entirely by Scotland Yard's anti-terrorist squad, but SAS members were on hand to give advice. The police cut off both the power supply and the telephone line to the flat, then settled down to negotiate a slow, peaceful end to the affair. From the outset it was made clear to the terrorists that no concessions would be made and surrender was the only possible course of action. Meanwhile, surveillance experts monitored the men's every move from adjoining flats. On the Friday, the female hostage was released in exchange for hot food, but it appeared that the terrorists were prepared to continue the stalemate for several more days at least.

At lunch time on the Friday, however, the gunmen heard a news report on the radio that the SAS was on standby to end the siege. Almost immediately they decided to negotiate a surrender to the police, preferring the certainty of a jail cell to the uncertainty of surviving an SAS assault. Hands held high, they walked out one by one to surrender in front of the cameras. Without even lifting a finger, the SAS had dealt a major propaganda blow to the IRA. The terrorists were later sentenced to a minimum of 30 years in prison after being found guilty of six murders.

Left: In the early hours of 18 October 1977, GSG 9 stormed the aircraft and killed three of the four Palestinian terrorists.

On Thursday 13 October 1977, a Lufthansa Boeing 737 departed Majorca on route for Frankfurt carrying 91 passengers and crew. Most of the passengers, including seven children, were holiday-makers returning home, but two of the couples were in fact terrorists. Armed with handguns and plastic explosives, the two males stormed the flight deck after take-off and ordered the pilot to divert to Rome, while their female colleagues held the cabin crew at gunpoint. Identifying themselves as members of the Red Army Faction, though they were of Arab descent, they broadcast their demands to Spanish air traffic control. In addition to wanting a ransom of nearly £10 million, they also demanded the release of 11 members of the Baader-Meinhoff gang imprisoned in West Germany.

GSG 9

After the Munich massacre, the West German government had formed a special counter-terrorist unit. Known as GSG 9 (*Grenzschutzgrüppe* 9) this special unit of about 50 men was linked to the Inner German Border Guard (*Bundesgrenzschutz*), and all of its personnel were volunteers. Most had seen prior service with the airborne and mountain divisions of the West German Army and all were keen shots. From the outset GSG 9 trained and worked alongside the SAS, adopting many of its methods and procedures. To this day the link is still maintained, with members of both units training side by side at NATO's Long Range Reconnaissance and Patrol (LRRP) and Mountain Warfare schools. As the Lufthansa hijackers actions became known, GSG 9 was activated and SAS personnel joined it.

After a refuelling stop at Rome, the 737 flew on to Cyprus, then headed for Bahrain, where it made an overnight stop. By morning the GSG 9 team had rehearsed its tactics and was about to leave Frankfurt on board a Boeing 707. The team, numbering about 30, was fully armed and had explosive charges to blow in aircraft doors and other specialist

The three most prominent international terrorist organisations during the mid-1970s were the West German Baader-Meinhoff gang, the Palestinian 'Black September' movement and the Red Army Faction, which had a world-wide membership. While Algeria, and later Libya, offered both a home and training facilities to members of these organisations, the Soviet Union and China gave financial assistance. Although, as mentioned above, in many ways politi-

cally opposed, these groups and their supporters all agreed with the old Arab maxim which states that 'my enemy's enemy is my friend'. Partly to cement their bond, but also to outwit the security services, this unusual alliance of extreme left and right frequently carried out operations on each other's behalf. The next time that SAS experts from the CTT went into action publicly, it was alongside West German colleagues fighting Arab terrorists in an African country.

Right: GSG 9 returns home in triumph. The SAS's involvement in the operation was far more covert.

equipment. Ahead of them, a three-man advance party had already flown out to the Gulf. The Germans had also asked their British opposite numbers for any help and advice they could give, particularly as the SAS was known to have a good working knowledge of the region and its security forces. In response, the SAS offered the services of its second-in-command, Major Alastair Morrison, and one of its most proficient NCOs, Sergeant Barry Davies.

The two British soldiers took some unique stun grenades with them. These pyrotechnics, which the SAS had specially designed, can be set off in confined spaces without permanently injuring hostages. They explode with a report which is loud enough temporarily to deafen anyone not wearing ear defenders, while simultaneously giving off an intensely bright flash which temporarily blinds those without eye protection. SAS and GSG 9 anti-terrorist team members are trained to operate in gas masks with tinted lenses and wearing radio headsets so the effect of stun grenades on them will be negligible. To unsuspecting hijackers in a dimly lit and confined area, the effect of stun grenades is disorientation and deprivation of sight and vision.

FINAL DESTINATION – MOGADISHU

On the Friday morning the hijacked jet left Bahrain for Dubai, where the West German ambassador tried all day to negotiate with the terrorists from the control tower, but met with little success. Realising that a specialist anti-terrorist team was probably being assembled, the hijackers decided to fly out before nightfall. They announced that they were going to the former RAF base on Masirah Island off Oman, though instead headed for Salalah in Dhofar Province. But when they tried to land they found that the runway there was blocked. Rather than heading for Masirah, where they possibly thought a reception committee had been arranged, they instructed the pilot to fly to Aden in Yemen.

After making a heavy landing the pilot, Captain Schumann, got out of the aircraft to inspect the undercarriage, then sprinted to the control tower to tell officials where explosives had been placed on the aircraft. The hijackers immediately demanded his return on threat of blowing up the jet, and the Yemenis complied. The pilot was then forced to take off again and once at cruising height told to hand over control to his co-pilot. The terrorist leader then dragged him into the main cabin and shot him in the back of the head in front of the horrified passengers. When the aircraft next touched down, at Mogadishu in Somalia, the pilot's body was thrown onto the tarmac. Having killed one hostage, the terrorists had gone beyond the point of no return – the shadowing GSG 9 team prepared for action.

As darkness fell on the evening of the 17th, with the 737 sitting on the apron, the anti-terrorist team made its final preparations for the assault. The entire team had only been together for a few hours, but everyone had practised this type of operation many times before in cabin crew training fuselages. At 0200 hours, 45 minutes before the hijackers' latest deadline for blowing up the jet and

the hostages, black-clad figures silently but rapidly approached the Lufthansa aircraft. Undetected, they grouped under cover of the fuselage, small squads beneath each access and emergency escape door. At a given signal, the doors were blown, stun grenades were lobbed in, lightweight ladders were placed against both sides and the assault team burst in.

FREEING THE HOSTAGES

Inside the aircraft, the terrorists were caught completely off their guard and all four were quickly identified and shot. Before dying of his injuries, the terrorist leader threw two grenades into the passenger cabin, but fortunately they exploded harmlessly under the seats. The second male terrorist and one of the females died instantly, but the other female lived despite several bullet wounds. None of 86 passengers or the four remaining crew members was seriously injured in the assault. Shortly afterwards, the British Government confirmed that the SAS had been involved both in planning the operation and in carrying out the raid as part of the GSG 9 team. In later anti-terrorist operations, GSG 9 loaned its personnel and planning skills to the SAS.

Princes Gate

On the morning of 30 April 1980, six armed terrorists of the Democratic Revolutionary Front for the Liberation of Arabistan burst into the Iranian Embassy in London and took all inside hostage. Six days later the SAS freed them in a stunning operation.

In response to lessons learned at Mogadishu, it was decided that rather than just having a small CRW team on permanent short-notice standby, every SAS trooper should be trained in rotation to undertake counter-terrorist duties. Each Sabre Squadron would now take a turn in the CRW role and provide instant response teams around the clock. Fully equipped helicopters and a C-130 Hercules transport aircraft would be kept at a few minutes' readiness to allow a troop to be flown anywhere in the British Isles within three hours maximum. Over the next two and a half years, the counter-terrorist teams quietly deployed several times without hitting the headlines, but on a sunny May evening in 1980 their existence was broadcast around the world in spectacular fashion.

THE TERRORISTS STRIKE

On the morning of 30 April 1980, a British policeman stood on duty in the doorway of the Iranian Embassy at No 16 Princes Gate, London. Inside the building were numerous embassy staff and members of the public, there to collect visas. In the past, under the deposed Shah's reign, relations between Iran and Britain had been very friendly, but they deteriorated considerably when the religious fundamentalist Ayatollah Khomeini seized power. Previously the SAS had advised the Shah's staff on security matters, but under the new regime this was the responsibility of the Iranian Revolutionary Guard. Being technically foreign territory under international law, the interior of the embassy was outside British jurisdiction, but by mutual agreement a lone armed policeman was stationed outside the door.

The six men walking towards PC Trevor Lock in the embassy doorway looked no different from any other Iranian visitors. Though they were well

wrapped up against the chill spring air, the constable could identify them as being of Arab descent, and only gave each one a cursory glance as they approached. This party, however, comprised Iraqis and Iranian dissidents backed by Iraq. Under their anoraks each carried a Browning handgun or a small Skorpion submachine gun, and their pockets were stuffed with ammunition and grenades.

As the constable courteously opened the outer door for the first man, the Arab

Above: A member of the Democratic Revolutionary Front for the Liberation of Arabistan at the door of the Iranian Embassy.

bumped into him and tried to draw a weapon, but the quick-thinking policeman slammed the door and blurted out a radio warning as he struggled with his assailant. Outside, one of the others pulled out a pistol and fired a number of shots through the glass as his accomplices forced the door. In seconds they were

through the inner security door, which the lax Iranians had not even been guarding, and a burst of machine gun fire alerted those staff who had not heard the first pistol shots that an armed assault on their building was under way.

THE SAS IS ALERTED

Two female staff members managed to slip out of the back door before the terrorists got to them, and two of their male colleagues tried to escape through upstairs windows. One made it to the safety of an office next door, but the other jumped to the ground and injured himself. The terrorists dragged him back inside before he could escape. The gang now had 26 hostages with which they hoped to bargain for the release of Arab prisoners in Iranian jails (Arabistan is a region of Iran not peopled by Iranians but by ethnic Arabs). They also wanted a safe passage for themselves once this had been achieved. What they did not appreciate was that the Iranian Government would hand the entire affair over to the British

Above: Moments before the SAS attack, frame charges are laid against the embassy's first-floor balcony windows.

and that the new Prime Minister, Margaret Thatcher, would never bow to terrorism. As specialist units began to arrive on the scene - D11 police marksmen, C13 anti-terrorist officers, the Special Patrol Group and members of C7, Scotland Yard's Technical Support Branch – the SAS was already on the move.

At its Hereford headquarters, the SAS squadron assigned to counter-terrorist duties keeps a 25-man Special Projects Team (SPT) on round-the-clock standby for immediate response to hostage incidents. A second identical SPT, on longer notice to move, alternates with them at regular intervals to keep reaction times to a minimum, with one team resting or training as the other watches and waits. Every member of these teams has spent hours in the 'Killing House' practising clearing rooms and killing terrorists without injuring hostages. At the time of

Below: The note authorising the Special Air Service to take over from the Metropolitan Police at Princes Gate on 5 May 1980.

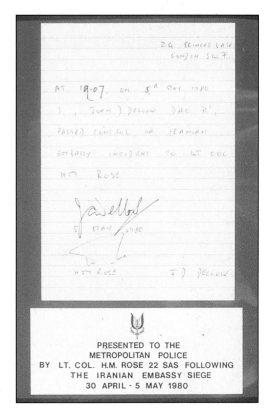

PRESENTED TO THE
METROPOLITAN POLICE
BY LT. COL. H.M. ROSE 22 SAS FOLLOWING
THE IRANIAN EMBASSY SIEGE
30 APRIL - 5 MAY 1980

Meanwhile, the Army built full-size replicas of each floor of the embassy at nearby barracks to allow the SAS men to familiarise themselves with the layout. 'Blue Team', another 25 men, the second SPT from Hereford, was also now on the scene and alternating with 'Red Team' at regular intervals. In the buildings next door to the embassy, surveillance teams were monitoring every sound made by captors and captives, to keep fully abreast of the ever-changing situation in the 50-room, six-storey building. From other vantage points, watchers logged every movement visible through the embassy windows and troopers carefully surveyed the building, including silently climbing over the roof.

The government's refusal to make concessions, coupled with the non-appearance of the Arab mediators demanded by the terrorists, created a volatile atmosphere inside the embassy.

Operation 'Nimrod', as the Iranian Embassy affair was codenamed, these sessions in the 'Killing House' used live ammunition with troopers in plain clothes playing the part of the hostages.

When 'Red Team', 24 troopers and one captain, from B Squadron, which was that day's duty SPT, arrived at the siege scene at Princes Gate in London, police negotiators had already established contact. At a higher level the Cabinet Office Briefing Room team (Cobra) under Home Secretary Willie Whitelaw, was about to lay down the ground rules. These equated to no surrender to terrorist demands and an armed rescue by the SAS if any of the hostages was killed. Until it became necessary to send in the troopers, the situation would be controlled by the police. Over the next six days, the negotiators patiently stalled the terrorists and gained minor concessions such as the release of five of the captives.

Right: 'Red Team' smashes its way into the Iranian Embassy using sophisticated equipment – sledgehammers!

The terrorist leader, Awn Ali Mohammed, codenamed Salim, sounded edgy and tense as he spoke to police negotiators on Monday 5 May.

'NIMROD' IS ACTIVATED

By the afternoon of the 5th, the terrorists, especially Salim, had reached the end of their tether, and one of the hostages was separated from the others. A few minutes later three shots rang out, to be followed by a phone call to the negotiators to say that the man had been killed. Men from both SAS special projects teams now prepared to move, but had to await final proof that a murder had indeed taken place and that the terrorists were not bluffing. Confirmation came at around 1900 hours, when three more shots were heard followed by a body being dumped out of the front door.

As the body of the embassy's chief press officer, Abbas Lavasani, was collected from outside the building, Sir David McNee, the Metropolitan Police Commissioner, telephoned Cobra and reported that he was handing over control

to the SAS. The SAS commanding officer, Lieutenant-Colonel Michael Rose, formally took control of the incident at 1907 hours. Operation 'Nimrod', the 'deliberate assault plan' for the freeing of the hostages (as opposed to an 'immediate action plan', which is what is implemented if there is no time to prepare), was about to begin. The plan was simple: for 'Red Team', two teams of four men would abseil down to the second-floor balcony at the back of the building, another group would assault the third floor, while more men would blow in the skylight on the fourth floor to enter that way; for 'Blue Team', the men were tasked with clearing the basement, ground and first floors. In addition, the whole assault would be covered by snipers.

THE ASSAULT BEGINS

On the given command, just after 1920 hours, three four-man sticks abseiled over the edge and crashed in through the second- and third-floor windows as a fourth stick took out the skylight and dropped through to clear the top floor. At the same

time, men from 'Blue Team' clambered over the first-floor front balconies from an adjacent building to place frame charges around the front windows (they were made of bullet-proof glass), and another four-man stick sledge-hammered their way through the rear basement French windows. At least 24 black-clad troopers wearing body armour and respirators and armed with Heckler & Koch MP5 submachine guns, were now entering the building, and about 20 others formed an outer cordon.

INSIDE THE EMBASSY

Inside the building, alerted by suspicious noises made by one of the abseilers accidentally breaking a window on his way past, the terrorists panicked. The 'Blue Team' front balcony stick split into two teams to clear the first floor. In one office PC Lock, who had managed to keep his own firearm hidden throughout the siege, had drawn his gun and was struggling with the terrorist leader. With a cry of 'leave off Trev', the SAS troopers pulled him off and killed the terrorist, who was armed with both a gun and a grenade, with a long burst of submachine-gun fire. At the same time, the other two troopers were about to enter a rear office when the door was violently thrown open by another terrorist, who was holding a pistol. One trooper shot him instantly, and he staggered back into the darkness of the inner office, mortally wounded, where he later died.

On the second floor, a stick from 'Red Team' had smashed their way into the main office, where most of the hostages had been held, only to find that the terrorists had transferred them to the telex room on the second floor at the front, and had locked the doors behind them. As they endeavoured to break through the locked and barricaded doors, one of their number climbed over the balcony to the adjoining room and forced an entry. One of the terrorists was trying to set fire to this room to delay the assault team. One of the SAS troopers tried to shoot him,

Left: 'Nimrod' is under way and the race is on to rescue the hostages being held in the embassy's second-floor telex room.

Above: As the fire took hold the embassy quickly filled with smoke and fumes, plus CS gas thrown in by the SAS.

but his Heckler & Koch jammed and his target escaped to the telex room.

THE TELEX ROOM

Inside the telex room itself, two of the four surviving terrorists began to shoot the hostages, of whom one was killed and two wounded before the SAS could reach them. One of the SAS soldiers who took part in the operation remembers hearing the shots: 'We heard the screams of the hostages coming from the telex room. "Shit, they're killing them all," I heard my mate shout. We raced into the room.' As the first trooper burst into the room, shooting with his pistol the terrorist who

Left: Five of the six terrorists were killed inside the embassy. The sixth was captured hiding among the hostages.

1. Operation 'Nimrod' begins. As a diversionary explosion rips through the third-floor skylight, 'Red Team' abseils from the roof (5) while 'Blue Team' gains entry to the library.

2. At the front, a four-man squad from 'Blue Team' blows in the window and rescues Sim Harris.

3. PC Trevor Lock tackles terrorist leader Awn, who is then killed by the SAS troopers.

4. Another terrorist runs into the Ambassador's office and is killed.

5. On the second floor, 'Red Team' gain entry into the back office, but their grenades set it on fire.

6. A member of 'Red Team' chases a terrorist heading for the telex room.

7. Three terrorists rush into the telex room and begin shooting the hostages.

8. A fourth terrorist enters the room, but is shot by a pursuing SAS soldier.

9. The rest of 'Red Team' burst out of the office and head for the telex room.

10. They discover one of the terrorists with a primed grenade and kill him.

11. Those hostages being held in the cypher room are freed.

12. As the hostages are being led away to the first floor, one of the terrorists is spotted. He pulls a grenade and is riddled with bullets.

13. The hostages are led out to the gardens behind the building. Here the last terrorist is found, wounded but alive.

The building has been cleared. The SAS operation has taken just **17 minutes.**

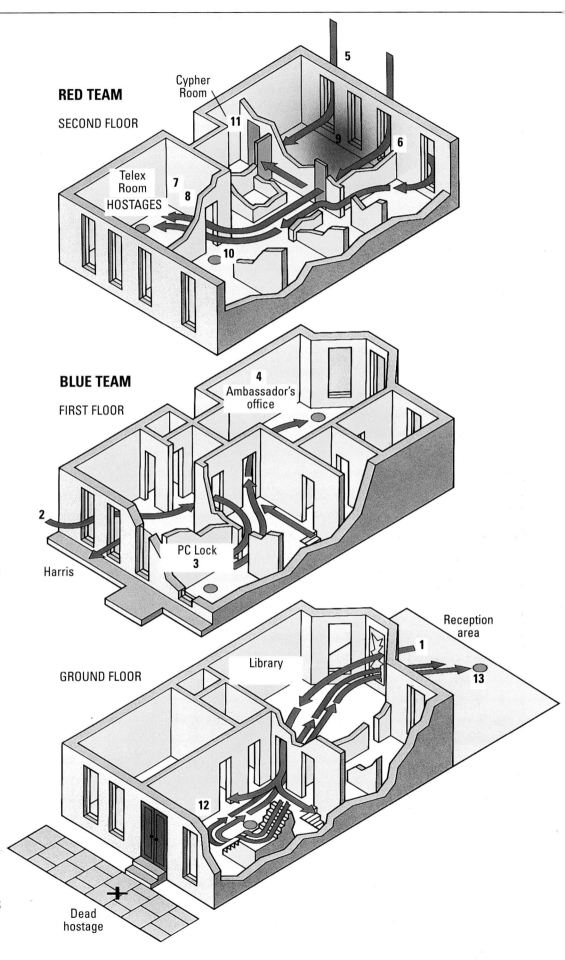

RED TEAM

SECOND FLOOR

Cypher Room

Telex Room
HOSTAGES

BLUE TEAM

FIRST FLOOR

Ambassador's office

Harris

PC Lock

GROUND FLOOR

Library

Reception area

Dead hostage

Left: The inside of the embassy after the rescue. The operation propelled the Regiment into the media spotlight.

tional responsibility back to the police at 1953 hours, having completed the job in only 46 minutes. The casualty toll was two hostages murdered, two hostages wounded and one trooper injured by burns, but none of the captives was killed or injured by their rescuers. Five of the six terrorists were killed, while the other was taken alive.

MEDIA HEROES

Much to the dismay of the SAS, television cameras had been smuggled into the area and much of the action was beamed live into just about every home in the country. Had Operation 'Nimrod' not gone to plan, this could have been extremely embarrassing, but in the event the publicity sent shock waves reverberating around the international terrorist community, and earned the admiration of democracies around the world. Britain was clearly no push-over for those determined to use violence to achieve political aims.

had just escaped when his submachine gun jammed, the other three tried to mingle with the hostages. By now the building was swarming with troopers, but it had also caught fire and was also full of CS gas, so everybody was evacuated as fast as possible. Two terrorists were posing as hostages. One was pulled out of the line of hostages leaving the building and made to lie on the floor. He then made a suspicious movement and was shot and killed.

His dead body was turned over, to reveal a Soviet hand grenade in his hand. The second armed terrorist was shot and killed trying to make his way downstairs with the hostages. The last man, who was unarmed, was searched and tied up. He was later sentenced to life imprisonment.

By 1928 hours, the first of the hostages had been led out of the Embassy and 12 minutes later the building was declared clear. The SAS formally handed opera-

For the Regiment there was not turning back. From being a relatively obscure specialist unit, it had suddenly been transformed into a world-famous force. One of those who took part in Operation 'Nimrod' sums up the effect it had on the SAS: 'Princes Gate was a turning point. It demonstrated to the powers that be what the Regiment could do and just what an asset the country had, but it also brought a problem we wished to avoid: the media spotlight. In addition, for the first few years after the siege Selection courses were packed with what seemed like every man in the British Army wanting to join the SAS. We just couldn't cope with the numbers who were applying, and so we had to introduce extra physicals on the first day just to get rid of the wasters. The same problem affected R Squadron, the reserve, and the sergeant in charge was overwhelmed with recruits.' Success can indeed be a double-edged sword.

Left: The hostages are bound and searched on the lawn to the rear of the embassy by the SAS. The operation took just 17 minutes.

Operations at home and abroad

In 1987, the services of the SAS were enlisted to gain the release of a prison officer held hostage by inmates of Peterhead Prison in Scotland. On this occasion, the troopers left their weapons at home, using staves instead to 'persuade' the hard men to give in gracefully. This type of operation would normally have been undertaken by Prison Officer MUFTI (Minimum Use of Force for Tactical Intervention) squads but, as the only safe access was over roof tops, it was felt that the climbing skills of the SAS would be more suited. When Strangeways Prison was taken over by rioters a few years later, the SAS was not used – a decision criticised by many inside and outside the service. If the SAS had been allowed to go in at an early stage, as it was prepared to do, inmates' lives may well have been saved.

Less than six months after the Peterhead Prison incident, SAS counter-terrorist operatives went into action against an Irish Republican Army (IRA) 'active service unit' in Gibraltar, but this operation was to bring bad publicity down upon the Regiment, despite its success. On Friday 4 March 1988, an IRA active service unit comprising two men and a woman flew independently into Malaga Airport in southern Spain. Their aim was to detonate a Semtex bomb during a regular 'changing of the guard' by British troops and bandsmen in nearby Gibraltar the following Tuesday.

The personnel involved were Mairead Farrell, who had served 10 years in prison in Northern Ireland for terrorist offences such as bombings and killings; Danny McCann, the hard man from the Lower Falls area of Belfast, who had masterminded a number of bombings and assassinations (the RUC had linked him to no less than 26 murders); and Sean Savage, the explosives expert.

Through good intelligence and observation work by the British and Spanish authorities, members of the team had been identified when undertaking a reconnaissance four months earlier, and they were under surveillance even before they left Ireland (there seems to have been another member of the team, one whose identity has never been fully established, but who travelled under the alias of Mary Parkin; it seems her task was to travel ahead of the team and gather intelligence concerning the target area, escape routes and when would be the best time to strike).

In the month prior to their arrival, another Irish woman – Mary Parkin – had been spotted monitoring troop movements at the regular Tuesday ceremonies in Gibraltar by alerted security forces, and the British quickly realised what the target was to be. As a reprisal for the Loughall ambush (8 May 1987) had been expected, security around Army targets in Ulster had been almost impregnable, so it made sense for the IRA to find a softer target overseas. After the appaling Enniskillen Cenotaph bombing (Remembrance Day, 1987), which had been aimed primarily at Protestant civilians, the British knew that the IRA had no hesitation in killing or maiming innocent bystanders, so the changing of the guard was recognised as being a prime target. As a consequence, before Farrell, McCann and Savage even arrived in Malaga, an SAS Special Projects Team was already in situ for Operation 'Flavius', the codename for the effort to stop the IRA team.

In nearby Marbella, the IRA rigged a hired Ford Fiesta with 65kg (140lb) of Semtex, which was enough to demolish a multi-storey building, then left it in a Spanish car park. Another hired car, a Renault, was driven into Gibraltar on the Saturday and parked to 'reserve' a space for the car bomb. At about the same time, the three identified terrorists also drove into Gibraltar in another hired car for a final recce, followed by members of a Spanish counter-terrorist unit. The following day they returned again, this time on foot, and headed for the Renault, which the British assumed contained the bomb. Two four-man SAS patrols were now tailing them, and when they headed back for the border one moved in to arrest them.

As the troopers closed in, a police car siren 'twitched' the terrorists and McCann turned round, immediately spotting his follower. Realising that he had been spotted by the look on McCann's face, and seeing him make a rapid arm movement, the SAS soldier opened fire. In court later the trooper stated that he thought the terrorist was about to trigger the bomb by radio. Farrell also made a suspicious movement and she was shot as well. Hearing the shots, Savage, who was walking alone, spun round and was gunned down by the troopers following him. When searched, however, all three people were found to be unarmed and had no bomb trigger device on them.

The outcry by some sectors of the press at the killing of unarmed terrorists was incredible. The Republican movement, many of whose members appear to condone cold-blooded murder of innocent civilians and security force personnel, yet object to their 'soldiers' being gunned down on an operational mission, made maximum capital from the affair. The troopers involved had to take part in the subsequent inquest into the shootings (September 1988), but no action was taken against them as they had acted only on information supplied to them and within their remit. The final verdict of the inquest was that the terrorists had been killed lawfully.

Irrespective of the perceived rights or wrongs of the Gibraltar killings, the SAS had successfully prevented a car bombing which could have killed and maimed scores. It also served as a timely deterrent to others intending to undertake similar attacks.

THE FALKLANDS WAR

Retaking South Georgia

The capture of South Georgia was the first part of Britain's strategy for regaining the whole of the Falkland Islands. A small flotilla of ships, codenamed Task Force 319.9, was despatched to take the island. On board the ships was D Squadron, 22 SAS.

The Falkland Islands in the South Atlantic Ocean, to the east of Argentina and 13,000km (8070 miles) from the British Isles, have been under continuous British occupation and administration since 1833, though the British first landed on the islands in 1690.

The islands' population in 1982, numbering less than 2000, was of British descent. They spoke English with a predominantly west-country accent, drank warm beer, drove on the left and considered themselves to be entirely British. Neighbouring Argentina, however, has long called the islands *Las Malvinas* and proclaimed them as hers. When Britain announced that her already minimal naval presence in the region was to be removed almost completely, the unpopular military junta in Argentina sought to divert public attention from the economic crisis at home by capturing the islands.

THE ARGENTINE INVASION

On Friday 19 March 1982, a group of Argentinians, posing as scrap metal dealers, landed on the Falklands dependency of South Georgia. At the time, as the harsh winter approached, the island was occupied only by a British Antarctic Survey team and two documentary film makers. Shortly after their arrival at the abandoned whaling station of Leith, the Argentinians ignored normal diplomatic formalities and raised their national flag, creating a diplomatic incident. With tensions rising, on 31 March the 22-strong detachment of Royal Marines from HMS *Endurance*, on ice patrol in the region, was ordered to provide a military presence on the island, to protect the survey team and observe the Argentinians.

Meanwhile, some 1100km (700 miles) to the northwest on East Falkland, the British military garrison was also put on alert when the news of the flag-raising reached the outside world. To call Naval Party 8901 a garrison is actually a bit of an overstatement, as its normal complement was a platoon-sized force of just over 30 Royal Marines. As luck would have it, however, the garrison was actually twice its normal size as the replacement Naval Party had just arrived for a period of acclimatisation prior to hand-over.

On 1 April, suspecting that trouble was brewing, the Royal Marines' commanding officer, Major Norman, deployed his small force on East Falkland to guard key points. He knew that they would not be able to hold off the full-scale invasion which the worried Falkland islanders were predicting. However, by covering all likely approach routes he could at least make the Argentinians use force to occupy the capital, Stanley. When the Argentinians made their move in the early hours of Friday 2nd in an operation codenamed 'Rosario', the Royal Marines were waiting for them. Outnumbered at least 15-1 by the invaders, Norman's men had little chance of beating off the amphibious and heliborne landings, but they put up a stout defence for three hours. At 0830 hours, though, the Governor of the islands, Mr Rex Hunt, ordered the surrender to save inevitable Royal Marine and civilian casualties.

Left: **HMS** Hermes *battles her way to the Falklands. She left Portsmouth on 5 April 1982 with SAS soldiers on board.*

Back in Hereford, as the incredible news broke on the BBC, the commanding officer of 22 SAS, Lieutenant-Colonel Michael Rose, immediately put D Squadron on standby. Typically, the crisis unfolded on a Friday afternoon, just as the men were due off on well-earned Easter leave. By late Saturday afternoon, cold weather equipment, specialist kit, weapons and ammunition were all being pulled out of store, even though at this stage only two men from G Squadron's Boat Troop were officially on standby for deployment. On Sunday morning, though, all of D Squadron was briefed, and the same afternoon the advance party flew out for what was to be the staging post on Ascension Island on the equator. They were followed next day by the rest of the squadron, plus all HQ staff and all available specialists from other squadrons.

THE FALL OF SOUTH GEORGIA

Down on South Georgia, the Argentine Navy tried to persuade Lieutenant Mills and his small detachment of Royal Marines to surrender on Saturday 3 April, but they naturally refused. The Argentinians then landed two parties of their marines by helicopter on both sides of the approaches to Grytviken harbour, and both opened fire on a British defensive position on King Edward Point. In reply, the Royal Marines shot down one of the two transport helicopters and damaged a light observation helicopter. When an enemy frigate then sailed into the bay, they holed it on the water-line with an anti-armour missile, put its gun turret out of action with 66mm rocket launchers, and raked the vessel with 1000 rounds of machine gun fire. Having made their point, and with no hope of escape, the Royal Marines then negotiated a ceasefire and ultimate surrender.

Just one week after the Argentinian invasion, a Royal Marine and SAS assault force was despatched by sea from Ascension with sealed orders for the recapture of South Georgia. Under command of Royal Marine Major Guy Sheridan, the

Right: Lying some 1100km (700 miles) southeast of the Falklands, South Georgia is subject to near Antarctic conditions.

combat group consisted of M Company 42 Commando, No 2 Special Boat Section (2 SBS) and D Squadron, 22 SAS. They were transported south in the Royal Fleet Auxiliary vessels *Fort Austin* and *Tidespring* under escort of the destroyer HMS *Antrim*, which was the command ship for the operation, codenamed 'Paraquet', and the frigate HMS *Plymouth*. The group of ships was given the name Task Force 319.9. Before the assault, they rendezvoused in mid-ocean with the

Above: Grytviken, South Georgia, which was assaulted by a combined force of SAS, SBS and Royal Marines on 25 April 1982.

survey ship HMS *Endurance* and the nuclear submarine HMS *Conqueror*.

Although South Georgia is in roughly the same latitude south of the equator as Aberdeen is to the north, its proximity to Antarctica, plus its mid-ocean position, give it a winter climate closer to that of northern Iceland. The few settlements on

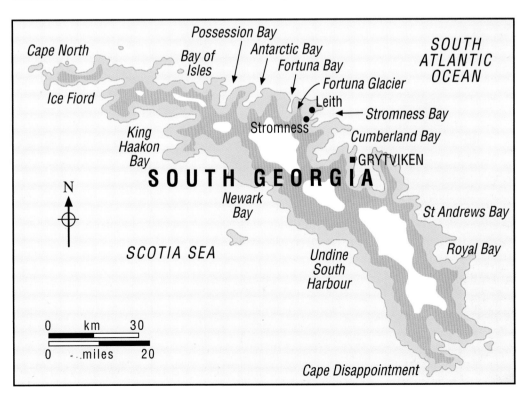

the island cling to the edge of deep fiords, while permanent glaciers running down to the sea fill the valleys between its mountain ridges. In the last half of April, the island is in the first throes of an Antarctic winter and daylight lasts for only a few brief hours. Once on the island, Argentinians believed that the weather alone made the island impregnable to anything other than an assault from the sea, and that they had more than sufficient men to guard the few suitable inlets.

THE SAS LAND ON FORTUNA GLACIER

Rather than mounting a blind amphibious assault, Major Sheridan, in consultation with Major Cedric Delves, the SAS commander, decided to put covert observation teams on the island to assess the strength of the enemy. Men of D Squadron's Mountain Troop would be flown in by helicopter to the west of the secondary objective of Leith. Simultaneously, the main advance party, from 2 SBS, would go ashore by inflatable well to the southwest of Grytviken, which would be the main objective. If all went to plan, the SAS and SBS would be used to launch diversionary raids as the main Commando force came ashore.

At first only one SAS troop was included by the Ministry of Defence in the Operation 'Paraquet' order of battle, but prior to leaving Ascension Delves persuaded the Royal Navy to transport all

of D Squadron to the South Atlantic, on the grounds that they would be of more use on board than kicking their heels on the island. With a full SAS squadron on attachment, plus 2 SBS, the Commando major now had nearly 300 highly trained men at his disposal for this tricky operation. Air support included Fleet Air Arm Wessex and Lynx helicopters, plus the Wasp from HMS *Endurance*.

At midday on Wednesday 21 April, less than three weeks after the Argentinian invasion and nearly 6000km (3700 miles) from the nearest British base, a troop of 16 SAS mountain warfare experts landed on a sub-Antarctic glazier in a blizzard. It had taken the naval helicopter pilots three journeys from ship to shore before eventually the blizzard lifted just enough to allow the troopers to de-bus. Within minutes, conditions returned to whiteout as the wind over the Fortuna Glacier picked up to gale force again. After battling against the elements for five hours, carrying 35kg (77lb) bergens and pulling four sledges (called *pulks*) each weighing 90kg (200lb), the troop had covered less than one kilometre when the light began to fail. When they tried to erect a pair of arctic tents for shelter, the wind swept one away and snapped the poles of the other. Most of the troop spent a freezing night on the glacier with just sleeping and bivvi bags for protection. The operation was starting to go very wrong.

After a pretty horrendous night in storm-force winds and temperatures well below zero, it was imperative to get the SAS soldiers off the glacier as quickly as possible. They radioed for extraction, but it was several hours after dawn before three helicopters, a radar-equipped anti-submarine version leading the way for the two troop carriers, were able to reach them during a short lull in the storm. The helicopters quickly picked up the 16 men between them and headed down and out towards the sea, but in whiteout conditions the second aircraft crashed, injuring one trooper and writing itself off. The other two helicopters returned to collect the survivors between them, but just after take-off the second troop carrier hit an ice ridge and also crashed.

On checking that there were no serious injuries from the second crash, the pilot of the remaining helicopter flew back to HMS *Antrim* to deposit his full load of passengers. He then collected medical supplies and blankets before returning immediately to the crash site, but the weather had closed in and he had to return to *Antrim* to refuel. It took Lieutenant-Commander Ian Stanley two more attempts that day before he managed to rescue the rest of the troop.

BOAT TROOP GOES INTO ACTION

With D Squadron's Mountain Troop recuperating from their ordeals, and any hope of a further landing on the Fortuna Glacier indefinitely postponed, the squadron's Boat Troop put a back-up plan into operation. This is where the decision to embark the full squadron at Ascension paid off. Five Gemini inflatable boats, each carrying a three-man team, were launched in darkness on the Friday morning to make their way to an offshore island, from where they could observe Leith and the other settlements around Stromness Bay. However, despite the engines having been warmed up prior to launch, three of the boats refused to restart, and two of the Geminis had to tow the other three towards the island.

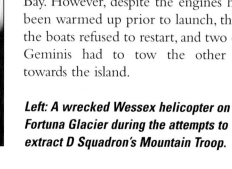

Left: A wrecked Wessex helicopter on Fortuna Glacier during the attempts to extract D Squadron's Mountain Troop.

Right: The Argentinian submarine Santa Fe *was disabled in Grytviken harbour after being hit by rockets and depth charges.*

When the wind suddenly picked up to gale force again on the run-in, two of the towed Geminis broke loose, though the crew of one was later rescued by helicopter. The troopers on the second drifting Gemini managed to swim ashore on a headland, and went to ground for several days to avoid compromising the mission. The other three teams made it to their objective and set up 'hides', from where they could observe the settlements. To the southeast, meanwhile, the SBS teams launched at the same time had also run into severe weather problems, and had to abort after ice punctured their inflatables. They were re-inserted by Wessex helicopter on the morning of the 25th.

All thoughts of taking the island by assault were temporarily put aside as the British ships discovered that an enemy submarine was heading in their direction. The flotilla scattered to increase their chances of survival.

THE ASSAULT ON GRYTVIKEN

As luck would have it, when returning from dropping off the SBS team, Wessex pilot Ian Stanley spotted the Argentinian submarine, the *Santa Fe*, on the surface, and dropped depth charges to disable it. The charges slightly damaged it, as did the Lynx and Wasp helicopters which subsequently strafed it with rockets and gunfire. Unable to submerge, the submarine limped into Grytviken, much to the dismay of the now panicking Argentinian defenders.

Seizing the initiative, and with any element of surprise now gone, the British decided to attack immediately, but as the main assault force of Royal Marines was too far out to sea, a scratch force was assembled on board HMS *Antrim*. Comprising two SAS troops, a second SBS team, 10 Royal Marines from the *Antrim's* company and all other available Royal Marines on the ship, this force numbered just over 70 in total. Against them they expected to find double the number of defenders. According to military doctrine, attackers should always outnumber

Right: The Argentinian submarine Santa Fe *was disabled in Grytviken harbour after being hit by rockets and depth charges.*

defenders by at least 3-1 to ensure success, but the SAS and Royal Marines don't worry about things like that.

Under cover of a naval bombardment from *Plymouth* and *Antrim*, which was carefully aimed to land near the defenders without hitting them, the first SAS troopers were landed in dead ground a couple of kilometres (1.2 miles) from the settlement. Subsequent Wessex and Lynx sorties brought in the rest of the force, and when all were assembled on the ridge overlooking Grytviken, one of the SAS troops advanced along the shoreline towards the settlement. Ahead of them, white sheets had been hung out by the Argentinians, to indicate they were very keen to surrender. The Union Jack flag was quickly run up by the SAS squadron sergeant-major, who had first pulled down the Argentinian national flag. The first battle of the Falklands conflict had been fought and won, with no major British casualties.

MOPPING-UP OPERATIONS

The next day, two SAS troops and one of the SBS teams flew to Leith by helicopter, where, upon considering his position fully, the Argentinian commander of the 16-man detachment surrendered without a fight. The combined SAS, SBS and Royal Marine assault force had now captured 156 military personnel and 38 Argentinians in civilian clothes. By the

following day, D Squadron was back at sea heading for the Falkland Islands proper. Meanwhile, the men of G Squadron were also sailing south, as was Lieutenant-Colonel Michael Rose with the Regimental Headquarters. The capture of South Georgia had given a huge boost to the morale of the whole Task Force, and had also confirmed the wisdom of having the SAS and SBS included.

Below: The note of surrender signed by the commander of the South Georgia garrison, Lieutenant Commander Alfredo Astiz.

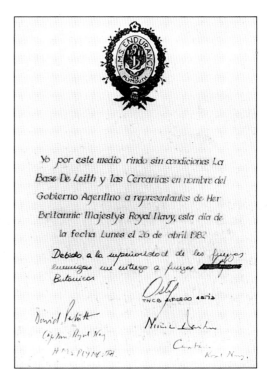

Intelligence Gathering

From the beginning of May 1982, SAS and SBS parties were put ashore on the Falklands to carry out a variety of missions, the most important of which was to determine which sites would be most suitable for a large-scale British landing.

Owing to the vast distance from the nearest British airfield at Ascension Island, and the lack of conventional aircraft carriers capable of taking reconnaissance aircraft, British intelligence on enemy troop dispositions on the Falkland Islands was almost non-existent. The precise location of the trailer-mounted French Exocet anti-shipping missiles, which could be shore-launched against the British assault ships, was also giving cause for concern. To provide the Commander of the Carrier Battle Group, Rear-Admiral Woodward, with as much accurate information as possible, and to try to locate the Exocet launchers, the men of the Mountain, Air and Mobility Troops from G Squadron were put ashore by helicopter all across the Falklands over three nights commencing on 1 May. Later, more patrols from D Squadron were also deployed to relieve some of the patrols from G Squadron, or to cover more locations.

When the initial plans were drawn up, high altitude, low opening (HALO) insertion by RAF Hercules flying at a height of 7400m (24,000ft) was considered as a way of getting SAS soldiers onto the Falklands. Much to the relief of the troopers, who realised how difficult it would be to land safely in the stormy conditions of the South Atlantic, this idea was scrubbed. However, if sufficient Hercules aircraft equipped with the new in-flight refuelling probes had been available only a few days earlier, this high-risk plan might have gone ahead. Instead, Royal Navy Sea King helicopters, their pilots using brand-new night vision goggles, inserted the Regiment's patrols in safe locations within one night's march of their objectives.

THE SAS AND SBS GO IN

All available SBS teams also went ashore over the same period as the SAS patrols to check possible landing beaches for suit-

ability. Even more publicity-shy than the SAS, the men of the Royal Marine Special Boat Service slipped silently ashore by canoes and inflatable boats to take soil samples, measure beach gradients, prepare tide tables and undertake a host of other survey tasks required to establish the best place for an amphibious landing. Like the SAS, they moved and worked at night, laying up in 'hides' during daylight hours to avoid being compromised. If there were Argentinian troops in the area, the SBS observed their numbers, movements and routines. At least three SBS sections, each similar in size to an SAS troop, were deployed during the conflict.

Between 30 and 40 troopers from G Squadron, working in four-man patrols, covered areas of actual and possible Argentinian deployment across the islands. On West Falkland, two patrols covered the main settlements of Port Howard and the Fox Bay area. On East Falkland, patrols observed the areas around San Carlos in the west, Port Salvador to the north, Goose Green on the narrow isthmus between Lafonia and the more occupied parts of the island, the capital Stanley, and three possible landing sites near it.

These last three locations, Cow Bay, Berkeley Sound and Bluff Cove, were the logical places for an amphibious assault as they offered relatively easy overland access to Stanley. However, as they were well within range of enemy artillery positions, and the defenders expected an attack from this direction, they were soon ruled out. However, the SAS patrols kept watch over all locations for anything from 15 to 26 days. During this period, the troopers had to exist on the whole without resupply, as this would have compromised their position, but unlike previous desert

Left: An SAS patrol waiting to be inserted behind Argentinian lines on West and East Falkland, early May 1982.

and mountain campaigns, on this job fresh water at least was plentiful.

The Falklands terrain is similar to that of Dartmoor so, from well-camouflaged observation posts (OPs) among the rocky tors and outcrops, the SAS patrols carefully monitored the unsuspecting Argentinians. Encoded messages were sent back at regular intervals to the operation command centre on the carrier HMS *Hermes* by state-of-the-art radio transmitters. Known as 'burst' radios, these computerised sets store the message in morse code form then 'squirt' it out in a high-frequency burst which lasts less than a second. So short is the transmission time that even if the enemy is locked onto the correct frequency, it is impossible for tracking stations to take an accurate fix. If, as is more usual, the enemy use frequency scanners, the chances are that they will not even 'hear' the burst. Safe in the knowledge that their transmissions were virtually untraceable, the SAS teams were able to broadcast from within a few hundred metres of major Argentine positions.

LIFE IN AN OBSERVATION POST

Once the British naval bombardment and Harrier ground attacks on enemy positions started in earnest, the SAS watchers were able to provide accurate target information to the gunners and airmen. For example, when a patrol dug in on Beaver Ridge above Port Stanley located a helicopter night dispersal site 30km (18 miles) to the west, it was able to call in an air strike. Several vital transport helicopters were destroyed or severely damaged on the ground. The troopers in this patrol spent a total of 25 days in their tiny 'hide' before being replaced on 25 May.

Lying in their cold, wet 'hides' in the peaty Falklands soil, or for the lucky few in the cover of a rock outcrop, the eight daylight hours were interminably long. Any movement was virtually impossible as Argentinian patrols, or even small groups of foraging soldiers, were a constant threat, and their helicopters crisscrossed the skies on re-supply and reconnaissance missions. Other than at dawn, before the Argentinians were out and about, stoves could not be used so rations had to be eaten cold. The dawn brew of

Michael Rose

Michael Rose was a lieutenant-colonel at the time of the Falklands War, being commander of 22 SAS Regiment. It was Rose, together with another SAS veteran, Brigadier Peter de la Billière, who was responsible for the SAS taking part in the British operation to retake the islands. This was most ironic, for only two months before the invasion he was informed that 'no scenario could be envisaged where it would be necessary to deploy the SAS to the Falkland Islands'. However, Rose lobbied Brigadier Julian Thompson, commander of 3 Commando Brigade, Royal Marines, for the SAS to be included in the Task Force. Rose was proved right, and the SAS took an active part in the war. Towards the end of the campaign, Rose conducted psychological warfare operations against the enemy, broadcasting on the radio their hopeless position. On the afternoon of 14 June, Rose flew into Stanley to begin surrender negotiations that would lead to the capitulation of the garrison.

warm tea and the occasional boil-in-the-bag hot meal soon became the highlight of the day. A member of G Squadron who lived in a 'hide' describes the conditions the men worked in: 'The weather was awful, it was either raining, drizzling or blowing a gale. It was a real problem getting and staying warm. The wet was the real killer for me, I don't like being wet. During observation at night I would break open a bar of chocolate and eat it. It was like someone turning on the central heating system, then, the next instant, you would be cold again.'

LIVING AMONG THE ENEMY

Although a patrol usually consisted of four men, only two normally manned the forward OP, with their colleagues covering them from a lying-up position (LUP) well out of sight of the enemy. The pairs would alternate after dark to vary the daily routine. During daylight hours in the OP both men would remain alert, but one of the soldiers in the LUP would try to have several hours uninterrupted sleep. This way every four days each man got a chance to recharge his batteries. At night all of the patrol would return to the LUP, each taking his turn to mount guard.

Incredibly, throughout nearly eight weeks of covert operations deep in enemy

occupied territory, only one SAS observation patrol was compromised. The officer in this patrol was killed trying vainly to cover his signaller's escape, but he was wounded and captured. This sad incident happened on West Falkland only four days before the end of the conflict.

Very early in May, a mysterious helicopter crash occurred in southern Chile. The whole incident has been shrouded in secrecy, by both Britain and Chile, but it is widely believed that the Sea King involved had been inserting SAS patrols into Argentina. The biggest threat to Britain's amphibious task force was the presence of long-range Super Etendard aircraft, operating from southern Argentinian bases and armed with anti-ship Exocet missiles. It was widely reported during and after the conflict that the SAS undertook observation of these airfields to provide advance warning of the Etendards' departure, but this has never been confirmed. Had the Royal Navy had an aircraft carrier capable of launching radar early warning planes, such an operation would not have been necessary.

Two weeks after the first G Squadron observation patrols were landed on the islands, a major SAS night attack was launched on Pebble Island to the north of West Falkland. The isolated settlement on

Above: SBS swimmer canoeists. The SBS worked closely with their SAS counterparts during the Falklands conflict.

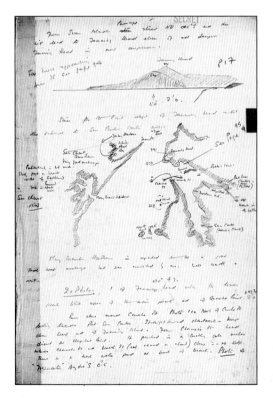

Left: British special forces made notes of all possible landing sites around the Falklands for the Task Force.

Pebble Island was served by a small grass airstrip, which the Argentinians were in the process of extending to give a night dispersal field for Pucara ground-attack aircraft. Some Argentinian military planners also thought that a British amphibious landing on sparsely populated West Falkland was the most likely possibility. Once the airfield on Pebble Island was completed, it would give them an operational base from where they could launch ground-attack operations on any such beachhead. In fact the British had decided to land at San Carlos on East Falkland, but the aircraft on Pebble Island still posed a grave threat to the landings.

At first, Admiral 'Sandy' Woodward would not approve Operation 'Prelim', as he felt that ships supporting the operation would be put unnecessarily at risk. A report from a Navy pilot of a possible radar emission from the island, however,

changed his mind, as such equipment might possibly detect the main assault fleet. On the night of 9/10 May, therefore, two four-man patrols, equating to half of D Squadron's Boat Troop, prepared to go ashore on a reconnaissance of the island by inflatable boats, but bad weather cancelled the mission. To save time, the following night they were inserted by helicopter on West Falkland, complete with collapsible canoes to enable them to cross to Pebble Island. They laid low on West Falkland for a day, before crossing to the island the following night.

PREPARING TO RAID PEBBLE ISLAND

With one patrol guarding the canoes, the other four men trogged (Marines 'yomp' and Paras 'tab', but SAS troopers 'trog') over the island to the airstrip. At dawn they observed no fewer than 11 Pucara ground-attack aircraft on the ground, then slipped away to lie low during daylight hours, though because of the flat terrain and lack of cover, they had to dump their bergens first. After darkness that

Captain John Hamilton

John Hamilton's exploits during the Falklands War are typical of the kind of audacity and courage displayed by SAS soldiers in the campaign. He joined 22 SAS in January 1981, joining D Squadron to lead Mountain Troop. He led his troop during the assault on South Georgia, failing on Fortuna Glacier but being ultimately victorious at Grytviken a few days later. He also took part in the raid on Pebble Island, leading his men and personally destroying four Argentinian Pucara aircraft. Later, his observation post above Port Howard, West Falkland, was discovered by the enemy. Heavily outnumbered, he gave battle for a lengthy period before succumbing to his fatal injuries. Throughout his short SAS career he displayed great courage and humour, and his actions earned the praise and admiration of the enemy commander of the garrison, General Mario Menendez. Hamilton was awarded a posthumous Military Cross for his actions near Port Howard, and his name was engraved upon the clock tower at Stirling Lines. Like so many before him, he had 'failed to beat the clock', which in SAS parlance means he failed to stay alive.

evening, they made their way back to join their colleagues, and then radioed their information to the Task Force early on the morning of the 13th. Out at sea, the raid was sanctioned and the rest of D Squadron made final preparations for departure on the night of the 14th.

THE PEBBLE ISLAND RAID

The attack force assembling on HMS *Hermes* was between 50 and 60 strong, and included a forward observation officer from 148 Commando Battery Royal Artillery to call in naval gunfire support from the destroyer HMS *Glamorgan*. The main attacking force was provided by Mountain Troop, with Air and Mobility Troops providing stop parties and a reserve. The men from Boat Troop not previously deployed on the recce acted as a screen party for a mortar team. In addition to personal weapons, ammunition, rocket launchers and spare ammunition for the GPMGs, each trooper carried two mortar bombs for the 81mm mortar that was taken along for support fire.

The transport to the island was provided by Sea King helicopters of 846 Naval Air Squadron. The aircraft themselves were equipped with a complete avionics suite which included doppler navigation radar, auto-pilot and auto-hover systems. As they are designed to fly in all weathers the SAS soldiers knew there would not be a problem with insertion.

Originally the objectives of the raid were the destruction of the enemy aircraft, their ground crews and the island's garrison. However, due to strong headwinds *Hermes* took longer to reach the flying-off point than expected. This meant that the SAS soldiers would only have a short time to carry out their mission. Because the Sea Kings had to be back on *Hermes* before daylight, so all three ships could be well east of the island to minimise the threat from Argentinian aircraft, the aircraft on the airstrip were the priority targets.

For the ships taking part in the raid, the weather was a problem. The frigate *Broadsword*, one of the escort ships for *Hermes*, made slow progress in the heavy winds. Then her Sea Wolf surface-to-air missile system became defective and she began to slip behind. *Glamorgan*, though, managed to sail to within 10km (six miles) of the shore to provide gunfire support and be on hand should any of the helicopters get into trouble. *Hermes* herself sailed to within 60km (36 miles) of the island to give the Sea Kings a shorter flight in the strong winds.

Each member of the SAS raiding party carried an M16 assault rifle, with three spare magazines plus another 200 rounds of 5.56mm ammunition. In addition, many of the men were carrying M72 Light Anti-tank Weapons (LAWs), which are light but have high-explosive warheads – ideal against grounded aircraft.

HIT AND RUN

When the three Sea Kings flew the attackers in to the landing zone about seven kilometres (three miles) from the airfield, they were met by the recce patrols from Boat Troop and led to their pre-designated start-line. Due to the

Below: Typically bleak Falklands terrain, notwithstanding the explosions. SAS teams had to dig covert 'holes' in such ground.

aforementioned difficulties with the weather, Operation 'Prelim' had got off to a late start, but the troopers managed to make up some time during the advance over the island.

At 0700 hours, Mountain Troop launched its attack accompanied by a 4.5in gun barrage on the enemy trenches from HMS *Glamorgan*. Due to the lack of time, the attackers commenced the operation by shooting and blowing holes in the aircraft with rifles, machine guns and 66mm LAW anti-armour weapons, but when they realised that the Argentinians were not firing back to any great extent or effect, they placed explosive charges on the airframes.

RETURN TO *HERMES*

In total six Pucaras, four trainers and a Short Skyvan light transport aircraft were destroyed before the team pulled back after 15 minutes of brisk action. Contact continued until 0730 hours, by which time the Squadron had regrouped and was withdrawing to the pick-up point to

await the return of their helicopters. With the Argentinian fuel and ammunition dumps destroyed by naval gunfire and 11 aircraft smouldering on the edge of the runway, the SAS departed two and a half hours after the first shot was fired. Their casualties were one man with concussion following a command-wire land mine blast and one trooper with a minor shrapnel wound, which did not prevent him continuing with the attack.

The raid had been a total success, and had dented Argentinian morale substantially, as well as raising the spirits of the British Task Force. In addition, there were no enemy aircraft on Pebble Island to interfere with the proposed landings at San Carlos Water.

While the Pebble Island raid was being planned and executed, SAS intelligence gathering continued unabated. Despite the fact that there were 11,000 Argentinian soldiers on the Falklands and 42 enemy aircraft and helicopters, both the SAS and SBS were able to insert teams onto the islands without difficulty. But

Above: A British Army patrol after the landings at San Carlos. D Squadron mounted a diversionary raid to support the landings.

the Regiment was to suffer a grievous loss while carrying out a simple transfer.

It was decided to transfer the special forces who had been housed in *Hermes* to *Intrepid*. As light started to fade on 19 May, Sea King ZA 294, with a crew of three and crammed with men from D and G Squadrons, made the last flight of the day. The helicopter approached *Intrepid* from directly astern, but then something hit the aircraft and it plunged into the sea. The crash killed over 20 men, 18 of them SAS soldiers. It was the Regiment's highest single loss since World War II.

The Regiment hardened its resolve and carried on. Unfortunately there were other tragedies, as a member of D Squadron explains: 'Working alongside our cousins in the SBS, we were given specific areas to work in. The concept, as in other theatres of war where friendly forces work in a confined area, was to

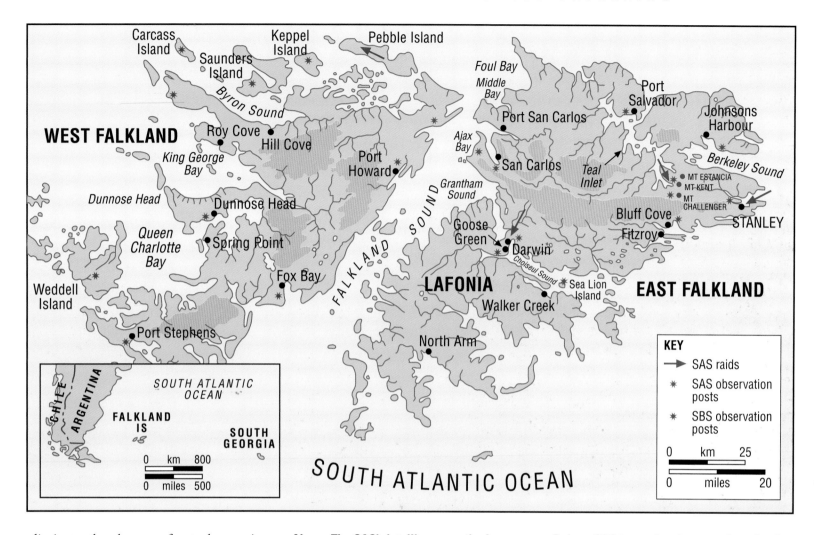

Above: The SAS's intelligence gathering ended after the landings on 21 May. After this the Regiment supported conventional forces.

Below: SAS teams fought several gun battles with members of the Argentinian garrison during the war.

eliminate the danger of patrols running into each other. This scenario, known as "blue on blue", happened several times in the Falklands, and patrols would open up on each other until both sides realised their mistake. Fortunately there were no casualties, that is until an SAS team ran into an SBS patrol. Exactly how they ran into each other is a mystery, but the consequence was a short, intense firefight in which one of the SBS men, Sergeant "Kiwi" Hunt, was mortally wounded. Great shame. He was one of the unsung heroes of the war, living ashore for weeks before the main landings.'

The work carried out by the Regiment before the British landings provided the Task Force with invaluable intelligence concerning enemy strengths and dispositions, as well as the geography of the islands themselves. The landings at San Carlos did not mark the end of the SAS's war in the Falklands, merely the beginning of another phase, in many ways a more dangerous phase, but one in which the Regiment would excel.

Battling through to Stanley

The SAS played a part in supporting the establishment of a beachhead at San Carlos Water, and then aided conventional units by conducting deep-penetration patrols to locate enemy forward positions and drive in their outposts. And the SAS finished the war with a flurry.

The effect of the Pebble Island raid had seriously undermined Argentinian morale. At dead of night on an isolated island, a garrison of more than 100 troops had been taken on by a daring team less than half their strength. In spite of Argentinian propaganda claims of a great success, news of the raid, often grossly exaggerated by young conscripts, spread the length and breadth of the Falklands. Few Argentinians slept at ease in their tents and trenches during the following nights as they waited for the now inevitable British landing.

The main landing was planned for the early morning of 21 May in the double inlet of San Carlos Water on the opposite side of East Falkland from Stanley. Three landing points were picked, Red and Blue Beaches near San Carlos Settlement, plus, a few kilometres to the north, Green Beach near Port San Carlos. To confuse the enemy and deter reinforcements, D Squadron was tasked with mounting a diversionary raid on a large Argentinian garrison at Goose Green, some 40km (25 miles) to the south. On the evening of the 19th the squadron cross-decked by Sea King from HMS *Hermes* to the commando assault ship HMS *Intrepid* to prepare for the attack.

DIVERSIONARY RAIDS

Eleven badged SAS men, including the sergeant-majors of both D and G Squadrons, plus nine dedicated members of the support arms all perished (see previous chapter). Many of the dead troopers had taken part in the successful Pebble Island raid only days before. Despite this tragedy, the following night the remaining men of D Squadron flew ashore to launch the diversionary raid.

While D Squadron, led by Major Delves, was making its epic night march on Goose Green, the SBS flew ashore at Fanning Head on the northern entrance

Above: Royal Marines (RM) on their way to Stanley, the location of an SAS diversionary raid on the night of the 13/14 June.

to San Carlos Water. Their task was to try to persuade an Argentinian force to surrender by fair means or foul, and they borrowed an SAS mortar team to help them do it. Back at Goose Green, the 40 or 50 troopers had spread themselves out overlooking the enemy and opened up with a disproportionately high number of machine guns, anti-armour missiles, mortars and grenade launchers. The 1200 defenders returned fire sporadically but did not dare counterattack, thinking that they were being attacked by at least a battalion. The odds against the SAS were literally 25 to 1, but 'Who Dares Wins'! Breaking contact at daybreak, the SAS marched off north to join up with the first wave of the main landing, stopping only to use a Stinger missile to shoot down a Pucara on its way to San Carlos.

With the men of G Squadron still manning observation posts throughout East Falkland, D Squadron was pressed into a more conventional role. When a G Squadron OP confirmed that the stra-

tegic central high ground of Mount Kent was not manned by the enemy, D Squadron deployed more than 60km (36 miles) into enemy territory to seize it. They held it for almost a week, despite numerous probing Argentinian patrols, until the arrival of the Royal Marines.

B SQUADRON FLIES IN

At about the same time B Squadron was flown into theatre as battlefield casualty replacements. They joined the Task Force by parachuting into the Atlantic after a 12-hour flight from Ascension, where they were picked up by *Glamorgan*. Over on West Falkland, now that their beach survey duties were over, the SBS ringed the island with covert observation posts to keep an eye on the Argentinians. They were joined in the first few days of June by five patrols from D Squadron, two of which relieved G Squadron patrols which had been there throughout May.

The battle to recapture the Falklands was now almost over, but on the night of 13/14 June the SAS mounted one last buccaneering raid. In an attempt to take some of the heat off 2 Para's attack on Wireless Ridge, one of whose companies was commanded by a well-respected former SAS officer, a diversionary seaborne raid was launched opposite Port Stanley. The original objective was an ammunition dump between Stanley and the eastern end of Wireless Ridge, with the attackers being landed by helicopter. However, when the weather closed in, four Royal Marine Rigid Raider assault boats were requisitioned instead.

RAID ON STANLEY

The defences in and around Stanley itself were quite formidable. There were some 8000 enemy soldiers in and around the town, plus 105mm and 150mm artillery, anti-aircraft guns and Panhard armoured cars to back them up.

The 60-strong force, comprising three SAS troops, a six-man SBS section and four Marine raiding squadron coxswains, raced eastwards along the inlet, under cover of fire from other SAS troops on the north shore (they had descended from Murrell Heights to lay down a barrage of GPMG and Milan fire). It was like an amphibious version of David Stirling's desert raids, and the founder would have loved it. Thinking that a full-scale amphibious landing was in progress, the Argentinians on Wireless Ridge, not to mention those in Port Stanley and on ships berthed in the harbour, turned their guns on the attackers. Although the SAS had to turn back before reaching their objective, their actions temporarily took some of the pressure off 2 Para. Despite the intense amount of incoming fire, only three of the raiders were slightly injured, though the Royal Marine craft were all badly holed.

The SAS soldiers in the boats were particularly aggrieved about the actions of the crew on board the hospital ship *Bahia Paraiso*, which was moored in Stanley harbour. The SAS men, following the rules of war, had not shot at the ship, but

it had used its searchlights to highlight the boats in the harbour. Justice was done, though, when the ship was hit by Argentinian gunfire.

The Stanley harbour raid was to be the last major SAS action of this diverse conflict, where every aspect of SAS training and procedures was put to good use.

SAS-BROKERED CEASEFIRE

On 14 June 1982, with a general ceasefire in effect, Lieutenant-Colonel Rose and a Spanish-speaking officer, Captain Bell, were helicoptered into Stanley to discuss surrender terms with General Mario Menendez, Argentinian governor of the Falkland Islands.

At first Menendez would consider only a limited surrender, as he could not speak for the garrison on West Falkland. However, Rose would have none of it, and informed the Argentinian that a half surrender was no surrender. Unknown to Menendez, the British Task Force high command would have settled for the surrender of East Falkland alone at this stage, as units were experiencing severe shortages. The Army, for example, was down to six rounds per gun.

Rose could have given way, but SAS officers are made of sterner stuff. He was daring, and he was going to win.

Menendez, demoralised and receiving no clear instructions from the Junta in Buenos Aires, capitulated in the face of such resolution. His surrender would encompass the whole of the islands.

Within two hours an agreement had been reached, and before midnight on 15 June Major-General Jeremy Moore, the British land forces commander, and the Argentinian commander-in-chief signed the official instrument of surrender. The SAS party then moved off to Government House, where they hoisted the small SAS Regimental Union Jack, which they had brought with them from Hereford (the possibility that Britain may have been defeated in the war was not even considered). Later this flag was hauled down and replaced by a much larger version, one brought from the UK by the Royal Marines.

Thus ended the Falklands War. For the Regiment it had been a well-fought campaign, in which it had had the opportunity to display its wide range of skills. Once again the men of the SAS displayed their cool professionalism, though 20 of them had died winning the war.

Below: The British flag flies in Stanley again. The Regimental SAS flag flew from Government House.

THE GULF WAR

False Start

Originally the SAS was tasked with rescuing the Western hostages being used as 'human shields' by the Iraqis. However, the release of the hostages marked a period of uncertainty with regard to the SAS having any role in the Gulf War at all.

On 2 August 1990 the Iraqi dictator, President Saddam Hussein, invaded the neighbouring country of Kuwait in a move which took the rest of the world by surprise, despite many warning signs being visible.

Fearing that Iraq's vast army would continue to advance on Saudi Arabia and her oilfields, the United States immediately dispatched rapid reaction forces to bolster that country's defences. Shortly afterwards, the United Nations Security Council passed resolutions in support of Kuwait, and an American-led coalition was formed under the 'Desert Shield' banner to protect Saudi Arabia. Britain and France also joined the Americans, and eventually 30 nations provided manpower and support.

When Iraq invaded Kuwait, most of A and G Squadrons, 22 SAS, were already in the Gulf undertaking routine training in extreme climatic conditions. From an operating base in the United Arab Emirates (UAE), the SAS was conducting vehicle patrols across the southeastern segment of the vast desert wilderness known as the Empty Quarter on Saudi Arabia's southern borders. As part of Britain's military assistance commitment to Oman and the UAE, the Regiment is allowed free access in northern Dhofar, western Muscat and

Below: An American Delta Force Chenworth Fast Attack Vehicle (FAV) is off-loaded from a Chinook during the Gulf War.

Above: A Scud surface-to-surface missile (SSM), like the ones used by the Iraqis to strike at Israel from western Iraq.

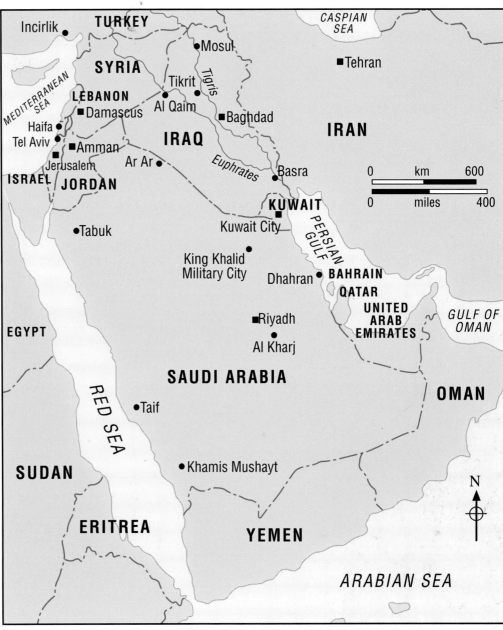

Above: From the expanses of western Iraq the mobile Scud launcher teams could wreak havoc upon Israeli cities.

southern Abu Dhabi to this near feature-less desert which stretches all the way from Yemen in the west to Qatar in the northeast. With daytime temperatures fre-quently exceeding 40°C during high summer, and few inhabitants for hundreds of kilometres, the Empty Quarter is the ideal training ground for long-range desert operations.

DESERT VEHICLES

Since the 1950s the SAS has regularly used heavily armed Land Rovers for long-range patrols, but by the late 1980s these vehicles were weighing in at nearly four tonnes when fully loaded with weapons, ammunition, kit, fuel and rations, and consequently were unwieldy.

To find a lighter option for raiding missions, the Regiment looked at the lat-est racing buggies to see if this type of vehicle could be successfully militarised. In the summer of 1990, a few of the new dune buggy-style Light Strike Vehicles (LSV) were delivered for user trials, and the Mobility Troops of both squadrons were looking forward to testing them out

in the desert conditions for which they were primarily designed.

Based loosely on the Chenworth Fast Attack Vehicle (FAV) procured a few years before by one of the US Army's Light Divisions, but now in service with Am-erican Special Forces, the LSV is a small and fast two-man vehicle. Manufactured to SAS specifications by an experimental engineering outfit in Sussex, the LSV has a lightweight tubular space frame incor-porating a weapons mount on the roll-cage over the crew. Power for the vehicle is provided by a rear-mounted Volks-wagen engine, which gives a top speed of 100km/h (60mph).

Later LSVs have been engineered with four-wheel drive, but those dispatched to the Gulf relied purely on their high speed

and low ground pressure for their mobil-ity. With the vehicles' centre of gravity finely balanced over the rear wheels, dri-ving technique was basically 'point-and-shoot', with rapid acceleration and a full length Makrolon underside skid plate allowing the vehicle to be powered up steep slopes and over ridges. However, high speed is not required in all situations, and for general recce work or stealthy final approaches the LSV was fitted with a crawler gear. An added advantage was that the overall loaded weight was suffi-ciently low to allow helicopters to insert these vehicles deep behind enemy lines.

Sir Peter de la Billière

De la Billière was commissioned into the Durham Light Infantry and served in the Korean War, Japan, Egypt and Jordan. He decided to join the SAS, went for SAS Selection and passed. He joined the Regiment as a captain in Malaya in 1955. During the campaign against the rebels holding out on the Jebel Akhdar, he won the Military Cross. He next went to Borneo, to help stop the Indonesian take-over of the Sabah and Sarawak regions of the island. His reorganisation of the SAS included the much-needed improvement of the transport of supplies to long-range jungle patrols. Now a major, he won his second Military Cross. Service in Oman in the 1970s resulted in him winning the DSO, and by the end of the 1970s he was in command of the SAS Group. A brigadier at the time of the Falklands, he ensured the SAS took part. He led the British forces in the Gulf as a lieutenant-general and retired in June 1991, a general and holder of the KBE and CBE.

In theory, a four-man patrol could now travel in a pair of LSVs at high speed over the desert at night using NVG (night vision goggles), creep quietly up to their target before dawn, then race through the objective loosing off 40mm grenades, machine-gun fire or even Milan missiles. Unfortunately, however, when the LSVs were trialled in operating conditions, it was discovered that their suspensions were not robust enough, and consequently none was actually deployed operationally during the Gulf War, though they were held in reserve at the SAS forward operations base in Saudi Arabia.

When news of the Iraqi invasion of Kuwait broke, the SAS troopers already in the region were put on standby, and more personnel flew out from Hereford at the earliest opportunity. As it was, the rapid deployment of US airborne forces, and the subsequent build-up using pre-positioned US war materiel, stopped Saddam Hussein in his tracks. The troopers were now left kicking their heels for several weeks, as the American, British and French conventional aviation, armoured and mechanised forces assembled. At this stage it appeared that no role could be found for the SAS, which was just one of the many special forces units in Saudi.

Of course the SAS did not take things lying down, and various officers were manoeuvred into positions, both in Britain and Saudi Arabia, where they could both glean information and put forward their case at every opportunity. The nomination of Lieutenant-General Peter de la Billière, who had had a long and distinguished career in the SAS, as the overall British commander also went in the Regiment's favour, but at first even he had difficulty in finding jobs for the boys. He was, however, able to ask the SAS to examine ways of rescuing the hundreds of British citizens being held hostage in Iraq and those still in hiding in Kuwait. There were around 1000 British citizens in Iraq when the invasion took place, with a further 800 trapped in Kuwait itself.

Although the SAS is well versed in hostage-rescue techniques, and on a wider scale trains with 5 Airborne Brigade and 3 Commando Brigade in Services Protected Evacuation procedures, freeing all the Britons in Saddam's clutches was well beyond anything it had trained for before. With hundreds of hostages spread around dozens of locations across two countries, even locating them all would be an impossible task, let alone getting them safely out. Several simultaneous clandestine parachute and helicopter insertions seemed to be the only half-viable option, followed up by assaults on the guards then a fighting retreat to a remote desert rendezvous for extraction by helicopter.

Saddam Hussein, in an effort to deter any Allied attack upon Iraq, had dispersed the hostages to sites throughout Iraq and

Below: The Allied air campaign knocked out the Iraqi air force and quickly established air supremacy, but the Scuds still operated.

Kuwait as 'human shields'. At the end of October 1990, for example, he placed 661 hostages at economic and military sites as protection against Allied air strikes (at this time he still had 3700 Western and Japanese hostages in his possession).

HOSTAGE-RESCUE PLANS

Even if Britain had every SAS trooper plus her entire Chinook helicopter fleet available for service in the Gulf (these helicopters did not arrive in-theatre until January 1991), it seemed unlikely that any more than half of the hostages could have been rescued. Nonetheless, the 'Kremlin' and the squadrons already in the Gulf carried on planning and training for such an eventuality, just in case this desperate course of action proved necessary.

Fortunately, on 6 December, the bulk of the British hostages being detained by the Iraqis were released. By this stage it was clear that only force would remove Saddam's troops from Kuwait, though high-level international diplomacy was still trying to find a compromise. With the next wave of British troops, including a second armoured brigade, now preparing to move, it seemed certain to most knowledgeable observers that a ground war was inevitable. With the hostages now no longer a factor, on 12 December Sir Peter de la Billière told the SAS it was time for them to start planning ahead for deep-penetration raids into Iraq and Kuwait.

DIVERSIONARY TACTICS

At this time, other than planning or secondment officers, few members of the Regiment were yet in Saudi Arabia, though just about every available trooper had been sent to the Gulf States for desert training and acclimatisation. On the basis that the balloon would almost certainly go up soon after New Year, those troopers not actually required in-theatre were flown home for Christmas leave, but the first orders to redeploy were issued on Boxing Day. Some went direct to Saudi Arabia in advance of their colleagues to set up a main operating base, but the bulk

returned to their Gulf State training base to perfect their desert skills.

According to Sir Peter's memoirs, it was to be the second week of January 1991, less than a week before the United Nations deadline expired on the 15th, before he finally identified a suitable role for the SAS in the forthcoming campaign. As they had done against Hitler in Europe in 1944, the SAS would infiltrate deep behind Iraqi lines to cut lines of communication and create diversions on the enemy's flank to convince him that the threat lay in the wrong direction. However, the overall UN Coalition commander in Saudi Arabia, US General Norman Schwarzkopf, had to sanction these actions, and so de la Billière invited the SAS planners to make the presentation themselves. Stormin' Norman was so impressed with their preparation, commitment and dedication that he immediately gave them his stamp of approval.

The Allied air war exceeded all expectations, and by the end of the day the Iraqis had surrendered control of the skies to the UN. However, on 18 January an Iraqi Scud surface-to-surface missile (SSM) was launched at Dhahran, Saudi Arabia. Then the Iraqis launched several at Israel from western Iraq, hitting a number

of towns and cities. The Israelis swore revenge, which would have undoubtedly shattered the UN Coalition. The Americans frantically diverted aircraft to hunt for the Scuds and their mobile launchers, but to no avail.

THE SAS GOES IN

As more and more Scuds hit Israel, the SAS was ordered to go into western Iraq and search them out and destroy them. The Regiment decided to tackle the Scud threat in three ways. First, static road watch patrols would be mounted to report the movement of Scud traffic, and direct American F-15 Strike Eagles onto the convoys. Second, fighting columns would roam western Iraq to hunt for the missile launchers. Finally, SAS parties would cut Iraq's concealed communications links to prevent orders being sent to the launch teams. The road watch patrols would be made up of three patrols of eight men each, and would monitor the three Main Supply Routes (MSRs) that went from the Euphrates valley to the Jordanian border. The men themselves would be drawn from B Squadron. From having a relatively minor role, the SAS was now tasked with saving the entire Coalition. As usual, it rose to the challenge.

Road Watch Patrols

The SAS road watch patrols were ultimately unsuccessful, but the exploits of one of the patrols, codenamed 'Bravo Two Zero', has since become famous for heroism and tenacity of the highest kind, plus the greatest feat of endurance in the history of the SAS.

The anti-Scud SAS road watch patrols were an answer to the problem of preventing Israel from entering the war. Saddam Hussein had pulled off a masterstroke in firing the Scuds at what he called the 'Zionist entity', and he temporarily wrested the initiative from the UN High Command in Riyadh.

Before the Coalition air campaign started, Lieutenant-General Peter de la Billière and General Norman Schwarzkopf went over the SAS's missions in western Iraq. At this stage the primary objective was still attacks on roads and communications centres, with general harassment as a secondary task. Well down the list was the hunt for Scud surface-to-surface missile (SSM) launchers.

The 'balloon went up' during the night of 16/17 January 1991. While Coalition aircraft began their attacks on the enemy, Colonel Andrew Massey, the commanding officer of the Regiment at that time, began to move the whole of the SAS to its forward operating base (FOB)

at Al Jouf in western Saudi Arabia. Men, their weapons, equipment and vehicles were moved by RAF Hercules transport aircraft to the FOB, which was situated 900km (1448 miles) northwest of Riyadh.

ALLIED OBJECTIVES

The overall objectives of the war, as dictated by Central Command (CENTCOM) in Riyadh, were as follows: to strike Iraq's political and military leadership, her command and control centres; to achieve and maintain air superiority in the skies over Kuwait and Iraq; to destroy Iraq's chemical, biological and nuclear capabilities; to destroy those Republican Guard units in the Kuwaiti theatre of operations; and to liberate Kuwait. The first part of the operation consisted of an air campaign, the initial targets of which were enemy radar sites, electrical plants, communications towers and command posts. To achieve these objectives, the Coalition had assembled a colossal air fleet, consisting of over 2000 aircraft. To

counter this threat, the Iraqi air force had around 750 fighters and ground-attack aircraft, plus a few Soviet bombers and transport aircraft. While these Iraqi air assets were not large or modern compared to those of the Coalition fleet, it was realised that Iraqi aircraft could inflict major damage on UN air assets and that they had to be neutralised.

THE AIR CAMPAIGN

Lieutenant-General Charles Horner, commander of the US 9th Air Force, and the man responsible for the Coalition's air war, planned accordingly. Horner split the air campaign into four phases. Phase one would last an estimated 7-10 days, and would have three main objectives: to gain air superiority over Iraq and Kuwait; to destroy Iraq's strategic attack capability, her nuclear, chemical and biological production facilities, and her Scud missile launch and storage sites; and to disrupt Iraq's command and control structure. Phase two, expected to last three days, entailed the suppression of the air defences of those Iraqi forces deployed in and around Kuwait itself. Phase three, which would last from the end of the second phase until the beginning of the ground offensive, involved Allied aircraft attacking those targets in the first two phases, but with the emphasis on striking Iraqi Army units in Kuwait. Phase four involved the provision of air support as and when required during the UN ground offensive. The first Coalition aircraft that would hit Iraq's comprehensive air-defence radar network were eight McDonnell Douglas AH-64 Apache attack helicopters from the crack US 101st Airborne Division, codenamed Task Force 'Normandy'. They took off just after dark on 16 January and

Left: An Iraqi transporter-erector-launcher (TEL) with its Scud stowed horizontally. It takes 45 minutes to prepare a launch.

Right: The thinking behind the road watch patrols was sound: to watch the Iraqi Main Supply Routes into western Iraq.

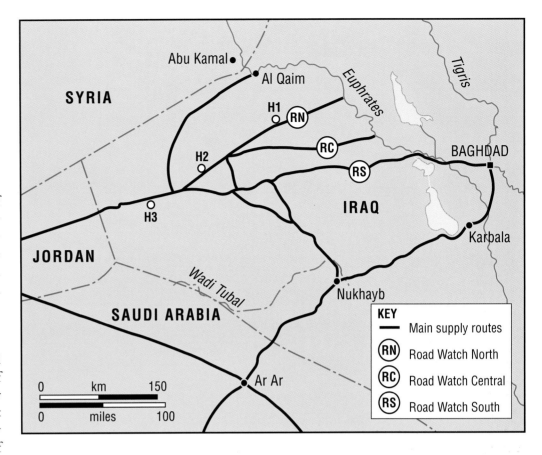

headed towards two Iraqi air-defence radars to the west of Baghdad, approximately 700km (435 miles) inside enemy territory. The destruction of such facilities was vital if the Iraqis were to be blinded as to the whereabouts of Coalition aircraft. Arriving within 3-6km (1.8-3.7 miles) of their targets, the Apaches started their attack with salvoes of Hellfire missiles. The radar sites erupted into flames as the missiles found their targets. The sites had been totally destroyed. The first aerial mission had been a success.

AIR ATTACK

At midnight on 16 January, Lockheed F-117 Night Hawk 'stealth' warplanes of the US Air Force's 415th Tactical Fighter Squadron took off from Khamis Mushait air base in the south of Saudi Arabia. They would be followed shortly by F-117s of the 416th Tactical Fighter Squadron, which took off from the same base.

The F-117s attacked 34 targets associated with the enemy's air-defence network. 52 Tomahawk cruise missiles launched from the battleships USS *Wisconsin* and *Missouri*, and the cruiser USS *San Jacinto*, also hit enemy strategic targets.

Their radar network seriously reduced in effectiveness, the Iraqis could do little to counter the second wave of Coalition fighters and attack warplanes which decimated Scud missile launch sites, missile storage bunkers and airfields.

The air war had begun superbly. The initial wave of air strikes consisted of 671 sorties. Despite the heavy flak that some of the Coalition aircraft had encountered, especially over Baghdad, there had been no losses. In addition, the Iraqi air force had hardly been seen. For example, up to midnight of 17 January the Allies had flown 2107 sorties compared to 24 combat missions undertaken by the Iraqis. It seemed that the war could be conducted and won by conventional air and ground forces alone. Schwarzkopf's beliefs seemed vindicated: there seemed little need for special forces.

On the second day of the war, 18 January, the Iraqis had fired one Scud missile at Dhahran, a major Saudi airport and military base. The threat to such high-value targets had been realised by the Coalition High Command, so 132 Raytheon MIM-104 Patriot surface-to-air missile (SAM) launchers had been positioned to protect Riyadh, Dhahran and other locations.

As an Iraqi Scud missile hurtled towards the air base at Dhahran at an estimated speed of 6400km/h (3975mph), a

Left: B Squadron's 'Bravo Two Zero', photographed just before they were inserted into Iraq on their fateful mission.

Left: The weather was appalling in western Iraq in January and February 1991. SAS soldiers like these therefore had to wrap up.

Patriot streaked from its launch canister and into the sky. The theory was simple enough: in the quarter of a millisecond in which the Patriot passed the Scud, the former would detonate, throwing out 300 ice-cubed sized cubes of metal that would destroy the Iraqi weapon. A split-second miscalculation would mean some of the Scuds slipping through. That night the Scud did not slip through, and the Patriot legend was born. While the Americans were congratulating themselves on the effectiveness of their Patriot system, in western Iraq several Iraqi Scud mobile launcher teams and their vehicle convoys were driving through the desert to speedily set up their missiles. They all managed to fire their missiles. Seven Scuds streaked into the sky and headed west towards Israel. Two struck Haifa, three landed on Tel Aviv and the rest fell in unpopulated areas. Although there were no serious casualties, Saddam had suddenly 'upped the stakes' in the Gulf conflict.

Although the missiles that hit Israel were armed with conventional warheads, the Israelis feared that subsequent ones would not be. Saddam had made frequent threats against the Jewish state. However, if Israel was to launch attacks upon Iraq, it might split the Coalition. In particular, it would have been doubtful that the Arab members, especially Egypt and Syria,

would allow themselves to become allies of Israel. Saddam had played a masterful stroke, but Schwarzkopf and de la Billière, with the help of the American administration in Washington, were to better it.

THE ISRAELIS THREATEN TO STRIKE

The Israelis were outraged by the missile attacks. They would clearly not dither while chemical and biological weapons landed among them. The Americans made frantic efforts to pacify the Israelis.

While the Israelis thought about moderation, more Scuds fell on their country. On 19 January, for example, two of them hit Tel Aviv, injuring 17 people, while another two fell into unpopulated areas.

The Americans had offered Patriot missile batteries as a defence against the Scuds. At first Arens refused them; now he welcomed them and asked that they be dispatched to Israel as quickly as possible. The first arrived on 20 January.

Meanwhile, over western Iraq, F-15E Strike Eagles had been designated to hunt for the Scuds and their mobile launchers. However, the 'great Scud hunt' reaped few rewards for the Eagles, and the frustration started to grow. The Iraqis became adept at hiding and masking their Scud launchers.

Israeli action seemed increasingly likely as January drew to a close and as more Scuds hit her cities: one on Tel Aviv on 22

January, causing three deaths, one the next day that fell on an unpopulated area, and eight on 25 January, all aimed at Tel Aviv but destroyed by Patriots, though debris from the missiles did kill two and injured a further 69.

The SAS was now ordered to search for the Scuds in western Iraq. The Regiment had gone from being one of the many special forces units in the area to being the Coalition's main hope of keeping Israel out of the war. The first men to go into enemy territory would be the road watch patrols, and would be drawn from B Squadron. After a briefing concerning mobile Scuds and the morale of the enemy troops, the men were issued with a warning order, a military term indicating they should be prepared to move at a moment's notice. As the time for the men to deploy neared, each patrol received its Orders Group (O Group) briefing. The three road watches were to be inserted by Chinook helicopter.

INSERTING THE ROAD WATCHES

The Chinooks took off and headed into enemy territory. When they reached their drop-off points, the aircraft disgorged their occupants. The commander of the South Road Watch team decided to abandon his mission. The ground he and his men would have to operate in was a gravel plain. There was no cover and they would have been compromised. The men left in the Chinook they arrived in.

The Central Watch was just as untenable, so its commander also had to evacuate his team, though not before he had called down an air strike on two enemy mobile radar systems that were positioned close by. The SAS soldiers then left the area at speed and began a 220km (140-mile) journey over four very cold nights before making it back to Saudi Arabia.

The story of the North Watch is one of heroism and tragedy. Dropped 300km (186 miles) from friendly lines, the men quickly settled down to a routine of keeping watch, sleeping and carrying out minor duties. On the second day an Iraqi convoy appeared and established itself nearby. Once set up, the SAS soldiers were alarmed to discover that it was a mobile anti-aircraft battery, complete with an array of anti-aircraft guns. Inevitably the SAS men were compromised, though not by Iraqi soldiers but by a group of civilians who were attached to the convoy (they were betrayed by a young goatherd, who they could have killed, but as the patrol leader, Sergeant Andy McNab, later asserted: 'We are SAS, not SS'). The SAS men did the only sensible thing: they ran like hell. Heavily laden down with their bergens, they bugged out. The Iraqi's fired on them and one trooper had his bergen ripped to shreds by machine gun fire.

EXPLOITS OF NORTH ROAD WATCH

They headed for the Syrian border, while all around Iraqi soldiers hunted for them. The weather conditions in the desert in January 1991 were desperately bad, and the SAS soldiers had to battle against freezing cold, rain and wind as well as evading the Iraqis. To avoid capture the group split up. One soldier, Sergeant Vince Phillips, got separated from his group and died of exhaustion and hypothermia in the snow-lashed hills. Another man of his three-man group was surrounded by enemy soldiers and forced to surrender. The third, Corporal Chris Ryan, escaped.

Chris Ryan walked for more than 300km (186 miles) in total during his flight to Syria. By the time he had reached safety he was in a poor state. His weight was down, he had a severe blood disorder and liver problems due to drinking water from a source near a uranium-processing plant. It would be two weeks before he could walk properly again, and six weeks before sensation returned to his fingers and toes.

The other five initially had better luck. They reached a town near the Jordanian border but then got into a skirmish with some Iraqi soldiers. One trooper, Robert Consiglio, was hit and killed. Two others were captured. The last two almost made

Right: The special forces effort – a Special Boat Service (SBS) observation post behind Iraqi lines in January 1991.

Chris Ryan

The philosophy of the SAS is 'train hard, fight easy' and a soldier who was the embodiment of this ethos is Chris Ryan. While on a Road Watch Patrol during the 1991 Gulf War his patrol was ambushed by Iraqi troops. Separated from his group whilst in flight, Ryan used his SAS training to conquer adverse conditions and survive.

Ryan had little water and food on him, and what he did have was soon used up. By the third day he was both mentally and physically shattered, but he drew on his mental reserves learned from his SAS training and he refused to give up and carried on. Soon his feet were cut and bleeding, but he carried on. By the sixth day he was severely dehydrated. He came across a stream and drank copiously from it. Unfortunately it was full of waste from a uranium processing plant and he developed blood and liver problems. He still carried on. After seven nights and eight days alone; he reached the Syrian border and safety. He had walked a total of 300km (186 miles).

it, but one, Lance-Corporal 'Legs' Lane, died of hypothermia and then the other soldier was captured.

A LEARNING EXPERIENCE

So ended the road watch patrols, an audacious plan but one which ultimately failed. All special forces operations are high risk, and some have to be aborted. That they failed was no reflection on the men concerned or their equipment. They simply could not perform their task in the terrain they were inserted into. Future operations would benefit from their experience. There it should have ended. But the experiences of the North Road Watch team, codenamed 'Bravo Two Zero', ensured that this particular part of the SAS's campaign in the Gulf War will always be remembered.

Fighting Patrols

The road watch patrols had failed, but the SAS did not give up its hunt for Iraqi Scuds, far from it. The heavily armed mobile fighting columns swept into western Iraq and began a campaign of destruction that effectively knocked Saddam Hussein's missiles out of the war.

The failure of the road watch patrols did not significantly affect the SAS's effort in western Iraq. They were, after all, just one strand of the Regiment's overall strategy. Whereas B Squadron had undertaken the road watches, it was the turn of A and D Squadrons to mount the mobile columns. The Regiment gathered together its vehicles at its forward base at Al Jouf and assembled its columns. Each one would consist of approximately 12 Land Rover vehicles plus motorcycle outriders. The vehicles were all heavily armed: GPMGs, 40mm M19 grenade launchers, Milan anti-tank weapons and Stinger surface-to-air missiles (SAMs). In addition, most of the weapons had thermal imaging night sights (passive infrared sensors that convert detected heat into video images - used mainly for night work), and the drivers wore night vision goggles.

There were four columns in all: two from A Squadron and two from D Squadron. Colonel Massey and his SAS soldiers were ordered to patrol one of the areas of western Iraq, the southern 'box', which straddled the Amman-Baghdad highway. The other two areas lay along the Syrian border, one being located near the town of Shab al Hiri, while the other lay near the town of Al Qaim, farther northeast. Clearing these two boxes would be the responsibility of the Americans, specifically the elite Delta Force.

PINPOINTING THE SCUDS

In the first few days of the war the Coalition believed that the majority of the Scuds being fired against Israel were from Iraqi bases numbered H1, H2 and H3. The Coalition had targeted these bases from the beginning of the air war. For example, H2 and H3 were hit by US Air Force aircraft on the night of 16/17 January, and on the next night it was the turn of US Navy jets. Nevertheless, the Israelis were not satisfied. To the horror of the Coalition, they were planning their own strikes. They would hit the area with their own jets, they informed the Americans, and would land their own troops in the area to hunt the Scuds. Frantic messages went to Israel from the Americans: we are doing all we can to destroy the Scuds, please do not use your own forces. For the moment, at least, the Israelis were appeased. But for how long?

In Riyadh it was realised that speed was critical. Therefore, the first SAS mobile columns started on 20 January. But they were not just hunting Scuds. Iraq had deployed hundreds of artillery pieces and multiple launch rocket systems capable of firing chemical warheads. They had a range of 30-40km (18-25 miles), which meant they could hit Allied units in Saudi Arabia. And the Iraqis were quite capable of using them. During the war with Iran, for example, Iraqi units had fired many chemical artillery shells during the 1988 offensive in the Fao peninsula. The SAS teams were ordered to knock out the Iraqis' battlefield chemical weapons delivery systems, as and when they found them.

THE FIRST FEW DAYS

The first day, 20 January, was uneventful, partly because the SAS limited its incursion into enemy territory to 40km (25 miles) into Iraq. This was because the Israelis had threatened to invade the area, and no one in the Regiment wanted to be killed by Israeli jets. When the invasion failed to materialise, the SAS columns pressed deeper into Iraq. The urgency of the mission had been increased: on 22 January a Scud hit Tel Aviv, killing three civilians. On the next day yet another was

Left: An SAS Land Rover 110 in western Iraq in typically wet conditions. The area was also subject to low cloud and snow.

launched at Israel, though fortunately it fell into an uninhabited area. These launches did nothing to appease the irate Israelis, who were itching to send in their own forces.

In desperation, Lieutenant-General Charles Horner and Brigadier-General 'Buster' Glosson, chief targeter and commander of all US Air Force wings in the Gulf, hatched a plan for all the combat aircraft available to the Allies – some 2000 warplanes – to be diverted to western Iraq. In a three-day campaign, the UN aircraft would completely flatten the area, particularly around Al Qaim, Rutba and other population centres. The enemy targets that faced destruction included police stations, service areas, and anything else that could support Scud operations. Also, bombers would sow mines on all the roads and destroy over 60 underpasses (these were favourite Scud hiding places). The plan was presented to Schwarzkopf, who rejected it for two reasons. First, it would result in the deaths of many civilians; and second, it would not shorten the war. In any case, by this time General Dynamics F-16 Fighting Falcons and Fairchild Republic A-10 Thunderbolt IIs had been diverted to the Scud hunt, and it was felt that more aircraft would just result in crowded skies, with no tangible results with regard to destroying Scuds.

FIRST KILL

Back on the ground in Iraq, the SAS initially had mixed fortunes. Its columns had not seen any Scud launchers for three days, and the men were getting frustrated, especially since another missile had been launched against Israel on 23 January (though fortunately it caused no casualties). However, on 23 January the Regiment had a stroke of luck. One of A Squadron's columns was operating between Nukhayb and Karbala, southwest of Baghdad, when the men ran into a group of four Iraqis driving across the desert. In a brief firefight three of the Iraqis were killed. The fourth was captured and interrogated. Being highly

Right: A heavily laden Land Rover from D Squadron deep inside Iraqi territory. Note the metal sand mat hanging on the side.

relieved that he was not going to be killed by the SAS soldiers, he began to impart some valuable information. This took the form of a map he was carrying, which detailed the positions of a previously unseen enemy brigade in western Iraq. The SAS soldiers immediately relayed this information to the Allied Tactical Air Co-Ordination Centre, and within a few hours the brigade was being pounded by Coalition aircraft.

FARTHER INTO THE 'SCUD BOX'

On 24 January the SAS began to push ever deeper into the 'Scud box'. Now the SAS soldiers began to encounter the enemy more, and there were frequent violent contacts. Whenever possible, SAS attacks were launched against the enemy at night. A Squadron itself suddenly became very busy, as a member of the squadron relates: 'We had spotted the

Above: An SAS fighting column from A Squadron behind Iraqi lines in early February 1991. Note the motorcycle used for scouting.

launcher two days earlier and had followed it, travelling at night over rough terrain until we had caught up with it and managed to plant explosives on it. The blast shattered the night's silence and sent a mushroom of flame high into the sky as our charges detonated, crippling the target and giving us the signal to kick off at anything that moved around the site.'

In the cold light of day the men discovered that it was not a Scud but a FROG surface-to-surface unguided artillery rocket. The two systems look very similar: the FROG has a cylindrical body, a conical nose and four large control fins. Ominously, Soviet FROGs were usually armed with nuclear warheads, and, as ever, they could also be armed with

chemical warheads. No one knew what the Iraqi warheads contained, but the worst scenario was feared. From their lying-up position (LUP), the SAS soldiers recognised the smaller rocket on its launcher, but no matter – they would destroy it: 'Scud or FROG, it had the capability to hit Allied targets and that was all that mattered to us.'

The SAS teams had been briefed as to the threat of Iraqi chemical weapons, but they had to take a chance and knock the missile out, chemical warhead or not. This contrasts sharply with 'Bravo Two Zero', the members of which specifically avoided damaging enemy missile warheads through fear of their contents – though the FROGs could not hit Israel (they were battlefield weapons), they could inflict damage on Allied units waiting for the ground offensive in Saudi Arabia.

Despite the fact that they had immobilised the launcher with charges, the SAS soldiers from A Squadron stayed where they were. 'Nothing was said when the explosion erupted; it's not like in the movies where the good guys all stand around cheering.' Like many contacts between the Iraqis and the SAS, the special forces soldiers were often forced to fight off Iraqi attacks. So it was this time. But, as on so many occasions, bluff and audacity saved the day:

'They were about 300m [330 yards] away and without delay we cracked off a couple of 66s [M72 66mm anti-tank weapons].' What the SAS soldiers had not realised was that there were several enemy trucks and armoured personnel carriers that lay undiscovered. They were about 100m (110 yards) from the FROG launcher, and had not been spotted by the team that had crept forward in the darkness to lay the charges. They now appeared, and around 150 Iraqi soldiers faced an eight-man SAS team. However, cool professionalism took over, and the SAS soldiers followed their drills exactly. First priority was to disable the first and last truck in the convoy:

'We banjoed the front and rear vehicles at the same time, but they had at least

three armoured personnel carriers and they quickly opened up on us. The thud of their heavy-calibre weapons seemed to get louder, probably because the rounds were ripping into the ground just in front of us. We knew we were on to a hiding, but they must have thought we were a much bigger unit. To our surprise they just raced away as quick as they could.'

The firefight had been fierce but short-lived – probably just a couple of minutes – and all that was left were two smouldering trucks. The SAS soldiers wasted no time. They left their LUP and sought their vehicles. Then they were away. As was standard operating procedure (SOP) in the Regiment, they wanted to put as much space between themselves and the enemy as possible.

DELTA FORCE LENDS A HAND

As January came to an end, the Regiment had more success. A fighting column spotted two Scud convoys and ordered in an air strike. The Americans obliged, and several F-15E Eagles from the US Air Force's 336th Tactical Fighter Squadron destroy the convoys totally. In addition, the SAS also spotted a Scud launch site, and once again the 336th TFS rendered it useless. The Coalition special forces were beginning to gain the upper hand, and the scales were tipped further in their favour by the arrival of Delta Force's 1st Squadron at King Fahd International Airport on 1 February.

The American elite unit was then rushed north to Ar Ar, from where it would be sent into the northern 'Scud box' to hunt for the Iraqi missiles. The man responsible for Delta Force's operations, Major-General Wayne Downing, head of the US Joint Special Operations Command at Fort Bragg, went to see the SAS commander in Riyadh, Colonel Massey, about Delta Force's operations. Massey briefed Downing about the difficulties his men would face in western Iraq. In particular, he warned him about the Bedouins, who would undoubtedly report the presence of any teams to the

Iraqis. Nevertheless, Downing was confident his men could perform just as well as the SAS (to get these men into Iraq, Delta Force had the services of Task Force 160, a helicopter unit that flew Sikorsky CH-53 Sea Stallion, Boeing Vertol CH-47 Chinook and Sikorsky UH-60 Black Hawk helicopters in a number of special operations variants).

When Delta Force was in the theatre, Massey's words proved to be true. Near Al Qaim there were many Bedouins, and they reported the American presence to the Iraqis. Very soon the American elite troops found themselves under attack. In early February, for example, nine Iraqi armoured vehicles pursued a Delta Force patrol across the desert. The special forces were on foot and would have been mown down were it not for the fact that an F-15 Eagle appeared and scattered the enemy. Then US helicopters managed to pick the men up. Two days later, another Delta Force team was chased by Iraqi helicopters, being saved only by the appearance of another Eagle, which destroyed one helicopter and chased off the rest. Though Delta Force had a tough time of it, its missions in Iraq made a valuable contribution towards the Scud hunt, as well as repairing Delta Force's reputation.

SCUD ALLEY

So pleased was Schwarzkopf with Delta Force's performance that he allowed another Delta Force squadron and an Army Ranger company to be deployed to Ar Ar. This meant the number of men operating in Iraq could be increased, and there were eventually over 200 US elite troops in Mesopotamia. Though the number of confirmed Scud kills was small, Delta Force's efforts did limit the launcher teams' endeavours, which stopped them hitting Israel. With the aid of Eagles, Delta sowed hundreds of Gator mines on roads, underpasses and other suspected concealment sites. In this way the Scud launchers were forced into areas that could be more easily watched. But what of the SAS?

Right: Unimogs were used as 'mother vehicles' by the SAS to carry extra fuel, water, ammunition, rations and clothing.

By the end of January the Regiment's activities had provoked a vigorous Iraqi response. On 29 January, for example, the Iraqis attacked an SAS column, damaging two of the latter's vehicles beyond repair, although losing 10 dead and three of their own vehicles in the process. One SAS soldier was also badly wounded, but was evacuated to Saudi Arabia and survived the war. From 30 January to 3 February the SAS was extremely active in 'Scud Alley'. On the latter date an SAS team from 1 and 17 Troops ordered an air strike on a Scud convoy. This preceded a prolonged contact, when it was realised that the aircraft had destroyed only one of the launchers. The SAS attacked the rest with their vehicle-mounted Milans, scoring a direct hit on a Scud missile and its launcher. However, the Iraqis counterattacked and drove off the SAS, though not before the latter had ordered a further air attack that destroyed most of the convoy.

Most of the SAS patrols that were operating in western Iraq at this time were vehicle-mounted, but not all. Some patrols were also sent in on foot, as a member of D Squadron relates: 'We had clocked up four patrols into Iraq and the squadron had bagged about a dozen targets, but there was no time to relax. The pressure was increasing from Riyadh for

more success, and just as soon as we had been debriefed and re-supplied we were back on the road. Some of the mobile teams had already chalked up their Scud scores by painting silhouettes of the launchers on their Land Rovers.

SCUD HUNTING

'US intelligence had monitored recent launcher activity in our sector, and after just 12 hours back inside Saudi we were preparing to attend another operational briefing, at which the Americans would outline full details of the potential targets they had tracked. We were to fly into Iraq and check out two areas identified by the US Air Force as "Iraqi operational sites" and eliminate both by means of the explosives we would be carrying, or by calling down air strikes. The briefing was followed by an O Group, which was headed by our boss [troop commander] and the squadron commander. The mission was simple: find the two launchers and mallet them by whatever means possible and then get out of the area as quickly as possible. The sector was believed to be alive with Republican Guard units en route to reinforce Iraqi forces in and around Kuwait.

'After a night's sleep we packed our bergens and prepared our kit for another

move into the field. For the trip we made sure we all carried tubes of ant-killer. The little bastards had earlier bitten us to bits, and came close to being more of a threat than the Scuds. I always shit myself when it comes to helicopter insertion – the actual point of drop-off is always the most dangerous, and you always think you're going to get bumped – but this time we were OK.

'Using the nearest MSR, which as I recall was to our right, as our key reference point, we tabbed out of the area to a new location. Here we were able to put in an OP on the road while resting up for the next move. Moving across such open terrain was made easier due to GPS [Global Positioning System].

'At dawn I remember seeing several jets flying low overhead, probably on a photo-reconnaissance of the area to examine the damage we had inflicted the night before. At this point we had been in the field for just four days, and to be honest we were knackered. It was a cold morning. The sky was overcast, and I remember being surprised to see aircraft flying in such weather.'

Despite the Coalition air activity, the Iraqis were often very careless and sloppy. An SAS foot patrol from D Squadron, for example, came across a Scud convoy in early February:

'We had just been on the comms net arranging a re-supply for the following morning to bring in more ammunition and food when we heard the distinctive sound of a convoy nearby, but nobody

could see anything. We were desperate for ammunition, particularly 66mm LAWs, and our immediate thoughts were that we would have to abandon our position.'

PUNISHING THE IRAQIS

The team was well camouflaged ('out of sight among the rocky scrapes we had made') and its members just sat and watched. Before long the Iraqis came into sight late in the afternoon. It was a sizeable target in the form of 'a column of about 25 vehicles in all, including two Scud launchers. In the main they were BMPs [Soviet-built infantry fighting vehicles] and BRDMs [Soviet-built armoured reconnaissance patrol vehicles], and they had all pulled into the side of the MSR.'

The SAS soldiers could not believe their luck: 'It appeared that one of the Scud launchers had broken down. Several mechanics or fitters were trying to sort out the problem while the vehicle crews stood smoking beside the road. As we monitored the situation through our scopes we couldn't believe what we were seeing.' The Iraqis made no attempt to pull any camouflage netting over their vehicles, they just parked them up on the side of the road in the open. They were a sitting duck. And yet the SAS team could do little by itself:

'Any question of mounting an attack was a non-starter. We were short of ammunition and would stand little chance against such a heavily armed unit. This was an opportunity for Uncle Sam

to earn some brownie points and blitz the whole convoy.'

One of the reasons the SAS is so successful is that its members can realistically appraise a situation: 'If we tried to take them on, it could have been "game over" for us, and the prospect of being taken prisoner did not appeal to any of us, for the simple reason that we knew the Iraqis would ignore the Geneva Convention when it came to special forces.' (The Geneva Convention regarding the treatment of prisoners of war makes provision for the humane treatment of captured service personnel. The convention gives prisoners certain rights, such as to be kept in a place of safety, to be given medical care when necessary, and to have access to food and water. A prisoner is also allowed to keep items of sentimental value, and is entitled to a receipt for any other personal items like money that is taken from him; prisoners are also allowed to write letters. All these provisions were blatantly ignored by the Iraqis.) The treatment meted out to the members of 'Bravo Two Zero' confirmed their anxiety.

IN FOR THE KILL

As the Scud convoy was making no apparent moves to go anywhere, the SAS team radioed for an air attack. For some of the men this was the first time they would witness a combat air patrol strike up close: 'I had only ever seen one from a distance in the past, during training in Scotland, but the attack would take place less than 500m [545 yards] from our position.' The message was passed back to the SAS's forward base, then to American AWACS aircraft, who passed the targeting details on to the Eagles loitering over western Iraq. By this stage of the war the F-15Es were armed with GBU-12 laser-guided bombs, which were deadly effective, and recent research has shown that the Coalition's 'smart' munitions in the war had a 90 per cent success rate against enemy targets.

'An hour or so before last light an F-15E screamed over the target area, pulling

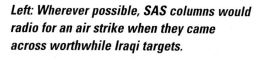
Left: Wherever possible, SAS columns would radio for an air strike when they came across worthwhile Iraqi targets.

high into the grey sky as it passed the convoy. I thought the pilot had taken a flypast as I couldn't see or hear anything – then there was a ball of flame and a thud as the high explosives detonated. It was strange to see it all unfold, it was just like being at the movies. Everything seemed to happen in slow motion. A second F-15 joined the attack, and as it swooped down to hit the convoy the Iraqis opened up with an anti-aircraft gun, but their efforts were wasted. After a third strike the whole convoy was decimated, and flames flickered from all the vehicles and smoke billowed into the darkening sky. Their war was over. Nothing moved – we presumed all the Iraqis had been either killed or wounded.'

The other SAS columns were also having good hunting in the desert. On 5 February, for example, A Squadron's Group 2 spotted a Scud convoy of two launchers and four escort vehicles, and immediately called down an air attack. The column later fought a gun battle with a force of Iraqis defending an observation tower, killing 10 of the enemy for no losses. Three days later D Squadron called down an air attack on an Iraqi 'Flat Face' radar installation. On the same day a team from A Squadron destroyed a microwave communications tower, then fought a 40-minute firefight with Iraqi troops before escaping.

THE IRAQIS HIT BACK

The worst encounter for the SAS occurred on 9 February, when a small patrol from A Squadron probed an enemy communications centre near Nukhayb. In a heavy firefight the SAS force was beaten off, though not before the patrol leader, a sergeant-major, was badly wounded. He had to be left by the other two and was captured. However, he survived the war and was awarded the Military Cross for his bravery.

The frequent firefights with pursuing Iraqis naturally sapped ammunition and fuel supplies. The Regiment had to find a way to replenish those supplies. To service the vehicle teams, the SAS organised supply columns to drive into Iraq and liaise with its teams in country. These columns consisted of 10 four-ton trucks manned

by SAS soldiers and Royal Electrical and Mechanical Engineers (REME) personnel. Six armed Land Rovers from B Squadron made up the escort, and the supply column was named E Squadron. It crossed the border on 12 February and rendezvoused with the Land Rovers from A and D Squadrons 145km (90 miles) inside Iraq. By 17 February it had returned, though not before it had spotted an enemy observation post and had used a laser rangefinder to direct an air attack upon it – this was the first and only time the SAS used a laser designator in the Gulf War.

THE FINAL PHASE

Re-supplied, the SAS continued to enjoy success against the enemy. On 18 February, for example, a D Squadron patrol discovered a Scud convoy and called down an air attack to wipe it out. The next day another SAS-directed air attack hit a second convoy. Tragedy struck on 21 February, however, when a running battle developed between a group of Iraqis and one of A Squadron's fighting columns. As the SAS vehicles were pulling back, Lance-Corporal David Denbury was shot and fatally wounded. Nevertheless, the SAS was making a valuable contribution to the battle against the Scuds.

What about the Americans? Delta Force had been concentrating its efforts

Above: One of the many congratulatory messages sent to the Special Air Service after the end of the Gulf War.

on several hundred square kilometres of enemy territory around H2 and H3. Typically, the US elite teams would consist of between 20 and 40 commandos, who would mount patrols of between 10 and 15 days in length.

But in the great Scud hunt the laurels belonged to the SAS and Delta Force. Downing telephoned Massey at the end of February and they congratulated each other for 'establishing Anglo-American dominion over western Mesopotamia'.

It was true that the SAS had not completely stopped the launch of Scud missiles from western Iraq against Israel, but it had made a major contribution in cutting them down severely. From an average of five launches per day during the first week of the war, the figure then fell to less than one launch per day. With the SAS fighting teams on the ground and the US Air Force in the air flying 75-150 anti-Scud sorties per day, the Iraqis found it almost impossible to set up and fire their surface-to-surface missiles. Above all, it had been the British special forces soldiers on the ground who made the biggest contribution. The men who wore the Winged Dagger had once again proved that they were second to none.

THE BALKANS AND SIERRA LEONE

Interventions

As somebody once said, 'The Balkans, the Balkans, never ever get involved in the Balkans' – advice that the British wished they had taken. World War I began there, and World War II saw several German divisions tied down there for the best part of the war; for the British, however, the Balkans was a vacuum into which they were sucked to carry out a humanitarian operation that would eventually cause immense frustration for the Army.

The Balkans conflict had enough ethnic hatred to fuel an orgy of unprecedented violence. This outbreak can be traced back to the summer of 1992, when the former Yugoslav republic of Bosnia Herzegovina found itself embroiled in a civil war involving Serbs, Croats and Muslims. Fearing that events in the area could have a domino effect impacting beyond the region, the United Nations authorized UNPROFOR (UN Protection Force) to escort aid convoys and their workers, who were being attacked and murdered as they tried to

help those in need. The first British troops to arrive were members of the Cheshire Regiment, who set up bases in Vitez, Gornji Vakuf and Tuzla.

Attached to the Cheshires were members of the SAS, who helped them with liaison officers and interpreters for the task of negotiating with the warring parties for permission to move aid through their territory. The situation was highly volatile, and in the UK there were genuine fears that British soldiers might be taken hostage by the warlords. Should this happen, the SAS were ready to perform a

rescue mission at a moment's notice with a troop based in Split, Croatia that was assigned to both HRT (hostage-rescue tasks) and general forces support duties.

SAS VETERAN

Around this time, former SAS commander Lieutenant General Sir Michael Rose was appointed commander of UN forces, Bosnia. Although he was reluctant to say anything in public about his UN colleagues, Rose was frustrated at the sheer lack of knowledge and purpose that seemed to dog this UN mission. To enable

him to operate with more confidence in Bosnia, Rose wanted eyes and ears on the ground that he could trust to provide him with well-informed, reliable intelligence, and the only unit qualified was the SAS.

The first task he set the SAS men was to monitor the newly-formed Bosnia-Croat alliance and its leader. In addition, they were to ensure that any difficulties between them and the Bosnian-Croats were quickly ironed out. To soften its true purpose in Bosnia, the force was called Joint Commission Observers (JCOs), and had permission to drive around the various warring factions in highly conspicuous, white Land Rovers. Their first major success came in March 1994, when they negotiated the withdrawal of Croat HVO forces from the Muslim town of Maglai.

Rose was pleased with the results and decided to send the SAS to the Muslim town of Gorazde, now surrounded by the

Left: The bombing campaign against the Serbs was directed in part by SAS teams on the ground, who identified Serb targets and, if necessary, laser-designated them for bombs dropped by UN aircraft.

Serbs. When the SAS arrived, they were shocked at what they saw: the place had been decimated by constant shelling from nearby Serbian artillery emplaced in the surrounding hills. The Serbs were also regularly sniping at the Muslim civilians as they went about their daily business.

On their way into Gorazde, the SAS team had sensed hostility from the Serbs as they passed through their check-points. The Serbs believed them to be casual UK liaison officers. To help with their cover, the seven men were armed only with standard British Army SA-80 assault rifles and wore normal uniforms. Once settled in Gorazde, they set up an observation post on top of the wrecked Hotel Gradina, which offered a good view of the surrounding hills and local roads. They chose an old bank for their HQ, the most secure building in the town. As standard operational procedure (SOP), the SAS began local patrols around the Serb positions in a bid to monitor their build-up and to report back to Rose on any significant activity.

The Serbs did not take kindly to the British snooping around their lines, and

Above: Regular British forces also played a key role in the Balkans. Here British paratroopers with their famous red berets stand guard at a political rally, watchful for any potential hostile threat.

opened fire on them on several occasions. In response, the SAS called in air strikes, and a confrontational mentality started to develop between the two sides. The situation finally came to a head on 15 April 1994, when an SAS patrol came under effective enemy fire and two SAS troopers were seriously wounded.

The SAS negotiated a ceasefire with the Serbs to allow a casevac helicopter time to land and extract the wounded soldiers. Not wanting to appear difficult, the Serbs agreed to a short pause in their shelling and one of the soldiers, Corporal Fergus Rennie, was evacuated but sadly later died of his injuries. The other wounded trooper refused to be evacuated and insisted on staying with his colleagues. The SAS decided to teach the Serbs a lesson and called in further air strikes against their tanks and artillery, but on this occasion the air attack backfired,

Left: An SAS radio operator in the Balkans, wearing a peaked cap to make it easier to use headphones. The SAS used radios that transmitted in a rapid 'burst', reducing the ability of the Serbs to track the unit's position.

The SAS would have been lucky to survive four hours, let alone four days. With this in mind, the officer went direct to General Rose and again asked for permission to withdraw. Thankfully, this time it was granted. It was impossible for a helicopter to land in Gorazde – the risks were just too great – so the men would have to make their way to an extraction site located for them in a valley. This site, however, was some distance away.

The main problem now was getting the team out of Gorazde with an injured trooper, downed pilot, and a local guide called Ahmed, all without being spotted by either the Muslims or the Serbs. It was decided that the best time to leave would be just after dark, as the SAS had good night-vision sights and the Muslims had none. With typical SAS stealth, the team and their guests slowly made their way out of the town without being seen.

VERTICAL CLIMB

After going through a forest and making good time, they suddenly found themselves facing a climb up a hill that was practically vertical in places. Even for the experienced men of the SAS, this climb was tough enough, but they also had a pilot and an injured trooper to think about. As the men were on a tight schedule, they had no choice but to climb it.

One person who impressed every member of the team was the injured trooper. Despite having lost a lot of blood from his injured arm – held together only by a few bolts and a couple of steel rods – he bravely carried on in agony.

Time was now running out for the SAS patrol, Alpha Two-One, and they knew it. As they struggled to make up the minutes, there was a further setback. All around the valley, the distant sound of artillery could be heard as the Serbs threw shell upon shell on Gorazde, and burning fires could be seen ahead of the SAS team. This meant only one thing: the area was crawling with Serb soldiers and there

---

with disastrous consequences for both the pilot and the SAS.

In modern air warfare, there is a simple rule: if you fail to hit a target on the first pass, you leave it; otherwise it is very likely that you will become a target yourself. Lieutenant Nick Richardson of the Royal Navy was flying a Sea Harrier on a practice air-support mission when he received a request for air support from the SAS in Gorazde. As he lined up for an attack on a number of Serbian tanks on a hillside, his HUD (head-up display) failed to lock-on when he tried to release his bombs. Forced to break away from the attack, he tried again, but when he lined up, his HUD failed again and he was forced to abort the attack run.

By now, the FAC was frustrated with the whole situation and asked the pilot to go around again. Richardson was, he realized, caught between a rock and a hard place – if he went around again, he really would be pushing his luck, but at the same time, he was not prepared to let his fellow countrymen down. As he rolled in

for a third attempt, disaster struck: he was hit by a Serbian SAM (surface-to-air missile) and forced to eject from his aircraft.

Fortunately for him, he landed near some friendly Muslim forces, who took him to the SAS in Gorazde. On arrival at the bank HQ, he was greeted by an SAS officer who explained that he had just jumped out of the frying pan and into the fire. It transpired that the SAS were in serious trouble as the local Muslims had turned against them due to NATO's failure to protect them from the Serbs.

As the SAS officer appraised the situation, a lynch mob gathered at the front door of the bank and began smashing it down. The situation was clearly untenable. Contacting his superiors, the SAS officer asked for permission to withdraw, reluctant to let his men get into a firefight with the very people that they were supposed to be helping. But permission to withdraw was refused, and the SAS were told to just tough it out for the next four days until a relief convoy could get through to Gorazde.

was no way that a rescue helicopter would be able to land. As they pondered their fate, a Serb patrol passed close by. In a firefight, the SAS could easily beat them, but once the shooting started, other Serbs would reinforce the patrol and the SAS would be cut off. After a few tense minutes, however, the Serbs moved on.

With this delay, there was no way that they could reach the original RV point, so they used their radios to try and make contact with the pilots, but there was no reply. They then worked out that they were roughly on the probable flight-path, so even without radio contact, they could place landing markers down for the helicopters. As they waited, however, it suddenly dawned on them that there was not going to be a helicopter, as nobody in Sarajevo would believe they had made it this far. Infuriated, the team set up their sat-net communications system and called General Rose in person. There was now only 30 minutes until dawn, and they knew that no rescue crew would fly in broad daylight over enemy territory. This time, their luck was in. General Rose personally arranged for a French rescue helicopter to come in and get them.

Thankfully for the rest of the Bosnia tour, nothing like this ever happened again. Eventually 400 British UN troops moved into Gorazde and some semblance of normality returned to the Muslim population. However, on another occasion, a JCO team was in the Bihac area and found itself under fear of attack from Serbian forces. Eventually the Serbians backed off after being threatened with NATO air strikes. General Rose favoured an aggressive line against the Serbs, but the UN wanted a softly, softly approach.

In May 1995, the UN paid heavily for its inconsistent policy in Bosnia when the Serbs seized hundreds of UN soldiers, including 40 British troops. To counter this, the United Nations' Rapid Reaction Force was formed, including two SAS Squadrons who were tasked with breaking through Serb lines and relieving the UN garrison in Sarajevo. Despite their best efforts, the United Nations failed to prevent the massacre of Muslim prisoners at Srebrenica, where over 8000 local citizens were murdered in cold blood by the

Serbs after Dutch troops had surrendered to them. Prior to this massacre, a JCO team had been with the Dutch forces, directing air strikes in support of the Srebrenican people, but the attacks failed to stop the Serbs' advance.

In August 1995, the UN retaliated against the Serbs by launching constant air attacks against their positions throughout Bosnia, causing considerable damage to their war effort. These attacks were supported with artillery barrages from both British and French guns on Mount Igman, the guns acting in response to SAS teams that were identifying targets for them. In addition, the SAS infiltrated deep behind Serb lines to act as Forward Air Controllers in support of NATO airstrikes, the primary task being to find and designate targets for the attacking aircraft, and act as a rescue force should a pilot be downed.

Eventually, the Serbs gave in to NATO and began a supervised withdrawal from Sarajevo. The SAS was given the task of supervising this process. Building on this success, the SAS helped the new NATO Peace Implementation Force (IFOR) by providing detailed information on the known troop lines and their levels of equipment, as required by the Dayton Accord. The SAS also played a key role in

keeping the various factions under observation until conventional forces were deployed to police the peace. On one occasion, an SAS team attached to US forces helped to diffuse a potentially dangerous situation after Muslim refugees attempted to re-occupy their village, now in Serb territory. Thanks to the team's tact and diplomacy, a crisis was averted.

KOSOVO

In March 1999, the storm clouds of war were gathering over Kosovo. Under the orders of Serbian President Slobodan Milosevic, Kosovo was invaded by both Serbian military and para-military police forces. In appalling acts of barbarity, the Serbs began systematically to 'ethnically cleanse' Kosovo. As a huge refugee crisis developed, NATO warned Serbia that it faced military action if it failed to rein in its military forces, who were carrying out human rights abuses on an unprecedented scale. A deadline was set for compliance – and was ignored by Milosevic. NATO now had no choice but to begin an intensive bombing campaign against Serbia and its forces in Kosovo.

As the air operations gathered pace, an unexpected factor began to hinder the safety and accuracy of the air strikes – the weather. These were now causing NATO

Rescue from Gorazde

The SAS team from Gorazde with the downed Harrier pilot waited for pick-up by a French Puma helicopter. With only minutes to go until first light and certain discovery by the local Serb forces, they heard the welcome sound of the helicopter as it made its way up the valley towards them. This photograph was taken by one of the helicopter crewmen with the aid of night vision equipment. Within minutes, they were safely on board and speeding back towards Sarajevo.

After landing, the unwounded members of the SAS team walked around to the front of the helicopter to thank the French crew for their bravery in risking their lives for them. They commented that it had been an uneventful flight back. At this point, the pilot showed them the bullet holes in his Puma: the men had been laughing and joking so much on board the Puma that they had failed to hear the Serb bullets hitting the airframe.

very 'severe operational problems, with many sorties being either cancelled prior to take-off, or aborted over their intended targets, as there was too much risk of causing collateral damage.

Obviously this situation could not be allowed to continue, so it was decided that special forces should be deployed to identify targets by using laser designators. Since the SAS had performed so well in Bosnia, it was considered to be the best placed to carry out this mission.

In response to the NATO request for SAS support, a number of squadrons were deployed, their key role being target designation for air strikes. Several four-man teams were sent into Serbia and Kosovo to find, identify and destroy targets of value. In addition, NATO was desperate for reliable and accurate information on Serbian troop movements within Kosovo. NATO's analysts were getting so much information from aircraft, UAVs (unmanned air vehicles), satellites and ground sensors that they were unable to cope. In some cases, they were taking three days to evaluate the information. By the time strike aircraft were assigned, the intended target had moved.

The SAS was also tasked with training and supporting the KLA (Kosovo Liberation Army) in its operations against the Serbian fielded forces in Kosovo. At first, the KLA struggled to make any headway against the Serbs, but with SAS direction and guidance, its men became a potent and highly effective force. Indeed, the SAS often used them as intelligence-gatherers; obviously they had intimate knowledge of their own country and its geography. One invaluable piece of intelligence the SAS discovered for NATO concerned the bridges in Kosovo.

INVASION PLAN

It was found that very few of these bridges could take the weight of modern tanks, a serious issue if a land invasion was launched. As a result, NATO decided to invade Kosovo by mounting a helicopter assault using British Paras from the 5th Airborne Brigade. After SAS recce missions near to the border with Macedonia, a number of invasion routes were identified as being suitable. Small teams were also deployed to the ridges overlooking the roads to ensure that the Serbs were not able to ambush NATO ground forces as they entered Kosovo on 12 June 1999. The invasion went smoothly and no resistance was encountered until British forces entered the city of Pristina, and even then it was very light.

There was, however, one incident that caused NATO immense concern, and that related to the Russians and their seizure of Pristina airfield. This led to a temporary stand-off between the Russians and NATO which was eventually resolved peacefully.

Shortly after the crisis ended, details emerged of an SAS mission that had been planned for 11 June 1999, against the Russian airborne forces occupying Pristina Airport. the plan was that two SAS teams were to be inserted into Kosovo ahead of the Russians advancing on Pristina. Their mission was to stop the Russian advance. However, as the RAF Hercules carrying the SAS team neared the airport, its cargo of SAS Landrovers and motorcycles shifted, causing the pilot to have severe control difficulties. An emergency landing was attempted, but the aircraft clipped a building on its approach and crash landed. Fortunately most of the SAS escaped with only light injuries, but one soldier was trapped in the wreckage and badly burned.

Eventually the Serbs agreed to leave Kosovo, and were supervised by the SAS to ensure that they complied with the withdrawal procedures as laid down by NATO. After the conflict ended, the SAS was involved in tracking down and apprehending known Serbian war criminals and their cronies. On one occasion, as they went to arrest a known suspect, a firefight broke out between the SAS and the Serbs, in which a war criminal was killed and one SAS soldier slightly injured. Kosovo will not go down in history as being NATO's finest hour, but the SAS did its bit, and did it well.

SIERRA LEONE 2000

On 6 May 2000, Britain launched Operation Palliser in response to the advance on Freetown, the capital of Sierra Leone, of rebel forces who were endangering the lives of British, Commonwealth and European citizens.

Their potential enemy was the Revolutionary United Front (RUF), a

Left: Thanks to the SAS's reconnaissance, NATO learnt that there were very few bridges in Kosovo capable of bearing the weight of a modern tank, so the decision was made to airlift forces in instead using helicopters like this RAF Chinook.

rebel group who took great pleasure in raping women and butchering young children. Although the RUF was large in number, there were also other maverick militias for the British to contend with, the most renowned being the 'West Side Boys' (WSB), a bizarre group who paraded around in odd clothing and frequently wore women's wigs. A motley crew made up of ex-RUF members and deserters from the Sierra Leone Army (SLA), they were almost perpetually drunk or high on drugs. Although at first treated as something of a joke, the WSBs were however good fighters, and a real menace, being totally unpredictable.

The first official British forces to arrive in Sierra Leone were members of the élite Pathfinders and two companies from the 1st Battalion of the Parachute Regiment. After flying into Lungi airport on 7 May, they secured the airport within hours and mounted patrols to reassure Freetown's citizens of their safety.

Prior to the arrival of 1 Para, Sierra Leone had, of course, received other unofficial visitors. These were members of the SAS; their job, to gather intelligence on the rebel forces and to recce good defensive positions for 1 Para. For mobility, the SAS initially used a number of locally commandeered Toyota pickup

trucks for liaison and utility duties. As soon as their role became more overt, however, they began driving around in heavily-armed Land Rover 110 Desert Patrol Vehicles (DPVs).

In a highly unusual procedure for the SAS, they patrolled during daylight hours, making no attempt to disguise who they were or their intentions. Their tactics were designed to intimidate the rebels and provoke them to make a move, and this would eventually pay off. One aspect of SAS operations, the 'hearts and minds' campaign to win over local people, was made easy for the British. In Sierra Leone, the locals despised the rebels and welcomed the British with open arms.

In a bid to set a trap for the WSBs, the SAS started to patrol aggressively near the rebels' favourite haunts, especially around Massiaka, where they had set up road blocks to loot passing traffic. Both the Paras and Pathfinders mounted extra patrols in set areas, and deliberately ignored others. The idea was that the WSBs would be encouraged to enter a designated trap area without realizing it.

Although the original plan was aimed at the WSBs, it was the RUF that took the bait and launched an attack against a patrol of Pathfinders at Lungi Lo, 16km (10 miles) east of Freetown airport. A

Above: At the height of operations against the 'West Side Boys', British forces mount a river patrol in Sierra Leone in a bid to cut off rebel supply routes. The rebels lacked the air support of the British and Sierra Leone forces.

fierce firefight developed and many rebels were killed. As the Pathfinders sprung their trap, reinforcements were flown in by Chinook helicopters, engaging the rebels with machine guns and mortars.

The overwhelming firepower broke the rebels' attack and they fled into the bush. However, the British had more surprises in store. Above the fleeing rebels were a number of heavily armed Chinooks, which opened fire with both their mini-guns and machine guns. The RUF's attack force was decimated, and their leader, Foday Sankoh, was captured by the SAS in Freetown.

For a time, everything settled down in Sierra Leone. Occasional rebel attacks were mounted against the UN peacekeepers. After a couple of weeks, the Paras were withdrawn and replaced by Royal Marines. For the SAS, however, it was business as usual, and the men continued to patrol the coastal areas in an effort to force the rebels back into the bush.

Just as everything seemed to be going so well for the British, disaster struck. On

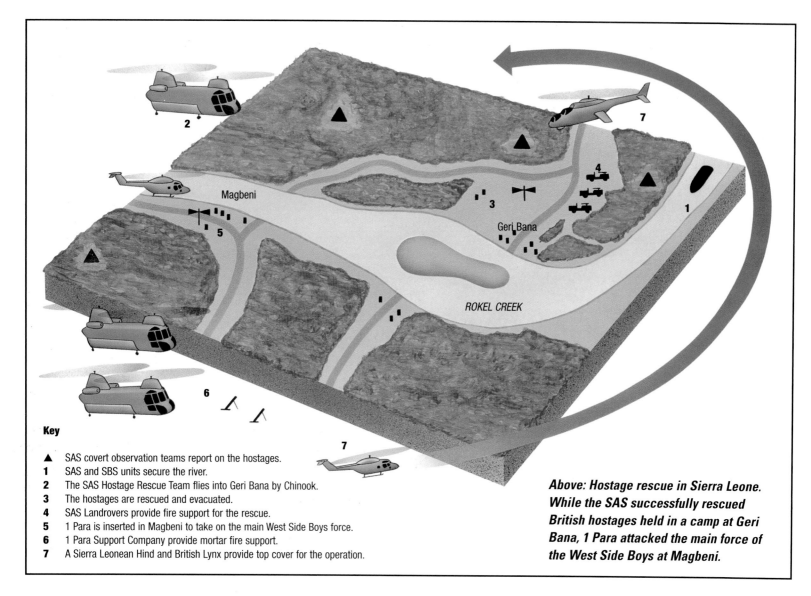

Key

▲   SAS covert observation teams report on the hostages.
1   SAS and SBS units secure the river.
2   The SAS Hostage Rescue Team flies into Geri Bana by Chinook.
3   The hostages are rescued and evacuated.
4   SAS Landrovers provide fire support for the rescue.
5   1 Para is inserted in Magbeni to take on the main West Side Boys force.
6   1 Para Support Company provide mortar fire support.
7   A Sierra Leonean Hind and British Lynx provide top cover for the operation.

Above: Hostage rescue in Sierra Leone. While the SAS successfully rescued British hostages held in a camp at Geri Bana, 1 Para attacked the main force of the West Side Boys at Magbeni.

25 August 2000, an 11-man patrol from the Royal Irish Regiment (RIR), along with a Sierra Leonean colleague, strayed into an area that was crawling with members of the 'West Side Boys', and were taken prisoner. 22 SAS were rapidly tasked with locating the rebels' base and mounting an OP (Observation Post). The British Government decided to see what transpired, while at the same time formulating a rescue plan.

Once contact had been established with the WSB, a dialogue developed, which was deliberately non-confrontational. At first the rebels' demands were quite modest – they wanted food and drink for themselves and the hostages – but once these demands were met, the rebels' confidence inevitably grew.

Deciding to be compliant, the British gave in, asking only that their soldiers be treated decently and humanely. As trust developed between the WSBs and the British negotiators, the British requested the release of some of their soldiers as an act of goodwill. Much to their surprise, on 30 August 2000 five members of the RIR were released unharmed.

PREPARATIONS

Negotiations continued with the rebels, while the SAS moved more troopers into the vicinity of the rebels' base in the hamlet of Geri Bana. Continuing with their observations, the SAS discovered that the rebels had another camp about 300m (328yd) away from where the hostages were being held. This was a hamlet called Magbeni, just south of Geri Bana, and it was well placed to provide mutual fire support to the other camp. The camps were divided by Rokel Creek.

As the planners, led by the future SBS commander Richard Van Der Horst, worked out a rescue strategy, the West Side Boys' leader, 24-year-old Foday Kallay – a former SLA NCO – started to make demands for the release of one of his men, known as Brigadier Bomb Blast, or Brigadier Papa. In addition, Kallay wanted a safe passage out of Sierra Leone, an education abroad – and an outboard motor for one of his dinghies.

Up till now, the British had tolerated the West Side Boys. Now they understood that matters were coming to a head. Fears for the safety of the hostages were growing; the WSBs were flaunting their power by carrying out mock executions on the British soldiers. The SAS requested permission to mount a rescue attempt as soon as possible.

As the British Government deliberated over what action to take, a serious new development made the decision for them. A UN helicopter strayed over the West

Side Boys' base by accident and the rebels, believing that they were about to be attacked, had dragged the prisoners out into the open as if to shoot them, but thought better of it. Fortunately for the hostages, the British negotiator managed to convince the rebels that this was a genuine mistake, and nothing more. Realizing that something like this could easily happen again – and next time they might not be so lucky – the British Government sanctioned a rescue mission, codenamed Operation Barras.

Time was now of the essence. The UK media was openly speculating about an imminent rescue attempt, further reinforced by the announcement that 1 Para was to return to Sierra Leone immediately. Well aware that the WSBs regularly listened to the BBC World Service, and would execute the hostages if they suspected something was in the air, the planners of Operation Barras took the decision to mount a tri-service operation on 10 September 2000.

At 0616 local time, elements of the SAS boat troop and members of the Royal Marines' Special Boat Service (SBS) sealed off the river leading to Rokel Creek. At the same time, members of the Jordanian UN battalion secured the main Massiaka highway to prevent the WSBs from escaping during the rescue. Once all security elements were in place, the operation's main thrust began with an assault on Magbeni and Geri Bana by three troop-carrying Chinook helicopters, supported by two smaller Lynx helicopters in the fire support role.

The timing of the operation was crucial. There had to be just enough light for the helicopters to see their target, but not enough for them to be seen by the rebels. Speed was essential: the hostages were all in one place, meaning that their captors could execute them very quickly, though this also made them easier to find.

As the helicopters swooped in at low level, the West Side Boys opened fire with

Right: A Landrover similar to those used in the attack on the West Side Boys' camp at Geri Bana. The hostage rescue was a perfect example of a small SAS operation that enhanced the unit's reputation yet further.

every weapon available, including captured heavy machine guns from the Royal Irish Regiment's vehicles. In a coordinated movement, the SAS opened fire on the rebels guarding the hostages, while the Paras, after being inserted by the Chinooks, made their assault.

Although initially taken by surprise, the WSBs lost no time in assuming their defensive positions surrounding both camps. To make matters worse, as the Paras moved forward, their assault temporarily stalled due to the terrain. They were moving through an area near Rokel Creek, which had looked from the air like a flat field covered in long grass. In reality, it was more of a paddy field, and the Paras were now laboriously wading through water up to chest level. Spotting their predicament, the West Side Boys opened fire with all their heavy weapons. The Paras sustained many casualties, but thankfully none that were fatal.

Seeing that the Paras were in serious trouble, the SAS directed their firepower at the WSBs, while the RAF Chinook pilots, risking their own lives, flew in front of the rebel positions to recover the injured soldiers. As they performed this brave act, the other helicopters involved in the operation directed their weapons at the rebels' main defensive positions in order to suppress their fire.

Within a few minutes, the officers and NCOs of 1 Para had rallied their men and were now assaulting the WSBs' main positions at Magbeni. As they did so, the SAS launched their assault on Geri Bana and secured the building where the hostages were held. After a short firefight, all the hostages were rescued unharmed.

HEAVY RESISTANCE

At Magbeni, the WSB were still putting up heavy resistance. To their credit, the WSBs were still fighting two hours later, and it was only when the Paras brought in mortars and extra firepower from vehicle-based weapons that they finally surrendered. Amongst those taken prisoner was the West Side Boys' leader, Foday Kallay, who later expressed regret for what he had done.

The WSBs were to pay a heavy price for crossing the British. The number of confirmed dead was put at 25, but later investigations showed that it was considerably higher. The WSBs were now a spent force in Sierra Leone and never recovered from the devastating British operation. But the British also paid a price for their victory. During the initial assault at Geri Bana, Bombardier Brad Tinnion, serving with 22 SAS, was fatally wounded. Despite desperate efforts to save him, he died before reaching RFA *Sir Percival*, which was berthed in Freetown. The Paras also suffered 12 casualties; all went on to make full recoveries from their injuries.

AFGHANISTAN AND AL-QAEDA

The War on Terror

The date 11 September 2001 will be etched in the minds of people around the world for decades to come. It marks the day that terrorism perpetrated its biggest and most spectacular attack on the world's most powerful nation, the United States of America. As a result, the SAS would once more be called to work alongside US special forces, this time in Afghanistan.

The attack began at 0845, US Eastern Standard Time, when a Boeing 767 of American Airlines crashed into the North Tower of the World Trade Center in New York. At first, it was assumed that this had been accidental; 11 minutes later, however, when another Boeing 767 from United Airlines hit the South Tower, it was clear that something was wrong. As millions of people around the world watched the events unfold on live television, the first of the two towers began a horrific and violent collapse. Barely 20 minutes later, the second tower imploded in the same way.

Giant clouds of grey dust filled New York's skyline, and a cold reality dawned on people around the world: they had just witnessed the worst terrorist atrocity in history. Thousands of innocent people from all walks of life and from many nations had been murdered in cold blood before their very eyes.

It was a sickening scene, but there was more still to come. News began to come in of a further two incidents involving airliners, and it was soon confirmed that a Boeing 757 of American Airlines had crashed at 0938 into the symbol of America's military power, the Pentagon.

All 58 passengers and 6 crewmembers were killed, along with 190 people on the ground. Later it was announced that a fourth aircraft had also crashed near Pittsburgh in suspicious circumstances.

OSAMA BIN LADEN

During the days and weeks after the attack, it was revealed that the aircraft had all been hijacked by Arab terrorists under the alleged leadership of America's arch enemy, Osama bin Laden. The attacks had been meticulously planned and executed by a very sophisticated and well-connected terrorist network. Naturally, this caused great embarrassment to the American Intelligence Agencies. They had failed to stop them, despite the growing evidence of an intended attack on the American mainland.

As the political and emotional fallout began over who was to blame for the events of 11 September 2001 – now being referred to as 'nine-one-one', or 'nine-eleven' – there was just one question: what was America and her allies going to do about it? In this highly charged and emotional period in America's history, there were fears of a

Left: The old, but highly effective B-52 executed most of the carpet bombing missions in Afghanistan. Large concentrations of Taliban fighters were best dealt with by using a B-52, which could suppress resistance over a wide area.

rash reaction from America's President George W. Bush, but he remained remarkably composed and rational.

As America considered its response to the attack, the world's media insisted that this atrocity had been suffered by America, giving little thought and sympathy to other countries who had also lost their nationals. Certainly, this was America's worst terrorist outrage, but it was Britain's, too, despite more than 30 years of terrorism emanating from the 'Troubles' in Northern Ireland.

On 4 October 2001, the British Prime Minister, Tony Blair, announced in the House of Commons that evidence had come to light linking Osama bin Laden and his Al-Qaeda (The Base) terrorist network to the attacks on the Pentagon and the World Trade Center on 11 September. Meanwhile, as military operations were being considered in response to the attacks, it was confirmed that Osama bin Laden was in Afghanistan under the protection of the Taliban regime.

OMANI EXERCISE

There was now no doubt that military action was on the cards, but what form it would take had yet to be decided. By sheer coincidence and good fortune, the British already had a massive force of air, sea and ground assets in the Gulf of Oman as part of Exercise Saif Sareea II (Swift Sword II), and the British Government put this entire force at the United States' disposal, literally inviting them to help themselves. Although appreciating this kind and generous offer, there were only two assets that the US decided it needed from Britain's armed forces: her RAF tanker aircraft and the Special Air Service Regiment.

In late September 2001, George W. Bush issued an ultimatum to the Taliban: either turn Osama bin Laden and his Al-Qaeda supporters in, or face the consequences. As the days ticked by, it became clear that the Taliban had no intention of complying with the Americans' request; instead, they defiantly threatened a Jihad (Holy War). Although there was no deadline for the commencement of military action, the planners in the

Pentagon were aware that they had only a short window of opportunity until the onset of the Afghanistan winter, when the weather conditions would became a serious factor impeding the execution of air strikes.

As the tension mounted, reports started to circulate that SAS units had been involved in firefights with the Taliban in Northern Afghanistan, but these were denied by the UK Ministry of Defence. Also around this time, the Taliban claimed that it had shot down an American spy aircraft flying over its territory. It was, in fact, a UAV (Unmanned Air Vehicle) lost due to control failure rather than enemy action, but it did, confirm that US forces were operating

Above: The impact of the second hijacked airliner on the World Trade Center on 11 September 2001. Within months, the SAS would be in Afghanistan, helping to evict the Taliban from power and hunting for Osama Bin Laden.

very close to Afghanistan. Obviously it would be only a matter of time before the shooting started.

On 7 October, the air war finally began with multiple attacks on Taliban air-defence systems, command-and-control centres, and fighter aircraft on airfields throughout Afghanistan. Although much of the intelligence for these initial air strikes came from air-based assets, some had clearly been obtained by covert ground forces operating from a base in Uzbekistan. Both British and American special forces were now operating in large numbers within Afghanistan, their main roles being recce, target designation, and 'shoot-and-scoot' operations.

For the SAS, Afghanistan was an old hunting ground. They had seen action there during the 1980s performing covert operations in support of the Mujahedeen against the Russians; in fact, at one point they were even training Afghanis in Scotland until locals assumed they were illegal immigrants and called the police. Although this put paid to the their training programme in the UK, the Afghanis now had access to western weapons and military intelligence, which proved invaluable in support of their cause. This experience would be an advantage when it came to training the anti-Taliban Northern Alliance, because the SAS already had a good rapport with many of their leaders.

NORTHERN ALLIANCE

The Northern Alliance forces were based primarily in North-Western Afghanistan and numbered around 15,000 men, while their enemy, the Taliban, dominated the eastern part of the country and had around 50,000 soldiers and several hundred Al-Qaeda terrorists.

Although enthusiastic and well intentioned, prior to the involvement of western special forces, the Northern Alliance had had very little military success for some years in their struggle against the Taliban after being ousted from power. However, within weeks of the western special forces' arrival, the Northern Alliance had made substantial gains in territory and gained more recruits.

On one particular training exercise, an SAS team were instructing the Northern Alliance in standard British Army tactics for assaulting an objective while under effective enemy fire. However, as the Northern Alliance men moved towards the real target, a Taliban-held village, they suddenly and without warning abandoned the British tactics and advice and, in a scene out of a Rambo movie, proceeded to attack using dozens of horsemen as cavalry. As they charged, the rest of the force sat down on rocks nearby and watched the

The SAS and its Allies

After the events of 11 September 2001, the special forces of the USA, the UK and Australia have worked ever more closely together. The SAS's high standing with the American military was based on its involvement in Iraq in 1991, where it had proved its worth despite initial US reservations, and the Australian SAS have earned a similar respect from the Pentagon.

In Afghanistan the SAS worked alongside US special forces and Australian SAS teams, as well as members of the SBS. With much commonality in training and equipment, especially as special forces soldiers have greater leeway in choosing their boots, camouflage and weapons than regular troops, it has become harder for the casual observer to distinguish which country the special forces unit belongs to. Furthermore during the operations in Afghanistan most special forces troops adopted local customs and dress in a bid to avoid drawing attention to themselves from either the locals or the media.

spectacle without firing any of their weapons at the defending Taliban forces. Fortunately for the Northern Alliance, the Taliban fled on this occasion, but the SAS was now concerned about the reliability of its new friends.

The SAS quickly learned that getting the best from the Northern Alliance required patience and understanding, and that you never told them what to do, but merely advised them. The operations in Afghanistan meant the deployment of almost every available SAS Squadron, as their mission tasking was growing by the day. The lack of roads hampered the speed at which SAS mobility columns could move; even by SAS standards, the going was tough.

In one operation near Mazar-e-Sharif, some vehicles got bogged down while driving off road, and as they tried to extract themselves a group of Taliban opened fire from a distant ridge with heavy machine guns and RPGs (Rocket-Propelled Grenades). The SAS responded with their vehicle-mounted GPMGs and 40mm grenade-launchers and after a fierce firefight, in which many Taliban were killed or injured, they withdrew.

For the SAS, the key task was to identify Taliban troop positions for the American bombers. The SAS men were

also to provide intelligence on tank and artillery assets, which could then be hit by US Navy strike aircraft flying local support sorties – or 'blat and splat' missions, as the SAS teams called them.

In addition to their original assignments, a further role was tasked to the SAS, one of a humanitarian nature. This was vitally important, as it was virtually impossible to get enough aid in by truck. America had promised to drop food aid packages from USAF transport aircraft to the starving Afghan people. There was, however, a serious problem with the aid drops. Afghanistan is littered with millions of anti-personnel mines, and these were killing dozens of people every day as they tried to reach the food packages. The SAS carried out surveys on suitable sites that were free of mines and marked these for the transport aircraft. It was a very successful mission, and saved many innocent lives. SAS Squadrons were now extremely active on several different fronts within Afghanistan, especially near the lower slopes of the southern Hindu Kush Mountains and around Bagram airfield near Mazar-e-Sharif.

As the combined air- and ground operations gathered pace throughout Afghanistan during late 2001 – part of a combined allied operation involving both British and American ground forces as well as the Northern Alliance – the SAS began direct attacks against Al-Qaeda and Taliban training camps. The camps were generally very well hidden, often featuring cave complexes that were virtually impossible to attack from the air.

One tactic the SAS used to great effect in the mountain regions involved a combination of Sabre Squadrons and US AC-130 Spectre Gunships. After identifying a training camp and watching it for a few days until satisfied that it was an important target, the SAS would summon a strike to deliver deep penetration bombs straight into the mouths of the cave entrances. Once this mission was completed, a Spectre Gunship would be called in to hit the dazed survivors of the first attack by strafing the ground with its deadly armament of mini-guns, 40mm (1.57in) cannon and howitzer.

The SAS recce team then plotted the predicted escape route of the enemy forces after the end of this attack, and arranged for the rest of their squadron to mount an ambush against them. If planned well, an enemy force could be decimated before they even realized what was happening to them. This highly effective tactic was based on the Russian 'Hammer and Anvil' concept, developed during the Soviet occupation of Afghanistan and used to good effect against the Mujahedeen.

The SAS was also able to draw on operational experiences in Aden and Oman for tactics, techniques and procedures in this conflict. This was to be of great importance. During the first few weeks of deployment in Afghanistan, the US special forces found operations difficult, as they had little comparable combat experience in such an environment, and so a small number of four-man SAS teams were assigned to them as advisors. It was during one of these combined operations that America suffered its first

Right: Masked SAS men arrive at the Qala-e-Jhangi fortress near Mazar-e-Sharif to help suppress a revolt by Taliban and Al-Qaeda prisoners, which left hundreds dead, including one CIA operative.

combat casualty while operating near Mazar-e-Sharif. After weeks of fighting between the Northern Alliance and the Taliban over the strategically important airfield of Bagram, it finally fell and many Taliban soldiers were taken prisoner. They were held in the stronghold of the Qala-e-Jhangi fortress, an impressive collection of mud-walled compounds just outside Mazar-e-Sharif.

TALIBAN REVOLT

One day, as the prisoners were being interrogated by the CIA, a revolt broke out, and Mike Spann, a CIA operative, was killed, along with many Northern Alliance and Taliban soldiers. It took several days of heavy fighting – including the calling in of air strikes – before order could be restored by the SAS and US special forces, who were acting as advisors to the Northern Alliance. At the height of the revolt, a number of SAS soldiers were seen on live television arriving at the fortress in white Land Rovers, bristling with machine guns. The soldiers quickly put on masks to protect their identities and wore a mixture of camouflaged combats and local Afghan dress. After the rebellion had been subdued, the SAS troopers withdrew to resume other tasks in the local area. They were lucky to escape without taking casualties, as it had been a ferocious and bloody action in which hundreds had died.

By now, the Taliban were in retreat and had very few strongholds left in which to take sanctuary. All the towns they had once occupied had fallen and were in the hands of the Northern Alliance. With the

Taliban now out of the way, the priority was to find Osama bin Laden and the remaining Al-Qaeda terrorists who were still putting up resistance, despite intensive American bombing on their known positions. One report suggested that bin Laden was holed up in an Al-Qaeda training camp near to Kandahar in southern Afghanistan; unfortunately, this could not be confirmed.

Nonetheless, the SAS were given the task of attacking the camp. After observing it for a few days, the higher powers deemed a ground assault to be more appropriate than an air strike, as part of the camp was underground and would be difficult to target from the air. Even by SAS standards, this would be a tough mission. The terrorists had sworn to fight to the death and previous experience suggested that they were not bluffing.

SURPRISE FLANK ATTACK

The SAS attacked with two full squadrons – A and G – comprising about 80 men who were well armed and highly experienced in this type of warfare. As they fought their way through Al-Qaeda's defensive positions, they were met by fierce resistance from well-placed machine guns positioned on a ridge set into the side of a deep gully. As the SAS tried to work their way around the posi-

tion, they were attacked by a large number of Taliban and Al-Qaeda fighters, who emerged suddenly from an underground bunker. This attack caught the SAS completely by surprise, and they were now in serious danger of being outflanked by a much larger enemy force.

With the threat of being overrun, the SAS advanced forward in a classic charge, which involved them coming face-to-face with their enemy at very close range, and included hand-to-hand combat. As the fighting continued, a number of SAS soldiers who had been manning the communications base saw what was happening and raced to the aid of their fellow troopers, who were now fighting for their lives.

After several minutes of intense fighting, the SAS turned the Al-Qaeda and Taliban fighters back and the action ended. One trooper commented later that 'Targets were being engaged at a distance of 10 feet. It was a case of who had the steadiest hand won.' Although they had been heavily outnumbered, the SAS suffered only 4 casualties but left 27 enemy dead and 35 wounded. Unfortunately one of the SAS wounded had to have his leg amputated after it was hit by an AK-47 bullet. A major commanding one of the squadrons had a lucky escape when his ceramic armour deflected two bullets which would probably have killed him.

Although the operation had been a success, many in the SAS felt that the regiment was not being used in the correct manner. A squadron commander involved in the attack claimed that a regular infantry company 'could have done [the mission] better'.

After this, SAS involvement in Afghanistan was limited to supporting the Northern Alliance rather than leading them in further operations. This was deliberate, as the SAS did not want to upstage the Northern Alliance in front of the Afghan people, or cause a lack of confidence in their ability to defend the country from further insurrection. The SAS was also asked to help in the destruction of the terrorists' opium fields, as this was their main source of income.

TORA BORA

The SAS in Afghanistan were next involved helping the Northern Alliance to clear the cave complexes of Tora Bora, located just south of Jalalabad. These caves were the last known hiding place of Osama bin Laden, and even though they had been continuously bombed for weeks, survivors remained inside them who posed a considerable threat. With experience in this type of warfare, the SAS showed the Northern Alliance how to clear caves and bunker complexes, and their expertise was greatly appreciated by all who took part in this extremely dangerous work.

Despite extensive searches for Osama bin Laden throughout Afghanistan, no trace was found of him. Many assumed at the time that he had been killed during the bombing campaign. During one of these search operations, an SAS team identified a fortified Al-Qaeda position in the mountain ranges of eastern Afghanistan. Under normal circumstances they would have called in an air-strike, but having observed the position for several days, they believed that Osama bin Laden was in hiding there, as there were

Left: American special forces soldiers return from a mission on horseback with friendly Afghan forces. It is likely that the SAS were also using such methods of transport in a country that lacks any kind of road network.

Right: A masked member of the British special forces departing on a patrol in Afghanistan. He wears a mixture of civilian and military clothing, along with a traditional form of Afghan headgear. His firearm has been heavily customized.

hundreds of Al-Qaeda terrorists guarding the site. By this time, the SAS had teams at both ends of the valley leading up to the position, but not enough men to launch an attack. As they called for reinforcements, they were ordered to withdraw, as the credit for capturing bin Laden was to be given to US forces for political reasons. The SAS withdrew to a nearby valley and awaited the Americans' arrival.

Finally, three days later, on 2 March 2002, the US launched Operation Anaconda, which lasted for 16 days. It hit problems from the word go, as most of the US forces were dropped in the middle of the target valley instead of outside it. As a result, the US troops were ambushed by a large Al-Qaeda force and suffered many casualties, including eight fatalities and 73 wounded. The firefight was so hot that every helicopter involved in supporting the ground forces was hit by effective enemy fire, resulting in the loss of two Chinooks and several others severely damaged. However, the US forces fought back with great determination and killed hundreds of Al-Qaeda before withdrawing. Although they failed to capture bin Laden or indeed any of his lieutenants, the operation was deemed successful as it forced Al-Qaeda out of Afghanistan.

The Special Air Service Regiment can be proud of the part they played in the war against terrorism; it was able to achieve so much with so little. As US Defense Secretary Donald Rumsfeld said of the SAS, 'They are amongst the best soldiers in the world, and are truly exceptional men.'

On 28 October 2002 the British Government released a list of military decorations for the campaign in Afghanistan. Four SAS soldiers were awarded the Conspicuous Gallantry Cross, believed to be members of the same patrol, who were wounded near Kandahar in November 2001. Another eight unnamed special forces soldiers

received other awards. There was also widespread media speculation in the UK that a Victoria Cross might be awarded to a Scottish SAS sergeant.

As preparations for the 2003 invasion of Iraq started in earnest, the SAS found their priorities changed. Most were inserted into Iraq, to gather intelligence and identify potential targets. To replace them, around 60 men from 21 and 23 SAS, the territorial units, were flown to Afghanistan and tasked with hunting down Al-Qaeda forces. After the cessation of military operations in Iraq and the successful capture of Saddam Hussein, Task

Force 121 was given the mission to find bin Laden. This elite unit is formed from members of the US Delta Forces, the US Navy SEALs, the SAS and their Australian equivalent, and the SBS.

In March 2004 100 men from 22 SAS were sent to take part in Operation Mountain Storm. This operation was intended to capture or kill the remaining Taliban and Al-Qaeda leaders hiding in the mountainous border area of South Waziristan, in co-operation with local Pakistani forces. Although there were a number of successes, Osama bin Laden remains at large.

OPERATION TELIC

The Fall of Saddam

Even as operations in Afghanistan became focused on hunting Osama bin Laden and Mullah Omar, the Taliban's leader, the world's attention was switched to Iraq. Large Western military forces were already present in the region, and speculation was rife in 2002 that the SAS were already in Iraq, seeking potential targets and trying to locate key Saddam loyalists.

The intervention in Afghanistan showed how special forces could successfully lead irregular troops and coordinate airstrikes, but it was realised that changes needed to be made to the UK's elite forces. A new Director of Special Forces was appointed, a brigadier commanding both the SAS and the Special Boat Service who had himself served with both units. At the same time the decision was taken to expand the SAS to cope with the greater demand for special forces. This was not welcomed by everyone, as some felt there was risk of dilution – traditionally the SAS had only accepted on average 10–15 new recruits a year, yet now another full squadron of approximately 80 men was proposed. The British Government believed that the demands on special forces troops would only increase due to the increasing specialisation of modern war. The SBS was also increased in size to three squadrons, or approximately 250 men.

WARNING

On 12 September 2002, while operations were still continuing in Afghanistan, President George W. Bush spoke to the UN General Assembly, asking the UN to disarm Iraq of its weapons of mass destruction (WMDs).

Twelve days later the British Government published a comprehensive dossier on Iraq's WMDs, including the claim that attacks could be mounted within 45 minutes. (This dossier is later largely discredited.) The UN Security Council passed Resolution 1441, declaring Iraq to be in material breach of past resolutions. Saddam Hussein was given the choice of complying immediately or face 'serious consequences'. Although Iraq allows weapons inspectors led by Hans Blix to return, the inspectors do not receive full cooperation from the Iraqis.

On 6 February 2003 Colin Powell addresses the UN Security Council detailing how Iraq has not fulfilled the

Left: Iraqi soldiers operating as part of the Free Iraq Forces with coalition special forces troops. A US Humvee armed with a .5in (12.7mm) machine gun is visible in the background. The SAS worked closely with the Kurds and US special forces in Iraq.

requirements of Resolution 1441. The US, UK and Spain prepare a draft resolution which would in effect authorise the use of force against Iraq. This meets strong opposition from France, Germany and others, and President Bush, determined to push ahead with the attack, decides that UN authority is unnecessary. The invasion is planned for late March.

SAS IN IRAQ

By this stage the SAS had already infiltrated Iraq. Two SAS squadrons and some SBS men were part of the 3000-man Combined Joint Special Operations task force in southern and western Iraq. The remainder of the task force are from Delta Force and other US SOCOM units, and about 100 members of the Australian SAS.

The SAS were tasked with identifying potential targets for the air strikes that will accompany the invasion, reconnoitering the approaches to Basra,

Above: For insertion into Iraq before the outbreak of war – and after – the SAS used Chinook helicopters capable of carrying a patrol and its equipment in one lift. The helicopters were fitted with machine guns for self-defence.

the main British objective, preparing to secure the southern oilfields, and searching western Iraq for SCUD missile launchers and potential launch sites.

Using friendly bases such as the Jordanian air base at Azraq al-Shishan, the SAS used long-range Chinook helicopters to fly into Iraq at low level. The large Chinooks were able to carry enough equipment for the patrols, including the infamous 'Pinky' Land Rovers, motorcycles and Supacat ATVs used to navigate the desert terrain of western Iraq. The patrols were between four and ten men in size, although patrols could join forces if required.

A smaller SAS force was involved with operations in the north of Iraq.

The original invasion plan called for US and UK forces to enter Iraq from Turkey, but permission to do so was refused by the Turkish government. The SAS forces instead hurriedly adopted the model used so successfully in Afghanistan, providing training, leadership and air support for the anti-Saddam Kurdish forces already active in the north of Iraq.

Events came to a head when President Bush announced on 17 March that Saddam Hussein and his two sons had 48 hours to leave Iraq. The following day a White House spokesman said that the US would invade Iraq regardless, 'the bottom line is, a coalition of the willing will disarm Saddam Hussein's Iraq, no matter what'. Some 90 minutes after the expiry of the deadline, on 20 March 2003, explosions were seen in Baghdad. The Iraq war had officially begun, and the SAS moved quickly into action.

While the SBS and the US Navy SEALs helped secure the offshore oil platforms and port facilities at Umm Qasr, SAS teams in the south of the country helped the supporting air strikes by using their laser designators to illuminate targets.

In western Iraq the SAS and their US and Australian colleagues eliminated the SCUD threat to Israel and rapidly denied a large area of their country to Iraqi forces. On 27 March the British Prime Minister, Tony Blair, announced at Camp David that 'We have disabled Iraq's ability to launch external aggression from the west'. Thanks to US intervention, the Israeli special forces teams that had been operating in western Iraq were withdrawn before the conflict, eliminating the risk of a tragic 'friendly-fire' incident.

Operating largely by night, and laying up in the day, as they had done in the first Iraq war in 1991, the SAS and other special forces had regular encounters with Iraqi forces and foreign fighters entering Iraq from Syria. Two forward bases were established for the special forces of the coalition deep in the desert of western Iraq, and well away from the eyes of the media, who were largely focusing on the events near Basra and the drive on Baghdad. These bases were former Iraqi air bases, known to the coalition as H2 and H3, and they rapidly became the focus of the special forces operations in western Iraq. After organized Iraqi opposition collapsed, the SAS mounted roadwatch patrols on the roads to Baghdad from Syria and the Jordanian capital, Amman.

A major row broke out between the SAS and the SBS after an operation went badly wrong. The Republican Guard ambushed an SBS patrol with an SAS officer on secondment. Badly outgunned and outnumbered, the SBS were forced to abandon their equip-

Left: A statue of Saddam Hussein in central Baghdad is attacked as US forces enter the city on 9 April 2003. Although Saddam's fall was popular with most Iraqis, for others it inspired fierce resistance to coalition involvement in Iraq.

ment during a six-hour fighting witdrawal. Two of the unit became separated, and made their way to the Syrian border, some 100 miles away. The equipment, including the Pink Panther Landrovers, was paraded on Iraqi TV, much to the embarrassment of the SAS.

BASRA

The SAS were actively involved in the capture of Basra. Regular British forces halted outside the city, hoping that potential resistance would melt away. Meanwhile the SAS were deep in the city, gathering intelligence and providing commanders with information on the location of potential strongpoints, gatherings of pro-Saddam forces, and arms and ammunition dumps. Snipers helped damage enemy morale.

A British journalist, Olga Craig, met a special forces soldier dressed in cargo trousers and a t-shirt on the bridge into Basra while it was being shelled by Iraqi mortars. After literally running into him during the confusion, the trooper asked, 'Who the **** are you?', not expecting to see a non-Iraqi. Once she had explained she was a journalist, the soldier told her what was going on in Basra. 'People who are getting information to us about what is happening. They are taking an enormous risk. The [Iraqi] militia are holding meetings in civilian homes, holding families at gunpoint and moving all the time. We realise that at home, people cannot understand why we are not being greeted as liberators, but the situation is much more complicated than that... There are some very brave people in [Basra].'

Using the vital information gathered by men such as this, the British commander of the assault on Basra was able to judge when the city was ready to fall with minimal resistance.

The SAS were also involved in the hunt for Ali Hassan al-Majid, known as 'Chemical Ali' for his role in the use of nerve agents against Kurdish rebels in 1988. Chemical Ali had been appointed commander of Iraqi forces in the south, and he was high on the coalition's wanted list. He was assumed killed after

The Hunt for Saddam

One of the prime objectives for the coalition was the capture of Saddam Hussein. Although he escaped the capture of Baghdad, a huge effort was made to track down his aides in the hope that they could reveal where he was hiding. The SAS were actively involved in this process, and British intelligence discovered that Saddam was using a battered taxi to drive around it. Sure enough, when Saddam was eventually located on a farm near the town of Ad Dawr, a taxi was found nearby. The capture was conducted by men of Task Force 121 and the US 4th Infantry Division. The former Iraqi president was found in a hole under a lean-to with a primitive ventilation device, two AK-47s, a pistol and around $750,000. Bedraggled and bearded, he was taken to Baghdad airport where he was cleaned up and his identity confirmed. At the time of writing only nine of the 55 Iraqis on the US most wanted playing cards are still at large.

his 'body' – actually a double – was found at his house, but he was later captured by US forces in August 2003.

The SAS did succeed in tracking down Watban Ibrahim Hasan al-Tikriti, a half-brother of Saddam who was caught trying to escape to Syria. A six-man patrol working with the Kurdish forces received a tip-off and intercepted Watban on the road from Mosul to the border on 13 April. An ex-Interior Minister, he had been fired in 1995 after arguing with Saddam's eldest son, Uday, who shot him in the leg.

THE END OF THE BEGINNING

The end of combat operations was declared by President Bush on 1 May 2003, standing on the deck of the aircraft carrier USS *Abraham Lincoln*. Despite the fall of Baghdad and the capture of Tikrit, in the months to come Iraqi resistance gradually grew in strength and effectiveness led by figures such as Abu Musab al-Zarqawi, a Jordanian with links to al-Qaeda. In particular the so-called 'Sunni Triangle' north-east of Baghdad became the centre of Iraqi resistance.

After the end of formal military operations, the SAS worked closely

with the SBS and their US and Australian counterparts in an effort to identify safehouses and routes used by Iraqi resistance groups while tracking down the important members of Saddam's former regime.

In November 2003 SAS and SBS troops fighting alongside US colleagues attacked a heavily fortified compound in the north of Iraq controlled by pro-Saddam fighters. An SAS soldier commented later that 'The guys were attacking a target they had been aware of for some time but they had no idea how many of them were in there. It was a hornet's nest.' Although 10 Iraqis were killed, Ian Plank, an SBS corporal, was killed and four SAS troopers wounded.

More bad news for the UK special forces followed when two SAS soldiers were killed in the early hours of New Year's Day 2004 while returning to their quarters in Baghdad's Green Zone, the special secure area within central Baghdad. Major James Stenner, 30, had been awarded the Military Cross for his actions as a troop commander in D Squadron, 22 SAS, earlier in the year. He was considered by some as a likely future commander of 22 SAS, and was serving as the operations

Left: Like their British counterparts, the Australian SAS were extremely proficient in desert operations, and they were heavily involved in patrolling western Iraq for SCUD missile launchers and escaping senior Ba'ath party members.

Dressed in civilian clothes, the 25 troopers kept a low profile despite their submachine guns. Plans were made for evacuating British ex-patriates, strengthening the embassy's protection against attack, and calling on other SAS stationed in nearby Qatar if needed.

Shortly afterwards two SAS and SBS teams were sent to Athens following a request by the Greek authorities for help in checking security arrangements for the 2004 Olympic Games. While the team from M Squadron of the SBS concentrated on maritime security, the SAS CRW team advised on the security arrangements for the Olympic stadium and village. An MOD spokesman, when asked about their presence, said, 'In the unlikely event of a terrorist incident it would be up to the Greek authorities to decide whether or not they wanted to use any British assets. It is not a case of Britain offering. It would be up to the Greeks to ask. That is how these things are done.' The teams remained as advisors until the successful conclusion of the games in late August.

IRAN NEXT?

The SAS remain stretched to the limit of their resources. Since the capture of Saddam Hussein and the free elections in Iraq, the security situation has improved, but the SAS remain dedicated to counter-insurgency warfare. In Afghanistan there has been a renewed emphasis on locating Osama bin Laden. There have also been repeated reports – denied by the Ministry of Defence – that the SAS have been active in Iran. The nuclear programme of Iran has caused concern for many Western countries, and the SAS may well be active in identifying potential nuclear sites for future intervention. Whatever the future holds for the SAS, its actions in Afghanistan and Iraq in recent years have added to its lustre and reputation.

officer for all British special forces in the Baghdad area when he died. His vehicle hit concrete barriers and both he and Sergeant Norman Patterson – who had only recently joined the SAS from the Cheshire Regiment – were killed instantly. The cause of the crash is still not publically known. In recent years six other SAS troopers have died in non-combat related accidents in Britain, Kenya and Oman.

Throughout 2004 leading up to the elections in Iraq there were a spate of foreign kidnappings that received significant amounts of media attention. The SAS were thrust into the spotlight again when Ken Bigley, a civilian contractor working in the country, was kidnapped by the Tawhid wal Jihad group led by Abu Musab al-Zarqawi on 16 September. Intensive efforts were made to track his kidnappers, and an SAS hostage rescue team was on standby if required. Unfortunately, shortly after an escape attempt, Mr Bigley was beheaded by his captors before the SAS could locate where he was being held.

The running sore that was Falluja was finally dealt with on 8 November 2004 when American forces entered the city. The SAS formed part of the screen that surrounded it, hoping to filter out any insurgents from the many thousands that left Falluja to escape the fighting and American bombing.

On 24 November 2004 the coalition expanded their operations against the insurgency, and a squadron of the SAS were involved in 'Plymouth Rock', a large-scale operation targeting the strongholds of the Iraqi resistance in central Iraq. Captain David Nevers of the 24th Marine Expeditionary Unit said that British forces – including the SAS – 'bring a wide range of capabilities to bear that will be enormously useful to us'.

ELSEWHERE

The situation in Saudi Arabia had been deteriorating for some time as the unrest continued in Iraq. In June 2004 an SAS team was sent to the embassy in Riyadh to advise on its protection.

THE SAS
ART OF
WAR

WEAPONS SKILLS

Every Bullet Counts

Since World War II SAS soldiers have been proficient in the use of a wide variety of firearms, of both allies and enemies. Because SAS units often operate behind enemy lines, troopers are taught to use fast, accurate fire to defeat an enemy attack.

It is imperative that Special Forces personnel are able to handle a range of weapons both of friendly and hostile manufacture. Although an elite soldier may have a favoured weapon system for a particular mission it may not always be available. More possibly, it may become damaged or jammed during the sortie, forcing him to rely upon a gun taken from the enemy. Expertise in the handling of many different types of hand-held weapons, from shotguns to sophisticated anti-aircraft systems, gained from multiple hours of training on the range and in the Hereford 'Killing House', has enabled the SAS to establish a reputation second to none in this field.

The SAS defence of the Omani town of Mirbat in July 1972 is perhaps the best example of the Regiment's skills in action, and is worth recording in detail. Mirbat is a small coastal town in western Oman, located some 65km (40 miles) east of the provincial capital, Salalah. At the time of the attack the town was defended by 30 Askaris from northern Oman armed with bolt-action .303in Lee-Enfield rifles, some *firqat* (local tribesmen, many of them ex-rebels), 25 Dhofar Gendarmerie in an old fort and armed with British 7.62mm SLR semi-automatic rifles, and an SAS training team.

WEAPONS SKILLS AT MIRBAT

The SAS team consisted of nine men based in the BATT (British Army Training Team) house, under the command of Captain Mike Kealy). Their heavy weaponry consisted of a single 25-pounder artillery piece dug in close to the fort, a .5in Browning machine gun and a 7.62mm General Purpose Machine Gun

Above: SAS soldiers are taught to use controlled fire, to make every shot count, as opposed to laying down a blanket of fire.

(GPMG), both on the roof of the BATT house. The position would have been far stronger, but 60 *firqat* had been dispatched to patrol the mountain overlooking the town to investigate an enemy sighting and had yet to return.

The enemy, or *adoo*, were guerrillas of the People's Front for the Liberation of the Occupied Arabian Gulf (PFLOAG), a Marxist-inspired organisation attempting to overthrow the pro-British Sultan. The *adoo* force which attacked Mirbat was considerably stronger than the defenders: 250 guerrillas armed with Soviet AK-47 Kalashnikov assault rifles, supported by 75mm recoilless rifles, rocket launchers and at least one battery of mortars. In addition, the attack would be launched during the monsoon period, making government intervention from the air difficult through the prevailing low cloud and

rain. The Mirbat defences consisted of flat-topped houses and mud-walled forts surrounded by a barbed-wire cattle fence. The terrain was open and relatively flat, affording the defenders excellent fields of fire during the battle.

The attack was launched in the early hours of 19 July 1972. The enemy's stealth-like approach was compromised when a firefight developed between the guerrillas and a small force of gendarmes in an outlying post, which gave the main body of defenders warning. Kealy gave the order for the SAS mortar to open fire, and then he and the other SAS soldiers opened up with a lethal combination of machine guns and assault rifles. The

the gunpit. Once there the scene which greeted them gave cause for alarm. The Omani gunner was seriously injured, as were both the Fijians. It seemed the gun-pit might fall, which would have meant the loss of the battle.

FIREPOWER DEFEATS THE *ADOO*

The 25-pounder, although momentarily silent, was still able to fire. As the unsuspecting *adoo* closed in for the kill Labalaba, who had now received basic first aid from Tobin, brought the 25-pounder into action once again. As he fell his place was taken by Tobin, covered as far as possible by Kealy, and supported by concentrated fire from the BATT house. The fanatical *adoo* continued to press a series of at times suicidally brave attacks, but to no avail.

The appearance of two Omani Strike-master jets stemmed the *adoo,* who began to withdraw in disorder. As they did they were met by the concentrated fire of the GPMGs manned by a rescue force from G Squadron, 22 SAS. The battle for Mirbat, one of the shortest but most savage in the history of the SAS, broke the Marxists' will to fight. It was also a testimony to the weapons skills of the SAS.

SLRs, GPMG and Browning found their marks with well-aimed shots and bursts, SAS training paying dividends as the full ferocity of the attack was blunted.

Fortunately, the *adoo* mounted their initial infantry assault against the Gendarmerie in the fort. Most of the SAS team were in the BATT house some 400m (1312ft) away. However, when Trooper Savesaki received a report that his fellow Fijian, Corporal Labalaba, who was himself beside the fort in the gunpit with the 25-pounder, was injured, he sought and was granted permission to run to his friend to offer medical assistance.

The initial attack was mounted by an extended line of some 40 *adoo*. Using a shallow wadi for protection, they skirted in front of the BATT house, turned towards the fort and broke into a run. As soon as they broke cover they were mown down with short bursts from the roof of the BATT house by Corporal Chapman manning the Browning.

The *adoo* now began to strafe the BATT house with machine guns and mortar rounds. Having radioed Salalah for assistance, Kealy took stock of the situa-

tion, and having failed to get a reply from the gunpit near the fort decided to go there himself. Leaving Corporal Robert Bradshaw in charge of the BATT house and the vital support weapons, he and Tommy Tobin, an SAS medical specialist, began their hazardous dash for the gunpit, one man sprinting, the other giving him cover. Miraculously, despite heavy enemy fire, the pair both made it uninjured to

Right: In a firefight SAS soldiers are instructed to fire first and accurately, as these dead Iraqis discovered in the Gulf War.

The standard personal weapon the SAS currently favours is the American M16 assault rifle, which is usually fitted with an M203 grenade launcher. The Regiment first used an earlier version of this weapon during its Borneo campaign (1963-66), where the advantages of its relatively short barrel and lightness were felt to outweigh the disadvantage of its lack of stopping power, i.e. the weight of the round hitting the target was less when compared to larger-calibre rounds. In addition, SAS soldiers found that the US 5.56mm M193 bullet was easily deflected by overhanging branches and other obstacles which occur in the jungle. They therefore adopted the heavier, slower-moving SS109 European round.

THE M16 ASSAULT RIFLE

The current version of the M16 is the M16A2, which differs in a number of ways from the original. It is slightly heavier than the original and has a far thicker profile. A three-round burst capability has been introduced, with new sights added and the non-metallic parts such as the butt, stock and pistol grip strengthened. More importantly, it has been adapted to accept the improved NATO 5.56mm ammunition, making it interchangeable with the SA-80 assault rifle carried by conventional units in the British Army.

The M203 grenade launcher is a significant force multiplier when fitted to an M16, and has become a tried-and-tested favourite with the SAS. The launcher is attached beneath the stock extending under the M16's barrel, and is fired by a separate trigger mechanism forward of the magazine. It increases a patrol's firepower enormously, and can fire a variety of 40mm high-explosive and anti-personnel grenades to a range of nearly 400m (1312ft). It is equally useful if a patrol is ambushed, as it can lay down heavy firepower and even smoke at short notice, enabling the patrol to withdraw.

However, it is as a fragmentation weapon for raiding that the M203 truly excels. The SAS raid on Pebble Island during the 1982 Falklands War exemplified the potential of the M203 used aggressively, as well as the devastating way SAS troopers use assault rifles. During the

Above: The Colt Commando, the compact version of the M16. Its size makes it ideal for SAS anti-terrorist operations.

SAS personnel have always used a wide variety of weapons, from heavy machine guns to pistols. Experienced soldiers before they transfer to the Regiment, they will have learned to handle a personal weapon, probably the 5.56mm SA-80, during basic training. Those with an infantry background may well also have learned to use platoon support weapons, such as the Milan, LAW-80 or GPMG, and will certainly have learned the rudiments of how to use a hand grenade. After Selection Training they are introduced to a wide variety of additional weapons, learn the strengths and weaknesses of each, how to strip, clean and reassemble them in the dark, and above all how to get the best from them.

MISSION CONSIDERATIONS

There are several considerations to be taken into account when choosing weapons for a particular special forces mission. As most will take place behind enemy lines, minimum weight, conservation of ammunition and compatibility with enemy weapon systems are crucial. Equally important, however, is firepower. Patrols are invariably small and require the ability to shoot their way out of trouble by bringing down maximum short-term fire to bear if compromised.

Falklands campaign, the Argentinians established an airstrip on Pebble Island off the north coast of West Falkland. A number of Pucara ground-attack aircraft were based there, which could have posed a considerable threat to the British landings at San Carlos. A force from D Squadron, supported by a Royal Naval gunfire observation team and three warships, was therefore tasked with destroying the aircraft, their ground crews and the garrison on the island.

Due to strong headwinds, the carrier *Hermes* was delayed and landed the main assault party by helicopter 60 minutes late. The mission was therefore reduced, and the aircraft became the main target. The attack on the airstrip was carried out by members of the Mountain Troop led by Captain John Hamilton. When the troops reached the perimeter of the airstrip they opened fire with M203 grenade launchers and 66mm LAWs (light anti-tank weapons), while heavier fire and illumination were provided by the cruiser HMS *Glamorgan*.

FIREPOWER ON PEBBLE ISLAND

The following is an extract from one of the SAS soldiers who took part in the raid, and is an excellent example of the weapons skills as used by the Regiment: 'My heart started pounding and I tightened the grip on my M16. Instinctively I slipped off the safety catch. We crept onto the airfield and laid charges on seven of the aircraft. Moments later the place erupted as we opened up with our small arms and LAWs. Using three-round bursts, I emptied a whole magazine into a Pucara, the bullets ripping into the nose and cockpit, sending shards of perspex into the air. Overhead para-flares from *Glamorgan* lit up the night sky.

'To my left a 66mm rocket slammed into the side of another Pucara, engulfing it in a fireball. The crackle of small-arms fire filled the air as the explosive charges started to detonate. I clipped a fresh mag into my M16 and looked around for fresh targets. By this time all the aircraft were

Right: In the field camouflaged SAS snipers must be able to hit targets up to a range of 1000m (3280ft) or more.

either burning or had been riddled with bullets, their undercarriages shot away and their fuselages full of holes.'

The Argentine defenders, taken completely by surprise, were unable to return accurate fire and caused only one minor casualty. When the raiders withdrew, six Pucaras, four Turbo-Mentors and a Skyvan transport aircraft lay destroyed on the grass. In addition, the SAS destroyed a large quantity of ammunition. Crucially, Pebble Island played no further part in the Argentine defence of the islands. The employment of fast, accurate firepower by the SAS soldiers on Pebble Island is typical of the Regiment's use of firepower.

Being able to use assault rifles is one part of being an SAS soldier, being a crack marksman is another. Sniping is integral to special forces missions, both on the battlefield and in the counter-terrorist role. The sniper, operating either alone or with a partner, can pin down a large enemy force by killing its leaders and communications personnel. Other targets may include enemy weapons specialists, machine gunners or electrical experts. Snipers can also inflict material damage on enemy radar and missile sites, turning a projectile into a bomb with one well-aimed shot.

SNIPING SKILLS

Marksmanship skills alone will not make a good sniper. Ice-cool nerves and excellent fieldcraft capabilities are also essential. A sniper must be able to move across open terrain without being spotted by the

Left: The 9mm Browning High Power. Though it is being slowly replaced by new handguns, it is still popular in the Regiment.

then introduced, and the Accuracy International PM was adopted for most purposes. Designated the L96A1, the rifle accepts 7.62mm ammunition fed either singly through the ejection port or from a detachable 10-round box-type magazine, and is accurate up to 1000m (3280ft). The butt and stock are of high-density green plastic manufacture, and an adjustable rubber butt-pad is fitted, an important factor when considering the length of time that an SAS sniper may have to lie motionless before firing.

THE ACCURACY INTERNATIONAL

The L96A1 is fitted with a bipod and spike on the rear of the butt, to enable the weapon to rest comfortably during long periods of observation. A Schmidt & Bender PM6x42 telescopic sight has been fitted, chosen for its high degree of ruggedness, excellent clarity and 93 per cent light transmission, enabling it to operate effectively in low-light conditions. Accuracy International have also introduced a suppressed version of the weapon, which is accurate up to a range of 300m (984ft).

HANDGUNS

Handguns are primarily used by SAS soldiers for counter-terrorist duties and hostage-rescue operations. However, they may also be carried on other missions, as a back-up for a larger weapon. The prime considerations in choosing a handgun, as with all weapon systems, are accuracy and first-round reliability. Although there are many newer systems available, the Browning High Power remains a favourite with the SAS. Designed and produced by Fabrique National of Belgium, the 9mm semi-automatic pistol will accept a magazine of 14 rounds, although less are usually loaded to prevent jamming, and is effective up to a range of 50m (164ft).

The High Power is an excellent weapon for engaging targets at short ranges, and its short barrel enables the SAS soldier to rapidly engage suddenly exposed targets with either hand.

enemy. He must then locate concealed firing positions which offer a good view of the target yet offer an avenue of escape, move in and wait for hours, perhaps days, for a target of opportunity to present itself. All SAS soldiers are taught weapons maintenance to a high degree, but for a trained sniper the standards are far higher. Sniper rifles are generally less robust than conventional weapons and must be especially well maintained to avoid any problems. Too much oil in the barrel, for

example, may create a telltale smoke 'signature', giving away the sniper's position to the enemy. This is also true of the sun glinting off a shiny barrel or any other part of the weapon.

The range of sniper rifles varies according to the weapon, the ammunition and the sights fitted. Until the mid-1980s, the British Army and SAS retained the L42A1 sniper rifle for field use, a Lee Enfield No 4 converted to 7.62mm calibre. However, trials for a new rifle were

However, because its barrel is short, the need to aim accurately is of paramount importance. For this reason SAS soldiers receive intense training in the use of handguns, especially in the use of the so-called double tap (two shots fired in quick succession).

THE BROWNING HIGH POWER

The High Power, despite its age, meets all SAS requirements: not only is it reliable and safe, but its compactness makes it ideal for undercover work, in Northern Ireland for example. It can be operated with either hand, has a rapid magazine-change function, and will work in all climates. The High Power was used extensively by the SAS during the Aden campaign, when SAS 'Keeni Meeni' patrols, disguised as Arabs, mingled with the local population in search of gunmen. They were also used at the Iranian Embassy siege in 1980, when they were carried as back-ups to the submachine guns employed by the SAS men in the successful rescue of the hostages.

Below: Damaged Argentinian aircraft on Pebble Island after the SAS raid. Many of the aircraft were shot-up with small-arms fire.

Gibraltar

The SAS operation against the three Irish Republican Army (IRA) terrorists in Gibraltar in March 1988 is an excellent example of the weapons skills employed by the Regiment. The SAS teaches its soldiers to use body-line shooting in their anti-terrorist operations. A double tap (two shots fired in quick succession) is often insufficient to stop a determined terrorist from detonating hidden explosives or pulling a weapon that can then be used to kill. It is drilled into SAS soldiers that sustained and accurate firepower will keep a terrorist's hands away from his body, thus making it impossible for him or her to push a button or reach for a gun. Forget the idea of shooting a gun out of a terrorist's hands, shots are always aimed at the trunk of the body, which contains the vital organs – heart, lungs and liver – but which is also a bigger target. One shot to the head, 'the suede' in SAS parlance, guarantees an instant kill, but the head is a much smaller target.

All the above must be borne in mind when analysing the events at Gibraltar. The SAS soldiers who were trailing them believed the IRA terrorists were armed and had remote-control devices on their persons, which they were going to use to detonate a car bomb. When confronted, the terrorists – Mairead Farrell, Sean Savage and Daniel McCann – all made movements which the SAS men on the ground interpreted as being threatening, and responded accordingly. In the space of a few seconds it was all over. All three terrorists were shot and killed at close quarters. Farrell was hit five times – two in the head and three in the torso – McCann was shot nine times and Savage was hit by 15 rounds. Such overwhelming firepower was explained by the SAS themselves at the later inquest. Soldier 'A' stated: 'I thought she [Farrell] was going for the button and I shot Farrell in the back. I then engaged McCann. His hands were away from his body.'

Force Multipliers

SAS patrols substantially increase their firepower by carrying weapons that act as force multipliers, such as machine guns, grenade launchers and light anti-tank weapons. This not only gives them protection against armoured vehicles, it means they can out-gun enemy infantry.

SAS teams operating behind enemy lines have always been faced with the dilemma of firepower versus mobility. Small-sized units far from friendly lines are vulnerable to enemy air and ground attack. The risk is partly offset by SAS soldiers' camouflage and concealment skills, but having sufficient firepower means compromises in other areas. SAS vehicle patrols can carry immense firepower, but they are obviously far more visible than foot teams. Foot teams, though, are restricted in terms of firepower by what they can carry.

SAS teams like to have heavier support weapons with them, both to add to the firepower of an attack or reinforce the defence. However, weight considerations are always a problem. Fortunately, modern anti-tank weapons and grenade launchers are compact and light enough to be carried by SAS foot patrols, and thus act as significant force multipliers.

MACHINE GUNS

Aside from rifles, SAS teams need fire-support weapons to provide small-sized units with destructive firepower and fire support. In highly trained hands the machine gun is a significant force multiplier. The most favoured machine gun in the SAS armoury is the L7A2 General Purpose Machine Gun (GPMG), which, until recently, was the principal section support weapon of the British Army. It was introduced following the adoption of 7.62mm calibre ammunition as the standard NATO round and was always regarded as an extremely reliable and accurate, if somewhat heavy, weapon. With its integrated bipod it has an accurate range of 800m (2624ft), and when attached to a tripod (in the sustained fire

role) it can fire 800 rounds per minute to a range of up to 1400m (4590ft).

A machine gun that has gained in popularity with the Regiment in recent years is the Belgian 5.56mm Minimi, which was carried by the patrol 'Bravo Two Zero' in the 1991 Gulf War. Its advantages for foot patrols are obvious: it weighs only

6.8kg (15lb) compared to nearly 11kg (24lb) of the GPMG, its ammunition weighs less than 7.62mm calibre rounds, and it has a second feed slot located below the first on the left side of the receiver. Thus if there is no belt-feed ammunition available, then any M16-type magazine can be fitted into the second feed slot.

Right: Machine guns, such as this 7.62mm GPMG, can give small-sized SAS patrols devastating firepower.

This interchangeability is an advantage for teams operating behind enemy lines.

SAS MACHINE GUNNERS

SAS troopers learn to operate machine guns from several positions, but unlike the conventional infantry, who serve the gun with a team of two, tend to operate it singly to save manpower. They will learn to fire the GPMG and Minimi from the hip, using the sling to maintain the weapon parallel to the ground and at waist height, and from the shoulder. This involves a great deal of physical strength, with the weapon being raised to the shoulder in the same way as a rifle. The ammunition belt is draped over the left arm, while the right supports the weight of the weapon, a not unsubstantial 10.4kg (24lb) unloaded. Only short bursts of up to four rounds or so can be fired in this manner, as the weapon becomes difficult to control, but even so this may prove devastating at short ranges. The 7.62mm disintegrating link ammunition fired by the GPMG is distributed throughout the patrol, lessening the weight to be carried by the weapon's gunner.

While the machine gun is capable of providing heavy accurate fire over great distances, its usefulness in urban environments, in the jungle, or at short range is limited. To fill this gap in its support armoury, the SAS introduced the shotgun during the Malayan campaign. Early models were standard, or had been introduced originally for police riot-control situations. As the potential of the shotgun as a weapon became more obvious, however, more thought was put into the acquisition of more specialist models.

Loaded with buckshot rather than the non-lethal birdshot used by riot police, shotguns can prove very effective in the hands of a patrol's lead scout, enabling him to put down a spread of deadly projectiles into a general area with a single shot. Different types of shotgun ammunition can be carried according to the circumstances. Small buckshot (either AAA or BB) is classified as short range, while large buckshot (SSG, SG or LG) has less of a spread, but is effective at ranges of 15-40m (50-131ft) and can stop a man at ranges up to 30m (98ft). An SSG car-

Above: Firing a machine gun like this US Navy SEAL is very tiring, but it is a technique that is taught to SAS soldiers.

tridge, which contains eight 9mm balls, has a spread of approximately 25mm per metre (1in per 39in), and is comparable in effect to a tight eight-round group fired from a sub-machine gun.

THE REMINGTON 870 SHOTGUN

The M203 grenade launcher can fire shotgun-type anti-personnel rounds and has largely superseded the conventional shotgun in the strictly military field. However, the SAS retains the shotgun for the CRW role, particularly to blow off door hinges. Civilian pump-action weapons have now largely been abandoned in favour of more modern purpose-built paramilitary models, such as the Remington 870, Mossberg 5-ATP-8 and the Franchi special-purpose automatic shotgun (SPAS) series. The Remington, based on a design introduced in 1949, has been officially adopted by the US Marine Corps as its combat shotgun, and by the British Army for its Close Observation Platoons (COPs) in Northern Ireland. Both the Remington and the Mossberg are of part aluminium construction to avoid weight.

The Luigi Franchi SPAS 11 and 12 models, on the other hand, were designed specifically for the military market, oper-

ate in both pump-action and semi-automatic mode, and in the case of the SPAS 12 can be fired with one hand if necessary. Tear gas rounds can be fired, and an attachment fitted to launch grenades to a maximum range of 150m (495ft). Using SSG rounds, the SPAS can place 48 shots per second into a target at 40m (132ft), and for extremely close-quarter shooting may be fitted with a shot diverter capable of widening the spread of shot. Crucially for CRW operations the SPAS will accept the British-made Hatton round, specially designed for shooting off hinges. The SPAS can even be loaded with a tungsten carbide, discarding-sabot 'penetrator' round and used at close range against the sides of light armoured vehicles.

22 SAS has maintained the tradition, begun by David Stirling, of enhancing its potency by using a wide variety of heavy support weapons in both the offensive and defensive mode. The weapons themselves must be the most effective systems available, and be light enough to be either man portable or mountable on Land Rovers or other types of small soft-

skinned vehicle. The equipment must also be air-portable or capable of being dropped by parachute.

Although anti-tank warfare is not a primary role of the SAS, patrols must be capable of neutralising heavy armour should they encounter it in an ambush. The tried-and-tested 84mm Carl Gustav recoilless anti-tank gun has always been a favourite with the SAS, although it is now being largely superseded by the American M72 66mm Light Anti-Armour Weapon (LAW), and the heavier 94mm LAW 80. Both are one-shot, throw-away weapons, and in the case of the LAW 80 can fire a fin-stabilised warhead capable of penetrating a defended bunker or an armoured vehicle at a range of 500m (1640ft).

MILAN AND STINGER

Medium-range anti-tank weapon systems such as Milan, which can be fitted with a MIRA thermal-imaging device for night use, may be deployed if greater accuracy over a longer range (1500m/4920ft) is required, but the weight of the weapon (23kg /51lb) means that its use is virtually limited to vehicle-borne operations.

The US-made FIM-92A Stinger anti-aircraft missile system was first deployed by the SAS offensively during the campaign to retake the Falkland Islands. Although only one aircraft was shot down using the system, its effectiveness was later proved by the Mujahedeen in Afghanistan. Armed with a limited number of CIA-supplied Stingers, they were able to destroy a large number of Soviet helicopters and force a complete re-evaluation of enemy tactics. Stinger fires a heat-seeking missile to a maximum range of 8000m (five miles) and is fitted with an IFF (Identification Friend or Foe) system which allows it positively to identify its targets, a crucial factor for special forces units working in close conjunction with friendly air forces.

Mortars have always been used by the SAS as a means of providing indirect fire support. The 51mm mortar can be carried and operated by one man, can fire an HE bomb to a range of 750m (2461ft), and can drastically increase a patrol's fire-power. The heavier and more powerful 81mm was used with great success on Pebble Island, and can fire an average of eight rounds of high-explosive rounds per minute to a maximum range of 5660m (3.5 miles).

THE STEYR AUG

New assault rifles themselves can be force multipliers especially if they pack more punch for the same weight. One such rifle is the Steyr AUG 5.56mm bullpup assault rifle, which has been adopted by the Australian SAS and is rapidly becoming a favourite with the British SAS.

Capable of putting down semi- or full-automatic fire, the Steyr is accurate, reliable and durable in all conditions (something which the M16 is not). In addition, it can be fitted with a three-round burst option, and can be turned into anything from a sub-machine gun to a light support weapon by swapping parts. It is extremely light, easy to maintain and has a clear magazine to show the user at a glance the number of rounds remaining.

GRENADE LAUNCHERS

Grenade launchers are now a favourite with special forces units worldwide, including the SAS, for a number of reasons. First, they can throw a projectile over a distance of up to 1600m (5248ft). Second, they fire fragmentation projectiles, which means they can lay down a large amount of firepower at a moment's notice. For SAS patrols this can be a godsend if they are ambushed.

However, there are a number of disadvantages with regard to grenade launchers. The grenade itself, for example, travels in a straight line, unlike one which is thrown by hand, which means it cannot go around cover. In addition, the grenade itself is around two-thirds fuse, which means the effect when it hits the target at the other end is not as great as one would imagine. Far more serious is that the grenades themselves lack punch against enemy bunkers and other strongpoints.

Despite all these problems, grenade launchers are significant force multipliers for vulnerable foot patrols, and in the M203 the SAS has a weapon that is compact and can be fitted beneath the barrel of an assault rifle. Weighing only 1.63kg (3.6lb), it was originally developed to overcome the problem with the M79 grenade launcher, which was a dedicated weapon. But with an M203 attached to every M16, an SAS four-man patrol has a substantial increase in overall firepower as well as an anti-armour capacity.

Of course the weapons themselves are only one part of the equation when it comes to explaining why SAS soldiers are

Left: The British 81mm mortar, which has been used by SAS teams, both at Mirbat and on Pebble Island, is a potent weapon.

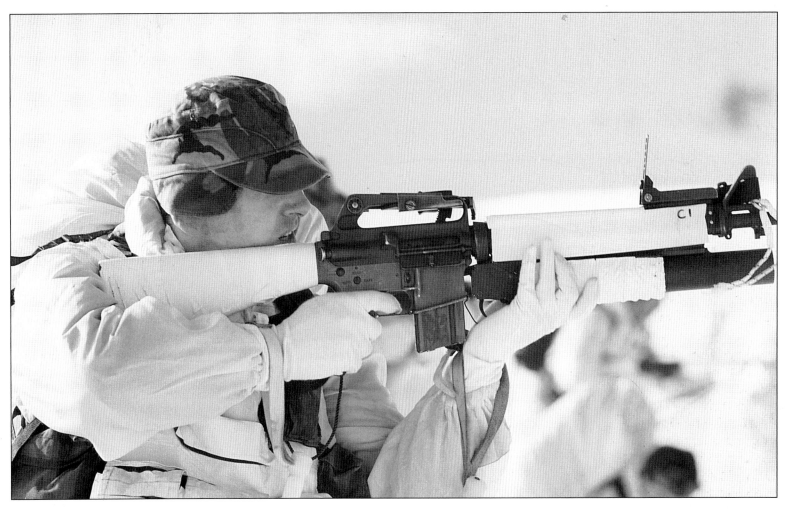

Above: The 40mm M203 grenade launcher, seen here attached to an M16 assault rifle, is an excellent force multiplier.

so good at weapons skills. As well as the hundreds of hours on the ranges and in the 'Killing House' firing thousands of rounds perfecting handling drills and marksmanship, SAS soldiers also learn the other skills associated with handling firearms, such as always keeping the weapon within arm's reach (the first few seconds of a contact decide the outcome), keeping it meticulously clean and learning how to deal with jams and stoppages. Being able to draw, aim and fire a 14-round Browning High Power magazine in under three seconds is proof, if proof were needed, that it is not so much the weapon that matters (the High Power has been in service since 1935), but the soldier who is firing it.

Right: The 84mm Carl Gustav anti-tank weapon is rather unwieldy for foot patrols, as this photograph illustrates.

THE FOUR-MAN PATROL

The Fundamental Unit

The SAS four-man patrol is one of the most effective special forces units in the world. It has evolved since World War II to become a self-contained, flexible formation that is filled with multi-skilled individuals capable of undertaking a wide variety of tasks.

The four-man patrol team has been the fundamental operational unit of the Regiment since 22 SAS was re-formed in the early 1950s. A small, completely self-contained unit, it forms the linchpin of the modern SAS. The four-man patrol, like the SAS itself, owes its existence to the vision of one man: David Stirling.

David Stirling had volunteered for Commando duty in the Middle East, and in the summer of 1941 had been injured in a disastrous parachute jump. During the period of forced inactivity which followed he had hatched the basic idea of the Special Air Service. Before this, though, he taken part in a number of ineffectual large-scale raids on the North African coast.

THEORY OF THE FOUR-MAN PATROL

He argued that five- (not four-) man teams of highly trained commandos could carry out strategic raids behind enemy lines on vulnerable targets such as airfields, vehicle parks, fuel dumps and lines of communication. His memo that he wrote while recovering in hospital stated: 'The scale on which the Commando raids are planned, i.e. the number of troops employed on the one hand and the scale of equipment and facilities on the other, prejudices surprise beyond all possible compensating advantages in respect of the defensive and aggressive striking power afforded. Moreover, the Navy has to provide ships to lift the force, which results in the risking of valuable naval units out of all proportion even to a suc-

cessful raid. It follows that 200 properly selected and equipped men, organised into these sub-units, will be able to attack up to 10 different objectives at the same time on the same night as compared to only one objective using the current Commando technique.'

He believed that SAS patrols could be inserted by parachute or, in coastal areas, by small boats launched from submarines. Because of their size the patrols would be difficult to detect, and would demand none of the massive logistics required of the larger, more orthodox Commando raids of which he had been a part. Stirling's teams would thus be able to attack a multitude of targets behind the lines simultaneously, as opposed to only one objective using the conventional commando method.

The first operation was a disaster. Due to adverse weather aircraft became lost, and many of the men who parachuted in were swept away. However, matters quickly improved, and between December 1941 and December 1942 SAS raids in North Africa destroyed hundreds of Axis aircraft on the ground, plus a number of supply depots, workshops and countless enemy vehicles.

SUCCESS IN NORTHWEST EUROPE

After operations on the Italian mainland, the SAS returned to England in 1944. After D-Day (6 June 1944) a number of strategic operations were carried out behind enemy lines, with reconnaissance parties operating within 80km (50 miles) of the advancing Allied armies. In the four months following D-Day a total of 43

Right: The four-man patrol is the smallest SAS operational unit and the cornerstone of the Regiment's art of war.

operations were conducted by the SAS. Although a few operations failed, the results achieved by most were out of all proportion to the manpower involved. Trains were derailed, vital supplies were destroyed and targets indicated for RAF bombing raids.

REFINING THE FOUR-MAN PATROL

Although the size of the SAS operational groups varied according to their individual mission, the concept of the four-man team gradually evolved within them. Four men came to be considered the optimum number for a variety of reasons. A patrol of less than four men was considered too vulnerable. It would be limited in its carrying capacity and firepower, would have difficulty in defending itself if attacked, and would almost certainly be rendered unoperational should one of its number be killed or wounded. Conversely, a patrol of more than four men might become unwieldy, and would certainly be harder to conceal from the enemy.

There were, in addition, extremely good psychological reasons for four-man patrolling. Soldiers are taught the 'buddy-buddy' principle from the earliest stages of their training, and will almost instinctively pair up to perform the majority of tactical and domestic tasks. Not only will a soldier instinctively offer mutual support to his 'oppo', but he will happily share the more mundane duties of brewing up, cooking meals, erecting a basha (as the SAS call their shelters), and camouflaging it thereafter.

PSYCHOLOGY OF THE PATROL

Soldiers who have trained and operated together for a long period grow to know each other's strengths and weaknesses, to call on the former and to compensate for the latter. Above all, they bond and gain absolute confidence in their partner, a factor crucial to the success of any special forces operation.

The concept of the SAS four-man patrol was refined and expanded during the Malayan 'Emergency'. In 1950, after

Right: Each SAS troop is made up of four four-man patrols, with each soldier being trained in at least one SAS patrol skill.

two years of stalemate during which conventionally trained British soldiers made little impact on the communist insurgents, Brigadier 'Mad Mike' Calvert was tasked with raising a force to take the war to the enemy.

A staff officer at Headquarters Far East and a former wartime commander of the since-disbanded 1st SAS Brigade, Calvert was a true disciple of David Stirling. He subjected his new all-volunteer force, known as the Malayan Scouts, to an exhausting training programme, much of which was planned by John Woodhouse, who was later to organise SAS Selection and Continuation training in Britain. It was from this somewhat unlikely beginning that 22 SAS Regiment was born in 1952. Mike Calvert was invalided out of Malaya that year and was replaced by John Sloane, an orthodox soldier who brought discipline to the new Regiment.

However, the concept of the four-man patrol survived, and was quickly developed to meet the challenges of counter-insurgency (COIN) warfare. The skills of each man were honed to enable him to fight and survive in the harsh jungle environment, while winning over the hearts and minds of a potentially hostile indigenous population.

During the Malayan campaign, the Regiment perfected its jungle operations.

It honed to a peak the arts of navigation, camouflage and survival. It learned preventative medicine and how to deal with various tropical diseases; and learned tracking from the Iban and Dyak tribesmen, some of them former headhunters brought as trackers from Borneo.

Above all, the SAS learned the need to win the trust and affection of the local people. Initially this involved such minor steps as ceasing to call the Malays 'sakai', or slaves. Later it developed into the implementation of a large-scale medical programme designed to eradicate malaria and tuberculosis, both curable diseases prevalent among the tribespeople.

Conversing with the natives in their own tongue became essential, and it quickly became the norm for a language specialist to be included in each four-man patrol. Not only could he gain the trust of the local population, making intelligence gathering far easier, but could assist the squad medic in his attempts to introduce basic health education to the more primitive villages.

SAS patrols often remained in the jungle for weeks on end, and quickly learned from experience how much ammunition and supplies to carry. It was discovered, for instance, that too much ammunition often resulted in its being expended wastefully, whereas much less would be

of Kuala Lumpur, D Squadron, under the command of Major Thompson, was given the dangerous task of searching out and destroying a guerrilla group under the command of the notorious Ah Hoi, nicknamed the 'Baby-Killer'. The squadron parachuted into the area, and through a combination of surprise and expert tracking achieved complete success.

One of the finest trackers of the day was a Yorkshireman, Sergeant Turnbull, who was also fluent in Malay and had excellent weapon skills. By the time that the campaign reached its successful conclusion in 1958 and the SAS was able to withdraw for a well-earned if short rest, men such as Turnbull had come to epitomise the ideal SAS patrol member.

INDIVIDUAL SKILLS

SAS patrol skills evolved over a period of time and will be examined in detail in the next section, but what individual qualities do SAS need as members of a four-man team? Being able to fire personal weapons accurately is a prerequisite, as is proficiency at ambush fire control procedures, contact drills, fire and movement when breaking contact, and shooting at night.

Individual navigation skills must also be of a high standard. Every member of the patrol is expected to be able to navigate using the minimum of natural and artificial aids. SAS troopers are taught basic map reading skills such as setting a map by inspection, use of the prismatic compass and to use compass bearings and the distance marched method (pacing) to reach a given destination either in daylight or in the dark. In addition, skills such as how to manufacture a compass from a needle or a razor blade are usually taught during Continuation Training.

Because there are only four men in the patrol, each member can end up carrying a back-breaking load. Personal equipment includes weapon, bergen and belt kit.

The SAS patrol codenamed 'Bravo Two Zero' that went behind Iraqi lines during the 1991 Gulf War was composed of two four-man patrols from B

used to greater effect, because soldiers were less physically exhausted and therefore more alert. As with most things in the Regiment, it was a process of evolution and learning from past mistakes.

INSERTING PATROLS

Patrols were often inserted by air. Initially each trooper jumped into deep jungle carrying 30m (97ft) of rope knotted every 450mm (18in). Once the jumper crashed through the top jungle canopy his 'chute was caught, leaving him hanging below the canopy. He then climbed down the rope hand over hand until safely on the ground. Later a crude form of lowering device was evolved based on a mountaineer's abseiling gear. Although this considerably reduced fatigue a number of snags were experienced.

In January 1953, as part of Operation 'Eagle', men of B Squadron successfully jumped into primary jungle with an abseiling device with a 73m (240ft) lowering line made of 45mm (1.75in) webbing with a 450kg (1000lb) breaking strain. However, three fatalities occurred in January 1954 when the equipment malfunctioned when used again as part of Operation 'Sword'. Further developments were introduced, and six months later a much improved system was used in Operation 'Termite', when 177 officers

and troopers were dropped into the Perak jungle with only four minor casualties.

'Tree jumping', although highly dangerous, was continued, even when the Regiment's new commander, Lieutenant-Colonel Oliver Brooke, was himself injured during a descent.

The highest standards of patrolling were demanded of the SAS. A patrol's top speed in the jungle was about 1.5km (one mile) an hour, although this 'rapid' rate of progress was discouraged as excessive since it might mean missing vital clues as to the passage of enemy forces. Slow, cautious, quiet, observant movement was preferred. Tracking in the swamps and jungles which comprised much of Malaya was particularly exhausting, requiring concentrated and constant observation, made more difficult by the heavy rains which all too often destroyed all traces of the trail.

Food supply was always a limiting factor for the duration of foot patrols. However, when a special 7-14 day SAS ration pack was introduced, which provided enough food for one man for a fortnight or for two men for a week, this became less of a problem.

The results of deep covert patrolling were often spectacular. In the spring of 1958, during an operation near Telok Anson, some 45km (28 miles) northwest

Right: SAS soldiers in Malaya in the 1950s. During this conflict the Regiment's patrol skills were expanded and refined.

Squadron. The personal equipment for the patrol was as follows: two weeks' supply of food and water; spare batteries for the radio, first aid kit containing suture kit, pain killers, rehydrate, antibiotics, scalpel blades and two syrettes of morphine; and belt kit containing ammunition in pouches, water, emergency food, survival kit, shell dressings, knife and prismatic compass.

The weapons, of course, also had to be carried. Four men carried M16 assault rifles with M203 grenade launchers, with 10 magazines of M16 ammunition plus 200 rounds each of Minimi ammunition. The other four had Minimis and carried 600 rounds for their weapons. Each man in the patrol also carried one 66mm LAW. The load came to an incredible 100kg (220lb) per man.

STRENGTH AND STAMINA

Carrying such a load meant that each man had to have massive reserves of stamina. This is the reason for the Regiment's stringent entry requirements. Unlike other special forces units around the world, the SAS does not accept direct entrants. Volunteers must have had prior military service, and then must pass Selection and Continuation. Fitness, endurance and mental toughness are all essential qualities which must be possessed by SAS soldiers if they are to become effective members of a four-man patrol. In conventional, larger formations, lazy or incompetent soldiers can hide, but there is nowhere to hide in an SAS unit.

Today's SAS four-man patrol is a self-contained unit which, like most of David Stirling's ideas, has withstood the test of time and many different theatres of war. SAS patrols were just as effective against the Iraqis in 1991 as they were against the *Afrika Korps* in North Africa in World War II. And the reason they are successful is the blend of skills within each patrol.

Right: An SAS four-man patrol in Malaya. Both Mike Calvert and John Woodhouse made the four-man unit much more flexible.

Patrol Skills

Each SAS four-man patrol member has his own patrol skill, either signalling, medicine, demolitions or languages. The combination of these skills allows a four-man team to become a self-contained unit in which these skills allow it to operate at maximum effectiveness.

SAS soldiering requires the highest state of physical and mental toughness. Malayan veterans Mike Calvert and John Woodhouse realised from the outset the need for supreme physical fitness, allied to mental alertness, and ensured that SAS Selection tested the applicant's ability not only to keep going, but to remain motivated well beyond the bounds of conventional human endurance. Though the criteria for Selection have changed somewhat in the last four decades, the basic principles have stayed the same, and the ability of the individual to remain a viable member of his patrol whatever the circumstances remains paramount.

Every patrol member has his own speciality, be it signals, demolitions, medicine or languages. All members of the Regiment are trained in communications to at least Regimental Signaller standard (that attained by the communications team

Left: As well as being trained in at least one patrol skill, SAS soldiers are also well versed in a wealth of other skills.

attached to an infantry battalion headquarters), in Morse transmission and ciphers. In addition to this general knowledge, each four-man patrol has its own specialist signaller, responsible for calling in aerial re-supply, casualty evacuation, target indication and exfiltration.

Patrols will keep in regular contact with their base, using voice or, in areas of difficult radio communication, Morse. High-speed transmissions will be used where the enemy is thought to have radio direction-finding equipment, or where signal-bursts of more than a few seconds might compromise the covert nature of the patrol itself.

MEDICINE AND 'HEARTS AND MINDS'

Arguably the most important patrol skill is medicine. Not only can the patrol-medic perform minor surgery if required, he is also an asset in the battle for the 'hearts and minds' of the population of the areas in which he operates (an SAS concept in which SAS soldiers attempt to gain the trust of the local inhabitants and then win them over to their side). In Malaya, for example, many of the more primitive aborigines had never seen a white man, and were naturally suspicious and hostile. The work of the medics in treating their tuberculosis, malaria and other illnesses did much to win them over to the SAS. Invaluable intelligence followed from the politically naive tribesmen, not because they hated (or even understood) the political aspirations of the communist insurgents, but because the SAS had won their trust.

In 1970 Lieutenant-Colonel Johnny Watts, then commanding 22 SAS, introduced the policy of 'hearts and minds' to the Oman. That year Sultan Qaboos bin

Said, a Sandhurst-trained Anglophile, overthrew his father in a bloodless coup and invited the British to assist him in preventing a group of Marxist-inspired guerrillas in the southern province of Dhofar and Yemen taking over his state.

Watts introduced an intelligence cell to monitor the activities and test the reaction of his enemy. He created an information team to counter their propaganda and to advise the locals of the very real gains to be made from siding with the government. He brought doctors and SAS paramedics to the villages to inoculate the tribesmen and their families against preventable, but to them previously lethal, diseases, and introduced veterinary teams to tend to their livestock (which was a masterstroke – Dhofaris are very attached to their livestock).

For several months four-man SAS teams lived with the local Dhofari tribesmen, many of whom were 'turned' rebels, gaining their trust and in many cases their admiration. Later, Watts established permanent bases on the Jebel Dhofar itself, a mountainous area previously considered safe by the rebels. From there SAS teams undertook a policy of aggressive patrolling, on one occasion fighting a 12-day battle and killing at least nine enemy before withdrawing.

The expertise of individual SAS soldiers in Oman, coupled with the Sultan's modernisation scheme, proved to be successful and led ultimately to the wholesale disintegration of the insurgents' campaign. The medical skills of the SAS had indeed reaped rewards (it is important to note that the provision of SAS medical facilities is a genuine attempt to improve the locals' quality of life, as opposed to cynical manipulation).

On operations it is essential that a patrol is not forced to abort its mission when a member is injured. All SAS troopers are therefore taught a secondary patrol

Above: Signalling is one of the four SAS patrol skills, and is crucial to relaying intelligence back to friendly headquarters.

skill, and great emphasis is placed on cross-training. The Regiment's troops, usually commanded by a captain, form the basis of the SAS's extensive special forces combat skills. Each of 22 SAS Regiment's four 'Sabre' Squadrons (A, B, D and G) is itself made up of four 16-man troops, each with its own specialist role: Boat Troop (amphibious warfare); Mobility Troop (Land Rovers and other vehicles, especially for desert operations); Air Troop (parachuting); and Mountain Troop (mountaineering and winter warfare operations).

Ideally, each SAS trooper is cross-trained in at least one other patrol specialisation and a secondary troop skill. Thus he may be a specialist linguist and paramedic, having trained primarily with his squadron's Boat Troop. He would then be ideally suited to a mission requiring both his personal and troop skills, such as a 'hearts and minds' operation in a coastal area in which he might be called upon to give medical advice to primitive tribespeople in their own language.

A second trooper might be a signals and demolition specialist from his squadron's Air Troop. Capable of military freefall (MFF) parachute deployment, he would be able to use his high altitude, low opening (HALO) or high altitude, high opening (HAHO) skills to drop covertly from a high-flying aircraft close to an enemy key point, which he would then be able to neutralise using his demolitions and explosives skills.

The four-man patrol is designed to operate primarily on its own, often in remote areas, and frequently behind enemy lines. It must be completely self-sufficient, and as well as performing routine reconnaissance and patrolling missions to the highest standards, must be able to undertake intelligence, sabotage and ambush missions if so ordered. The four-man patrol is not in itself an aggressive fighting or combat patrol, although it is very capable of extracting itself from danger if attacked. Large-scale ambushes are normally conducted by either half or complete troops, comprising eight or 16 personnel.

'TRAIN HARD, FIGHT EASY'

Nowhere is the maxim 'train hard, fight easy' more adhered to than in the SAS. Basic patrol skills and personal specialisations are honed to perfection by rigorous training and extensive experience. Complacency is never tolerated; there is simply no such thing as a fully trained trooper. Where possible four-man patrols train for a mission together, not just to perfect individual skills but also to learn to gel as a team. 'Lofty' Large, an SAS veteran of northern Oman and the campaigns in the Far East, puts it thus: 'Complete, unwavering trust in each other is essential to any patrol on operations.'

Only by trusting each other will each member of a patrol feel safe in giving his best, secure in the knowledge that he is in the company of three experts upon whom he can rely for his life. Occasionally patrols will be asked to undertake relatively short but extremely dangerous

Right: The disadvantage of SAS four-man patrols is that each patrol member can be weighed down with a lot of equipment.

operations, such as behind the lines in Iraq during the 1991 Gulf War. At other times they will be asked to undertake patrols deep into the jungle, with no contact with the outside world for up to three months. Whatever the mission, it is essential that internal friction is never allowed to surface. One of the founding principles of the SAS, as laid down by David Stirling, that all ranks should possess humour and humility, ensures that SAS men are not arrogant prima donnas.

SAS CROSS-TRAINING

Occasionally an SAS patrol will be tasked with specialist reconnaissance and intelligence gathering. This may include collecting geological information on the state of a river bed, selecting sites for a rendezvous (RV), establishing potential gun positions or ambush sites or identifying safe helicopter landing zones. It is imperative that such a patrol is able to pin-point its position precisely.

Unlike a reconnaissance patrol, which rarely exceeds four men in strength, a standing patrol may vary from a four-man team to in excess of a troop, dependent upon its role. It may be designed to warn of an enemy's advance, prevent cross-bor-

der infiltration, protect a key point or vulnerable area, or direct fire onto the enemy from friendly artillery guns or ground-attack aircraft.

Since its formation, 22 SAS has gained considerable experience in border protection. In January 1963 A Squadron, under the command of Major John Edwardes, was posted to Borneo to help secure the border with neighbouring Indonesia. A total of 21 patrols were spread out along the 1500km (930-mile) border. The border itself was difficult to define, but A Squadron were aided by two factors: first, because of the terrain there were only a limited number of crossing points; and second, the local tribesmen provided the patrols with excellent intelligence.

PATROL SKILLS IN BORNEO

The tried-and-tested policy of 'hearts and minds' and the skills possessed by four-man patrols proved highly successful in Borneo. After keeping a village under observation to establish where its allegiance lay, patrols would visit and speak with the headman. They would then move back to their jungle hideout, and return a day or a week later to pick up where they had left off. Visits were never hurried, and the business of establishing friendships never rushed. Once a mutual respect was established, the tribesmen

often provided food, shelter, transport and trackers, and the patrols reciprocated with gifts, medical treatment and, occasionally, construction work. One patrol member, Gipsy Smith, even constructed an improvised hydro-electric generator in one village, and is reputed to have built a still in another, although this has always been denied by official sources!

FIGHTING PATROLS

The local natives proved so invaluable, and provided such key intelligence, that the SAS was soon able to mount fighting patrols against Indonesian insurgents. Fighting patrols tend to be larger than reconnaissance patrols, and may comprise two four-man teams or even an entire troop. Their primary tasks are to harass the enemy, to raid for intelligence and prisoners for interrogation, to neutralise key targets and to protect friendly forces from attack.

In Borneo the SAS often operated as guides for much larger fighting patrols drawn from the 14,000 conventional British and Gurkha troops in the area. In late 1964, the SAS was given permission to carry out secret cross-border operations. Four-man reconnaissance patrols would penetrate Indonesian territory up to a distance of 10km (six miles). Ambush patrols would then be sent out to cover

the trails and rivers used by the Indonesians to catch the enemy unawares when he thought he was still safe.

Although aggressive operations invariably demand larger numbers, the four-man patrol remains the most versatile for intelligence gathering. During the 1982 Falklands campaign, and later in 1991 in the Gulf, small SAS reconnaissance patrols were extremely active, providing military commanders with vital and accurate information as to the disposition of enemy forces.

Patrolling is always divided into three parts: rehearsal, execution and de-briefing. Where possible the patrol commander is given at least a day to prepare, make his plan, brief his team and conduct a daylight or night-time rehearsal. Ideally he will supplement his map with recent aerial photographs and current intelligence reports, and may even over-fly the area.

PATROL TACTICS

Once the patrol commander has sorted out the equipment he will ensure that it is tested thoroughly. Radios and batteries will be checked, ammunition cleaned and weapons test-fired, grenades will be primed and rations drawn. Each patrol member will take responsibility for his own personal and specialist kit, while the commander will check the specific-to-task equipment, dividing it equally among the patrol members while ensuring that each knows what the others are carrying.

Each individual will carry his personal weapon, a bergen and belt kit. He will carry spare ammunition for his personal weapon, water, emergency rations and an escape tin with his survival aids on his belt. If the patrol is compromised and forced to withdraw in a hurry he will then have the option of discarding his bergen while retaining sufficient material to survive on his belt. In addition, the patrol commander will carry more detailed maps (which he will take care not to mark), navigational equipment, a spare radio and where relevant night-vision goggles.

Left: Medicine, one of the patrol skills, is useful not only for treating other patrol members, but also for 'hearts and minds'.

The patrol's order of march will depend on a number of factors, but will usually comprise the lead scout followed by the commander and signaller, with the second-in-command (2IC) acting as 'tail end Charlie'. Conventional patrol formations will be used. The team will proceed in single file or diamond formation depending on the light, the ground and the proximity of the enemy. In jungle, for example, single file is best.

The lead scout, who in addition to his personal equipment may also carry a night-vision aid, wire cutters and perhaps an M203 grenade launcher, is responsible for ensuring that the route chosen is not booby-trapped, while maintaining the required route and speed.

Patrolling requires high levels of concentration. 'Lofty' Large again: 'They must keep their eyes open to left and right for any sign of problems, and make sure the man behind is still where he should be. They must keep in sight of the man in front but must remain far enough back not to be caught in the same burst of automatic fire, mine or booby trap. In a contact with the enemy they must react instantly, guided by the actions of the man in front of him, or what happens to him.'

CONTACT DRILLS

Each man will keep in visual contact, communicating through a series of hand signals. As the patrol progresses rendezvous will be allocated by the commander. If the patrol is attacked its members will break off, returning independently to the last rendezvous where they will re-form and carry on with the mission.

An SAS four-man patrol needs slick contact drills to survive an encounter. The Regiment has therefore devised a number of procedures to increase a patrol's chances of survival. The head-on contact drill is one such tactic.

If a patrol is 'bumped' by the enemy, patrol members instantly flank left and right to get themselves into positions from where they can direct fire at the enemy without hitting their comrades. If the patrol is advancing in file, for example, and the lead scout makes contact, then the other patrol members will break left and right to bring their weapons to

Above: For SAS four-man patrols operating behind enemy lines, camouflage and concealment skills are imperative.

bear on the enemy. If the enemy force is destroyed in the contact, then the patrol may wish to continue, but if the men wish to withdraw then two patrol members will lay down covering fire while the other two withdraw some distance. These will cover the withdrawal of the other two, and so on (SAS patrols have no interest in holding ground).

'Shoot and scoot' is another patrol tactic. Designed by John Woodhouse as a way of preventing casualties, when a patrol is fired upon it returns a barrage of fire, then, while the enemy is trying to work out what is going on, 'scoots' to an emergency rendezvous, with each trooper taking a different route to confuse the enemy. Any SAS casualties have to make their own way to the rendezvous.

The four-man patrol has stood the test of time, and has proved itself in many different types of terrain, from the frozen wastes of the Falklands to the sands of the Middle East. There can be little doubt that the four-man patrol, as envisaged by David Stirling, will continue to form the core of SAS operational thinking for many years to come.

The five-man patrol

The Australian SAS employs the five-man patrol as its smallest operational unit. The Australians' experience in Vietnam revealed that five men were better for them. In a contact, for example, they did not like the idea of any wounded making their way back to an emergency rendezvous. Instead, they preferred the other patrol members to carry them to the rendezvous. But this reduced a four-man's patrol firepower to just two weapons. In such circumstances the patrol might not be able to break contact, let alone make it to the rendezvous, especially if the enemy attempts to out-flank the patrol (which lightly armed and equipped Viet Cong guerrillas did in Vietnam). Obviously the additional patrol member means that its firepower is slightly more than its British counterpart. Australian patrol skills include tracking, which is geared towards the terrain of northern Australia and the islands off the north coast.

BEHIND THE LINES

Intelligence Gathering

The SAS's wartime role is primarily one of gathering intelligence behind enemy lines by using small self-contained groups which observe the enemy from concealed 'hides'. The work is uncomfortable and very dangerous, but is strategically vital to the war effort.

The SAS was devised by David Stirling in World War II specifically to serve behind enemy lines, and this task remains integral to the Regiment's operational *raison d'être*. In a conventional conflict, SAS teams can be inserted behind the lines to cause maximum disruption through raids, sabotage and ambushes. However, they primarily act as intelligence gatherers, and where relevant assist in the organisation of resistance groups and escape lines. SAS teams are trained to strike at the enemy's relatively lightly defended rear areas and main supply routes (MSRs), often returning to underground 'hides' to avoid detection. Mission over, they will attempt to 'escape and evade' through the enemy front line to the safety of their own forces.

Operating behind the lines requires specialist skills and individual qualities. Despite the 'glamour' of such actions as the Pebble Island Raid in the Falklands War, when an SAS team raided an Argentine airstrip and destroyed the aircraft there, the SAS is expected to provide specialist reconnaissance units to provide a constant stream of accurate and timely intelligence.

MISSION PARAMETERS

SAS teams must be capable of operating for long periods with little or no support, and in close proximity to the enemy. Working in four-man units, they are equipped with long-range communications equipment to allow them to keep up a flow of timely and accurate intelligence back to commanders at corps level or above.

As stated above, the primary role of these SAS teams is not one of being a combat soldier. To be effective they must remain hidden from the enemy. Their role is to observe, identify and communicate what they see. This naturally demands superb fieldcraft skills. If a team has to move it does so at night.

Like most things concerning the SAS, the purely intelligence-gathering role has evolved over time. Though David Stirling always envisaged the SAS having a strategic role, he originally cast it in the deep-raiding role.

Targets in North Africa in 1941-43 varied according to circumstances, but included airfields, headquarters, workshops, command, control and communications (C3) centres, vehicle parks and supply dumps. Traditionally such targets have offered themselves as easy targets to a regiment keen and able to live up to its motto 'Who Dares Wins'. In November 1941, for example, during the North African campaign, SAS teams carried out four weeks of coastal raiding, destroying large quantities of trucks and their cargoes. By 1943 the Regiment had expanded its area of interest to incorporate Italy and the Balkans, infiltrating singly or in groups from the air and by boat, to arm and train local partisan groups. Almost single-handedly Ambrose McGonegal, later to become a Northern Ireland High Court judge, operating in the hostile mountains of central Yugoslavia, turned a disparate and highly suspicious rabble into a coherent fighting force.

BEHIND THE LINES IN EUROPE

The SAS was heavily involved in the Northwest European campaign. Between D-Day (6 June 1944) and the end of November 1944, the SAS organised some 780 air drops and supply sorties of which 600 were successful. Most supply drops took place from heights of less than 100m (328ft), with six aircraft being lost in the process. Of the 2000 SAS participants, 330 became casualties. Enemy killed or severely wounded numbered 7753; 4764 were taken prisoner and 18,000 cut off. Motor vehicles destroyed numbered 7600, with 29 locomotives and 89 railway goods wagons. German-controlled railways were cut in 164 places.

Such actions clearly irritated Hitler who, in response to raids undertaken by British Commando units in North Africa,

Left: The SAS is a unit which specialises in gathering intelligence by using small groups deep behind enemy lines.

Left: The CH-47 Chinook twin-rotor helicopter, which is frequently used for inserting SAS teams behind the lines.

establish the feasibility and report back. If the SAS gets permission to proceed, the 'Kremlin' will begin the preparation of detailed plans for ultimate submission to the proposed sortie commander.

The intelligence required to make an assessment is gleaned from a number of agencies, including several American and West European sources. Satellite and aerial reconnaissance photographs will be studied in detail, as will press reports, radio stations (from the Government Communications Headquarters at Cheltenham), bulletins and debrief reports from political opposition groups and dissidents from the target country. In the area of Counter Revolutionary Warfare (CRW) operations, the SAS will liaise closely with a number of further agencies both within NATO and other friendly non-aligned intelligence services. These will include a number of overt and covert counter-intelligence groups, such as Italy's NOCS, Germany's GSG 9 and America's CIA and FBI.

Once an operation has been planned, it will be discussed fully with all the proposed participants. Not all plans are well

issued his infamous 'Commando Order'. This gave them licence to execute any captured members of such units, including the SAS: 'I therefore order that from now on all opponents...in so-called Commando operations...are to be exterminated to the last man in battle or flight...Even should these, on their being discovered, make as if to surrender, all quarter is to be denied on principle.' In France in 1944, many captured soldiers were handed over to the Gestapo because of the order, after which they were executed as terrorists.

Not all SAS raids were successful. During Operation 'Bulbasket', which took place between 6 June and 7 July 1944, 55 men from 1 SAS under the command of Captain Tonkin were dropped in the area of Chateauroux. Initially all went well, the railway was cut in some 12 places while 20 casualties were inflicted on the enemy. Success, however, turned to tragedy when the SAS base was compromised by unknown elements of the local population (security among the French Resistance, the *Maquis*, was notoriously lax). The base was subsequently attacked, resulting in 37 casualties, of whom 33 were captured and executed.

Right: One of the most important aspects of working behind the lines is the ability to infiltrate unseen into hostile territory.

Modern operations mounted by the SAS require a very high level of prior planning and preparation. The SAS's Operational Intelligence (OP/INT) cell, based at Stirling Lines in Hereford, is responsible for the collation and timely dissemination of relevant intelligence to the operational planners. If an operation is anticipated, the Director Special Forces (DSF), based in London, will task the Op/Int cell (known as the 'Kremlin') to

Left: Some of the SAS soldiers of Operation 'Bulbasket', photographed behind German lines in France in June 1944.

at the time, the participation of the SAS was unheralded.

The SAS system of covert operations has changed little in 50 years; the target will be identified, a plan formulated and agreed, a force will be inserted to infiltrate the target and finally, if an attack is required, will assault using surprise coupled with intense speed and maximum available firepower before withdrawing to an agreed rendezvous (RV) to begin the often difficult process of exfiltration. Once behind enemy lines, the standard operational procedures (SOPs) for SAS patrols are, in theory at least, relatively simple. Yet their execution places a great strain upon the personal resources of the soldiers taking part. They must keep constantly alert, endeavouring to move as silently as possible without leaving any tell-tale signs. Rubbish, food scraps, and even human waste must be disposed of so as not to give away their presence.

MOVEMENT BEHIND THE LINES

Where possible movement is at night to reduce the possibility of compromise. When travelling through hilly terrain SAS teams, whether on foot or vehicle-borne, will keep clear of ridges to avoid the danger of being skylighted. Bridges, roads and tracks will also be avoided where possible to minimise the danger of mines, booby traps or ambushes, while maps will never be marked, nor even folded in such a way as to suggest the area of patrol interest in the event of patrol members being captured. If agents are to be met during the mission, the rendezvous and passwords will be memorised and never committed to paper.

It will often be necessary to carry heavy loads, yet this must never be allowed to interfere with a patrol's crucial timings. During the night climb prior to the final assault on Jebel Akhdar, for example, Watts found that a few of his men, who were particularly laden, were unable to keep up with the others. Knowing that it was crucial for the main force to be in position for the final assault

received. When, during the Falklands War, the then Director of the SAS, Brigadier Peter de la Billière, approved a plan for a troop to land in Chile, move east into Argentina and attack enemy aircraft on the ground, his plan ran into considerable opposition, so much so that the sortie commander was replaced. The operation was ultimately abandoned for reasons beyond SAS control.

The SAS organisational system, with its four specialist troops within each of its four squadrons, provides the planners with a high degree of flexibility. They can select soldiers with experience of at least one speciality: Mobility, Boat, Mountain or Freefall parachute operations, and with subordinate skills in at least one other. All SAS personnel remain at the peak of fitness, both physical and mental, and can expect to move virtually overnight from one theatre of operations to another if required. In late 1958, for example, Major John Watts and 70 officers and men from D Squadron were moved amid the greatest secrecy from the jungles of Malaya to the mountain wastes of northern Oman, and with little time to acclimatise set about the capture of Jebel Akhdar, the mountain headquarters of the leader of a tribal revolt against the pro-British Sultan. The operation was as successful as, by daybreak, he ordered the stragglers to remain behind, preferring to reduce the size of his force rather than allow it to arrive in position late. In 1970, during a subsequent SAS operation in Oman, patrol members ordered to attack an enemy airfield found themselves moving through rocky terrain on foot in high temperatures. Each man carried 400 rounds of machine gun ammunition around his body, 600 more rounds in his bergen, as well as four SLR magazines for his personal weapon, each holding 20 rounds. In all each trooper carried 40kg (88lb) of weapons and ammunition, in addition to three water bottles, rations and personal kit, yet all made it to the final RV and the assault was successful.

SECURE OPERATIONAL BASES

After insertion the first requirement for an SAS 'Sabre' Squadron is to establish a secure operational base. Usually this process is started by an advance party, although in the case of long operations it may be possible to take over the facilities left by the previous squadron. There are normally two types of base: a headquarters base area, which is often co-located with a major strategic terminal such as a port or airfield and which will be close to the overall command structure, and a forward operational base (FOB), normally sited on or near a tactical landing strip. During the 1991 Gulf War, for example, the SAS's FOB was at Al Jouf near the Iraqi border. By their nature SAS operations are covert, and it is important that the FOB be secure, not just from the enemy but from the prying eyes of allied personnel and the media.

All additional equipment, spare weapons, fuel and ammunition will be flown directly to the FOB as and when required. During the Malayan campaign in the 1950s, Blackburn Beverley aircraft were used to drop supplies to SAS teams operating deep in the jungle. With their range of 2080km (1292 miles) and payload capacity of 20,500kg (45,195lb), the Beverley was an extremely capable aircraft. Today the SAS uses the Lockheed C-130 Hercules transport aircraft. Not only is its payload twice that of the Beverley and its range far greater, it is

capable of in-flight refuelling and, in the hands of an experienced crew, can low-drop pallets with amazing accuracy.

Increasingly helicopters, such as the Boeing MH-47E Special Operations Chinook, will be pressed into service to transport the patrols to and from the FOB. The MH-47E was designed to complete a 5hr 30min covert mission over a range of 556km (345 miles), at low level, day or night, in adverse weather, over all types of terrain, with a 90 per cent probability of success. Capable of operating from ships or land, it features advanced terrain-avoidance/terrain-following radar and a removable air-to-air refuelling probe. It has a troop capacity of up to 44 men, an internal cargo handling system, an on-board oxygen-generating system for the pilot and co-pilot, and provision for two 0.5in heavy machine guns.

Often the SAS will work with other special forces units. The Regiment and the Special Boat Service (SBS), for example, worked in close cooperation during the Falklands War. The islands themselves, situated some 13,000km (8070 miles) from the United Kingdom, are prone to

Right: Just some of the pieces of military kit needed for a long-term observation post inside enemy territory.

Above: Working covertly behind enemy lines demands the highest levels of military professionalism.

extremes of climate. Wet and windy and comprising mostly moorland and rocky hills, they do not easily lend themselves to covert activity. These conditions posed many dangers for the SAS and SBS teams that were put ashore from the beginning of May 1982, not least the hazard of being discovered by enemy patrols and aircraft.

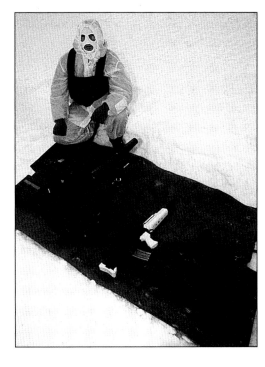

Left: The construction of observation posts requires a thorough understanding of siting, discipline and construction.

Sheer professionalism prevailed, and the SBS was able to set up a number of excellently sited covert hides, some of them under the noses of the enemy.

SAS Captain Aldwin Wight was able to set up an OP on Beaver Ridge, overlooking the capital, Stanley. His four-man team remained in position for 26 days, using burst transmissions to report on helicopter movements from a dispersal area between Mounts Kent and Estacia, destined to become an early (and successful) target for the Fleet Air Arm's Sea Harrier jets. Another patrol positioned itself on a sunken hulk in Stanley harbour, and from there was able to pass invaluable information on shipping activity and on aircraft overflying the capital.

LIFE INSIDE A 'HIDE'

The conditions within the OPs were atrocious, the discomfort being compounded by the constant threat of compromise. The men were permanently cold and wet, movement, talking and cooking during the day was impossible, resulting in aching limbs and frozen bodies. Only at night did the occupants have the chance of a hot meal, and even then they had to be on their guard for the possibility of an enemy patrol sighting their 'hexi' fires or smelling their cooking.

A member of G Squadron describes the daily routine inside a Falklands 'hide': 'If we had a chance for re-supply one of the first things we would request would be thick plastic to line the shallow "hides" we dug. Anything to keep out the bloody wet. The procedure in each team was the same: one man would get his head down while the other kept watch. There would be no movement or talking during the day. At night we would walk to the rear of the position and carefully cut a hole in the peat bog using a foldaway US-issue shovel – this was our latrine.

'It was impossible to cook during the day because the smell might alert a passing Argentinian, if one strayed that close, and so we only had a brew at first light. We would fish out a couple of tins of

Insertion proved the first problem. A landing from a submarine would have been fraught with danger. The coastal waters are shallow, thus forcing any submarine in the area dangerously close to the surface. Given that, at the time, the Argentines enjoyed undisputed control of the air in the region, the chances of a submarine being spotted and depth-charged were considered unacceptably high. Airborne insertion was a possibility, indeed a plan was considered to drop the whole of G Squadron onto the sparsely inhabited southern tip of West Falkland from a C-130 Hercules transport aircraft, but realistic counsel prevailed and ultimately the plan was abandoned as over-ambitious. Helicopters were regarded as more realistic; not only was 846 Squadron within striking distance aboard the carrier HMS *Hermes*, but the inhospitable nature of the area more than countered the problems caused by the noise and relatively slow speed of its Sea Kings.

The role of the SBS was not unlike that traditionally afforded the SAS: their four-man teams were to report on the strength and location of Argentine defences, identify suitable landing sites for the main British force, and find a base where the Royal Marines of 3 Commando Brigade, supported by the Paras of 2 and 3 Parachute Battalions, might establish a

Brigade Maintenance Area. The first SBS team left HMS *Hermes* on 30 April. In absolute darkness the helicopter pilot, who was equipped with night vision glasses, skimmed the sea to avoid radar detection. He headed for the Falkland Sound between the two main islands, and from there south to San Carlos Water. The first SBS team to land was laden with weapons, food and ammunition, and high-powered binoculars, night sights and spare clothing, all essential for operating an observation post (OP) under the eyes of the enemy. Movement was made more difficult by the terrain, the rocks and uncharted bogs slowing progress to a meagre 250m (820ft) an hour, while the constant wind and rain made the experience all the more uncomfortable.

FALKLANDS OPS

Daylight movement was too risky, forcing the Royal Marines to dig camouflaged shell scrapes as dawn approached. This entailed cutting out sods of earth and laying them on chicken wire, then scraping out the uncovered earth to a depth of 500mm (20in), scattering it over a wide area to disguise the fresh soil, and covering the 'hide' with the sods supported by the chicken wire. Each morning great care was taken to ensure that the patrol had left no indication of its earlier occupation.

bacon burgers, or whatever came to hand, and put them in the water we were heating. When they were heated up we took them out and had the food, leaving plenty of water for a brew of tea or coffee.'

OBSERVING THE ENEMY NEAR DARWIN

Being so close to the enemy was dangerous and uncomfortable, but there was a wealth of targets. However, the patrols were there to watch and report, nothing else: 'Our first position was near Darwin, East Falkland, and the forward OP was situated near the edge of an inlet. Little happened at first, but after a few days had passed we logged enemy helicopters buzzing the ground immediately to our front. We stayed there 10 days before we received our first re-supply and fresh orders. The targets were really tasty, and it would have been very easy to take a pot at them, but our role was to sit and watch and that's what we did. Later it emerged that the aircraft we had reported were bringing in troops from Stanley to garrison the Goose Green settlement.'

Living in confined spaces for long periods has a detrimental affect on personal hygiene, as one former SAS soldier who took part in an OP exercise remembers: 'Exfiltration from the operational area was to be by air. The move out was undertaken by Royal Navy helicopters. They came in to pick us up and, as we moved to our helo and jumped in, the RN aircrew physically moved away from us and kept us at arm's length. We couldn't figure out why at the time. We had been out in the field for about five days. We had no idea how disgusting we smelt, because we were used to it. In the shelter, we had to crap and piss into different bags which were then sealed together in a plastic bag. Do both together in the same bag and it is prone to explode. Before the exercise they tended to explode inside the shelter, a problem that has since been ironed out, but you could end up covered in the stuff, with no real way to clear up the mess. We were also hot-bunking, using two sleeping bags between the four

Right: A destroyed village in Bosnia. SAS teams have worked behind Serb lines on behalf of both the UN and NATO.

Behind the lines in Bosnia

The SAS has, and still does, operate in war-torn Bosnia. In 1994, for example, under the direction of UN commander Lieutenant-General Sir Michael Rose, a 10-man SAS team was sent into the Serb-besieged Moslem town of Maglai on 15 March to assess the situation and locate drop zones for US Air Force food drops. When, a few days later, a British relief force drove through Serb lines, SAS forward controllers directed NATO fighter aircraft to provide air cover. The SAS was also used on 6 April at another besieged Moslem town, Gorazde. A seven-man SAS team directed air strikes against Serb positions using laser range finders to pinpoint enemy positions, which were relayed to NATO F-16 fighter aircraft, which then pounded Serb positions. Unfortunately, during their retreat from Gorazde, through Serb lines, one SAS soldier, Corporal Fergus Rennie, was killed. In August 1995 the SAS was in action again, when its men, who had infiltrated Serb lines that ringed Sarajevo, reported the exact location of Serb armour, artillery and anti-aircraft units. When the UN was forced to take action, the intelligence supplied by SAS teams on the ground ensured that the NATO aircraft air strikes which took place on the 30th were deadly accurate.

of us, surrounded by all our kit and with absolutely no room to move. The food was appaling and, probably because of the overriding stench, tasted awful.'

SAS four-man patrols will usually be commanded by a senior non-commissioned officer, or a corporal. A larger patrol will be commanded by a troop leader, usually a captain. Once a base has been established, missions can be mounted. During the Malaya campaign, one patrol

spent 103 consecutive days in the jungle winning the 'hearts and minds' of the local tribesmen while gaining intelligence on enemy movements, its only contact with the outside world being by radio. Such operations are testimony to the skill the Regiment has in operating behind enemy lines. Although the majority of SAS missions involve long-range reconnaissance, the Regiment is also adept at inserting deep-penetration fighting patrols.

Fighting Patrols

Intelligence gathering is one of the most important missions for SAS patrols behind enemy lines. However, as the Regiment's actions from World War II to the Gulf War proved, it is also adept at mounting effective fighting patrols.

Although the main role of SAS teams behind the lines is intelligence gathering, the Regiment will on occasion mount deep-penetration fighting patrols to strike at enemy targets.

During the Borneo campaign, for example, towards the end of 1964, the SAS was given permission to take the offensive by mounting clandestine cross-border operations into Indonesia. Code-named 'Claret', these incursions took the form of reconnaissance missions up to an attributable distance of 10km (6.2 miles) into enemy territory. Intelligence was gathered on a massive scale, but force was used only selectively, causing enough punishment to the front line Indonesian troops to demoralise them yet not enough to provoke their government into escalation. Publicly neither side admitted to this new and bloody phase in the

Confrontation, as adverse reaction might have affected either. To ensure anonymity, SAS troopers carried United States-manufactured Armalite rifles (not then on general British issue), wore non-regulation boots and carried no personal identification. To avoid compromise, the movement on patrol was painfully slow. Patrols would pause for up to twenty minutes after often less than ten minutes' movement to watch and listen intently for anything unusual.

SERGEANT LILLICO'S PATROL

Although the SAS did not seek combat, (unless leading Gurkha fighting patrols to their targets), there were a number of occasions when two- and four-man patrols were forced to shoot their way out of trouble. On an occasion, in February 1965, a small patrol probing an old

Indonesian terrorist camp was itself ambushed. The leading scout, Trooper Thompson, and the second man in the patrol, the leader, Sergeant Lillico, were both hit. As the rest of the patrol went to ground Thompson managed to crawl back to Lillico's position to join him in returning the enemy fire. Thompson, who had shattered a bone in his left thigh and could hardly move, crawled back along the trail, from where he engaged the enemy with a few bursts of fire. Fearing that the bursts represented the arrival of reinforcements, the Indonesians, who had suffered several casualties, temporarily withdrew.

Both men took advantage of the situation. Thompson continued to crawl to where he expected to find the rest of the patrol. He applied a tourniquet, remembering to release it regularly, took morphia and bandaged the wound as best he could. He rested the night, and in the morning continued on his way. He had covered some 1000m (3280ft), about half of the distance to safety, when he was located by a rescue party shortly before last light on the second day. For his part Lillico, who was in a worse physical state, succeeded in pulling himself into cover before collapsing. He rested that night, and during the course of the second day succeeded in dragging himself some 400m (1312ft) to a ridge, from where he was able to fire a burst of signal shots. His shots were immediately answered by a series of automatic bursts from the enemy, from whom he was able to hide until rescued by helicopter that night. For their bravery Lillico was awarded the Military Medal, while Thompson was mentioned in dispatches.

The success of SAS operations behind the lines can often depend upon the abil-

Left: SAS fighting patrols operating behind the lines are invariably equipped with overwhelming firepower.

ity of the patrol to move rapidly from one area to another, both to avoid enemy forces and to hit targets in quick succession. Where possible fighting patrols will infiltrate their targets silently, lay delayed-action charges against key areas and withdraw without being seen, thus enabling them to move to a second target before the enemy has become alerted to their presence. Since the earliest SAS raids in December 1941, the Regiment has used a wide variety of special vehicles for mobile operations.

JEEP RAIDS IN NORTH AFRICA

In North Africa SAS teams used jeeps to attack enemy targets. Fast, highly mobile and very manoeuvrable, the Jeep was originally designed to carry a crew of two, but by 1945 had been substantially modified. Armour plate was strapped to the front of the bonnet to protect the engine, and mounts fitted for two twin Vickers 'K' machine guns, one pointed fore and one aft. In a large patrol every third or fourth vehicle carried a .50in Browning heavy machine gun, while the drivers had easy access to a Bren gun. SAS raiding parties wrought havoc upon enemy supply columns, troop concentrations and headquarters, causing severe destruction in the rear areas. Parked aircraft were a favourite target of Lieutenant-Colonel 'Paddy' Blair Mayne, an Irish former rugby international of larger than life proportions who was reputed personally to have destroyed more than 100 enemy aircraft on the ground.

Modern transport for covert operations includes a variety of special-purpose Land Rovers, modified for long-range activity. These vehicles have now replaced the venerable SAS Land Rover 'Pink Panthers', so-called because they were painted in matt pink camouflage for desert operations.

LAND ROVER FIGHTING PATROLS

The Land Rovers which went behind the lines in Iraq in the 1991 Gulf War were, like their World War II counterparts, heavily armed. The weapons carried on each vehicle included GPMG machine guns, 40mm Mark 19 grenade launchers, Milan anti-tank missile launchers and

Stinger manportable surface-to-air missiles (SAMs).

The Gulf War demonstrated the diversity of covert missions capable of being undertaken by the SAS. Although the number of Iraqi Scud surface-to-surface missiles (SSMs) actually destroyed by the SAS was not high, the fact that the Iraqis were forced to keep constantly on the move did much to reduce their potency.

Despite their heavy armament, SAS mobile fighting columns in the Gulf still had to follow standard operating procedures (SOPs) for operations behind the lines. These included laying-up during the day to reduce the risk of being spotted by the enemy (especially his air force), hit hard and fast and then withdraw quickly to put as much space between themselves and the enemy. That was why the Milan was so popular among the troopers, as one SAS soldier who fought in the Gulf War relates: 'accurate, reliable and has excellent armour-penetration capabilities. It also has an effective range of 2000m [6566ft], which means you don't have to get too close to the opposition to score a direct hit.'

Occasionally an SAS fighting column would break the rules if the risks were acceptable. One such instance was when SAS Land Rovers were sent into enemy territory to destroy an Iraqi listening sta-

Above: An SAS team behind enemy lines on a so-called 'Claret' mission in Indonesian Kalimantan in the mid-1960s.

tion close to the border. One of the men who took part in the mission states what happened: 'The boss wanted everyone to be ready. We were to go in as fast as possible and hit them hard. His orders had been very clear: "If it looks good we'll go straight in and hope that our sand trail doesn't compromise us."

'Travelling fast and furious in a column of Land Rovers is not SAS standard operating procedure – you give your position away and risk falling into an enemy ambush. Nevertheless, we were confident that the odds were in our favour.' The patrol's luck held, and they came across the site some 20 minutes later. Once again the method of attack was with Milan missiles, and the site was totally destroyed.

The SAS normally operates covertly behind the lines, but there are occasions when the Regiment's soldiers will deliberately make the maximum amount of noise and disruption as a diversion for other missions. One such example was during the Falklands War, just prior to the main British landings at San Carlos Water. The SAS and SBS were tasked with mounting a diversionary attack against

concealment and camouflage skills must be first class. From early on in their SAS careers, therefore, troopers are taught the principles of concealment and how to apply them in the field.

On operations SAS bases will be arranged in such a way that they include defensive positions that will absorb any attack. In the 1991 Gulf War, for example, SAS Land Rover columns would deploy in a circle while not on the move to provide all-round defence. The vehicles themselves were hidden under camouflaged netting.

Individual defensive positions are concealed from both the air and the ground. Careful preparation and proper use of the ground results in any attacking enemy being caught unawares, and suffering accordingly. One of the most suitable sites for a defensive position, for example, is on a reverse slope, just behind the crest of a hill, so that direct enemy fire can only be brought to bear once the enemy has crossed the skyline and presented the defender with an ideal target.

CAMOUFLAGING WEAPONS

To blend in naturally with his local environment, an SAS soldier must have highly developed personal concealment skills. To disguise the shape of his equipment and to merge into the background, a trooper will use both artificial and natural aids. The rifle, for example, is one of the most distinctive features carried by the modern soldier on the battlefield. One of the easiest ways of camouflaging it is with paint. In the Falklands, SAS men could often be seen carrying green-painted M16 assault rifles, while in the Gulf their weapons were sand-coloured. Aside from paint, another effective way of distorting the outline of a weapon is by wrapping it with strips of cloth dyed to match the background. Cloth strips can also be used to break up the outline of the barrel, while the magazine, pistol grip and top can be covered with tape.

Fighting patrols in the Gulf War consisted of Land Rover vehicles and motor-

the Argentinians. One of these missions involved 40 men of D Squadron, led by Major Cedric Delves, attacking the enemy garrison in the Darwin/Goose Green area to keep it away from San Carlos. One of those who took part recalls what happened: 'We were sent to keep the opposition's heads down at Goose Green. We knew the Argies had a sizeable garrison there but we didn't know how many. What we did know was that we were heavily outnumbered. Still, we were armed with GPMGs, Milans, grenade launchers, mortars and a Stinger surface-to-air missile. Our orders were to convince the Argies they were being attacked by a whole battalion. We were told to "just blast them", though any close-quarter fighting was out because if we got too close they would suss us. This battle would be from a safe distance.

'We were flown in by Sea Kings, each man carrying a great big load of armaments. We left the choppers and had to trudge 30km (18 miles) to our positions: the low hills to the north of Darwin/Goose Green. We stopped regularly to adjust our bergens, as well as the Milans we were carrying. The weight was unbelievable. I remember thinking it was a good job we were going to fire most of

the ammo because I for one didn't fancy the idea of marching back with it.

'When we reached our position we spaced ourselves out and then the boss gave the signal to open up. The next minute the night sky was illuminated with tracer rounds as the GPMGs began firing. Then the 66mm LAWs streaked across the ground and found their targets, quickly followed by the Milans. The noise was deafening. We would move from spot to spot to give the impression there was a multitude of firing positions. The Argies never knew what hit them. They did return fire, but it was wild and inaccurate and we never took any casualties. God knows how many rounds we fired that night, but the enemy never ventured from their positions and we were well pleased with ourselves.'

After the action the Argentinian garrison reported that they had been attacked by a battalion of British troops, but had prevented them from moving towards the main landing area!

The success of many SAS missions, including fighting patrols, can depend on the ability to remain hidden from the enemy. Stealth and secrecy allow SAS teams to remain concealed until it is too late. However, in order to achieve this end

cycles, which require skilled vehicle camouflage techniques. Ideally when parked the vehicles should be under natural cover, but in Iraq this was not possible, hence the use of netting. However, netting has to be used with care. In snow areas, for example, netting requires excessive maintenance, it cannot support a heavy snow load and, when wet, becomes frozen and bulky, and therefore very difficult to handle.

SAS PRISONERS

Special forces soldiers, by the nature of their employment, are prone to capture. They are often operating against unscrupulous enemies, and cannot expect to receive the protection of the Geneva Convention once in captivity (the Geneva Convention regarding the treatment of prisoners of war makes provision for the proper treatment of captured personnel. It gives prisoners certain rights – to be kept in a place of safety, to be given medical care, food and water – as well as the right to write letters home). The best hope of survival is to effect an immediate escape, or should this not be possible to

Right: During the Gulf War, SAS columns operating in Iraqi territory also called in air strikes against enemy targets.

disguise their status by acting as 'grey men', ordinary soldiers of no immediate political or intelligence value to their captors. Most prisoners will be questioned before they are incarcerated or killed. Adhering to a few simple rules can mean the difference between being broken by, or resisting, their interrogators. They are taught not to resist being tied, and to act

more submissively and tired than they actually are. All prisoners suffer 'the shock of capture', their interrogators will know this and will thus expect their victims to be subservient. This will enable the SAS captives to husband their strength and potential for escape. All SAS personnel go through in-depth resistance-to-interrogation training. It is far from pleasant, yet cannot begin to simulate the atrocities which a special forces captive may suffer at the hands of a sadistic enemy. Every SAS soldier knows that the best way to avoid lasting pain is not to be captured.

For the SAS, fighting behind enemy lines has been a major part of operations since late 1941. The individual skills of SAS soldiers, from their weapons proficiency to camouflage expertise, means that small-sized teams can inflict great damage on the enemy, while at the same time having the ability to get back to friendly lines with the minimum of casualties. Over 50 years of practice has ensured that the British Special Air Service today is probably the most proficient special forces unit to mount missions behind enemy lines.

COUNTER-INSURGENCY
Malaya and Borneo

First developed during the Malayan campaign in the 1950s, the SAS's counter-insurgency skills, more commonly referred to as 'hearts and minds', proved their worth in subsequent campaigns in Oman and on the island of Borneo.

There is an average of around 25 wars, large and small, going on in the world at any one time. Many of them are insurgency/counter-insurgency (COIN), actions in which small, dedicated and usually brutal groups are attempting to overthrow an established government. In the period of de-colonisation which followed World War II, a number of nationalist organisations understandably balked at the idea of returning to colonial rule. Britain and the Netherlands in particular had suffered a series of humiliating reversals at the hands of the Japanese, and their return to influence in the Far East was far from universally popular. By the early 1950s, communism seemed an unstoppable world force. It had taken over much of Eastern Europe, all of China and Russia, and had gained crucial footholds in Korea and Vietnam.

THE SPREAD OF COMMUNISM
Communist guerrillas used their new power bases to export their ideology. To do so they relied upon guerrilla warfare and subversion, not conventional warfare. Their aim was to replace the existing government with one of their own choosing. To do so they levied taxes, demanded conscripts and amassed intelligence, dealing ruthlessly with anyone who they regarded as a challenge. Most rural populations were apolitical, and were relatively easy to convert, if not by persuasion then by terror. Conventional military efforts to destroy the insurgents invariably proved costly and ineffective, and in many cases succeeded only in turning the neutral peasantry against the government.

According to United States Army teaching, 'Resistance, rebellion or civil

Above: SAS soldiers with aborigines during the war in Malaya, where the Regiment's 'hearts and minds' concept was developed.

war begins in a nation where political, sociological, economic or religious division has occurred.' Such divisions, it is argued, occur when one dominant force threatens the perceived rights or privileges of the populace as a whole. Resistance may develop if the once-welcomed liberators fail to improve an intolerable economic or social situation. Resistance may be active or passive, and may well take the form of smouldering resentment which requires no more than the catalyst of political or physical persuasion to turn into an active guerrilla campaign.

Between 1948 and 1960, however, the British in Malaya showed that communist guerrillas could be taken on at their own game and comprehensively beaten, not just in terms of policing and firepower, but in the battle for the hearts and minds of the people. During the war the British

had supported the Malayan Communist Party (MCP) and its leader Chin Peng. Almost entirely Chinese, the MCP had fought not just to expel the Japanese but to achieve equality for the minority Chinese population in post-war Malaya, which numbered over two million people. When this was not forthcoming, Chin Ping re-formed his fighters as the Malayan Races Liberation Army (MRLA) and began a campaign of intensifying terrorism in June 1948.

Classically the MRLA attempted to undermine every aspect of normal life under British colonial rule. Estate owners, colonial officials and police were murdered, estates, mines and factories destroyed, and the rural population intimidated into cooperation. The guerrillas, referred to originally as bandits but later as CTs (Communist Terrorists), used their wartime weapons caches (many of which, ironically, had been supplied by the British) and jungle fighting expertise to operate from jungle bases. An organisation of underground sympathisers, the Min Yuen, supplied Chin Peng's guerrillas with money, intelligence, food and medicines. For the first two years the MRLA's campaign proceeded without any serious check from the British. The will to defeat the CTs was not lacking, but the policy of policing roads, manning towns and villages and making a few arrests was not enough, though the post-war British forces in Malaya were trained for little else. They lacked the experience, as National Servicemen, to seek out and destroy the CTs in their jungle bases.

THE 'BRIGGS PLAN'

All this changed in April 1950 when Lieutenant-General Sir Harold Briggs was appointed the new Director of Operations. From the methodical assessment which Briggs brought to the problem of communist terrorism, he produced not only a master plan for the defeat of the MRLA but a blueprint for the destruction of similar counter-insurgency groups for decades to come (in this he had been helped by the report written by Mike Calvert on how to defeat the communists and win the 'Emergency'). In essence, the 'Briggs Plan' took Mao Tse-tung's theories of guerrilla war and turned them against the guerrillas, starting with 'the sea of the people in which the guerrillas would swim like fish'. If guaranteed normality and security, the people would effectively leave the communists and return, at least passively, to a pro-government stance. To leave the 'fish' high and dry, Briggs arranged for Malaya to be combed, sector by sector from south to north, in a rigorous collaboration between the military, the police and the civil administration. 'New villages' were built for those most at risk; those who lived on the edge of the jungle (in total 410 villages – many inhabited by Chinese squatters – were uprooted and moved).

To starve the CTs, Briggs introduced rigorous controls over the sale and distribution of food, with every crop harvest recorded in minute detail.

When the civilian High Commissioner, Sir Henry Gurney, was assassinated in October 1951, he was replaced by a highly experienced soldier, General Sir Gerald Templer. Templer wasted no time in putting the 'Briggs Plan' into action. Templar was a man of some vision who understood the theory of counter-insurgency clearly. For example, when asked in June 1952 if he had sufficient, he replied: 'The answer lies not in pouring more soldiers into the jungle, but rests in the hearts and minds of the Malayan people.' Operational details were delegated to Major-General Sir Rob Lockhart, who by 1952 had 45,000 men in 24 battalions under command, 25,000 of them British. Special hunter-killer platoons of Gurkhas were created to seek out and destroy the CTs in the jungle, while the assistance of the newly re-formed SAS was actively sought. The energy and practicality which Templer brought to the war was almost immediately effective. The stringent new food regulations, by which every tin sold had to be punctured to prevent hoarding, had by the end of 1953 reduced the

Above: One of the new villages built under the 'Briggs Plan' in Malaya, designed to deny support to the Communist Terrorists.

MRLA to a position where it was forced to spend an estimated 90 per cent of its time organising food supplies. At the same time the protected 'new villages' became models of excellence, good administration and self-sufficiency.

The aggressive new style of jungle patrolling was backed up by helicopter supply flights to extend the duration of the patrols, and was supported by intelligence in unheard of depth. Dossiers were built up on all CT leaders and their groups, and the creation of White Areas, freed of communist influence, accelerated by the insertion of intelligence and psychological warfare teams. Massive rewards were offered for information, £30,000 for Chin Peng himself. If Templer's methods brought about a drastic reduction in the MRLA's freedom of operations and effectiveness, they also carved steadily into the MRLA's manpower at a steady 1000 CTs killed per year between 1951 and 1953 – excluding the unknown number of CT casualties who died unrecorded in the jungle. Equally importantly, they increased the number of CT surrenders;

Left: A New Zealand SAS trooper in Malaya. The New Zealanders proved particularly adept at winning over the natives.

As ever, it was the work of the patrol medics which was the most important part in the building of relationships between the natives and SAS patrols. Sick parades were held to allow the natives to come forward and be treated, and the RAF dropped medical supplies and even arranged helicopter flights for the headmen. In this way British strength was demonstrated, but more importantly the aborigines came to trust the SAS soldiers. Soon they began to pass on intelligence concerning the whereabouts of the CTs, and became the 'eyes and ears' of the security forces, even in the remotest areas.

THE LEARNING PROCESS

Of course it was not all plain sailing. Mike Calvert, in an effort to attract recruits to the Malayan Scouts, had travelled to Rhodesia, where he selected 100 volunteers. These men became C Squadron, Malayan Scouts. They were excellent soldiers, and stayed in Malaya for two years, returning home in December 1952. The Rhodesians had a slight attitude problem when it came to non-whites, which did little to assist 'hearts and minds'. Their replacements, a squadron from New Zealand, were much more adept at dealing with the natives. Their number included a number of Maoris, which facilitated good relations between troopers and natives.

The Malayan campaign highlighted a number of areas where the SAS was deficient. Patrol medics, for example, needed to be dentists and midwives as well as military doctors. In addition, the Regiment's language skills needed to be expanded. Being able to talk to the natives in their own tongue greatly helped to win them over. Above all, there proved no substitute for actually living among the locals, for sharing their problems and helping them out when it came to planting crops, building and repairing shelters and learning their everyday existence.

As a result of the Malayan campaign the policy of 'hearts and minds' was expanded, particularly by the SAS, who

men who could no longer stand the ever more wretched existence which the British and their Malay supporters were inflicting upon their would-be 'liberators'.

In 1957, when the new state of Malaysia gained its independence, there were no more than 1500 CTs still operational. Of these 331 were killed that year and 209 surrendered. By 1960, when Chin Peng finally abandoned the struggle and withdrew into Thailand, he had only about 500 effectives left. The policy of 'hearts and minds', supported by vigorous patrolling and intensive intelligence gathering, had proved an unmitigated success.

SAS 'HEARTS AND MINDS'

For the SAS, its 'hearts and minds' campaign involved going deep into the jungle and winning over the native aborigines.

The way in which this was achieved became a blueprint for later SAS 'hearts and minds' efforts.

The process of winning over the natives was long and often frustrating, but its long-term aim compensated for any short-term disappointments. Initially, a number of jungle forts were built by the SAS. Attracted by free food, medical treatment and protection from the CTs, natives would come into the forts and set up shelters next to those of the SAS soldiers. These forts eventually became permanent, and provided a safe haven for locals from a wide surrounding area. Once a fort had been established the SAS would hand over its running to the police or security forces and then build another. In this way a chain of forts was built around the country, thus further denying ground to the enemy.

Right: 'Hearts and minds' in action. An SAS trooper treats a Dyak in a remote region on the island of Borneo.

exported it to a number of subsequent counter-insurgency actions. Above all, 'hearts and minds' requires large quantities of tact, courtesy and patience, attributes all too often sadly lacking in professional soldiers. Soviet Spetsnaz units in Afghanistan in the 1980s, the French Foreign Legion in Algeria in the 1960s and the Royal Marines in Borneo in the 1960s all established short-term military superiority over their enemy, but because none had been trained in the policy of 'hearts and minds', were unable to exploit their advantage fully.

'HEARTS AND MINDS' IN BORNEO

By the time the Regiment had to fight on the island of Borneo in 1963, it was well equipped to deal with winning 'hearts and minds', having acquired new skills. The standard procedure was for a patrol to establish contact with the local inhabitants and gain their trust. This took time and patience, but again the patrol medic proved his worth. The experience of a patrol from A Squadron is typical of the many contacts between SAS and locals during the Borneo war. The patrol was led by Sergeant 'Tanky' Smith: 'When

we arrived at this village near the border a baby looked as if it was dying and I said to my medic, "You'd better get this right or we'll be kicked out." He gave it a quarter of an aspirin dissolved in milk and it got better, so we were made welcome and that was a good start. It was a happy time, better then Malaya because although I loved the abos they weren't so civilised as the Muruts, who took us into their hearts and homes.'

As the bond grew between natives and SAS, the latter were frequently invited to local celebrations, though this could be a mixed blessing. Smith again: 'What they [the Muruts] do is split a length of thick bamboo and fill it with uncooked port, salt and rice; then they bury it for a month, and when they dig it up it's called "jarit" and, oh God, the pong. But we had to eat it. You just could if you'd drunk enough "tapai".'

In Malaya, Major Dare Newell, who later became the SAS's regimental adjutant and secretary of the SAS Regimental Association, warned troopers to stay away from the native women. In Borneo SAS soldiers faced a similar problem, as 'Tany' Smith relates: 'After a month the headman said we'd been away from home a long time and would we like to refresh ourselves with four of their girls who rather fancied us? I said we'd be delighted' – and there is no reason to disbelieve him for these people were primitive only in consequence of their environment, and he would have been less than a man who was not awakened by the girls' intelligent sweetness and bare-breasted charm – but there's a snag. Even if they themselves

Left: SAS troopers in native shelter in Borneo. Once trust had been established with villagers, the patrol would move in.

fancy us, they've probably each got a boyfriend so we've made four enemies when we're supposed to be here making friends. Besides I didn't want a blowpipe dart in my back and my head added to their collection. My youngest unmarried trooper said, "Speak for yourself, I think it would be impolite to refuse"; but I told him, "No", and that was an order. It was a talking point for an evening and then we got on with something else; though I did just wonder which one fancied me.'

Keeping the natives on their side benefited the SAS in many ways, as a former trooper who fought in Borneo relates: 'They [the Ibans] were state of the art at tracking. On occasion their skill even boggled my mind. We were moving towards an enemy force and the tracker, who had been following the tracks of three or four people all morning, returned and said, "One of the patrol is an officer and he is wearing brown boots, carrying a pistol, has an assault rifle, a bush hat..." I said, "Hold on, wait. I mean I know you're very good at tracking and I know that you're much better at reading

signs than we are but how, in the name of Christ, do you know what sort of hat he's got on, what sort of weapons he's carrying?" And the tracker said, "Oh, he's over there." And through a thin screen of trees was a clearing in which stood an Indonesian regular army officer.'

FIGHTING WITH THE IBANS

Of course, it was not the intention of the SAS to Westernise the natives, who still retained their customs and pastimes, as an SAS soldier who fought with one testifies to: 'The contact was over in seconds and the jungle fell silent. We had killed one Indonesian but there might be more nearby. By this time I had taken cover and, like everyone else, scanned the area for signs of any more of the opposition. Then we quickly bugged out and moved downstream, taking up defensive positions and waiting for the Indos to mount a follow-up ambush. However, they didn't bother and we speedily crossed the river. There is one interesting postscript to the story. Our tracker, who spoke English, said he would check the body. Before we

Above: SAS troopers with villagers in Borneo. The work of patrol medics was the key to winning 'hearts and minds'.

knew what he was up to, he came running back with a big smile on his face. He had cut off the Indo's head and stuffed it into his bag! "Good money, good money," he kept repeating, referring to the bounty he would receive from the Brunei government.

'Ibans were natural trackers and several patrols developed a strong rapport with their own man. Ours would always carry an old pack he had acquired from an infantry battalion. It was full of what appeared to be tree bark and animal skin, which he often chewed on, giving his teeth a tobacco-stained look. They were great blokes, though their headhunting habits were a little disconcerting. We had to continually remind ourselves that it was part of their culture and had been going on for years. It was naturally encouraged by the Brunei government, who wanted as many Indonesian soldiers dead as possible, hence the bounty. The

Ibans then suddenly stopped acquiring heads and started to collect ears (the heads were taking up too much space in their bergens!). Mind you, their habits stopped anyone going into their backpacks!'

There were some setbacks concerning the 'hearts and minds' campaign in Borneo, especially in 1964 following an increase in the number of Indonesian incursions. The Muruts who lived along the border became rather hostile to the SAS, no doubt thinking that the British troops could not protect them against the Indonesians, and so they would switch allegiances. The Regiment had to do something, and quick.

PSYCHOLOGICAL WARFARE

The answer came via Major Peter de la Billière, who hit upon the idea of turning Step-up exercises into psychological warfare (Step-up was a drill evolved by the SAS during the Borneo war to counteract Indonesian incursions. Once an incursion was discovered, the SAS would radio for infantry reinforcements to be flown into the area to land on cleared landing sites by helicopter, and would then guide the infantry to an ambush point to await the enemy force).

Major de la Billière continues the story: 'It was a great game and we only cheated a little by making sure the Gurkhas and helicopters were at split-second readiness. "Look," we said to the Muruts, "when you see any sign of the Indos, come and tell us straight away and we'll use our magic radio box to bring masses of soldiers in to clobber them." Well that was a bit unconvincing at first so we said, "Let's try it tomorrow; you pretend you've found some footprints, anywhere you like, and see what happens." So along they came and told us there were signs where the tracks cross just south of Bukit Oojah; and this bit wasn't cheating because our patrols knew their areas intimately and landing points with lateral tracks had been cut wherever tactically expedient, so within an hour or two a hundred Gurkhas bristling with weapons would be right on the spot and the locals' eyes boggled. The Muruts were thus impressed that the British were more efficient than the Indonesians, as

well as a good deal nicer; but the most telling effect was to the headman's prestige. That factor was crucial because had it just been a matter of troops arriving arbitrarily in his domains, his authority might have been shaken and his displeasure incurred.'

In this way the allegiances of the border villagers were restored to the SAS. By the middle of 1966 the war had been largely won, thanks in large part to the SAS's 'hearts and minds' campaign. SAS veteran George Lea, who was Director of Operations in Borneo, sums up the campaign thus: 'Success therefore was first and foremost a military one. It had been argued that the new regime in Djakarta coupled with the parlous Indonesian economy brought about the Bangkok Accord; those were certainly important factors, but the significance of our military contribution can best be judged by asking what would have happened if we had not given it. There can be no doubt that Borneo certainly and Malaya possibly would now be under the complete control of the Indonesians.

Above: An Iban being transported to hospital in Borneo. 'Hearts and minds' worked because it provided genuine help to the locals.

'Many voices were raised in favour of what was called a political solution, believing there could be no valid military one. This was dangerous muddled thinking because it posed a political solution as an alternative to a military, whereas in fact the two were complementary. Peace follows war. When one side seeks a solution by force it has to be convinced by force that it can't succeed, and only then does a political settlement become possible. *But side by side with military action it is very important to remove the economic, political or sociological sources of discontent on which subversion flourishes* [author's italics]; though, again, in order to do that you must provide a basis of security so that the police, administrators and ordinary people can go about their business without fear.' The SAS's 'hearts and minds' campaign had helped contribute towards the eventual defeat of the Indonesians, as well as recruiting many native friends.

South Oman

In South Oman in the early 1970s, the SAS's counter-insurgency skills proved instrumental in preventing the fall of the regime of Sultan Qaboos to the communists, thereby preserving the free flow of the West's oil through the waters of the Gulf of Oman.

As a maritime nation, Britain long ago learned the significance of the Gulf to her position as an international trader. A Treaty of Friendship was signed with the Sultan of Muscat in 1789. The treaty continued into the twentieth century, and by the late 1950s had taken on a new significance with the discovery of oil.

Oman's borders were (and still are) largely undefined. This, compounded by her proximity to Marxist Yemen in the south, made her vulnerable to subversive influences, and thus indirectly threatened the supply of oil to the West. Britain supported the aged and despotic Sultan Said bin Taimur in 1959, when a squadron of SAS was secretly diverted from Malaya to neutralise a group of rebels on the Jebel Akhdar. However, the oppressive policies of the Sultan resulted in rebellion flaring up again in 1962, this time in the south of the country, in Dhofar Province. The party which spearheaded the revolt was the Dhofar Liberation Front (DLF).

Essentially traditionalist in nature, emphasising the Moslem religion and the tribal structure, the DLF's aims were modernisation and the rather nebulous 'Dhofar for the Dhofaris'. Its fighters were hardy, but for the most part poorly equipped and armed. As such, they were no match for the Sultan's Armed Forces. However, in neighbouring Yemen another, more powerful, guerrilla group, the People's Front for the Liberation of the Occupied Arabian Gulf (PFLOAG) made overtures to the DLF and suggested a merger, promising weapons and money.

The DLF accepted, and the PFLOAG, using the neighbouring People's Democratic Republic of Yemen (PDRY) as a base, began a successful campaign against the small government presence in Dhofar. In 1970 the unpopular and by now totally out of touch Sultan fell victim to a British-inspired, bloodless palace coup and was replaced by his only son, the Sandhurst-trained Sultan Qaboos.

Qaboos requested and was immediately granted British assistance to crush the insurrection. SAS teams were introduced within days, and at once began to implement Operation 'Storm', the regaining of the initiative in the south. The Dhofari people were, and still are, very different to the Omanis of the more affluent north. The town tribes of the coastal plain were basically of Kathiri origin, industrious and comparatively sophisticated. The Jebalis of the mountains, on the other hand, were hot tempered, highly intelligent and fiercely independent. Drawn from the Qarra peoples, they were unswervingly loyal to self, livestock, family and tribe in that order. As the SAS was to discover, they made loyal friends but bitter enemies. The Bedu of the Negd, a flat desert between the mountains and the Empty Quarter to the west, had their own languages and were equally independent. Nomadic, they derived their wealth almost exclusively from camels and goats.

THE 'FIVE FRONTS' CAMPAIGN

Lieutenant-Colonel Johnny Watts, commanding officer of 22 SAS and a veteran of the Jebel Akhdar campaign, realised that his greatest battle was for the 'hearts and minds' of the much-abused indigenous population. If he could successfully convince them that their future lay with the regime of the young Sultan Qaboos and not with the *adoo*, or Marxist rebels, he could starve the rebellion of manpower making the task of the conventional infantry operating in support of the Sultan much easier. Fortunately, because of its expertise built up in Malaya and Borneo, the SAS was well placed to wage an effective counter-insurgency war, one which would become a classic mission.

Left: SAS with Dhofari tribesmen in southern Oman. The ability of troopers to speak local dialects greatly aided 'hearts and minds'.

Watts decided to wage the campaign on five 'fronts', and to this end introduced his 'Five Fronts' campaign, a local extension of the tried-and-tested SAS 'hearts and minds' concept. An intelligence cell was created to monitor the activities and test the reaction of the enemy. An information team was formed to counter the propaganda of Radio Aden, while advising the locals of the very real material benefits of participating in the embryonic civil aid development schemes. Doctors and special forces paramedics were brought to the villages to inoculate the tribesmen and their families against previously lethal diseases, and veterinary teams were introduced to tend the livestock.

Above all, the Dhofaris were given the opportunity to take up arms and protect themselves against the increasingly brutal *adoo*. Initially many Dhofaris had given at least tacit support to the rebels in their prosecution of a war in which the mountain tribes had no real interest. Most, however, had become disenchanted by the rebels' uncompromising denial of God and family – two crucial tenets in Dhofari society – and their brutal methods to make everyone conform

Increasing numbers of Moslem fighters defected from the rebels, and were eagerly snapped up by the SAS. They were formed into groups of fighters to be trained, armed and paid but not directly commanded by the SAS. Known as *firqat,* they were allowed to elect their own leaders, after which they were given almost total autonomy.

CULTURAL PROBLEMS

The SAS in the Dhofar found themselves facing some fundamental problems. The Dhofaris believe that all things came from God, and that it was therefore little short of blasphemous to thank a fellow man for his largesse. They also held that they should ask for anything that they might want – it would, after all, come from God, and if it was His will they would receive it. When the first *firqat* units were formed the SAS had no option but to listen to each individual demand, however unrealistic, so as not to offend. Not until the trust between the SAS and *firqat* had been forged in battle were the Britons able to

insist that all demands came through elected *firqat* leaders.

Tony Jeapes fought as an officer in Oman, and later wrote a book about his experiences in the war. He describes a typical example of the Dhofaris' attitude when asked to the wedding of the first firqat leader, Salim Mubarak: 'I felt under my shirt and produced a brand new Smith and Wesson .357 magnum, fully loaded. The pistol gleamed blue-black in my hand, accentuating the whiteness of its ivory handle.

' "It's too big," he said. "I want one

Above: SAS teams in Oman lived among the Dhofaris, sharing their lifestyle to fully integrate themselves into local communities.

smaller, an automatic."

'I was staggered. It was a beautiful and expensive pistol which I had gone to much trouble to get for him. I had thought he would be delighted with it, or if not, would have had the courtesy to pretend to be.

' "Well, take it now," I said lamely, "and I will see if I can get an automatic, but it will not be easy."

Left: 'Hearts and minds' in action. A makeshift SAS surgery in Oman. As ever, patrol medics greatly helped the COIN effort.

made by an SAS team led by Captain Branson, who with two *firqat* units climbed the jebel to the east, the main force under Watts, with a squadron of SAS, a number of Baluchis and two other *firqats*, *A'aasifat* and *Salahadin*, climbed up to seize the deserted airfield at Lympne. Having secured the airstrip, Watts seized the village of Jibjat and began to patrol along the sides of the Wadi Darbat, dislodging the unsuspecting *adoo* from the plateau. On 9 October a secure base was established at 'White City', from which Watts was able to control the entire plateau above the coastal plain (leaflets had been dropped into the Wadi Darbat to try to persuade rebels to throw in their lot with the government; it was a powerful message, stating that the communists did not 'recognise the Prophet Muhammed (blessing upon his name) and others of God's prophets).

THE *FIRQATS* PROVE DIFFICULT

At this point the *firqats* decided to stop fighting and observe the religious festival of Ramadan. As this meant that they were not able to eat or drink between dawn and dusk, their military effectiveness was inevitably compromised. Watts was enraged (especially as they had been granted dispensations to fight), but had no option but to respect local sensibilities. During November Watts resumed hostilities, though the *firqat* again proved difficult and demanded that their animals be brought off the jebel and transported to a government-organized market. Watts now implemented his most audacious plan. On 27 November he organized a 'Texas-style' cattle drive, supported by jet fighter cover and 5.5in artillery pieces. Over 1400 goats and several hundred cattle were either airlifted or driven from the plateau to the coastal market in Taqa. Most of the animals belonged to *firqat* families, but many allegedly belonged to men serving with the *adoo*, and were therefore 'confiscated' by the *firqat*.

By the end of 1971, Watts had established a government presence on the

'It was my first experience of that Dhofari forthrightness which in the early days was to cause some friction between [the SAS] and the firqats.'

The behaviour of the communists towards the local Dhofari tribesmen did much to assist the government to establish its 'hearts and minds' policy. Their hardline Marxist ideology was in marked contrast to the religious fundamentalism of the locals. In an attempt to export their ideals, the insurgents forcibly removed children from their parents and sent them for schooling in the Yemen, tortured the old for refusing to deny the existence of God, and sent the young to training camps in China and the Soviet Union. The full extremes of 'people's power' were introduced into the mountains as revolutionary courts were set up and began the summary execution of known or suspected government sympathisers. The policy wholly backfired. Between September 1970 and March 1971, 200 *adoo* surrendered to the government which had declared a general amnesty, and were formed into *firqat* units by the SAS.

The defection of Salim Mubarak was particularly welcomed by the SAS. He was a hardened fighter, a nationalist and the second-in-command of the rebels' eastern area. After discussions with Major

Tony Jeapes of 22 SAS, Mubarak was invited to form the two dozen men he had brought with him into the *Firqat Salahadin*, a particularly potent group which began training at Mirbat. The SAS realised that, however steady the trickle of defections, if it was to be turned into a torrent nothing less tangible than a victory in the field would be required. It was imperative for the SAS to prove to the *adoo* and Dhofaris, as well as to the *firqat* themselves, that they could more than match the Marxist guerrillas in battle. The coastal town of Sudh was carefully selected for the blooding. A mixed force of 100 SAS and *firqat* were landed by boat and quickly took the town. The victory was somewhat marred by the fact that the town was empty of *adoo* at the time. Nonetheless, it was hailed as a victory and regarded as a turning point.

The SAS leaders were more realistic, and realised the need to exploit the momentary euphoria by taking the war firmly to the enemy. In October 1971, immediately after the monsoon, Watts launched Operation 'Jaguar', an offensive onto the Jebel Dhofar, with precisely that in mind. A mixed force of 100 SAS, 250 Omani regulars, a few northern tribesmen and five *firqat* (300 men) – in all some 800 troops – was gathered. While a feint was djebel, had freed the plain of Adoo, and had convinced over 700 Dhofaris to join the *firqat*. When the Marxist attack on Mirbat was bloodily repulsed in July 1972, the sovereignty of Sultan Qaboos over Dhofar became indisputable. The influence of the Marxists steadily waned, until by 1975 the survivors had been pushed back to the Yemeni border, and the war was all but over.

THE CIVIL AID PROGRAMME

As ever, the civil side of affairs contributed towards ultimate victory. SAS teams established clinics for the people and their animals, and the gossip picked up from these places was often first-class intelligence. In addition, advanced drilling equipment was brought into Dhofar from the United Kingdom to drill for new wells and to reopen those which had been sealed on the orders of the old Sultan.

The SAS fight against disease and ignorance was conducted on the strict understanding that the Omani government would take over the tasks started by the British soldiers. In this way the Dhofaris were convinced that their government was sincere in its wishes to aid them (and the government did indeed honour its promises).

The SAS's counter-insurgency effort in Dhofar was neatly summed up by Jeapes himself: 'If the *firqats* were the most important Government department to be created to win the war, Civil Aid must run them a close second. The Civil Aid Department (CAD) was, I believe, the one new lesson the Dhofar Campaign provided in the study of counter-revolutionary war, yet it came about almost by default. The Dhofar Development Department could not provide aid fast enough to follow in the wake of the rapid SAF successes of 1973-74. The Department was, in any case, undermanned, but civil development is a long-term business. Roads cannot be built nor wells drilled overnight. It takes time. But time was something the Government did not have... The Government had to demonstrate immediate bounty. The CAD was created initially to fill a gap. It seldom had an executive staff of more than three or four, but its impact on the war was enor-

mous. CAD's fingers reached into practically every wadi on the jebel before the war was over.'

Another reason why the Dhofar war was won was that the major power in the region, Saudi Arabia, was pro-Western (in any COIN campaign if a major power in the region backs the insurgents the odds are stacked against eventual victory). However, this is not to detract from the SAS's achievements in southern Oman. In

Above: Part of the 'Five Fronts' campaign was the provision of veterinary skills, which was greatly appreciated by the Dhofaris.

six years of war (1970-76) the Regiment lost only 12 soldiers killed. In addition, its actions had guaranteed the survival of a pro-Western regime in a very sensitive area of the world. It also confirmed the SAS to be the most expert counter-insurgency unit in the world.

The American experience

The American Special Forces have also had wide experience of counter-insurgency warfare, though have not had the same success. During the Vietnam War the Special Forces' Civilian Irregular Defense Group (CIDG) Program was an attempt to win over the Montagnard tribesmen of Vietnam's Central Highlands to the cause of the South Vietnamese government. Begun in December 1961, by the end of 1963 the Green Berets had trained 18,000 strike force troops and over 43,000 hamlet militiamen. The Montagnards proved their worth during the 1968 communist Tet Offensive, but the whole programme was handed over to the South Vietnamese in 1970 and was ended. The Green Beret-trained militiamen were absorbed into the South Vietnamese army. Ironically, the Green Berets had done their hearts and minds work too well. The tribesmen were totally loyal to them, but they never extended the same sentiments to the South Vietnamese government (who tended to look down on the Montagnards anyway) or its servants. With the lack of political will on the part of the government, the CIDG Program, through no fault of the Green Berets, ultimately failed.

HOSTAGE-RESCUE

The Munich Legacy

The murder of 11 Israeli athletes at the 1972 Olympic Games in Munich prompted many Western governments to establish dedicated counter-terrorist units. In Britain, for example, the SAS refined its hostage-rescue tactics to prepare for any eventuality.

There are currently more than 90 counter-terrorist/hostage rescue units (CT/HRUs) in the world. Many of these have been established and trained by the SAS and other Western CT formations, and have thus adopted their equipment and tactics. The need for such units became apparent in the 1960s, when a plethora of international terrorist groups, many of them with Palestinian sympathies, began to attack Western and Israeli targets. These ranged from the bombing of both hard and soft targets to hostage taking and the assassination of political and military figures. The one incident above any other which provided the catalyst for the formation of dedicated Western counter-terrorist units was the massacre of 11 Israeli athletes at the 1972 Munich Olympics.

On 5 September 1972, armed members of the Palestinian terrorist group 'Black September' seized 11 Israeli sportsmen at the Olympic village in Munich. Having demanded the release from prison of 234 of their compatriots, the terrorists and their hostages were flown by helicopter to Fürstenfeldbrük military airport, from where, they were promised, they would be given safe passage to Cairo. However, as they left the helicopters hidden snipers opened fire, killing two terrorists and wounding others, as well as two helicopter crewmen. The surviving terrorists managed to get back to the helicopters, whereupon the authorities mounted an assault with troops and armoured cars. In the resultant carnage the Palestinians executed five of their hostages in one helicopter before blowing it up, while the other helicopter exploded in the firefight. Five terrorists were killed and three captured, but at the price of 11 Israeli hostages murdered.

THE WEST FIGHTS BACK

The massacre sent shock waves throughout Western Europe and the United States. Munich had demonstrated that local police forces, however well trained, could not hope to combat a determined terrorist attack, while the intervention of conventional troops, far from providing a solution, was likely to lead to an escalation in violence. The necessity for dedicated hostage-rescue units was accepted. Once formed these would have to operate at a complete disadvantage; they would rarely be able to choose their combat ground and would not always be able to take time to plan their assault.

Only highly skilled individuals would be suitable for such units. For example, candidates would have to be excellent combat marksmen with a variety of weapons, and would need to be highly competent in the skills of fighting in a built-up area (FIBUA). They would need to be fit and resourceful, capable of operating on their own or in small groups. They

Left: The hijacked Lufthansa Boeing 737 at Mogadishu Airport, where GSG 9, with SAS assistance, freed the hostages.

would need to be trained in hostage management, close personal protection and insertion techniques. They would need nerves of steel and be able to demonstrate total coolness under fire. In short, they would be too precious to waste on the daily mundanities of conventional soldiering or ordinary police duties. Many countries turned to their special forces to supply these units, while others, notably West Germany and France, created special-purpose forces from within their police services. The Soviet Union, drawing on its unique politico-military structure, created units from within the KGB and Interior Ministry (MVD). In Britain, the government was indeed fortunate to have an organisation whose members already possessed the required skills: the SAS.

GERMANY'S GSG 9

West Germany's *Grenzschutzgrüppe* 9 (GSG 9) was formed by government order on 26 September 1972. Prior to the Munich outrage, post-war Germany had found it difficult to introduce effective counter-terrorist measures, which were often questioned by the country's powerful left wing. These problems were compounded by West Germany's attempts to forge relationships with Third World countries, particularly in the Middle East. Consequently, the government was not prepared to authorise controversial 'high-profile' security arrangements at the Munich Olympics. However, in the aftermath of the massacre new laws were passed creating new anti-terrorist agencies. Originally formed by Colonel (later General) Ulrich Wegener, GSG 9 has evolved into one of the finest HRUs in the world. It draws the majority of its members from the *Bundesgrenzschutz* (BGS), the paramilitary border protection service, now responsible for the protection of all German borders and ports of entry, the security of government buildings and embassies.

The entry qualifications for GSG 9 are exacting. An initial interview selects candidates with a high proficiency in conventional police work, coupled with self-confidence, intelligence and the social ability to mingle comfortably if required to act as a future close-protection officer.

Thereafter, practical training lasts for four months and is followed by an operational posting. Proficiency is maintained by practising a series of simulated hostage-rescues from cars, trains, aircraft, boats and buildings. Marksmanship skills are honed during three half-days and one additional evening per week spent on the range, during which each combat team expends in excess of one million rounds of ammunition per year.

THE FRENCH RESPONSE

GSG 9 achieved an outstanding success in October 1977, when hostages being held in a Lufthansa Boeing 737 at Mogadishu Airport, Somalia, were rescued and their Palestinian captors 'neutralised'.

France's crack HRU, the *Groupement d'Intervention de la Gendarmerie Nationale* (GIGN), was created from the paramilitary. France has long been the focus of terrorist activities. Pre-war France was riven by political intrigue, polarised further during World War II when communist and nationalist *Maquis* groups often fought each other for future peacetime sovereignty. Subsequent conflicts in Vietnam and Algeria, particularly the latter when violence between the Algerian *Front de la Libération Nationale* (FLN) and the right wing *Organisation de l'Armée Secrète* (OAS) spilled onto the streets, did nothing to improve matters. In the first

Above: Fighting fire with fire. French GIGN men storm the hijacked Airbus at Marseilles Airport on 26 December 1994.

week of May 1962 alone France suffered over 200 murders.

President Charles de Gaulle responded by reorganising and extending the powers of the intelligence service, the *Service de Documentation Extérieure et de Contre Espionnage* (SDECE). Legalised telephone tapping, semi-official assassinations and even torture began to take their toll as France introduced her own distinctive system of 'counter-terror'.

Other troubles also found their way to France in the 1970s. The seizure of the Saudi Arabian Embassy in Paris in 1973 led to the French security services preparing to retaliate. However, the numerous French counter-terrorist agencies were ineffective and began to squabble among themselves. Exasperated, the French government decided, in November 1973, to create an independent counter-terrorist unit from the ranks of one of the oldest regiments in the French Army, the *Gendarmerie Nationale*.

After training and a successful period in the Gendarmerie, candidates may apply to transfer to GIGN. Their records are then scanned for disciplinary offences before they are granted initial interviews. All have to complete basic parachute and

Left: 5 May 1980. The SAS storms the Iranian Embassy in London and establishes itself as one of the world's top hostage-rescue units.

Responsibility for domestic hostage-rescue within the United States lies with the FBI, which maintains its own HRU. Known as the Hostage Response Team, the 50-strong unit is reputed to be among the best in the world. The Bureau also maintains small counter-terrorist teams in each US state, although localised hostage-rescues, resulting from purely criminal activity, are likely to be dealt with by state, county or city police Special Weapons and Tactics (SWAT) teams. Other anti-terrorist intervention teams are maintained by the Secret Service Executive Protection Division, the National Park Police and the United States Marshal's Service. United States overseas army and air force bases are protected by the Military Police and Security Police respectively, the latter reputedly having been trained by GSG 9.

Counter-terrorist operations abroad, including hostage-rescue, are the responsibility of the Army's 1st Special Operational Detachment, called Delta Force. Activated in November 1977 after GSG 9's successful hostage-rescue mission at Mogadishu, it was formed by Colonel Charles Beckwith, a US Special Forces veteran who had served with the SAS in the early 1960s. Under Beckwith's command the Delta Force structure, selection and philosophy closely mirrored that of the SAS. However, it is thought that since he relinquished command these have been further refined to take into account Delta's more specialist role.

DELTA FORCE

All potential transferees to Delta must attend a lengthy and very searching interview with a number of serving officers and NCOs of the group, and must undergo psychological assessment before they are even accepted for selection. This is to ensure that they are self-assured and mature enough to endure the hours, possibly days, of extensive monotony which invariably precede the few minutes of naked aggression which mark the final stages of most hostage rescues. Training

diving courses before selection for the training course, which itself emphasises mental and physical fitness, strength, raw courage and marksmanship. On average, GIGN agents fire 9000 rounds of pistol and 3000 rounds of rifle ammunition on the range annually. They are expected to hit a moving target at 25m (82ft) or more in two seconds; faced with multiple targets they must hit a vital spot on six targets at 25m (82ft) within five seconds.

Diver training continues in the unit and the men progress to become combat swimmers, spending four hours a week underwater. Much of the training is conducted at night and in murky conditions, as experience has shown that the best time for the insertion of swimmers during a hostage-rescue operation is under cover of darkness. To help prepare the men for night diving, the team sits on the muddy bottom of the River Seine, listening to the heavy barges passing overhead. This allows the individuals to get used to the sound of passing ships, which appear larger and closer than they actually are. The GIGN's expertise in swimming proved invaluable in May 1977, when combat swimmers were deployed during a train hijack! A Dutch train was seized by South Moluccan terrorists, who halted it

at De Punt. Combat swimmers managed to swim up a canal running close to the track and attach heat detectors and listening devices to the outside of the train. These enabled the planners to establish the precise whereabouts of the gunmen prior to the final assault.

GIGN SUCCESSES

GIGN enjoyed its greatest success at Djibouti in February 1976, when, in conjunction with the paratroopers of the Foreign Legion's 2ème REP, it rescued French school children from a terrorist-held bus. In January 1978, it intervened when two inmates at Clairvaux prison seized a deputy warden and two prison officers. The incident ended successfully with precision sniper fire, which did much to enhance the GIGN's reputation for uncompromising action in the face of terror. And when French diplomats were taken hostage at the French Embassy in El Salvador, the 'leaked' news that a GIGN team had arrived in the country convinced the terrorists that it was time to surrender. In late 1994, GIGN again achieved success when it stormed a terrorist-held airliner at Marseille airport, rescuing all the hostages from the hands of Algerian extremists.

covers all aspects of conventional soldiering, with particular regard being paid to the handling of foreign weapons and deep reconnaissance, together with the more esoteric skills of vehicle theft, aircraft refuelling and hostage reassurance. The size and organisation of Delta is secret, although it is considered to have an establishment of approximately 400 personnel, of whom about half are combat operators organised into two squadrons. Delta's most famous action was Operation 'Eagle Claw', the ill-fated attempt in 1980 to rescue the United States hostages from Iranian hands. As a direct result, a top-level re-evaluation was made of all counter-terrorist resources, after which a new Joint Special Operations Control (JSOC) was established at Fort Bragg.

THE SAS AND CRW

In 1969, the SAS was tasked with the formation of training teams to protect friendly overseas heads of state. The Counter Revolutionary Warfare (CRW) Wing at Hereford was officially created in 1973 with a permanent staff of 20 when the Regiment formally adopted the counter-terrorist role in response to the Munich Olympics massacre, although the SAS had in fact been exploring this area of operations before it was sent to Northern Ireland in 1969.

It made sense to give the SAS the hostage-rescue brief, as the Regiment always had a CRW responsibility. As applied to the SAS, CRW missions involve infiltrating areas by land, sea or air; collecting intelligence about the location and movement of enemy guerrilla forces; ambushing and harassing insurgents; undertaking demolition and sabotage operations; border surveillance; implementing a 'hearts and minds' policy; and training and liaising with friendly guerrilla forces. Hostage-rescue was now added to the list.

Of all the operations carried out by the SAS since its re-establishment, none has captured the imagination of the world, nor been carried out on so public

Right: One of the terrorists is brought out of the Iranian Embassy. The SAS operation has deterred any other hostage takers.

a stage, as the operation to end the siege at the Iranian Embassy in May 1980.

The details of the siege and its outcome have been described in an earlier chapter, but it is worth recounting some incidents in the operation to illustrate the SAS's hostage-rescue skills. The SAS had an 'immediate assault plan', but this would have meant storming the building without knowing the precise whereabouts of the hostages, a blueprint for a large number of casualties. Fortunately, this turned out to be unnecessary, and the SAS were given an opportunity to formulate a detailed 'deliberate assault plan'.

PRINCES GATE

Intelligence is the key to all successful military operations, and is also essential when hostages have to be rescued. As the negotiations went on at Princes Gate, the building and its surrounds were thoroughly scrutinised by the SAS. Thermal imagers were used to determine which rooms were in occupation, and by how many individuals. Further intelligence was steadily added by Scotland Yard's C7 Technical Support Branch using micro-

phones and surveillance devices in the chimneys and walls of adjoining buildings. A large-scale model of the embassy was constructed by the Royal Engineers at the old Royal Corps of Transport barracks in Albany Street, near Regent's Park, which also became the secure headquarters for the SAS. And the Regiment had a godsend when the caretaker of the building was able to provide a thorough briefing on its interior.

The SAS was therefore able to formulate a plan for the rescue of the hostages which had an excellent chance of succeeding. Four-man teams would abseil down the rear of the building to the ground and first floors while a second team would enter the building from the front. The teams would use frame charges to effect their entry and would then lob in stun grenades to disorientate the terrorists (again intelligence came into play, for it was discovered that the front first-floor windows were bulletproof; they would not have succumbed to sledge-hammers like those at the rear). As was standard operation procedure (SOP), team members were to be dressed in

of the assault; to call off the operation would have resulted in more hostage deaths). Once inside the building, the SAS troopers showed the effectiveness of the Regiment's hostage-rescue training.

Carefully and deliberately they moved through the building in search of the terrorists. They meticulously cleared the building using standard room-clearance drills; shoot off the lock, kick in the door, throw in a stun grenade, enter the room and clear it. The weapons skills of the SAS also manifested themselves: five of the six terrorists were located, shot and killed inside the building, while the sixth only escaped because he hid among the hostages. The entire operation took no more than 17 minutes. The hostages and remaining terrorist were evacuated from the by now burning building, allowing the SAS to depart as they had come, in almost complete secrecy.

NEW EQUIPMENT FOR RESCUES

In 1987 the SAS extended the scope of its support to the civil powers when it successfully rescued a prison warder held at knife point in HM Prison, Peterhead. In the process they demonstrated a powerful new hostage-rescue armoury. This includ-

ed a high-powered cannon capable of breaching walls with water-filled shells, a thermal lance designed to cut through prison bars in seconds and a range of new disabling gases. All these piece of equipment, plus the clothes worn by SAS troopers during a rescue, would have been thoroughly tested and evaluated beforehand by the Regiment's Operations Research Wing at Stirling Lines.

THE HRU BROTHERHOOD

The SAS has close links with other HRUs across the globe, and this interaction has resulted in the exchange of ideas, tactics and equipment in the fight against international terrorism. Holland, for example, has 7 (NL) SBS, the Special Boat Section of the Royal Netherlands Marine Corps, which has an enviable reputation. Working in conjunction with the Dutch Close Combat Unit, it demonstrated its expertise on 23 May 1977 when, after a three-week siege, its members stormed a Dutch train which had been hijacked by South Moluccan terrorists. SAS advisers, who had been invited to the scene, had offered stun grenades to the Marines for their assault, but in the event the terrorists were distracted by fighter aircraft flying low over the train.

The interchange of information between the various counter-terrorist units is now immense. During the planning

black anti-flash suits, bulletproof jackets and respirators, and would be armed with Heckler & Koch MP5 submachine guns and Browning High Power pistols. Following the deterioration of the situation inside the embassy, the terrorists murdered one of the hostages on 5 May. The SAS was ordered to bring the siege to and end, and the assault went in.

Unfortunately, the SAS men at the rear were unable to detonate their frame charges as their commander had got caught up on his harness. They were forced to use sledgehammers to effect entry (in such a situation the most important thing is to maintain the momentum

stages of Operation Eagle Claw, for example, the CIA, not for the first time, was hampered by the lack of human intelligence (HUMINT) assets on the ground. GSG 9 offered to infiltrate a team of operators, using the cover of a television team, into Tehran to establish the whereabouts of the hostages. Although ultimately the offer was rejected, the very fact that it was made demonstrates the extent to which one Western country will come to the aid of another in the fight against their common enemy.

The SAS has strong links with other CT units. In its efforts to keep tabs on over 300 active terrorist cells internationally, it freely exchanges intelligence with its allies, and positively encourages the hosting of exchange officers from, among others, GIGN, GSG 9 and the various

United States agencies. In 1978, the Italian Red Brigades killed former prime minister Aldo Moro after a mock trial conducted by a so-called 'people's tribunal'. While the hunt for Moro was being conducted, the SAS was helping the Italians to create a specialist anti-terrorist unit, *Nucleo Operativo Central di Sicurezza* (NOCS). The Italians were very quick learners, and today NOCS, with its 50 members drawn from the Carabinieri, provides the principal intervention unit in the country.

TRAINING FOREIGN UNITS

Such is the esteem in which the SAS is held that numerous allied governments have asked it to help them establish their own counter-terrorist units. Spain's *Grupo Especial de Operaciones* (GEO), NOCS,

Above: A member of GSG 9 practises aircraft assaults. The legacy of Munich has been the establishment of crack anti-terrorist units.

Delta Force, Singapore's Police Tactical Unit, Philippines' Aviation Security Commando, Pakistan's Special Services Group, Sri Lanka's Army Commando Squadron, Malaysia's Special Strike Unit, Bahrain's U-Group, Jordan's Special Forces Battalion, Oman's Sultan's Special Force and Morocco's GIGN. Cumulatively, over 10 per cent of all CT formations have been set up with the considerable assistance of Hereford.

This is testimony to the excellence of the SAS, but to maintain its position the Regiment needs to constantly train for all hostage eventualities; it does so by putting its members through the 'Killing House'.

Training in the 'Killing House'

All SAS troopers are rotated through hostage-rescue training at Hereford when they are part of the Special Projects Team. This means spending many hours in the 'Killing House', the building where many different hostage-rescue scenarios can be realistically created.

At Stirling Lines in Hereford, the SAS's UK base, there is a long, window-less building with a corridor running down the centre. On one side of the corridor there are a variety of different-sized rooms, while on the other side there are two large rooms. There are also video cameras and screens to allow interaction between different rooms and to record the action, the footage of which can later be used in debriefs. Each day the building is filled with SAS soldiers shooting off thousands of rounds of ammunition as they refine their weapons skills and reaction times. This is the 'Killing House', where the Regiment's men perfect their hostage-rescue skills.

At any one time there is an SAS 'Sabre' Squadron on 24-hour standby for anti-terrorist and hostage-rescue operations. The squadron is divided up into operational troops called Special Projects Teams. Each team consists of a captain

Left: Members of France's hostage-rescue specialists, GIGN, with some of the equipment they use during rescues.

and 15 soldiers, but for the purposes of an actual assault to free hostages it will be divided further into four-man assault teams. The amount of time a squadron will spend on hostage-rescue duties will depend entirely on the Regiment's commitments, but every six months is the norm. If the Regiment is stretched, though, then a squadron may face an interval of 18 months before assuming anti-terrorist duties once more.

THE PURPOSE OF THE 'KILLING HOUSE'

Each member of the Special Projects Teams must be able to burst into a room full of hostages and terrorists, identify the terrorists, and kill them before they can harm the hostages. All this has to be done in a matter of seconds. Such skill has to be learnt, and so all SAS soldiers have to undergo training in the 'Killing House'.

A member of the SAS describes the reasoning behind the creation of the 'Killing House': 'The aim is to slowly polish your skills as a team so that everyone is trained up to the same level, thinking on the same wavelength and aware of each other's actions.'

The 'Killing House' course itself lasts four weeks and is designed to improve the personal reaction times of individual SAS soldiers, to sharpen team drills and overall room combat effectiveness.

The staff of Training Wing are in charge of the course and they ensure that it is as realistic as possible. The layout of the rooms in the building can be changed to represent different scenarios, such as a railway carriage, an aircraft fuselage or even a cinema. By moving partitions and putting in chairs and seats an almost endless number of scenarios can be created, all designed to sharpen the skills of indi-

viduals. A member of G Squadron remembers his first impressions: 'The "House" is full of corridors, small rooms and obstacles, and often the scenario demands that the rescue be carried out in darkness (a basic SOP [standard operating procedure] on a live mission is for the power to be cut before the team goes into a building). The rooms are pretty barren, but they can be laid out to resemble the size and layout of a potential target.'

Like everything in the Regiment, the course in the 'Killing House' starts with basics. Each man will learn how to enter a room and take out targets to his front – nothing complicated. Once he has mastered this the drills get more difficult. Multiple entries will be practised, whereby two or four men will burst into a room and clear it of targets. Once an individual has mastered working in a team, the team itself will practise clearing several rooms at a time, and then a whole floor.

ROOM-CLEARANCE DRILLS

As the men get more proficient at room clearing, the number of targets within each room will also increase. This sharpens reaction times – something that is vital to the success of a real operation. At first there will be just one target in a room, but then the instructors will put three or more in one room. In another the terrorists and hostages will be mixed together. The SAS team will, in a split-second, have to identify the terrorists and take them out, though making sure they don't hit any hostages. One favourite trick is to have three or more figures in a room with their backs to the assault team as it enters. Suddenly, all the figures will move but only one will be armed. The SAS troopers have no time at all to shoot the armed target.

As the course continues added complications are added. The environment within the 'Killing House' is totally controllable, so the SAS teams will be faced with having to shoot in poor light, in bad light and in complete darkness. Then smoke will be added to simulate fire in the building (during the Iranian Embassy rescue in May 1980, the building caught fire during the assault, filling it with smoke, and the SAS team also used CS gas, which further added to the poor visibility). Other distractions include recordings designed to simulate the shouts of terrorists and the screams of hostages, and heavy rock music being played at a high volume – all designed to throw the SAS soldiers off balance.

EVER-CHANGING SCENARIOS

Because the layout of the 'Killing House' is constantly being changed by the instructors, no one knows what to expect each day – everyone is deliberately kept on their toes. One team might be told one day that they are going to clear a house, the next day an airliner and so on. Even if they practise clearing buildings two days in a row, the layouts of the rooms will be entirely different on the second day. Other problems introduced by the instructors include ordering team leaders to stand down minutes before a rescue is due to take place, thereby forcing the other team members to carry out an assault on their own.

In addition to the partitions, chairs, tables and other physical obstacles, the 'Killing House' also has cine-projection screens for sharpening reaction times. A film will be projected onto a screen representing a particular scenario. As soon as a terrorist appears on the screen he will be shot. The film is then stopped and the screen examined to see where the shot impacted on his body.

The 'Killing House' is in constant use, and at any one time there could be 10-20 men practising their hostage-rescue skills in the building. Despite the fact that they are firing live rounds, there is no chance of any rounds going through walls. The walls of each room are covered in thick absorbent rubber, with metal, wooden railway sleepers and bricks behind, to absorb the impact of rounds.

In the 'Killing House' all the men wear the full combat kit they would if it was a

live operation. This means Nomex flame-proof assault suit, assault vest, respirator, ballistic helmet, spare ammunition, medical kit, radio, armour plates, pistol and Heckler & Koch MP5 submachine gun. This means each man carries 36.3kg (80lb) of equipment on him when he is bursting into rooms. This is a lot, but there is no way around it, as a member of Training Wing explains: 'We have to train harder than we fight. It's no use taking away the armour plates to allow individuals to bend and get through windows and around other obstacles during training. When it comes to the real thing they will have to go through the same spaces and around the same obstacles wearing the

Above: A GEO member practising hostage-rescue shooting and abseiling drills. The SAS helped establish Spain's CT unit.

restrictive heavy ceramic plates. You have to train exactly as you're going to fight.'

Training in the 'Killing House' does have its dangers. Because the men use live rounds, the building soon fills with toxic fumes (bullets are lead lined), despite the expensive extraction system that has recently been installed. It is so bad that the men of squadron on anti-terrorist duty undergo monthly blood tests to check for levels of toxicity. Though respirators are worn during training, toxins are absorbed through the skin. Because of this, training is undertaken outside the building where possible.

Because everyone is heavily 'psyched up' during hostage-rescue training, accidental discharges often happen. The Regiment has lost one killed and others shot in the feet as a result of weapons going off accidentally – a price that has to be paid for realism.

WEAPONS AND AMMUNITION

The weapons used in the 'Killing House' are 9mm pistols and submachine guns – the guns that are used by SAS teams during real hostage-rescue operations. The targets the men shoot at are old diving suits stuffed with rags – crude but sufficient to simulate real people.

The Regiment also uses the 'Killing House' to experiment with new types of ammunition. Hostage-rescues invariably take place within confined spaces, such as inside rooms and aircraft cabins. In such areas there is a real danger of hostages being killed by a ricochet. A member of the Regiment describes the kinds of ammunition tried: 'New weapons and ammunition are continually being tested in the "House", and among the latest introductions is a new fragmentation round. It explodes on impact, so if a team has to storm a boat it will hit the bulkheads and burst without ricocheting, unlike ball rounds.'

When a squadron takes over the anti-terrorist role it has a four-week handover period, during which time it has a chance to put its men through the four-week course and introduce those new members to hostage-rescue training. But do SAS soldiers like training in the 'Killing House'? A member of B Squadron gives his view: 'Initially it's good fun, but then the novelty wears off. All the fumes and the gear quickly reduce the enjoyment factor. Also, there's the noise. With all the rounds being fired and the special sound effects it's deafening inside the building.'

Be that as it may, the 'Killing House' is essential to getting squadrons up to the required level. But what is that level? An experienced instructor gives his view: 'We are never satisfied with times – one second to draw and fire is too long in SAS reckoning. But it's not just about being

able to fire quickly. Guys must be able to identify the bad guys and also prioritise threats. So, when you go into a room you have to clear the doorway – you don't want to get silhouetted – and take the point of dominance so you can sweep the room. You shoot whoever shows intent first. Speed with accuracy, that's what it's all about.'

EMERGENCY DRILLS

Only the training carried out in the 'Killing House' allows SAS soldiers to learn the 'tricks of the trade' inside out, drills that can mean the difference between success and failure, as an SAS

Above: Live ammunition is used in the 'Killing House'. This gives a degree of unmatched realism and fosters confidence.

soldier recounts: 'If the front man of the team has a problem with his primary weapon, which is usually a Heckler & Koch MP5 submachine gun, he will hold it to his left, drop down on one knee and draw his handgun. The man behind him will then stand over him until the problem with the defective weapon has been rectified. Then the point man will tap his mate's weapon or shout "close", indicating that he is ready to continue with the assault. Two magazines are usually carried

Above: A trooper in the 'House' with the SAS's primary hostage-rescue weapon: the MP5 submachine gun. Note the two mags.

Above: Pump-action shotguns are part of the hostage-rescue armoury, being used to blow door hinges to allow access to rooms.

on the weapon, but magnetic clips are used as opposed to tape. Though most of the time only one mag is required, having two together is useful because the additional weight can stop the weapon pulling into the air when firing.'

At the end of the day, all the training has only one purpose: to refine each SAS trooper's speed, reaction times, drills until they become second nature. It is not unusual for an individual to fire over 5000 rounds of ammunition during his training

in the 'House' as part of the current Special Projects Team.

The 'Killing House' at Hereford is the most realistic hostage-rescue training ground in existence, and it has been copied by dozens of hostage-rescue units around the world. Realism is the key in the 'Killing House', using blank rounds is counterproductive. Live rounds increase the danger, and therefore focuses everyone's minds on the task at hand. In a real hostage-rescue the team will be firing live rounds, so they do so in training. The instructors believe that using live rounds fosters confidence, especially when live hostages are also used. It is all part of mak-

ing hostage-rescue training as near to the real thing as possible.

Since it was built the 'Killing House' has achieved some remarkable results: it is unmatched for realism, variety and surprise with regard to hostage-rescue training; it has honed the SAS's anti-terrorist capability to perfection; and it is large enough for many teams to train inside it at any one time.

But what does the training in the 'Killing House' achieve? It produces soldiers who can handle weapons with a skill that is extraordinary. Being able to identify, hit accurately and fire a full magazine of pistol or submachine gun ammunition in under three seconds is remarkable by any standards. SAS troopers 'own' the first four, critical, seconds of an encounter with terrorists.

The real test, however, for a hostage-rescue unit is its performance during a real rescue attempt. To date no SAS hostage-rescue operation has resulted in large-scale losses among the hostages. This shows how effective the training carried out inside the 'Killing House' is.

HOSTILE ENVIRONMENTS

Jungle

From very early on in their SAS careers, troopers are taught how to live and fight in the jungle, an environment that saps stamina and is full of threats. However, as the Regiment demonstrated during its wars in Malaya and Borneo, it has mastered jungle warfare.

One of the great strengths of the SAS is its ability to operate anywhere in the world, a skill shared with few other special forces units. All candidates hone their skills in survival during Continuation Training, and thereafter undertake a 4-6-week jungle training course in the Far East, usually Brunei, in which they are taught basic standard operating procedures (SOPs) and patrol skills. The course culminates in a final exercise which all students must pass. They are split into four-man patrols and given a specific task

designed to test all their newly acquired skills. Even at this stage a man can fail and be returned to unit (RTU'd). The SAS realises that this can be a cruel blow to a student who has come so far, but the Regiment is jealous of its reputation for jungle fighting gained during the Malayan and Borneo campaigns in the 1950s and 1960s, and is adamant that it will not compromise its standards.

Jungles are characterised by high temperatures, frequent heavy rainfall and high humidity. Primary jungle contains trees

that can grow to a height of over 60m (200ft) before forming a canopy of foliage so thick that very little light penetrates. The lack of sunlight means that there is little undergrowth to prevent movement, but equally the attendant gloom reduces visibility to 50m (164ft) or less. Secondary jungle occurs where the canopy is less thick and sunlight reaches the ground, as

Below: Jungle training in Brunei. In the jungle the humidity is oppressive and the threat of ambush ever-present.

on river banks, or where primary jungle has been cleared by man. Here the ground is covered in grasses, ferns, vines and shrubs which can reach a height of 3m (10ft), making visibility poor and movement slow and arduous.

Individuals sweat a great deal, particularly when carrying heavy loads, while water, although usually plentiful, is often contaminated. Disease is rife in the jungle, and a soldier operating in it has constantly to guard against infection. However, providing he has become acclimatised, has an adequate knowledge of where and how to obtain food and water, and is capable of constructing a rudimentary shelter, he should have little problem in remaining fit to fight. Physical and mental preparedness are essential. Wading through swamp for long periods with full kit is exhausting, yet the soldier must remain alert at all times, not just to the possible presence of the enemy but to the very real dangers posed by insects, snakes and other wild animals.

JUNGLE BASICS

SAS jungle training starts with the basics. Upon arriving at their jungle training camp the recruits are informed that they only need two sets of clothing – one wet and one dry. The training staff tell them to sleep in the dry set and wear the wet ones during the day. It is constantly wet in the jungle, either from humidity or rain, so staying dry is impossible. A simple plastic bag keeps the other set of clothes dry to sleep in.

Other SOPs taught to recruits are simple but very effective. They include learning how to construct an A-frame shelter to sleep on and that it is imperative to sleep under a mosquito net. The Regiment takes the view that a man who is comfortable and has had a good night's sleep will be more effective in combat. Thus the troopers are instructed to apply liberal quantities of mosquito repellent first thing in the mornings on their faces, clothes and arms. Then they take their Paludrin anti-malaria tablets.

One of the most important aspects of jungle warfare is learning how to navigate properly. This is done by using a compass, pacing and being able to match features

on a map to how they actually appear on the ground.

Andy McNab describes the intricacies of SAS jungle navigation: 'The jungle canalises movement. The dense vegetation, deep gullies, steep hills and ravines, and wide, fast rivers are obstacles which make cross-country movement very difficult. However, it's got to be done. High ground and tracks are where every Tom, Dick and Harry moves, and where ambushes are laid.

'We navigated across country, using a technique called cross graining. Up and down, up and down, not keeping to the high ground. It took us much longer to travel a small distance, but tactically it was much better: we weren't getting ambushed, we weren't leaving signs, and we weren't going to bump into any opposition.'

The jungle is full of food, and so in a survival situation an individual can find plenty to eat. The training staff instruct the recruits on what is safe to eat and how to subject plants and animals to the taste test (to determine if something is edible, it is first rubbed on the skin to see if there is a reaction; if there is not, then after at least two hours it is rubbed on the lips; again, if there is no reaction it is tasted, and then a little eaten and so on).

Above: SAS troops crossing a river in Belize. Immersion in water in the jungle usually results in being covered with leeches.

On operations, however, it is SOP not to catch lizards and snakes to eat. For one thing it takes up valuable time that could otherwise be spent on more military matters. In addition, there is the risk of catching diseases and stomach complaints from such sources, which would compromise a mission. SAS soldiers therefore rely on the rations they carry and those which are air-dropped to them.

FINDING WATER

One of the crucial aspects of jungle craft is the ability to locate and prepare water, which is in abundance in the jungle. A soldier's daily water requirement is far greater than in temperate climates; indeed, during acclimatisation, a newcomer may require up to seven litres (12 pints) per day, plus additional salt tablets, just to keep going. Water may usually be obtained from rivers or streams, being treated with water purification tablets before it is drunk. Should this not be possible a jungle still may be built, or a Milbank bag, a canvas container used by the SAS since Malaya, employed to collect water for sterilisation.

Left: Since the 1960s, SAS troopers have learnt many jungle tricks, such as wearing bandanas to keep sweat out of the eyes.

enemy, each patrol member takes great care where he steps. He has to watch for twigs and dried leaves, which will make a cracking sound when stepped on. He will also have to watch for snakes, as well as scorpion, ant and spiders' nests. In the sapping humidity of the jungle this calls for a special kind of soldier.

To be a jungle fighter an SAS soldier has to be supremely fit. Wading through a swamp for hours on end, carrying a rifle above your head, is a severe test of physical fitness. Even out of the water you get wet. Wet through sweating continuously. The high humidity soaks clothes through, and the body's fluid loss is very high. Each men can be carrying up to 36.3kg (80lb) in weight, enough to sustain him for 14 days in the jungle, or *ulu* as it is known in the Regiment ('ulu' is the Malay word for jungle). Each day is a trial of strength: get up at 0530 hours, move for an hour, halt for a brew, another halt at 1300 hours, then patrol again until 1600 hours. Then prepare camp and the one meal of the day. This routine can go on for up to two months – each patrol member must be extremely fit.

SAS jungle training stresses silent movement and superior weapons skills. Firefights in the jungle, and contacts in general, take place at close range – around 5m (16ft) is the norm – and involve small groups. Noise discipline is crucial to survival, especially when moving through dense jungle where visibility is poor. Special forces soldiers do not hack through the jungle. They move silently and stealthily. They move at a rate of 100m (328ft) an hour, sometimes slower. Every 20 minutes the whole patrol stops and listens. As well as scanning for the

CAMOUFLAGE

Training stresses the importance of avoiding using foliage as camouflage. It may seem like a good idea to cut branches and leaves off tress and bushes and stick them on webbing and headgear. However, as soon as it is cut foliage starts dying and fading. It then contrasts sharply with its surroundings, making individuals stick out like a sore thumb.

The instructors will always stress that holding ground in a contact has no place among SAS SOPs. Therefore, contact drills revolve around the ability to lay down a lot of instantaneous fire to allow the patrol to escape.

The contact drills taught in training are the result of hard-learned lessons in

Left: Contacts in the jungle are usually at ranges well under 50m (164ft), and thus require razor-sharp reflexes.

Right: The group photograph at the end of an SAS jungle course in Belize. SAS jungle training begins after Continuation Training.

Malaya in the 1950s and Borneo in the 1960s. In the jungle SAS four-man patrols move in file, one man behind the other. When contact is made with the enemy, it is always the trooper at the front, the lead scout, who makes contact first. Therefore, the head-on contact drill was devised. When a contact is made the other patrol members were trained to move into positions each side of the lead scout to pour fire at the enemy. Another tactic is 'shoot and scoot' (see Fighting as a Four-Man Patrol Chapter)

WEAPONS SKILLS

But for these tactics to work, SAS soldiers have to learn to fire their weapons to great effect in a split-second. As a result, weapon skills are the most important part of jungle training. SAS soldiers can only become effective jungle fighters if their personal weapons become an integral part of themselves, almost like an extension of their bodies.

SAS soldiers prefer the M16 assault rifle in the jungle. The weapon is light, which means it is easy to bring to bear in a firefight. It has little recoil. This makes it both easy and comfortable to fire. It is relatively short – 990mm (39in) – always a bonus in the jungle.

Contrary to popular myth SAS men do not fire from the hip. In the jungle the men have to learn instinctive point firing. To do this they must carry their personal weapons in a different way. There are no rifle slings. Each man holds his weapon in his hands. The butt is always in the shoulder, the rifle always ready to bring to bear. The index finger used to fire the weapon is always resting on the trigger guard. Each men leans into his weapon, a position that makes firing easier.

Instinctive point stresses that troopers must shoot only when a target is visible. Wild shooting only wastes ammunition. Both eyes remain open. The instructors teach the men how to pivot to fire at a target. It is no good swinging to fire, they are told, you will miss. When they open fire, SAS soldiers always use the double

tap. This is two shots fired in quick succession – usually a split-second. However, in that split second the trooper must make an adjustment to ensure that the second round is dead on target.

Weapons must work first time every time, and so SAS soldiers are taught the importance of keeping their rifles and machine guns clean. The jungle is humid. Everything goes rusty very quickly without the proper maintenance. Troopers have to clean their weapons every day, and make sure they are oiled. However, there is a problem with oil, as a member of Training Wing explains: 'If you oil the barrel, and don't dry-clean it before you shoot, the first round you fire will go high because it will be tight in the barrel. In addition, it will produce a lot of smoke, which can be disastrous in an ambush.'

Though weapons are cleaned every day, they are never cleaned all at the same time. There is always one patrol weapon that is loaded and ready to fire. And SAS SOPs demand that each patrol member has his personal weapon within arm's reach at all times. Weapons are stripped thoroughly during cleaning, with the working parts cleaned first and then the barrel pulled through with oil. Magazines

can be a problem with regard to stoppages. Training stresses the importance of their maintenance. As well as keeping them clean, they must always be changed frequently to keep their springs working. The M16's magazine takes 30 rounds, but SAS soldiers will only load them with 29. In this way the magazine's spring is not fully compressed. If a magazine has 30 rounds and it is full over a long period, the spring will not operate properly. Improper feeding of rounds into the chamber can cause a stoppage – potentially fatal in a firefight. Every five days, therefore, the magazine is taken out of the weapon, the rounds are taken out and put in a fresh magazine, which is loaded into the weapon.

Only one weapon is carried by SAS jungle patrols. This is for practical reasons. If each man was issued with a handgun this would mean carrying a different type of ammunition. The handgun used by the SAS is the Browning High Power, which is 9mm calibre. The last thing foot patrols want is additional weight. So it's one weapon per man. But how good are SAS jungle drills? This may be judged by one fact: not one patrol has been ambushed while following SAS jungle SOPs.

Mountains

Each SAS 'Sabre' Squadron has a Mountain Troop which specialises in mountaineering and winter warfare operations. Fighting among the high rocks is extremely hazardous, but it is an art that the SAS has gained much experience in.

Mountain regions are characterised by high winds, inclement weather, difficult terrain and virtually no food, shelter or water. They are among the most inhospitable to places to fight in, but special forces units such as the SAS must know both how to live and fight in them. To this end each SAS 'Sabre' Squadron has a Mountain Troop that specialises in mountain and winter warfare operations.

Mountain regions have severe climates, and sometimes the weather alone can defeat an elite team. During the 1982 Falklands War, for example, members of D Squadron's Mountain Troop were landed on Fortuna Glacier during Operation 'Paraquet', the codename for the mission to retake South Georgia. As is standard operating procedure (SOP), all the troop-

ers were equipped with climbing kit, sleeping bags, warm clothing and bivi-bags. However, once on the glacier they were so buffeted by 80km/hr (50mph) winds that they were unable to establish any form of even semi-permanent shelter. They had to abandon the mission and be extracted the next day by helicopter, when hurricane-force winds threatened them with hypothermia and frostbite. Just one example of how the weather can affect mountain operations.

MOUNTAIN WARFARE TRAINING

To operate in mountain areas, SAS soldiers must be skilled in a number of specialist techniques, including rock climbing, rappelling, belaying and obstacle negotiation. Movement through mountainous terrain can be hazardous, with the dangers of rock falls and avalanches ever present. All troopers therefore receive instruction in the skill of mountain walking, whereby, among other things, they learn the need to step over, rather than on top of, obstacles. Not only does this greatly reduce noise, which can carry for vast distances in the clear air of the mountains, but lessens the likelihood of injuries.

To hone their skills in mountain and arctic warfare SAS men attend courses run by the Royal Marines, and by a number of NATO allies. One of the finest courses is run by the German Army Mountain and Winter Warfare School at Luttensee, near Mittenwald, Bavaria. The course begins with an initial selection week, followed by five weeks of intensive rock training at Oberreintal on the Wendelstein. The troops live in tents high in the Bavarian Alps, where they spend up to 10 hours a day conducting climbs. The course then moves to Chamonix in the

French Alps, where the students receive instruction in ice-climbing techniques, culminating in a difficult climbing exercise in the Mont Blanc area. Those who succeed then move on to the skiing sector, which many of the SAS participants, some of whom have never skied before in their lives, find the most difficult. Lack of experience is not taken into account, and within six weeks students have to pass the German Ski Association's Instructor's Test. Those who succeed spend a further three to four weeks on a high alpine course in the Gran Paradiso region of Italy before returning to Luttensee for the final test.

SAS AND ROYAL MARINES

SAS soldiers also attend training courses run by Britain's Royal Marines. The Royal Marines remain heavily committed to the defence of NATO's northern flank. Elements of 3 Commando Brigade still conduct exercises in Norway, during which all participants must pass the Arctic Warfare Training Course, which is also attended on occasion by SAS soldiers.

The three-week course teaches survival and fighting in arctic conditions, and includes elementary skiing tuition given by the Mountain Leaders (MLs) and Military Ski Instructors (MSIs). The MSIs also teach cold-weather survival and the art of building 10- and four-man shelters and snow holes, after which the students spend 11 days and four nights in the field. Ski-qualified personnel who have not deployed to Norway within the previous 12 months, and those who require any form of refresher training, undertake a seven-day course, run during the first month of the Brigade's three-month deployment to Norway. The three-month training schedule includes section and individual battle drills, patrolling, camouflage and concealment, ambush and anti-ambush drills, and an exercise in which

Left: Each SAS 'Sabre' Squadron has a Mountain Troop that specialises in winter warfare operations and mountaineering.

Left: *Rocky terrain on the Jebel Akhdar, northern Oman, which A and D Squadrons conquered in January 1959.*

more simple because many of the men live in the same area as their 'regular' brigade. It is not unusual for SAS troopers to be seen among Italy's rock soldiers.

TRAINING WITH AMERICAN UNITS

The US Marine Corps (USMC) has a cold-weather operational requirement due to the possibility of conflict in Korea, the need to be able to undertake 'out of area' operations, and the USMC's recently established special operations/intervention role. The Corps' Mountain Warfare Training Center, situated at Pickle Meadows in the Sierra Nevada mountains, is an all-year facility which conducts cold weather training and skiing in the winter and mountaineering and high alpine operations in the summer. Up to 10,000 troops a year undertake the 28-day courses which comprise ski instruction, forced marches in the mountains – 10km (six miles) with light packs weighing 13-18kg (29-40lb), and 15km (nine miles) with 22-32kg (49-70lb) packs – and among those troops are British SAS soldiers. The training is extremely realistic, with a number of Marines evacuated with frostnip and acute mountain sickness annually.

All this training ensures that the Regiment's squadrons are fully equipped to undertake mountain campaigns anywhere in the world.

the Commandos play both defenders and the enemy.

Mountain Leaders are provided by the Mountain and Arctic Warfare (M&AW) Cadre, which in time of war also provides 'tactical reconnaissance' for 3 Commando Brigade. Selection and training for the M&AW Cadre is among the toughest in the world, and is a great tester for aspiring SAS mountain warfare specialists. The course lasts over eight months and begins with a seven-day selection phase in Devon and Cornwall. The initial part of the course is so strenuous that a failure rate of 60 per cent is not unusual. The successful candidates then move to the Black Mountains, and from there to Plymouth and ultimately to Rjuken in Norway, where the students undertake the Military Ski Instructor (MSI) course. Usually the students spend six days a week living and training in the field. They learn to survive in sub-zero temperatures, to break trails and cross obstacles. The course finishes with an 11-day exercise, during which the skills learned in the United Kingdom and Norway are tested.

Outside the United Kingdom, the SAS trains with other mountain warfare specialists to further hone its skills. The Italian Alpini are primarily responsible for the defence of NATO's southern flank. The five Alpini brigades are largely made up of conscripts who are doing their 12-month national service. All complete a three-month basic training course before undergoing mountain warfare training with the brigade to which they are posted. Training is very intensive, with much emphasis placed on physical fitness, a factor of obvious importance to mountain troops. A number of men go on for further training as gunners, sappers or radio operators, but the majority serve most of their conscription as infantrymen. Although the majority of Alpini serve for a very short period, most live and work in the mountains and retain their skills and fitness. They could, therefore, be recalled with comparative ease, a factor made

The Jebel Akhdar

In late 1958 and early 1959, A and D Squadrons, 22 SAS were involved in a mountain campaign in northern Oman, specifically on the Jebel Akhdar, a mountain plateau surrounded by high peaks and access via narrow passes. Fresh from the jungles of Malaya, the SAS soldiers had to learn new skills. These included long-range shooting and climbing sheer rock faces. For those who took part, the environment was hard on men and equipment alike. 'Lofty' Large was one of those who fought on the Jebel Akhdar: 'Our boots, which had rubber soles, were worn down so that the screws which had held the soles on were like football boot studs with rubber washers under them. The toe caps were mostly worn away and some of us had our toes showing through. After six weeks a re-supply of boots was most welcome.' Despite the conditions, a combination of supreme stamina and courage led to the SAS storming the plateau after a gruelling night march in the face of the enemy.

Snow and Ice

The 1982 Falklands War proved that SAS soldiers could fight in environments characterised by extremes of cold and wet. Such terrain demands specialised training and equipment to allow the Regiment's men to operate at optimum efficiency.

SAS soldiers receive intensive training in Arctic warfare, an exacting and uncompromising area of combat in which the smallest mistake can prove fatal. In polar regions the body can only operate effectively as long as its temperature is kept within certain limits. Intense cold numbs the brain as well as the body, increasing lethargy and lengthening the reaction time required for even the simplest of tasks. The wind can freeze exposed flesh in minutes, even seconds,

and immersion in cold water can mean death for even the well protected in under 20 minutes.

Cold weather affects every aspect of the soldier's daily routine: the clothing required to withstand the windchill factor (the combination of cold, wind and humidity which can prove lethal at even relatively 'normal' temperatures), the specialist equipment he must take with him, the food he must eat to maintain his strength and the shelter he must construct to pro-

tect him from the elements. High levels of fitness and personal hygiene are paramount, though a balance has to be struck over the latter. Shaving, for instance, is often discouraged as it removes natural oils that protect the face from frostbite. Severe cold can cause frostnip, superficial or deep frostbite, and shock, the latter two being potentially lethal, while wet socks can lead to the incapacitating condition known as trench foot.

The need to keep the whole body covered, especially the hands and feet, is of paramount importance when operating in extreme cold weather. Not only has clothing to be tough, light, windproof and waterproof, it also has to provide insulation down to minus 40 degrees C, while remaining suitable for work in temperatures above zero. Natural fabrics, such as wool and fur, are ideal for cold temperatures as they trap air and maintain a barrier of warm air close to the body. Ideally several layers of relatively thin clothing should be worn, since not only is insulating air trapped between the various garments, but they can be added or removed according to the temperature.

ARCTIC CLOTHING

The SAS has tested a variety of the clothing now commercially available. Choice is largely subjective, but most members of the Regiment favour thermal-knit cotton 'long johns' (although silk 'long-johns' and vests are sometimes purchased privately), wool and nylon socks, heavy wool or wool/nylon blend trousers, Goretex smocks, jackets made from synthetic insulation material, gloves and woolly hats or balaclavas. It is customary to wear wool socks next to the skin and a nylon or Goretex pair on top. Goretex clothing is

Left: Well-wrapped SAS soldiers on an Arctic warfare course in Norway. The beige berets would not be worn on operations.

expensive, but its ability to keep rain out while allowing sweat and moisture to escape outward is considered so beneficial that many servicemen have invested in privately purchased outer jackets. Thermal liners, comprising a green quilted jacket and trouser set, are occasionally worn beneath windproof clothing to supply additional warmth, especially when the soldier is not involved in hard physical activity. They can be worn with or without outer garments, depending on the level of protection required, and over, or instead of, long wool/cotton mix issue underwear.

PROTECTING HANDS AND FEET

Inner mittens are usually worn beneath a windproof and waterproof outer set, although the latter may be replaced for short periods by water-resistant gloves when working in wet conditions. Proper headgear is vital in Arctic conditions, as an estimated 50 per cent of an individual's body heat can be lost through an uncovered head. The standard issue Arctic cap with fold-down ear flaps is popular, although many experienced soldiers have a natural aversion to wearing anything which might interfere with their hearing.

Footwear depends on the particular mission. However, the issue ski-march boot is fairly basic, and many Arctic specialists prefer to invest in the more comfortable and versatile German *Bundeswehr* ski-mountaineering boot. The SAS Arctic warfare rig includes a bergen, snow shoes and cross-country skis. The standard SAS bergen is sometimes replaced with an 'Arctic bergen', which has a light tubular aluminium H-frame, allowing the sac to be carried high on the back, the most effective position for ski-mountaineering. The SAS has a relatively generous budget and can therefore afford to purchase equipment privately when it considers an issue item to be sub-standard. Equally, it is often approached by manufacturers and asked to 'trial' new equipment free. It has therefore been able to abandon the rather inferior standard issue ski with cable bindings in favour of an Alpine tourer/downhill type with ski-mountaineering bindings. Snow shoes are generally small, and their use confined to

close-quarter work, such as a target attack or the completion of routine tasks around the camp.

Not all movement in the Arctic is conducted on foot, and so the SAS makes extensive use of Snow Cats and helicopters when available. However, bad weather and poor visibility can often keep helicopters grounded for days on end, and can also restrict surface traffic. It can also make the maintenance of vehicles and weapons extremely difficult, indeed in extremely cold conditions it can even cause lubricants to thicken or freeze, causing weapon stoppages and sluggish actions. Weapons have therefore to be stripped completely and thoroughly cleaned to remove any excess lubricants. Snow and ice must be kept out of the working parts, sights and barrel, which will otherwise rust. A weapon taken into the warmth of a shelter will sweat for up to an hour. After this period it must be thoroughly cleaned before being taken outside again. Otherwise the condensation will freeze, rendering the weapon unusable. An example of what Arctic conditions can do to weapons occurred during the SAS operation on South Georgia in April 1982. As the men of D Squadron's Mountain Troop struggled across Fortuna Glacier to establish observation posts around Stromness, Husvik and Leith, they were lashed by high winds,

Above: SAS soldiers attend Arctic warfare courses in both Bavaria and the French Alps, as well as here in northern Norway.

which blew snow and ice into their equipment. Very soon ice was found in the feed trays of their GPMGs, effectively rendering them inoperable.

CARE OF AMMUNITION

Ammunition must likewise be cleaned of oil, and all ice, snow and condensation removed. Stored ammunition must be left in its boxes, raised off the ground and covered to protect it from the elements. In the extreme cold certain radio components can become brittle and fail, battery strength is reduced and condensation becomes a problem for all general electrical equipment.

During the winter months almost all cross-country movement in the Arctic is restricted to specialist skis or snow shoes, although using the latter for long periods uses up valuable reserves of stamina. All SAS soldiers who deploy to the area on exercise therefore receive in-theatre ski training on arrival as part of their Arctic warfare (AWT) and Arctic survival (AST) training. During their two- to four-week course they are taught snow-shoeing, fast military skiing and trail-breaking, all essential to successful special forces operations in Arctic regions.

Deserts

The SAS has a long association with the desert. Its first campaign was fought among the sandy wastes of North Africa, while 50 years later SAS soldiers were again fighting in the desert, this time in Iraq. The Regiment has learned to respect this inhospitable environment.

The SAS fought its first and latest campaigns in the desert, an environment in which it has come to feel entirely at ease. Operations in the desert are physically demanding. The dangers of dehydration, sunstroke and sunburn, coupled with the extremes of temperature and the absence of water, have led the SAS to evolve a lifestyle which permits its men not only to survive in the desert but to fight. Attributes required in the desert include good water discipline, thorough personal hygiene and a high standard of physical fitness and stamina. Drinking and eating the correct quantities is crucial, as thirst and appetite are adversely affected by heat. It is not unusual for a trooper to consume up to 14 litres (three gallons) of water a day. In addition to plenty of water, extra salt must be added to the food to replace that lost through evaporation.

DESERT DANGERS

Other dangers to the individual derive from the various types of dangerous animal inhabiting the desert. Snakes dislike the cold, and have an unfortunate dangerous habit of crawling into a part-open sleeping bag at night to enjoy the body-warmth of the unsuspecting occupant. Equally, spiders and scorpions are renowned for crawling into boots, which must be shaken well before being donned in the morning. Lice, mites and flies can carry diseases such as scrub typhus and dysentery. Good sanitation is therefore essential to keep their presence to a minimum. The proper cleaning of cooking and eating utensils, and the correct disposal of garbage and human waste must never be neglected, however exhausted a patrol may be. Feet, which often provide the SAS soldier with his only source of

Right: In a desert environment SAS soldiers have to be constantly on their guard against dehydration, sunstroke and sunburn.

mobility, require particular attention in the desert. They tend to overheat when encompassed in standard combat boots. Most SAS soldiers therefore favour desert boots, with suede uppers, rubber soles and ankle support.

SAS Land Rover vehicles and cross-country motorcycles are specially modified for the desert. The conditions encountered require greater attention to maintenance than normal; vapour locks occur in the fuel systems, batteries become unreliable, and fuel, oil and coolant filters get blocked by sand and dust. Due to the distances involved, and the need for mobility, good driving skills are essential. Prior to the Gulf War, D and G Squadrons held exercises in the Empty Quarter of Saudi Arabia. Drivers learned, when traversing a dune, to climb it on foot first, to ensure that the vehicle would not get stuck on the top, that the slopes were not

too steep nor the sand too soft. They learned that tyres could be partly deflated to improve traction, though too much driving on deflated tyres would lead to overheating. SAS vehicle training in Saudi Arabia, Oman and the United Arab Emirates continues to keep the men up to the high standards required, and helps them combat the exhaustion which inevitably accompanies long-distance desert driving.

The effects on weapons and ammunition of the relentless sun and sand must also be considered. Weapons must be kept covered when not in use as a clogged barrel may lead to dangerous malfunctions. After a rifle is cleaned all excess oil must be removed from the working parts, otherwise sand will adhere and create an abrasive paste which will quickly damage the weapon. Domestic cling film, and even condoms, can be used as a makeshift

barrier against sand and dust intrusion. The desert heat can also adversely affect radio equipment. Solder may become brittle and connections loose. In addition, batteries require re-charging more frequently, a factor which only serves to add to the signaller's already heavy workload.

CAMOUFLAGE

Camouflage is crucial in the flat, featureless desert. Nets are used to conceal both men and vehicles, and should ideally have hessian or cloth sown into them to provide shade from the sun. They also provide a degree of protection when using optical equipment such as binoculars, which might otherwise glint in the sun. Harbour areas must be camouflaged as soon as they are occupied. Where available, natural features such as caves and dead ground provide protection both from the elements and prying eyes, but deep wadis should be avoided if at all possible. Deserts are prone to sudden heavy downpours which may result in flash floods. Special forces soldiers have drowned in the desert.

However, it is the absence, rather than the abundance, of water that is generally a problem. SAS troopers are trained in

The Gulf War

The 1991 Gulf War was a triumph for the SAS, but the conditions the men faced on the ground were a long way from the popular image of a desert terrain. Though it was undoubtedly sandy and rocky, the weather was very cold in western Iraq in January and February. All those SAS soldiers who took part in missions in Iraq spoke of the cold and the wet, of being lashed continually by rain and sleet, and of the whole region being 'worse than the Falklands'. The desert clothing issued to the men was insufficient, and so improvisation was the order of the day. In photographs of SAS soldiers on operations in Iraq, they are invariably clothed in Goretex jackets, jumpers, blankets, gloves, Arctic smocks and woolly hats. Hypothermia is usually associated with mountain and Arctic warfare, but two of the Regiment's men – Sergeant Vince Phillips and Lance-Corporal 'Legs' Lane – died of hypothermia as they tried to escape from Iraqi troops. The Gulf War brought home just how unpredictable and dangerous a desert environment can be.

emergency situations to construct a desert still which will provide sufficient water to sustain life. Stills are comparatively easy to construct and can provide up to a litre (1.8 pints) of drinkable water per day. A site is chosen where water might be expected to collect. A hole is then dug one metre (39in) deep and two metres (6.5ft) wide and filled with old vegetation, waste water, urine and any other liquid available. A container is then placed

in the centre, together with a drinking tube extending to the side. The hollow is then covered with a plastic sheet with a rough outer surface, with one or two placed in the centre. Condensation will form, and drip into the container. Just one of the tricks taught to SAS soldiers.

Below: An SAS Mobility Troop in the United Arab Emirates, one of the countries used by the Regiment for desert warfare training.

INSERTION TECHNIQUES

Over Land

Since the campaign in North Africa in World War II the SAS has had to solve the problem of how to transport its men on land. Today each 'Sabre' Squadron has a Mobility Troop that specialises in vehicles, and the SAS is among the best when it comes to insertion over land.

The SAS was among the first allied units to be deployed in the Gulf theatre of operations during the UN conflict with Iraq in 1991. The SAS preceded the Royal Marines onto the Fortuna Glacier during Operation 'Paraquet', the taking of South Georgia, and paved the way for 3 Commando Brigade's landing at San Carlos Water. None of this would have been possible had the SAS not become expert in the art of covert insertion.

The method by which an SAS patrol is taken to, and removed from, enemy occupied territory is determined by its specific mission. If speed is of the essence the attack force may be inserted close to its objective. When, during the Gulf War, a combined US-British strike force was tasked with the capture and return for analysis of an enemy SAM missile and launcher system, it was dropped almost on top of its target, and relied upon speed and surprise to secure its objective. Egyptian helicopters of Soviet manufacture, painted in Iraqi colours, were used, and were so successful in their deception that upon their return to base their presence started a rumour that a sizeable part of the Iraqi helicopter fleet had defected.

SAS patrols may be inserted by a variety of means, either by land, sea or air. Less often they may adopt disguises and false identities for undercover operations. In Aden in the 1960s, for example, SAS 'Keeni Meeni' patrols adopted local dress to infiltrate on foot the local markets which provided cover for insurgent groups. More recently, SAS patrols have operated in plain clothes in Northern Ireland, gaining intelligence on the movement of terrorist cells. Land-borne insertion has always been a popular method of getting the SAS to their targets.

MOBILITY TROOPS

Many borders are poorly monitored or consist of difficult terrain, facilitating vehicle-borne covert insertion. In July 1942, the SAS began its tradition of riding into battle when it adopted the US-made Willys jeep. Today, the Mobility Troop attached to each 'Sabre' Squadron may call upon a variety of vehicles, including converted Land Rovers, motorcycles and even specially adapted Range Rovers (used by hostage-rescue teams). Where possible, vehicles are designed to operate in any climate, although in reality they are most likely to be used in desert or open grassland conditions.

Left: The SAS 'Pink Panther', first used in the 1960s. The pink camouflage helped the vehicle blend into its desert surroundings.

Units such as the SAS and their close foreign counterparts, the Australian SAS and the US Special Forces, which often operate behind the lines, require light, reliable vehicles which are capable of giving maximum mobility while carrying a heavy weapons load. The requirements for lightness and speed on the one hand and maximum payload on the other are conflicting, with the result that individual units have had to prioritise their needs. Thus the SAS, which does not train to hold ground and uses its weapons mainly on targets of opportunity, concentrates on vehicles capable of transporting the vast quantities of food and water required to carry out long-range reconnaissance deep inside enemy territory.

Other special forces units have developed vehicles for their very different needs. Thus the French Foreign Legion, as part of France's *Force D'Action Rapide* (Rapid Reaction Force), is equipped for combat against all but heavy forces. Ideally suited to service in Africa and the Middle East, the armoured cars of its 1st Cavalry Regiment (*Regiment Etranger de Cavalerie*) and a battalion of its 1st Infantry Regiment served with the 6th Light Armoured Division during the Iraq War. At other times the Legion has served to show the French flag on numerous high-profile peacekeeping missions and in a number of 'out of area' operations. Never far from logistical support, it uses its heavily armed reconnaissance vehicles according to French military doctrine, for scouting and screening. As such its needs are wholly different from those of the British SAS.

AMERICAN VEHICLE DOCTRINE

At the moment the SAS is far ahead of American units when it comes to vehicles. The United States has yet to develop a comprehensive land insertion policy. Until the Gulf War, the Green Berets had gained most of their experience in the jungle and had thus learned to rely on airborne or seaborne insertion (the SAS had also much experience of the jungle, but had not neglected its vehicle capabilities). It was only after Operation 'Eagle Claw', the abortive attempt to free the Iranian hostages in 1980, that the United

States began to accept the need for a dedicated covert operations road vehicle. The Chenworth Fast Attack Vehicle (FAV) was developed, and saw considerable service in the Gulf, but its usefulness has still to be accepted by many at Fort Bragg, the Headquarters of the Green Berets. Unlike the SAS, the US Green Berets have no specialist courses in vehicle operation and maintenance. Although Delta Force, the elite counter-terrorist unit, received some training in the maintenance of its FAVs before deployment to the Gulf, the overall US attitude towards vehicle-mounted insertion remains sadly lacking. It must be said, however, that US Special Forces are trained in both vehicle tactics and movement, which closely mirror the operating procedures of more conventional reconnaissance units. The lead vehicle is halted in a surveillance position to observe the

Above: Heavily armed Land Rovers give the SAS the ability to launch long-range land operations behind enemy lines.

road ahead. While it offers cover, the second vehicle moves forward, passes it and adopts a surveillance position some way forward. Thus the vehicles leap-frog forward, each offering the other some degree of protection.

Only the US Rangers make full use of vehicle infiltration. In snow and ice areas they make excellent use of Snow Cats, motorised sledges, skis and snow shoes, and in the desert and other flat terrain employ jeeps to mount raids and interdiction missions. Until recently the Rangers relied on Ford M151 utility trucks, or 'gun jeeps', to provide the short-distance mobility and high firepower required. These might be armed with a variety of

Left: SAS Jeeps in northwest Europe in early 1945. The SAS Willys Jeep had an unrefuelled range of 460km (285 miles).

weapons, including two 7.62mm M60 machine guns, 90mm recoilless rifles, M72 Light Anti-Tank Weapons (LAWs) and Claymore anti-personnel mines. Currently they employ the High Mobility Multi-purpose Wheeled Vehicle (HMMWV), which is designed to operate in all types of terrain and climate. Through the use of common components and kits it can be turned into a number of variants, including a cargo-troop carrier, armament carrier, ambulance or TOW missile carrier.

TRAINING OTHER UNITS

The land-borne insertion doctrine of the SAS naturally means devoting huge resources to training. But this produces soldiers who are experts at their craft, and who are in great demand around the world to train other elite units. The SAS, for example, has helped establish a land-borne insertion doctrine of its Australian counterpart. One of the main tasks of the Australian SAS is the defence of northern Australia. In the event of invasion, SAS vehicle groups would either remain in stay-behind positions or infiltrate themselves behind the lines via the old cattle stock routes which crisscross the area. Their mission requirements would be to provide reconnaissance and intelligence on the enemy's flanks and rear, and to

execute harrying raids against his lines of communication. The Australians turned to Hereford for instruction in solar and astro-navigation.

Australian vehicle training incorporates many of the skills taught at Hereford: negotiating inclines, crossing rivers, winching vehicles over obstacles or out of soft ground, navigation, and vehicle service and repair. Vehicle tactics, such as scouting and contact drills, are taught, as are communications and mission planning. Patrol leaders must become adept at assessing their fuel requirements and payload priorities, locating checkpoints and lying-up positions, the location of friendly forces, and the sheer problems of survival in one of the most uncompromisingly brutal desert terrains in the world. Experience has taught the SASR to rely on the tried-and-tested long-wheelbase Land Rover. Despite its comparative lack of sophistication it is one of the few vehicles able to cope with the vast distances involved, the amount of kit to be carried and the need to service the vehicle under operational conditions.

Like most things concerning the British SAS, the use of vehicles has been a process of evolution. The Regiment used heavily armed jeeps in World War II, and then progressed to Land Rovers in the early 1960s. Despite the occasional flirta-

tion with other vehicles, the Regiment has remained loyal, and still favours the Land Rover for most circumstances. During the Gulf War, for example, specially adapted SAS Land Rover 110s usually carried a crew of three, and were armed with varied combinations of heavy machine guns, GPMGs, 40mm automatic grenade launchers, Milan anti-tank missiles and Stinger surface-to-air missiles. Some of the Land Rovers did not have the fixture to mount Milans, but this did not worry their crews, as an SAS soldier states: 'We used a homemade bracket improvised from wood and para-cord and strapped to the roll bar.'

Although not employed in the Gulf, the Land Rover Special Operations Vehicle (SOV) aptly provides for the Regiment's future needs. Capable of carrying a crew of six, it can be fitted with machine guns front and rear (in addition to the twin mounts on the pulpit), an 81mm mortar, a 51mm mortar and has mounts for individual weapons. A Milan or Tube-launched, Optically-tracked, Wire-guided (TOW) anti-tank missile or a 30mm cannon can be mounted on the pulpit instead of the twin machine guns if required.

GULF WAR TESTING GROUND

The adoption of the FAV by the US Special Forces caused the SAS to reappraise its attitude towards light vehicles. A number of Longline Light Strike Vehicles (LSVs) were taken to the Gulf, but their limited payload was found to be inadequate for long-range operations, and they were relegated to reconnaissance along the border area.

The Gulf War fully tested the various special forces land insertion techniques. The SAS and US Special Forces were tasked with locating mobile and static Iraqi Scud sites for Allied air interdiction. The SAS adopted two methods to find the missiles, one of which was markedly more successful than the other. Three road watch patrols were sent into Iraq to watch main roads. All three patrols had to abandon their missions.

Above: Nearly 50 years later, SAS Land Rover 110s were transporting SAS soldiers behind the lines in Iraq during the 1991 Gulf War.

The vehicle patrols were more successful. The fighting columns comprised 12 or more heavily armed Land Rovers, each carrying a total of 1525kg (1.5 tons) of supplies and accompanied by motorcycle scouts. The SAS's operational area ran from Karbala, 80km (50 miles) southwest of Baghdad, to Iraq's border with Syria and Jordan. The fighting columns had sufficient firepower to fend off Iraqi attacks and take on targets themselves should no Allied aircraft be available for air strikes (though it was standard operating procedure to keep as far away from Iraqi units as possible). However, the frequent contacts and speedy withdrawals severely reduced supplies of fuel and ammunition (a perennial problem for vehicle-mounted patrols is the compromise between

loading down vehicles with weaponry and ammunition for defence and trying to make them as light as possible to extend range and speed).

The SAS fighting columns were re-supplied by a convoy of 10 four-ton trucks escorted by armed Land Rovers from B Squadron. The convoy drove 145km (90 miles) inside Iraq to establish a replenishment base. The effort was well worth it, for the SAS fighting columns achieved some significant results: a number of Scud surface-to-surface missile (SSM) sites and convoys were located and designated for air attack. Other targets of opportunity destroyed included high observation towers, microwave repeater towers and buried fibre-optic cables.

Meanwhile, the US Delta Force undertook a similar role to the north of the SAS. The limited range of their FAVs – around 400km (250 miles) – forced them to undertake short, penetrating raids

rather than long-range missions. Delta was equally successful, but was forced to rely on re-supply from the air, and its operations would have been severely compromised had the Allies not enjoyed complete air superiority over the area of operations from the beginning.

The SAS has the expertise to take its vehicles anywhere in the world. They can do this because of two things. First, it has highly trained vehicle operators who can service their vehicles and repair battle damage without the need for garage facilities. Second, in the Land Rover the Regiment has a vehicle that can operate in any terrain with the minimum of needs. Land Rovers also provide SAS Mobility Troops with the ideal combination of mobility, range, payload requirements and firepower. And as the 1991 Gulf War proved, when it comes to insertion over land, the SAS is one of the best and most experienced.

By Water

SAS Boat Troops are experts when it comes to working with small boats and canoes. This is part of David Stirling's original belief that SAS soldiers should be trained to reach their targets by land, sea or air. Today the SAS works closely with its maritime counterpart, the SBS.

The Special Air Service (SAS) and the Special Boat Service (SBS) both come under the operational control of the Director Special Forces (DSF). Although they work closely they are separate units, and their roles should not be confused. In time of war the SBS, a five-squadron force drawn from the ranks of the Royal Marine Commandos, would undertake reconnaissance, small raids and maritime and coastal sabotage. They regard the water as their natural habitat rather than as a means of access to the land, and many of their operations take place completely submerged. They will reconnoitre a beach prior to an amphibious landing to identify the slope of the beach, the depth of the water, underwater obstacles, sea conditions and enemy defences. They will go ashore to investigate the composition and gradient of the beach, but will avoid contact with the enemy unless specifically ordered to do otherwise.

To destroy ships in harbour, SBS teams will carry their equipment and explosives in a buoyancy bag partly filled with water to make it weightless when submerged. Once inside the harbour the divers will try to use the prevailing currents to drift from target to target, thereby avoiding creating telltale swirls in the water. The precise position in which the limpets are placed will depend on the size of the ship and the configuration of the hull, factors which the divers will have learned to take into account during training.

SAS BOAT TROOPS

There are only four Boat Troops in the SAS – some 64 men – yet their contribution to Britain's amphibious warfare effort is immense. During Operation 'Paraquet', for example, the retaking of South Georgia during the Falklands War, they undertook a seaborne landing at considerable personal risk in appalling weather conditions. Their boats were overturned, flooded and suffered damage, and one was swept away to sea, but all the SAS personnel involved were eventually recovered

safely. Subsequently, during the battle for the Falklands, SAS personnel arriving by air from Ascension Island with their equipment were parachuted into the sea to be picked up by submarines or surface vessels. Patrols were then inserted by the boat close to the shore to begin their reconnaissance activities.

SAS patrols landing by sea along a hostile shoreline are usually inserted by Rigid Raider boats piloted by members of the specialist 539 Assault Squadron, Royal Marines. The boats themselves are 5m (16.4ft) long with glass-fibre hulls, and are powered by 140hp Johnson outboard engines giving maximum speeds of up to 35 knots. Their low silhouette, coupled with their modified, quiet engines, make them ideally suited to the clandestine infiltration and extraction of SAS patrols along enemy-held coastlines. Each 16-man Boat Troop will usually be carried in three Rigid Raiders. One will beach first, while the others 'stand-off' to offer covering fire in the case of any enemy resistance.

Canoes have been associated with the SAS since its inception, and are still used when the employment of Rigid Raiders is considered impractical. Wooden-framed Kleppers have been in service since the 1950s, and still remain operational with the SAS and SBS. For example, they were used by the SAS during the build-up to the raid on Pebble Island in May 1982. A reconnaissance team from D Squadron's Boat Troop was dropped by Sea King helicopter on 10 May and had to march across a ridge at the end of the Mare Rock headland, carrying their Klepper canoes and bergens with them. Throughout the next day they watched Pebble Island for Argentine activity, before pad-

Left: SAS soldiers in Borneo in the 1960s steer their canoes through choppy waters. Such craft are ideal for silent approaches.

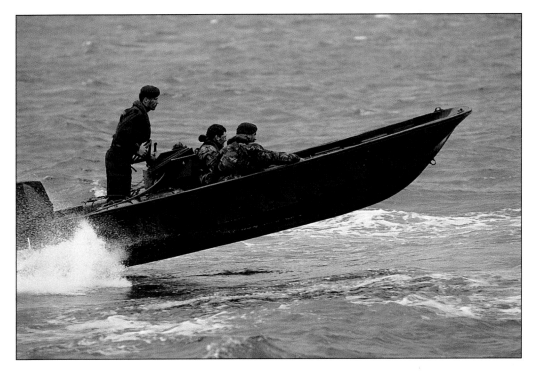

dling across under cover of darkness to carry out their mission.

Later, during the final stages of the battle for East Falkland, the SAS volunteered to put in a diversionary raid from the sea to take the pressure off 2 Para who were about to assault Wireless Ridge. The target was a large Argentinian ordnance depot, and the approach was by a narrow strip of water immediately to the north of the capital, Stanley. The mission was risky, there were about 8000 heavily armed soldiers in and around the town. The infiltration team – two troops from D Squadron, one from G Squadron and six members of the SBS – approached the target in Rigid Raiders. They were supported by naval gunfire from the frigate *Antrim*, and by an SAS mini-diversion launched from Murrell Heights on the northern shore of the harbour approach. The raiders were compromised when searchlights from the hospital ship *Bahia Paraiso*, which was moored in the harbour, spotted the Rigid Raiders. The attackers came under immediate sustained fire. Faced with annihilation, they did the only sensible thing and withdrew. The SAS reached the safety of the shore after sustaining three minor casualties.

Right: The two-man Klepper canoe, which was used for reconnaissance prior to the Pebble Island raid during the Falklands War.

Larger landing craft, again crewed by Royal Marine Commandos from the task force's landing craft, assault and raiding squadrons, were also involved in the insertion and extraction of SAS and SBS reconnaissance patrols. The Landing Craft Vehicle/Personnel (LCVP) had a greater range – 140km (87 miles) – if slower speed – 9.5 knots – than the more agile Raiders, but were more heavily armed and armoured, and were capable of conducting a fighting withdrawal if attacked.

The SAS and SBS have always worked closely together. In 1972, for example, a combined SAS/SBS team parachuted into the Atlantic Ocean to deal with a bomb threat to the luxury liner *Queen Elizabeth II*. Fortunately it turned out to be a hoax, though it did highlight the problems of maritime security.

Today the SAS's Boat Troops are responsible for Maritime Counter Measures, which entails providing security for Britain's oilfields against terrorist attack. This necessarily means working closely with the SBS. The two units continue to use the Rigid Raiders for fast insertion, but insertion from under the waves is also practised. This involves combat diving training at Poole in Dorset and in Horsea Lake near Portsmouth.

A new item of equipment to be recently tested by the Boat Troops is the submersible recovery craft, an inflatable which can submerge and deliver a team to the target below the waves. It can also be parked on the bottom and left by the team until after the mission. This piece of kit gives SAS Boat Troops greater flexibility when it comes to clandestine insertion onto an enemy shore.

By Air

The airborne role of the Special Air Service is to insert teams into and out of enemy territory as and when required. To this end all troopers are parachute trained, but each 'Sabre' Squadron has an Air Troop that specialises in methods of airborne delivery.

SAS specialists from the 'Sabre' Squadrons' Air Troops are all fully parachute trained. Before any recruit can wear the Winged Dagger badge, he must pass the static-line parachute course at RAF Brize Norton in Oxfordshire. All the Regiment's soldiers have to be parachute-trained from day one. Every member of the 'Sabre' Squadrons wears the famous SAS wings on his chest, indicating he is a trained parachutist.

The parachute course lasts four weeks, and is held at least four times a year. As well as potential SAS soldiers, recruits from the Parachute Regiment also attend. It is run by RAF Parachute Jump Instructors (PJIs), and they teach an average of 30 on each course.

STATIC-LINE DROPS

The aim is very simple: the PJIs teach the recruits how to make a static-line jump from an aircraft. A static-line jump is where the parachute ripcord is pulled automatically when a soldier jumps from the aircraft. To pass the course, each potential SAS soldier must make eight jumps, including one at night. All straightforward stuff.

But those who think that they will be jumping from an aircraft on day one will be disappointed. The PJIs are among the best in the world at their job. They have to ensure that each man is thoroughly trained and briefed before he can make a jump. And that means starting right at the beginning – on soft mats in one of the aircraft hangars.

The first week consists of learning how to make parachute landings. This involves practising parachute rolls, attending lectures concerning aircraft flight techniques, the theory of parachute aerodynamics and the types of aircraft the men will be jumping from. The talks are designed to give the men a rest from all the physical exercises.

Landing correctly is very important to airborne soldiers. Getting him to the drop zone (DZ) is fine, but if he is wounded when he lands then he will be useless to his unit. In fact, he will be worse than useless because he will require looking after. Therefore, the first week starts with the PJIs teaching the recruits how to land correctly. They are taught the proper position for landing: chin on chest, elbows in, legs together, knees bent and feet flat to the floor. They will then practise rolling on the mats: rolling to the right, to the left and forward.

Then the PJIs introduce them to flight drills. The men are taught that they must look up immediately after the parachute opens to check their canopy. If their rig lines are twisted they will have to untangle them. They are taught the procedure.

During the second week the students are introduced to the aircraft mock-ups. These are precise representations of the Hercules transport aircraft, the type they will be making the real drops from. They go through the drills in the aircraft, such

Above: British special forces kitted up in all the equipment needed to make a high altitude, low opening (HALO) jump.

as hooking-up their 'chutes, checking their equipment and exit drills.

Exiting an aircraft correctly is crucial. The students are therefore instructed on the procedure using the exit trainer. This consists of a 22.8m- (75ft-) high tower, from which the men drop. Their harnesses are connected to a wire, which allows them to drop as they would were they making a proper jump. As well as giving them a 'feel' for a jump, it allows the PJIs to get a look at how they make landings. This is where the students first really appreciate the hours they put in learning how to land and roll.

During the second week the men are also introduced to their equipment. This includes their parachutes – the Irwin PX1 Mark 4 main parachute, worn on the back, and the PR7 reserve, worn on the chest – and their bergens. The bergens are carried under the reserve 'chute when the men exit the aircraft. During the descent they are released and are suspended underneath each man at the end of a 12m (40ft) line. The line is secured to the chest webbing by way of two hooks. In this way they hit the ground first. As each bergen weighs at least 18.18kg (40lb), to put it on a man's back will substantially increase his chances of a landing injury. In addition, there is his weapon, which is carried in a sleeve on the side of the bergen. The men will also be introduced to the life jackets, which will be worn if they are making a jump near water.

JUMP TRAINING

This familiarisation training takes all of the second week. The third week is when the men make their first jump. The first jump is made without any bergen. The men just wear their main 'chute and the reserve. By now they are fully briefed as to the procedure.'

Some 20 minutes into the flight the order is given to check kit. The men stand up and check their reserve 'chutes. Then each man checks the main 'chute of the man in front. The command 'action station' is given, and the men file down the aircraft towards the two doors at the rear of the aircraft. They are located on each side of the fuselage. They hook up their 'chutes. They will make their jump in two lines, or 'sticks', one from each door. When they leave the aircraft the lines will automatically open their parachutes.

When the light over each door changes from red to green the aircraft is then over the DZ. The instructors scream 'go, go, go!', and the men throw themselves out of the aircraft.

The first jump over, they then prepare for drops with bergens. The jumps are made from an altitude of 300m (984ft). For the SAS on the course this is a gentle introduction: SAS operational jumps can be as low as 120m (400ft)!

The rest of weeks three and four are taken up with the other seven jumps. The men are briefed on wind speed and direction, height of jump, rally points after they have hit the ground, weather conditions, visibility and the exact time they will leave the aircraft. The final jump is the night one with full kit. This does cause

some jitters, as an SAS soldier explains: 'Even in the Regiment blokes are terrified of parachuting at night, especially the bigger guys. They come down heavier, you see. If they drop you in the wrong place, over power lines and water, you can drown or break your neck. Having said that, at the end of the day it's the coward's option to jump. Does that sound surprising? You have to remember that you are frightened of what people, your mates, are thinking about you. At the end of the day it's easier to jump, despite the risks.'

The main parachuting injuries are broken ankles and legs, sprains and damaged knees and backs. Leg injuries are

Above: The Sea King helicopter, seen here lifting a Light Strike Vehicle, is used by SAS teams for airborne insertion.

particularly common when students get tangled rig lines and attempt to untangle them by flailing around with their legs. If they land with their legs apart they risk broken bones.

Problems in the air are very rare these days. Canopies used to be made of silk. When they got wet sometimes they wouldn't open. The parachute used to 'Roman candle', plummeting to earth and killing its wearer. Occasionally men would collide in the air and get tangled

Above: A four-man Pathfinder team exits a Hercules to make a HALO jump. This is the procedure followed by SAS Air Troops.

– which meant death for both of them. A further problem was one parachutist getting underneath another and 'stealing' his air, causing the top canopy to collapse.

However, all these are freak accidents, and the SAS has only had one fatality on parachute training in its entire history. The failure rate at Brize Norton is less than one per cent – testimony to the excellence of the tuition.

Once they are deployed to their squadrons, SAS soldiers are trained to drop on to targets from heights of 11km (6.8 miles) above sea level. HALO (high altitude, low opening) is the parachute insertion technique most commonly used by the SAS. Patrols leave the aircraft from

Left: Flat canopy ramair parachutes are controllable, and allow SAS team members to land in close proximity to each other.

high altitude, usually off the back ramp of a C-130 Hercules, and descend in freefall as a group, before deploying their 'chutes at low altitude and landing normally. HALO has many advantages. The aircraft will be able to fly high enough to be invisible to the naked eye and safe from hand-held SAM systems; the team being inserted will be able to stay together, an important consideration during night descents; and will be able to descend to a minimum height comparatively fast. Automatic parachute release mechanisms are used where possible. The parachute will usually deploy at about 760m (2500ft), giving the parachutist the chance to pull his reserve should the main canopy fail.

HALO jumping has its risks. Parachutists may face stress-induced hyper-ventilation and barometric trauma, caused by the lower air pressure at great heights. In addition there is a danger of wind-chill as individuals plummet at a rate of 192km/hr (120mph). Ice may form on goggles and altimeter, which may cause the freefaller to lose symmetry as he tries to rub it off. Should his load shift as a result he may go into an uncontrollable spin, with fatal results.

HAHO (high altitude, high opening) insertions are also employed by the SAS. Exit procedures from the transport aircraft are at about 10,000m (32,800ft) and standard, with members of the patrol deploying their parachutes at about 8500m (27,887ft) after a delay of eight to 10 seconds. Downwards speed will normally be at a rate of 8-10m (26-33ft) per second, depending on height, temperature, air density and equipment carried.

HAHO INSERTION

The military benefits of HAHO parachuting are obvious. An aircraft can unload its human cargo well outside the borders of a hostile country, yet the landing area can be well inside. With the introduction of remotely steered parachutes, containers can be dropped with the parachutists, who will be able to guide them safely to land. Yet there are also a number of attendant risks. There is a danger of the team drifting off course. Chest-mounted navigation packs, based on the Global Positioning System (GPS), allow each parachutist to check his position and amend his glide path, but can do nothing in the face of unexpected wind changes or thermals. The team must try to stick together in order to land in a tight formation. Some parachutes have panels coated with a luminous material that emits a dull glow, but even this can be difficult to see and mid-air collisions remain a constant threat. Finally, there is the danger of asphyxiation and frostbite. Temperatures can be as low as minus 45 degrees C (minus 50 degrees F) at 10,000m (32,800ft), and layers of warm clothing are essential if the parachutists are not to sustain serious injury.

Helicopters are now in regular use by special forces throughout the world, and the SAS has its own Army Air Corps flight. The flight employs a number of

Right: Lynx helicopters such as these have been used for the infiltration and exfiltration of SAS personnel, especially in Ulster.

Parachutes

A standard parachute canopy with its low glide-ratio would keep its wearer in the air for about 10 minutes after being dropped from a height of 10,000m (32,800ft) and would land no more than 5km (3.1 miles) from the release point. However, a fully-laden SAS trooper HAHO (high altitude, high opening) jumping from 10,000m (32,800ft) using a GQ 360 nine-cell flat ramair main canopy, which has the same aerodynamic properties as an aircraft wing, can travel up to 24km (14.9 miles) before touching down. At these high altitudes oxygen will be required for the initial part of the glide, which may well last from 70 to 80 minutes. Both HAHO and HALO (high altitude, low opening) SAS parachutists wear oxygen-breathing equipment, helmet with headset and altimeter as standard, in addition to his two 'chutes. The latter are fully steerable, allowing the team to land together. In addition, they can be stalled by their wearer on landing to make for a safer landing. Many SAS troopers, because of their parachuting skills, take part in international events.

rotary-wing aircraft, including Chinooks retrofitted with air-to-air fuelling probes for long-range insertions. During the Falklands War, helicopters were used for, inserting and recovering SAS reconnaissance and fighting patrols from various parts of the islands. Sea Kings of 846 Squadron, Royal Navy, were used to transport the men of D Squadron to Pebble Island to raid the enemy airstrip located there. And two Wessex helicopters of 845 squadron were lost during the ultimately successful attempt to recover a patrol trapped on South Georgia's Fortuna Glacier.

Though all SAS are parachute trained, it appears that parachute insertion has been down-graded by Hereford in favour of helicopter insertion. However, there are no plans to drop parachute training.

SABOTAGE

Targets

As well as collecting intelligence, other SAS missions behind enemy lines include sabotaging key vulnerable military and industrial targets with explosives. In this way a small-sized SAS team can achieve results out of all proportion to its size.

The men of the SAS are masters in the use of demolitions and sabotage. The Regiment was created by David Stirling in July 1941 as a hit-and-run force, ideally suited to small-scale raids behind the lines, but equally ill-equipped for conventional battle. From September 1941 to the end of the North African campaign in May 1943 it operated in the desert, attacking main supply routes, airfields,

ammunition and fuel dumps, indeed any target of opportunity which would cause the enemy distress. During one successful raid in December 1941, for example, a four-man patrol destroyed no less than 37 Axis aircraft at Agedabia airfield. Under the cover of darkness they infiltrated the airfield and placed small delayed-action charges on the fuselage of each aircraft before withdrawing unseen. From North

Africa the SAS moved to Italy, and ultimately to the Northwest European theatre. Although its targets altered as the war evolved its principles were never compromised. Boldness and surprise remained two of its basic tenets.

Where possible its members infiltrated their targets covertly, laying delayed-action explosive charges timed to go off only after they had effected their escape. Occasionally, multiple charges were laid on the same night, each timed to explode simultaneously to effect maximum confusion. In all the SAS undertook over 40 independent missions in France between June and December 1944. Although many were costly in terms of lives, none was a complete failure. Whole German divisions were diverted from the front to counter the infiltrators and their *Maquis* (French Resistance) supporters. No more than 2000 SAS personnel were employed in France, yet their contribution, particularly in terms of disruption to enemy railways by sabotage, was immense.

MODERN SAS SABOTAGE
Modern SAS sabotage operations usually involve the disruption of enemy services, supplies or industrial output by violent means. Targets may be chosen for their political, social or economic impact, or as part of a larger military strategy to confuse, hamper and tie down troops engaged in the static defence of vital installations or the search for saboteurs. Occasionally targets will be non-attributable to avoid escalation or to prevent the alienation of

Left: Half a kilo (1lb) of Semtex plastic explosive detonates underneath a standard motorcar during a demolitions test.

neutral third parties. During the covert infiltration of SAS patrols into Indonesia during the Borneo campaign in the 1960s, enemy forward bases and supply routes were frequently sabotaged, but the fact was kept a closely guarded secret by both sides to avoid the possibility of adversely affecting international opinion.

Later, during the campaign to recover the Falklands in 1982, plans were laid to land an SAS troop in Chile, from where it would have moved eastwards to attack Argentine air assets on the ground. The plan was eventually abandoned for a number of reasons, not the least being the effect that carrying the war to the South American mainland might have had on Argentina's neighbours.

SPECIAL FORCES DEMOLITIONS

The SAS, along with other special forces units, has discovered that the most effective sabotage is that committed against strategic targets. The risks, though, can be very high.

In 1985 France was forced to concede secret service complicity in the sinking of the Greenpeace ship *Rainbow Warrior* in Auckland harbour. On that occasion France took a hawkish stance. Although defence minister Charles Henru resigned and Admiral Lacoste, head of the security services, was sacked, the government remained largely unrepentant. When two agents, Major Alain Tourand and Captain Sophie Turenge, were arrested, France threatened New Zealand with economic sanctions to secure their release. As a result they were transferred to French military custody and deported to the Pacific island of Hao to complete their sentences. Despite New Zealand protests, Tourand and Turenge were returned to France on the grounds of ill health and released well before their sentences were completed. Both made 'surprising' recoveries.

The propensity of Israel to resort to overt sabotage when she feels her security to be imperilled is well known. The Israeli Intelligence and Security Services have always been unorthodox in their interpretation of international law. *Shin Beth*, the Security and Counter-Espionage Service, and *Mossad le Aliyah Beth*, the Institution for Intelligence and Special

Services, were both founded in 1949, the latter by Eliahu Golomb and Shaul Avigur, the founders of the 1940s Haganah intelligence service, Shai. They quickly developed a remarkable reputation for ruthlessness, but without doubt helped to secure the embryonic state of Israel. Mossad suffered a series of reverses in 1954, when a number of sabotage operations within Egypt and Syria ended in disaster. However, with limited, and at the time top secret, CIA support it was able to recover. Today Mossad receives help and support from the American Central Intelligence Agency (CIA) and MI6, the British intelligence-gathering service, as well as the French and German security services. However, it is probably fair to say that none of these institutions fully trusts it, and would certainly no longer support it in acts of sabotage.

SAS TARGETS

In a conventional war SAS targets for sabotage will include the enemy's means of nuclear release if any; his command, control, communications and intelligence centres; and his headquarters and vulnerable points along his main supply routes (MSRs). These may take the form of bridges, rail junctions or even dykes pro-

Above: The tremendous power of modern explosives becomes abundantly clear after the dust has settled.

tecting low-lying areas from flooding. Often these will be more easily interdicted from the air. However, occasionally geographical constraints, the presence of heavy anti-aircraft defences or the small size of the target, will make this impossible. When this occurs specialist teams like SAS patrols will be inserted to destroy the target from the ground.

Where circumstances permit, these teams may be given multiple missions, not all of them relating to sabotage. Thus, during the Iraq War three SAS teams, including the ill-fated 'Bravo Two Zero', were helicoptered into enemy territory with orders to locate and report the movement of enemy Scud surface-to-surface missiles (SSMs) along the MSRs, while destroying the underground communication links between Baghdad and northwest Iraq.

'Bravo Two Zero' was given a strategic task in locating and destroying the underground landlines. These landlines were the only way that the Iraqi dictator, Saddam Hussein, had of getting orders to his Scud mobile launch teams in western Iraq. All other communications methods

had been destroyed by United Nations aircraft when the pylons and transmitters above ground had been knocked out. The team was also ordered to destroy the mobile Scuds if they could. The SAS soldiers decided to do this by disabling the control centre in the middle of the Scud launcher with explosives.

The landlines themselves were to be destroyed by making four or six cuts along the cables and packing each with explosives, each charge timed to detonate at different times over a number of days. The charges would all be laid in one night, with small Elsie anti-personnel mines used to booby trap the actual manhole covers.

Sometimes sabotage teams will be positioned during the period of transition to war, when a degree of freedom of movement is still permissible. They will cross the border unarmed and in plain clothes, singly or in small groups, and will meet at a safe house where they will collect their weapons and explosives. They will then use the period of confusion which follows the outbreak of hostilities to lay their demolitions and then escape.

Reconnaissance is all important and static targets, such as bridges and power stations, will almost certainly be surveyed in peacetime. Prior to the disintegration of the Soviet Union, for example, it is widely believed that *Spetsnaz* (special forces) teams frequently toured the West in the guise of sporting clubs and other organisations. When not participating in their chosen event they would slip into the countryside to examine the perimeters of their proposed targets for vulnerable points and means of entry. It was not unusual for such teams to get lost en route to a sports event, and to arrive at their destination having driven suspiciously, and wholly unnecessarily, close to a power station or other site of strategic interest. Little could be done to stop them, even though the abuse was well known within NATO, and it is likely that prior to the ending of the Cold War the Soviet Union could boast some very comprehensive plans of a large number of extremely important strategic centres throughout western Europe.

NON-LETHAL USE OF EXPLOSIVES

There is another aspect to the SAS use of explosives, and that is as an aid to medical evacuation and clearing landing sites in the jungle. In Borneo in the 1960s, for example, wounded SAS soldiers were often extracted by helicopter from landing sites that had been cleared with explosives. Learning to clear landing sites with explosives is taught to prospective SAS troopers during the jungle phase of their Continuation Training, even before they have become fully fledged SAS men.

Andy McNab was one of those who received this instruction: 'We learned more or less straightaway how to blow landing sites [LS] and winch holes, because we might have to do it. If somebody broke his leg, we'd have to stabilize him, cut a winch hole and wait for the

helicopter. "When blowing an LS for a long-term base, you can put direction on the way the tree falls," the DS [Directing Staff] said. "The higher the ground the better, because as the taller ones fall they'll take the smaller ones with them. The explosive pack is called 'packet echo' – ask for it and a big wad of chainsaws and explosives and augers will be dropped, enough to blow a site." We went out one day with explosives to practise blowing trees.' The use of explosives is both an art and a science, as McNab discovered after setting charges to a tree that looked as though it might require a substantial quantity of explosives: 'There was a massive explosion that shook the ground. The tree went straight up in the air and disappeared from sight.'

QUANTITIES OF EXPLOSIVE

The precise use of explosives against a target is very important, and is taught to SAS soldiers from day one. 'Bravo Two Zero', for example, went over the design and layout of Iraqi Scud missiles and their launch vehicle in detail. Above all, the team members did not want to blow up the missile itself, as its warhead could be filled with chemical, biological or nuclear agents (the team did not want to kill themselves in the process of knocking out the Scuds). The decision to destroy the launcher's fire control station demanded placing enough explosive to do the job without damaging the missile itself.

It is a myth that large quantities of explosives are required to achieve results. Enemy aircraft, for example, can be rendered inoperable by the precise placement of charges on their nose cones, engines, propellers, air intakes and undercarriages. The trick is to place them in such a way that the detonation will cause the maximum damage. This calls for prior intelligence and assessment of the target so that the team on the ground will be able to achieve the best results. Fortunately, the Regiment possesses much more effective explosives than when it first tried sabotage in World War II.

Right: A wrecked aircraft control tower. A few kilos of explosives can reduce a tower such as this to a charred ruin.

The Lewes Bomb

In North Africa during World War II, David Stirling's SAS patrols targeted Axis airfields behind the lines. If they could destroy enemy aircraft on the ground, so the reasoning went, the SAS could have a strategic impact on the war. Once a team had breached an airfield's security and reached the aircraft, the men needed an effective way of destroying them. One of the original members of the SAS, Lieutenant 'Jock' Lewes, came up with the answer. He invented a simple explosive device for disabling enemy aircraft. Named after him, the Lewes bomb consisted of half a kilo (1lb) of plastic explosive rolled in a mixture of thermite from an incendiary bomb and old engine oil. It was detonated by means of a time pencil and detonator, which were carried separately on the approach to the target. The time pencil itself consisted of different strengths of acid, which ate through a wire connected to the plunger of the detonator at different rates: between 10 minutes and two hours.

Types of Explosive

SAS soldiers use a variety of high explosives on operations, ranging from British Army PE4 to Semtex. To use such materials requires a thorough knowledge of the properties of the explosives themselves and detonation sequences.

SAS soldiers are introduced to the use of explosives during Continuation Training, and while a proportion of NCOs and troopers will go on to become demolition specialists, all will undergo the basic introductory course. They are instructed by their own experts in Hereford and elsewhere, and by outside specialists drawn from the Royal Logistic Corps (formerly the RAOC), and from Royal Engineers EOD (Explosive Ordnance Device) Teams.

An explosive is defined as a solid or liquid substance which, on application of a suitable stimulus (such as an exploding detonator), is converted in a very short time into other, more stable substances, usually gases, with the development of high pressure (an explosion). Explosives greatly increase the potential for sabotage. They may be of commercial manufacture or improvised, and may be adapted to fulfil particular criteria. Thus a simple bomb can be given a deadly shrapnel effect by packing the explosives with nails, stones or broken glass. However, military explosives are used mainly for demolition tasks and fall into two categories: high explosives and low or incendiary explosives.

HIGH EXPLOSIVES

Upon detonation, high explosives are converted instantaneously to heat and gas, with the production of a high-pressure, high-speed shock wave which, when properly harnessed, can be highly destructive. As explosive charges may have to be stored safely in unsatisfactory conditions, may be dropped and will almost certainly have to be carried to their target they must be made inert and safe to handle. Substances such as TNT (trinitrotoluene), Tetrytol, Composition C3 and C4 (plastic explosive/PE), Semtex, Amatol, PE4 and dynamite have therefore been specifically designed not to explode without the prior introduction of a primer. A deto-

Above: Elsie anti-personnel mines, which were carried by SAS teams behind the lines during the 1991 Gulf War.

nator or blasting cap is embedded in the primary charge. When this explodes, it produces a shock wave that sets off the main charge. Occasionally the primary explosive is so inert that even this is not sufficient to effect an explosion. In this instance a hole is made in the primary charge and filled with a wad of more volatile explosive or 'primer'. The detonator now explodes the primer, which in turn activates the main charge.

FUSES

An 'initiator' is required to set off high explosives. There are in fact two main types of initiator, electrical and non-electrical. In a non-electrical firing system detonation is effected via a time fuse connected to a non-electric blasting cap – a thin aluminium tube 250mm (9.8in) long – which is embedded in the explosive charge. The blasting cap provides the detonating impulse required to ignite the charge. The fuse itself can either be a safety fuse or a

detonating cord. Safety fuse is flexible cord about 5mm (0.2in) in diameter which comprises black powder encased in a fibre wrapping, itself covered with a waterproof material. Once lit, the fuse burns at a rate of 36-47 seconds per 300mm (11.8in).

Detonating cord, or 'det cord', provides the second, non-electrical firing system. It comprises a small high-explosive core protected by six layers of material, and detonates at the rate of 6-8000m (19,680-26,250ft) per second. The det cord, like the safety fuse, is connected to a non-electric blasting cap. However, unlike the safety fuse it cannot be ignited by a match or igniter, but must be fired by tapping it together with two primers and a detonator, which are then set off either by a safety fuse or an electrical current. In electric firing systems the blasting cap contains two wires which are connected in the cap by a bridge wire. When a current is passed through the wires the bridge wire becomes hot and ignites the charge within the cap, thus detonating the main explosive charge.

Once placed, charges can be ignited in one of three ways: by the firer lighting the fuse or detonating the charge in close proximity to the target; by means of a timer, whereby a charge detonates according to a pre-set timing device (a favourite with the SAS); or detonation by remote control. Timers may be improvised or mechanical, and are not always very reliable.

TIMERS

During World War II, for example, Lieutenant 'Jock' Lewes invented the so-called Lewes bomb. In this the explosive was detonated by means of a 'time-pencil', in which acid eroded through a metal wire in the pencil to release a spring which caused the explosion. Variations of wire thickness resulted in bombs with fuses of between 30 seconds, and 30 minutes, duration. But the time pencils on Lewes bombs were notoriously unreliable. More recently, various terrorist groups have introduced the 'condom fuse'. Acid is placed inside a condom which is then tied up at the end. It is then packed among combustible material and placed against the explosive. As the acid burns through the rubber walls of the condom it ignites the combustible material which in turn detonates the main explosive.

Electrical detonators are not always reliable. They are susceptible to mechanical damage, for example, and need to be well greased to keep them waterproofed, something that is often difficult for SAS teams operating in adverse conditions. A short-circuit or a break in the circuit anywhere will render them useless, making it advisable to have a back-up form of detonation available. In addition, they are susceptible to random frequency hazard (RFH), a phenomenon by which a near-

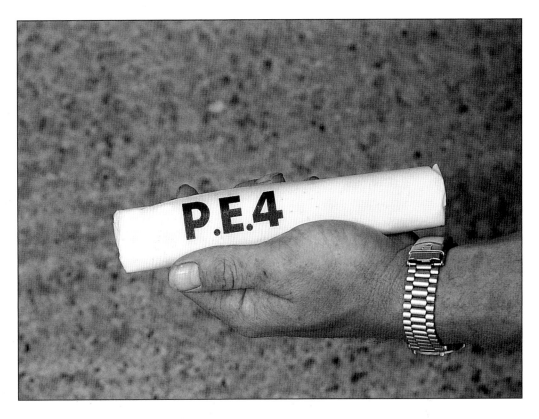

by radio transmission detonates the charge prematurely.

Despite all the disadvantages, though, electronics has revolutionised timers. They can now be set for any time from nine seconds to 99 years. And to increase their capabilities and destructive potential, they can also lie dormant, restarting themselves at various times in order to

Above: PE 4 plastic explosive, as used by the Special Air Service. It is very inert: it will burn like a candle if set alight.

recharge. At any given time they can be activated by a radio signal, releasing a charge that will set off the explosive.

Military explosives come in all shapes and sizes, each with a designated task.

explosions. The main charge is covered by wheat flour, gasoline or coal dust, which is dispersed or vaporised by the first explosion before igniting and saturating the atmosphere inside the building with burning material in a second explosion.

To achieve the maximum effect, a favoured trick among SAS soldiers is to place a charge of plastic explosive in what is known as a 2:1 shape. This means that on the target the charge is twice as high as it is wide. In this way the shock waves go down into the target. Likewise with the detonator. If it is placed at the end of a flat charge, then a lot of the force of the subsequent explosion will be lost sideways. The most effective way is to place the detonator on top of the charge so that the shock waves go down into the target and thus create the most destructive effect.

PICKING THE RIGHT TARGET

A knowledge of explosives is not enough for a special forces operator. It is essential that he chooses his targets well to produce maximum damage and inconvenience to the enemy. Too much explosive used against one target is wasteful and denies its use against another. As the SAS quickly discovered in North Africa, while a slab of explosive might obliterate a single aircraft, a series of smaller delayed-action charges, strategically placed on the undercarriage, cockpit or wings, may disable an entire squadron. The destruction of the control tower or fuel stocks may deprive the enemy of aircraft cover for a few vital hours, enabling a friendly air strike to be mounted against ground assets.

A section of railway track, unless it is blown with a train on it, is replaced relatively easily by teams of track layers. The destruction of track at multiple points, over a bridge or at the entrance to a tunnel, however, will maximise the damage and greatly hinder repairs (wrecked points and intersections mean that two lines at least will be temporarily out of action), as well as disrupt the enemy's communications systems.

Inevitably, such targets will be well guarded, and it will thus be necessary for the bomber to be an expert in infiltration. Under certain circumstances it may be possible to detonate a small, subordinate

Above: Charges will be set to cause maximum target damage, which includes burning as well as cutting.

Simple slab explosive must be positioned carefully if it is to cut through steel or reinforced concrete as intended. Formulae are employed to calculate that just sufficient explosive is used, while care is taken to channel the explosive into, and not away from, the intended demolition. An explosion is, in effect, an escape of energy and, if allowed to, will seek the easiest route of escape. If, therefore, a charge is placed in the open much of its force will be dissipated into the surrounding atmosphere and away from the target. A long length of explosive, such as a 'rib-

bon charge', placed properly may produce a fissure in concrete or slice through a steel beam. It will also prove excellent in clearing a route through massed barbed wire if fired along the ground.

A 'saddle charge' funnels the shock waves to produce a cross fracture, while a 'diamond charge' cuts at right angles to the explosives. Shaped charges, such as the 'beehive', concentrate the shock waves onto a small target area to produce a linear tubular fracture. The simultaneous activation of two diametrically opposite charges, known as 'counter-force', produces twin shock waves which meet inside the target to cause internal destruction. Buildings may be destroyed by dust initiators which produce two distinct charge some distance away to draw the guards from the main target, but this may prove counterproductive, particularly if it causes enemy reinforcements to be rushed to the area.

Faced with a target such as a bridge, the demolitions expert must identify the weakest points which can be cut with explosives to topple the structure. It is often not necessary to destroy a bridge to render it unusable to the enemy. For example, a bridge on an MSR which is so weakened that it can no longer bear the weight of armour or tracked artillery may completely close that route to the enemy. Cutting the load-bearing piers may require an inordinate amount of explosive, but charges laid carefully on the roadway close to the ends of a cantilever bridge may cause the collapse of the suspended span. Equally, the destruction of the pylon-carrying towers on a suspension bridge, or the girder arms of a continuous span truss bridge, will cause instability and often collapse. Ironically, older masonry bridges often cause the greatest problem. Their usually massive piers and relatively narrow spans require not only the application of a considerable amount of explosive, but necessitate the charges being drilled into the fabric for greatest effect, a noisy and cumbersome exercise under the eyes of the enemy!

HOW MUCH EXPLOSIVE?

The development of more sophisticated demolition methods has meant that SAS teams can hit more targets with the explosives they carry with them. The aforementioned 'diamond charge', for example, meant that a charge weighing only 1.36kg (3lb) has the same explosive effect as a solid mass of explosive some five times larger.

High explosives carried on missions can be surprisingly inert. PE4, for example, which was used by SAS teams in the 1991 Gulf War, can even be set alight without danger of it exploding. It can be moulded in the hands, jumped up and down upon and hit with a hammer. It will not explode, though, not without a detonator. This means that SAS teams do not have to worry about the explosive they are carrying.

SAS soldiers tasked with the demolition of a bridge or other structure will be able to call upon a considerable number of resources in deciding where best to place their charges. Where possible the target will be overflown and stereoscopic photographs taken. These will be analysed by imagery analysts to establish weak points in the structure, and the strength and positioning of the guard force. Engineers will then advise on the best position for the charges to be laid. However, the world of the saboteur is far from perfect, and in the final analysis the assault team will be on its own, reliant on its skills and daring to carry out its mission.

The SAS continually trains its men in demolitions and sabotage. This training

Above: A white phosphorus grenade detonates. Carried by SAS patrols, it is a device that can cause horrific injuries.

includes making dummy attacks against nuclear and conventional power stations in the United Kingdom, as well as industrial facilities on mainland Europe. As well as brushing up on the Regiment's skills, these exercises help in the planning of defensive measures for these establishments. For the individual SAS soldier, to get the most out of modern explosives he has to be many things, not least a structural engineer and mathematician. He must also be an electrician to set detonators and timers. And he must do all this under the noses of the enemy.

Booby Traps and Mines

All SAS soldiers are taught how to improvise explosives and set booby traps. For small-sized teams operating behind the lines, it is vital to be able to generate explosive materials from locally available materials, and to set traps for an unwary enemy.

SAS teams operating behind the lines cannot run the risk of sustaining injuries in unnecessary encounters with the enemy. They will therefore often resort to the laying of mines and planting of booby traps along tracks and suspected supply routes. Such weapons are, however, totally undiscriminating. They will kill or maim the first living creature of sufficient weight and size to encounter them and will prove extremely unpopular with the local, possibly neutral, civilian population. Equally, they will remain charged long after the battle has moved on, possibly causing inconvenience to friendly troops advancing.

Mine-laying techniques will vary according to circumstance. Pressure mines such as the American Claymore and Russian PMN may be left along a route taken by regular patrols or around the perimeter of enemy bases. They may even

be placed along the anticipated route of a reinforcement party likely to be dispatched from its base camp to the site of a major demolition. Second- and third-generation jumping mines, such as the AP Bounding Mine, which are activated by trip wire, may also be employed. The slightest disturbance to the wire will cause the ignition of a minor charge in the base of the mine. This will be sufficient to propel the mine into the air, but not ignite the main charge. The main charge will be connected to the base by a second wire, perhaps one metre (39in) in length. Once this has become taut it will activate a trigger mechanism which will cause the mine to explode in the air, killing or severely maiming not only the unfortunate victim who set it off, but also those in the immediate vicinity.

ANTI-PERSONNEL MINES

It has never been the purpose of anti-personnel mines to kill. Rather, they are intended to maim. A soldier who is badly wounded will require immediate attention, almost certainly necessitating his evacuation to the rear area. This will necessitate the release of two of his colleagues to carry him, thus removing three personnel from the immediate battlefield. During the 1991 Gulf War the SAS patrol 'Bravo Two Zero' took Elsie anti-personnel mines into enemy territory, to plant them on booby-trapped manhole covers.

Anti-tank mines by their nature are large, and are therefore less employable in conventional sabotage. However, an anti-tank mine planted on an main supply route (MSR) may cause havoc, particularly if it is of second-generation manufacture and has been fitted with a trembler fuse. The first vehicle to touch the

Left: A simple but effective booby trap. A hand grenade on a stick with its pin attached to a trip wire.

mine activates the fuse and not the mine itself. It is only when a second vehicle comes into contact with the mine that it explodes. Although such mines were designed primarily to combat flails in front of tanks, they are equally effective against second and subsequent vehicles in a convoy.

Explosives can be fashioned by an expert into very effective booby traps. These may be placed along tracks known to be used by the enemy, in buildings about to be evacuated, or in the vicinity of more obvious and conventional demolitions. An inexperienced soldier finding a demolition is likely to panic. He is likely to be so mesmerised by it, and so intent on neutralising it before it explodes, that he will forget to look for anything else unusual in the immediate area. Thus it may be possible to disguise a booby trap as a lump of wood, or other object placed over the demolition in a vain attempt to hide it. The soldier will be so excited by his find that he will move the wood, ignite the booby trap, and possibly set off the demolition with it.

BOOBY TRAPS

SAS soldiers are issued with a variety of percussion detonators for use in improvised explosives or booby traps. Essentially these are camouflaged tubes which are screwed into the explosive charge. When the devices are activated, perhaps by moving an innocent-looking log, a powerful spring drives a striker or firing-pin into the percussion primer. The resulting mini-explosion is funnelled through the narrow mouth of the firing device and into the main charge.

Recently improvised explosive devices have made their appearance on the streets of Northern Ireland. Typically, the spring of an otherwise conventional booby trap is secured in place by a poster or other propaganda item pasted to a post or wall.

Right: Inserting a fuse and trip wire into a Claymore mine. Claymores are used by the SAS for perimeter defence and booby traps.

The poster is torn down by a disapproving member of the security forces, the spring is released, the device activates and explodes in the face of the hapless target. In a few instances the spring has been replaced by a light-sensitive igniter. The poster is removed, light strikes the igniter and the bomb is activated.

Primitive animal traps were adapted as anti-personnel devices by the SAS in Borneo and by both sides in Vietnam. Concealed pits, lined with punji stakes and smeared with pig excrement, were capable of inflicting deep leg wounds, with the attendant risk of blood poisoning. Man-traps, activated by a trip wire and designed to impale an unwary enemy, were constructed from sharpened bamboo or hardwood spikes mounted on scaffolding and concealed in the foliage.

During World War II, numerous small acts of sabotage were undertaken, particularly by railway workers in Nazi-occupied Europe. Sand poured into axle grease chambers brought rolling stock to a grinding halt. Later sugar, thrown into the cement mix destined for building Nazi coastal defences, ensured that it failed to set properly, and in some extreme cases dissolved in the rain. Logs and coal bricks, hollowed out and filled with explosive rigged to a detonator and match-head fuse, when left to be shovelled into factory furnaces caused considerable damage to the German economy. There is no reason why a future resistance movement, properly motivated and trained by such as the SAS, could not wreak havoc among an invading enemy again.

LOW EXPLOSIVES

Low explosives, although less dramatic, when properly employed are as effective as high explosives in the world of sabotage. Low explosives, more usually known as incendiary devices, are used to start fires in buildings, stores, oil-depots or

ammunition dumps. They are easy to ignite, burn with a very intense heat and are difficult to extinguish. Most are also small, and therefore relatively easy to conceal. Military incendiaries use a fuse consisting of a mixture of chemicals known collectively as the 'first-fire mixture'. These ignite easily and slowly reach a combustion temperature which is sufficient to ignite the main charge or 'main-fire mixture'. By the time the incendiary

device is consumed, the target should be a roaring inferno.

On operations SAS soldiers will fashion booby traps as and when required. For example, a trip wire attached to the pin of a standard-issue hand grenade is enough to cause severe injuries to a pursuing enemy patrol, as is a simple spear track along a trail. One of the most important aspects of being able to fashion booby traps is an active imagination.

Right: The Claymore mine consists of 350 metal balls embedded in a convex charge of plastic explosives.

COMBAT SURVIVAL

Polar Regions

All SAS soldiers are instructed how to survive in polar regions. This is part of their training against one of the deadliest foes of all special forces soldiers: nature. In the freezing wastes of polar regions life can be extinguished in a matter of minutes.

All prospective SAS soldiers receive combat survival instruction during Continuation Training, and throughout their careers in the Regiment will attend refresher courses so that they can survive in any terrain in the world. One such environment is snow and ice terrain. Nowhere in the world is the windchill factor more potentially lethal than in areas such as the Arctic, where exposed skin can freeze in seconds.

The rules for surviving in such areas are simple: movement should be kept to a minimum, as a survivor will burn off a huge number of calories and will sweat far more than usual. Improvised snow-shoes, made of willow or other spongy wood, are essential. Poor visibility makes navigation difficult. In summer the mass of thawing bogs and swamps will make movement difficult, and in winter white-outs (when the clouds are so dense that they cause the sky to merge with the land to cause total disorientation) are common. In the Arctic itself the proximity of the Magnetic North Pole makes navigation by compass impossible.

MOVEMENT

Routes have to be chosen carefully to avoid natural obstacles such as bogs. Where possible they should follow the route of a river, as there will be fish in the stream and plant life on the banks to eat. However, the survivor should not attempt to make a raft. Many Arctic rivers are fast and dangerous, and all are extremely cold. It is unwise to rely on landmarks; snow-

Right: In Arctic terrain SAS soldiers must guard against hypothermia, frostbite and, curiously enough, sunburn and sunstroke.

falls and resultant whiteouts can obliterate them in seconds.

It is important to keep the body well covered at all times and to protect the fingers (frostbite is a dangerous enemy and can lead to gangrene; it can be staved off by wrinkling the face to stop stiff patches forming, dressing inside the sleeping bag, brushing snow off clothing before entering the shelter and not touching metal with bare hands).

There are other dangers besides frostbite, such as dehydration, and hypothermia (which leads via violent shivering and irrationality, to loss of purpose, unconsciousness and death). It is not easy to recognise the onset of hypothermia in oneself, and it is therefore essential that survivors, when travelling in pairs, look out for the signs in each other. Attention to personal hygiene is also essential if trench foot (caused by damp clothing) is to be avoided.

Arctic survivors require a constant supply of food and water. Water is abundant, but must be purified before drinking. Survivors are told not to eat snow or ice if they are thirsty (melt them first), since this lowers the body's temperature, and to avoid consuming frozen sea water unless it is old, has turned bluish or blackish and shatters easily (it is then salt-free).

FOOD AND SHELTER

In the hunt for food the SAS survivor must be careful of animals. Many are extremely dangerous and should be avoided at all costs. Bear, walrus and musk ox in particular can inflict lethal injuries if provoked. However, if a large animal is caught some of the meat should be preserved for future use by freezing, but it is important to skin and gut the carcass while still warm. Ice fishing can prove highly successful in the hunt for food; a hole should be cut above deep water, a hook baited and lowered. However, the line should be attached to a stout stick to avoid it being pulled into the water.

Getting out of the wind and into temporary shelter, however basic, as quickly as possible is essential in polar regions. SAS soldiers are therefore taught how to build all kinds of shelter from materials available. If manufacturing a tree shelter, for

example, they will remember that the superstructure poles must be the strongest as everything else rests on them. Once the shelter has been built, the trooper will sleep on insulating material such as spruce or dry grass and not on the ground.

Survival above the tree line involves making shelters from snow blocks. Again the rules are simple: each block should be about 45 x 50cm (18 x 20in) and 10-20 cm (4-8 in) thick; ideally blocks should be cut from vertical surfaces to reduce strain. Keep the entrance as small as possible to minimise heat loss, and if circumstances permit dig a connecting snow cave for

Above: SAS soldiers are instructed on how to construct improvised Arctic shelters, as well as how to find food in snow and ice regions.

use as a toilet. Watch out for snow accumulating on the shelter roof, as this may cause a cave-in.

Inside the shelter survivors should be able to see their breath; if not it means the interior temperature is too warm, which will result in condensation and melting. With these basics SAS soldiers are fully equipped to live and survive in polar regions, and to get back to friendly lines in one piece.

Mountains

Ever since the Jebel Akhdar campaign in the late 1950s, SAS soldiers have shown they can fight in the high peaks. But it is very difficult to survive in mountain regions, and the first priority is to get down out of danger to remain out of harm's way.

Weather conditions in mountain regions are erratic. A survivor will encounter snow, ice and high winds; he must also be aware of avalanches, rock falls and crevasses. Avalanches occur most commonly during winter, usually on the leeward side of slopes ranging from 30-45 degrees. If caught in an avalanche the

Regiment advises its men to discard their backpacks and skis and try to work towards the side. They are told to turn their backs to the force, keep their heads up and their mouths shut. In addition, they should save their strength until the avalanche loses momentum, when they may be able to dig slowly to the surface.

Movement during periods of poor visibility or at night is inadvisable. During daylight hours the survivor must survey the entire area thoroughly and then head for a valley. Glaciers should be avoided if possible, since the crevasses they contain are often invisible to the naked eye. If in a group SAS soldiers will rope themselves together, like they did when on Fortuna Glacier on South Georgia during the Falklands War. If a survivor falls into a crevasse speed is essential to rescue him, but it may take three people to haul an unconscious person to safety. SAS soldiers are taught to be wary of bridges over crevasses, to always cross them singly, sending the lightest person over first. When in doubt one man will slither across on his stomach to distribute the weight over a larger area.

CLIMBING AND DESCENDING

In mountain regions zigzag routes are used on steep slopes, which is less tiring and safer than a straight uphill or downhill climb. The lead person should be changed frequently, as he has to choose the route of travel and will get tired more quickly than the rest. The other travel rules are: keep an experienced person at the rear to check the route; do not assume that the lead man cannot get lost; ensure all items of equipment, especially ice axes, are secured whether in use or not; and if possible travel in the early morning after a cold night, as snow and ice will be more stable and less exhausting, because they will be firmer.

Survivors attempting rock climbing should conserve energy by keeping the centre of gravity over the feet, thus passing the strain to the legs and not the arms. For the same reason the hands should be

Left: Mountainous regions are full of life-threatening dangers, such as snow avalanches, ice and high winds.

no higher than shoulder level. It is important to watch where the feet are placed and to keep three points of contact with the rock, and to think ahead, to move slowly and rhythmically and always test holds for stability.

Mountainous areas are predominantly rock, snow and ice and offer little help in the construction of natural shelters. SAS soldiers are told to dig into the snow if there is no shelter among the rocks, to sleep with the head uphill, and on stony

Below: On the high slopes SAS soldiers have to beware of crevasses, as well as keeping watch for the enemy.

ground on the stomach for greater comfort. A sleeping bag can be improvised from a plastic bag or other material.

Because of the wind, it is imperative to try to get into some sort of shelter. If the mountain side is covered in snow it may be possible to build a snow cave. Another important point is the building of a fire, which will provide warmth and also be a psychological support.

Food is another problem in mountains, because there is little to be had (and none at all on the high peaks). SAS soldiers have their survival packs in their belt kits, but it may be necessary to supplement them. The only food to be had in

the mountains are mountain goats and sheep on the lower slopes. To kill them requires all the stealth-like qualities of an SAS soldier. These animals are very wary and difficult to approach. That said, they can be surprised by moving quietly downwind when they are feeding with their heads lowered. However, survivors are told not to chase these animals as they are extremely sure-footed and this can result in twisted ankles or worse.

A major danger in the mountains is the threat of being hit by lightning. It is attracted to summits and pinnacles, and survivors are told to avoid summits, exposed ridges and gullies containing water and lone trees in a thunderstorm. Overhangs and recesses in cliffs do not offer protection against a discharging current, and wet ropes and metal equipment will attract lightning. In a thunderstorm survivors are instructed to adopt a sitting position with the knees drawn up against the chest, which is the best protection against earth currents.

The soldiers on Fortuna Glacier had to be evacuated by helicopter to save their lives, and the advice to survivors in mountainous terrain is to get down to civilisation as quickly as possible.

Below: The high winds in the mountains can freeze flesh during the winter. Gore-tex clothing can help prevent this danger.

Desert Regions

Desert regions are extremely harsh environments, characterised for the most part by high temperatures and lack of water. SAS survival doctrine teaches its men to get out of the sun as quickly as possible, as well as to stay alive from the meagre resources to hand.

Deserts occupy approximately one-fifth of the earth's land surface. Not all are composed of sand, although in other respects they share common physical characteristics. Their average annual rainfall may vary from between zero and 25cm (10in) and is completely unpredictable. Flash flooding, when normally dry streams (wadis) fill with fast-flowing water and empty almost at once, are very common and should never be discounted. Vegetation is generally scarce, but where it does exist may indicate the presence of a high water-table. Cactus and common sage have no bearing on the water level, but palm trees indicate the presence of water within 0.6-0.9m (2-3ft) of the surface.

Temperature extremes are profound in the desert and vary according to latitude. In the Gobi Desert in China the temperature may drop to minus 10 degrees C (minus 50 degrees F) in the winter. On the other hand, the North African Sahara may experience summer highs of 58 degrees C (136 degrees F). These, however, will fall drastically at night as the surface rapidly cools beneath the clear night skies. The low cloud density will compound with the abnormal daylight brightness to offer amazing visibility, a characteristic which may lead to the formation of mirages in which non-existent hills, lakes and mountains can be 'seen' in the distance. For the survivor mirages should be ignored at all times; they have often caused unsuspecting travellers to wander deep into the desert, where they have become hopelessly lost.

DESERT TRAVEL

SAS soldiers get many opportunities to train in desert environments throughout their careers, mostly in the United Arab Emirates and Oman. Wherever they train, though, they learn survival principles that are common to all deserts. For example, most deserts are criss-crossed by man-made features such as roads, railways and pipelines. They also contain rudimentary trails for the local nomadic tribesmen. They will be taught to be constantly on the look out for these as they are a source of potential civilisation, although rescue may still be some considerable distance away.

Travelling in the desert can be extremely hazardous. SAS troopers are told not to underestimate the climate or the terrain and to remember that distances may be much further than they seem to the untrained eye. Other travel rules in the desert are: avoid the midday sun, travel if possible in the evening or at night; be careful if the ground is rocky or mountainous, since a twisted ankle may make further movement impossible; avoid loose sand or rough terrain, which will only add to fatigue; and seek shelter on the leeward side of hills and do not try to move through sandstorms.

At night it is possible to navigate by the stars and moon; by day with a compass. However, in certain deserts localised magnetic rock piles may lead to considerable inaccuracy, so it is important to use landmarks to prevent walking in circles, though with the warning that local features will vary considerably after a sandstorm. If a storm is imminent troopers are told to mark the route – a simple stick to indicate direction will suffice – and above all to look at what is there, not what they want to see.

DESERT CLOTHING

Clothing is extremely important when moving in desert areas. The entire body, especially the head, should be covered against sunburn, heat, sand and insects. During SAS desert training, for example, the instructors make sure that the men are protected as much as possible from the hostile environment. This means all the body is covered. Desert camouflage clothing is worn at all times, and the instruc-

Left: Deserts are very harsh environments in which to fight, being subject to wide temperature extremes and lack of water.

tors make sure that sleeves are rolled down and legs covered (not only is sunburn painful it's also an offence in the Regiment). All flesh is covered: hats or *shemaghs* (Arab headgear) are worn, and camouflage cream is applied to the face.

During desert survival training the instructors impart other useful information: ensure that the neck is covered at all times; boots and socks should be removed only in the shade, and should be thoroughly shaken before being put back on in case a scorpion or spider has crawled into them; sunglasses or goggles should be worn if possible (they can be improvised from spare clothing or bark); and do not neglect eye protection in general, even if only to smear soot below the eyes to avoid damage from glare.

DESERT CLOTHING

Food and water are crucial to survival in the desert. Without water the strongest man will die within 60 hours in the extreme heat of the Sahara. At 48 degrees C (120 degrees F) he will be able to walk no more than perhaps 8km (5 miles) without collapsing. To preserve water an SAS soldier is told to remain fully clothed and move as slowly as possible, to avoid washing and to drink in sips only to avoid wastage and stomach cramps.

Water in the desert frequently flows underground. It flows downhill, encourages vegetation and creates grooves, creek beds and canyons when flash-flooding. Survivors therefore seek out dry river or lake beds, locate the lowest point and then dig into the ground with a spade, stick or rock (if the sand appears wet, digging should cease at once to allow the water to collect). Greenery and vegetation often indicate the presence of permanent water sources, and cacti, although not indicators of water, may prove valuable sources of water in themselves. The leaf stems of other desert plants, such as pigweed, produce a limited supply of water while affording much-needed nutrition.

The men are instructed to eat only when necessary in a survival situation, and then avoid protein-rich foods which require water for digestion. The desert produces many edible foods, such as figs and dates, which can be found in the areas of oases and dry lakes. Less conventional plants, such as wild gourds, prickly pears and carrion flowers, also make good eating, but flowers that have milky or coloured sap should be avoided because they are poisonous.

All desert animals are edible but have first to be caught. Insects may be attracted at night with a small light, or gathered by lifting up stones. If circumstances permit, rabbits and birds may be trapped, and rabbits smoked from their lairs by building a fire at the entrance. Snakes are edible but are also often venomous.

Cooking may be improvised with a little imagination. Boiling pots may be made by scooping a hole in hard ground, filling it with leaves, adding hot stones from the fire and filling with water. Although they take longer to make, Dutch ovens are excellent and protect the meat from the unwelcome attention of flies and birds. Their construction is taught to SAS soldiers: dig a hole and place hot stones in the bottom, the meat should be placed on top of the coals and covered with a damp cloth; the hole should then be filled in and left for several hours. When retrieved the meat will not only be tender but often tasty.

DESERT CLOTHING

The main dangers in the desert are occasioned by heat, poisonous vegetation and dangerous animals. Many plants are protected by sharp thorns or spines, which can cause intense skin irritation if touched. Although most insects are edible, ants' nests, centipedes and caterpillars, some of which are poisonous, are all to be avoided by the survivor.

There is no immediate effective treatment for scorpion bites, the effects of which are immediate. The best remedy is to remain calm – most adult victims of scorpion bites recover. Likewise with spider bites: although extremely painful, they are rarely lethal. Many varieties of venomous snakes may be found in the desert. The survivor's best protection is to take care, wear boots and keep hands away from crevices (most bites are below the knee or on the hand or forearm).

Dehydration is a major danger in the desert. In high temperatures and low

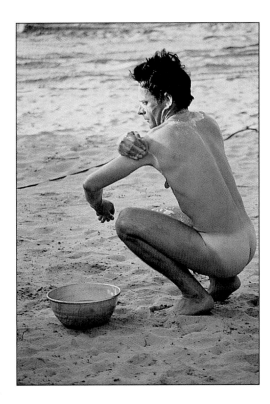

Above: When serving in desert conditions, it is imperative to maintain personal hygiene to avoid contracting any diseases.

humidity sweating will not always be apparent. It will nonetheless occur, and should be kept to a minimum. Remaining fully clothed at all times will help. Heat exhaustion, caused by an excessive loss of water and salt, can be fatal if untreated. The victim should be placed in the shade, his legs should be elevated and he should be massaged to return blood to the heart. Where possible he should be given large quantities to drink. Heatstroke, caused when the body loses its ability to cool itself by sweating, is equally potentially fatal. The patient should be placed in the shade and his body temperature lowered as quickly as possible. His clothing should be removed and his body sprinkled with water from head to foot.

It is impressed upon all troopers that shelter is very important in the desert. The best time to build a shelter is during the early morning, late evening or at night when the temperature is relatively cool, in this way the survivor preserves energy. By relying on their thorough knowledge and survival kits, every SAS soldier is fully equipped to deal with all the hazards that a desert environment can throw at him.

Tropical Regions

The SAS was 'reborn' in the tropical jungles of Malaya in the early 1950s. The jungle survival skills it has amassed since then have been the result of many often hard-learned lessons which SAS soldiers have endured. Today the Regiment's jungle survival skills are second to none.

There are two SAS jungle training areas: Malaya and Belize. Of these Malaya is the most important, reflecting the SAS's strong ties with that country and its people. There are two types of jungle, primary and secondary. Primary jungle consists of tall trees up to 60m (200ft) in height, with their leaves forming a dense jungle canopy that stops sunlight reaching the floor. As a result, there is little undergrowth, it is dark and damp, with visibility down to 50m (164ft). Secondary jungle is where sunlight reaches the ground (usually in clearings and around river banks). As a result there is often thick undergrowth, with ferns, grasses and vines growing to a height of 2-3m (7-10ft). Moving through such terrain is often slow and exhausting.

Left: SAS belt kits are an important aid to tropical survival as they contain water bottles and a survival kit.

The first thing that the SAS instructors do when the new recruits arrive on their jungle survival course is to try to get them acclimatised to the jungle. For many this will be their first time in such an environment, and it comes as a shock. Everything is different: the climate (high humidity), the trees and plants, and the animals. As a jungle instructor states: 'You're wet all the time from the humidity, and the jungle is full of creepy-crawlies. As a result, a lot of people can't hack it.'

FINDING FOOD AND WATER

During their 4-6 weeks in the jungle, the recruits are taught how to find food and water in the jungle. Though they will be equipped with personal equipment, it is imperative that they learn how to live off the land in the event of an emergency. Water is not much of a problem in the jungle. As well as the surface water from streams, lakes and swamps, there are several plants that provide drinking water. These include vines, bamboo, coconuts and banana plants. The instructors will stress the importance of purifying water obtained from streams and the like.

There is also an abundance of food sources in the jungle, though some are more easily obtained than others. Many jungle plants are edible, such as tropical fruits, yams, coconuts and papaya. Similarly, snakes and insects can also be eaten. The men will be instructed how to kill snakes, and for larger animals, how to construct spear and pit traps to catch wild pigs and deer.

For men in SAS squadrons about to undergo jungle training, the normal procedure is for the instructors to construct a survival camp as part of the squadron's two-week acclimatisation programme. The instructors collect all the edible plants, fish and animals from the jungle and lay them all out for the men to see. In this way the men know what they can and cannot eat. The rules are fairly simple. For example, the men are urged to stay away from anything that is brightly coloured. This is usually an indication of toxicity. Brightly coloured frogs, for instance, are extremely poisonous.

Though the men are issued with ground sheets, ponchos and sleeping bags, the instructors will teach them how to construct shelters from locally available materials, as well as providing information on where to sleep. Large animals, reptiles and insects use the jungle floor to travel on. Therefore, recruits are advised to build a raised shelter to enable them to sleep off the ground. They will also be advised to look above before selecting a site. Dead wood in trees can be lethal if it comes crashing down, and hornet and wasp nests are to be avoided at all costs, as are coconut trees – a falling coconut can kill!

Shelters themselves can be made from atap, a vine that has barbs at each end, three-lobed leaves, elephant grass and bamboo. Recruits will be taught how to make them waterproof by arranging the leaves in a thatched fashion, or by cutting bamboo stems in half and laying them alternately to interlock with each other.

JUNGLE DANGERS

The instructors spend a lot of time impressing upon the men the main dangers they will face in the jungle. Though snakes and large wild animals are considered the main threats in the jungle, and they are of course ever-present, an SAS soldier's main adversaries, aside from the enemy, are insects that transmit diseases or have poisonous bites and stings. The main threats therefore come from fleas, mites, spiders, mosquitoes, leeches, scorpions,

Right: The jungle abounds with food, the trick is to catch it. Here, an Iban tribesman shows off his monkey trap in Borneo.

wasps, bees and ants. In the jungle everything thrives, and that includes bacteria and infections. It is therefore imperative to cover up to prevent being scratched, stung and bitten.

In addition, the diseases prevalent in the jungle pose a constant threat. These include bilharzia (a disease of the bowel or bladder), hookworm (larvae that penetrate the skin), amoebic dysentery (transmitted via contaminated water and uncooked food), malaria (an insect-borne disease), and typhus (transmitted by body lice or raft fleas).

PERSONAL HYGIENE

Before they go to the jungle the soldiers are immunised against infections, but the instructors stress the importance of personal hygiene. Scratches and cuts must be cleaned and dressed at the earliest opportunity, and each man must keep his groin area as dry and clean as possible to prevent fungal infections. In addition, human waste must be dealt with efficiently. 'We tell the recruits to shit in a river if they can, just like the locals do. That way the fish will eat it. Alternatively, if you are in the jungle, scrape away the earth with your boot, have a crap, then smooth over the earth. It's important to clean your arse afterwards. Some guys use four-by-two rag, what we use to clean the weapons with, for toilet paper, while others tear one of their pockets off and use that.'

By the end of their survival course, SAS soldiers will be fully able to live in a tropical environment. Over 50 years of jungle warfare and survival experience has made the SAS one of the best jungle units in the world, and it is therefore not surprising that the Americans and Australians send their best men to attend SAS courses in the Far East and Latin America. It is no boast to say that the soldiers who wear the Winged Dagger have made the jungle their own.

Right: A golok, the extremely useful long jungle knife carried by every SAS soldier involved in tropical missions.

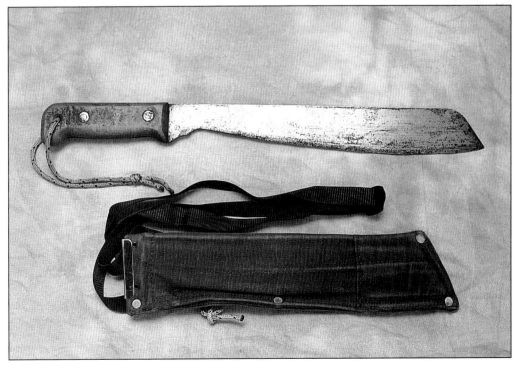

Survival at Sea

The sea has claimed the lives of many SAS soldiers over the years, some on operations and others due to training accidents. It is the most unforgiving of environments, and the Regiment's soldiers accord it a great deal of respect.

Nearly three-quarters of the earth's surface is covered by water, and man does not find it a natural environment. However, SAS instructors stress that it is still possible to survive at sea by adhering to a few golden rules. First, never give up hope; armed with his resources, and a degree of luck, there is no reason why a trooper should not reach safety. The actions taken before going into the water can often be the difference between living and dying. Putting on warm clothing, wrapping a towel around the neck, taking a torch, and grabbing some sweets and chocolate can increase the odds of survival. In addition, throwing something wooden which will float and jumping close to it will save precious energy.

Once in the water a survivor should keep calm – a relaxed body is more buoyant – and try to swim on the back, which is less tiring than swimming face-down. If the water is cold, survivors are urged to

try to get into a raft, and once secure look for other survivors. In a raft it is important to both relax and try to keep the mind occupied. If a group is in the raft then everyone can be given different jobs to do. Rafts themselves need regular attention, such as bleeding off the air if the raft expands in hot weather, and top up the air if it contracts in the cold or at night. If there is no raft, survivors are urged to huddle together with other survivors for warmth, or cross the legs and pull them gently into the stomach, which will reduce body heat loss considerably.

DANGERS AT SEA

There are many dangers at sea, such as hostile fish, starvation, thirst and hypothermia. Sharks can be a major threat in tropical waters; the SAS rules for dealing with them if in the water are as follows: if in a group in the water bunch together and face outwards; stay as quiet as possible. If swimming is essential use regular strokes, never frantic irregular movements, which remind the shark of an injured fish. If threatened move towards, not away from, the shark. People have succeeded in warding a shark off by kicking it, or by vigorously striking it with a hard object on the snout.

Many other fish in the oceans are poisonous or dangerous to touch. Troopers are told: if in doubt leave unknown species alone. Jellyfish should be avoided, many of which can inflict painful stings. If stung remove the tentacles from the wound immediately but do not suck the wound or rub it with anything abrasive. Soap, lemon juice, baking powder and even urine may alleviate the pain.

Fresh water is a most precious commodity, and the survivor must preserve it

Left: It is a little-known fact that the SAS has lost more men training in the water than it has on live operations.

at all costs. Fluid intake must be severely controlled. For example, it is advisable to drink nothing on the first day adrift, and then no more than 400cc (14oz) per day. Fluid loss can be reduced by eating minimally, sleeping and resting as much as possible. Drinking alcohol and smoking should be avoided; instead, the survivor should suck on a button to stimulate saliva and reduce the desire to drink. The golden rule at sea is never drink sea water.

Fortunately the oceans are full of edible fish, which can be caught by passing a net under the raft; fish and turtles often shelter in the shade there. Use a torch to attract fish at night with improvised hooks, and bright objects such as buckles for bait. Offal from caught fish may also be used as bait, but not in such quantities that it attracts sharks! All birds are potential food if they can be attracted to the raft. Seaweed is rich in nutrition, but it may act as a violent laxative if the body is not used to it! In addition, since seaweed absorbs water, it should not be eaten when drinking water is scarce.

RAFTING SHORE

One of the dangers concerning survival at sea is beaching a raft. SAS soldiers are taught how to make a shore landing on a raft, which can be more difficult than expected. For example, if the surf is strong there is a risk that the raft will capsize. If this is so the crew should look for a beach that has a sandy, sloping surface and where the surf is gentle.

When making a landing it is important not to do so with the sun shining into the eyes, or to attempt a landing where there are coral reefs and rocky cliffs. In colder climates landings should only be made on sea ice when the floes are large and stable, while icebergs should be avoided at all costs. It is ironic that many survival fatalities occur when salvation is in sight. But SAS soldiers always maintain their focus.

ARSENAL OF AN ELITE

SMALL ARMS

Since its creation in World War II, the SAS has made use of many different types of small arms, from bolt-action rifles to full-automatic submachine guns. But the one criterion demanded by the Regiment of its small arms is that they are, above all, reliable.

The SAS is a unit designed and trained for operations deep behind enemy lines. It is therefore imperative that the weapons carried are totally reliable. One malfunctioning weapon may jeopardise the safety of the whole team. In addition, the weapons carried by the SAS must be capable of putting down concentrated firepower in a short space of time, which requires the weapons themselves to have automatic fire modes. SAS small arms must also be able to withstand a lot of harsh treatment, and be able to work after being covered in mud, sand and snow.

Small arms must also be compatible with the team's role. Submachine guns, for example, with their high volume of fire, are excellent for hostage-rescue duties but useless for long-range missions inside hostile territory. In addition, their fearsome rate of fire – over 900 rounds per minute – would quickly exhaust the team's supply of ammunition.

Ammunition supply has been a perennial problem for SAS patrols. Whether of short or long duration, all operations need to be re-supplied. This was carried out by air during World War II, when reinforcements, light vehicles and Jeeps were para-dropped to troops on the ground. Since 1945, the SAS has made extensive use of rotary-wing aircraft to supplement the re-supply work done by fixed-wing aircraft. However, this method of delivery often compromises the ability of the recipient unit to operate clandestinely in the enemy's rear areas, and the more frequent the re-supply missions, the greater the chance that the enemy has of finding the position of the SAS unit in question.

AMMUNITION CONSERVATION

In order to allow the SAS operation to continue effectively, re-supply must be kept to the absolute minimum, and every effort is made to reduce the quantity of additional supplies that have to be delivered. SAS parties enter the operational area with as much equipment as possible and live off the land as far as possible. One bulky and weighty item that is always required, however, is ammunition, and its expenditure is generally proportional to the duration and success of the mission.

One of the reasons for the great marksmanship skills of SAS troopers in battle is the need to conserve ammuni-

Left: The 5.56mm Colt M4, a shortened version of the M16 assault rifle, and a weapon that is used by the SAS.

tion. Quite apart from the military advantage of 'making every round count', the logistic advantage of expending as few rounds as possible reduces the need for constant replenishment of the unit's ammunition supplies. Even so, the nature of modern warfare demands a moderately high rate of ammunition expenditure, especially in automatic weapons, and this raises the possibility of an SAS party running out of ammunition in the field.

The most ready source of re-supply in the field is, of course, the enemy. It is unlikely, however, that the enemy's ammunition is compatible with the American, British and German weapons generally used by the SAS. The SAS is trained, therefore, to handle weapons used by most actual and potential enemies. This allows the SAS party to discard their original weapons when they become unserviceable or run out of ammunition in the field, to be replaced by weapons and ammunition seized from the enemy. The important factor here is not just the possibility of using the enemy's weapons, which most soldiers would be capable of

doing after a little thought, but rather of using these weapons immediately and in a highly effective manner.

SAS WEAPONS SKILLS

This flexibility of thought is one of the great strengths of the SAS, for its troopers are capable not only of adapting to large numbers of small arms, but also to other weapons, so that each trooper is, in a sense, a sort of 'force multiplier'. The classic example of this remains the action fought at Mirbat in Oman in July 1972, when a nine-man SAS team, aided by some local police and irregulars, fought off attacks by some 250 communist insurgents. The key to this success was twofold: first, the SAS troopers proved their ability to hit long-range targets with their first shots, and second, they were able to operate a number of weapons, including assault rifles, machine guns, mortar, and even a 25-pounder field gun.

It is worth emphasising that while the ability to use a number of different weapon types is in itself a major advantage, it is not by any means the whole

Above: An SAS Land Rover and its crew in the 1991 Gulf War. Note the M16 with M203 carried by the trooper standing on the left.

story. Where the SAS has a significant advantage is the ability of its troopers to use their weapons with both cool determination and great technical skill. The small arms used by the SAS are, for the most part, not exotic items, but standard weapons from which they can extract the best and most economical performance.

The ability of SAS soldiers to hit individual targets at long range is often the crucial factor in a firefight, that and shooting first. But there are also other tricks that are integral to SAS success. These include having tracer rounds as the last two bullets in a magazine. When the first tracer is fired the second round is automatically chambered, thus letting the firer know that it is time to change magazines but he still has another round left in the breech. SAS soldiers know how to get the most performance out of the small arms they use, which, combined with their proficiency, gives them the edge.

Rifles and Assault Rifles

The SAS makes use of a wide variety of assault rifles, and has an in-depth working knowledge of the rifles of many foreign nations. Among the most popular rifles currently in use with the Regiment is the 5.56mm M16 and its more compact version, the Colt Commando.

The most common weapon used by SAS troopers is the rifle in both its standard and assault forms. The assault rifle delivers fully automatic fire and, in its most modern incarnations, its overall design as a 'bullpup' weapon, with a straight line through from the muzzle to the shoulder, reduces the weapon's length and weight, which improves 'aimability' and accuracy in the automatic-fire mode.

Such rifles are the standard weapons of the conventional infantryman, but there is a major difference between the tactical approach of the infantryman and that of the SAS trooper. Whereas the infantryman is generally trained to fire his assault rifle with modest expenditure of ammunition at groups of targets within a range of 200m (656ft), the SAS trooper is trained to fire with the minimum possible expenditure of ammunition (single shots or two/three-rounds bursts) at individual targets and, wherever possible, at a range of 200m (656ft) or over except, of course, where conditions such as jungle or urban fighting make this impossible.

AK-47

The Kalashnikov AK-47 was the first member of a long series of Soviet infantry weapons designed for efficient use, despite the attentions (or perhaps lack of attentions) of the poorly trained and technically illiterate infantrymen of the USSR, its European satellites and Third World clients. The great virtues of the AK-47 are therefore its 'soldier-proof' nature, its simplicity, and a combination of robustness and reliability. The AK-47's main limitations are its lack of accuracy at any range over 300m (984ft), and the noisiness of its safety/fire selector lever. Nevertheless, the ubiquitous availability of the weapon, of which more than 50 million were produced, means that it is one of the opposition weapons with which every SAS trooper is familiar.

Type: assault rifle
Calibre: 7.62mm
Weight: 4.3kg (9.5lb) empty
Length: 0.869m (2ft 10in) with butt extended, and 0.699m (2ft 4in) with butt folded

Effective range: 300m (984ft)
Rate of fire: 600 rounds per minute (cyclic)
Feed: 30-round box magazine
Muzzle velocity: 710m (2329ft) per second

AK-74

The Kalashnikov AK-74 is the version of the AKM revised to fire the 5.45mm round that was developed as the Soviet counterpart to the NATO 5.56mm round. The weapon is notable for its effective muzzle brake and compensator, which make it possible to deliver fully automatic fire with the muzzle unlikely to move away from the firer's line of sight, and in combination with lower recoil forces and an improved bullet shape, the AK-74 is a more accurate weapon than the AK-47 and AKM.

Type: assault rifle
Calibre: 5.45mm
Weight: 3.6kg (7.9lb) empty
Length: 0.93m (3ft 1in)
Effective range: 400m (1312ft)
Rate of fire: 650 rounds per minute (cyclic)
Feed: 30-round plastic box magazine
Muzzle velocity: 900m (2953ft) per second

AKM

The Kalashnikov AKM is a modernised version of the AK-47. It differs in no fundamental feature and is produced in two forms, as the AKM with a wooden stock and the AKMS with a folding stock.

Type: assault rifle
Calibre: 7.62mm
Weight: 3.15kg (6.9lb) empty
Length: 0.876m (2ft 11in)
Effective range: 300m (984ft)

Left: The Russian AK-74 assault rifle. Designed to fire the 5.45mm round, it is one of the Kalashnikov family of assault rifles.

Rate of fire: 600 rounds per minute (cyclic)
Feed: 30-round box magazine
Muzzle velocity: 715m (2346ft) per second

ARMALITE

The Armalite assault rifle is a close relative of the M16 assault rifle, and was designed in the USA by Eugene Stoner during 1956 when he was employed by Armalite Inc., a division of the Fairchild Engine and Airplane Corporation. The production of the weapon was licensed to Colt, and after it had evaluated the type as the XM16, the US Army adopted the new rifle as the M16 series that entered service in 1967. The basic Armalite weapon was produced in modest numbers as the AR-15 and, because of its compact dimensions and light weight, is admirably suited to jungle warfare. The weapon was used by the SAS during the Indonesian Confrontation in Borneo, (1963-66), and its primary advantages over the standard FNL1 series rifle of the British army are the fact that it is some 150mm (5.9in) shorter, 2kg (4.4lb) lighter, and fires a 5.56mm round whose

Below: The Colt Commando assault rifle. Compact and light, it has been used for SAS anti-terrorist missions in Northern Ireland.

bullet offers greater short-range lethality than the 7.62mm bullet of the L1 series. For details of the Armalite, see the M16 entry below.

COLT COMMANDO

The Colt Commando is an American weapon, and the smallest, lightest and most compact derivative of the basic Armalite assault rifle. It differs from the M16 series mostly in its telescopic butt

Above: The Armalite was first adopted by the SAS during the Borneo campaign, when the Regiment needed a light and compact rifle.

and short barrel, which is fitted with a removable flash hider. The primary advantages of this are that in, combat, the weapon can be brought to bear on its target with great speed, and in counter-terrorist operations it is both easy to conceal and handy to use in a confined space. The

weapon has been used by the SAS in Northern Ireland.

Type: assault rifle
Calibre: 5.56mm
Weight: 2.44kg (5.4lb) empty
Length: 0.76m (2ft 6in) with butt extended, and 0.68m (2ft 3in) with butt retracted
Effective range: 400m (1312ft)
Rate of fire: 700-100 rounds per minute (cyclic)
Feed: 20- or 30-round box magazine
Muzzle velocity: 820m (2720ft) per second

FN FAL

The Fabrique Nationale FAL (*Fusil Automatique Léger*, or light automatic rifle) is a Belgian weapon that was used by the SAS in the Malayan campaign (1948-60). The weapon is basically similar to the L1 series rifle that was developed from it for the British army, but had the advantage for the SAS that in its baseline Belgian form the weapon is capable of automatic as well as semi-automatic fire. It is worth noting, however, that some SAS troopers

felt that the accuracy of the FAL was degraded to an unacceptable degree in full automatic-fire mode.

Type: assault rifle
Calibre: 7.62mm
Weight: 4.25kg (9.4lb) empty
Length: 1.09m (3ft 7in)
Effective range: 650m (2130ft)
Rate of fire: 650-700 rounds per minute (cyclic)
Feed: 20-round box magazine
Muzzle velocity: 840m (2756ft) per second

HECKLER & KOCH G3

The Heckler & Koch G3 is a German (originally West German) rifle, and has been the standard weapon of the German and many other armies since the late 1950s. The most important attributes of this almost ubiquitous weapon are its excellent engineering and robust construction. The G3 is an extremely reliable weapon that continues to function well under virtually all climatic and geographical conditions. It is this factor that has made the weapon attractive to a number of special forces around the world, including the US Army Rangers and US Navy SEALs in the USA, and the SAS in the UK, where the weapon has been extensively used in Northern Ireland.

Type: assault rifle
Calibre: 7.62mm
Weight: 4.4kg (9.7lb) empty
Length: 1.025m (3ft 4in)
Effective range 400m (1312ft)
Rate of fire: 500-600 rounds per minute (cyclic)
Feed: 20-round box magazine
Muzzle velocity 780-800m (2559-2624ft) per second

HECKLER & KOCH G8

The Heckler & Koch G8 is a German weapon of considerable versatility: it is capable of single-shot, three-round burst and fully automatic fire, and can readily be adapted to fire from a magazine or belt. Other features are a quick-change heavy barrel, a telescopic sight and a

bipod. The weapon was designed specifically for use in counter-insurgency operations, and is used most notably by the German GSG 9 counter-terrorist unit, as well as the SAS.

Type: assault rifle optimised for the counter-terrorist and counter-insurgency roles
Calibre: 7.62mm
Weight: 8.15kg (17.97lb) empty with bipod
Length: 1.03m (3ft 5in)
Effective range: 800m (2624ft)
Rate of fire: 800 rounds per minute (cyclic)
Feed: 20- or 50-round box magazine, or belt
Rate of fire: 800m (2624ft) per second.

HECKLER & KOCH G41

The Heckler & Koch G41 is another German weapon, in this instance essentially the G3 revised to fire 5.56mm ammunition. Other changes include provision for a fixed or retractable butt, a 30-round magazine and a three-round burst capability. The type is made even more attractive to special forces, including the SAS, by its low noise signature and its dustproof ejector port.

Type: assault rifle
Calibre: 5.56mm
Weight: 4.1kg (9lb) empty with fixed butt, or 4.35kg (9.6lb) empty with retractable butt
Length: 0.997m (3ft 3in) with fixed butt, or 0.806m (2 ft 8in) with retractable butt retracted
Effective range: 400m (1312ft)
Rate of fire: 850 rounds per minute (cyclic)
Feed: 30-round box magazine
Muzzle velocity: 800m (2624ft) per second

LEE-ENFIELD

The SMLE (Short Magazine Lee-Enfield) was the standard British rifle of World Wars I and II and evolved through five major variants. One of the finest military bolt-action rifles ever produced, the SMLE was comparatively weighty, but relatively handy, and for a bolt-action rifle had a high rate of fire. The type was accurate and reliable, and one of its main

attractions was a magazine holding 10 rounds rather than the five rounds typical of most other rifles of its period. The SMLE was used in World War II by both the SAS and the Long Range Desert Group.

Type: bolt-action rifle
Calibre: 0.303in
Weight: 4.13kg (9.1lb) loaded
Length: 1.132m (3ft 9in)
Effective range: 800m (2624ft)
Feed: 10-round detachable box magazine
Muzzle velocity: 738m (2421ft) per second

M1 CARBINE

The M1 Carbine was made in very large numbers in World War II for the US forces. They needed an intermediate-power weapon that offered greater range and lethality than the M1 and M3 sub-machine guns, but was lighter and smaller than the M1 rifle. Easy to clean and maintain, the M1 Carbine was reliable and offered a moderately high rate of fire, and for these reasons was much favoured by the SAS for use in the Malayan 'Emergency' (1948-60). It became clear during this campaign, however, that the M1 Carbine was a far from ideal weapon; it had poor accuracy at ranges of more than 100m (328ft), and the limited lethality of its low-powered round at all except the shortest ranges was another drawback. The bullet was based on that of a pistol, and therefore possessed a poor ballistic shape, and this combined with a low muzzle velocity to result in a rapid loss of

speed and low kinetic energy on impact with the target.

Type: semi-automatic rifle
Calibre: 0.3in
Weight: 2.48kg (5.5lb) empty
Length: 0.905m (3ft)
Effective range: 300m (984ft)
Feed: 15- or 30-round detachable box magazine
Muzzle velocity: 593m (1945ft) per second.

M16

The Colt M16 is one of the world's most widely used weapons, and came into existence as a result of the US Army's need for a weapon firing ammunition lighter than the 0.3in and 7.62mm rounds used in the rifles of the M1 and M14 series. The M1 had been the standard American rifle of World War II, and the M14 was developed from it, with the M1's awkward eight-round ammunition clip replaced by a detachable box magazine holding 20 rounds of the NATO standard 7.62mm ammunition. The smaller, and therefore lighter, round meant reduced recoil, which would improve accuracy at the shorter ranges becoming typical for infantry combat. In addition, the soldier would be able to carry a considerably larger number of rounds for a given weight, especially as the new rifle would itself be lighter than its two predecessors. The US Army's first thought in the direction of a lighter weapon was the AR-10, designed by Eugene Stoner to fire the 7.62mm standard NATO round, but trials revealed that this rifle, employing plastic

Above: The M16A2 assault rifle. In SAS use it usually comes with an M203 grenade launcher attached under the barrel.

and aluminium wherever possible, was too light for the powerful 7.62mm round. The AR-10 first appeared in 1955, and modest numbers were made until 1962, when the type was followed by the AR-15, which fired a high-velocity round in the new 5.56mm calibre. This proved altogether more successful, and was standardised for production as the M16, which entered service in 1959.

The weapon was thought to be self-cleaning, but experience in Southeast Asia soon convinced the US Army that daily maintenance of the gas passages was required, and that a thumb-operated plunger was needed on the right of the receiver to ensure that the bolt was fully closed in muddy conditions. This turned the M16 into the M16A1, which became the first definitive model of an increasingly ubiquitous weapon whose current version is the M16A2 with a number of improved features.

The SAS felt that the M16A1 was ideal for its purposes in jungle fighting and adopted the weapon for the Indonesian Confrontation in Borneo (1963-66). The weapon was then used in Aden (1964-67) and Oman (1970-76), and later in the Falklands War (1982). Experience in the jungles of Borneo was not altogether successful, the SAS finding that the light weight of the bullet fired by the M16A1's standard M193 round made it ineffective at ranges of more than 400m

(1312ft), and it was also prone to deflection by twigs and thick foliage. They generally adopted the slightly heavier European SS109 round, even though this resulted in a certain loss of muzzle velocity. This bullet improved the M16A1's capabilities in the jungle, but the weapon's success in the Aden and Oman campaigns was notably poor because of its tendency to jam under sandy and dusty conditions; in addition, the long-range accuracy of the light bullet was poor.

The version of the M16A2 used by the SAS has the capability to fire three-round bursts as well as single shots, but lacks the capacity for fully automatic fire found in some export versions of the M16 series.

Type: assault rifle
Calibre: 5.56mm
Weight: 3.4kg (7.5lb) empty
Length: 1.0m (3ft 3in)
Effective range: 400m (1312ft)
Rate of fire: 700-900 rounds per minute (cyclic)
Feed: 20- or 30-round detachable box magazine
Muzzle velocity: 991m (3250ft) per second with the M193 round, or 948m (3110ft) per second with the SS109 round

RUGER MINI 14

The Ruger Mini-14 is an American weapon developed by Sturm, Ruger &

Co. in 1973 as a scaled-down version of the M1 Garand rifle and fires a 5.56mm rather than 0.3in round. The lighter weight of the bullet and the reduced propellant load of the round yield a significant reduction in recoil force, meaning that a fair degree of accuracy can be maintained even when the weapon is firing in fully automatic mode, and this is particularly important for the SAS's counter-terrorist role. The version of the Mini-14 used by the SAS is the AC-556, which is a selective-fire weapon with single-shot, three-round burst and fully automatic fire options.

Type: assault rifle
Calibre: 5.56mm
Weight: 2.89kg (6.4lb) empty
Length: 0.984m (3ft 3in)
Effective range: 300m (984ft)
Rate of fire: 750 rounds per minute (cyclic)
Feed: 5-, 20- and 30-round box magazines
Muzzle velocity: 1058m (3470ft) per second

SA-80

The L85A1 is the assault rifle version of the British army's SA-80 weapon that

Right: The SLR, until recently the standard-issue rifle of the British Army. A real 'soldier's weapon', it was liked by the SAS.

entered service in 1984 as replacement for the L1A1. The type has suffered a number of in-service problems, including a tendency for the magazine to become detached and the for-end to break, but the weapon is potentially excellent in terms of its light weight, ease of handling, accuracy up to a range of 300m (984ft), and good sights. The weapon is in limited service with the SAS, but remains somewhat suspect because of its unreliability.

Type: assault rifle
Calibre: 5.56mm
Weight: 3.8kg (8.4lb) empty without sight unit
Length: 0.765m (2ft 7in)
Effective range: 300m (984ft)
Rate of fire: 650-800 rounds per minute (cyclic)
Feed: 30-round box magazine
Muzzle velocity: 940m (3085ft) per second

SLR

The L1A1 was the British Army's standard weapon until the advent of the SA-80 (L85) assault rifle. It was otherwise

Right: Used by the SAS in Northern Ireland, the Steyr AUG is reliable, accurate and very robust – ideal for special forces operations.

known as the SLR (Self-Loading Rifle) after its introduction in the mid-1950s as a variant of the Belgian FAL with single-shot rather than automatic fire capability. The weapon was reliable and accurate, although both the basic rifle and the ammunition were somewhat on the heavy side. It was used by the SAS from the early 1960s until the early 1980s, proving notably successful in the fighting of the Aden and Oman campaigns (1964-67 and 1970-76 respectively), in which its reliability and long-range combination of accuracy and stopping power were highly admired.

Type: assault rifle
Calibre: 7.62mm
Weight: 4.3kg (9.5lb) empty
Length: 1.143m (3ft 9in)
Effective range: 600m (1968ft) with SUIT (Sight Unit Infantry Trilux)
Feed: 20-round box magazine
Muzzle velocity: 838m (2750ft) per second

STEYR AUG

The Steyr AUG (*Armée Universal Gewehr*, or army multi-role weapon) is one of the most advanced weapons currently in service. It is an Austrian weapon of the 'bullpup' type that has been used by the SAS in Northern Ireland in both of its two forms: one has single-short and fully automatic capability, and the other possesses the ability to fire single shots or bursts of three rounds. Despite its distinctly futuristic appearance, which might persuade some that the type was designed for impressive looks rather than first-rate performance, the AUG is an excellent weapon. Its inbuilt optical sight unit provides excellent accuracy, it is reliable and is rugged enough to withstand the type of punishment that would either destroy or render inoperative virtually every other assault rifle. The AUG is also extremely versatile, for it can be turned into a sub-machine gun or light support weapon merely by the change of a few parts.

Type: assault rifle
Calibre: 5.56mm
Weight: 3.6kg (7.9lb) empty
Length: 0.79m (2ft 7in)
Effective range: 500m (1640ft)
Rate of fire: 650 rounds per minute (cyclic)
Feed: 30- and 42-round box magazine of plastic construction so that the firer can see how many rounds remain
Muzzle velocity: 970m (3182ft) per second

TYPE 56

The Type 56 is a Chinese assault rifle based on the Russian Kalashnikov AK-47 and, in common with most other Chinese weapons that SAS troopers are trained to use, it is a weapon of indifferent quality because of its cheap manufacture. It is capable of semi- and full-automatic fire.

Type: assault rifle
Calibre: 7.62mm
Weight: 3.8kg (8.4lb) empty
Length: 0.874m (2ft 10in)
Effective range 300m (984ft)
Rate of fire: 600 rounds per minute (cyclic)
Feed: 30-round box magazine
Muzzle velocity: 710m (2329ft) per second

TYPE 68

The Type 68 is another Chinese assault rifle whose action is modelled on that of the Soviet Kalashnikov AK-47. The weapon is capable of semi-automatic and automatic fire but, while slightly more accurate than the Type 56 because of its longer and slightly heavier barrel, it is more cumbersome.

Type: Type 68 assault rifle
Calibre: 7.62mm
Weight: 3.5kg (7.7lb) empty
Effective range 400m (1312ft)
Rate of fire: 750 rounds per minute (cyclic)
Feed: 15- and 30-round box magazines
Muzzle velocity: 730m (2395ft) per second

Machine Guns

The machine gun is a rapid-fire weapon that can use up vast quantities of ammunition. In the hands of SAS soldiers, however, the machine gun is a firearm that can be fired in short, accurate bursts to take out enemy personnel at long ranges.

Despite its high rate of ammunition consumption, which is always a problem for foot patrols with their limited weight-carrying capabilities, the machine gun has always played a prominent part in SAS operations. In the hands of a well trained trooper it can offset many aspects of an enemy's numerical superiority. In this capacity the machine gun is a vital fire-support weapon: the light machine gun provides support for the squad, and covers troopers as they advance, the medium machine gun lays down sustained fire in an area in which enemy movement is thus impossible, and the heavy machine gun provides multiple capabilities in offensive and defensive operations. A weapon of this type is fundamental to the typical four-man SAS patrol for fire support in tactical manoeuvres, providing destructive power in raiding operations, and protection against both fixed- and rotary-wing aircraft in all types of operation.

Below: The 7.62mm L4 light machine gun, a modernised version of the famous Bren, which was used by the SAS in World War II.

AMELI

The Ameli looks like a scaled-down German MG42 machine gun from World War II, and is based on the same action as the G3 rifle.

Type: light machine gun
Calibre: 5.56mm
Weight: 5.2kg (11.5lb)
Length: 0.97m (3ft 2in)
Effective range: 1000m (3280ft)
Rate of fire: 900 rounds per minute (cyclic)
Feed: 100- or 200-round box magazine, or belt
Muzzle velocity: 875m (2871ft) per second

BREN GUN

The Bren Gun was possibly the best light machine gun of all time, and was widely used by the SAS in World War II and in the post-war period until the late 1970s. The weapon was originally chambered for the 0.303in round of the World War II era, but it was later revised in its L4 version for the 7.62mm NATO round.

Type: L4A4 light machine gun
Calibre: 7.62mm

Weight: 8.68kg (19.15lb)
Length: 1.156m (3ft 11in)
Effective range: 600m (1968ft)
Rate of fire: 520 rounds per minute (cyclic)
Feed: 30-round box magazine
Muzzle velocity: 838m (2750ft) per second

BROWNING M1919

The classic Browning M1919A4 medium machine gun was often used in the Jeep-mounted role in World War II and for a time after. A belt-fed, air-cooled weapon it was notable for its accuracy, reliability and ease of maintenance.

Type: medium machine gun
Calibre: 0.3in
Weight: 14.06kg (31lb)
Length: 1.044m (3ft 5in)
Effective range: 1510m (4953ft)
Rate of fire: 400-500 rounds per minute (cyclic)
Feed: belt
Muzzle velocity: 860m (2820ft) per second

BROWNING M2

The 0.3in Browning machine gun was often replaced or complemented in World War II by its larger brother, the 0.5in Browning M2, a heavy machine gun that is arguably the finest machine gun ever to have been produced and which is still in widespread service. It can be mounted on a vehicle or used in the ground role as a sustained-fire weapon mounted on a tripod; it possesses an excellent capability against light armour as it fires an effective armour-piercing round as well as ball and tracer. A Browning was used by the SAS at the Battle of Mirbat in July 1972.

Type: heavy machine gun
Calibre: 0.5in
Weight: 38.1kg (84lb)
Length: 1.654m (5ft 5in)
Effective range: 1805m (5921ft)

Rate of fire: 450–575 rounds per minute (cyclic)
Feed: belt
Muzzle velocity: 884m (2900ft) per second

GPMG

From the late 1950s, these older weapons were complemented in SAS service by the General Purpose Machine Gun, which is the medium machine gun counterpart of the L1 semi-automatic rifle and designated L7 in British army service. The GPMG is extremely sturdy and is notable for its accuracy, especially in the delivery of the short bursts that can be so effective in broken engagements common to the SAS. The weapon is generally used on a bipod, but can be installed on a tripod for the sustained-fire role.

Type: L7A2 light/medium machine gun
Calibre: 7.62mm
Weight: 10.9kg (24lb) with a bipod
Length: 1.232m (4ft) in the light role, or 1.048m (3ft 5in) in the sustained role
Effective range: 1805m (5920ft)
Rate of fire: 750–1000 rounds per minute (cyclic)
Feed: belt
Muzzle velocity: 838m (2750ft) per second

HECKLER & KOCH 13E

The Heckler & Koch 13E is based on the action of the G3 assault rifle, can fire three-round bursts as well as fully automatic fire, and can be fed from a belt or double drum as alternatives to the standard box magazine.

Type: light machine gun
Calibre: 5.56mm
Weight: 6kg (13.2lb) including bipod
Length: 0.98m (3ft 3in)
Effective range: 400m (1312ft)
Rate of fire: 750 rounds per minute (cyclic)
Feed: 25-round box magazine
Muzzle velocity: 950m (3117ft) per second

LSW

In more recent years, the SAS has used small numbers of modern light machine guns chambered for the 5.56mm round, including the British Light Support Weapon (LSW), German Heckler & Koch 13E, Singaporean Ultimax 100 and Spanish Ameli. The Light Support Weapon is the machine gun member of the SA-80 series of weapons, and differs from the L85 assault rifle mainly in having a heavier barrel. The weapon is very accurate, but lacks an interchangeable barrel and cannot, therefore, be used in the sustained-fire role.

Type: L86A1 light machine gun
Calibre: 5.56mm
Weight: 6.58kg (14.5lb)
Length: 0.9m (2ft 11in)
Effective range: 1000m (3280ft)
Rate of fire: 700–850 rounds per minute (cyclic)
Feed: 30-round box magazine

Above: The Browning 0.5in heavy machine gun, one of the finest machine guns ever built. It is a favourite with SAS soldiers.

Muzzle velocity: 970m (3182ft) per second

MINIMI

In recent years the Belgian Minimi machine gun has become a firm favourite with SAS foot patrols. It is light, accurate and can take an M16-type magazine via one of its two feed slots. SAS soldiers do have a couple of complaints about the Minimi, as Sergeant Andy McNab states: 'The plastic prepacked boxes of ammo for the weapon are not its best design feature. As you're patrolling the box is

Above: The GPMG, nicknamed 'Gimpy' in the SAS. Reliable, robust and accurate, it will remain in SAS use well into the future.

across your body; it can bang against you and fall off. Another problem can be that the rounds are not completely packed in the boxes and you get a rhythmic banging noise, which is bad news at night as noise travels more easily.'

Type: light machine gun
Calibre: 5.56mm
Weight: 6.8kg (15lb)
Length: 1.04m (41in)
Effective range: 600m (1968ft)
Rate of fire: 750–1000 rounds per minute (cyclic)
Feed: 30-round box magazine or 200-round metal belt
Muzzle velocity: 915m (3000ft) per second

RPK

The RPK is the light machine gun version of the Russian AK-47 assault rifle with a longer barrel and a bipod attached, and combines all the virtues of the Kalashnikov AK-47 with the ability to serve as an effective squad automatic weapon.

Type: light machine gun
Calibre: 7.62mm
Weight: 5kg (11lb)
Length: 1.035m (3ft 5in)
Effective range: 800m (2624ft)
Rate of fire: 650 rounds per minute (cyclic)
Feed: 40-round box magazine or 75-round drum magazine
Muzzle velocity: 732m (2402ft) per second

SGM

The SGM is an obsolescent weapon out of Russian (ex-Soviet) service, but is still encountered in many parts of the world.
Type: medium machine gun
Calibre: 7.62mm
Weight: 13.6kg (30lb)
Length: 1.12m (3ft 8in)
Effective range: 1000m (3280ft)
Rate of fire: 700–850 rounds per minute (cyclic)
Feed: 250-round belt
Muzzle velocity: 800m (2624ft) per second

TYPE 56

The SAS also trains in the use of a number of Chinese and Soviet machine guns. The two principal Chinese types are the Type 56 and Type 74. The Type 56 is a belt-fed weapon optimised for the sustained-fire role, and the use of a powerful round provides good range.
Type: medium machine gun
Calibre: 7.62mm
Weight: 7.1kg (15.6lb)
Length: 1.036m (3ft 5in)
Effective range: 800m (2624ft)
Rate of fire: 700 rounds per minute (cyclic)
Feed: 100-round belt
Muzzle velocity: 700m (2297ft) per second

TYPE 74

The Type 74 is still comparatively little known, but is a useful weapon based on a

modified Kalashnikov action.
Type: medium machine gun
Calibre: 7.62mm
Weight: 6.2kg (13.7lb)
Length: 1.07m (3ft 6in)
Effective range: 600m (1968ft)
Rate of fire: 150 rounds per minute (cyclic)
Feed: 101-round drum magazine
Muzzle velocity: 735m (2411ft) per second

ULTIMAX 100

The Ultimax 100 is notable for its reliability and soft recoil, the latter resulting in considerable accuracy.
Type: light machine gun
Calibre: 5.56mm
Weight: 4.9kg (10.8lb) including bipod
Length: 1.024m (3ft 3in)
Effective range: 1000m (3280ft)
Rate of fire: 400-600 rounds per minute (cyclic)
Feed: 20- or 30-round box magazine, or 100-round drum magazine
Muzzle velocity: 970m (3182ft) per second

VICKERS GUN

The final machine gun used by the SAS in World War II was the 0.303in Vickers

Gun, a classically reliable water-cooled weapon, with enormous capability in the sustained-fire role. The Vickers Gun was extremely versatile, and it was also possible to lay down indirect fire with it.
Type: heavy machine gun
Calibre: 0.303in
Weight: 18.1kg (40lb)

Above: The Minimi light machine gun was used by SAS foot patrols in the Gulf War, who found it an excellent weapon.

Length: 1.156m (3ft 10in)
Effective range: 2010m (6593ft)
Rate of fire: 450-500 rounds per minute (cyclic)
Feed: belt
Muzzle velocity: 744m (2440ft) per second

VICKERS 'K'

Another weapon used by the SAS in World War II, generally side by side on Jeeps, was the Vickers 'K' or Vickers GO gun. It usually fired a mix of ball, tracer and armour-piercing ammunition.
Type: light machine gun
Calibre: 0.303in
Weight: 9.5kg (21lb)
Length: 1.016m (3ft 4in)
Effective range: 1800m (5904ft)
Rate of fire: 1000 rounds per minute (cyclic)
Feed: 96-round drum magazine
Muzzle velocity: 745m (2445ft) per second

Left: A World War II SAS Jeep sporting Vickers 'K' machine guns, which had a fearsome rate of fire of 1000rpm.

Submachine Guns

Primarily a weapon for SAS hostage-rescue teams, the Heckler & Koch submachine guns used by the Regiment have a high rate of fire. More importantly, they are superbly engineered and therefore work first time, every time.

The submachine gun is a pistol-calibre weapon designed to deliver selective or automatic fire, and is generally associated with close-range combat and a firing position at the shoulder or the waist. In World War II, the SAS used the submachine guns of the period, most notably the British Sten gun and captured German weapons of the *Maschinenpistole* (machine pistol) series – which were extremely popular among SAS soldiers – alongside rifles and pistols to provide additional volume of fire in 'conventional' fighting. After the end of that war, however, the general replacement of the bolt-action rifle, first by the semi-automatic rifle and then by the assault rifle with its capability to deliver fully automatic fire, rendered the submachine gun obsolete as a mainstream weapon for battlefield use. Submachine guns were still produced, generally in modest numbers and in specialised forms, for deployment to paramilitary and police forces of several nations. However, a revival in the fortunes of the submachine gun began in the mid-1960s with the reappearance onto the world stage of international terrorism.

This growing terrorist threat persuaded many governments to create specialist hostage-rescue units or, as happened in the United Kingdom, task some of their elite forces with an anti-terrorist role in addition to their more standard military tasks. These new or revised forces soon discovered that they needed a short-range weapon capable of delivering a high volume of fire, yet one compact enough for easy concealment and light enough to be brought to bear on a fleeting target with only the smallest of delays. The answer was, inevitably, the submachine gun in a form optimised for the anti-terrorist role

and therefore unsuitable for battlefield use. Such weapons are characterised by a short effective range – around 200m (656ft) – and a very high rate of fire (typically 800 to 1000 rounds per minute to ensure the killing of a terrorist by one squeeze of the trigger). This heavy and sustained firepower means that the magazine can be emptied very rapidly. In addition, the submachine gun almost invariably fires from an open-bolt position in the type of action in which the movement of the reciprocating parts makes accurate fire very difficult. However, as indicated below, the SAS has solved this.

As with other types of small arms, SAS soldiers are fully trained in the use of friendly and hostile submachine guns, some of which are listed below.

AKSU-74

The Kalashnikov AKSU-74 is the submachine gun counterpart of the Russian AK-74 assault rifle, and shares the same advantages and disadvantages as its half-parent. The weapon is therefore very reliable and rugged, but suffers from a high level of muzzle blast and flash as it fires a rifle round from a short barrel.

Type: submachine gun

Right: The Heckler & Koch MP5 submachine gun, as used by the SAS. This is the A3 version, which has a retractable butt.

Calibre: 5.45mm
Weight: not known
Length: 0.675m (2ft 3in) with stock extended, or 0.42m (1ft 5in) with stock retracted
Effective range: not known
Rate of fire: 800 rounds per minute (cyclic)
Feed: 30-round box magazine
Muzzle velocity: 800m (2624ft) per second

HECKLER & KOCH 53

A weapon much favoured by the SAS for use in Northern Ireland, as it can be operated as a submachine gun or as an assault rifle, is the Heckler & Koch HK53, which is, in essence, a derivative of the MP5 revised for the 5.56mm round.
Type: submachine gun
Calibre: 5.56mm
Weight: 3.05kg (6.72lb) empty
Length: 0.755m (2ft 6in) with stock extended, or 0.563m (1ft 10in) with stock retracted
Effective range: 250m (820ft)
Rate of fire: 700 rounds per minute (cyclic)
Feed: 25-round box magazine
Muzzle velocity: 750m (2461ft) per second

HECKLER & KOCH MP5

The main submachine gun used by the SAS for its hostage-rescue operations is the Heckler & Koch MP5 series. It is available in a number of forms, and all are excellent weapons with the safety and reliability typical of good German design and manufacture. The baseline weapon is the MP5, which has the advantage of firing from a closed-bolt position: when the trigger is pulled the bolt is already in the forward position against the breech, meaning that activation of the trigger merely releases the firing pin to fire the already-chambered cartridge, so there is no forward movement of the gun's centre of mass and thus no disturbance of the aim. The MP5 is delivered with a good open sight, but can alternatively be fitted with an optical, image-intensifying, infra-red or aiming projector sight to suit the particular tactical situation. The main variants of the MP5 series are the MP5A2

with a fixed plastic butt and the MP5A3 with a sliding butt that can be extended or retracted on a single strut. The MP5 is altogether a superb weapon.
Type: submachine gun
Calibre: 9mm
Weight: 2.55kg (5.62lb) empty
Length: 0.68m (2ft 3in) for the MP5A2; 0.66m (2ft 2in) for the MP5A3 with the butt extended, or 0.49m (1ft 4in) with the stock retracted
Effective range: 200m (656ft)
Rate of fire: 800 rounds per minute (cyclic)
Feed: 15- or 30-round box magazine
Muzzle velocity: 400m (1312ft) per second

Above: The MP5SD, the silenced version of the MP5. Its silencer means that its muzzle velocity is lower than the standard version.

HECKLER & KOCH MP5K

The Heckler & Koch MP5K is the MP5 model designed for paramilitary and counter-terrorist use. It is therefore shortened to allow easy concealment in clothing or easy use in a confined space.
Type: shortened submachine gun
Calibre: 9mm
Weight: 2kg (4.41lb) empty
Length: 0.325m (1ft 1in)
Effective range: 200m (656ft)
Rate of fire: 900 rounds per minute (cyclic)

Feed: 15- or 30-round box magazine
Muzzle velocity: 375m (1230ft) per second

HECKLER & KOCH MP5SD

The Heckler & Koch MP5SD is the silenced version of the MP5 specifically intended for special forces' use, and therefore designed so that the bullet and propellant gases leave the muzzle at subsonic speed.
Type: silenced submachine gun
Calibre: 9mm
Weight: 2.9 kg (6.39lb) empty
Length: 0.55m (1ft 10in)
Effective range: 200m (656ft)
Rate of fire: 800 rounds per minute (cyclic)
Feed: 15- or 30-round box magazine
Muzzle velocity: 285m (935ft) per second

HECKLER & KOCH MP5/10

The Heckler & Koch MP5/10 is a version of the basic MP5 firing the 10mm Auto cartridge which, with a hollow-point bullet, had significantly greater stopping power than the bullet fired by the standard 9mm Parabellum round.

Left: An SAS trooper in Malaya prepares for an operational jump in January 1953. His weapon is an Australian Owen.

INGRAM MODEL 10

Until the adoption of the MP5 in 1980, the SAS mainly used the Ingram Model 10 for counter-terrorist operations. Although this is a compact weapon that can be fitted with a silencer (both attributes important in the counter-terrorism role), it is a comparatively clumsy weapon that is also inaccurate especially when fired one-handed. The SAS still used the Model 10 into the early 1990s in Northern Ireland, where its small overall size and high rate of fire still made it attractive.
Type: submachine gun
Calibre: 9mm
Weight: 3.46kg (7.63lb) loaded
Length: 0.548m (1ft 2in) with stock extended, or 0.269m (11in) with stock retracted
Effective range: 40m (131ft)
Rate of fire: 1090 rounds per minute (cyclic)
Feed: 32-round box magazine
Muzzle velocity: 366m (1200ft) per second

OWEN

The Owen submachine gun was used by the SAS during the Malayan 'Emergency' (1948-60). It was particularly suitable, partly because of its ready availability from Australian supplies and partly because its overhead magazine made it easy to use in low-lying jungle ambush positions. The weapon was also reliable and accurate.
Type: submachine gun
Calibre: 9mm
Weight: 4.815kg (10.6lb) empty
Length: 0.813m (2ft 8in)
Effective range: 150m (492ft)
Rate of fire: 700 rounds per minute (cyclic)
Feed: 33-round box magazine
Muzzle velocity: 421m (1380ft) per second

STEN GUN

Older weapons used by the SAS included the British Sten and Sterling, the American Thompson, and the Australian Owen

---

submachine guns. The Sten gun was developed and introduced in World War II as a cheap, yet effective weapon that was reliable under extreme weather conditions and easy to strip for cleaning or repair purposes. The weapon's primary failings were a lack of accuracy and a tendency for rounds to jam in the magazine.
Type: Sten Mk II submachine gun.
Calibre: 9mm
Weight: 3.7kg (8.16lb) empty
Length: 0.762m (2ft 6in)
Effective range: 160m (525ft)
Rate of fire: 550 rounds per minute (cyclic)
Feed: 32-round box magazine
Muzzle velocity: 366m (1200ft) per second

STERLING

From 1956 the Sten was replaced by the Sterling submachine gun. A rugged and reliable gun, it has only just been retired from service. The L34A1 Sterling Mk V was the silenced version. This is based on a shorter barrel with perforations that bleed off propellant gas, so that those emerging from the muzzle are subsonic. The weapon also has its barrel enclosed in a sound suppressor, and the result is a very useful weapon whose main drawbacks are moderate length and a cumbersome physical presence.
Type: L2A3 Sterling Mk 4 submachine gun
Calibre: 9mm
Weight: 2.72kg (6lb) empty
Length: 0.68m (2ft 3in) with the butt extended, or 0.483m (1ft 7in) with the butt retracted
Effective range: 200m (656ft)
Rate of fire: 550 rounds per minute (cyclic)
Feed: 34-round box magazine
Muzzle velocity: 390m (1280ft) per second

THOMPSON

The Thompson, or 'Tommy', gun remains one of the most celebrated weapons of all time. An accurate and reliable weapon, its main drawbacks were its considerable weight, the tendency of the bullets to move around noisily in the magazine, and the propensity of the barrel to climb as a

Above: An old photograph of two SBS soldiers coming ashore from a Klepper canoe. The weapon is a silenced Sterling.

sustained burst is fired. The two main variants were the original M1928 with the classic drum magazine holding 50 rounds, and the definitive M1 with a box magazine.

Type: submachine gun
Calibre: 0.45in
Weight: 4.74kg (10.45lb) empty
Length: 0.813m (2ft 8in)
Effective range: 150m (492ft)
Rate of fire: 700 rounds per minute (cyclic)
Feed: 20- or 30-round box magazine
Muzzle velocity: 280m (920ft) per second

UZI

The two other submachine guns of western origin used by the SAS are the Israeli Uzi and the American Ingram. The Uzi is an extremely reliable weapon, notable for

Right: A French frogman armed with a Mini-Uzi. The standard version of the weapon has been used by the Special Air Service.

its overall compactness and ease of use in the dark, as its magazine is in the grip.
Type: submachine gun
Calibre: 9mm
Weight: 3.70kg (8.16lb) empty
Length: 0.65m (2ft 2in) with butt extended, or 0.47m (1ft 7in) with butt

retracted
Effective range: 150m (492ft)
Rate of fire: 600 rounds per minute (cyclic)
Feed: 25- or 32-round box magazine
Muzzle velocity: 400m (1312ft) per second

Handguns

The SAS has come a long way from the aged Webleys its men used to carry. The modern handguns used by the Regiment are high-powered semi-automatics that have large magazine capacities – ideal for counter-terrorist work.

The SAS has always used pistols or handguns, but in two widely different forms. In World War II, the handgun was carried in its standard role as a side arm for personal protection, but in more recent years it has become a weapon associated with counter-terrorist operations (killing of terrorists and rescue of hostages). There has been considerable argument about the relative merits of the submachine gun and handgun for this role, some arguing that the submachine gun offers greater capability through its higher rate of fire and single-shot accuracy. Others point to the advantages of the handgun's rapid fire capability at ranges up to 30m (98ft), easy 'pointability', and more effective single-handed use. Critics of the handgun also aver that the pistol has so high a recoil force that any second shot is generally less accurate than the first, but the SAS has circumvented this problem with specialised training.

Recently, there has been speculation that the SAS has taken possession of a new handgun produced by the Belgian firm. Called the Five-seveN, it reportedly has around 20 times the range and penetrative power of the most powerful military handguns currently in service. The details for the Five-seveN are impressive: its round can punch through 48 layers of Kevlar armour at 200m (656ft), has a muzzle velocity of 650m (2132ft) per second and has a magazine capacity of 24 rounds. One interesting point about this new handgun is that the lightweight bullets and the design, which enables the gas pressures created when the gun is fired to cancel each other out, has only a modest recoil. One thing is certain, the Five-seveN's smooth shape and lack of levers, which means it is less likely to catch on clothing when it is pulled from clothing, makes it ideal for SAS plainclothes operations in Northern Ireland (should the tortuous peace process collapse).

BROWNING HIGH POWER

The Browning High Power, made in Belgium by Fabrique Nationale and now the standard handgun of the SAS, is one of the classic pistols of all time. It first entered service in the 1930s. The weapon has a semi-automatic action, very considerable stopping power, and a large magazine. The High Power has been produced and used in a number of forms, but the current model is the BDA (Browning Double Action), in which the hammer can be cocked manually before the trigger is pulled to fire the weapon, or alternatively the hammer can be cocked and the weapon fired by continuous pressure on the trigger.

Type: FN BDA semi-automatic pistol
Calibre: 9mm
Weight: 0.905kg (2lb) empty
Length: 20cm (8in)
Effective range: 40m (131ft)
Feed: 14-round box magazine

Above: The Browning High Power handgun, still used by SAS hostage-rescue and anti-terrorist teams despite its age.

Muzzle velocity: 253m (830ft) per second

COLT M1911

Since World War II, the SAS has used a number of American and European handguns, most notably the American-designed Colt M1911A1 and Browning High Power, and the European-designed Glock and SIG-Sauer weapons. The Colt M1911A1 is a large and heavy weapon with a semi-automatic action. The weapon is reliable in the extreme, easy to strip for cleaning, and possesses very considerable stopping power.

Type: semi-automatic pistol
Calibre: 0.45in
Weight: 1.13kg (2.5lb) empty
Length: 21.9cm (9in)

Effective range: 40m (131ft)
Feed: eight-round box magazine
Muzzle velocity: 253m (830ft) per second

GLOCK GUNS

Made in Austria and notable for their light weight, resulting from the use of a high-strength polymer material for the receiver, the Glock range of handguns are very well suited to the anti-terrorist role; they do not have a conventional safety catch, but rather a safety system built into the two-pressure trigger mechanism. The Glock 17 is a semi-automatic 9mm weapon with a 17-round box magazine, and the Glock 19 is a smaller and lighter version of the Glock 17 with a 15-round box magazine. The Glock 18 is a development of the Model 17 with full automatic as well as semi-automatic fire capability, as well as provision for larger magazines. The Glock 18 is really only suited to special forces use, as it requires intensive training in its proper use.

Type: Glock 18 automatic and semi-automatic pistol
Calibre: 9mm
Weight: 0.636kg (1.4lb) empty
Length: 22.3cm (9in)
Effective range: 50m (164ft)
Rate of fire: 1300 rounds per minute (cyclic)
Feed: 17-, 19- or 33-round box magazines
Muzzle velocity: 360m (1181ft) per second

SIG-SAUER GUNS

Made in Switzerland, the SIG-Sauer family of handguns is notable for its excellent manufacture and extreme reliability. There are a number of models, including the P226 and more compact P228 semi-automatic weapons of the single- or double-action types. SIG-Sauers are now in SAS use. They are very reliable; indeed, in one famous Royal Canadian Mounted Police test, 10 separate P226s discharged a total of 150,000 rounds. The malfunction rate was an incredible 0.007 per cent. There are other reasons why SIGs are so popular with units such as the SAS. For one thing, they are compact, easy to point and shoot, and all have double-action

trigger devices and magazine catches that can be reversed for left-handed firers.

There seems little reason to doubt that the SIGs will eventually replace the High Power as the handgun used on hostage-rescue missions. This is because they fulfil all the criteria looked for in a handgun by the SAS: reliability, safety (there must be no risk of an accidental discharge before an assault takes place), good magazine capacity, compactness, suitability for both left- and right-handed firers, rapid magazine change function, speedy operation and the ability to work under adverse weather conditions. The only challenger seems to be the Five-seveN (see page opposite).

Type: SIG-Sauer P226 semi-automatic pistol
Calibre: 9mm
Weight: 0.75kg (1.65lb) empty
Length: 19.6cm (8in)
Effective range: 50m (164ft)
Feed: 15- or 20-round box magazine
Muzzle velocity: 350m (1148ft) per second

Above: The SIG-Sauer P228 handgun, one of the excellent series of weapons produced by the Swiss firm, which are now in SAS use.

WEBLEY

During World War II, the standard pistol of the SAS was the British army's Webley revolver, which was notable for its strength, reliability and accuracy. Widely used by SAS officers during that conflict, at the time the Webley represented the best there was in handgun design. The maufacture was of an extremely high standard, and the weapon could take a lot of punishment. Its only fault was the six-round magazine, which was often insufficient for the task in hand.

Type: Webley Pistol Mk VI revolver pistol
Calibre: 0.45in
Weight: 1.09kg (2.4lb) empty
Length: 28.6cm (11in)
Effective range: 40m (131ft)
Feed: six-round revolving cylinder
Muzzle velocity: 199m (653ft) per second

Sniper Rifles

The SAS uses sniper rifles during field operations and for anti-terrorist duties. But whatever the mission, only the best is chosen, and in the Accuracy International PM the Regiment has a sniper rifle that is one of the world's top models.

The SAS uses the sniper rifle for two different and highly contrasting roles. The first is in 'conventional' warfare, and demands that the sniper be capable of operating in the field to score a first-round hit (but not necessarily a kill) on a head-sized target at a range of 300m (984ft), or a torso-sized target at a range of between 600 and 1000m (1968 and 3280ft). The second is for use in counter-revolutionary and counter-terrorist operations, and places less emphasis on movement and concealment skills, but more on a first-round kill rather than hit at a range that may be as short as 100m (328ft).

ACCURACY INTERNATIONAL PM

After evaluating several weapons, the SAS decided on the Accuracy International PM. It entered service as the L96A1 bolt-action rifle with a plastic stock, a light bipod under the barrel and a monopod under the stock so that the rifle can be laid on the target for long periods without tiring the firer, and a Schmidt & Bender telescopic sight providing accuracy out to a range of 1000m (3280ft).
Type: L96A1 sniper rifle

Calibre: 7.62mm
Weight: 6.5kg (14.3lb) empty
Length: 1.124m to 1.194m (3ft 5in to 3ft 11in)
Effective range: 1000m (3280ft)
Feed: 10-round box magazine
Muzzle velocity: 914m (2998ft) per second

L42

The oldest sniper rifle used by the SAS is the L42A1, which is a conversion of the SMLE No.4 bolt-action rifle with a heavier barrel chambered for the 7.62mm rather than 0.303in round.
Type: L42A1 sniper rifle
Calibre: 7.62mm
Weight: 4.43kg (9.7lb) empty
Length: 1.181m (3ft 11in)
Effective range: 800m (2624ft)
Feed: 10-round box magazine
Muzzle velocity: 838m (2750ft) per second

SSG 69

Although the L42 rifle was used up to and during the Falklands War (1982), it had become clear that a more modern weapon of improved accuracy was now required, and the SAS investigated three European weapons that were all used in small numbers. The SSG 69 is an Austrian bolt-action rifle notable for its reliability and very considerable accuracy.
Type: sniper rifle
Calibre: 7.62mm
Weight: 4.6kg (10.14lb) empty
Length: 1.14m (3ft 9in)
Effective range: 800m (2624ft)
Feed: five-round rotary magazine
Muzzle velocity: 860m (2820ft) per second

M55

The Tikka M55 is a bolt-action rifle of Finnish design and manufacture, and is notable for its ability to fire a number of ammunition types.
Type: Tikka M55 sniper rifle
Calibre: 0.223in, 0.243in or 7mm
Weight: 3.27kg (7.21lb) empty
Length: 1.01m (3ft 4in)
Effective range: 550m (1804ft)
Feed: 4-round box magazine
Muzzle velocity: 900m (2953ft) per second

SSG 3000

The SSG 3000 is a Swiss weapon, and as a product of the SIG Sauer company is notable for its excellent manufacture. The weapon has a bolt action and is fitted with a bipod.
Type: SSG 3000 sniper rifle
Calibre: 0.308in
Weight: 6.2kg (13.7lb) empty
Length: 1.18m (3ft 10in)
Effective range: 650m (2130ft)
Feed: 5-round box magazine
Muzzle velocity: 750m (2461ft) per second

Left: The Accuracy International PM sniper rifle, currently in service with the SAS. Its accuracy is outstanding.

Combat Shotguns

In the anti-terrorist armoury the SAS has found a use for the combat shotgun. Totally unsuitable for use in a room full of terrorists and hostages, it is an effective tool for blowing open doors and the like to allow SAS teams entry.

The SAS first used shotguns in action during the Malayan 'Emergency' (1948-60), initially using the Browning auto-loader, a civilian weapon which worked well under jungle conditions and proved effective in close combat. Shotguns were also used in Borneo in the 1960s, though there were problems with cartridges. They were paper and tended to swell up in the humid atmosphere. Even carrying them in a plastic bag didn't solve the problem. The only way round this was to use plastic cartridges. It was customary for the lead man in a four-man patrol to be armed with a shotgun, allowing him to release a good spread of shot if contact was made with the enemy. This would hopefully keep enemy heads down, giving enough time for the other patrol members to return fire. The SAS now uses the shotgun for counter-terrorist operations, principally for blowing off door hinges at the moment an assault team moves into a room to kill terrorists and free hostages. Modern military shotguns are optimised for this type of role through their ability to fire a number of different cartridges, including buckshot, armour-piercing, CS gas, Hatton (hinge-removing) and others. The three types of shotgun currently used by the SAS are two Franchi Special-Purpose Automatic Shotguns (the SPAS 12 and SPAS 15), and the Remington 870.

FRANCHI SPAS 12

The SPAS 12 has a skeleton butt with a device that allows single-handed firing, a choke that ensures a short spread of 0.9m (2ft 11in) at a range of 40m (131ft), and provision for semi-automatic or automatic fire (the latter at an initial four rounds per second). There is also provision for a muzzle device that ensures an early spread of the shot for indoor firing.
Type: combat shotgun
Calibre: 12 gauge

Weight: 4.2kg (9.25lb) empty
Length: 0.93m (3ft 1in) with stock extended, or 0.71m (2ft 4in) with stock folded
Effective range: 50m (164ft)
Rate of fire: 24-30 rounds per minute (practical)
Feed: seven-round internal magazine
Muzzle velocity: dependent on the type of round used

FRANCHI SPAS 15

The SPAS 15 is a development of the SPAS 12. It has a box rather than a tubular magazine, and can be operated in semi-automatic or pump-action modes.
Type: combat shotgun
Calibre: 12 gauge
Weight: 3.9kg (8.6lb) empty
Length: 0.915m (3ft)
Effective range: 50m (164ft)
Rate of fire: 24-30 rounds per minute (practical)

Above: The Remington 870 pump-action shotgun, used by the SAS to gain entry to rooms during a hostage-rescue mission.

Feed: six-round internal magazine
Muzzle velocity: dependent on the type of round used

REMINGTON 870

The Remington 870 is the main combat shotgun of the SAS, and having been designed for this task is considerably more robust than any shotgun designed initially for civilian use. It is also used by the US Marine Corps.
Type: Remington 870 combat shotgun
Calibre: 12 gauge
Weight: 3.6kg (7.94lb) empty
Length: 1.06m (3ft 6in)
Effective range: 40m (131ft)
Feed: seven-round internal magazine
Muzzle velocity: dependent on the type of round used

SUPPORT WEAPONS

Anti-Tank Weapons

Modern hand-held anti-tank weapons are ideal tools for significantly increasing the firepower of SAS patrols. During the 1991 Gulf War, SAS foot and vehicle teams made effective use of such weapons as the M72 and Milan anti-tank systems.

Given that its primary tasks have been hit-and-run raids and deep reconnaissance, it may seem that the SAS had, and continues to have, little need for anti-tank weapons. During World War II, however, the SAS operated anti-tank weapons in small numbers for area defence and in ambush operations. Since 1945, light-weight anti-tank weapons have been used to provide a capability against light armoured vehicles and field fortifications.

In World War II, the primary anti-tank capability of the SAS was provided by two pieces of British artillery, namely the 6-pounder dedicated anti-tank gun and the 25-pounder gun/howitzer; the British PIAT anti-tank projector; and one specialised American anti-tank rocket launcher, the so-called 'bazooka'. The two British weapons were generally used in the course of the SAS reconnaissance and blocking operations undertaken in France and the Low Countries after June 1944, when SAS parties were parachute-landed in strategic areas. They established a base from which they could contact and organise the local resistance forces and harry the German lines of communication to prevent the movement of German reserves to threatened sectors of the front. Given that a measure of local security could be provided by the local resistance elements, and that the weapons could be delivered by air and maintained with ammunition via the same route, it was felt that the potential advantages of using such artillery outweighed the risks of losing them to a German attack.

6-POUNDER ANTI-TANK GUN

The British 6pdr anti-tank gun, more formally known as the Ordnance, QF, 6-pounder 7cwt, was introduced to service in September 1941 and proved an effective tank killer for only a short time. The type was thought suitable for allocation to the SAS in 1944, as it had been replaced in first-line service by the altogether more powerful 17-pounder anti-tank gun. It could be delivered easily by air, was light enough for comparatively straightforward towing by SAS Jeeps, and

Left: The 25-pounder field gun manned by Corporal Labalaba at the Battle of Mirbat. It is now on permanent display at Woolwich.

still provided a useful capability against lighter armoured vehicles and all soft-skinned vehicles.

Type: Ordnance, QF, 6pdr 7cwt Mk IV medium anti-tank gun
Calibre: 57mm (2.2in)
Weight: 1112kg (2,471lb)
Projectile weight: 2.84kg (6.28lb)
Muzzle velocity: 823m (2700ft) per second
Armour penetration: 68.5mm (2.7in) at 915m (3001ft) at a 20-degree angle.

25-POUNDER MKII

A similar rationale was applied to give the SAS small numbers of the 25-pounder field guns, more formally known as the Ordnance, QF, 25-pounder Mk II. This was an extremely capable weapon able to provide a full range of field artillery capabilities, including a limited anti-tank facility. The type was used in very small numbers by the SAS in World War II, but enjoyed its great success in the action at Mirbat in Oman on 19 July 1972, when a single example of this weapon was used to very considerable effect to help a small party of SAS men, supported by some police and irregulars, to drive off a considerably larger assault group of communist insurgents. During that battle one man ensured that the 25-pounder would forever be linked to his name in the Regiment's folklore. The Fijian Corporal Labalaba manned and fired the gun for the most part single-handedly before being mortally wounded, but his efforts saved the day.

Type: Ordnance, QF, 25pdr Mk II field gun/howitzer
Calibre: 87.6mm (3.45in)
Weight: 1800kg (3968lb)
Maximum range: 12.255km (7.6miles)
Projectile weight: 11.34kg (25lb) for the HE round
Muzzle velocity: 532m (1745ft) per second

CARL GUSTAV

It was the hollow-charge warhead, relying on chemical factors rather than kinetic energy for the penetration of armour, that emerged from World War II as the lightest and therefore best way for infantry to be provided with an anti-armour capability,

and it later become clear that such warheads also had a devastating effect on field fortifications and other obstacles. Considerable development has since gone into the evolution of such weapons, which today provide the infantrymen, and for that matter the SAS trooper, with a formidable if somewhat short-range capability against all but the most heavily armoured tanks. The weapon of this type most generally associated with the SAS since the later 1950s has been the Swedish Carl Gustav M2-550 recoilless gun. This is sturdy, reliable, accurate and versatile, the last factor being generated by the Carl Gustav's ability to fire an anti-personnel round as well as an anti-tank round. Some indication of the weapon's tactical flexibility is provided by the fact that during the Falklands War a Royal Marine used his Carl Gustav first to shoot down an Argentine helicopter, and then put a hole though the side plate of an Argentine destroyer!

Type: Carl Gustav M2-550 man-portable anti-tank recoilless gun
Calibre: 84mm (3.31in)
Weight: 15kg (33.1lb)
Length: 1.13m (3ft 8in)
Round weight: 3kg (6.61lb) for the hollow-charge projectile
Muzzle velocity: 380m (1247ft) per second

Above: The 84mm Carl Gustav anti-tank weapon. It is an effective anti-armour tool, though heavy compared to modern systems.

Maximum range: 1000m (3280ft)
Armour penetration: 400mm (15.75in) at any range

LAW 80

The LAW 80, designed and produced by Hunting Engineering, is another single-shot weapon with a discardable launcher tube, and like the M72 suffers from a large firing signature in terms of noise and smoke. The type is designed to tackle main battle tanks, and the fact that this requires a substantial warhead means that the LAW 80 is a somewhat weighty and cumbersome item of equipment.

Type: LAW 80 man-portable single-shot anti-tank rocket launcher
Calibre: 94mm (3.7in)
Weight: 9.5kg (20.9lb)
Length: 1m (3ft 3in) closed, or 1.5m (4ft 11in) extended for firing
Rocket weight: 4kg (8.8lb)
Effective range: 500m (1640ft)
Armour penetration: 600mm (23.6in) at any range

M9 BAZOOKA

The 'bazooka' was an American weapon based on the concept of delivering the

Above: The LAW 80, the replacement for the Carl Gustav. It has an effective warhead, but its firing signature is very visible.

Above: The M72, a one-shot, throw-away anti-tank weapon that is light enough to be carried by SAS foot patrols.

same type of hollow-charge warhead as the PIAT. This warhead performs its armour-penetration 'trick' most effectively when not spinning and moving at the lowest possible velocity, so the Americans decided that the best way to deliver it was not in the form of a horizontally fired mortar bomb (as in the PIAT) with all its weight and considerable recoil, but on the front of a rocket that could be fired from a hollow tube and thus generate no recoil at all. The weapon was originally delivered in 1942 as the 2.36in Rocket Launcher M1, but by 1944 this early version had been replaced by the tactically improved 2.36in Rocket Launcher M9 in which the reloadable launcher tube could be broken down into two sections for ease of transport.

Type: 2.36in Rocket Launcher M9 man-portable anti-tank rocket launcher
Calibre: 60mm (2.4in)
Weight: 6.01kg (13.25lb) empty
Length: 1.55m (5ft 1in)
Rocket weight: 1.53kg (3.4lb)
Muzzle velocity: 83m (270ft) per second
Maximum range: 640m (2099ft)

Armour penetration: 119.4mm (4.7in) at any range

M72

During the 1960s there were many who felt that a reloadable weapon such as the Carl Gustav was unnecessarily complex, too heavy and also too expensive, and as a result many countries developed single-shot weapons of the anti-tank type: once the launcher had been fired the empty tube was discarded, and the operator then picked up a fresh unit, delivered as a certified round ready for battlefield use. The two weapons of this type to have served with the SAS have been the American M72 and British LAW 80. Accurate and fitted with a potent warhead, the M72 is light enough that several complete units can be carried by a single man; its main disadvantage, shared by many weapons of the same type, is a prominent firing signature that forces a rapid departure of the operator after he has discharged the weapon and discarded the spent launch tube. Nevertheless, for SAS foot patrols the M72 is a godsend, and its advantages far outweigh any bad points.

Type: M72A2 man-portable single-shot anti-tank rocket launcher
Calibre: 66mm (2.6in)
Weight: 2.36kg (5.2lb)

Length: 0.655m (2ft 2in) closed, or 0.893m (2ft 11in) extended for firing
Rocket weight: 1kg (2.2lb)
Muzzle velocity: 145m (475ft) per second
Maximum range: 1000m (3280ft)
Armour penetration: 305mm (12in) at any range

MILAN

With their low velocities, such rockets are highly susceptible to atmospheric conditions such as crosswinds, and being unguided, they can also be defeated, or at least degraded in effect, by any sudden change in course by the target vehicle after the rocket has been fired. It is for this reason that guided missiles were developed for use in the surface-to-surface role against tanks. The sophistication and capabilities of these weapons have increased dramatically since they were first introduced in the 1950s, but the size and weight of such systems generally precludes their use by fast-moving, lightly equipped units such as SAS patrols, who would run rather than stand in the face of main battle tank opposition.

The one weapon of this type that has been used by the SAS is the Euromissile Milan (*Missile d'Infanterie Léger Anti-char*, or light infantry anti-tank missile). It was fired in small numbers during the Falklands War while the SAS provided a diversion for the main British amphibious landing on the eastern side of San Carlos Water. During the Gulf War SAS Land Rover columns would often engage Iraqi targets with their vehicle-mounted Milans. The great advantage with the system is that it is difficult to detect in battle because of its reduced noise and flash compared to other systems. In addition, the fact that the missiles are wire-guided means that they are not vulnerable to electronic countermeasures. The Milan is launched from a ground-based firing unit that can be reloaded without difficulty, and uses semi-automatic command to line-of-sight guidance: the operator has merely to keep the target in his sight and the launcher's fire-control subsystem tracks the missile and generates guidance commands that are transmitted to the missile via a trailing wire system. The Milan is widely used and has been developed through three main variants with longer range and improved warheads.

Type: Euromissile MILAN ground-launched anti-tank missile
Diameter: 90mm (3.5in)
Length: 0.769m (2ft 6in)
Weight: 6.65kg (14.66lb)
Speed: 720km/h (447mph)
Maximum range: 2000m (6566ft)
Armour penetration: 650mm (25.6in)

PIAT

The only other British anti-tank weapon used by the SAS in World War II was the PIAT (Projector, Infantry, Anti-Tank). This superseded the Boys anti-tank rifle in the early part of the war as the primary anti-tank weapon of infantry units, and was based on the spigot mortar principle to fire a short-range grenade carrying a hollow-charge warhead. Despite its obvious obsolescence and clumsiness, the weapon was used with some success by the SAS in the Northwest European campaign of 1944-45, usually in the type of ambush situation in which the weapon's limited effective range of 91m (298ft) was

no great liability.
Type: PIAT man-portable anti-tank projector
Weight: 14.52kg (32lb) empty
Length: 0.99m (3ft 3in)
Grenade weight: 1.36kg (3lb)
Muzzle velocity: 76-137m (250-450ft) per second
Maximum range: 685m (2247ft)
Armour penetration: 110mm (4.33in) at any range

RPG-7

The SAS, as part of its standard practice of training with enemy weapons that may become available to SAS parties behind the enemy lines, also has experience of Soviet anti-tank rocket systems, most particularly the RPG-7 that entered Soviet service in 1962 and has since become one of the most ubiquitous anti-tank weapons in the world. It is based on a firing tube with sight and trigger group, which can be loaded with a slim rocket carrying an oversize hollow-charge warhead. There is also a rocket with an anti-personnel warhead.

Type: RPG-7 man-portable anti-tank rocket launcher
Calibre: 40mm (1.57in) for the launcher tube
Weight: 7kg (15.43lb)
Length: 0.99m (3ft 3in)
Rocket weight: 2.25kg (4.96lb) for the anti-tank type
Effective range: 500m (1640ft)
Armour penetration: 400mm (15.75in) at any range

Below: An SAS Land Rover and its crew photographed behind the lines during the Gulf War. Note the Milan on the roll bar.

Mortars

SAS teams generally operate far beyond the support capability of friendly artillery, so the mortar has become, and will continue to be, an important support weapon in both offensive and defensive operations.

As a unit designed for operations deep in the enemy's rear areas, the SAS cannot rely on support from the heavier weapons of associated units. It is optimised for speed and agility to minimise the chances of interception by heavier enemy forces, and always operates in the lightest possible condition; it cannot carry organic heavy support weapons such as heavy mortars or field artillery. The SAS is intended primarily to provide a reconnaissance and intelligence-gathering capability, and as such should avoid major engagements with the enemy, but is inevitably required to stand and fight on occasion. For this reason, it requires light support weapons to increase the chances of its subordinate units' survival.

The mortar is traditionally associated with the provision of close fire support for infantry units up to battalion size. Such fire support can also be provided by field artillery, but the availability of the mortar as a basic element of the infantry unit offers greater flexibility and a faster response time.

2IN MORTAR

In World War II, the SAS used three types of mortar for the provision of light, medium and heavy support fire. Light fire support was provided by the Ordnance, ML, 2in Mortar, which was adopted for British service in 1937 as a development of a Spanish design by ECIA and entered production and service in 1938. The weapon was developed through a large numbers of variants for a host of applications, and remained in service until 1980, when it was replaced by the 51mm mortar. The primary versions used by the SAS were the Mk II, Mk VII and Mk VIII weapons, which could fire high explosive (HE), smoke and flare rounds.

Type: 2in Mortar Mk VII light support mortar
Calibre: 51.2mm (2in)
Weight: 3.32kg (7.3lb)
Maximum range: 320m (1050ft)
Bomb weight: 1.02kg (2.25lb) for the HE round

3IN MORTAR

The medium support weapon of the SAS in World War II was the Ordnance, ML, 3in Mortar. This weapon was developed in the 1920s to equip infantry battalions so that the Royal Artillery's light regiments, then equipped with 3.7in (94mm) pack howitzers in the infantry support role, could be re-equipped with heavier weapons and thereby become more versatile field regiments. The most important of these weapons was the 3in Mortar Mk II, which was a useful piece of equipment in terms of the weight of bomb fired, but was generally inferior to contemporary German and Italian mortars in terms of range, even after the introduction of more advanced propellants boosted the maximum range from the original figure of 1465m (4805ft). The weapon was accurate but somewhat heavy, and was

Left: The 81mm mortar currently used by the SAS. It was used by D Squadron during the Pebble Island raid in the Falklands War.

replaced in the late 1970s by the 81mm mortar.

Type: 3in Mortar Mk II medium support mortar
Calibre: 76.2mm (3in)
Weight: 57.2kg (126lb) in action
Maximum range: 2.5km (1.5 miles)
Bomb weight: 4.54kg (10lb) for the HE round

51MM MORTAR

In the 1970s the 2in Mortar was replaced by the Mortar, ML, 51mm, which was designed as a simple light support weapon that could be operated by a single man. The weapon is essentially an improved and updated version of the 2in Mortar, firing a useful assortment of bombs (HE, flare and smoke) to a greater range and with superior accuracy.

Type: 51mm Mortar light support mortar
Calibre: 51.25mm (2 in)
Weight: 3.25kg (7.2lb)
Maximum range: 800m (2624ft)
Bomb weight: 0.79kg (1.74lb) for the HE round

81MM MORTAR

Over much the same period, the 3in Mortar was superseded by the Mortar, ML, 81mm, otherwise known as the L16. This is an advanced weapon capable of delivering its bombs accurately over a long range as a result of its nicely engineered barrel and the use of a plastic sealing ring to trap the propellant gases behind the bomb with minimum leakage. This weapon was used to support the SAS on Pebble Island in the Falklands War.

Type: 81mm Mortar medium support mortar
Calibre: 81mm (3.19in)
Weight: 34.6kg (76.28lb)
Maximum range: 5.65km (3.5 miles)
Bomb weight: 4.26kg (9.39lb) for the HE round

Surface-To-Air Missiles

Because of their weight, SAS foot patrols in general do not carry hand-held surface-to-air missiles (SAMs). However, vehicle-mounted patrols, such as those in the 1991 Gulf War, have found they are compact enough to provide defence against air attack.

The most important anti-aircraft weapon currently used by ground forces is the surface-to-air missile (SAM), and the particular type generally issued to infantry units is the shoulder-launched SAM. This usually comprises a comparatively small missile (with solid-propellant rocket propulsion and an infra-red guidance package) carried in a disposable sealed container/launcher tube.

In general, SAS patrols are not equipped with such weapons for three reasons. Firstly, SAS patrols rarely operate from static bases that require defence against fixed- and rotary-wing warplanes: even when such a base is used, SAS practice is to camouflage the base so that it is effectively invisible to warplanes. Secondly, SAS patrols carrying even lightweight shoulder-launched SAMs would find their ability to move rapidly severely compromised. Thirdly, the fieldcraft and camouflage skills of the SAS make the use of shoulder-launched SAMs generally superfluous in mobile operations. Occasionally, notably in arctic and desert warfare, shoulder-launched SAMs are useful, especially for vehicle patrols.

BLOWPIPE
The Shorts Blowpipe is a capable weapon proved in combat against targets as difficult as high-speed crossing aircraft. The weapon comes in a sealed container, weighing 13kg (28.7lb), and is clipped to an 8.9kg (19.6lb) aiming unit. The operator acquires the target visually with his monocular sight, fires the missile and then guides it to the target with a thumb controller before discarding the launcher tube and clipping on another round.
Type: Shorts Blowpipe man-portable point defence tactical surface-to-air missile
Diameter: 76mm (3in)
Length: 1.39m (4ft 7in)
Weight: 11.1kg (24.5lb)

Warhead: 2.2kg (4.85lb) proximity- and impact-fused shaped-charge and blast/fragmentation
Maximum speed: Mach 1.5
Maximum range: 4km (two miles)

JAVELIN
The Shorts Javelin is a development of the Blowpipe designed to deal more effectively with battlefield targets such as combat helicopters, which may launch their anti-tank missiles at ranges of more than 4km (two miles). To provide the necessary range, a more powerful sustainer rocket motor is fitted, and destructive capability is enhanced by the provision of a new-pattern warhead. Targeting at greater range is aided by the use of semi-automatic command to line-of-sight guidance, requiring the operator merely to keep the target centred in his sight.
Type: Shorts Javelin man-portable point defence tactical surface-to-air missile
Length: 1.39m (4ft 7in)
Weight: 11.1kg (5lb)
Warhead: fragmentation
Maximum speed: supersonic
Maximum range: more than 4km (two miles)

Above: The Stinger surface-to-air missile (SAM), which was carried by SAS Land Rover patrols during the 1991 Gulf War.

STINGER
The General Dynamics FIM-92 Stinger has all-aspect engagement capability, greater performance and manoeuvrability, an IFF system and enhanced resistance to electronic countermeasures. It was introduced in 1981 and has proved generally successful with .its passive infra-red homing system. Incorporating the Identification Friend or Foe (IFF) system, the Stinger-POST is the current production model. It has a Passive Optical Scanning Technique seeker to provide better discrimination between the target and the ground for low-altitude engagements.
Type: General Dynamics FIM-92A Stinger man-portable point defence tactical surface-to-air missile
Diameter: 70mm (2.75in)
Length: 1.52m (5ft)
Weight: 10.1kg (22.3lb)
Warhead: 3kg (6.6lb) proximity-fused blast/fragmentation
Maximum speed: more than Mach 2
Maximum range: 5km (three miles)

GRENADES & EXPLOSIVES

Since World War II the SAS has made use of explosives in its operations, and today all SAS troopers are trained to use a wide variety of explosives and grenades, both for defence and offence, plus perimeter defence weapons such as the Claymore mine.

The grenade is a small bomb designed to be thrown by hand and generally comprises a small explosive charge contained in a thick metal casing that shatters into a large number of fragments on the detonation of the explosive charge. The casing is usually corrugated or otherwise scored to ensure that fragments of basically similar mass expand evenly from the point of detonation; the grenade is always fitted with a delay mechanism that provides time for the thrower to find cover after throwing the bomb. The mass of most grenades is between 0.5 and 1kg (1.1 and 2.2lb), and their blast/fragmentation effect possesses a lethal radius in the range of 10-20m (33-66ft).

In the course of its career to date, the SAS has used too large a number of grenade types to be listed conveniently, so the types mentioned below are meant to convey an impression of the capabilities possessed by those most commonly used.

It is also thought that the SAS may use a number of the specialised grenades produced by the Haley & Weller company. The types include fragmentation and incendiary, and their primary advantage over the British army's standard grenades is their use of an electric rather than pyrotechnic fuse: the latter is characterised by an enemy-warning fizz or crack as the priming lever is released, while the former is silent.

EXPLOSIVES

The use of explosives has been associated with the SAS since its origin; David Stirling's original concept for the unit was the sabotage of installations and vehicles of all types behind the enemy lines. There are two basic types of explosive, namely low explosive and high explosive. Typical of low explosives, which burn at subsonic speed, is gunpowder. The type of explosive generally used today, and invariably used by special forces such as the SAS, is high explosive. This is relatively insensitive to prevent premature detonation, is resistant to heat and humidity, and when initiated burns at supersonic speed (anything between 2000 and 8500m/ 6566 and 27,887ft per second) so that the gases released create shock waves that shear and shatter nearby objects.

High explosive is initiated by electrical or non-electrical means. In the electrical method, the passing of a current through wires in the blasting cap ignites the small charge within the cap to set off the main charge. In the non-electrical method, a time fuse is connected to a non-electric firing cap (perhaps black powder in a fibre wrapping) whose ignition again sets off the main charge.

The SAS and other special forces generally use the plastic type of high explosive, such as PE4, RDX and PETN. The basic explosive material is mixed with a plasticising agent that improves the mix stability and resistance to factors such as shock, heat and humidity (high explosives can be hit with a hammer and set on fire without exploding). High explosive of this type is being constantly improved, particularly to meet the ever more demanding needs of special forces. The result is a series of new high-explosive compounds which combine lower volume with greater destructive effect. A good example of this is provided by the American PAM (Penetration Augmented Munition) programme, which has produced an aluminised RDX of which some 15kg (33.1lb) can achieve the same bridge-destroying effect as 90kg (198.4lb) of previous-generation C4 explosive.

Left: The Claymore anti-personnel mine. It is an ideal weapon for perimeter defence, as well as for use in ambushes.

CLAYMORE

The Claymore mine was used by SAS troopers in the Indonesian Confrontation (1963-66) and is still in the SAS inventory. Initiated electrically or mechanically (by hand or tripwires), the Claymore is an oblong weapon that is located on the ground with its face towards the enemy. When fired, the weapon hurls some 350 metal balls outward in a fan shape to a range of 100m (328ft), the size and velocity of these metal balls ensuring that anyone in the way is shredded.

L2

The SAS currently use the standard British army grenade, the Grenade, Hand-Rifle, Anti-Personnel, L2, which was designed for delivery by hand-throwing or rifle projection, although problems with the latter mean that the grenade is only used in hand-thrown mode. The weapon is basically a copy of the American M26 grenade and thus of the typical 'pineapple' configuration. Although it has a smooth outer casing of tinned plate, the interior is filled with a long length of coiled wire 2.39mm (0.094in) in diameter and notched every 3.175mm (0.125in) to ensure even fragmentation and dispersion on the detonation of the 170g (6oz) explosive filling which occupies the centre of the grenade.

NO 36

In World War II, the SAS used mainly the British Grenade No.36M and the German Stielgranate 24. The No.36M grenade was of the standard 'pineapple' type with a four- to seven-second delay fuse, a weight of 0.773kg (1.7lb) and dimensions that included a diameter of 0.055m (2.2in) and a length of 0.097m (3.8in). The Stielgranate 24, on the other hand, was of the typical German 'potato masher' type with a four-and-half-second delay fuse, weight of 0.506kg (1.3lb) and dimensions that included a diameter of 70mm (2.75in) and length of 0.356m (1ft 2in). This German weapon was based on a hollow wooden handle with the screw-on warhead at one end and a screw-off cap at the other. To prepare and use it, the thrower removed the warhead, inserted the detonator, replaced the warhead,

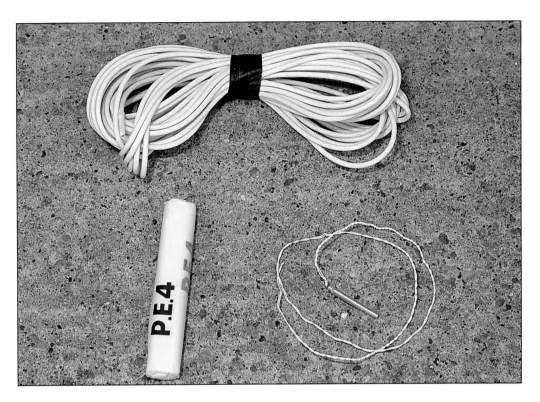

unscrewed the end cap, pulled the string initiator thus revealed, and finally threw the grenade.

NO 80

A later type of British grenade, used with considerable success by the SAS in the Aden and Oman campaigns of the 1960s and 1970s, was the Grenade No.80 WP Mk 1. This is filled with white phosphorus and was designed to provide smokescreens, but also proved effective in the anti-personnel task. The type is based on a tinned plate body of cylindrical shape, and has a delay of between two and a half and four seconds.

M79

The M79, which was used operationally by the SAS in Oman during the 1970s, is a single-shot weapon of American design and manufacture. The gun is of the break-open breech-loading type, and was the first of its breed to be designed for use with the fin-stabilised 40mm grenade. Relatively light, strong and accurate, the weapon has the added advantages of possessing only moderate recoil and being capable of lobbing its grenade over cover. One major disadvantage is the fact that it is a dedicated single-role weapon, which means that its operator is defenceless during the time it takes to load a fresh

Above: PE4 plastic explosive, as used by the SAS, and the agents needed to detonate it: detonating cord and electric detonator.

grenade, but in general the tactical utility of the M79 outweighs its disadvantages.
Type: M79 single-shot grenade launcher
Calibre: 40mm
Weight: 2.72kg (6lb) unloaded and 2.95kg (6.5lb) loaded
Length: 0.737m (2ft 5in)
Effective range: 350m (1148ft) against area targets or 150m (492ft) against point targets
Muzzle velocity: 76m (250ft) per second

M203

The M203 was designed after the tactical limitations of the M79 had become apparent, and was therefore conceived for attachment under the barrel of the M16 assault rifle, although the current M203PI can be fitted under the barrel of any assault rifle. The effect of this installation feature is that the operator of the M203 has a weapon that can be used between the firing of 40mm grenades, and that larger numbers of men within each squad can be equipped with this weapon without detriment to the squad's conventional firepower. The M203 is light, and can fire an assortment of grenades, including

Above: The British Army L2A2 hand grenade. Used by SAS soldiers, it is a typical fragmentation anti-personnel grenade.

high explosive, anti-armour, anti-personnel and buckshot. The last is perhaps the most important single round, for it provides the relatively inaccurate M203 with an effective capability against personnel and other soft-skinned targets. The M203 will remain in SAS service for many years to come because it substantially increases the firepower of small-sized teams operating in hostile territory, and also gives them an anti-armour capability.

Type: M203 single-shot grenade launcher
Calibre: 40mm
Weight: 1.63kg (3.6lb) loaded
Length: 0.38m (1ft 3in)
Effective range: 400m (1312ft)
Muzzle velocity: 76m (250ft) per second

MARK 19

The SAS is not a major user of the automatic grenade launcher as it is generally bulky and weighty, but troopers are trained in the use of this type of weapon, which has been used operationally on occasion, such as mounted on SAS Land Rovers in the Gulf War.

The Mark 19 is an air-cooled and fully-automatic American grenade launcher, that can fire a variety of 40mm grenades, including high explosive, anti-personnel and dual-role armour-piercing and anti-personnel. The 'gun', which is blowback-operated, is mounted on a tripod, and is usually fed from a 20- or 50-round ammunition container.

Type: Mk 19 automatic grenade launcher
Calibre: 40mm
Weight: 34kg (75lb)
Length: 1.028m (3ft 5in)
Effective range: 1600m (5248ft)
Rate of fire: 325-375 rounds per minute (cyclic)
Muzzle velocity: 239m (785ft) per minute

Above: Used by the Regiment until the introduction of the M203, the M79 grenade launcher was both accurate and light.

SB 40 LAG

The Santa Barbara 40 LAG is a weapon designed and produced in Spain, and is a belt-fed grenade launcher that, as a result of its modest weight, is mainly operated as a general-purpose weapon in the field. Another advantage of the weapon is its ability to use left- or right-hand feed as the situation demands.

Type: Santa Barbara 40 LAG automatic grenade launcher
Calibre: 40mm
Weight: 30kg (66.1kg) for the gun, 22kg (48.5lb) for the tripod, and 10.5kg (23.15lb) for the cradle mount
Length: 0.98m (3ft 3in)
Effective range: 1500m (4920ft)
Rate of fire: 200 rounds per minute (cyclic)
Feed: 25- or 50-round linked belt
Muzzle velocity: 239m (785ft) per second

RIFLE GRENADES

Grenades can also be fired from the muzzles of standard rifles, as noted above, and such rifle grenades help to provide small patrols with a significant increase in fire power for the support role. During the 1960s MECAR, a Belgian company, developed a number of grenades that could be fired with the aid of conventional ball ammunition, whereas early rifle-launched grenades required the use of blank cartridges. MECAR's Bullet Trap Universal (BTU) system traps the bullet in the tail of the rifle grenade and uses the bullet's kinetic energy to propel the grenade. The MECAR range of rifle grenades is currently the best in the world, and is produced for use on 7.62mm and 5.56mm rifles.

The current range is moderately extensive, and comprises a range of grenades for tasks from anti-armour to smoke, via blast/fragmentation for use against light structures, matériel and personnel; dual-purpose anti-armour and anti-personnel; delayed blast/fragmentation with a four-second delay allowing the grenade to be launched through a light structure to detonate inside it; and incendiary with the ability to penetrate a light structure before detonating to produce a fireball 6m (20ft) in diameter. The MECAR grenades are accurate and easy to shoot, and in the hands of a skilled soldier such rifle grenades can be highly

effective force multipliers. As such, they are attractive to units such as the SAS.

Another Belgian company with a range of rifle grenades is Fabrique Nationale Nouvelle Herstal with its FN Bullet-Through series. The particular advantage of this series of rifle grenades for units such as the SAS is the light weight and compact dimensions of the grenades, which permit the individual soldier to carry several of the type. When required for use, the grenade has its tail extended and placed over the muzzle of the rifle, but as the grenade leaves the muzzle the tail is retracted by a spring-loaded mechanism and the weapon is armed by the bringing into alignment of the firing pin and detonator. The FN Bullet-Through series currently includes anti-vehicle, anti-personnel and smoke grenades, and like the MECAR series can be used effectively over a range bracket between a minimum of 25m (82ft) and a maximum of 300m (984ft).

The rifle grenade concept is too complex for effective use at the instinctive

level in combat, and thus in the early 1960s there emerged grenade launchers designed to fire their payloads to a range of about 300m (984ft). The SAS grenade launchers are listed above. But they are not the panacea for all ills: the main problems with the grenade launcher are basically the flat trajectory of the fired grenade, which cannot, therefore, pass over cover, and the more complicated fusing of the weapon, which generally means that about two-thirds of the grenade is occupied by fuse and only the remaining one-third by explosive. Despite these two disadvantages, however, the grenade launcher has developed into an extremely popular weapon, largely as a result of the fact that in its fully developed form it is an automatic weapon that can lay down an effective barrage of blast/fragmentation explosions in situations such as an ambush.

Below: An SAS Land Rover and its crew behind the lines in the Gulf War. Note the Mark 19 grenade launcher on the vehicle.

COMMUNICATIONS

To be effective behind enemy lines, SAS teams need reliable and secure communications equipment to stay in contact with their operational base. Today the Regiment is equipped with state-of-the-art communications hardware to fulfil its mission.

One of the primary roles undertaken by the SAS in war is the penetration of the enemy's front line so that hidden observation posts can be established in the enemy rear areas. From these, SAS troops observe the movements and dispositions of the enemy's forces, and send the information back to headquarters, where it helps to build up as complete an impression as possible of the enemy's strength and location; this in turn helps to reveal the enemy's intentions.

Within the context of this operational role, good communications equipment is vital to the success of the SAS in transmitting timely intelligence. Such communications equipment must be rugged and reliable under all field conditions, and must also offer the capability for wholly secure transmission of messages. This last factor is particularly important, for secure transmission capability is the main key to sustained operations in the enemy's rear without electromagnetic detection.

Radio equipment has therefore been an essential part of the operational equipment used by the SAS since its establishment in 1941. Before considering such equipment, however, it is useful to establish in the most basic possible terms the workings of a radio system for military purposes. Radio equipment works in the electro-magnetic spectrum, which is the frequency range of electro-magnetic radiation between zero and infinity. Matter of every kind emits, reflects and absorbs electro-magnetic radiation, whose frequency is directly proportional to its energy state. Electro-magnetic radiation is both measured and classified by its wavelength (measured in metres) and by the frequency of its oscillation (measured in Hertz, one Hertz being one cycle per second): as the wavelength lengthens the frequency decreases, and vice versa. This

overall spectrum is divided arbitrarily into 'regions' ranging from the lowest to the highest frequencies and comprising the radio, infra-red, visible light, ultraviolet, X-ray and gamma ray regions.

RADIO FREQUENCIES

The radio frequency region, which is also used for radar and navigation aids, is subdivided into nine frequency bands. These bands are Extra Low Frequency (ELF with a frequency between 300Hz and 3KHz and a wavelength between 1000 and 100km) used for communication with submerged submarines; Very Low Frequency (VLF with a frequency between 3 and 30KHz and a wavelength between 100 and 10km), again used mainly for communication with submerged submarines; Low Frequency (LF with a frequency between 30 and 300KHz and a wavelength between 10 and 1km) used mainly for 'long-wave' civil radio com-

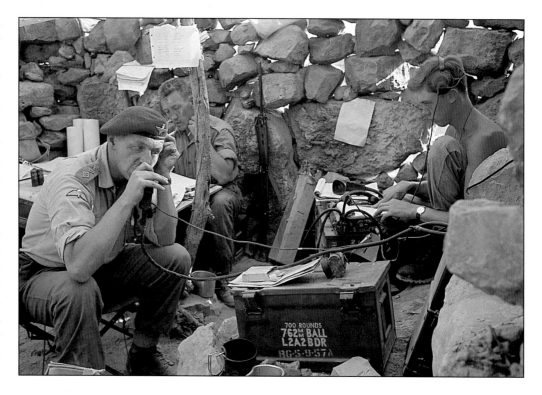

Above: The A41 wireless set, the standard British Army and SAS tactical radio set until 1978, seen here in action in Aden.

munications; Medium Frequency (MF with a frequency between 300KHz and 3MHz and a wavelength between 1km and 100m) used mainly for 'medium-wave' civil radio communications; High Frequency (HF with a frequency between 3 and 300MHz and a wavelength between 100 and 10m) used mainly for 'short-wave' civil radio communications over long ranges as the signals can travel by both a ground wave and a sky wave, the latter bouncing between the Earth and the ionosphere; Very High Frequency (VHF with a frequency between 300 and 300MHz and a wavelength between 10 and 1m) used mainly for television, civil short-range radio communications, and military short-range radio communications at low command levels as it is easily

Above: British Pathfinders using a Magellan Global Positioning System receiver in the field. It is also used by the SAS.

Above: The hand-held GPS receiver. The positional information can be displayed according to user requirements.

intercepted and jammed; Ultra High Frequency (UHF with a frequency between 300MHz and 3GHz and a wavelength between 1m and 10cm) used for military communications at higher command levels as it has a tighter and therefore less jammable beam whose range can be increased by bouncing the beam off the troposphere in the 'tropospheric scatter' phenomenon; Super High Frequency (SHF with a frequency between 3 and 30GHz and a wavelength between 10 and 1cm), otherwise known as the 'centrimetric band' or 'microwave band' and increasingly used for military communications, despite the fact that it needs an unobstructed line of sight for its fine beam, as it is largely unjammable and is ideally suited for satellite relay purposes; and Extremely High Frequency (EHF with a frequency between 30 and 300GHz and a wavelength between 1cm and 1mm), otherwise known as the 'millimetric band' and used for short-range military communications as many of its sub-bands are weakened by the atmosphere.

Communications are wholly essential to modern military operations, but it has to be admitted that radio communica-

tions have two major disadvantages. Firstly, radio transmissions (of either the direct or satellite-relayed types) can be intercepted by the enemy using ESM (Electronic Signal Monitoring) systems based on broad-band receivers that can be turned to the enemy's specific radio wavelengths. These receivers are linked to powerful signal processors and computers containing a library of all known emitter characteristics. In this way ESM systems, working in association with direction-finding equipment, can rapidly locate and identify the source of any given radio signal. Secondly, radio transmissions are vulnerable to ECM (Electronic Counter Measures) of the type that can deceive or drown the latter by using high-power continuous-wave transmissions.

MESSAGE TRANSMISSION

The initiative does not lie exclusively with the signal interceptor, however, for the signal transmitter can use a number of ECCM (Electronic Counter-Counter Measures) to reduce the chance of his transmissions being intercepted or jammed by the enemy or, if the signals are intercepted, being understood by the enemy. The main method of preventing interception is 'frequency hopping', in which the transmitting radio automatically changes frequency many times per sec-

ond in a pattern known only to itself and the receiver radio. The system is not foolproof, however, for modern computers can eventually discern the pattern of the apparently random frequency hops, and another disadvantage is the fact that frequency hopping takes up many frequencies. The encryption of communications is an important means of denying the enemy use of intercepted communications, though the encrypted messages use a much greater bandwidth than any non-secure system.

Data can be transmitted in any one of several forms. The most common is voice transmission, which suffers from the twin disadvantages of possible misunderstanding between the sender and receiver, and the increased probability of the enemy's interception of the transmission the longer it lasts. The most common method of avoiding these twin pitfalls is the use of a data entry device, which is in essence a mini-computer into which the transmission is entered in alphanumeric or Morse form. The data entry device is then attached to the radio transmitter and the message is sent in compressed or 'burst' form whose extremely short duration

Left: The PRC 319 radio system currently used by the SAS. It was designed with long-range reconnaissance forces in mind.

a rotor erected on a 3m (10ft) pole, and another was a generator driven by a small two-cylinder steam engine powered by a boiler suspended over a brazier.

GLOBAL POSITIONING SYSTEM

The SAS also uses the American-developed Global Positioning System, in which signals from a series of satellites in fixed orbits are processed by a lightweight hand-held unit (in the case of the SAS the Magellan GPS NAV 1000M known in military terms as the Small Lightweight GPS Receiver) to provide the operator with a read-out of his position to within 25m (82ft). The GPS receiver, by measuring the time interval between the transmission and the reception of a satellite signal, calculates the distance between the user and each satellite. It then uses the distance measurements of at least three satellites to determine the exact position of the user on the ground.

The system proved extremely reliable in the Gulf War (1991), in which most of the 400 receivers available to the British forces within the United Nations effort were allocated to the SAS for operations deep in Iraq, where they were used to pinpoint enemy columns and locations. It was particularly useful for navigation in the featureless and poorly mapped areas of Kuwait and Iraq, where sandstorms often reduced visibilty to zero. The SLGR is soon to be replaced by the Precise Lightweight GPS Receiver, which is accurate to 16m (53ft).

MCR 1

The best radio equipment available to the SAS in World War II was the MCR 1, otherwise known as the 'biscuit receiver' as it was installed in a container that looked like a Huntley & Palmer biscuit tin. This equipment entered service late in the war, and was based on five miniature tubes for long-range communication. The equipment was supplied with two or three batteries, each able to provide 30 hours of operation, and four interchangeable coil units that were plugged onto

makes interception highly problematical.

In World War II, the activities of the SAS were hampered to a modest degree by the sheer size and weight of the radio equipments of the time. Based on thermionic valve rather than transistor technology, a transmitter which could weigh up to 30kg (66 lb), and the large batteries that powered it were generally dispersed throughout the patrol to make the signaller's load manageable.

A41 WIRELESS SET

In 1960 the SAS started to use the A41 equipment that remained in British army service until 1978. This was a tactical radio equipment which weighed just under 5kg (11lb), and was generally carried as a backpack. The SAS operated the A41 in Aden (1964-67), the Indonesian Confrontation (1963-66) and Oman (1970-76).

EUREKA BEACON

The S-Phone was generally used with the Eureka beacon, which was a portable radar transponder that served as homing beacon and paradrop indicator. Both the S-Phone and Eureka beacon were powered by 6-volt batteries, and the recharging of these units was entrusted to any one of several systems developed by the British in the course of World War II: one was a wind-driven generator powered by pins at the end of the receiver to provide operability in different frequencies.

NO.11 WIRELESS SET

The No.11 Wireless Set was used by the British army between 1935 and 1945, and its size and weight made it wholly unsuitable for use by men on foot. The equipment, whose transceiver alone weighed 26kg (57lb), was therefore restricted to Jeep-mounted SAS operations close to the front line as its range was only a poor 19km (12 miles).

NO.22 WIRELESS SET

The No.22 Wireless Set was used by the SAS in North Africa and the Mediterranean region between 1941 and 1943, and was also bulky and weighty. The range was only 16km (10 miles), and the whole equipment included a 16.5kg (36lb) transceiver unit and a 9kg (20lb) power unit.

PRC 319

The most modern radio equipment in service with the SAS is the PRC 319 set, which is microprocessor-based and offers five times more transmission power per kilogram of weight than any other military radio. The whole equipment comprises four detachable units (transceiver, electronic message unit, and two antenna tuners), and also possesses a 0.7kg (1.5lb) pocket-sized electronic message unit that can be removed from the radio for independent use. The PRC 319 is powered by a small battery carried internally, and can store messages for up to 500 hours. Other tactical features include the storage of up to 20 pre-set channels in its electronic memory and a burst message transmission capability, the latter sending messages that are loaded via a keyboard, displayed, checked and then sent by the operation of a single key; the message can also be encrypted before transmission. One of the things which makes the PRC 319 such a bonus for SAS patrols is its 'soldier-proof' qualities. It can withstand salt contamination, dust, immersion in water and rain. It can also be dropped by parachute and take being roughly handled by soldiers on the ground – all important attributes for special forces missions.

PRC 320

A unit of the British army's clansman tactical communications system optimised for operation in all geographical and climatic conditions, the PRC 320 is a backpack radio weighing only 5.6kg (12.3lb) and using nickel-cadmium batteries that provide a 12-hour working life but which can be recharged. The radio can also be worked off a hand generator, and possesses a 3km (1.86-mile) remote operation facility. This is an important item of equipment which is admirably suited to the needs of the SAS: its small size and weight leaves the operator's hands free for the carriage and use of a personal weapon, and features include a choice of 280,000 frequencies, a ground-wave range of 40km (25 miles) and a sky-wave range of between 50 and 2000km (31 and 1243 miles).

S-PHONE

As the SAS evolved from deep-penetration missions in an assortment of wheeled vehicles towards truly clandestine operations, with the members of the SAS party dropped by parachute and later receiving reinforcements and essential supplies by the same method, a lightweight communication system became essential. It was realised that lightweight, secure and compact communications systems were needed for SAS teams behind German lines. It was also imperative for the men on the ground to be able to link up with the aircraft dropping supplies or reinforcements, using a narrow emission beam and ultra-short waves which could not be detected by the enemy. The result was the S-Phone, which was developed in World War II as a radio-telephone, aircraft homing beacon and paradrop indicator in a 6kg (13.2lb) package in an aluminium container only 0.51m (1ft 8in) long, 20cm (8in) wide and 25cm (10in) deep. The S-Phone could be used to contact an aeroplane flying at 150m (500ft) at a range of 20km (12 miles) or at 3050m (10,000ft) at a range of 100km (62 miles). The S-Phone was usually used in conjunction with the Eureka beacon, which were both used to guide in aircraft during operations in northwest Europe throughout 1944–45.

Above: The SARBE (surface-to-air rescue beacon), a radio used for communications between aircraft and people on the ground.

SARBE

In the mid-1950s, the SAS was able to turn in the last of its World War II beacon equipments for the new 1.45kg (3.2lb) SARBE (surface-to-air rescue beacon) equipment, a beacon with a 75-hour battery life (less if the voice facility was used), which allowed supporting aircraft to link up accurately with ground patrols. The equipment's range was highly dependent on the type of terrain in which it was used and the altitude of the receiving aeroplane, but typical figures were a range of 95km (60 miles) with an aeroplane at 3050m (10,000ft) or between eight and 24km (five and 15 miles) with an aeroplane at an altitude of 305m (1000ft) in the beacon mode, or in the voice mode 8km (5 miles) with an aeroplane at a height of 305m (1000ft). In jungle terrain the SARBE has been the salvation of stranded SAS soldiers.

VEHICLES

Light Vehicles

In World War II the SAS perfected the use of specialist light vehicles for its operations. The light vehicles used by the Regiment today consist of Land Rovers, which give the SAS a combination of range, good payload capacity and ultra reliability.

The SAS is essentially an infantry unit, but from its very beginnings was designed for delivery into operational areas by land, sea or air. SAS troopers usually operate on foot or, wherever possible, in light vehicles which increase the speed, scope and flexibility of their activities and the overall efficiency of the reconnaissance or sabotage unit. David Stirling, the founder of the SAS, believed that this method of operation combined minimum manpower with maximum surprise to make feasible a force of 200 highly trained men who could operate in five-man teams to launch simultaneous attacks on up to 30 different targets. Until mid-1942 the SAS was reliant on the Long Range Desert Group (LRDG) for transport to and from its targets. This was not altogether a bad thing, for the LRDG had considerable experience in long-range, clandestine movement behind the enemy's lines, and had an intimate knowledge of the best possible routes to and from potential enemy targets. The cooperation between the SAS and LRDG was effective, and also had the beneficial effect of allowing the SAS to build up its own knowledge of motor transport. The SAS made good use of this in the hinterland of North Africa, and it came into its own when it acquired its own vehicles.

The SAS decided that it needed vehicles that would be thoroughly reliable under all terrains and weather conditions, that could be cannibalised in emergency situations to keep other vehicles in operation, and that would make minimum

Right: A Land Rover 90. Several of these vehicles were used by the SAS in the Gulf War, nicknamed 'Dinkies' by the men.

demands on POL (Petrol, Oil and Lubricant) supplies that were generally carried on operations, usually in 'Jerry Cans', which were copied from captured German equipment.

The primary vehicle used by the LRDG was the 30-cwt Chevrolet truck, a 4x2-drive vehicle armed with a 0.303in Lewis machine gun or Vickers 'K' drum-fed machine gun, and sometimes with a 0.3in Browning belt-fed machine gun as well. Standard equipment on these vehicles included a sun compass, radio equipment, metal sand mats and channels for crossing areas of soft sand, water condensers to minimise demands on external water supplies, a larger radiator and fan, sand tyres, and special filters to reduce the ingress of dust.

In mid-1942, the SAS began to acquire its own motor transport in the form of Jeeps and trucks. The Jeeps were the primary vehicles for operational purposes and the trucks, although sometimes used on operations when it was necessary to move larger numbers of men or greater quantities of supplies, were generally used to move supplies from the SAS's rear area depot to forward-area bases, which were often behind enemy lines.

SAS LAND ROVERS

The other light vehicle most famously associated with the SAS is the Land Rover, which replaced the Jeep during the 1950s. It is an eloquent testimony to the overall capabilities of the Land Rover, especially in terms of payload-carrying

Left: The Land Rover 110, the standard SAS patrol vehicle. The whole SAS 110 fleet was used for operations in the Gulf War in 1991.

doors, smoke canisters, and an overall pink colour scheme designed to make the vehicles blend into the typically pink haze often encountered in the deserts of North Africa and the Middle East.

The features that particularly attract the SAS, and of course other military operators, to the Land Rover are the vehicle's power and agility at low speed in muddy and sandy conditions, relatively high speed for road travel, excellent power/weight ratio, good ground clearance, good traction on soft surfaces as a result of its evenly distributed weight, a very high level of serviceability. Finally the aluminium bodywork can take a lot of punishment before crumpling - rather than breaking as would generally be the case with steel bodywork.

The SAS currently uses a modest number of short-wheelbase Land Rover Defender 90 vehicles nicknamed 'Dinkies', and a larger numbers of long-wheelbase Land Rover Defender 110 vehicles. Offering a better ride, greater stopping power and an improved turning circle than their predecessors, the Defender 110 incorporates the coil-spring suspension pioneered by the Range Rover civilian vehicle, front-wheel disc brakes and a revised steering system.

The armament of the SAS's Land Rovers varies according to the specific mission being undertaken, but is generally on a lighter scale than that used on the Jeeps of World War II. The forward-facing armament is generally one 7.62mm General Purpose Machine Gun, and the rearward-facing fit usually comprises one 0.5in Browning heavy machine gun (of World War II vintage), one 7.62mm Minigun, or two 7.62mm GPMGs on power-assisted mountings with a swivel seat. Further armament capability seems to be in the offing with the probability of the SAS's adoption of the Land Rover Special Operations Vehicle (SOV). This combines the firepower of the Light Strike Vehicle (see below) with the payload of the Land Rover in a six-man machine based on the Defender 110, with

capability and reliability, that the SAS, who can choose from any such vehicle in the world, has opted for so long for the British-made Land Rover series.

The first Land Rover 4x4 vehicles for military use, the Land Rover Series I, were built between 1948 and 1958 initially in petrol-engined variants, but later in diesel-engined models. From 1954 the original short wheelbase Land Rover was complemented by a long wheelbase model offering significantly increased payload capacity. Introduced in 1958, the Land Rover Series II introduced a number of improved features and was delivered in both petrol- and diesel-engined models. A lightweight version was added to the Series II range in 1968 and, known as the Lightweight, the Half-Tonne and the Airportable, the last model introduced cut-down wings and removable panels as a means of reducing weight to the point at which the vehicle could be carried by a medium-lift helicopter.

Between 1971 and 1983 production switched to the Land Rover Series III, whose sole major change was the relocation of the headlamps to the front wings to satisfy Ministry of Transport regulations. The main variant of the Series III standard utility vehicle was the Forward Control or One Tonne type that was produced between 1975 and 1978, mainly as

an air-portable artillery tractor and observation post vehicle. In 1984 production switched to the renamed Land Rover 90 and Land Rover 110 series with short and long wheelbases respectively, and these are the current mainstays of the Land Rover force in service with the British forces, which also uses the stretched Land Rover 130 as an ambulance and artillery tractor. Shortly before the Iraqi invasion of Kuwait in August 1990, which sparked the UN response that culminated in the 'Desert Storm' campaign of January-February 1991, Land Rover renamed its military vehicles in the Defender series, which is the designation currently in use during the mid-1990s.

THE 'PINK PANTHER'

While the standard vehicle of the British Army has generally been the short wheelbase variant of the relevant Land Rover series, largely because it is so manoeuvrable, the SAS has mostly used the long-wheelbase variant because of its greater payload-carrying capability. The most famous SAS customisation is the 'Pink Panther', which has served faithfully as the Regiment's long-range desert patrol vehicle. Operated since the early 1960s, the 'Pink Panther' is a long-wheelbase Land Rover Series II with a spare wheel mounted over the front bumper, no

Left: The Longline Light Strike Vehicle (LSV), which was tested by the Regiment in the Gulf War but suffered mechanical problems.

an intercooled, turbo-charged diesel engine. The massive armament comprises the standard machine gun fit (forward- and rearward-facing weapons) as well as two 7.62mm machine guns in the 'pulpit' and a variable fit of a LAW (Light Anti-armour Weapon), 81mm (3.2in) mortar, 51mm (2in) mortar, two personal weapons, two submachine guns, two grenade launchers and ammunition for all these weapons. The SOV's 'pulpit' position can also be used to carry a 25mm cannon or an anti-tank missile launcher for weapons such as the Milan or TOW.

Type: Land Rover Defender 110 4x4 utility light truck
Weight: 3050kg (6725lb)
Dimensions: length 4.669m (15ft 4in); width 1.79m (5ft 11in); height 2.035m (6ft 8in)
Payload: driver, and up to eight passengers or freight
Engine: one Rover 3.528-litre petrol engine delivering 95.4kW (128hp) to four wheels
Fuel capacity: 79.5 litres (17.5 imp gal)
Performance: speed 121km/h (75mph; range 748km (465 miles); ground clearance 0.216m (8.5in)

LIGHT STRIKE VEHICLE

In the 1991 'Desert Storm' campaign, the SAS made limited use of the Light Strike Vehicle (LSV) 'dune buggy' light attack

vehicle for reconnaissance duties. A similar vehicle was also used by US special forces units, and its origins can be traced to the requirement of these forces in the early 1970s for a small and very light vehicle optimised for the reconnaissance or deep attack roles. This marked a considerable shift of emphasis from the type of heavily laden Jeep and Land Rover vehicles traditionally used by the SAS and similar units toward a cheaper type that would offer significant advantages in features such as easier air portability, simpler concealment in the field, the ability to operate on smaller tracks, the facility to be manhandled by its crew if necessary, a lower visual silhouette, and smaller thermal and electromagnetic signatures as a result of its open-frame type of construction. Trials of vehicles adapted from civilian 'dune buggies' revealed all these advantages, but its considerably smaller load-carrying capability was a major disadvantage. The 'dune buggy' is unable to carry large loads of fuel, water, weapons, ammunition and other supplies, and is therefore restricted to comparatively short missions from its base. Resupply is, of course possible from the air, or from a larger and therefore less mobile and more visible 'mother truck'.

Despite its limitations, the 'dune buggy' can effectively undertake a number of roles including weapons' carriage,

reconnaissance, forward observation and laser designation for artillery and aircraft operating in the anti-tank role, and command and control. In the armed role, the 'dune buggy' carries some 601kg (1325lb) of equipment and supplies, including petrol, food, water and up to 295kg (650lb) of ammunition in the form of 2000 small arms rounds and 500 larger grenade rounds.

THE LSV'S ARMAMENT

The LSV has wishbone suspension, four-wheel drive and a frame fabricated from seamless steel tube for great structural integrity and strength. The LSV can carry a wide assortment of weapon combinations whose individual members can include the 0.5in GAU-19 three-barrel heavy machine gun, the 0.5in Browning heavy machine gun, two 7.62mm machine guns, the 40mm M19 grenade launcher, a 25 or 30mm cannon, a Milan anti-tank missile launcher, FIM-92 Stinger surface-to-air missiles, and an 81 or 51mm (3.2 or 2in) mortar. Unfortunately, the LSVs suffered a number of mechanical problems in the Gulf.

Type: Longline Light Strike Vehicle light multi-role vehicle
Payload: driver and up to one passenger
Engine: one 1.9-litre Volkswagen four-cylinder inline petrol engine
Performance: speed 129km/h (80mph); range 401km (250 miles)

WILLYS JEEP

More formally known as the Truck, Utility, 4x4, M38, the American Willys Jeep was one of the most important light vehicles of World War II, and as such was vital to the Western Allies, especially after 1943. Production totalled 639,245 vehicles, and the first reached North Africa in June 1942, entering service with the SAS soon after.

The origins of the vehicle can be found in the US Army's 1940 requirement for a 'go anywhere' field car. The design competition was won by the Bantam Car Company with a vehicle using many components derived from its pre-war runabout automobile. Bantam was too small a company to produce the very large numbers of such vehicles under consideration by 1941, however, and the production programme was entrusted to the Willys Overland Company, which incorporated into the Bantam design a number of the best features from its unsuccessful contender in the 1940 competition. Ford later joined the production effort and delivered some 277,896 of these excellent vehicles.

Although intended primarily for use as a reconnaissance and liaison vehicle, and armed with a 0.3in Browning M1919 pintle-mounted machine gun, the Jeep was so versatile that it was also pressed into service as a frontline ambulance (two types of conversion kits were used), mobile observation post, military police vehicle, radio vehicle, recovery vehicle, and cargo carrier. In this last capacity, the Jeep was produced in an alternative amphibious form, with a boat-hull body modelled on that of the DUKW amphibious truck, and a power take-off to drive a rear-mounted propeller. The Jeep could also be used to tow the Trailer, M100. This weighed 256kg (565lb) and could carry a load of 340kg (750lb) on roads, or 227kg (500lb) across country.

SAS WILLYS JEEPS

As used by the SAS in World War II, the Jeep was considerably revised from its production standard. The fuel tankage was enlarged to provide a larger radius of action, all non-essential equipment was removed to reduce weight and to enable it to carry specialised equipment (water condensers, sand mats and channels, and POL), and provision was made for the two or three men and their food and water, together with the required weapons and their ammunition. The on-board weapons initially comprised up to four 0.303in Vickers 'K' guns, but these were later supplemented by a single 0.3in Browning machine gun.

In North Africa the Jeep proved highly effective if somewhat uncomfortable, and its main operational attributes, in addition to its four-wheel drive and great reliability, were its speed and agility.

For service in northwest Europe from the middle of 1944, the SAS used a somewhat different version of the Jeep without provision for the water condenser system and a reduced complement of on-board equipment and supplies. This was possible because the SAS was operating over shorter ranges (generally from concealed bases behind the German lines) and was also supplied from the air by the RAF, which used converted Handley Page Halifax bombers to para-drop Jeeps to SAS parties that had established bases and linked up with the local resistance forces.

Late in 1944, the SAS began to receive an improved version of the Jeep with a windscreen that could stop the standard rifle bullet, a covering of amour over the forward half of the vehicle, provision for a wire-cutting device projecting upward from the front bumper, and provision for a more varied assortment of on-board weapons. The standard fit was two 0.303in Vickers forward-firing machine guns, two 0.303in Vickers rearward-firing machine guns, and one 0.303in Bren forward-firing machine gun for the driver, but some vehicles had one 0.5in Browning forward-firing heavy machine gun and one 0.303in Lewis rearward-firing machine gun; also included in the armament fit were the crew's personal weapons, large numbers of grenades, and considerable quantities of ammunition for the machine gun and personal weapons.

Type: Willys Jeep 4x4 utility light truck
Weight: 1247kg (2750lb)
Dimensions: length 3.55m (11ft 1in); width 1.60m (5ft 2in); height 1.32m (4ft 4in) to top of steering wheel in open condition, or 1.77m (5ft 10in) overall with cover erected
Payload: driver, and up to three passengers or 363kg (800lb) of freight across country increasing to 544kg (1200lb) of freight on roads
Engine: one Willys four-cylinder inline petrol engine delivering 44.7kW (60hp) to four wheels via a gearbox (one reverse and three forward ratios) with two transfer speeds
Fuel capacity: 56.8 litres (12.5 imp gal) standard
Performance: speed 88.5km/h (55mph); range 363km (225 miles) increased to 460km (285 miles) in North African vehicles with enlarged fuel tankage; ground clearance 0.235m (9.25in); fording 1.88m (6ft 2in) with a fording kit

Below: An SAS Jeep in North Africa in World War II. Its armament includes Browning and Vickers 'K' machine guns.

Trucks

The trucks of the Long Range Desert Group were used to transport SAS teams to and from their targets in North Africa in World War II, and the Regiment has continued to make use of truck transport for mundane but vital logistic tasks.

Once it started to acquire its own vehicles in World War II, the SAS initially found itself with an assortment of trucks that were not all ideally suited to the SAS's task. This miscellany of medium vehicles, generally inherited from other units in North Africa, was gradually whittled down to the small number of types which experience suggested were best suited for the role of the SAS.

The Ford F60 and Bedford QL were used in the largest numbers. The Ford F60 was based on the Canadian Military Pattern Chassis, and could carry a 3048kg

Below: A Chevrolet truck of the Long Range Desert Group in North Africa in World War II. These vehicles transported SAS teams.

(6720lb) payload over a range of 274km (170 miles) at a maximum speed of 80km/h (50mph). It had a Ford V-8 petrol engine, which delivered a maximum of 70.8kW (95hp).

Although they were generally successful in World War II operations, the trucks of the period were limited by the power of their engines and their comparatively limited size/payload ratios. When new trucks were designed to replace the vehicles that had survived the war, considerable emphasis was placed on greater payload (between four and five tons rather than between two and three tons), and larger wheels and tyres which provided greater ground clearance and improved ability to traverse rough terrain. All-wheel

drive became standard for improved cross-country mobility, and diesel rather than petrol engines provided better fuel consumption and a reduced risk of fire from low-volatility diesel fuel.

BEDFORD MK

Having decided to replace the Bedford RL in the early 1960s, the British army chose the Bedford MK to replace it. It was a military version of another Bedford civil truck, the 4x2 TK. The military type entered production as the MK with 4x4 drive and was taken into service as the FV138 series, of which the two main variants are the FV13801/13802 cargo truck, and FV13803/13804 cargo truck which has a 3500kg (7716lb) capacity winch and 76m (250ft) of cable. Both of these basic variants can be converted into flat-bed models, and another feature is the facility for the single-tyred rear wheels to be replaced by twin-tyred wheels for improved traction under adverse cross-country conditions.

Based on a steel frame chassis with coil-spring front suspension and leaf-spring rear suspension, the MK has a two-man fully enclosed cab with a separate steel body covered with a removable tilt carried on bows and with access provided by a drop gate at the rear. A spare wheel is carried under the chassis to the rear of the silencer box on the near-side.

Type: Bedford MK utility medium truck
Weight: 9650kg (21,275lb) loaded
Dimensions: length 6.579m (21ft 7in); width 2.489m (8ft 2in); height 3.404m (11ft 2in) to top of tilt; body internal dimensions include a length of 4.28m (14ft 1in) and width of 2.01m (6ft 7in)
Payload: driver and up to two passengers in the cab and a variable numbers of passengers or 4000kg (8818lb) of freight in the body
Engine: one 5.42-litre Bedford six-

cylinder inline diesel engine delivering 79kW (106hp) to four wheels via a gearbox (one reverse and four forward ratios)

Fuel capacity: 150 litres (33 imp gal)

Performance: speed 73km/h (45mph); range 563km (350 miles)

BEDFORD QLT

The Bedford QLT, or more formally the Lorry, 3-ton, 4x4, Troop Carrier, was introduced in 1941 and remained in service until well after World War II. Production totalled 3373 vehicles, which had a General Service-type body over boxed wheel arches. Constructed of a welded steel tube with sheet metal panels, it had a hardwood floor, a detachable tilt and bows, two forward doors that opened inward with a fixed step below, and full-width rear doors with an arrangement of two hinged steps for maximum ease of boarding and debussing. Folding seats were installed along the sides and on a support frame extending along the centreline for a maximum of 29 passengers, with one more passenger to the left of the driver in the fully enclosed cab. There was a hip ring in the roof of the cab over the passenger's seat to permit the use of a machine gun in the anti-aircraft role, and an anti-aircraft gunner's platform with a gun mounting and a roof hatch in the forward part of the body. For the carriage of a payload other than personnel, the side seats could be folded and the central support frame removed and stowed on the off-side. A spare wheel was carried under the chassis frame at the rear of the vehicle.

The SAS made extensive use of this vehicle. One of its most important attributes was the 4x4 drive that generated excellent mobility under adverse cross-country conditions, but could also be switched to 4x2 mode for reduced tyre and gearbox wear on paved roads.

Type: Bedford QLT utility medium truck

Dimensions: overall length 6.65m (21ft 10in); width 2.29m (7ft 6in); height 2.05m (9ft 8in); internal body dimensions included a length of 4.83m (15ft 10in), width of 2.17m (7ft 1.5in) and height of 1.83m (6ft)

Payload: driver, and up to 30 passengers or 3048kg (6720lb) of freight

Engine: one 3.518-litre Bedford six-cylinder inline petrol engine delivering 53.7kW (72hp) to four wheels via a gearbox (one reverse and four forward ratios) with two transfer speeds

Performance: speed 61km/h (38mph); range 371km (230 miles); ground clearance 0.305m (12in)

BEDFORD RL

The two vehicles that have seen the widest service with the British Army, as well as with the SAS, have been two Bedford products, namely the RL or 4-tonne Truck and the MK 4-tonne Truck.

The Bedford RL was introduced to service in 1952 and was subsequently developed in a large number of specialised forms including the FV13101 General Service Cargo Truck, FV13105 Cargo Truck (dropside with winch), FV13109 General Service Cargo Truck, FV13112 Cargo Truck (dropside), and FV13142 Cargo Truck (dropside, airportable). The RL can also tow several types of trailer, and this considerably enhances its logistic and tactical utility for operators such as the SAS.

When first issued, these useful vehicles were classified in the 3-tonne type, but in 1968 the classification was uprated to the 4-tonne type. The truck was derived from

Above: Modern British Army Bedord trucks. They are used to transport prospective SAS soldiers during Selection Training.

a commercial chassis, and production up to 1969 totalled 73,135 vehicles. It is based on a steel frame chassis with coil-spring front suspension and leaf-spring rear suspension. It has a two-man fully enclosed cab with a separate steel body which is covered with a removable tilt carried on bows, and with access provided by a drop gate at the rear. A spare wheel is carried under the chassis to the rear of the silencer box on the near-side.

Type: Bedford RL utility medium truck

Weight: 8800kg (19,400lb) loaded

Dimensions: length 6.36m (20ft 11in); width 2.39m (7ft 9in); height 3.11m (10ft 3in) to top of tilt; internal body dimensions include a length of 4.237m (14ft) and width of 2.178m (7ft 2in)

Payload: driver and up to one passenger in the cab and a variable number of passengers or 4000kg (8818lb) of freight in the body

Engine: one 4.93-litre Bedford six-cylinder inline engine delivering 96.9kW (130hp) to four wheels via a gearbox (one reverse and four forward ratios)

Fuel capacity: 118 litres (26 imp gal)

Performance: speed 75km/h (47mph); range 401km (250 miles)

SHIPS AND BOATS

Each SAS 'Sabre' Squadron has a Boat Troop that specialises in all aspects of amphibious warfare. This usually entails operations with small assault craft, though on occasion the Regiment's soldiers have had to make use of larger naval vessels.

Despite the fact that it has generally conducted its operations on land within the context of a land war, the SAS is fully aware of the need for an amphibious capability for operations anywhere in the world, including places where the securest access is provided by the sea, either on or under the surface. Moreover, the SAS may also find itself fighting an enemy in an inhospitable part of the world in which riverine transport is the best method of surface movement (such was certainly the case in the Indonesian Confrontation of 1963-66, for example). As a result, each of the Regiment's four 'Sabre' Squadrons includes a Boat Troop that specialises in amphibious warfare in all its aspects.

AIRCRAFT CARRIERS

The largest vessel from which the SAS has operated is the aircraft carrier HMS *Hermes*, which was the flagship of the Task Force despatched from the UK to recap-

ture the Falkland Islands from Argentine occupation in 1982. The ship was laid down in World War II as the light fleet carrier *Elephant*, but was completed only in 1959 as the *Hermes*. It was reconstructed in 1964-66 with an angled flightdeck and missile armament, converted in 1971-73 to a commando carrier, and then adapted in 1976 as an anti-submarine carrier. In the Falklands War, *Hermes* could have embarked the whole of No 3 Commando Brigade, but in fact sailed from the UK with only a company of Royal Marines, a number of Special Boat Service (SBS) personnel, and a small party of SAS men who were reinforced in mid-Atlantic by the delivery of additional men flown to Ascension Island and then lifted by helicopter to *Hermes*.

The ship also carried BAe Sea Harrier multi-role Short Take-Off and Vertical Landing) STOVL warplanes and Westland Sea King helicopters, and it was the latter, operated by 846 Squadron, that inserted

part of G Squadron, 22 SAS, for reconnaissance of the Argentine strength and disposition in the Falklands. They also carried part of D Squadron, 22 SAS, for the destruction of several Argentine air force Pucara attack aircraft on Pebble Island.

Type: *Hermes* multi-role aircraft carrier
Displacement: 23,900 tons standard and 28,700 tons full load
Dimensions: length 226.87m (744ft 4in); width 48.77m (160ft) over flightdeck; draught 8.69m (28ft 6in)
Armament: two quadruple launchers for Seacat short-range surface-to-air missiles
Aircraft: six BAe Sea Harrier FRS.Mk 1 multi-role STOVL warplanes and seven Westland Sea King helicopters out of a maximum possible 37 aircraft
Propulsion: four boilers supplying steam to two sets of geared steam turbines delivering 56,675kW (76,000hp) to three shafts
Performance: speed 28kn
Complement: 1350 men, including air group

DESTROYERS

During the Falklands War, the SAS also operated from a number of Royal Navy destroyers, even though these comparatively large vessels were designed mainly for the anti-submarine and anti-aircraft roles without the capacity to carry or support ground forces. The exigencies of the situation, however, demanded that the 'County' class guided-missile destroyer HMS *Antrim*, which possessed an advanced command and control centre, be used as the leader of the force detailed to recapture South Georgia Island as a pre-

*Left: The multi-role aircraft carrier **Hermes**, which was used as a base for SAS operations during the Falklands campaign.*

cursor to the main assault on the Falkland Islands. In this capacity the *Antrim* therefore became the mobile base and headquarters for three types of troops in the form of 22 SAS's D Squadron, a party of SBS and No 42 Commando's M Company, nicknamed 'the Mighty Munch'.

Type: *Antrim* guided-missile destroyer

Displacement: 5440 tons standard and 6200 tons full load

Dimensions: length 158.65m (520ft 6in); beam 16.46m (54ft); draught 6.25m (20ft 6in)

Armament: two 114mm (4.5in) dual-purpose guns in one twin mounting, two 20mm anti-aircraft cannon in single mountings, four MM.39 Exocet anti-ship missiles in two twin mountings, 32 Seaslug Mk 2 long-range surface-to-air missiles launched from one twin launcher, and 32 Seacat short-range surface-to-air missiles launched from two quadruple launchers

Aircraft: one Westland Wessex helicopter

Propulsion: two boilers supplying steam to two sets of geared steam turbines delivering 22,370kW (30,000hp) and four English Electric G.6 gas turbines delivering 22,370kW (30,000hp) via a COSAG (COmbined Steam And Gas turbine) arrangement to three shafts

Performance: speed 30kn; range 6440km (4000 miles) at 28kn

Complement: 480 crew

FOLBOT

The SAS has also made extensive use of light assault craft of various types. The first of these was the Folbot, which was a two-man canoe used in World War II. This had a wooden frame inside a rubberised fabric cover, and although designed to be collapsible for easier stowage, was seldom, if ever, collapsed and usually had the joins in the wooden frame bound with heavy-duty tape to prevent any accidental disconnection. The boat was 1.52m (5ft) long and its rudder could be operated by lines running to each of the two paddler positions. The type was moderately effective, but its main tactical limitation was the fact that it was too lightly built to be pulled across mud in the fully laden condition.

GEMINI

For the operation to retake South Georgia Island in the 1982 Falklands War, the SAS used the Gemini with a rigid bottom and inflatable sides. The Gemini comes in three sizes with a length of 5.2m (17ft 1in) to carry 12 men, 3.8m (12ft 6in) to carry ten men, and 1.6m (5ft 3in) to carry eight men. They can be powered by a 13.4 or 29.8kW (18 or 40hp) outboard petrol engine.

INFANTRY RECONNAISSANCE BOAT

The Infantry Reconnaissance Boat, of which small numbers were used in the middle years of World War II, was inflatable and made of black rubber, with a hand pump for inflation. It could carry six men, but was unmanoeuvrable in windy

Above: The 'County' class destroyer **Glamorgan,** *which, with her sister* **Antrim,** *served in the Falklands War.*

conditions. The boat was 2.6m (8ft 6in) long when inflated and weighed 28kg (62lb); when deflated it could be fitted into a canvas bag measuring 1.1m (3ft 7in) by 0.56m (1ft 10in) by 0.23m (9in).

KLEPPER CANOE

In the 1950s the SAS adopted the Klepper canoe, and this is still in service. The canoe is of German design and manufacture, and is a two-man collapsible type made of ash and birch with a covering of cotton woven with hemp for the deck, and of polyester-reinforced rubber for the hull. The skin is slack until the two

Above: The Gemini inflatable assault craft, seen here in French Foreign Legion use, is used by SAS Boat Troops.

air sponsors under each gunwale are inflated, which produces a length of 5.2m (17ft 1in) and width of 0.68m (2ft 3in).

LANDING CRAFT ASSAULT

The Landing Craft Assault was a small vessel designed to take on its load of troops from a larger ship offshore and then to make the run into the assault beach, where the troops were disgorged over a single bow ramp, which was armoured to provide protection from short-range direct fire for the embarked troops during the run in to the beach. The type was built in large numbers, and was notably uncomfortable.

Type: LCA infantry assault craft
Displacement: 13 tons loaded
Dimensions: length 12.65m (41ft 6in); beam 3.05m (10ft); draught 0.69m (2ft 3in)
Armament: three 0.303in machine guns (two Lewis guns forward and one Vickers 'K' gun aft) and, in some craft during 1943-44, two 2in (51mm) mortars
Payload: 35 troops and 363kg (800lb) of freight
Propulsion: two Thornycroft

(converted Ford) diesel engines delivering 96.9kW (130hp) to two shafts
Performance: speed 7kn; range 129km (80 miles)
Complement: 4-5 crew

LANDING CRAFT INFANTRY

In the period between the middle of World War II and the present, the SAS has operated from too many different types of specialised amphibious warfare vessels to mention in full. The two types used most

frequently by the SAS in World War II, especially during the amphibious landings undertaken in Sicily and southern Italy after July 1943, were the Landing Craft Infantry (LCI) and Landing Craft Assault (LCA). The Landing Craft Infantry (Large) was designed to transport troops who disembarked over the bow via two external ramps or, in later vessels, one inboard ramp. Production of the LCI(L) was undertaken in the USA, and totalled 913 vessels (220 of them for the Royal Navy) completed to the originally specified personnel transport standard, and another 337 as gunboats, flotilla leaders and other special craft.

Type: LCI(L) infantry assault vessel
Displacement: 387 tons loaded
Dimensions: length 48.26m (158ft 4in); beam 7.09m (23ft 3in); draught 1.47m (4ft 10in)
Armament: up to five 20mm cannon
Payload: 205 infantrymen and 32 tons of freight
Propulsion: eight diesel engines delivering 1730kW (2320hp) to two shafts
Performance: speed 14.4kn; range 14,805km (9200 miles) at 12kn
Complement: 24-28 crew

Below: In SAS use since the 1950s, the two-man Klepper canoe is ideal for a clandestine approach onto a hostile shore.

LANDING PLATFORMS

SAS troopers used a number of considerably more advanced and capable ships in the Falklands War. The most sophisticated of these was the 'Fearless' class assault ship *Intrepid*, which is formally classified as an LPD (Landing Platform, Dock), as the stern of the vessel can be flooded to allow landing craft to use a large docking well built into the stern. Each of the two 'Fearless' vessels was planned for the carriage and assault delivery of a brigade, and possesses an integrated command facility for the control of the land, sea and air battle round the assault beach.

Type: *Intrepid* assault vessel (landing platform, dock)
Displacement: 11,060 tons standard and 12,120 tons full load
Dimensions: length 158.5m (520ft); beam 24.38m (80ft); draught 6.25m (20ft 6in)
Armament: two 40mm Bofors anti-aircraft guns in single mountings and four quadruple launchers for Seacat short-range surface-to-air missiles
Aircraft: five Westland Wessex or four Westland Sea King medium-lift helicopters as well as three Aérospatiale Gazelle or Westland Lynx light helicopters
Payload: 370 troops normal, but 670 troops maximum, together with 15 main battle tanks, seven 3-tonne trucks and 20 Land Rovers or 2100 tons of stores; these are all delivered by four LVCPs carried in davits and four LCM(9)s carried in the docking well
Propulsion: two boilers supplying steam to two sets of geared steam turbines delivering 16,405kW (22,000hp) to two shafts
Performance: speed 21kn; range 9250km (5750 miles) at 20kn
Complement: 663, including an air detachment of 25, and 88 Royal Marines

MOTOR TORPEDO BOAT

The SAS also made occasional use in World War II of the motor torpedo boat for the high-speed delivery of small parties to the coast, generally in darkness. A type that can be taken as generally typical of the breed was the Vosper 72ft class, of which 26 were built.

Type: Vosper 72ft class motor torpedo boat
Displacement: 47 tons
Dimensions: length 22.1m (72ft 6in); beam 5.87m (19ft 3in); draught 1.68m (5ft 6in)
Armament: two 0.5in and four 0.303in machine guns, and two 533mm (21in) torpedoes
Propulsion: three Packard petrol engines delivering 3020kW (4050hp) to three shafts
Performance: speed 40
Complement: 12 crew

REPLENISHMENT SHIPS

During the Falklands War, the SAS also made use of three other types of ship, all of them operated by the Royal Fleet Auxiliary. These were the fleet replenishment ships *Fort Austin* of the 'Fort' class, the *Resource* of the 'Resource' class, and the landing ship logistic *Sir Galahad* of the 'Sir Bedivere' class. The *Fort Austin* has a full-load displacement of 22,800 tons and is designed to carry up to 3500 tons of palletised stores in four holds, served by three 10-ton and three five-ton cranes; there are also two sliding-stay constant-tension transfer rigs to allow the simultaneous underway replenishment of two warships, one on each beam. The ship has an armament of two 20mm cannon and provision for four Westland Sea King helicopters on a large aft platform with its

Above: **Intrepid** *under attack in the Falklands. During cross-decking to* **Intrepid** *the SAS suffered its greatest loss of the war.*

own hangar. The *Resource* has a full-load displacement of 22,890 tons and is designed to carry ammunition, explosives, food and general stores. Its armament comprised two 40mm Bofors anti-aircraft guns, and up to four Westland Sea King helicopters, the latter on a platform on the after superstructure. Both of these ships were used for the movement of the SAS to the Falklands operational region.

The *Sir Galahad* was designed for the delivery of all the weapons and equipment required by landed troops to stabilise a beach-head and begin its inland extension into a secure lodgement. The ship is therefore of the 'ro-ro' (roll-on/roll-off) ferry type with stern and bow doors allowing straight-through movement of vehicles and other equipment. There was a small party of SAS troopers on board the ship when it received direct hits from Argentine attack aircraft near Fitzroy Inlet. Although the subsequent fires gutted the main part of the ship and resulted in the loss of 45 men, most of them Welsh Guardsmen, and injuries to another 150, the SAS troopers escaped major injuries are they were located near the bows of the ship.

Type: *Sir Galahad* assault vessel (logistic landing ship)

Left: Sir Galahad *burns after being hit by Argentinian aircraft near Fitzroy on 8 June, which killed 48 of those on board.*

Displacement: 3270 tons light and 5674 tons full load
Dimensions: length 125.6m (412ft 1in); beam 18.24m (59ft 10in); draught 3.96m (13ft)
Armament: two 40mm Bofors anti-aircraft guns in single mountings
Aircraft: three Westland Wessex or two Westland Sea King medium-lift helicopters, or alternatively three Aérospatiale Gazelle or Westland Lynx light helicopters
Payload: 340 troops normal, but 534 troops maximum, together with 16 main battle tanks, 34 mixed vehicles, 120 tons of POL (Petrol, Oil and Lubricants) and 30 tons of ammunition
Propulsion: two Mirrlees diesel engines delivering 7010m (9400hp) to two shafts
Performance: speed 17kn; range 14,805km (9200 miles) at 15kn
Complement: 68 crew

RIGID RAIDER

One of the most important assault craft currently in service with the SAS is the strong and fast Rigid Raider. The type can carry eight men and is powered by a 104kW (140hp) outboard engine; its high speed makes it ideal for the delivery and extraction of small teams, and for the resupply of stay-ashore parties.

SUBMARINES

During World War II, the SAS made some use of submarines for the landing of small parties on hostile coasts. The Regiment has since maintained a capability for landing from submarines, which have the advantage of being able to reach an operational area more rapidly and with a greater level of secrecy than is ever possible for a surface vessel. Moreover, while the submarine's capacity to carry additional men is strictly limited, the fact that the SAS is designed to operate in small parties means that the submarine was, and also remains, a viable method for the delivery of small parties of elite soldiers onto a hostile shore.

In modern conditions, the SAS has a choice of delivery by nuclear-powered or conventionally-powered submarine. Nuclear submarines have considerably higher sustained underwater speed and can carry a larger and better equipped party. However, this is at the expense of greater noise; because of its considerable size, it is unable to close well into the coast in areas where the continental shelf is shallow. Conventional submarines can move close into the coast extremely quietly, with a smaller and more lightly equipped party.

Left: The Rigid Raider assault craft. Able to carry eight soldiers at speed across the water, it is used by SAS Boat Troops.

Right: The Submersible Recovery Craft, which can transport teams of combat divers both above and below the waves.

The 'Trafalgar' class of fleet (attack) boats, of which seven were commissioned between 1983 and 1991, are typical of the nuclear-powered submarine type used for SAS purposes.

Type: 'Trafalgar' class submarine
Displacement: 4700 tons surfaced and 5210 submerged
Dimensions: length 85.395m (280ft 2in); beam 9.78m (32ft 1in); draught 8.2m (26ft 11in)
Armament: five 533mm (21in) torpedo tubes for 25 Mk 24 Tigerfish and Spearfish wire-guided torpedoes, of which up to five can be replaced by UGM-84 Sub-Harpoon submarine-launched anti-ship missiles, or up to 50 Mk 5 Stonefish or Mk 6 Sea Urchin mines
Propulsion: one Rolls-Royce PWR-1 pressurised water-cooled reactor supplying steam to two sets of General Electric geared steam turbines delivering 11,185kW (15,000hp) to one pump-jet propulsor
Performance: speed 20kn surfaced and 32kn submerged; diving depth 400m (1312ft) operational and 600m (1968ft) maximum; range effectively unlimited
Complement: 97 crew

The 'Upholder' class of patrol (attack) submarines is a good example of the conventionally-powered submarine type used by the SAS. The successor to the classic 'Oberon' class of conventionally powered boats, the 'Upholder' class is highly advanced by conventionally powered submarine standards, and can remain submerged through the use of its 'snorting' system, in which only the head of a mast carrying the air inlet and exhaust valve is extended above the surface of the water.

Type: 'Upholder' class submarine
Displacement: 2160 tons surfaced and 2455 tons submerged
Dimensions: length 135.6m (230ft 8in); beam 7.62m (25ft); draught 5.41m (17ft 9in)
Armament: six 533mm (21in) torpedo tubes for 18 Mk 24 Tigerfish and

Spearfish wire-guided torpedoes, of which up to four can be replaced by UGM-85 Sub-Harpoon submarine-launched anti-ship missiles, or alternatively up to 44 Mk 5 Stonefish and Mk 6 Sea Urchin mines
Propulsion: diesel/electric arrangement with two Paxman/GEC Valenta 1600 RPA-200 SZ diesel generators supplying current to one GEC electric motor delivering 4030kW (5400hp) to one shaft
Performance: speed 12kn surfaced and snorting, and 20kn submerged; diving depth 300m (984ft) operational and 400m (1312ft) maximum; range more than 14,805km (9200 miles) at 8kn snorting and 315km (195 miles) at 3kn

submerged
Complement: 44 crew

SUBMERSIBLE RECOVERY CRAFT

Finally, there is the Submersible Recovery Craft (SRC), which can operate as a high-speed surface craft or as a lower-speed submersible. The whole boat is flooded down to submerge it, and it can also be operated in the 'snorting' mode with only the air inlet, exhaust pipes and divers' heads above the surface of the water. The SRC can be 'parked' on the sea bed during missions, the crew exiting and entering as divers, and propulsion is provided by one 67.1kW (90hp) piston engine for surfaced movement or two 24-volt electric motors for submerged movement.

HOSTAGE-RESCUE KIT

Clothing

Rescuing hostages from flame-filled buildings with enemy bullets flying around demands specialist equipment for SAS counter-terrorist teams. The Regiment has therefore ensured that its men has the best clothing and breathing equipment there is to do the job.

When 11 Israeli competitors were murdered by Palestinian terrorists of the 'Black September' group at the 1972 Olympic Games in Munich in southern Germany, the repercussions around the Western world regarding security were considerable. It was now apparent that terrorism had finally emerged as a major weapon in the arsenal of so-called 'liberation fighters', and was a very real threat to the security of every country.

The first response of West Germany, where the atrocity had taken place, was the establishment of GSG 9 as the country's primary counter-terrorist unit. In the UK, the experience of the SAS in counter-terrorist operations during the Malayan 'Emergency' (1948-60) made the SAS the inevitable choice for the development and implementation of a similar British capability. Several senior SAS officers had advocated the development of

such a capability since the late 1960s, and in 1973 the SAS was formally instructed to develop a full counter-terrorist capability. The Counter Revolutionary Warfare Wing was formed at the Regiment's Hereford base. This wing has a permanent staff of about 20 men, and on a rotational basis, trains each of the Regiment's 'Sabre' Squadrons in every aspect of the counter-terrorist role.

THE REQUIREMENT

Two of the key techniques to be mastered by everyone involved in counter-terrorist operations are rapid entry into any building occupied by terrorists, and the rescue of any hostages held inside. These are tasks that are constantly practised and refined by exercises in the 'Killing House', a series of specially-built rooms where SAS troopers rehearse scenarios they may encounter during counter-terrorist operations. Early and continuing experience has shown that the entry into such buildings (and also the individual rooms), which are often filled with smoke and CS or other similarly incapacitating gas, in order to overpower or kill terrorists and rescue their hostages, demands not only exceptional human skills, but also a wide range of specialised equipment and weapons. The lives of the counter-terrorist team and the hostages depend on the weapons, which must work reliably, first time and every time; they must also be light and handy, efficient and rugged. The same strictures apply to the clothing worn by the counter-terrorist team. Early

Left: All SAS assault suits are manufactured from flame-resistant materials to provide protection against heat, fire and smoke.

Right: Underneath his assault suit an SAS hostage-rescue trooper wears assault underwear to increase overall protection.

experiments revealed that standard British Army clothing was too bulky for fast entry into a building, as it tended to catch on items such as splintered door frames, and was also flammable.

The response of the SAS was the creation, also at its Hereford base, of the Operations Research Wing. The men of this small but highly professional organisation test, evaluate and design every type of specialised equipment needed by the Regiment's counter-terrorist teams.

The counter-terrorist role falls into two main categories: the rescue of hostages and the killing of terrorists, usually of foreign nationality, on the British mainland, and the tackling of the Irish Republican Army (IRA) and, to a lesser extent, the Irish National Liberation Army (INLA), in Northern Ireland. Whatever the political situation, the SAS maintains its counter-terrorist capability at a very high level of instant response, with work on improved weapons, equipment and techniques continuing as a matter of the highest priority.

THE REGIMENT'S CT ROLES

The very secret nature of the SAS's counter-terrorist capability is greatly enhanced by its targets' lack of concrete information about its weapon, equipment and techniques. Even less has been revealed about this facility than other aspects of the SAS's operational capabilities. The fact that the modern world is faced with the problem of countering terrorism has spawned a moderately large international industry to service the needs of counter-terrorist forces. The most that one can say is that the SAS probably uses the best of this industry's products, together with a number of its own developments, which may be pure SAS improvements or alterations to commercially available products.

The SAS's two primary counter-terrorist roles demand a number of different capabilities. The Northern Ireland task places a considerably greater emphasis on sustained surveillance in rural area (often

requiring the trooper to hide for days on end in a cramped and highly uncomfortable 'hide' to watch for terrorist movements and observe arms dumps), uniformed or plain clothes operations on the streets of Northern Irish towns, and, on occasion, ambushing Republican units.

ASSAULT SUITS

If an SAS team has to make an assault on a terrorist-held building, it is faced with the very real problems of the heat, fire, blast and smoke generated by the assault, not to mention the bullets fired by the terrorists. The team seeks to secure the utmost tactical surprise in the assault, and then to move through the building as fast

as possible in an effort to keep the terrorists off balance and as poorly placed as possible to use their weapons. Until the building has been secured and all the terrorists captured or killed, there always remains the possibility of hostile counterfire. Each member of the SAS assault and rescue team, therefore, wears an assault suit and underwear made of flame-resistant material.

The SAS currently uses the G.D. Specialist Supplies assault suit, which is made of Nomex and reinforced by the regiment itself with Kevlar inserts to provide additional protection to the knees and elbows (Kevlar is a synthetic fibre of very high tensile strength – far greater

Useful as the combination of assault underwear, assault suit and fireproof gloves certainly is, it provides no protection as such from bullets and flying fragments. Body armour is moderately effective in this role, but only at the expense of considerable weight and a major reduction in the mobility of the wearer.

BODY ARMOUR

Body armour, which had been so much a feature of medieval warfare and only disappeared in its final vestigial forms at the outset of the Industrial Revolution, made its reappearance in World War I. Steel helmets were worn to protect the wearer from the fragments generated by the overhead detonation of shells (and saved many lives in the process). Sappers and assault troops were issued with torso armour made of overlapping plates to protect the upper and lower torso and, in some cases, the upper part of the thighs. Comparable armour was issued to the crews of early tanks, which suffered much from high-velocity spall (fragments flaked off the interior of the tank's armour by the impact of a projectile outside it) and splash (hot lead penetrating the gaps between plates after being liquefied by impact with the tank's exterior surface); tank crews were also equipped with face armour against the same threats.

With the exception of the helmet, armour disappeared once more in the period between the wars, but was then revived in World War II in the form of 'flak jackets', which were issued to bomber crews. These consisted of steel plates carried in an upper-body garment, and were both weighty and limited the wearer's movement.

MODERN BODY ARMOUR

Armour became more widespread after World War II with the development of 'soft' armour made from fibreglass and ballistic nylon. Such armour was lighter than the 'flak jacket' and did not impede the wearer's mobility. It worked by reducing the velocity of the impacting body,

than steel – which can be woven into a tough cloth that provides armour protection in bulletproof vests; with an epoxy resin Kevlar can be moulded into solid sheets of lightweight armour. Originally developed for the US space programme, it is also widely used in aircraft manufacture). It incorporates an integral respirator hood and flame barrier felt pads in the elbow and knee sections. Together with the Kevlar inserts, this padding offers protection against sharp objects and also permits the wearer to crawl over hot surfaces without suffering injury. The basic protection afforded by the assault suit can be increased as the situation demands by wearing items of assault underwear under the assault suit. It is standard to wear fireproof gloves to protect the hands and wrists and also to ensure a continuous grip on miscellaneous items of equipment as well as weapons.

whose momentum was reduced by being spread over many layers. 'Soft' armour worked moderately well against lower-velocity items such as shell and grenade fragments, but was significantly less effective against high-velocity items such as rifle bullets.

Greater capability was provided against high-velocity items by the invention of Kevlar, which is a lightweight fibre of immense tensile strength and highly suitable for the creation of tightly woven material that is both flexible and able to absorb the impact of bullets. The SAS uses Kevlar body armour with ceramic inserts to provide a high level of protection against all types of bullets, including high-velocity rounds and even armour-piercing rounds.

The type of body armour used by the SAS for the hostage-rescue role is the Dowty Armourshield vest. Available in two styles, for general-purpose wear and restricted-entry tasks, both these types incorporate the so-called blunt trauma shield, which is designed to prevent the wearer from suffering serious injury from a round that fails to penetrate the armour. In a normal vest, the bullet may be prevented from reaching and penetrating the wearer, but this may be achieved only at the expense of a depression in the armour so deep that a large amount of shock energy is transferred to the wearer as the type of blunt trauma that can cause serious injury or even death. The blunt trauma shield, which is worn underneath the armour vest, absorbs and dissipates the energy of the incoming round, though the impact of the round may still knock down and wind the wearer.

DEFEATING ENEMY ROUNDS

The SAS currently use the Dowty Armourshield General-Purpose Vest 25, which is 18mm (0.7in) thick, including the blunt trauma shield. This offers wrap-around protection, and also features high under-arm protection that allows the wearer to raise his firing arm without fear of exposing a vulnerable area. Ceramic composite plates can be worn over the basic vest, which provide protection against all NATO and Soviet (now Russian) high-velocity and armour-piercing rounds. The weight of this additional protection is considerable, however, for each plate of Dowty Armourshield armour weighs around 4kg (8.8lb), although these can be replaced by 3kg (6.6lb) plates of Protec Armour System's 'uparmour plate', a ceramic tile over an inner layer of laminate and under an outer layer of rubberised foam.

Another British company producing such armour protection is Meggitt Composites, whose Type 18 armour jacket was designed for special forces' use. Its modular and lightweight construction permits a high level of mobility, and it is fitted with double-curvature ceramic plates that offer a higher-than-average level of protection.

At present there is a race between manufacturers of body armour and small arms, which the latter appears to be winning. During the Eurosatory '96 at Paris in 1996, for example, the small arms company FN displayed its new Five-seveN handguns (see Handguns section). Its 5.7mm round is designed to defeat targets on the battlefield of the future. For example, while a 9mm round (used in the

Protection for the head was therefore considered as a matter of urgency, an early conclusion being that standard military helmets were unsuitable for the hostage-rescue role as they were too heavy, provided only an inadequate level of protection, and tended to become dislodged or skewed during the assault. Manufacturers therefore set about the conceptually simple, but practically difficult, task of designing a lightweight helmet that could be worn over a gas mask, was difficult to dislodge or skew, offered a high level of protection and, when worn with a visor or gas mask, prevented dust, tear gas, smoke, grit and debris from getting into the eyes, nose and mouth. The main difficulties with such headgear, however, are their general clumsiness, especially in the pre-assault phase of the mission as the assault team tries to get into position silently, and the limitation it imposes on the wearer's all-round vision.

ASSAULT HELMETS

The helmet currently used by the SAS in the hostage-rescue role is the Courtauld Aerospace Advanced Materials Division AC100/1. Designed to be worn over a headset and respirator, it is fabricated from multiple layers of ballistic-resistant composite materials. Such construction offers a higher level of protection against small arms ammunition than the standard military helmet, which is of single-layer construction, and the helmet is made as comfortable as possible by its completion with webbing and support elements of natural fibres and high-quality leather. The helmet also has an inbuilt high-impact trauma system liner to dissipate the energy of impacting rounds before it can be passed to the wearer's head.

RESPIRATORS

The nature of a hostage-rescue operation demands the utmost speed to throw the terrorists off balance and keep them in a disoriented state, and for this reason the SAS makes extensive use of explosives, shotguns and sledgehammers to gain

majority of today's pistols and submachine guns) will dent but not penetrate a Kevlar helmet at a distance of 10m (33ft), the 5.7mm bullet will penetrate the helmet at a range of 200m (656ft). In addition, the cartridge will also penetrate up to 48 layers of Kevlar at the same distance, whereas a 9mm round will not penetrate more than six or seven layers at point-blank range. Though there is speculation that the SAS will be equipped with the new pistol, it could also get into the hands of terrorists. If it does, hostage-rescue teams will need better armour vests and shield from the manufacturers.

COMMUNICATIONS

The communications system used by the SAS for counter-terrorist operations is the Davies Communications CT100 harness system. It includes the CT100E electronic ear defender headset with earphone and a socket for the CT100L body-worn microphone, which has a large front-mounted press-to-talk button, but is disabled when the SF10 respirator (with inbuilt microphone) is worn.

For counter-terrorist operations in open areas such as Northern Ireland, the SAS uses any of several types of small 'walkie talkie' systems with covert earpieces and microphones.

HELMETS

The first major hostage-rescue undertaken by the SAS was that of those persons held in the Iranian Embassy in London by six terrorists of the Democratic Revolutionary Front for the Liberation of Arabistan during May 1980. The rescue was a considerable success: all the hostages were freed and five of the six terrorists killed, while the sixth was wounded and captured. Assessment of the operation after its completion looked closely at ways in which the equipment of the SAS could be improved, and an early conclusion was that some form of head protection was needed. In the Iranian Embassy operation the assault team had worn anti-flash hoods that provided limited protection against heat, dust and smoke, but no protection at all against bullets, fragments and falling masonry.

Right: The SF10 respirator gives the wearer protection against gases and smoke, and the design stops fogging inside the mask.

access, and then uses stun, CS gas and smoke grenades as the assault team moves in. This means that the room(s) or airliner fuselage will generally be filled with dust, debris, gas and smoke, particularly if any flammable materials are ignited during the assault; it is standard procedure, however, to cut off the electricity and gas supplies to an occupied building. Survival and continued operational capability in these conditions can only be ensured by wearing a respirator.

THE SF10

The respirator currently used by the SAS is the Avon Polymer Products SF10, a British product that entered service in 1986 in succession to the S6 respirator. This unit provides full protection for the eyes, nose and mouth, and is also characterised by low breathing resistance, which reduces the physiological burden on the wearer and is a decided advantage in any operational situation. The filter (mountable on either the left- or right-hand sides according to operational dictates or personal preference) protects against gases, aerosols and smoke; the small oral/nasal chamber that exhausts used air leaves only very low levels of carbon dioxide behind, and the nose-guide channels indrawn air up the sides of the face and over the eyepieces to minimise fogging. The eyepieces themselves are of sturdy polycarbonate construction resistant to scratching and attacks by chemical or solvents, and can be fitted externally with flash-resistant protective lenses (this tinting, combined with the black colour of the other clothing worn by each SAS hostage-rescue trooper, supposedly adds to the overall impression of menace, and is thought to provide a psychological edge). This respirator allows two types of communication: direct speech at short range, and by radio at longer range through use of a microphone mounted in front of the lips.

Right: New hostage-rescue clothing is continually subjected to rigorous tests to ensure it will perform well in action.

Support Equipment

*As well as proper clothing, SAS hostage-rescue teams must have hardware to allow them to
gain entry to buildings, boats and aircraft to reach the hostages. Fortunately, Hereford has
equipped its men with a whole range of hostage-rescue support equipment.*

An assault is generally launched from the roof of an occupied building, which offers the best chance of assembling the team in secrecy. An accurate and speedy arrival at a window or door from the roof is vital, and here abseiling equipment is generally used. This equipment comprises three main units in the form of the rope, the harness worn by the SAS trooper, and the descendeur that connects the harness to the rope and allows control of the rate of descent. Descendeurs currently available include the Rollglis locking-brake system that can be operated with one hand to allow the other to be used for a weapon. The Inter Risk Abseil 3 Speed Descendeur is hand operated for pre-set slow, medium or fast descents, but automatically brakes the wearer when released; the IKAR AS1 allows descent speeds of up to 5.5m (18ft) per second.

AMMUNITION

With the choice of weapon made, the assault team then has to choose the ammunition to be used. The ammunition must be powerful enough to stop individual terrorists before they can harm any of the hostages or the assault team, yet not so forceful as to pass right through the terrorist, possibly hitting a hostage behind the real target. From the beginning of the SAS's counter-terrorist role it was clear that standard ammunition was not suited to the task, largely because any round sufficiently powerful to halt a terrorist could send its bullet through him or her to strike a hostage, either directly or after a ricochet.

Specialised ammunition was clearly required by the SAS as much as by all other counter-terrorist and armed law-enforcement agencies in the world. The one standard type of round that could be retained was the high-velocity round used by sniper rifles. With a velocity of more than 900m (2953ft) per second, such rounds are fired with extreme deliberation, preferably to the head or torso, to cause the type of massive tissue damage, followed by hydrostatic shock, that results in almost instantaneous death. The skills of the sniper are all-important with this type of ammunition, for the bullet almost invariable passes through the target body with high residual velocity. The choice of shot is vital not only to the target, but also any hostage in the vicinity. For this reason, therefore, the sniper prefers a down-

*Left: Abseiling equipment is often used to
allow teams to descend from above unseen
to force entries during a rescue.*

ward shot that will continue into the floor and not into hostages.

Most of the specialised ammunition devised for counter-terrorist use in weapons of 5.56mm or 9mm calibre falls into two basic categories: one with a bullet that breaks up in the body, and the other with a bullet with some sort of hollow-point or unconventional shape that will tumble in the body and thereby lose velocity very rapidly. The design of such bullets has profited considerably from the use of composite materials.

SPECIALIST ROUNDS

Several manufacturers produce bullets based on the Hydra-Shok principle developed in the USA. Made almost entirely of lead, with a hemispherical recess in the nose, they have an upstanding peg to ensure a mushrooming of the nose for massive damage and rapid deceleration. The Glaser Safety Slug, also developed in the USA, has a thin casing filled with compressed bird shot that penetrates thin inanimate objects without breaking up, but on impact with soft tissue, fragments into some 330 sub-projectiles. The KTW has a Teflon coating over a brass core. The French cone-pointed copper Arcane is capable of penetrating body armour and walls.

The Arcane round is made of solid copper, is cone-pointed and has a special propellant charge which gives it high velocity. This means it can be fired from short-barrelled pistols. It will literally go through anything, though a major drawback with regard to hostage-rescue work is that against soft targets such as flesh it will cause severe wound cavities but will pass straight through the body.

The THV (also French) contains a stack of bollard-shaped sub-projectiles to provide excellent penetrative power, but then very rapid deceleration. The British Cobra High Safety Ammunition incorporates a number of flechettes which are released from their casing only after impact with the target. Finally, the British Conjoy CBX Low Penetration type loses between 65 and 100 per cent of its energy on hitting the target to cause an enormous wound with no possibility of passing through the target.

ASSAULT LADDERS

When they cannot abseil down to their entry point, the members of the assault team often have to climb up to it, and it is in this situation that the assault ladder comes into its own. The SAS uses the W. J. Clow series of sectional assault ladders made in the UK. The sections are fabricated of lightweight aluminium and are deeply serrated to provide the best possible grip for the hand and foot and also against walls or airliners. There is also a double-width ladder that can support six troopers at a time, and other features include a hooked top for additional grip. The ladders can be carried on a large number of vehicle types, can double as bridges and sniper platforms, and can be readily assembled into units of the right length. The SAS (together with other European special forces) maintains a database of the height of the windows of vulnerable buildings, the wings of the main airliner types, and the doors of airliners and trains. Assault ladders may seem a trivial item, but it was the silent placing of rubber-coated assault ladders against the fuselage of the hijacked Boeing 737 airliner at Mogadishu in October 1977 that played a significant part in the success of the GSG 9 operation.

Among the tools carried by the assault team can be a number of comparatively simple yet highly effective items such as sledgehammers, bolt cutters, glass cutters, axes, wrecking bars and grappling hooks.

EXPLOSIVES

Once it is in place for the assault, the SAS team decide on the optimum method for effecting a fast entry into the building; if this cannot be achieved with a sledgehammer or other basic tool, they usually resort to explosives, usually of the 'frame charge' type that can be bent and shaped to exactly the right configuration for the selected point of entry. The two best-known types of 'frame charge' are those manufactured in France by SNPE and in the USA by Accuracy Systems. The SNPE system is based on a cutting detonating cord and an adhesive explosive strip charge. Accuracy Systems offers an explosive door cutter system capable of blowing open hollow or solid wood doors, as

Above: The stun grenade. When detonated it emits a blinding flash and loud bang which incapacitates all those in close proximity.

well as standard industrial hollow metal doors, and uses charges wrapped in soft flexible foam which can be bent to the desired shape.

GRENADES

As the explosive charge works and the team enters the building, train or airliner, it is common practice to throw either stun or CS gas grenades. The stun grenade was devised by the SAS, and is essentially a diversionary device that explodes with a deafening bang and blinding flash. It is now available in single- or multiple-bang types, and the main European manufacturers of this device are the German firm PPT and the British companies Royal Ordnance and Brocks Pyrotechnics. PPT's range includes the Type A, which produces a loud bang as well as an intense light that lasts for 15 seconds, the Type B, that issues eight loud bangs in quick succession; and the Type C that has no bang. There are few details of the Royal Ordnance stun grenades, which include the G60 type optimised for the loudest possible bang, and the Brocks' grenades

Left: The Browning High Power handgun may not be the most modern around, but its reliability endears it to SAS users.

under the barrel of most rifles, submachine guns, shotguns and pistols to project a small but powerful line along the weapon's line of fire. Typical of the latter are the American Law Enforcement International LEI-100 unit and the British Electro Prismatic Collimators system, both of which project a beam of red laser light along the line of fire.

WEAPONS

Once it has entered the target structure and temporarily disoriented or incapacitated the terrorists, the SAS assault team has to be ready to engage any resistance with their personal weapons. Given that such operations almost invariably take place at short range and within a confined area, the choice of weapons is constrained by maximum lethality (requiring a high rate of fire, a large magazine and the utmost accuracy) and minimum encumbrance to the firer (the shortest possible weapon length and the fewest possible features that can catch on clothing, etc., as the weapon is brought to bear). In these circumstances, the preferred SAS weapons are the Heckler & Koch MP5 submachine gun, the Remington 870 pump-action shotgun, and the Browning High Power and Glock 18 semi-automatic pistols, all of which are examined at greater length in the Small Arms section.

When selecting a weapon, the SAS looks for a number of attributes in the weapon. These are, in order of priority: reliability, accuracy, compactness, full-automatic fire capability and good balance. The MP5 submachine gun meets all these requirements.

One of the most important members of a hostage-rescue team is the sniper. The sniper gives a team the opportunity of resolving the siege with one shot. During a siege the sniper's job is to identify and track targets. Both the sniper and his rifle need to have certain qualities. Hostage-rescue snipers are selected for their stability, calmness, patience and marksmanship. In addition, they must be able to observe and gather intelligence, for their optics

include the MX5 with five simultaneous flashes and bangs, the MX7 which delivers a mix of flashes, bangs and smoke, and the MX8, with a rapid series of eight very loud bangs.

The stun grenade is designed to disorient the terrorist(s), but the CS gas grenade is intended to put him or her out of action by causing severe lachrymation, coughing and difficulty of breathing with a tightness of the chest. The CS gas grenade can be very useful, but has to be used with caution as it affects the hostages as much as the terrorists, and at short

range or in a confined space can have long-term adverse effects.

SIGHTS

Aiming the weapons accurately is also of paramount importance in situations involving hostages. This is made more difficult as the structure is likely to be without power, and will therefore be dark, or at least gloomy. The two most common sighting aids are the torch type and the aiming dot type. Typical of the former is an American item, the Laser Products Sure-Fire Tactical Sight that can be added

Right: Spanish GEO personnel practising with Heckler & Koch MP5 submachine guns, the favoured hostage-rescue weapon.

and vantage points give them access to information that the team on the ground is denied. It is standard operating procedure (SOP) for snipers to be trained in pairs: one acts as the observer and the other is the shooter. This means that the two can rotate duties, thus lessening fatigue somewhat.

Snipers always use the same rifle. In this way they can learn its every feature and characteristic. In addition, he needs to be skilled in covert infiltration so he can deliver the unexpected first shot with deadly effect. The sniper rifle itself must have certain characteristics to fulfil its role. These are: a free-floating barrel, adjustable trigger pull, capacity for a bipod and monopod, good accuracy over long ranges, excellent optics and ability to withstand rough treatment.

The current SAS sniper rifle is the Accuracy International PM, a bolt-action model of 7.62mm calibre (sniper rifles have traditionally been bolt-action models, though increasingly many hostage-rescue units throughout the world are using highly accurate semi-automatics, which allow snipers to deal with multiple targets during an assault).

WEAPONS FOR ULSTER

For counter-terrorist operations in Northern Ireland, where outdoor operations were more the norm, a larger assortment of weapons were used by the Regiment, including the L1A1 (or SLR) rifle, the Colt commando assault rifle, the silenced version of the Sterling submachine gun, the Heckler & Koch 53 submachine gun and the Ingram submachine gun, as well as a number of the weapons habitually used by the IRA and INLA, including the Kalashnikov AK-47 assault rifle, Armalite assault rifle and M1 carbine. SAS soldiers even experimented with the Ingram submachine gun, though it was found to be slightly erratic.

Right: At the end of the day a successful rescue is a blend of training, the right equipment and accurate firepower.

AIRCRAFT

Fixed-wing Aircraft

Fixed-wing aircraft have always played a crucial part in the SAS's operational doctrines, either for the delivery of men and equipment to the zone of operations, or the dropping of supplies to men on the ground, especially in jungle terrain.

The SAS has always been associated with the use of aircraft for the delivery of parties behind enemy lines, either by parachute or by landing on extemporised airstrips, for the receipt of reinforcements, supplies and other equipment, or for extraction at the end of a mission when required. Initially the aircraft were all of the fixed-wing type, but since World War II the rotary-wing aeroplane has become increasingly important in military operations. It is now one of the most important methods for the delivery of SAS parties, who can be landed or collected from sites little larger than the helicopter's rotor diameter or, failing the availability of such a site, abseil to the ground from the hovering helicopter.

Each of the SAS's 'Sabre' Squadrons has one Air Troop that specialises in all aspects of parachute operations, and parachute training is an fully integrated part of the Regiment's Continuation Training.

A fixed-wing aeroplane needs several specific attributes to make it suitable for the needs of the SAS. It must have long-range potential (which is now provided by inflight-refuelling techniques) so that remote spots can be reached directly, or closer sites can be approached by a circuitous route to avoid enemy air defences and radar coverage; STOL (Short Take-Off and Landing) capability means that the aeroplane can operate into and out of short airstrips that are often in areas such as jungles, with tall trees limiting the airstrip's approaches. A sizeable fuselage that will accommodate the right number of men and all their equipment is vital, and should be fitted with doors and/or ramps to facilitate the loading and unloading of bulky items. Finally, the aircraft must be rugged and reliable enough to operate safely and effectively in conditions ranging from the extreme cold of an Arctic night to the scorching heat of the desert day, via the oppressive humidity of many jungle regions.

The aircraft initially allocated to the SAS in World War II seldom managed all or even many of these attributes, for they were generally superannuated bombers converted for the purpose. Essentially, they were available and possessed the ability to lift the required load in terms of weight, even if they were not perfect in terms of access and egress and accommodation. Later in the war, the situation improved with the availability of larger numbers of aircraft that had been designed for the transport role in general, if not the airborne or special forces roles in particular. After the war the introduction of the Lockheed Hercules answered all the requirements of the SAS. It is a classic tactical airlifter, with long range and moderately high speed, genuine STOL capability, a large fuselage accessed by lateral doors and a ventral ramp and door arrangement that can be used in flight, and is also enormously reliable and rugged.

ARMSTRONG ALBEMARLE

The Armstrong Whitworth Albemarle was used for the delivery of SAS parties into occupied France after June 1944, and was originally designed as a reconnaissance bomber. It was notably underpowered for this demanding role, and was therefore adapted for the associated roles of glider towing and paratroop dropping.

Right: The Armstrong Whitworth Albemarle, used by the SAS as a troop carrier in the weeks after the D-Day landings in June 1944.

Above: The Blackburn Beverley, a heavy transport aircraft used by the Regiment in the support role in the 1950s and 1960s.

The paratroops were carried in the fuselage, and launched themselves from a coffin-shaped exit hatch in the belly of this unit. The shape of this exit and the nature of the airflow beneath the Albemarle's fuselage had to be approached with great care if the dropping man was not to suffer a broken nose or the loss of his front teeth, which was known as 'ringing the bell'. The Albemarle had a notional capacity of 10 men, although this was generally reduced to just four or five men when they were fully laden with operational equipment. Production of the Albemarle, which was built largely of non-strategic materials such as steel and wood, totalled 600 aircraft.

Type: Armstrong Whitworth Albemarle Mk II five-crew paratroop transport
Powerplant: two Bristol Hercules XI radial piston engines each rated at 1185kW (1590hp)
Dimensions: span 23.47m (77ft); length 18.26m (59ft 11in); height 4.75m (15ft 7in)
Weight: maximum take-off 16,556kg (36,500lb)
Performance: maximum speed 427km/h (265mph) at 3200m (10,500ft); range 2092km (1300 miles); service ceiling 5485m (18,000ft)

Armament: two 0.303in Vickers 'K' guns in the dorsal turret
Payload: up to 10 paratroops

AUSTER

The Auster series of light planes entered service in World War II as the military counterpart of the Taylorcraft braced high-wing light planes, and was designed for the roles of tactical reconnaissance and air observation. The series remained in service up to the 1960s, and the type was found especially useful in its AOP.Mk 6 and AOP.Mk 9 variants by SAS troopers operating against insurgent forces in Aden, Borneo and Malaya. Here, a close liaison system was evolved so that visual sighting of insurgent forces was relayed to ground patrols which were of 10 spearheaded by SAS troopers.

Type: Auster AOP.Mk 9 two/three-seat tactical reconnaissance and air observation post aeroplane
Powerplant: one Blackburn Cirrus bombardier 203 inline piston engine rated at 134kW (180hp)
Dimensions: span 11.10m (36ft 5in); length 7.23m (23ft 9in); height 2.57m (8ft 5in)
Weight: empty 663kg (1461lb); maximum take-off 966kg (2130lb)
Performance: maximum speed 204km/h (127mph) at sea level; range 396km (246 miles); service ceiling 5640m (18,500ft)
Armament: none
Payload: none

BRITISH AEROSPACE ANDOVER

The British Aerospace (Hawker Siddeley/Avro) Andover was widely used by the SAS from the late 1960s to the late 1970s, especially in the Middle East. The type was designed as a civil transport by Avro, and was then developed into the Andover for the STOL military transport

Below: The Beaver light reconnaissance and utility aircraft, which was used to support SAS operations in the Middle and Far East.

Above: The legendary Douglas Dakota, which dropped SAS teams into northwest Europe in World War II, and later Malaya.

role. It had low-pressure tyres to facilitate operations from poor airstrips, a strength-ened floor, a longer fuselage, a raised tail allowing the incorporation into the underside of the rear fuselage of clamshell doors providing straight-in access to the hold, and landing gear whose height could be adjusted on the ground to place the fuselage floor at any of several truckbed heights to facilitate the loading and unloading of bulky items. The fuse-lage was large enough to carry light vehi-cles, and the rear doors could be opened in flight for the paradropping of men and equipment.

Type: British Aerospace (Hawker Siddeley/Avro) Andover C.Mk 1 three/four-crew tactical transport
Powerplant: two Rolls-Royce Dart RDa.12 Mk 201C turboprop engines each rated at 2420kW (2280hp)
Dimensions: span 29.95m (98ft 3in); length 23.75m (77ft 11in); height 9.17m (30ft 1in)
Weight: empty 12,569kg (27,709lb); maximum take-off 20,185kg (44,500lb)
Performance: maximum speed 486km/h (302mph) at 4570m (15,000ft); range 602km (374 miles) with maximum payload; service ceiling 7255m (23,800ft)
Armament: none
Payload: up to 44 troops, or 30 paratroops; or 18 litters, five seated

casualties and three attendants; or 6350kg (14,000lb) of freight

BLACKBURN BEVERLEY

The Blackburn Beverley was an ugly, but thoroughly utilitarian heavy transport aeroplane designed by General Aircraft Ltd before its take-over by Blackburn. The type was notable for its all-metal construction, with a high-set wing, tail unit with endplate vertical surfaces, and fixed tricycle landing gear, including two wheels on each unit. The fuselage was of the pod-and-boom type, with accommo-dation for men, vehicles, pieces of light artillery and equipment in the pod. Access was via large clamshell rear doors, each containing an inset door, and accommo-dation for men was in the boom that sup-ported the tail unit. The type first flew in 1950, and production for the RAF totalled 47 aircraft that remained in ser-vice until 1968. The SAS used it in the Middle East and the Far East, mainly for the delivery of men and vehicles into poor airstrips where the Beverley's semi-STOL capability proved very useful.
Type: Blackburn Beverley C.Mk 1 four-crew tactical transport
Powerplant: four Bristol Centaurus 273 radial piston engines each rated at 2125kW (2850hp)
Dimensions: span 49.38m (162ft); length 30.30m (99ft 5in); height 11.81m (38ft 9in)
Weight: empty 35,941kg (79,234lb); maximum take-off 61,236kg (135,000lb)
Performance: maximum speed

383km/h (238mph) at 1735m (5700ft); radius 371km (230 miles) with maximum payload; service ceiling 4875m (16,000ft)
Armament: none
Payload: up to 94 troops, or 70 paratroops, or 20,412kg (45,000lb) of freight

BRISTOL BOMBAY

The Bristol Bombay was designed to meet a 1931 requirement that reflected the parsimonious nature of British aircraft procurement at the time. It demanded a single type that was optimised for the roles of troop transport and freighting, but would still be capable of undertaking bombing in lesser theatres such as the Middle East. The result was an angular machine of all-metal stressed skin con-struction, with a high-set cantilever wing, a fuselage whose hold was accessed by a large port-side door, a tail unit with twin vertical surfaces, and fixed tailwheel land-ing gear. The prototype first flew in June 1935, and the RAF eventually received a total of 50 aircraft that remained in ser-vice until the middle years of World War II. The SAS used the type for a number of North African operations.
Type: Bristol Bombay Mk I three-crew bomber and transport
Powerplant: two Bristol Pegasus XXII radial piston engines each rated at 753kW (1010hp)
Dimensions: span 29.18m (95ft 9in); length 21.11m (69ft 3in); height 6.07m (19ft 11in)
Weight: empty 6260kg (13,800lb); maximum take-off 6096kg (20,000lb)
Performance: maximum speed 309km/h (192mph) at 1980m (6500ft); range 1416km (880 miles) with standard fuel or 3589km (2330 miles) with additional tankage; service ceiling 7620m (25,000ft)
Armament: single 0.303in Vickers 'K' machine guns in the manually operated nose and tail turrets, and up to 907kg (2000 lb) of bombs carried externally
Payload: up to 24 troops or freight

DE HAVILLAND CANADA DHC-2 BEAVER

The de Havilland Canada DHC-2 Beaver was designed in Canada as a braced high-wing monoplane. Basically of all-metal construction for 'bushplane' operations that required a highly reliable engine, the plane's sturdy construction allowed operations into and out of primitive airstrips with heavy payloads. It was also able to operate on skis or floats as an alternative to the standard wheels. The type first flew in 1947, and secured moderately good sales to military forces who were attracted by its reliability, goods payload capability, STOL field performance, and ability to operate under any and all geographical and climatic conditions. The British Army bought 46 of these aircraft with the designation Beaver AL.Mk 1, and these saw service until the 1970s in Aden, Borneo, Northern Ireland and Malaya – operational areas in which the SAS was re-supplied by such machines.

Type: de Havilland Canada DHC-2 Beaver one/two-crew utility STOL transport

Powerplant: one Pratt & Whitney R-985-AN-6B/14B Wasp Junior radial piston engine rated at 336kW (450hp)

Dimensions: span 14.62m (48ft); length 9.24m (30ft 4in); height 2.74m (9ft)

Weight: empty 1294kg (2850lb); maximum take-off 2313kg (5100lb)

Performance: maximum speed 257km/h (160mph) at 1525m (5000ft); range 1180km (783 miles); service ceiling 5485m (18,000ft)

Armament: none

Payload: up to seven passengers or 613kg (1350kg) of freight

DOUGLAS DAKOTA

The Douglas Dakota was the British counterpart of the US Army Air Forces' Douglas C-47 Skytrain and C-53 Skytrooper, themselves military developments of the classic Douglas DC-3, the airliner that may be said to have ushered in the era of modern air transport. The type was of all-metal construction with a cantilever low-set wing. Among its advanced features were the combination of an enclosed cockpit and fully enclosed passenger accommodation in a separate

Right: The Hercules long-range transport aircraft, which the SAS currently uses to support its long-range operations.

cabin, trailing-edge flaps, tailwheel landing gear with retractable main units, provision for de-icing, and a powerplant of two fully cowled radial piston engines each driving a variable-pitch propeller. The DC-3 first flew in December 1935, and the C-53 and C-47 entered military service in October 1941 and January 1942 respectively. More than 10,000 were built in World War II, some surviving in military service to this day, and more than 1900 of these were transferred to the RAF, under the terms of the Lend-Lease Act, in four variants. The type was widely used during and after World War II for the delivery and supply of SAS, and was retired from British service in 1970.

Type: Douglas Dakota Mk I three-crew transport, glider tug and paratroop aeroplane

Powerplant: two Pratt & Whitney R-1830-92 Twin Wasp radial piston engines each rated at 895kW (1200hp)

Dimensions: span 28.96m (95ft); length 19.66m (64ft 6in); height 5.16m (16ft 11in)

Weight: empty 7650kg (16,865lb);

maximum take-off 14,062kg (31,000lb)

Performance: maximum speed 371km/h (230mph) at 2590m (8500ft); range 2414km (1500 miles); service ceiling 7070m (23,200ft)

Armament: none

Payload: up to 28 troops, or 20 paratroops, or 3538kg (7800lb) of freight

HANDLEY PAGE HALIFAX

The Handley Page Halifax was designed as the UK's second four-engined heavy bomber of World War II. Later in the war it was developed in specialised forms for the support of airborne forces after the primary heavy bomber role had been assumed by the Avro Lancaster. The fuselage of these specialised models was revised for the carriage of up to 16 paratroops who exited via a floor hatch, and the bomb bay was altered to carry paradropped freight items such as equipment and even light vehicles like Jeeps. The Halifax was used extensively in the later stages of the war for supplying SAS parties with additional weapons, ammunition, equipment and vehicles. The main

variants involved in these tasks were the Halifax A.Mk III that was a conversion of Halifax B.Mk III bombers; the Halifax A.Mk VII, of which 378 were built, and which was the glider-tug development of the Halifax B.Mk VII bomber; and the Halifax A.Mk IX, a more fully optimised post-war airborne forces variant, of which 145 were delivered.

Type: Handley Page Halifax A.Mk IX five-crew paratroop transport and supply dropping aeroplane
Powerplant: four Bristol Hercules XVI radial piston engines each rated at 1249kW (1675hp)
Dimensions: span 31.75m (104ft 2in); length 21.82m (71ft 7in); height 6.32m (21ft 9in)
Weight: empty 18,031kg (39,750lb); maximum take-off 29,484kg (65,000lb)
Performance: maximum speed 459km/h (285mph) at optimum altitude; range 1851km (1150 miles); service ceiling 7315m (24,000ft)
Armament: two 0.5in Browning machine guns in the power-operated tail turret
Payload: up to 16 paratroops and freight

LOCKHEED HERCULES

The Lockheed Hercules, now a product of the combined Lockheed Martin Corporation, was the airlifter that in the early 1950s introduced the definitive tactical airlift configuration. It has a high-set wing carrying powerful turboprop engines on its leading edges, and a combination of ailerons and flaps across the full span of its trailing edges for STOL capability. With a fuselage of considerable diameter it can incorporate a large hold, which is pressurised for high-altitude flight. It has an upswept tail unit allowing the rear fuselage to be fitted with a ventral ramp and door arrangement for straight-in loading and unloading, as well as the paradropping of large loads or paratroops in flight. The landing gear is of the multi-wheel tricycle type that keeps the fuselage level and close to the ground for loading and

Right: The Skyvan was used extensively by the SAS during its campaign in southwest Oman as a troop transport.

unloading, and whose main units retract into external blisters so that no inroads are made into internal volume. The C-130 prototype made its first flight in August 1954, and the type has been in development and production ever since. From December 1966 the RAF received 66 examples of the C-130K British version of the C-130H that introduced a significantly uprated powerplant, and these Hercules C.Mk 1 aircraft have performed wonders as the core of British tactical transport capability. Some of the aircraft have since been adapted to improved forms such as the Hercules C.Mk 1K (six aircraft equipped as inflight-refuelling tankers), the Hercules C.Mk 1P (an initial 16, but later more aircraft with an inflight-refuelling probe for longer range), the Hercules C.Mk 3 (30 aircraft with the fuselage lengthened by 4.57m/15ft to increase their payload to 128 troops or 92 paratroops), and the Hercules C.Mk 3P (Hercules C.Mk 3 transports revised with an inflight-refuelling probe). The Hercules is the type most generally associated with current SAS operations, and this situation is certain to continue with the new C-130J Hercules II version ordered by the RAF. It has a new engine and propeller combination, more advanced flight and operational electronics, and a host of other improvements,

Type: Lockheed Martin Hercules C.Mk 1 five-crew tactical transport
Powerplant: four Allison T56-A-15 turboprop engines each rated at 3661kW (4910hp)
Dimensions: span 40.41m (132ft 7in); length 30.01m (98ft 9in); height 11.66m (38ft 3in)
Weight: empty 34,827kg (76,780lb); maximum take-off 79,379kg (175,000lb)
Performance: maximum speed 592km/h (368mph) at 9145m (30,000ft); range 3911km (2430 miles) with maximum payload; service ceiling 13,075m (42,900ft)
Armament: none
Payload: up to 92 troops, or 64 paratroops, or 74 litters plus two attendants, or 20,820kg (45,900lb) of freight

SHORT STIRLING

The Short Stirling was the first four-engined heavy bomber to enter British service in World War II, but was soon rendered obsolete by the advent of the more capable Handley Page Halifax and Avro Lancaster bombers. The type was therefore adapted to the airborne forces role as successor to the Albemarle, and was used mainly to tow gliders, although it could also carry 22 paratroops who dropped through a floor hatch. A number of the aircraft were adapted for the carriage and paradropping of vehicles, and as such were useful to the SAS. The main variants

for the airborne forces support role were the Stirling Mk IV, 579 of which were built with nose and tail turrets, and the Stirling Mk V, of which 160 were built with no armament.

Type: Short Stirling Mk IV six/seven-crew transport

Powerplant: four Bristol Hercules XVI radial piston engines each rated at 1230kW (1650hp)

Dimensions: span 30.20m (99ft 1in); length 26.59m (87ft 3in); height 6.93m (22ft 9in)

Weight: empty 21,200kg (46,900lb); maximum take-off 31,790kg (70,000lb)

Performance: maximum speed 434km/h (270mph) at 4420m (14,500ft); range 3240km (2010 miles); service ceiling 5180m (17,000ft)

Armament: two and four 0.303in Browning machine guns respectively in the power-operated nose and tail turrets

Payload: up to 22 paratroops or 6364kg (14,000lb) of bombs

SHORT SC.7 SKYVAN

The Short SC.7 Skyvan first flew in January 1963 as a utility light transport with full STOL capability, and although not adopted by the RAF, was bought in small numbers by the Sultanate of Oman's Air Force, which used it for the support of SAS parties involved in defeating the communist insurgency in the southwest of the country (1970-76). The type has a high-set braced wing, fixed tricycle landing gear, and a rectangular-section fuselage with a rear ramp and door arrangement facilitating parachute operations.

Type: Short Skyvan 3M two-crew utility STOL transport

Powerplant: two Garrett TPE331-2-201A turboprop engines each rated at 533kW (715hp)

Dimensions: span 19.79m (64ft 11in); length 12.60m (41ft 4in); height 4.60m (15ft 1in)

Weight: empty 3357kg (7400lb); maximum take-off 6577kg (14,500lb)

Performance: maximum speed 325km/h (202mph) at 3050m (10,000ft); range 386km (240 miles) with a 2268kg (5000lb) payload; service ceiling 6705m (22,000ft)

Armament: none

Payload: up to 19 passengers, or 12 litters and attendants, or 2268kg (5000kg) of freight

VICKERS VALETTA

The Vickers Valetta first flew in June 1947 as a medium-range transport and remained in service until the mid-1960s. The type was of all-metal construction with a low-set cantilever wing and retractable tailwheel landing gear, and was used to support SAS operations in Borneo, Malaya and Oman despite the fact that it had only one door, a large unit located on the port side of the fuselage, just forward of the tailplane.

Type: Vickers Valetta C.Mk 1 four-crew transport

Powerplant: two Bristol Hercules 230 radial piston engines each rated at 1473kW (1975hp)

Dimensions: span 27.20m (89ft 3in); length 19.18m (62ft 11in); height 5.94m (19ft 6in)

Weight: empty 11,274kg (24,854lb); maximum take-off 16,556kg (34,500lb)

Performance: maximum speed 415km/h (258mph) at 3050m (10,000ft); range 579km (360 miles) with maximum payload; service ceiling 6765m (22,200ft)

Armament: none

Payload: up to 34 troops, or 20 paratroops, or freight.

WESTLAND LYSANDER

The Westland Lysander was designed as a STOL type for the army cooperation

Above: The inflight refuelling probes on British RAF Hercules means that they can deploy SAS parties anywhere in the world.

role. It was characterised by its oddly shaped wing, which was set in the high position and braced on each side by a Vee strut. It carried machine gun armament and could be fitted with stub 'winglets' for the carriage of light bombs. It entered service in 1938, but was soon revealed as wholly obsolete. Production continued to January 1942. The type was then used for the support of special operations, in which its STOL and slow-flying capabilities were useful for clandestine operations in France and the Low Countries.

Type: Westland Lysander Mk I cooperation and special operations aircraft

Powerplant: one Bristol Mercury XII radial piston engine rated at 664kW (890hp)

Dimensions: span 15.24m (50ft); length 9.30m (30ft 6in); height 3.51m (11ft 6in)

Weight: empty 1844kg (4065lb); maximum take-off 2685kg (5920lb)

Performance: maximum speed 352km/h (219mph) at 3050m (10,000ft); range 966km (600 miles); service ceiling 7925m (26,000ft)

Armament: two 0.303in Browning fixed forward-firing machine guns, one 0.303in Lewis trainable rearward-firing machine gun, and up to 54kg (120lb) of bombs carried externally

Payload: up to one passenger and stores when used in the special operations role

Helicopters

Since their introduction into military service during the 1950s, helicopters have had a major impact on the battlefield. For the SAS, they have provided the means to insert and extract teams into any terrain, and today they are as important to the Regiment as fixed-wing aircraft.

The helicopter has revolutionised special forces warfare. Its ability to take off and land vertically, hover and fly at low speeds makes it ideal for inserting elite teams into enemy territory. First used by the SAS in Malaya in the 1950s, helicopters have been used in all of the Regiment's campaigns ever since. So successful has the helicopter been that it has replaced parachuting as the primary SAS airborne insertion technique (during the Gulf War, for example, SAS teams inserted by air were done so by Chinook helicopter; there were no parachute drops).

AÉROSPATIALE GAZELLE

The Aérospatiale Gazelle (now supported by Eurocopter France) was designed as successor to the highly successful Alouette series of multi-role light helicopters, and first flew in April 1967. It is a trim machine with a fully enclosed fuselage of the pod-and-boom type, twin-skid landing gear and an anti-torque tail rotor set into the vertical fin. The type was adopted by the British forces in a number of forms for operational as well as training and liaison roles, and has been used by the

SAS in the Falklands and Northern Ireland.

Type: Aérospatiale Gazelle AH.Mk 1 two-crew light multi-role helicopter
Powerplant: one Turbomeca Astazou IIIN turboshaft engine rated at 440kW (590hp)
Dimensions: main rotor diameter 10.50m (34ft 6in); length 11.97m (39ft 3in); height 3.18m (10ft 5in)
Weight: empty 920kg (2028lb); maximum take-off 1800kg (3968lb)
Performance: maximum speed 264km/h (164mph) at sea level; range 360km (223 miles) with a 500kg (1102lb) payload; service ceiling 5000m (16,405ft)
Armament: generally none, although provision is made for a fixed forward-firing cannon, or machine gun and/or rockets pods, or air-to-surface missiles, or anti-tank missiles
Payload: up to four passengers or 700kg (1540kg) of freight

AÉROSPATIALE PUMA

The Aérospatiale Puma (now supported by Eurocopter France) was developed as

an all-weather tactical helicopter and first flew in April 1965 before entering large-scale production for French and export sales. There is little that is remarkable in the basic design, although modestly high performance is provided by the type's clean lines and retractable tricycle landing gear. It was adopted by the RAF with the designation Puma HC.Mk 1 for the tactical transport role, which includes the insertion and extraction of SAS parties.

Type: Aérospatiale Puma HC.Mk 1 one/three-crew multi-role medium helicopter
Powerplant: two Turbomeca Turmo IIIC4 turboshaft engines each rated at 990kW (1328hp)
Dimensions: main rotor diameter 15.00m (49ft 3in); length 18.15m (59ft 7in); height 5.14m (16ft 11in)
Weight: empty 3615kg (7970lb); maximum take-off 6400kg (14,109lb)
Performance: maximum speed 258km/h (160mph) at optimum altitude; range 550km (341 miles); service ceiling 4800m (15,750ft)
Armament: generally none, although pintle-mounted weapons can be installed in the cabin doors
Payload: up to 20 troops; or six litters and six seated casualties; or 3000kg (6614lb) of freight

AGUSTA A109A

Two examples of the Agusta A109A were captured from the Argentine forces in the Falklands War and allocated to the SAS, which now operates additional machines of the same type. It is a trim, light helicopter of Italian design and manufacture, with high performance as a result of its advanced rotor, clean lines and retractable landing gear. The type can be used in a

Left: The Puma has been used by the SAS for transport duties in Northern Ireland. It can carry up to 20 fully equipped troops.

number of unarmed and armed roles.

Type: Agusta A 109A Mk II two-crew light utility helicopter

Powerplant: two Allison 250-C20B turboshaft engines each rated at 258kW (346hp)

Dimensions: main rotor diameter 11.00m (36ft 1in); length 13.05m (42ft 9.8in); height 3.30m (10ft 10in)

Weight: empty 1560kg (3439lb); maximum take-off 2600kg (5732lb)

Performance: maximum speed 285km/h (177mph) at optimum altitude; range 593km (368 miles); service ceiling 5485m (18,000ft)

Armament: a large assortment of fixed and disposable weapons can be carried on four hardpoints under two optional outriggers

Payload: up to six passengers or 1180kg (2601lb) of freight

BOEING CHINOOK

The Boeing Chinook is currently the RAF's medium/heavy-lift helicopter, and as such is very important to the SAS. The type first flew in September 1961 and is still in development and production. It is notable for its tandem-rotor design, fixed quadricycle landing gear, and rectangular-section fuselage whose internal volume is maximised for payload by the location of the fuel tanks in external pannier fairings. Access to the hold is through forward doors and a rear ramp and door arrangement that can be opened in flight. There is provision for the carriage of external loads on up to three hooks. The baseline British model is the Chinook HC.Mk 1, based on the CH-147 version of Canada's CH-47C. This has been revised, firstly with an uprated powerplant as the Chinook HC.Mk 1A, and secondly, with a number of CH-47D features, as the Chinook HC.Mk 2.

Type: Boeing Chinook HC.Mk 1A two/three-crew medium/heavy-lift helicopter

Powerplant: two Lycoming T55-L-512 turboshaft engines each rated at 3356kW (4500hp)

Right: Used to insert SAS road-watch patrols during the Gulf War, the Chinook is an important asset in the Regiment's armoury.

Dimensions: rotor diameter, each 18.29m (60ft); length 30.18m (99ft); height 5.68m (18ft 7.8in)

Weight: empty 10,475kg (23,093lb); maximum take-off 24,494kg (54,000lb)

Performance: maximum speed 302km/h (188mph) at sea level; radius 185km (115 miles) with maximum payload; service ceiling 6735m (22,100ft)

Armament: generally none, although provision is made for pintle-mounted machine guns

Payload: up to 55 troops, or 24 litters plus two attendants, or 12,701kg (28,000lb) of freight

BRISTOL BELVEDERE

The Bristol Belvedere was the first tandem-rotor helicopter developed in the UK, and 26 helicopters of this type were operated by the RAF with indifferent success between 1961 and 1969, supporting SAS operations in Aden and Borneo.

Type: Westland Belvedere HC.Mk 1 two-crew short-range tactical helicopter

Powerplant: two Napier Gazelle NGa.2 turboshaft engines each rated at 969kW (1300hp)

Dimensions: rotor diameter, each 14.83m (48ft 8in); length 16.56m (54ft 4in); height 5.26m (17ft 3in)

Weight: empty 5167kg (11,390lb); maximum take-off 8618kg (19,000lb)

Performance: maximum speed 222km/h (138mph) at optimum altitude; range 121km (75 miles) with maximum payload; service ceiling 5275m (17,300ft)

Armament: none

Payload: up to 18 troops, or 2722kg (6000lb) of freight

WESTLAND DRAGONFLY

The Westland Dragonfly was the British-built version of the American Sikorsky S-51. Of the pod-and-boom design, with a three-blade main rotor and fixed tricycle landing gear, the Dragonfly offered limited capabilities, but supported SAS operations in Malaya during the 1950s with supply and casualty evacuation facilities.

Type: Westland Dragonfly HC.Mk 4 one-crew utility helicopter

Powerplant: one Alvis Leonides 50 radial piston engine rated at 410kW (550hp)

Dimensions: main rotor diameter 14.94m (49ft); length 12.50m (41ft); height 3.94m (12ft 11in)

Weight: empty 1726kg (3805lb); maximum take-off 2495kg (5500lb)

Performance: maximum speed 166km/h (103mph) at sea level; range not known; service ceiling 4115m (13,500ft)

Armament: none

Payload: up to three passengers, or two litters, or freight

WESTLAND LYNX

The Westland Lynx was designed in the 1960s in two versions. The land-based model had twin-skid landing gear, and the naval model had fixed tricycle landing gear, together with different electronic and armament fits. It first flew in March 1971 and entered service in 1977. Since that time the type has been built in substantial numbers, and the baseline Lynx AH.Mk 2 for the British Army has been upgraded in several forms. The SAS has used the Lynx AH.Mk 7 for operations in Northern Ireland.

Type: Westland Lynx AH.Mk 7 two-crew multi-role light helicopter

Powerplant: two Rolls-Royce Gem 42-1 turboshaft engines each rated at 835kW (1120hp)

Dimensions: main rotor diameter 12.80m (42ft); length 15.165m (49ft 9in); height 3.505m (11ft 6in)

Weight: empty 2787kg (6144lb); maximum take-off 4536kg (10,000lb)

Performance: maximum speed 259km/h (161mph) at sea level; range 630km (392 miles); service ceiling not available

Armament: several types of trainable and fixed guns can be carried in cabin doors and on the sides of the fuselage, and a wide assortment of disposable stores can be carried on optional outriggers

Payload: up to 10 troops or paratroops; or six litters plus one attendant; or 907kg (2000lb) of freight

WESTLAND SCOUT

The Westland Scout was the first turbo-shaft-powered helicopter to enter British Army service, and had twin-skid landing gear as the land-based counterpart of the Wasp naval helicopter, which had quadri-cycle landing gear. The type entered service in 1963, and was used for SAS purposes in Aden, Borneo and the Falklands.

Type: Westland Scout AH.Mk 1 two-crew utility light helicopter

Powerplant: one Rolls-Royce Nimbus 102 turboshaft engine rated at 511kW (685hp)

Dimensions: main rotor diameter 9.83m (32ft 3in); length 12.29m (40ft 4in); height 2.72m (8ft 11in)

Weight: empty 1466kg (3232lb); maximum take-off 2404kg (5300lb)

Performance: maximum speed 211km/h (131mph) at sea level; range 505km (314 miles); service ceiling 4085m (13,400ft)

Armament: provision for machine guns, rocket launcher pods and light air-to-surface missiles

Payload: up to three passengers, or four litters (two external), or freight

WESTLAND SEA KING

The Westland Sea King is the British licence-built development of the Sikorsky S-61 that serves the US forces as the H-3 series. It was initially developed for service with the Fleet Air Arm in the anti-submarine role, but has since evolved into airborne early warning, search-and-rescue, land-based tactical transport, and sea-based tactical transport forms. The Sea King HC.Mk 4 (used as marine transport) retains the amphibious capability and folding rotors of the naval variants, with the fixed tailwheel landing gear of the Commando land-based derivative. The Sea King has been extensively used by the SAS, especially in the Falklands War.

Type: Westland Sea King HC.Mk 4 two/three-crew tactical transport helicopter

Powerplant: two Rolls-Royce Gnome H.1400-1 turboshaft engines each rated at 1238kW (1660hp)

Dimensions: main rotor diameter 18.90m (62ft); length 22.15m (72ft 8in); height 4.72m (15ft 6in)

Left: The Sea King is one of the finest tactical transport helicopters in service. It was used by the SAS in the Falklands.

Weight: empty 6201kg (13,672lb); maximum take-off 9525kg (21,000lb)
Performance: maximum speed 208km/h (129mph); range 1230km (764 miles); service ceiling 1220m (4000ft) on one engine
Armament: generally none, although provision was made for pintle-mounted machine guns and/or rocket launcher pods
Payload: up to 28 troops, or 3629kg (8000lb) of freight

WESTLAND SYCAMORE

In 1951, the Westland Sycamore was the first practical helicopter of British design to enter service with the RAF. It remained in use until the mid-1970s, and supported SAS operations in Borneo, Malaya and Oman.
Type: Westland Sycamore HC.Mk 14 two-crew utility light helicopter
Powerplant: one Alvis Leonides 73 radial piston engine rated at 410kW (510hp)
Dimensions: main rotor diameter 14.81m (48ft 7in); length 14.07m (46ft 2in) with rotors folded; height 3.71m (12ft 2in)
Weight: empty 1728kg (3810lb); maximum take-off 2540kg (5600lb)
Performance: maximum speed 204km/h (127mph) at sea level; range 510km (317 miles); service ceiling not available
Armament: generally none, although

some helicopters were fitted with a 7.62mm Bren light machine gun in one door
Payload: up to three passengers, or two litters, or freight

WESTLAND WESSEX

The Westland Wessex was the British licence-built development of the Sikorsky S-58 that served the US forces as the HSS, HUS and CH-34. The Wessex had a turboshaft powerplant in place of the baseline American model's piston engine. The type was developed through a number of forms, but the models most frequently associated with SAS operations were the Wessex HAS.Mk 1, which was operated in stripped-out transport form in the Borneo campaign. The better equipped Wessex HAS.Mk 3 and Wessex HU.Mk 5 both had a powerplant of two Rolls-Royce Gnome 110/111 turboshafts, and were used in the Falklands War and for operations in Northern Ireland.
Type: Westland Wessex HAS.Mk 1 one/three-crew anti-submarine and tactical transport helicopter
Powerplant: one Napier Gazelle NGa.13 Mk 161 turboshaft engine rated at 1081kW (1450hp)
Dimensions: main rotor diameter 17.07m (56ft); length 20.04m (65ft 9in); height 4.93m (16ft 2in)
Weight: empty 3447kg (7600lb); maximum take-off 5715kg (12,600lb)
Performance: maximum speed

Above: First used by the SAS during its Borneo campaign in the 1960s, the Westland Wessex is still in RAF service.

212km/h (132mph) at sea level; range 628km (390 miles); service ceiling 4300m (14,100ft)
Armament: generally none, but provision was made for machine guns as well as rocket launcher pods
Payload: up to 16 troops; or eight litters; or 1814kg (4000lb) of freight

WESTLAND WHIRLWIND

The Westland Whirlwind was the British licence-built development of the Sikorsky S-55 that served the US forces. The type was used to support the SAS in the Malaya and Borneo campaigns, generally in the re-supply and evacuation roles.
Type: Westland Whirlwind HC.Mk 10 three-crew tactical light helicopter
Powerplant: one Bristol Siddeley (later Rolls-Royce) Gnome H.1000 turboshaft engine rated at 783kW (1050hp)
Dimensions: main rotor diameter 16.15m (53ft); length 19m (62ft 4in); height 4.76m (15ft 7.5in)
Weight: empty not available; maximum take-off 3629kg (8000lb)
Performance: maximum speed 140km/h (104mph) at optimum altitude; range not available; service ceiling 4815m (15,800ft)
Armament: generally none
Payload: up to eight troops, or freight

CLOTHING

The right clothing is essential to the success of special forces operations. Because the SAS is trained to fight in any terrain in the world, it requires a wide variety of clothing and personal equipment to equip its 'Sabre' Squadrons.

Although it is not as 'glamorous' as other items of his equipment, the importance of using clothing and equipment best suited to the campaign is fully recognised by every SAS trooper. Numerous experiences have confirmed that the success of any mission, at any level, can suffer or even fail from the lack of the right clothing and personal equipment. The SAS knows it is likely to undertake demanding missions in areas of geographic and climatic extremes, and accordingly places very great importance on the selection of the right clothing and personal equipment for each mission. At the time of its creation in 1941, the SAS wore standard British Army clothing or variations of this, and also used standard personal equipment, but from its revival after the end of the war has become increasingly free to select what it deems best. While this is often standard British Army kit, sometimes it is not.

This section cannot hope to list all the types of clothing and personal equipment ever used by the SAS, and instead con-centrates on the kit currently used by the SAS for operations in the geographical and climatic regions in which it works.

The three main dangers faced by any special forces trooper on active duty are the threat posed by the enemy, disease and injury, and the dangers posed by the environment in which he is operating. The last type of threat is divided into two sub-categories: 'thermal insult' in the forms of extremes of temperature, and 'nutritional insults' in the form of lack or toxicity of food and water. SAS training teaches that there are three 'containers' in which a soldier can carry the equipment that defends against these threats. Firstly, there is himself: items are carried in the seams and pockets of smocks, but not of the trousers, as this inhibits movement. Secondly, there is the belt kit, which is an important carrying tool (braces are essential so that in hot weather the trooper can take off his belt and hang it, together with the equipment attached to it, over his shoulders rather than having to have it tight round his waist). Thirdly, there is the bergen (back-carried rucksack) for the carriage of large loads.

ARCTIC CLOTHING

The snow and ice of polar regions offer two main threats: extreme cold and harsh winds. The 'windchill' factor drives air temperature down: a 32km/hr (20mph) wind will reduce a temperature of -14 degrees C (7 degrees F) down to -34 degrees C (-30 degrees F), which can freeze exposed flesh in 30 seconds. The primary task of the clothing worn by the SAS trooper in Arctic conditions is therefore to provide protection against the effects of cold and wind. This protection is best afforded by wearing multiple layers of clothing, rather than thick weighty items. Loose-fitting clothes worn in layers promotes a free circulation of the blood, and this helps to prevent frostbite, which is the freezing of body parts exposed to temperatures below freezing point.

Arctic conditions demand the protection of the whole body, including the feet, hands and face. The keys to survival in extreme Arctic conditions are the cleanliness of the clothing, as dirt and grease block air spaces and thus reduce ventilation, the avoidance of over-exertion – sweat can freeze more rapidly than it can evaporate – the looseness of the clothing to promote a free circulation of air, and the avoidance of moisture on the interior or the exterior of the clothing.

Next to the skin, the trooper wears green cotton 'long johns'. These are tight from the ankle to the knee, and baggy from the knee to the groin so that a layer of insulating air is trapped. Over the upper part of the body he wears a high-

Left: For an SAS four-man patrol, clothing on operations must provide protection against the cold, wet and high winds.

Right: In polar regions all troopers wear a white nylon cover over all their clothing and bergen to aid camouflage.

Right: In polar regions all troopers wear a white nylon cover over all their clothing and bergen to aid camouflage.

necked cotton vest with long sleeves and elasticated wrists to trap the air and thus prevent heat loss.

The task of keeping the feet both warm and dry is particularly difficult in Arctic conditions. Troopers generally wear two pairs of mountaineering socks: a woollen pair is worn next to the skin (sweat builds up inside a waterproof boot, and cotton is significantly worse than wool as it absorbs moisture more readily and the foot becomes colder). Worn over the socks are seals of Gore-tex, which is a breathable material that allows the exit but not the entry of moisture. Over the Gore-tex seals are drawn the boots, which are typically of the Berghaus mountain type. These boots are preferred because they have an outside cleat that allows the use of Gore-tex gaiters if desired. Any boot used by an SAS trooper must also be capable of carrying a ski and snow shoe.

The trousers of the SAS trooper are the Royal Marine cotton DPM (Disruptive Pattern Material) trousers, as these have a Velcro-closed slash between the ankle and the knee to allow a quick change, and also have Velcro-closed pockets and large buttons, the latter designed for ease of use by gloved fingers.

In general, the SAS trooper in Arctic conditions wears a Gore-tex smock with a hood for head protection instead of a shirt. When a patrol is moving slowly or has stopped, a 'fitzroy' jacket is worn under the smock, and white light nylon trousers, smock and bergen cover are worn over the whole kit.

Gloves are absolutely essential to prevent the loss of fingers to frostbite. The options here are the standard-issue Northern Ireland glove or commercial ski gloves, even though these present some problems with weapon firing because of the thickness of the fingers, or superimposed pairs of thin cotton gloves under white nylon gloves. Some troopers like to wear a pair of mittens over their gloves, although they must be prepared to rip off the right mitten if they have to fire their weapon. Some men attach the mitten to

the torso with a length of tape that allows it to be yanked off very rapidly.

The two types of headgear most frequently used by SAS troopers in Arctic conditions are a woolly hat and a balaclava, the latter being less popular as it muffles the wearer's hearing. Face masks are also standard, especially at night, and are of two-layer construction with silk next to the skin under an outer layer of cotton. Snow blindness is also a problem in Arctic conditions, and tinted goggles are therefore standard. These goggles are the same as those worn in the desert, but are camouflaged with white tape. Finally, the worst effects of sunburn are mitigated by the liberal application of sunblock or chapstick to all exposed areas of the face, especially the lips, nose, and eyelids.

DESERT CLOTHING

For desert operations the SAS has generally worn two types of footwear, although is should be noted that during the Oman campaign of the 1970s individual members of the Regiment tended to purchase commercial footwear. The first of the standard types is the ankle-length desert boot, which is comfortable but has a marked tendency to split along the seams. The second, and that currently preferred by the Regiment, is the high-neck desert boot. Socks are never worn with such

footwear as they help the foot to sweat, and also rot very quickly in these conditions. It is not uncommon for troopers to wrap their feet in masking tape before pulling on their boots. It is also worth noting that sandals, which might be considered most suitable for desert operations as they are loose and therefore allow the feet to breathe, are never worn as they leave the upper part of the feet liable to sunburn, and open to biting insects or, more seriously, those that burrow beneath the skin to lay their eggs.

The trousers usually worn in the desert are the lightweight cotton desert

Right: Desert clothing must cover the whole body to prevent sunburn, and the wearer also needs protection from sand and dust.

Left: An SAS trooper in Borneo in the 1960s. Note his floppy hat, a favoured item of clothing in the Regiment for jungle missions.

DPM type; nylon is never worn as it becomes extremely hot. The DPM trousers are loose and give the wearer excellent protection against the effects of the sun. Shorts are also worn on occasion, generally during stand-down periods, but are very seldom worn on operations as they expose the legs to sunburn and also promote the wearer's tendency to lose water. Sweat evaporates rapidly from exposed skin, whereas skin covered by loose trousers is surrounded by a body of insulating air that allows any sweat to cool the wearer more efficiently. It is also worth noting that the desert can become very cold at night, and here trousers are better than shorts for the retention of warmth.

The desert shirt is a long-sleeved cotton DPM type, and the reasoning behind this choice is exactly the same as that for the trousers. The cold of desert nights is ameliorated by wearing the desert 'woolly pully' and the 'fitzroy' jacket, the latter being made of green nylon with a hollow-fill stuffing, and generally carried in a stuff sack at the bottom of the bergen. A variety of gloves is also used, the two most popular being US Army pilot's gloves of Nomex, and fingerless mittens.

With sunburn and sunstroke a constant threat in the desert, some form of headgear is vital. Probably the most effective type is the local *shemagh* head cloth, which is often dyed yellow. It traps a layer

of cooler air over the head and provides protection for the neck. The shemagh is also large enough to be used as an improvised shelter if required. Sunglasses are generally avoided in favour of tinted goggles, which are less likely to slip or fall off.

JUNGLE CLOTHING

The tropical regions in which the SAS is trained to operate are characterised by dense jungle, heavy rainfall, extreme humidity and very high temperatures. In these circumstances it might seem sensible for the SAS trooper to wear as little as possible, which is the standard for the local populations. In order to protect themselves from scratches, bites and stings, however, SAS troopers have to wear extensive clothing. The combination of exertion, heat and humidity causes men to sweat and their clothing soon becomes saturated. The impossibility of drying the clothing effectively inevitably causes it to rot.

First-class footwear is essential for jungle operations, for it is the boots that offer the best protection against scorpions, spiders, leeches and centipedes. The type generally used is of rubber and canvas manufacture, often with a metal plate inserted in the sole as protection against sharp (or indeed sharpened) sticks.

Because of the threat of infection from bites and scratches, SAS troopers never

wear shorts in the jungle, but rather long trousers of cotton DPM that are loose, baggy and fitted with a drawcord waist (to allow for the inevitable loss of weight on protracted patrols), cross-overs and button flies. The shirt is also of cotton DPM material, long-sleeved with buttoned cuffs and, like the trousers, baggy.

The favourite headgear for jungle operations is the Hat, DPM, Tropical, which is a floppy item of the 'banana leaf' variety and generally attached to the smock or short with a length of nylon cord. SAS troopers also have a penchant for lengths of olive green veil material worn round the head to prevent sweat running into the eyes, or alternatively worn round the neck to prevent sweat running down over the torso.

TEMPERATE CLOTHING

With a wider range of terrain and climatic possibilities than any of the extremes represented by the desert, Arctic or jungle, the temperate zone presents the SAS trooper with a more difficult choice of clothing options to counter conditions that may include heat, cold, heavy or intermittent rain and wind.

The boot most commonly used is the standard British Army issue type, but some men buy their own. Of the commercial types, the most popular is the Danner boot, which is made of full-grain leather and cordura nylon, with a Goretex lining. The trousers are most frequently the standard British Army DPM windproof tight-weave cotton variety, and the smock is also the standard British Army DPM combat smock that is baggy, big and loose. Some form of headgear is also common, the most popular type being the peaked camouflage combat cap.

Members of the SAS Regiment also operate in civilian clothes on some covert operations on occasion, most notably in Northern Ireland.

Trained to operate for extensive periods behind enemy lines, or alternatively to secure tactical advantages from their ability to move far and fast before engaging in a major firefight, the men of the SAS Regiment have acquired a considerable and thoroughly justified reputation for self-sufficiency in the field. They are also respected for their ability to carry large loads of the equipment and supplies in which they cannot be self-sufficient, most notably ammunition, explosives and communications gear.

BERGENS AND BELTS

The two key items for carrying major loads over long distances are the bergen and the belt, the former being used for basic equipment and supplies, and the latter for emergency items. The bergen is a back-packed rucksack, and while the British Army uses the PLCE (Personal Load-Carrying Equipment) bergen, the SAS prefers either of two commercial external square-frame equipments, the 60-litre (13-gallon) Cyclops and the 80-litre (17.5-gallon) Crusader. However, individual troopers tend to load the bergen with as much as it will accommodate, and its weight then becomes one of the constraints on the trooper's ability to move far and fast over a sustained period.

The order of priority for loading the SAS bergen is ammunition, water, food and clothing. Any spare space is filled by spare radio batteries (patrol signaller), a medical pack (patrol medic), explosives and detonators (patrol demolitions expert), extra machinegun ammunition, Claymore mines, mortar bombs and, only exceptionally, a laser designator.

Rations are an important part of any trooper's load, and men start on patrol with rations for 14 days and the knowledge that two days' food can be squeezed out of a single day's ration allocation if necessary. Most of the food is of the high-energy type, and is packed in plastic containers rather than tin cans to lighten the load and make the packs easier to open. The food, mostly rice and stew-type meals, are pre-cooked so that they only need to be heated, rather than cooked, or may be eaten cold.

The belt is divided into a clear front (as an aid to movement) and a load-carrying rear from hip to hip. On the left are the pouches for spare ammunition magazines, and on the right are a compass pouch, an

escape and evasion pouch, a survival and utility knife, two or three aluminium water bottles and a water filter, a pouch for the 'bivvy bag', a bayonet, and two ammunition pouches.

British combat training for the medical attendant places a higher priority on life support (airways, breathing and circulation) than on trauma management (arterial bleeding, broken bones and burns), and this is reflected in the standard medical kit. It generally includes a paediatric mucus extractor (used to suck debris from a wound), a blood volume expander, infusion fluid, wound and burn dressings, forceps to clip off bleeding arteries, a suture kit and fracture straps. There is also a pharmaceutical pack which includes

Above: Bergens must be big enough to contain all the equipment needed for a long-range patrol behind enemy lines.

antibiotics in tablet and injection forms, pre-packed and pre-dosed counter-NBC injections, pain killers (aspirin and morphine), flamazine cream to prevent infection of burns, and anti-fungal creams.

The survival kit is small, but potentially life-saving, and is therefore carried by all SAS troopers. It contains ready-to-eat emergency rations for two days, vacuum-compressed plastic sheets, a map of the operational area, a compass, a fishing line and weights, snares, nylon cord, flint and steel, a utility knife, marker chemicals, and a pencil.

SAS Organisation

22nd Special Air Service Regiment and the TA units, 21 and 23 SAS, are part of the UK Special Forces Group, which is commanded by the Director of Special Forces, an Army brigadier. A new SAS regiment is in the process of being formed, as is a new intelligence-gathering regiment.

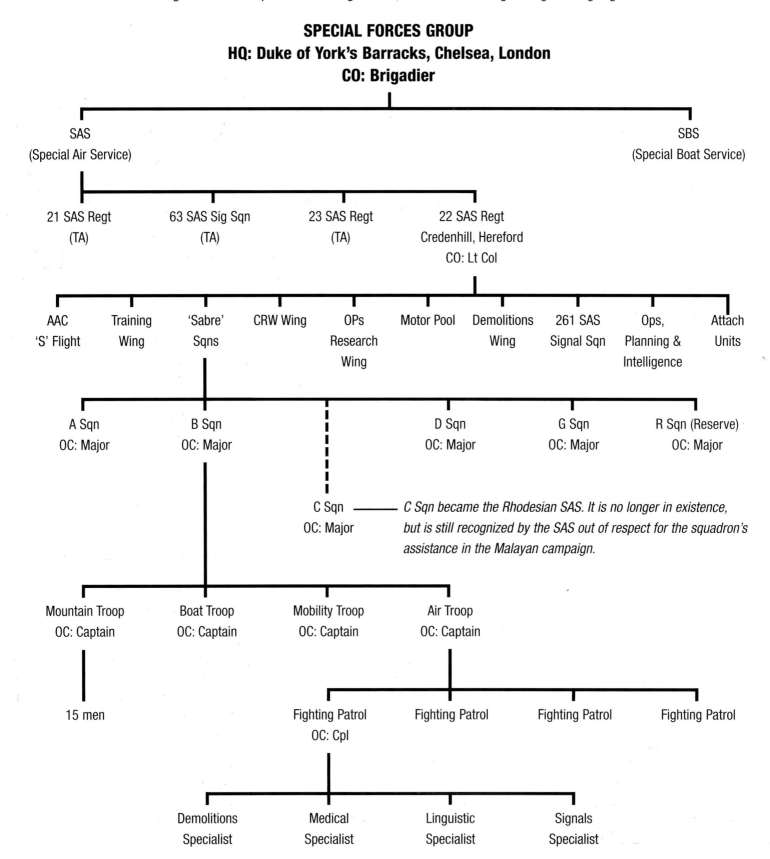

SPECIAL FORCES GROUP
HQ: Duke of York's Barracks, Chelsea, London
CO: Brigadier

SAS
(Special Air Service)

SBS
(Special Boat Service)

21 SAS Regt
(TA)

63 SAS Sig Sqn
(TA)

23 SAS Regt
(TA)

22 SAS Regt
Credenhill, Hereford
CO: Lt Col

AAC
'S' Flight

Training
Wing

'Sabre'
Sqns

CRW Wing

OPs
Research
Wing

Motor Pool

Demolitions
Wing

261 SAS
Signal Sqn

Ops,
Planning &
Intelligence

Attach
Units

A Sqn
OC: Major

B Sqn
OC: Major

D Sqn
OC: Major

G Sqn
OC: Major

R Sqn (Reserve)
OC: Major

C Sqn
OC: Major

C Sqn became the Rhodesian SAS. It is no longer in existence, but is still recognized by the SAS out of respect for the squadron's assistance in the Malayan campaign.

Mountain Troop
OC: Captain

Boat Troop
OC: Captain

Mobility Troop
OC: Captain

Air Troop
OC: Captain

15 men

Fighting Patrol
OC: Cpl

Fighting Patrol

Fighting Patrol

Fighting Patrol

Demolitions
Specialist

Medical
Specialist

Linguistic
Specialist

Signals
Specialist

Badges and Insignia

LIke all other regiments in the British Army, the SAS has its own badges and insignia. Of these, the Winged Dagger badge is probably the most famous military badge in the world, and is also worn by the Australian and New Zealand SAS Regiments.

The SAS feels that as one of the most capable and respected elite units anywhere in the world, it has little need of distinction in the form of special badges and other insignia. The Regiment's rank and specialist badges are therefore the same as the rest of the British Army, and its only distinguishing features are its beret and badge. In fact, these are seldom seen outside the Regiment's barracks at Stirling Lines as concealed identities are essential for the safety of individuals and the success of the regiment as a whole.

BEIGE BERET

The beret is the standard British Army beret, although uniquely it is beige. The SAS's beret was originally white when the unit was first formed in 1941. However, this colour was derided by other units, especially the Australians and New Zealanders, and so it was withdrawn. It was replaced by a khaki forage cap and then a beige beret.

PARACHUTE WINGS

The SAS's parachute ('Sabre') wings were originally designed by Lieutenant 'Jock' Lewes in late 1941. He supposedly got the idea after seeing a fresco of an ibis, a large wading bird with a long curved bill, in an Egyptian hotel. During World War II, those members of the SAS who had made three parachute drops behind enemy lines were allowed to wear the wings over the left breast pocket instead of on the sleeve, which was the standard British military custom at the time. They are now worn on the right shoulder.

REGIMENTAL COLLECT

'O Lord, who didst call on Thy disciples to venture all to win all men to Thee, grant that we, the chosen members of the Special Air Service Regiment, may by our works and our ways, dare all to win all, and in doing so render special service to Thee and our fellow men in all the world. Through the same Jesus Christ, Our Lord, Amen.'

SAS MOTTO

'Who Dares Wins' was reportedly invented by the founder of the SAS, David Stirling, in 1941.

WINGED DAGGER

On the beige beret is worn the famous Winged Dagger badge. This is a black shield, on which is a pale gold dagger with two upswept pale blue feathered wings supported by red centres. The wings extend from the upper part of the

Left: A modelled photograph of the SAS beige beret and Winged Dagger cloth badge worn with standard British Army field dress.

Above: The SAS Winged Dagger badge. The dagger is meant to be the sword Excalibur.

blade, just below the hilt, and lower down the blade is a scrolled black ribbon bearing the motto 'Who Dares Wins' in the same pale blue as the wings. The badge was reportedly the creation of Sergeant Bob Tait, who won a competition for the choice of a badge for the new unit in North Africa at the end of 1941. The dagger is in fact meant to be the sword Excalibur, the symbol of truth and justice. The colours of the wings are Cambridge and Oxford blue, so chosen because in the original L Detachment 'Jock' Lewes had rowed for Oxford and Lieutenant Langton for Cambridge.

The Winged Dagger is also the cap badge of the New Zealand and Australian SAS. In addition, it is worn by members of the Belgian Para-Commando Regiment, though it is sported on a maroon beret, not the khaki of the New Zealanders and Australians.

Selection and Training

Becoming an SAS soldier takes over six months, and requires determination and high levels of intellectual and physical stamina from every student. Most don't make it, which suits the Regiment fine – it wants only the best of the best.

The SAS Regiment accepts for training only those officers and other ranks who have passed a highly rigorous selection procedure. It is designed to weed out the unsuitable, leaving only men with the qualities that the Regiment believes to be essential: physical and mental strength, self-reliance, and the intelligence to work his way through a problem regardless of the situation and conditions in which he finds himself.

The Regiment considers only those men who have volunteered after service

Below: Pen-y-Fan, the highest peak in the Brecon Beacons, which prospective recruits to the SAS must conquer on Selection.

with a regular unit of the British Army. This immediately eliminates civilian volunteers who might think that the SAS offers the sort of 'glamour' previously attached to units such as the French Foreign Legion or even mercenary organisations. As a result of this unalterable rule, the SAS is generally faced with men who are in their mid-twenties, already versed in the basic skills required of the soldier, and still with at least three years and three months of service left from the time they pass Selection Training.

The course is run twice a year, once in summer and once in winter, and each volunteer must wait until he is called upon to fill a vacancy in the programme.

Naturally, any man with the resourcefulness to volunteer for the SAS appreciates the realities of the physical and mental task ahead, and is likely to spend as much time as possible in preparing his body and mind before he is summoned to the training programme.

SELECTION TRAINING

The Selection Training programme, which lasts for one month, is run by the Training Wing of 22 SAS at Hereford, and is based on the programme designed in 1953. It starts with a build-up period (two weeks for officers and three weeks for other ranks), for although each volunteer must have been certified as fit by his own

Above: Selection Training is all about mental and physical stamina. The SAS is looking for men who can think even when exhausted.

regimental medical officer, the SAS feels that it is only sensible and fair to give each man a chance to come up to the Regiment's physical requirements. During the first week, therefore, volunteers start with a series of road runs that increase in length over the week. Each volunteer must be capable of passing the standard Battle Fitness Test in the time allotted for infantrymen and paratroops, but this is seen by the SAS as a minimum. As the Selection Training programme continues, the volunteers are sent on a number of strenuous cross-country marches over the Black Mountains and the Brecon Beacons of South Wales. The object is not only to assess their physical condition and resilience, but also to prove their capabilities in map reading and navigation. At this stage in the programme, the men are divided from their original pairs and are individually assigned marching and map reading tasks, with bergen packs steadily increased in weight from 11 to 25kg (24 to 55lb). These tasks must be completed within time limits which are unknown to the volunteers.

At the end of their two- or three-week build-up period, many of the volunteers have dropped out, some at their initiative and others through rejection by the selectors. Thus it is only a smaller number who embark on the final stage, known as Test Week. This is an intensive weeks of tests and assessments culminating in the 'Long Drag' or 'Fan Dance', which is a 60km (37-mile) land navigation exercise over the highest points in the Brecon Beacons. It must be completed in 20 hours no matter what the weather conditions may be – and these conditions may be appalling even in the summer. Once he has successfully completed the 'Fan Dance', the would-be SAS trooper has passed Selection, he will be one of five or six out of every hundred.

CONTINUATION TRAINING

The next hurdle, Continuation Training, which lasts 14 weeks and is designed to teach recruits basic SAS skills. The skills are those required for any new troops to be integrated successfully into a four-man patrol (the smallest of the SAS's operational units). These Standard Operating Procedures (SOPs) include movement through hostile territory, the arcs of fire of each patrol member, and contact drills. Each student also receives training in the art of signalling, which is vital to the task of four-man patrols. All students must achieve the British Army's Regimental

Signaller standard, which includes the ability to send and receive Morse code at the minimum rate of eight words per minute. Other elements of this preliminary stage of training include field medicine and basic demolition skills.

With these fundamental abilities taken on board, the student moves forward to the Combat and Survival Training programme for instruction in every aspect of survival in a hostile environment (shelter building, the finding of food and water, laying traps and making fire). The training ends with an Escape and Evasion exercise, in which the prospective trooper has to avoid capture by an 'enemy' (generally a battalion of locally based infantry). At the end of the exercise every man still at liberty must 'surrender' himself for transfer to an interrogation centre for a 24-hour 'Resistance to Interrogation' exercise. In this he is subjected to a wide range of mental stresses designed to make men yield information. This is a particularly difficult part of the would-be trooper's training, and any man that fails the test is rejected.

Survivors to this stage next undergo Jungle training, which lasts between four and six weeks and is undertaken in the Far East (typically Brunei), the object being to teach the student basic jungle survival capabilities such as the construction of a shelter, the finding of food and water, and navigation in the jungle. The course ends with an exercise that must be successfully completed if the student is to go forward to parachute training at No.1 Parachute Training School at RAF Brize Norton in Oxfordshire.

The static-line training course lasts four weeks. All students must make a total of eight jumps, including one at night, though those recruits who are already parachute trained are excused the course.

It is only at the successful completion of this stage that the student is awarded his 'Sabre' wings and, on return to Hereford, is finally accepted as a 'badged' member of the SAS. His training, though, is only just beginning. He goes on to receive intensive training in both patrol and troop skills. Furthermore, all SAS troopers are rotated through counter-terrorist training at Stirling Lines.

SAS Operations: World War II to the present

1941

Sirte airfield
Date: 8 December 1941
Unit: L Detachment
Commander: Captain Stirling
Location: North Africa
Objective: to destroy Axis aircraft
Outcome: unsuccessful

Tamit airfield
Date: 12 December 1941
Unit: L Detachment
Commander: Captain Mayne
Location: North Africa
Objective: to destroy Axis aircraft
Outcome: 24 aircraft destroyed

Agheila airfield
Date: 14 December 1941
Unit: L Detachment
Commander: Lieutenant 'Jock' Lewes
Location: Gulf of Sirte, North Africa
Objective: to destroy Axis aircraft
Outcome: no aircraft at airfield; some Italian vehicles destroyed

Agedabia airfield
Date: 21 December 1941
Unit: L Detachment
Commander: Lieutenant Fraser
Location: Cyrenaica, North Africa
Objective: to destroy Axis aircraft
Outcome: 37 Italian CR44 fighter-bombers destroyed

Marble Arch airfield
Date: 24 December 1941
Unit: L Detachment
Commander: Major Fraser
Location: Tripolitania, North Africa
Objective: to destroy Axis aircraft
Outcome: no aircraft at airfield

Tamit airfield
Date: 24 December 1941
Unit: L Detachment
Commander: Captain Mayne
Location: North Africa
Objective: to destroy Axis aircraft
Outcome: 27 aircraft destroyed

Sirte airfield
Date: 25 December 1941
Unit: L Detachment
Commander: Captain Stirling
Location: North Africa
Objective: to destroy Axis aircraft
Outcome: unsuccessful

Nofilia airfield
Date: 26 December 1941
Unit: L Detachment
Commander: Lieutenant Lewes
Location: Gulf of Sirte, North Africa
Objective: to destroy Axis aircraft
Outcome: only two aircraft destroyed

1942

Bouerat
Date: 23 January 1942
Unit: L Detachment and Special Boat Section
Commander: Captain Stirling
Location: port on North African coast
Objective: to blow up shipping in the harbour
Outcome: no shipping in harbour, several warehouses and petrol tankers destroyed

Barce airfield
Date: 8 March 1942
Unit: L Detachment
Commander: Major Fraser
Location: Gulf of Sirte, North Africa
Objective: to destroy Axis aircraft
Outcome: only one aircraft and several trucks knocked out

Benina airfield
Date: 8 March 1942
Unit: L Detachment
Commander: Captain Stirling
Location: Gulf of Sirte, North Africa
Objective: to destroy Axis aircraft
Outcome: no aircraft present

Berka airfield
Date: 8 March 1942
Unit: L Detachment
Commander: Captain Mayne

Location: outskirts of Benghazi, North Africa
Objective: to destroy Axis aircraft
Outcome: 15 aircraft destroyed

Benghazi
Date: mid-March 1942
Unit: L Detachment
Commander: Captain Stirling
Location: North African coast
Objective: to destroy Axis shipping in the harbour
Outcome: SAS canoe damaged, mission aborted

Benina airfield
Date: 25 March 1942
Unit: L Detachment
Commander: Captain Stirling
Location: Gulf of Sirte, North Africa
Objective: to destroy Axis aircraft
Outcome: five aircraft destroyed

Benghazi
Date: 21 May 1942
Unit: L Detachment
Commander: Captain Stirling
Location: North African coast
Objective: to destroy Axis shipping in the harbour
Outcome: dinghies damaged, mission aborted

Benina airfield
Date: 13 June 1942
Unit: L Detachment
Commander: Major Stirling
Location: Gulf of Sirte, North Africa
Objective: to destroy Axis aircraft
Outcome: two aircraft and several workshops destroyed

Berka airfield
Date: 13 June 1942
Unit: L Detachment
Commander: Lieutenant Zirnheld
Location: outskirts of Benghazi, North Africa
Objective: to destroy Axis aircraft
Outcome: 11 aircraft destroyed

Derna airfield
Date: 13 June 1942
Unit: L Detachment
Commander: Captain Buck
Location: Cyrenaica, North Africa
Objective: to destroy Axis aircraft
Outcome: party betrayed before it reached the airfield

Martuba airfield
Date: 13 June 1942
Unit: L Detachment
Commander: Captain Tourneret
Location: North Africa
Objective: to destroy Axis aircraft
Outcome: unsuccessful

Bagoush airfield
Date: 7 July 1942
Unit: L Detachment
Commander: Major Stirling
Location: North African coast
Objective: to destroy Axis aircraft
Outcome: 37 aircraft destroyed

El Daba airfield
Date: 7 July 1942
Unit: L Detachment
Commander: Captain Jellicoe
Location: North Africa
Objective: to destroy Axis aircraft
Outcome: failed to breach airfield defences; a number of trucks destroyed

Fuka airfield
Date: 7 July 1942
Unit: L Detachment
Commander: Captain Mayne
Location: North Africa
Objective: to destroy Axis aircraft
Outcome: 14 aircraft destroyed

El Daba airfield
Date: 11 July 1942
Unit: L Detachment
Commander: Captain Jellicoe
Location: North Africa
Objective: to destroy Axis aircraft
Outcome: unsuccessful

Fuka airfield
Date: 12 July 1942
Unit: l Detachment
Commander: Major Stirling
Location: North Africa

Objective: to destroy Axis aircraft
Outcome: 22 aircraft destroyed

Sidi Barrani airfield
Date: 12 July
Unit: L Detachment
Commander: Captains Warr and Schott
Location: North Africa
Objective: to destroy Axis aircraft
Outcome: unsuccessful

Bagoush airfield
Date: 26 July 1942
Unit: L Detachment
Commander: unknown
Location: North African coast
Objective: to destroy Axis aircraft
Outcome: unsuccessful

Sidi Haneish airfield
Date: 26 July 1942
Unit: L Detachment
Commander: Major Stirling
Location: North Africa
Objective: to destroy Axis aircraft
Outcome: 40 aircraft destroyed

Benghazi
Date: 13 September 1942
Unit: L Detachment
Commander: Major Stirling
Location: North African coast
Objective: to destroy Axis shipping in the harbour
Outcome: SAS column shot up before reaching port

1943

Operation 'Snapdragon'
Date: 28 May 1943
Unit: 2 SAS
Commander: unknown
Location: island of Pantelleria
Objective: reconnaissance
Outcome: unsuccessful

Operation 'Marigold'
Date: 30 May 1943
Unit: 2 SAS (eight SAS men plus three SBS men)
Commander: Captain Dudgeon
Location: Sardinia
Objective: to snatch a prisoner for intelligence purposes

Outcome: unsuccessful

Operation 'Narcissus'
Date: 10 July 1943
Unit: 2 SAS (40 men)
Commander: Major Scratchley
Location: southeast Sicily
Objective: to seize an enemy battery to support Allied landings
Outcome: successful (though no guns were present)

Operation 'Chestnut'
Date: 12 July 1943
Unit: 2 SAS
Commander: Captain Pinckney and Captain Bridgeman-Evans
Location: northern Sicily
Objective: to disrupt enemy communications while Allies invaded the island
Outcome: parties widely scattered, unsuccessful overall

Operation 'Baytown'
Date: 3 September 1943
Unit: Special Raiding Squadron (1 SAS temporarily renamed)
Commander: Lieutenant-Colonel Mayne
Location: Bagnara, southern Italy
Objective: to disrupt German communications in southern Italy
Outcome: Bagnara was captured, though enemy remained in immediate area

Operation 'Speedwell'
Date: 7 September–mid-November 1943
Unit: 2 SAS (14 men)
Commander: Captains Pinckney and Dudgeon
Location: Spezia/Genoa, northern Italy
Objective: to cut railway lines
Outcome: successful

Operation 'Begonia'
Date: 2–6 October 1943
Unit: 2 SAS (61 men)
Commander: Lieutenant McGregor
Location: between Ancona and Pescara, eastern Italy
Objective: to collect escaped Allied POWs
Outcome: because of poor planning only 50 POWs were rescued

Operation 'Devon'
Date: 3 October–5 October 1943
Unit: Special Raiding Squadron
Commander: Lieutenant-Colonel Mayne
Location: Italy's Adriatic coast
Objective: to capture Termoli to help
    British Army break the Termoli line
Outcome: port taken, though only after
    sustained enemy resistance

Operation 'Jonquil'
Date: 2–12 October 1943
Unit: 2 SAS
Commander: unknown
Location: between Ancona and Pescara,
    eastern Italy
Objective: to round up large numbers of
    freed POWs
Outcome: complete disaster

Operation 'Candytuft'
Date: 27 October–2 November 1943
Unit: 2 SAS
Commander: Major Farran
Location: east coast of Italy
Objective: to cut railway lines between
    Ancona and Pescara
Outcome: railway severed and roads mined

Operation 'Saxifrage'
Date: 27 October–1 November 1943
Unit: 2 SAS
Commander: Major Farran
Location: between Ancona and Pescara,
    eastern Italy
Objective: to sever local railway line
Outcome: railway cut in several places

Operation 'Sleepy Lad'
Date: 18 December 1943
Unit: 2 SAS
Commander: Major Scratchley
Location: Italian east coast
Objective: to disrupt German road and
    road communications between
    Ancona and Pescara
Outcome: much damage inflicted

1944

Operation 'Maple'
Date: 7 January 1944
Unit: 2 SAS
Commander: unknown
Location: Italian east coast

Objective: to cut rail communications on
    Italian east coast
Outcome: railways attacked successfully,
    though many SAS men captured

Operation 'Pomegranate'
Date: 12–17 January 1944
Unit: 2 SAS (six men)
Commander: Major Widdrington
Location: San Egidio airfield, Italy
Objective: to destroy Axis aircraft
Outcome: seven aircraft destroyed

Operation 'Baobab'
Date: 30 January 1944
Unit: 2 SAS
Commander: Lieutenant Laws
Location: between Pesaro and Fano,
    eastern Italy
Objective: to support Anzio landings by
    severing strategic railway line
Outcome: vital bridge destroyed

Operation 'Bulbasket'
Date: 6 June–10 August 1944
Unit: 1 SAS and a Phantom patrol
    (56 men)
Commander: Captain Tonkin
Location: Vienne area, southern France
Objective: to disrupt enemy movements
towards Normandy beachhead
Outcome: limited successes, Germans
    very active

Operation 'Dingson'
Date: 6–18 June 1944
Unit: 4 SAS (160 men)
Commander: Commandant Bourgoin
Location: Vannes, Brittany
Objective: to organise *Maquis* and interfere
    with enemy movements
Outcome: limited success

Operation 'Houndsworth'
Date: 6 June–6 September 1944
Unit: 1 SAS (144 men)
Commander: Major Fraser
Location: west of Dijon, France
Objective: sever railway lines and disrupt
    enemy communications
Outcome: railway lines cut and 220
    Germans killed or wounded

Operation 'Samwest'
Date: 6–9 June 1944
Unit: 4 SAS (116 men)
Commander: Captain El Blond
Location: northern Brittany, France
Objective: to prevent German forces
    moving towards the Normandy
    beachhead
Outcome: party scattered owing to poor
    Maquis security

Operation 'Titanic'
Date: 6 June–10 July 1944
Unit: 1 SAS (six men)
Commander: Lieutenants Poole
    and Fowles
Location: south of Carentan, France
Objective: to fool the Germans into
    believing a full-scale drop was
    taking place
Outcome: unsuccessful

Operation 'Cooney'
Date: 7 June 1944
Unit: 4 SAS (54 men)
Commander: unknown
Location: Brittany, France
Objective: to sever railway lines
Outcome: a number of railway lines cut

Operation 'Gain'
Date: 7 June–15 August 1944
Unit: 1 SAS
Commander: Major Fenwick
Location: southwest of Paris, France
Objective: severing railway lines and
    enemy lines of communications
Outcome: railway lines cut on many
    occasions

Operation 'Lost'
Date: 23 June–18 July 1944
Unit: 4 SAS (eight men)
Commander: Major Elwes
Location: Brittany, France
Objective: to establish contact with
    'Dingson' party
Outcome: very successful; large-scale
    damage inflicted on the enemy

Operation 'Haft'
Date: 8 July–11 August 1944
Unit: 1 SAS (seven men)
Commander: unknown
Location: Le Mans, northwest France

Objective: to collect intelligence and establish contact with *Maquis*
Outcome: useful intelligence gathered

Operation 'Dickens'

Date: 16 July-7 October 1944
Unit: 3 SAS (65 men)
Commander: Captain Fournier
Location: Nantes/Saumur, western France
Objective: to sever railway lines and gather intelligence
Outcome: good; railways cut, 500 enemy killed and 200 vehicles destroyed

Operation 'Defoe'

Date: 19 July-23 August 1944
Unit: 2 SAS (22 men)
Commander: Captain McGibbon-Lewis
Location: Argentan, Normandy
Objective: reconnaissance
Outcome: unsuccessful

Operation 'Rupert'

Date: 23 July-10 September 1944
Unit: 2 SAS (58 men)
Commander: Major Symes
Location: Metz area, eastern France
Objective: to cut as many railway lines as possible
Outcome: unsuccessful

Operation 'Gaff'

Date: 25 July-15 August 1944
Unit: 2 SAS (seven men)
Commander: Captain Lee
Location: Rambouillet, southwest of Paris
Objective: to kill Field Marshal Rommel
Outcome: unsuccessful

Operation 'Hardy'

Date: 27 July-1 September 1944
Unit: 2 SAS (56 men)
Commander: Captain Hibbert
Location: northwest of Dijon, France
Objective: gather intelligence
Outcome: intelligence gathered and enemy attacked

Operation 'Chaucer'

Date: 28 July-15 August 1944
Unit: 5 SAS (22 men)
Commander: Captain Hazel
Location: Le mans, northwest France
Objective: to harry retreating Germans
Outcome: party dropped too late

Operation 'Shakespeare'

Date: 31 July-15 August 1944
Unit: 5 SAS (23 men)
Commander: Lieutenants Debefre and Limbosen
Location: northwest of Le Mans, France
Objective: to harry retreating Germans
Outcome: harried Germans and helped rescue 150 downed Allied airmen

Operation 'Bunyan'

Date: 3-15 August 1944
Unit: 5 SAS (22 men)
Commander: Lieutenant Kirschen
Location: Chartres, west of Paris
Objective: to harry retreating enemy forces
Outcome: damage inflicted and intelligence collected

Operation 'Dunhill'

Date: 3-24 August 1944
Unit: 2 SAS (59 men)
Commander: Captain Bell
Location: eastern Brittany, France
Objective: collect intelligence
Outcome: US breakout overran the SAS soldiers and they were withdrawn

Operation 'Moses'

Date: 3 August-5 October 1944
Unit: 3 SAS (48 men)
Commander: Captain Simon
Location: around Poitiers, southwest France
Objective: disrupting enemy communications
Outcome: much damage inflicted on the enemy

Operation 'Derry'

Date: 5-18 August 1944
Unit: 3 SAS
Commander: Captain Conan
Location: Finisterre, Brittany
Objective: to hinder enemy movements and stop destruction of two viaducts
Outcome: both objectives achieved

Operation 'Haggard'

Date: 10 August-23 September 1944
Unit: 1 SAS (53 men), reinforced later by troop from 3 SAS
Commander: Major Lepine
Location: between Nevers and Gien, France

Objective: harry retreating Germans and sever their lines of communication
Outcome: a few targets attacked, but overrun by advancing Allied forces

Operation 'Samson'

Date: 10 August-27 September 1944
Unit: 3 SAS (24 men)
Commander: Captain Le Blond
Location: west of Limoges, southern France
Objective: to disrupt road traffic and bolster local *Maquis*
Outcome: moderately successful; 100 Germans killed

Operation 'Marshall'

Date: 11-24 August 1944
Unit: 3 SAS (32 men)
Commander: Captain Wauthier
Location: Correze, southern France
Objective: to raid enemy units and stiffen *Maquis*
Outcome: very successful

Operation 'Loyton'

Date: 12 August-9 October 1944
Unit: 2 SAS (91 men)
Commander: Lieutenant-Colonel Franks
Location: Vosges, eastern France
Objective: gather intelligence and attack enemy
Outcome: limited; large number of German troops in area

Operation 'Barker'

Date: 13 August-19 September 1944
Unit: 3 SAS (27 men)
Commander: Lieutenant Rouhan
Location: Saone-et-Loire, central France
Objective: to disrupt enemy movements and support the *Maquis*
Outcome: inflicted large-scale damage, including 3000 enemy casualties

Operation 'Harrod'

Date: 13 August-24 September 1944
Unit: 3 SAS (86 men)
Commander: Commandant Conan
Location: Saone et Loire, central France
Objective: disrupt enemy movements and bolster *Maquis*
Outcome: enemy targets destroyed; very successful

Operation 'Kipling'
Date: 13 August-26 September 1944
Unit: 1 SAS (107 men)
Commander: Major Marsh
Location: west of Auxerre, central France
Objective: to aid Allied airborne landings in the Orleans Gap
Outcome: caused many enemy casualties, and assisted in surrender of 3000 German troops

Operation 'Snelgrove'
Date: 13-24 August 1944
Unit: 3 SAS (28 men)
Commander: Lieutenant Hubler
Location: around Creuse, eastern France
Objective: to disrupt enemy movements and bolster *Maquis*
Outcome: successful

Operation 'Jockworth'
Date: 15 August-9 September 1944
Unit: 3 SAS (58 men)
Commander: Captain Hourst
Location: southeast France
Objective: disrupt enemy movements and organise *Maquis*
Outcome: major damage inflicted on the Germans

Operation 'Noah'
Date: 16 August-13 September 1944
Unit: 5 SAS (42 men)
Commander: Captain Blondeel
Location: French Ardennes
Objective: to gather intelligence
Outcome: very successful; additional damage inflicted on enemy

Operation 'Trueform'
Date: 17-26 August 1944
Unit: 1, 2 and 5 SAS (102 men)
Commander: Lieutenant-Colonel Franks
Location: northwest of Paris, France
Objective: to harry retreating Germans
Outcome: partly successful

Operation 'Newton'
Date: 19 August-11 September 1944
Unit: 3 SAS (58 men)
Commander: Lieutenant de Roquebrune
Location: Champagne/Burgundy area, central France
Objective: to harry retreating Germans
Outcome: casualties inflicted on enemy

Operation 'Wallace'
Date: 19 August-19 September 1944
Unit: 2 SAS (60 men)
Commander: Major Farran
Location: Vosges mountains, eastern France
Objective: strengthening existing SAS bases and attacking Germans
Outcome: very successful, including 500 Germans killed or wounded

Operation 'Wolsey'
Date: 26 August-3 September 1944
Unit: 2 SAS (60 men)
Commander: Lieutenant McDevitt
Location: around Soissons and Compiègne, northeast France
Objective: to gather intelligence
Outcome: very successful

Operation 'Abel'
Date: 27 August-22 September 1944
Unit: 3 SAS (82 men)
Commander: Captain Sicand
Location: Vosges and Jura mountains, France
Objective: to assist Allied capture of the Belfort Gap
Outcome: numerous attacks against German forces in conjunction with *Maquis* and troops of French First Army

Operation 'Benson'
Date: 28 August-1 September 1944
Unit: 5 SAS (seven men)
Commander: Lieutenant Kirschen
Location: near Amiens, northeast France
Objective: to collect intelligence on German troop strengths and movements
Outcome: detailed information regarding enemy deployments collected.

Operation 'Spenser'
Date: 29 August-14 September 1944
Unit: 4 SAS (318 men)
Commander: Commandant Bourgoin
Location: around Bourges, central France
Objective: to inflict damage on retreating Germans
Outcome: very successful, including 2500 prisoners taken

Operation 'Bergbang'
Date: 2-12 September 1944
Unit: 5 SAS (41 men)
Commander: Captain Courtoy
Location: Liege-Aachen-Maastrict, Belgium
Objective: to aid Resistance and sever enemy communications
Outcome: unsuccessful

Operation 'Brutus'
Date: 2-15 September 1944
Unit: 5 SAS (19 men)
Commander: Captain Blondeel
Location: east of River Meuse, Belgium
Objective: to link up with Resistance and other SAS troops
Outcome: unsuccessful

Operation 'Caliban'
Date: 6-11 September 1944
Unit: 5 SAS
Commander: Lieutenant Limbosch
Location: northeast Belgium
Objective: to sever German communications west of River Meuse
Outcome: mostly unsuccessful

Operation 'Pistol'
Date: 15 September-3 October 1944
Unit: 2 SAS (51 men)
Commander: Captains Scott and Holland
Location: Alsace/Lorraine, eastern France
Objective: to cut enemy communications between Rivers Rhine and Moselle
Outcome: partly successful, though local population hostile

Operation 'Fabian'
Date: 16 September 1944-14 March 1945
Unit: 5 SAS (five men)
Commander: Lieutenant Kirschen
Location: around Arnhem, Holland
Objective: to collect intelligence regarding enemy dispositions and V-2 sites
Outcome: useful intelligence gathered

Operation 'Gobbo'
Date: 27 September 1944-17 March 1945
Unit: 5 SAS (seven men)
Commander: Lieutenant Debefre
Location: northern Holland
Objective: to gather intelligence
Outcome: unsuccessful

Operation 'Franklin'
Date: 24 December 1944–25 January
  1945
Unit: 4 SAS (186 men)
Commander: Captain Puech-Samson
Location: Belgian Ardennes
Objective: to support left flank of US
  VIII Corps
Outcome: much reconnaissance and
  fighting undertaken

Operation 'Galia'
Date: 27 December 1944–15 February
  1945
Unit: 2 SAS (35 men)
Commander: Captain Walker-Brown
Location: between Genoa and La Spezia,
  northern Italy
Objective: disrupting enemy
  communications and liaising with
  partisans
Outcome: extremely successful; casualties
  inflicted and a large number of
  Germans troops tied down

Operation 'Regent'
Date: 27 December 1944–15 January
  1945
Unit: 5 SAS
Commander: Captain Blondeel
Location: the Ardennes
Objective: supporting British armoured
  units during German offensive
Outcome: successful

1945

Operation 'Cold Comfort'
Date: 17 February–31 March 1945
Unit: 2 SAS (13 men)
Commander: Captain Littlejohn
Location: Verona, northern Italy
Objective: to block the railway line leading
  to the Brenner Pass
Outcome: unsuccessful

Operation 'Tombola'
Date: 4 March–24 April 1945
Unit: 2 SAS (50 men)
Commander: Major Farran
Location: around La Spezia and Bologna,
  northern Italy
Objective: to stiffen Resistance and harry
  Germans
Outcome: very successful; 600 enemy dead

Operation 'Archway'
Date: 25 March–3 May
Unit: 1 and 2 SAS (430 men and 75 jeeps)
Commander: Lieutenant-Colonel Brian
  Franks
Location: east of the River Rhine to Kiel,
  Germany
Objective: to assist advance of British 21st
  Army Group
Outcome: achieved its objective

Operation 'Canuck'
Date: April 1945
Unit: 2 SAS
Commander: Captain McDonald
Location: Italian Riviera
Objective: disrupt enemy communications
Outcome: partisans equipped and garrison
  of Alba overrun

Operation 'Larkswood'
Date: 3 April–8 May 1945
Unit: 5 SAS
Commander: Captain Blondeel
Location: northeast Holland and into
  Germany
Objective: to recce for the Canadian
  II Corps
Outcome: moderately successful

Operation 'Howard'
Date: 6 April–6 May 1945
Unit: 1 SAS
Commander: Lieutenant-Colonel Mayne
Location: Oldenburg, northwest Germany
Objective: to recce for the Canadian 4th
  Armoured Division
Outcome: SAS suffered heavy casualties;
  only partially successful

Operation 'Amherst'
Date: 8–16 April 1945
Unit: 3 and 4 SAS (700 men and 18 jeeps)
Commander: Colonel Prendergast
Location: Groningen, Coevordon and
  Zwolle, northeast Holland
Objective: to prevent Germans establishing
  a defensive line against the advancing
  Canadian First Army
Outcome: mostly successful. SAS harried
  enemy and inflicted 270 killed, 220
  wounded and 187 captured

Operation 'Keystone'
Date: 11–18 April 1945
Unit: 2 SAS
Commander: Major Druce
Location: south of Ijsselmeer, Holland
Objective: to interfere with enemy
  movements and capture bridges over
  the Apeldoorn Canal
Outcome: some damage and casualties
  inflicted upon the enemy

Operation 'Apostle'
Date: 12 May–31 August 1945
Unit: 1 and 2 SAS, HQ SAS Brigade
  (845 men)
Commander: Brigadier Calvert
Location: Norway
Objective: to disarm 300,000 German
  troops in Norway following end of
  World War II
Outcome: successful

1950-60

The Malayan 'Emergency', in which
British forces were heavily committed to
defeating the threat of communist insur-
gency, undertaken largely by disaffected
Chinese elements, resulted in major jun-
gle operations for which the SAS was re-
formed and proved highly effective.
Significant dates are as follows:
November 1950-February 1952: the
  Malayan Scouts (A, B and C Squad-
  rons) operate against Communist
  Terrorists in the jungle interior
February 1952-February 1958: A, B, D, the
  New Zealand and Parachute Squad-
  rons of 22 SAS help defeat the
  guerrillas in a long-range jungle war

NOVEMBER 1958-JANUARY 1959

A and D Squadrons are committed to the
war against rebels in northern Oman who
are based on the formidable Jebel Akhdar
plateau. On 27 January 1959 the SAS
storms the plateau and brings the rebellion to an end.

1963-66

The SAS is heavily involved in the successful British effort to defeat rebel guerrillas and Indonesian forces in the jungles
of Borneo who are opposed to the formation of the Federation of Malaysia.

Significant dates are as follows:

January 1963: A Squadron arrives on the island of Borneo

April 1963: Indonesian incursions begin into Sarawak and Sabah

May 1963: D Squadron replaces A Squadron and mounts long-range patrols along the border with Indonesian Kalimantan

January 1964: B Squadron is re-formed

June 1964: top-secret cross-border SAS 'Claret' raids into Kalimantan begin

1965: A, B and D Squadrons are active along and across the whole border

1966: G Squadron is formed

March 1966: President Sukarno of Indonesia is toppled in a coup

August 1966: Indonesia makes peace

APRIL 1964-NOVEMBER 1967

A, B and D Squadrons are involved in the Aden campaign against tribesmen in the Radfan area of the interior and guerrillas in the port of Aden (the so-called 'Keeni Meeni' operations).

1969-94

22 SAS is involved in operations to check the terrorists operating in Northern Ireland. Significant dates are as follows:

1969: D Squadron deploys to Ulster for a brief tour

1976: the British government announces that the SAS is to be deployed to South Armagh to fight terrorism

19 March 1978: SAS Lance-Corporal David Jones is mortally wounded in a firefight with an IRA terrorist.

2 May 1978: SAS Captain Richard Westmacott is shot and killed by IRA gunmen in Belfast

10 July 1978: schoolboy John Boyle is mistakenly shot and killed by the SAS in Dunloy, County Antrim

8 May 1987: the SAS wipes out the East Tyrone Brigade of the IRA in an ambush at Loughall in Northern Ireland.

6 March 1988: an SAS team shoots dead three IRA terrorists in Gibraltar.

3 June 1991: the SAS shoots and kills three IRA terrorists in Coagh, County Tyrone.

1970-76

The SAS is instrumental in the defeat of communist guerrillas seeking to overthrow the government of Oman, and is responsible for the highly successful 'hearts and minds' effort that proves decisive in preventing larger numbers of Omanis joining the insurgency. Significant dates are as follows:

23 July 1970: Sultan Qaboos overthrows his faher, Said bin Taimur, in a bloodless coup

late July 1970: SAS teams begin arriving in Oman to support the new regime, they are titled British Army Training Teams

January 1971: first *firqat* unit formed, titled *Firqat Salahadin*

24 February 1971: SAS and *firqat* troops assault and take the small fishing village of Sudh

2 October 1971: Operation 'Jaguar' begins.

It is a combined SAS, *firqat* and Sultan's Armed Forces (SAF) operation to establish a presence on the Jebel Dhofar, and ends in success

19 July 1972: the Battle of Mirbat, a nine-man SAS team defeats a large guerrilla force in a one-day battle.

1973: the SAS clears the area between Salalah and the Thamrait road

1974: SAS, *firqat* and SAF clears the enemy from all the valleys in central Dhofar

5 MAY 1980

Operation 'Nimrod' is the SAS operation to free hostages and kill and/or capture their terrorist captors in the Iranian Embassy in London.

JULY 1981

The SAS helps to restore President Jawara to power in the Gambia.

APRIL-JUNE 1982

The SAS undertakes intelligence-gathering and raiding operations against the occupying Argentine forces in the Falklands War. Significant dates are as follows:

23 April: D Squadron's Mountain Troop has to be evacuated from Fortuna Glacier, South Georgia, but Boat

Troop manages to establish several observation posts (OPs) around Leith

25 April: a combined Royal Marines, SBS and SAS force assaults and takes Grytviken, and thus retakes South Georgia

from 1 May: SAS and SBS patrols are inserted onto East and West Falkland to establish OPs and collect intelligence

14-15 May: D Squadron attacks and destroys enemy aircraft on Pebble Island

19 May: 18 members of D Squadron are killed in a helicopter crash

20 May: D Squadrons mounts a diversionary raid in the Goose Green area

30 May: SAS assists 42 Commando in taking Mount Kent

14 June: members of D and G Squadron, plus SBS, mount a diversionary raid in Stanley harbour.

1989-

22 SAS is committed to the anti-cocaine war, and thereupon starts to provide training and other assistance to the government forces in Colombia.

AUGUST 1990-FEBRUARY 1991

A large SAS contingent is heavily involved in the UN-led campaign to oust Iraqi occupation forces from Kuwait, and operates mostly behind the lines in Kuwait and Iraq. Significant dates are as follows:

end of 1990: A, B and D Squadrons, plus a small contingent from R Squadron, are deployed to the Gulf as part of the British special forces group

17 January 1991: the whole of the SAS force is moved to its forward operating base at Al Jouf in northwest Saudi Arabia

19 January 1991: three patrols from B Squadron are inserted by helicopter into Iraq to watch three highways in the Euphrates Valley; all are either aborted or end in failure

20 January 1991: SAS Land Rover columns from A and D Squadrons enter western Iraq to locate and target mobile Scud launchers

12 February 1991: a re-supply column is sent 145km (90 miles) into Iraq to replenish A and D Squadron's patrols

1994–95

Small SAS teams gather intelligence on the Serbian forces in Bosnia and provide target designation for RAF strike aircraft.

1997

Six-man SAS team sent to Lima, Peru, along with US Delta Force operators, following the takeover of the Japanese Ambassador's residence in January.

FEBRUARY 1998

The SAS deploy a squadron to Iraq when Saddam Hussein briefly threatens war. Its role is reconnaissance and rescuing downed pilots.

MARCH 1998

A four-man team rescues a British aid-worker, Robert Welch, from Albania. The team locate him and secure his rescue by driving to the coast in Land Rovers. There, two helicopters are waiting, one to provide a security force while the other extracts the team and its vehicles.

1999

After Serbian forces invade Kosovo, the SAS helps find and designate targets for NATO aircraft and rescues downed aircrew. It also supports the Kosovo Liberation Army (KLA) and helps apprehend Serbian war criminals.

MAY-SEPTEMBER 2000

The SAS is initially called in to provide overt support for UN peacekeepers in Sierra Leone. Then British soldiers are captured by a ruthless militia, known as the 'West Side Boys'. In response, the SAS launches a joint rescue operation with 1 Para and secures the hostages for the loss of one soldier.

SEPTEMBER 2001-

After the terrorists attacks on the US of 11 September 2001, the SAS supports operations against terrorism. It carries out recce and targeting missions for US forces against Taliban and Al-Qaeda soldiers and their equipment. It also supports the Northern Alliance and helps to find safe areas for delivering humanitarian aid. It plays a key role in this war and is extremely successful, though operating in difficult and demanding conditions. After the end of formal military operations, the SAS are involved in the hunt for Osama bin Laden and other al-Qaeda and Taliban senior figures.

2002

SAS teams sent to Mogadishu in Somalia following an intelligence tip-off that al-Qaeda are setting up a base with Somali warlords.

2002

SAS teams are deployed in Zimbabwe on covert reconnaissance missions to explore evacuation possibilities following death threats to British nationals living there.

2002-

SAS teams deploy on the Iraqi border during August following the threat of a new war with Iraq.

end of 2002: the SAS are active in Iraq alongside the SBS, US and Australian special forces

20 March 2003: the war begins and the SAS are involved in the capture of Mosul and Kirkuk in the north, Basra in the south, and extensive roadwatch patrols throughout western Iraq

1 May 2003: as official operations end, the SAS switch to the task of hunting insurgents and senior figures of the former regime

November 2004: the SAS are involved in operations around Falluja

2004

SAS teams are sent to Saudi Arabia and Greece to advise on anti-terrorist precautions against the threat of al-Qaeda.

2004-

SAS teams are reported to be active in Iran, identifying nuclear sites and providing hard intelligence for Western planners on Iran's armed forces and infrastructure.

INDEX

INDEX

PICTURE CREDITS